The Law of Global Custody

Legal Risk Management in Securities
Investment and Collateral

The Law of Global Custody

Legal Risk Management in Securities
Investment and Collateral

Fourth Edition

Madeleine Yates
and
Gerald Montagu

Bloomsbury Professional

Bloomsbury Professional Ltd, Maxwelton House, 41–43 Boltro Road, Haywards Heath, West Sussex, RH16 1BJ

© Bloomsbury Professional Ltd 2013 (other than in relation to Chapter 10: UK Taxation)
© GFH Montagu 2013 (Chapter 10: UK Taxation)

All rights reserved. No part of this publication may be reproduced in any material form (including photocopying or storing it in any medium by electronic means and whether or not transiently or incidentally to some other use of this publication) without the written permission of the copyright owner except in accordance with the provisions of the Copyright, Designs and Patents Act 1988 or under the terms of a licence issued by the Copyright Licensing Agency Ltd, Saffron House, 6–10 Kirby St, London, England EC1N 8TS. Applications for the copyright owner's written permission to reproduce any part of this publication should be addressed to the publisher.

Warning: The doing of an unauthorised act in relation to a copyright work may result in both a civil claim for damages and criminal prosecution.

Crown copyright material is reproduced with the permission of the Controller of HMSO and the Queen's Printer for Scotland. Any European material in this work which has been reproduced from EUR-lex, the official European Communities legislation website, is European Communities copyright.

A CIP Catalogue record for this book is available from the British Library.

ISBN 978 1 84766 877 6

Typeset by Phoenix Photosetting, Chatham, Kent
Printed and bound in Great Britain by CPI Group (UK) Ltd, Croydon, CR0 4YY

Preface to Fourth Edition

In the context of ongoing uncertainty and lack of confidence in the financial markets, the continuing widespread impact of large numbers of insolvency proceedings (including the administration proceedings relating to Lehman Brothers International (Europe) and other extensive associated litigation), and ever-increasing amounts of legislation and regulation at both international and domestic levels, the financial world has significantly changed since the third edition of *The Law of Global Custody*. Unsurprisingly, the focus by regulators on the significance of holding assets through intermediaries and the protection of client assets has increased hugely. Moreover, in times of financial hardship, governments have not been slow to try to increase the scope of tax legislation, as evidenced by FATCA and similar initiatives. As a result, it is essential for any intermediary holding assets for clients, and clients holding assets through intermediaries, to understand the nature of the rights and obligations where one person holds assets on behalf of another, and the implications of related issues. As with the third edition, this new edition is based on Dr Joanna Benjamin's valuable approach to analysis of the relevant issues, but incorporates appropriate updates and discussion of relevant developments since 2009 (including reference to MiFID and MiFID2, case law generated by the administration proceedings respecting Lehman Brothers International (Europe), and other relevant developments such as EMIR and FATCA), accompanied by an updated review of various related UK tax issues. The law and practice are generally stated as of 1 December 2012, although we have endeavoured to include reference to new developments prior to the book going to press.

Madeleine Yates
Gerald Montagu
January 2013

Contents

Preface	v
Table of Statutes	xv
Table of Statutory Instruments	xix
Table of European Legislation	xxiii
Table of Cases	xxvii
List of Abbreviations	xxxv
FSA Handbook	xliii

Chapter 1 Introduction — 1
- 1.1 Overview — 1
  - 1.2 International securities portfolios — 1
  - 1.4 Global custody — 1
  - 1.6 The global custody industry — 2
    - 1.6 Background — 2
    - 1.7 Challenges and opportunities — 2
    - 1.10 Development of the service — 4
    - 1.11 Other custody functions — 4
- 1.13 The legal analysis — 5
  - 1.13 Electronic, intermediated, cross-border securities markets — 5
  - 1.15 Analytic and law reform context — 6
  - 1.16 Scope — 6
  - 1.17 Changes from the third edition — 6
- 1.18 Fundamental concepts — 7
  - 1.20 The nature of securities — 7
    - 1.21 Debt and equity — 7
    - 1.23 Bearer and registered securities — 8
    - 1.24 Computerisation — 8
  - 1.25 Securities trading, clearing and settlement — 8
    - 1.25 Trading — 8
    - 1.26 Clearing — 9
    - 1.27 Settlement — 9
  - 1.28 Personal rights, property rights, and insolvency — 9
    - 1.29 Personal rights — 9
    - 1.30 Property rights — 10
  - 1.33 Securities collateral — 10
  - 1.35 Possession — 11
  - 1.37 Legal categories of assets — 11

Chapter 2 Securities in the electronic environment – how transfers occur — 13
- 2.5 Immobilisation and dematerialisation — 13
  - 2.6 Book entry transfer — 14
  - 2.7 Immobilisation — 14
  - 2.10 Dematerialisation — 15
- 2.14 Bearer securities in the electronic environment — 16
  - 2.15 Negotiability — 16
  - 2.17 A new class of negotiable instrument? — 17
  - 2.18 Arguments against negotiability — 17
    - 2.18 Indirect — 17
    - 2.20 Intangible — 17
    - 2.25 Conclusion — 19

viii Contents

	2.29	The benefits of negotiability	19
		2.30 Ease of transfer	19
		2.32 Security of transfer	20
		2.34 Conclusion	20
2.35	Registered computerised securities		20
2.37	Interests in securities		21

Chapter 3 Custodian as trustee – The custody relationship in the electronic environment — 23

3.2	The accounts		23
3.3	Cash		23
	3.3	The debtor/creditor principle	23
	3.5	Trust over cash	24
3.10	Interests in securities, bailment and trust		26
	3.14	Possession	28
	3.16	Trust	30
3.23	The allocation question		30
	3.24	Fungible custody and equivalent redelivery	31
	3.27	The requirement for allocation	31
	3.30	The cases	33
		3.31 *Re London Wine (Shippers) Ltd*	33
		3.33 *Re Stapylton Fletcher Ltd*	33
		3.35 *Re Goldcorp Exchange Ltd (in receivership)*	33
		3.37 *Hunter v Moss*	34
	3.42	Equitable tenancy in common	36
	3.43	Two lines of cases	36
	3.47	Conclusions	37
3.50	Shortfalls		38
	3.51	Shortfalls and commingled accounts	38
	3.55	Allocation of shortfall	39

Chapter 4 The use of the custody portfolio as collateral — 41

4.4	Overview		41
	4.4	Nature of collateralisation	41
	4.6	Financial institutions as collateral takers	42
	4.10	Financial assets as collateral	43
	4.11	Collateral and the global custodian	43
		4.12 The global custodian's settlement exposures	43
		4.15 Collateral management products	44
4.23	Legal structures of collateral		46
	4.24	Security interests	46
	4.30	Outright collateral transfers	48
4.33	Sensitivities		49
	4.35	For all types of collateral assets	50
		4.36 All collateral structures	50
		4.47 Security interests	54
		4.57 Outright collateral transfers	57
	4.62	For collateral comprising securities held in custody	60
		4.63 In all structures – intermediation and lex situs	60
		4.68 In favour of global custodian	60
		4.73 In favour of prime broker	62
4.76	Regulatory restrictions		63
4.79	The Financial Collateral Directive		63
	4.80	Progress	64
	4.81	Overview	64

Contents   ix

	4.84	Removing formal requirements	65
	4.86	Insolvency protection	66
	4.89	Enforcement	67
	4.91	Right of use	68
	4.93	Recharacterisation risk	68
	4.95	Criteria	69
	4.99	Floating charges	71
	4.107	Policy issues	73
	4.108	Governing law	74
	4.111	General comments	75

Chapter 5   Cross-border questions   77
5.5   The conflict of laws   77
    5.7   Jurisdiction   78
        5.7   Overview   78
        5.9   Jurisdiction – non-insolvency   78
        5.15   Jurisdiction – insolvency   80
    5.25   Choice of law   84
    5.29   Enforcement   86
5.30   Sub-custodian insolvency issues   86
    5.31   Trust and bailment   86
    5.33   Risks of sub-custodian insolvency   87
    5.35   Local ring-fence opinions   88
    5.37   Other risks   88
5.38   Cross-border collateral issues   89
    5.38   Overview   89
    5.39   Conflict of laws analysis of collateral arrangements   89
    5.42   Property rights   90
        5.43   Property rights in intangible assets   90
        5.46   Jurisdiction   91
        5.48   Choice of law – the lex situs rule   91
        5.51   Applicability to intangibles   92
    5.54   PRIMA   93
        5.57   Settlement Finality Directive   95
        5.58   Other EU measures   96
    5.59   Hague Convention on Securities held with an Intermediary   96
    5.63   UNIDROIT   97
        5.66   Conceptual issues   101
        5.68   Interests in securities and cash   102
    5.69   Securities Law Directive   102
    5.73   Set off   103

Chapter 6   The global custodian's duties   105
6.2   Overview   105
6.5   Limitation clauses   106
    6.5   Generally   106
    6.9   Negligence and gross negligence   106
    6.10   Wilful default   107
    6.11   Statutory restrictions   108
        6.11   Unfair Contract Terms Act 1977 ('UCTA')   108
        6.15   Unfair Terms in Consumer Contracts Regulations 1999   108
        6.16   Contractual duties   108
6.21   Tortious duty of care   109
6.24   Trustee's duties   110

		6.29	Trustee's duty of care		111
			6.29	Trustee Act 2000	112
			6.30	Case law	112
			6.32	Limitation clauses	112
		6.36	Fiduciary duty		115
6.56		Liability for third parties			122
		6.57	Liability for sub-custodians		122
		6.64	Fraudulent instructions		124
		6.69	Nexus		125
6.70		Particular clauses			126
		6.71	Force majeure		126
		6.72	Consequential damages		126
		6.73	Erroneous instructions		127
		6.74	Information		127
		6.75	Indemnities for breach of duty		128
6.76		Corporate actions			128
		6.77	What do we mean by 'corporate action'?		128
		6.78	Generally		129
		6.80	Issues for the client		130
		6.86	Issues for the custodian		133

Chapter 7 Regulatory duties — **135**

7.2	Custody as a regulated activity				135
	7.2	Regulation of custody			135
7.5	UK regulatory authorities				136
	7.5	Financial Services Authority			136
	7.6	Financial Conduct Authority and Prudential Regulatory Authority			138
7.10	UK regulatory framework				139
	7.10	MiFID and MiFID2			139
		7.10	MiFID		139
		7.14	MiFID2		140
	7.15	Regulated activities			141
	7.17	Specified activities			142
	7.18	Meaning of 'safeguarding' and 'administration'			142
	7.20	Nominees			143
	7.21	Relevant rules			144
	7.22	Context – MiFID business or non-MiFID business			144
	7.23	General principles and 'treating customers fairly'			145
	7.30	Protection of client assets			147
	7.32	General provisions			149
	7.33	Client classification			149
	7.34	Custody services			149
		7.35	Sub-custodians		150
		7.36	Content of custody agreements		151
		7.38	Protection of client assets		152
		7.39	Stock lending		152
		7.41	Lien and set-off rights		153
		7.45	Maintenance of records		154
		7.46	Risk warnings		155
		7.49	Registration of title		156
		7.59	Affiliates		158
	7.58	Client money			158
		7.61	Application of rules		159
		7.62	Disapplication of rules		160

		7.66	Holding of cash by custodian	161
		7.68	Opting out	162
		7.74	Trustee firms	163
		7.76	Use of a non-approved bank	164
		7.77	Prior written notice	164
		7.78	Unclaimed funds	165
		7.83	BCOBS and set-off	166
	7.85	Client money and case law		167
		7.87	When client money trust applies	167
		7.92	Adequate arrangements and set-off rights	168
		7.95	Commingling	169
		7.98	Relevance of MiFID	169
		7.100	Reconciliations	170
		7.101	Reliability of Client Money Rules	170
		7.102	Deductions from client money	170
	7.109	Further client money developments		172
	7.117	Collateral		174
		7.119	Compliance	175
		7.120	Extension of Rules	175
	7.121	CASS Resolution Pack		176
	7.123	Control and custodians		178
	7.127	Trustees and custody		179
	7.130	Outsourcing		180
7.139	Related issues			183
	7.139	Clients' right of action		183
		7.141	Breach of FSA rules	184
		7.142	Breach of regulatory requirements	184
	7.144	Unclaimed assets		185
	7.145	EEA passport arrangements		186
	7.151	Rights of indirect holders?		187
	7.154	Prime brokerage		188
	7.159	Further amendments to CASS?		190
7.162	International regulatory developments			192
	7.164	AIFMD		192
		7.165	Depositary's liability for loss	192
		7.171	Implications for Depositary's delegates	195
7.177	Securities Law Directive			197
	7.178	Rights granted to persons other than legal owner		197
	7.182	Loss of securities		198
	7.185	Non-discrimination regarding securities rights		199
	7.187	Further developments		200
		7.189	Nature of ownership	201
		7.190	Rights of use	201
		7.191	Omnibus accounts	202
		7.192	The future?	202

Chapter 8	**Overview of post-trade infrastructure**			**203**
8.2	Background			203
8.3	Overview			203
	8.4	Nature of settlement		204
		8.5	Delivery and payment	204
		8.6	Book entry transfer	205
	8.11	Nature of clearing		206
		8.12	Central counterparty	206
		8.13	Netting	206

	8.16	Challenges	207
8.20	Risk management	208
	8.21	Key risks in post-trade infrastructure	208
		8.22	Credit risk – principal risk	208
		8.23	Credit risk – replacement cost risk	208
		8.25	Liquidity risk	209
		8.27	Operational risk – generally	210
		8.28	Operational risk – legal risk	210
		8.29	Systemic risk	210
		8.30	Risk in cross-border trades	211
	8.31	Basic risk management techniques	211
		8.32	DVP	211
		8.39	Shorter settlement cycles	214
		8.40	T+1	214
		8.41	STP	215
		8.46	Central counterparty	216
		8.48	Collateralisation	217
		8.49	Default provisions	217
		8.51	Benefits of clearing for market participants	218
		8.53	The development of clearing	218
	8.56	Leading studies and reports	219
8.85	Consolidation	229
	8.86	Current fragmentation of post-trade infrastructure	229
	8.88	Consolidation of settlement	231
	8.90	Consolidation of clearing and/or CCP services	232
8.99	Underlying legal principles	234
	8.100	Property rights	235
	8.101	Insolvency	235
		8.103	Collateral	236
		8.104	Netting	236
		8.106	The conflict of laws	237
	8.107	Law reform initiatives	237
		8.108	The Settlement Finality Directive	238
		8.110	EU Insolvency Regulation and Banking Winding Up Directive	239
		8.111	Financial Collateral Directive	239
		8.112	Hague Convention	239
		8.113	European Securities Code	239
		8.114	Lisbon Treaty 2009	240

Chapter 9   UK settlement systems   **243**
9.1	CREST	243
	9.1	Introduction	243
	9.5	Core legal structure	244
		9.5	Dematerialisation	244
		9.6	Legal and equitable ownership	245
		9.7	Settlement structure – UK securities	245
		9.11	Settlement structure – non-UK securities	246
		9.12	Payments	246
		9.25	Regulation	252
	9.31	Custody accounts	253
		9.33	Pooled accounts	254
		9.34	Designated accounts	254
		9.36	Sponsored membership	254
		9.40	Visibility	256

Contents xiii

	9.42	Risk		257
		9.42	Credit	257
		9.49	Bad deliveries and fraudulent transfers	259
		9.61	Custody agreements	264
	9.66	Cross-border issues		266
	9.69	International securities		266
	9.75	Collateral and securities lending		268
		9.77	Security interests	268
		9.88	Securities lending and repos	270
	9.94	Corporate actions		271
	9.95	Central sponsor arrangements		272
	9.106	Funds		274
	9.107	Gilts		274
		9.110	Transfer of title	275
		9.111	Stamp duty and SDRT	275
		9.112	Gilt title finance (stock lending and repos)	275
		9.119	Eligible debt securities	276
	9.125	CREST – further developments		278
	9.135	Conclusions		282
9.136	Further issues for consideration in relation to CREST			283
	9.136	Operator register of title, record of title and issuer register		283
	9.137	Capacity and liability of registrar		285
9.141	Extract from old CGO membership agreement			286

Chapter 10   UK taxation **287**
10.1	Introduction			287
10.6	Stamp duty			288
	10.8	Bearer instrument		289
	10.10	Transfer on sale		289
		10.11	Exempt loan capital	290
		10.12	Call options	291
		10.14	Other exemptions	292
		10.16	Depositary receipts	293
	10.17	Transfer of any other kind		294
	10.20	Contract or agreement chargeable as a transfer on sale		294
	10.21	Depositary receipt and clearance service charge – EU law aspects		295
	10.22	Depositary receipts		297
	10.24	Clearance service		298
		10.25	One-off charge	298
		10.26	Election to pay stamp duty or SDRT	298
		10.27	Exempt agreements to transfer	299
	10.28	Investors		299
	10.29	Custodians		300
	10.30	Evidence		301
10.30	Stamp duty reserve tax (SDRT)			301
	10.31	Chargeable securities		301
	10.32	Excluded securities		303
	10.33	Charges to SDRT		304
		10.34	Principal charge	304
		10.39	Depositary receipt charge	308
		10.43	Clearance service	310
	10.45	Settlements and direct assessment		312
		10.47	Income Tax (Trading and Other Income) Act 2005, ss 687 and 689	314

xiv Contents

		10.49	UK representatives and disregarded income	314
10.52	Enforcement in the UK of tax assessed under the laws of another jurisdiction			315
10.56	Situs			317
10.59	Withholding tax			322
	10.61	Payers and paying agents		323
	10.65	Collecting agents		326
10.69	Information reporting			327
10.72	European Union Directive on the taxation of savings income			329
	10.74	Transitional period		330
	10.79	Reform of the EUSD		331
	10.80	Implementation of the EUSD by the UK		332
10.82	FATCA			333
	10.82	Overview		333
	10.83	Compliance under the UK IGA		336
	10.84	Account identification and review obligations for UK RFIs		339
		10.85	Pre-existing accounts held by individuals and opened on or before 31 December 2013	339
		10.86	Pre-existing Entity Accounts	342
		10.87	New Individual Accounts opened on or after 1 January 2014	344
		10.88	New Entity Accounts opened on or after 1 January 2014	344
	10.89	Reporting obligations for UK RFIs		345
		10.89	US Reportable Accounts	345
		10.90	Reporting in relation to payments to Non-participating Financial Institutions	347
	10.91	Account review, monitoring and reporting by a UK Non-reporting Financial Institution		347
10.92	Value added tax			348
	10.93	Scope		348
	10.94	Exemptions		348

Chapter 11 Conclusions **351**
11.1   Preceding chapters   351
11.5   Managing legal risk   351
11.7   Interests in securities   352
11.10 The future?   352

Bibliography   **355**

Index   **361**

Table of Statutes

All references are to paragraph number

Bank of England Act 1998	7.6	Dormant Bank and Building Society	
Banking Act 1987	7.3	Accounts Act 2008	7.82
Banking Act 2009	1.15; 3.13; 7.6	Electronic Communications Act 2000	
Bills of Exchange Act 1882		s 8	2.23, 2.31
s 29(1)	2.15; 4.45	European Communities Act 1972	
83	2.16	s 2(2)	4.97
Civil Jurisdiction and Judgments Act		(a)	4.97
1982	5.9	Fair Trading Act 1973	9.125
Civil Procedure Act 1997	6.83	Finance Act 1930	
Companies Act 1985		s 42	10.34
s 360	9.34	Finance Act 1942	
395	4.50	s 47	10.20
Companies Act 1989		Finance Act 1946	
Pt VII (ss 154–191)	5.24; 8.108; 9.23, 9.56	s 57	10.31
		(1)	10.31
s 207	9.5, 9.50	Finance Act 1965	
(4)	9.50	s 90	10.11
Companies Act 2006	4.46, 4.52; 6.84; 9.138	Finance Act 1976	
		s 131	10.56
s 112	9.136	Finance Act 1977	
113	9.139	s 11	10.54
(8)	9.139	Finance Act 1986	10.31
114	9.139	s 67	10.21, 10.22
115	9.136	(6)	10.21
126	9.34	(9)	10.18
127	9.6	70	10.21, 10.24
145–153	6.83; 9.40	(6)	10.21
303	6.77	(9)	10.18
744	10.58	71	10.28
769, 770	9.5	72A	10.18
785	9.5; 10.32	78	10.40
793	9.40	(7)	10.9
859A(3)	4.54	79(2)	10.9
(6)	4.52	(4)–(6)	10.11
859G	4.54	(7A), (7B), (8A)	10.11
Pt 25 (ss 860–894)	4.50, 4.51	80A	10.35
s 860	4.85; 5.39; 9.86	80C	10.15
1052	4.50	(6)	10.15
1157	6.26	80D	10.15
Contracts (Applicable Law) Act		87	10.35
1990	5.25, 5.48	88(1A)	10.38
Contracts (Rights of Third Parties)		88A(1)–(1C), (2A)–(2C)	10.35
Act 1999	6.19, 6.69	(4), (5)	10.35
s 1(1), (2)	6.19	89AA, 89AB	10.35
Corporation Tax Act 2009		90(3)(a)	10.35
s 3(1), (2)	10.47	(3A)–(3F)	10.35
507	10.9, 10.35	(4)	10.36
Corporation Tax Act 2010		(5)	10.21, 10.36, 10.44
Pt 22 Ch 6 (ss 969–972)	10.49	(6)	10.35, 10.36
s 1122	10.15	(7)	10.36
1146	10.51	91(1)	10.34

Finance Act 1986 – contd
s 92	10.37
93	10.21
(1)–(3)	10.39
(4)	10.39, 10.43
(7)–(9)	10.39
94(1)	10.39
95(1)	10.21, 10.40
(2)–(2D)	10.40
(3)–(5)	10.40
96	10.21
(2)	10.40
(5)–(7)	10.43
97	10.44
(1)	10.21
97A	10.42, 10.44
(3)	10.26, 10.44
97AA	10.44
97B	10.42, 10.44
(1)	10.21
97C	10.36, 10.42, 10.44
(4)(a), (b)	10.21
97C1	10.21
99(3)	10.31
(4)–(4A)	10.32
(5)–(5ZA), (6), (7)	10.32
(10)	10.41
186	10.38
Finance Act 1987	10.31
s 50	10.11
87	10.34
Finance Act 1989	
s 178	10.6
Finance Act 1991	10.35
s 116, 117	10.35
Finance Act 1996	10.59
s 186	10.19
(1)	10.32
Finance Act 1999	
s 112	10.10
119	10.32
Sch 13	
para 1	10.10
(3A)	10.10
2–4	10.10
7	10.20
24	10.14
Sch 15	
para 1	10.8
2	10.6, 10.8
11	10.8
13	10.9
16	10.40
17	10.9
23	10.6
Sch 19	10.31
para 14	10.31
Finance Act 2000	10.62, 10.65, 10.69
Finance Act 2001	10.68
s 85	10.63, 10.68

Finance Act 2002	10.54, 10.63, 10.68
s 134	10.54
Sch 39	10.54
Finance Act 2005	
s 48A	10.9
Finance Act 2006	10.55
Pt 9 (ss 170–177)	10.53
s 173	10.55
Finance Act 2007	10.62
Sch 21	10.15
Finance Act 2008	10.11, 10.56
s 98	10.10
99	10.17
Sch 32	10.17
para 6–8	10.18
Finance Act 2010	10.21
s 54	10.21
65	10.35
Finance Act 2011	
s 84	10.32
Sch 23	
para 12(2)	10.70
Finance Act 2012	10.56
Finance Bill 2013	10.59, 10.82
Finance (No 2) Act 2005	
s 68	10.54
Finance (No 2) Act 2010	10.45
Financial Services Act 1986	6.36; 7.2, 7.3, 7.4, 7.20, 7.23; 10.31
s 36	9.25
Sch 1	
para 13A	7.2
Sch 4	
para 2(4)	9.25
Financial Services Act 2010	6.83; 8.84
Financial Services and Markets Act 2000	1.15; 3.8; 6.1, 6.36, 6.83; 7.1, 7.5, 7.6, 7.15, 7.17, 7.20, 7.22, 7.120, 7.124, 7.127, 7.149; 9.25; 10.31
s 19(1)	7.3
22	7.15
118	7.5
150	7.141
Pt XII (ss 178–192)	6.90; 7.123
s 181(1), (2)	7.124
182, 183	7.124
184(3)	7.125
190, 191F	7.123
235	10.62
(2)	10.31
237(1)	10.31
Pt XVIII (ss 285–313)	9.25
s 285	9.25
Income Tax Act 1842	10.48
Income Tax Act 2007	
s 9	10.45
12	10.47

Table of Statutes   xvii

Income Tax Act 2007 – *contd*		Sale of Goods Act 1979	
s 19	10.45	s 6(1)	3.27
81	10.47	16, 20A	3.27
479, 491	10.45	61(1)	3.27
564G	10.9	Sale of Goods (Amendment) Act 1994	
578	10.59	s 1(1)	3.27
809A–809Z7	10.56	Scotland Act 2012	10.58
811	10.50	Stamp Act 1891	
814	10.50	s 5	10.29
(4)	10.51	13(4)	10.6
825, 826	10.50	14(4)	10.6
Pt 14 Ch 2B (ss 835C–835S)	10.46, 10.49	15A(3), (4)	10.6
		15B	10.6
s 874	10.59, 10.61, 10.66	17	10.6, 10.29
882	10.62	55, 57	10.10
899	10.59	60	10.13
919, 920	10.59	117	10.28, 10.30
930	10.63, 10.68	122	10.20
(9)	10.64	State Immunity Act 1978	5.14
933–936	10.61, 10.63	s 3(1)	5.14
937	10.61, 10.63	Stock Transfer Act 1963	9.107
(6)	10.63	Stock Transfer Act 1982	9.107
987	10.62	Taxation (International and Other Provisions) Act 2010	10.9
989	10.50		
999	10.61	Taxation of Chargeable Gains Act 1992	
1005	10.62		
Income Tax (Trading and Other Income) Act 2005	10.47	s 4	10.45
		60	10.58
Pt 4 Ch 3 (ss 382–401B)	10.45	(1)	10.45
s 430–436	10.70	68	10.45
683	10.59	151N	10.9
687, 689	10.46, 10.47, 10.48	265, 266	10.56
		Pt VIIA Ch I (ss 271A–271D)	10.49
Inheritance Tax Act 1984		s 275(1)(c), (d), (da)	10.58
s 3(1), (2)	10.56	(2)(b)	10.58
6(1)	10.56	275A(3)	10.58
43, 48	10.45	275B(2)	10.58
64	10.45, 10.56	275C	10.58
65	10.56	Trustee Act 1925	7.144
Insolvency Act 1986	9.23	s 30(1)	6.10
s 117	5.22	61	6.26
127	4.37; 9.82	Trustee Act 2000	6.10, 6.29, 6.51, 6.62
144	5.23		
220, 221	5.22	s 1	6.29
238, 239	4.37	(1)	6.29
240, 245	4.37	2	6.29
283(3)(a)	1.30; 3.17	17	6.5, 6.50, 6.59, 6.60
423	10.55		
426	5.28	(3)	6.5
Law of Property Act 1925		20(2), (3)	6.50
s 53(1)(c)	2.31; 8.100; 9.6	22(1)(a), (b)	6.59
136	2.31; 8.100; 9.6	23(1)	6.59
Lloyd's Act 1982	4.52	29(1), (3), (5)	6.51
Local Government and Housing Act 1989		30(1)	6.60
		31	10.30
s 47(7)	4.68	(1)	6.51
OECD Support Fund Act 1975	10.56	32	6.51
Public Trustee Act 1906		Sch 1	
s 4(2)	6.64	para 1, 3	6.29
(3)	3.15	7	6.29, 6.59
Recognition of Trusts Act 1987	5.31		

xviii *Table of Statutes*

Unfair Contract Terms Act 1977	6.13, 6.15, 6.35, 6.73
s 2	6.12
(2)	6.14
3	6.11, 6.12
4	6.12
11	6.14
Sch 1	
para 1	6.12
Value Added Tax Act 1994	10.92
s 3	10.92
Sch 1	
para 1(1)	10.92
Sch 5	10.93
Sch 9	
Group 5	10.94

BELGIUM

Royal Decree No 62 of 10 November 1967	2.33

CAYMAN ISLANDS

Mutual Funds Law (2007 revision)	
s 5	10.81

IRELAND

Companies Act 1990	
s 239	9.2

ISLE OF MAN

Companies Act 1992	9.2

LUXEMBOURG

Grand Ducal Decree of 17 February 1971	
art 7	2.33

UNITED STATES

Hiring Incentives to Restore Employment Act 2010	10.82
Inland Revenue Code	
s 501(a)	10.82
1441	10.83
1471	10.83
(d)(1)	10.83
(e)(2)	10.83
(g)	10.83
4979(a)(1)	10.82
6045(c)	10.82
Investment Companies Act 1940	10.82
r 17f-5	5.35
Tax Equity and Fiscal Responsibility Act 1993	10.67
Uniform Commercial Code	5.55
Pt 8	1.15
art 8	5.32; 8.113; 11.8
8-313(1)(d)(ii), (iii)	5.32
(2)	5.32
9	4.107

Table of Statutory Instruments

All references are to paragraph number

Civil Procedure Rules 1998, SI 1998/3132	5.12, 5.13
Companies Act 2006 (Consequential Amendments) (Taxes and National Insurance) Order 2008, SI 2008/954	10.32
Credit Institutions (Reorganisation and Winding Up) Regulations 2004, SI 2004/1045	5.21
Cross-Border Insolvency Regulations 2006, SI 2006/1030	5.24
Data-gathering Powers (Relevant Data) Regulations 2012, SI 2012/847	10.70
Dormant Bank and Building Society Accounts Act 2008 (Commencement and Transitional Provisions) Order 2009, SI 2009/490	7.82
Double Taxation Relief and International Tax Enforcement (Taxes on Income and Capital) (New Zealand) Order 2008, SI 2008/1793	10.55
Double Taxation Relief and International Tax Enforcement (Faroes) Order 2007, SI 2007/3469	10.55
Double Taxation Relief (Taxes on Income) (General) Regulations 1970, SI 1970/488	10.61
Double Taxation Relief (Taxes on Income) (The United States of America) Order 2002, SI 2002/2848	
art 27	10.82
Financial Collateral Arrangements (No 2) Regulations 2003, SI 2003/3226	1.35; 4.52, 4.79, 4.85, 4.88, 4.97, 4.98, 4.100, 4.102, 4.104, 4.105, 4.106, 4.111; 5.24; 7.40, 7.117; 9.86
reg 3	4.83, 4.97, 4.110
(1)	4.98
(2)	4.104
4	4.85
(4)	4.85
5–7	4.85
12	4.88
Financial Collateral Arrangements (No 2) Regulations 2003 – *contd*	
reg 16	4.92
(2)	4.92
17	4.90
18	4.90
(1)	4.90
19	4.110
(4)(b)	4.100
Financial Markets and Insolvency Regulations 1996, SI 1996/1469	9.23
Financial Markets and Insolvency (Settlement Finality) (Amendment) Regulations 2001, SI 2001/997	5.57
Financial Markets and Insolvency (Settlement Finality and Financial Collateral Arrangements) (Amendment) Regulations 2010, SI 2010/2993	8.109
Financial Markets and Insolvency (Settlement Finality) Regulations 1999, SI 1999/2979	5.24, 5.57; 9.53
Pt II (regs 3–12)	8.108
reg 14(1)	9.54
23	5.27
Financial Markets and Insolvency (Settlement Finality) (Revocation) Regulations 2001, SI 2001/1349	5.57
Financial Services Act 1986 (Extension of Scope of Act) Order 1996, SI 1996/2958	7.2
Financial Services and Markets Act 2000 (Carrying on Regulated Activities by Way of Business) Order 2001, SI 2001/1177	7.15, 7.16
Financial Services and Markets Act 2000 (Consequential Amendments and Repeals) Order 2001, SI 2001/3649	7.28
art 3(1)(c), (d)	7.3
Financial Services and Markets Act 2000 (Exemption) Order 2001, SI 2001/1201	9.25
reg 5	9.25
Schedule	
Pt III (paras 26–39)	9.25

xx *Table of Statutory Instruments*

Financial Services and Markets Act 2000 (Regulated Activities) Order 2001, SI 2001/544 .... 7.3, 7.15, 7.17, 7.61, 7.127
   art 4(4A) 7.127
   5(2) 7.16
   10 .... 7.141
   40 .... 3.8; 7.4, 7.19
   (1) 7.127
   41 .... 7.20
   45 .... 9.29
   64 .... 7.4
   66 .... 7.127
   (4A) 7.127
   67 .... 7.127
   74–88 .... 7.15
   89 .... 7.15, 7.19
Financial Services and Markets Act 2000 (Rights of Action) Regulations 2001, SI 2001/2256
   reg 3 .... 7.141
Government Stock Regulations 2004, SI 2004/1611 .... 9.107
   reg 15 .... 9.107
   16 .... 9.50
Insolvency Rules 1986, SI 1986/1925
   r 4.90 .... 4.59
Insurers (Reorganisation and Winding Up) Regulations 2003, SI 2003/1102 .... 4.39
Insurers (Reorganisation and Winding Up) Regulations 2004, SI 2004/353 .... 4.39; 5.22
Investment Bank Special Administration (England and Wales) Rules 2011, SI 2011/1301 .... 1.15
Investment Bank Special Administration Regulations 2011, SI 2011/245 .... 1.8, 1.15; 3.13
   reg 10(1), (2) 3.13
   11, 12 .... 3.13
   14 .... 7.122
MARD Regulations 2011, SI 2011/2931 .... 10.54
Money Laundering Regulations 2007, SI 2007/2157 .... 6.35
Open-Ended Investment Companies Regulations 2001, SI 2001/1228 .... 7.74
Overseas Companies (Execution of Documents and Registration of Charges) (Amendment) Regulations 2011, SI 2011/2194 ...... 4.50
Overseas Companies (Execution of Documents and Registration of Charges) Regulations 2009, SI 2009/1917 .... 4.50
Overseas Companies Regulations 2009, SI 2009/1801 .... 4.50

Recovery of Duties and Taxes etc Due in Other Member States (Corresponding UK Claims, Procedure and Supplementary) Regulations 2004, SI 2004/674 .... 10.54
Recovery of Foreign Taxes (Amendment) Regulations 2010, SI 2010/794 .... 10.55
Recovery of Foreign Taxes Regulations 2007, SI 2007/3507 .... 10.55
Reporting of Savings Income Information Regulations 2003, SI 2003/3297
   reg 3, 8–13 .... 10.80
Stamp Duty Reserve Tax (Amendment of section 89AA of the Finance Act 1986) Regulations 2008, SI 2008/3236 .... 10.35
Stamp Duty and Stamp Duty Reserve Tax (Eurex Clearing AG) Regulations 2011, SI 2011/666 .... 10.35
Stamp Duty and Stamp Duty Reserve Tax (European Central Counterparty Limited) Regulations 2011, SI 2011/667 .... 10.35
Stamp Duty and Stamp Duty Reserve Tax (European Multilateral Clearing Facility NV) Regulations 2011, SI 2011/668 .... 10.35
Stamp Duty and Stamp Duty Reserve Tax (LCH Clearnet Limited) Regulations 2011, SI 2011/669 .... 10.35
Stamp Duty and Stamp Duty Reserve Tax (SIX X-CLEAR AG) Regulations 2011, SI 2011/670 .... 10.35
Stamp Duty Reserve Tax Regulations 1986, SI 1986/1711 .... 10.31, 10.34
   reg 4A 10.34
Stamp Duty Reserve Tax (UK Depositary Interests in Foreign Securities) (Amendment) Regulations 2000, SI 2000/1871 .... 10.32
Stamp Duty Reserve Tax (UK Depositary Interests in Foreign Securities) (Amendment) Regulations 2001, SI 2001/3779 .... 10.32
Stamp Duty Reserve Tax (UK Depositary Interest in Foreign Securities) (Amendment) Regulations 2007, SI 2007/12 .... 10.32
Stamp Duty Reserve Tax (UK Depositary Interests in Foreign Securities) Regulations 1999, SI 1999/2383 .... 10.32

Stock Transfer (Gilt-edged Securities) (CGO Service) (Amendment) Regulations 1999, SI 1999/1208 .... 9.50
Stock Transfer (Gilt-edged Securities) (CGO Service) Regulations 1985, SI 1985/1144 .... 9.107
   reg 3 .... 9.50
Stock Transfer (Specified Securities) Order 1991, SI 1991/340.......... 9.107
Taxes and Duties (Interest Rate) (Amendment) Regulations 2008, SI 2008/3234................. 10.6
Taxes (Interest Rate) Regulations 1989, SI 1989/1297
   reg 3 .... 10.6
Uncertificated Securities (Amendment) Regulations 2000, SI 2000/1682 .... 9.4

Uncertificated Securities Regulations 1995, SI 1995/3272 .... 9.4
   reg 29 .... 2.32; 9.120
Uncertificated Securities Regulations 2001, SI 2001/3755 ..... 2.31; 9.4, 9.5, 9.69; 10.19
   reg 3(1).. 10.32
   35 .... 2.32
   38(5).. 2.31
Unfair Terms in Consumer Contracts (Amendment) Regulations 2001, SI 2001/1186................. 7.28
Unfair Terms in Consumer Contracts Regulations 1999, SI 1999/2083 .... 6.15; 7.28
   reg 3(1).. 6.15
Value Added Tax (Finance) (No 2) Order 2008, SI 2008/2547........ 10.94

Table of European Legislation

All references are to paragraph number

TREATIES AND CONVENTIONS
Convention for the Protection of Human Rights and Fundamental Freedoms (Rome, 9 November 1950)
  Protocol 1
    art 1 .... 10.55
Convention on Jurisdiction and the Enforcement of Judgments in Civil and Commercial Matters (Brussels, 27 September 1968) 5.10
Convention on Jurisdiction and the Enforcement of Judgments in Civil and Commercial Matters (Hague, 1 February 1971) 5.12
  art 1 .... 5.12
    2(e) 5,12
    4 .... 5.12
    12(1) 5.12
    18(2) 5.12
    30 .... 5.12
Convention on Jurisdiction and the Enforcement of Judgments in Civil and Commercial Matters (Lugano, 16 September 1988) .. 5.9, 5.10
Convention on Substantive Rules for Intermediated Securities (Geneva, 9 October 2009) 5.64, 5.65
  art 1(b)–(e) 5.64
    6, 7 .... 5.64
    9(1)(a) 5.64
      (i) 5.64
      (b) 5.64
    11(1) 5.64
    12 .... 5.64
    15(1)(a) 5.64
    18, 19 .... 5.64
    22 .... 5.64
      (3) 5.64
    24–26 .... 5.64
    31–38 .... 5.64
Convention on the Law applicable to Certain Rights in Respect of Securities (Hague, 5 July 2006) 5.49, 5.59, 5.62, 5.63; 8.112
  art 2 .... 5.60
    (1) 5.61
    4–6 .... 5.61
    19(1) 5.59

Convention on the Law Applicable to Contractual Obligations (Rome, 19 June 1980) 5.48
  art 8, 9 .... 5.39
    15 .... 5.25
Convention on the Law Applicable to Trusts and on their Recognition (Hague, 1 July 1985) 5.31
Treaty amending the Treaty on European Union and the Treaty establishing the European Community) (Lisbon, 13 December 2007) 8.114

DIRECTIVES
Dir 69/335/EEC 10.21
Dir 76/308/EEC 10.54
Dir 85/611/EEC 6.53; 7.1
Dir 93/6/EEC 6.53; 7.1
Dir 93/13/EEC 6.15
Dir 93/22/EEC 6.53; 7.1, 7.10, 7.145
Dir 98/26/EC 4.81; 5.57, 5.58, 5.59, 5.60; 8.108, 8.109, 8.112; 9.23, 9.28, 8.53
  art 1(a) 8.108
    2(a), (i), (k) 8.108
    3(1), (2) 8.108
    4 .... 8.108
    8 .... 8.110
    9(1) 8.108
      (2) 5.57
    10 .... 8.108
  Recital 2 .... 8.107
Dir 2000/12/EC 6.53; 7.1
Dir 2001/17/EC 4.8; 5.22
  art 2(a), (c), (d),(k) 4.8
Dir 2001/24/EC 4.34, 4.37, 4.56, 4.59, 4.62, 4.64; 5.21, 5.22, 5.28, 5.58, 5.73; 8.110
  art 1(1), (2) 5.21
    3(1) 5.21
    9 .... 8.110
      (1) 5.21
    10(2)(c) 5.73
    21 .... 5.49
      (4) 5.49
    23(1), (2) 5.73
    27 .... 8.110
  Recital 16 .... 5.16

Dir 2002/47/EC	1.15; 4.23, 4.34, 4.40, 4.49, 4.56, 4.59, 4.62, 4.71, 4.74, 4.79, 4.83, 4.108, 4.109, 4.111; 5.24, 5.58, 5.59, 5.60, 5.62, 5.64, 5.69, 5.71; 7.163; 8.109, 8.111	Dir 2004/39/EC – contd	
		art 2(1)(b)	7.10, 7.13
		(h)	7.10
		4(1)	7.13, 7.165
		(18)	7.165
		13(7), (8)	7.11, 7.42
		16(1)(d)	3.10
art 1	4.81	(10)	7.73
(2)	4.81, 4.95, 4.97	18	3.10
(a)–(d)	4.95	19, 21, 22, 25	7.147
(e)	4.95, 4.96	26	6.53
(3)	4.95, 4.96	27, 28	7.147
(4)	4.107	34(1), (2)	8.63
(a), (b)	4.81	Recital 27	4.107
(5)	4.84, 4.91	Annex I	10.35
2	4.81	s A	7.13, 7.14, 7.136, 7.137, 7.145, 7.146
(1)(a)–(c)	4.83		
(g), (h)	4.108	B	7.137, 7.146
(o)	4.81	C	7.13, 7.165
(2)	4.42, 4.84, 4.99	Dir 2005/60/EC	6.35
3	4.82	Dir 2006/46/EC	7.149
(1)	4.84	Dir 2006/48/EC	7.58, 7.62, 7.149
4	4.82, 4.84, 4.89, 4.90	art 4(1)	4.81, 7.149
(1)(a), (b)	4.89	28	7.149
(2), (3)	4.89	Dir 2006/73/EC	3.10; 6.53; 7.107.38, 7.46, 7.49, 7.58, 7.143
(6)	4.107		
5	4.91, 4.92	art 13	7.135
(1)–(5)	4.91	(2)	7.137
6	4.82, 4.93, 4.94	(b)	7.135
(1), (2)	4.93	14	7.135
7	4.82, 4.86, 4.93	16–18	7.12
(1)(a), (b)	4.86	19	7.12, 7.39
(2)	4.86	29(3)	7.42
8	4.82, 4.87	30(1)(g)	7.46
(1)(a), (b)	4.87	31(2), (3)	7.148
(2)	4.87	32	7.12, 7.46
(3)(i), (ii)	4.87	(6)	7.42, 7.47
9	4.82	43	7.12
(1)	4.108	Dir 2008/7/EC Capital duty directive	
(2)(a), (b)	4.108	art 11(a)	10.21
Dir 2003/48/EC	10.60, 10.71, 10.72, 10.78, 10.79, 10.80	12	10.21
		Dir 2008/551/EC	10.54
art 2(2)	10.73	art 7	10.54
4	10.73	(2)(a), (b)	10.54
(3)	10.73, 10.79	Dir 2009/44/EC (amends settlement finality dir)	8.109
6	10.73		
10(1)	10.74	Dir 2009/65/EC	1.9
(2)	10.77	Dir 2010/24/EU	10.54
(3)	10.74	Dir 2011/61/EU	1.9; 4.112; 7.164, 7.165, 7.171
15	10.78		
(1)	10.78	art 3(1)(n)	7.165
18	10.79	21	7.175
Dir 2004/39/EC	1.9, 1.16; 6.8, 6.53; 7.1, 7.3, 7.10, 7.14, 7.22, 7.35, 7.38, 7.49, 7.50, 7.57, 7.58, 7.60, 7.61, 7.69, 7.75, 7.76, 7.77, 7.98, 7.136, 7.137, 7.143, 7.146, 7.147, 7.158, 7.177, 7.182; 8.63; 8.51; 10.35	(8)(a)	7.168, 7.175
		(b)	7.175
		(10)	7.175
		(11)	7.169, 7.173, 7.175
		(12)	7.165, 7.166, 7.168, 7.170
		(13)	7.168, 7.173, 7.176
		(14)	7.168

REGULATIONS	
Reg 1346/2000/EC............	4.34, 4.37, 4.56, 4.59, 4.62; 5.17, 5.20, 5.21, 5.22, 5.28, 5.58, 5.73; 8.101, 8.110
art 1(1)..	5.20
(2)..	5.21
2(a)...	5.20
(g)...	5.19, 5.50
(h)...	5.18
3(1)...	5.17, 5.50
(2)...	5.18, 5.28
4(1)...	5.28
(2)(d)......................................	5.73
5	5.19, 5.49
(1)...	5.50
(4)...	5.29
6(1), (2)....................................	5.73
7	5.19
10(1)...	5.28
14	4.37
16(1), (2)....................................	5.19
17(1), (2)....................................	5.19
18(1)...	5.19
26	5.19, 5.28
Reg 1346/2000/EC – *contd*	
art 27	5.28
28	5.28
31	4.37
44(3)(b)	5.28
Recital 11	8.101
25	5.49
33	5.17
Reg 44/2001/EC............................	5.9
art 1	5.11
(2)(b), (d)	5.11
2(1)...	5.11
3(1)...	5.11
8–21	5.11
22	5.11
(1).......................................	5.11
23	5.11
Recital 13	5.11
Reg 1287/2006/EC..........................	7.10
Reg 864/2007/EC............................	5.25
Reg 593/2008/EC............................	5.25
art 10, 11	5.39
20	5.25
Reg 648/2012/EU.............	1.9, 1.26; 7.109; 8.92

Table of Cases

All references are to paragraph number

A

A-G v Bouwens (1838) 4 M & W 171, 150 ER 1380 .... 10.57
A-G v Johnson [1907] 2 KB 885 .... 5.54
A-G for Hong Kong v Reid [1994] 1 AC 324, [1993] 3 WLR 1143, [1994] 1 All ER 1 .... 5.54
A-G v South Wales Electrical Power Distribution Co [1920] 1 KB 552 .... 10.31
AIC Ltd v ITS Testing Services (UK) Ltd (The Kriti Palm) [2006] EWCA Civ 1601, [2007] 1 All ER (Comm) 667, [2007] 1 Lloyd's Rep 555 .... 6.9
Agnew v IRC *see* Brumark Investments Ltd, Re [2001] UKPC 28, [2001] 2 AC 710, [2001] 3 WLR 454
Alcock v Smith [1892] 1 Ch 238 .... 5.52
Alloway v Phillips (Inspector of Taxes) [1980] 1 WLR 888, [1980] 3 All ER 138, [1980] STC 490 .... 5.51
Anders Utkilens Rederi A/S v O/Y Lovisa Stevedoring Co A/B & Keller Bryant Transport Co Ltd (The Golfstraum) [1985] 2 All ER 669, [1985] STC 301 .... 10.45
Andrabell Ltd (in liquidation), Re [1984] 3 All ER 407 .... 6.40
Armitage v Nurse [1998] Ch 241, [1997] 3 WLR 1046, [1997] 2 All ER 705 .... 6.9, 6.10, 6.32, 6.33, 6.34, 6.37
Associated British Engineering Ltd v IRC [1941] 1 KB 15, [1940] 4 All ER 278 .... 10.16

B

BA Peters plc (in administration), Re [2008] EWHC 2205 (Ch), [2010] 1 BCLC 110, [2008] All ER (D) 392 .... 3.6
BHP Petroleum v British Steel [2000] 2 All ER (Comm) 544, [1999] 2 Lloyd's Rep 583 .... 6.72
Baker (Inspector of Taxes) v Archer-Shee [1927] AC 844 .... 5.25, 5.54
Bank of Credit & Commerce International SA (in liquidation) (No 8), Re [1995] Ch 46, [1994] 3 WLR 911, [1994] 3 All ER 565 .... 4.89
Bank of Credit & Commerce International SA (in liquidation) (No 11), Re [1997] Ch 213, [1997] 2 WLR 172, [1996] 4 All ER 796 .... 5.73
Bank of England v Cutler [1907] 1 KB 889 .... 2.40
Bankers Trust International Ltd v Todd Shipyards Corpn (The Halcyon Isle) [1981] AC 221, [1980] 3 WLR 400, [1980] 3 All ER 197 .... 5.40
Barclays Bank Ltd v Quistclose Investments Ltd [1970] AC 567, [1968] 3 WLR 1097, [1968] 3 All ER 651 .... 1.30; 3.17
Barlow Clowes International Ltd (in liquidation) v Eurotrust International Ltd [2006] UKPC 37, [2006] 1 WLR 1476, [2006] 1 All ER 333 .... 6.67
Barlow Clowes International (in liquidation) v Vaughan [1992] 4 All ER 22, [1992] BCLC 910 .... 3.55
Barnes v Tomlinson [2006] EWHC 3115 (Ch), [2007] WTLR 377, [2006] All ER (D) 95 .... 6.33
Bartlett v Barclays Bank Trust Co Ltd (No 2) [1980] Ch 515, [1980] 2 WLR 430, [1980] 2 All ER 92 .... 6.31
Bechuanaland Exploration Co v London Trading Bank Ltd [1898] 2 QB 658 .... 2.16
Bennett v Ogston (1930) 15 TC 374 .... 10.59
Bentinck v London Joint Stock Bank [1893] 2 Ch 120 .... 2.16
Berkeley Applegate (Investment Consultants) Ltd (No 1), Re [1989] Ch 32, [1988] 3 WLR 95, [1988] 3 All ER 71 .... 3.53
Bishopsgate Investment Management Ltd (in liquidation) v Maxwell (No 1) [1994] 1 All ER 261, [1993] BCC 120, [1993] BCLC 1282 .... 6.25, 6.37

Bogg v Raper (1998) 1 ITELR 267 .... 6.7
Bolkiah v KPMG [1999] 2 AC 222, [1999] 2 WLR 215, [1999] 1 All ER 517 .... 6.48
Bonham v Fishwick [2007] EWHC 1859 (Ch), (2007-08) 10 ITELR 32 .... 6.7
Booth v Ellard [1980] 1 WLR 1443, [1980] 3 All ER 569, 53 TC 393 .... 10.45
Brandao v Barnett (1846) 12 Cl & Fin 787, 8 ER 1622, 3 CB 519 .... 4.72
Brassard v Smith [1925] AC 371 .... 5.52; 10.57
Braybrooke v A-G (1861) 9 HL Cas 150, 11 ER 685 .... 10.16
Brickenden v London Loan & Savings Co [1934] 3 DLR 465 .... 6.25
Bristol & West Building Society v Mothew (t/a Stapley & Co) [1998] Ch 1, [1997]
  2 WLR 436, [1996] 3 All ER 698 .... 6.2, 6.25, 6.36, 6.37, 6.38, 6.47
British Eagle International Airlines Ltd v Compagnie Nationale Air France [1975]
  1 WLR 758, [1975] 2 All ER 390, [1975] 2 Lloyd's Rep 43 .... 4.38; 5.33; 8.102
British Road Service Ltd v Arthur V Crutchley & Co Ltd (No 1) [1968] 1 All ER 811,
  [1986] 1 Lloyd's Rep 271 .... 6.24
Brooke Bond & Co's Trust Deed, Re Brooke Bond & Co [1963] Ch 357, [1967]
  2 WLR 320, [1963] 1 All ER 454 .... 6.40, 6.51
Brown v Davies (1789) 3 Term Rep 80, 100 ER 466 .... 2.15
Brown v IRC [1965] AC 244, [1964] 3 WLR 511, [1964] 3 All ER 119 .... 3.15
Brown Shipley & Co v IRC [1895] 2 QB 598 .... 10.20
Brumark, Re sub nom Agnew v IRC [2001] UKPC 28, [2001] 2 AC 710, [2001]
  3 WLR 454 .... 4.29, 4.50, 4.71
Buckley v Gross (1863) 3 B & S 566, 122 ER 213 .... 3.45
Bulmer v CIR [1967] Ch 145, [1966] 3 WLR 672, [1966] 3 All ER 801 .... 10.45
Burdick v Garrick (1869-70) LR 5 Ch App 233 .... 3.15

C

C & E Comrs v Everwine Ltd [2003] EWCA Civ 953, [2003] All ER (D) 97, (2003)
  147 SJLB 870 .... 3.27
C & E Comrs v Guy Butler (International) Ltd (No 1) [1977] QB 377, [1976] 3 WLR
  370, [1976] 2 All ER 700 .... 2.16
CA Pacific Finance Ltd (in liquidation), Re [2000] 1 BCLC 494 .... 3.41, 3.42
Cammell v Sewell (1858) 3 Hurl & N 617, 157 ER 615 .... 5.48
Cammell v Sewell (1860) 5 Hurl & N 728, 157 ER 1371 .... 5.67
Carlos Federspiel & Co SA v Charles Twigg & Co Ltd [1957] 1 Lloyd's Rep 240 ...... 3.27
Carl Zeiss Stiftung v Rayner & Keeler Ltd [1967] 1 AC 853, [1966] 3 WLR 125,
  [1966] 2 All ER 536 .... 5.39
Carr v Carr (1811) 1 Mer 541n, 35 ER 799 .... 3.3
Chapman, Re sub nom Cocks v Chapman [1896] 2 Ch 763 .... 6.10
Charge Card Services Ltd (No 2), Re [1987] 1 Ch 150, [1986] 3 WLR 697, [1986]
  3 All ER 289 .... 4.89
Cigala's Settlement Trusts, Re (1878) 7 Ch D 351 .... 5.54
City Equitable Fire Insurance Co Ltd, Re [1925] Ch 407, [1924] All ER Rep 485 ...... 6.10
Clarke Boyce v Mouat [1994] 1 AC 428, [1993] 3 WLR 1021, [1993] 4 All ER
  268 .... 6.44, 6.47
Coggs v Bernard (1703) 2 Ld Raym 909, 92 ER 107 .... 3.11
Collins v Martin (1797) 1 Bos & P 648, 126 ER 1113 .... 2.22
Colonial Bank v Whinney (1886) 11 App Cas 426 .... 2.36
Commonwealth Bank of Australia v Smith (1991) 102 ALR 453 .... 6.47
Comr of Stamp Duties (Queensland) v Livingston [1965] AC 694, [1964] 3 WLR 963,
  [1964] 3 All ER 692 .... 5.54
Comr of Stamps v Hope [1891] AC 476 .... 5.51
Concorde Construction Co Ltd v Colgan Co Ltd (1984) 29 BLR 120 .... 3.40
Cooper v PRG Powerhouse Ltd (in creditors'voluntary liquidation) [2008] EWHC
  498 (Ch), [2008] 2 All ER (Comm) 964, [2008] BPIR 492 .... 3.6
Cosslett (Contractors) Ltd, Re [1998] Ch 495, [1998] 2 WLR 131, [1997] 4 All ER
  115 .... 4.26, 4.29
Crouch v Crédit Foncier of England Ltd (1872-73) LR 8 QB 374 .... 2.18, 2.25

D

Dearle v Hall (1828) 3 Russ 1, 38 ER 475 .... 4.45
Deddington Steamship Co Ltd v IRC [1911] 2 KB 1001 .... 10.20

Dollfus Mieg et Compagnie SA v Bank of England (No 1) [1949] Ch 369, [1949]
1 All ER 946, 66 TLR (Pt 2) 559 .... 3.10
Drexel Burnham Lambert International BV v Nasr [1986] 1 Lloyd's Rep 356............ 4.60
Dunderland Iron Ore Co Ltd, Re [1909] 1 Ch 446 .... 10.20

E
Edelstein v Schuler & Co [1902] 2 KB 144, [1900-3] All ER Rep 884 .... 2.16
Euro Hotel (Belgravia) Ltd [1975] 3 All ER 1075, [1975] STC 682, 51 TC 293 .... 10.59

F
F & K Jabbour v Custodian of Israeli Absentee Property [1954] 1 WLR 139, [1954]
1 All ER 145, 1953] 2 Lloyd's Rep 760.. 5.51
Favorke v Steinkopf [1922] 1 Ch 174.. 5.54
Foley v Hill (1848) 2 HL Cas 28, 9 ER 1002 .... 3.3
Friedlander v Texas 130 US 416 (1889) 2.21

G
Galmerrow Securities Ltd v National Westminster Bank plc [2002] WTLR 125 ..... 6.32, 6.67
Garnett v IRC (1899) 81 LT 633, 48 WR 303 .... 10.16
General Estates Co, ex p City Bank, Re (1867-68) LR 3 Ch App 758 .... 2.16
George Wimpey & Co Ltd v IRC [1975] 1 WLR 995, [1975] 2 All ER 45, [1975] STC
248.. 10.12, 10.13, 10.31
Glencore International AG v Metro Trading International Inc (No 2) [2001] 1 All ER
(Comm) 103, [2001] Lloyd's Rep 284, [2001] CLC 1732 .... 3.27, 3.45
Global Trader Europe Ltd (in liquidation), Re [2009] EWHC 602 (Ch), [2009]
2 BCLC 18, [2009] BPIR 446.. 7.85
Glynwill Investments NV v Thomson McKinnon Futures Ltd (unreported, 13 Febru-
ary 1992)... 6.54
Goldcorp Exchange Ltd (in receivership), Re [1995] 1 AC 74, [1994] 3 WLR 199,
[1994] 2 All ER 806... 3.27, 3.35, 3.36; 6.36, 6.44; 10.13
Goodman v Harvey (1836) 4 Ad & El 870, 111 ER 1011 .... 6.9
Goodwin v Robarts (1874-75) LR 10 Exch 337.. 2.16
Gorgier v Mieville (1824) 3 B & C 45, 107 ER 651 .... 2.16
Government of India, Ministry of Finance (Revenue Division) v Taylor [1955] AC
491, [1955] 2 WLR 303, [1955] 1 All ER 292 .... 10.52
Gray v G-T-P Group Ltd sub nom F2G Realisations Ltd (in liquidation), Re [2010]
EWHC 1772 (Ch), [2011] BCC 869, [2011] BCLC 313.................... 1.35; 4.102, 4.104
Great Northern Rly Co v IRC [1902] 1 KB 416.. 10.13
Grosvenor Casinos Ltd v National Bank of Abu Dhabi [2008] EWHC 511 (Comm),
[2008] 2 All ER (Comm) 112, [2008] 2 Lloyd's Rep 1 .... 6.9

H
HMRC & Comr of South African Revenue Service v Ben Nevis (Holdings) Ltd [2012]
EWHC 1807 (Ch), [2012] STC 2157, [2012] BTC 240.. 10.55
HSBC Holdings plc & The Bank of New York Mellon Corpn v HMRC [2012] UKFTT
163 (TC), [2012] SFTD 913 .... 10.16, 10.21, 10.23, 10.27,
10.40, 10.44, 10.58
HSBC Holdings plc & Vidacos Nominees Ltd v HMRC (Case C-569-07) [2008] STC
(SCD) 502, [2008] STI 190 .... 10.21, 10.23, 10.27, 10.40, 10.44
Hadley v Baxendale (1854) 9 Exch 341, 156 ER 145 .... 6.17, 6.72
Hallet's Estate, Re sub nom Knatchbull v Hallett (1880) 13 Ch D 696.............. 3.3, 3.5, 3.10
Hamlet International plc (in administration), Re sub nom Trident International Ltd v
Barlow [2000] BCC 602, [1999] 2 BCLC 506 .... 4.72
Harrods (Buenos Aires) Ltd (No 2), Re [1992] Ch 72, [1991] 3 WLR 397, [1991] 4 All
ER 334 .... 5.14
Harvard Securities Ltd (in liquidation), Re [1998] BCC 567, [1997] 2 BCLC 369...... 2.40; 3.41
Healy v Howlett & Sons [1917] 1 KB 337.. 3.27
Hedley Byrne & Co Ltd v Heller & Partners Ltd [1964] AC 465, [1963] 3 WLR 101,
[1963] 2 All ER 575.. 6.21
Henderson v Merrett Syndicates Ltd (No 1) [1995] 2 AC 145, [1994] 3 WLR 761,
[1994] 3 All ER 506 .... 6.22, 6.23, 6.44

Higgs v Northern Assam Tea Co Ltd (1868-69) LR 4 Exch 387 .... 2.16
Hinton v Dibbin (1842) 6 Jur 611, 114 ER 253, (1842) 2 QB 646 .... 6.9
Horsfall v Thomas Hey (1848) 2 Ex 778, 154 ER 705 .... 10.16
Hospital Products International Pty Ltd v United States Surgical Corpn (1984) 156 CLR 41 .... 6.41
Hotel Services v Hilton International Hotels [2000] All ER (D) 331 .... 6.72
Hunter v Moss [1993] 1 WLR 934; *aff'd* [1994] 1 WLR 452, [1994] 3 All ER 215, (1994) LSG 38 .... 2.40; 3.28, 3.37, 3.41, 3.42; 10.13

I

ILG Travel Ltd (in administration), Re [1996] BCC 21, [1995] 2 BCLC 128 .... 3.6, 3.40
IRC v Clarkson-Webb [1933] 1 KB 507 .... 10.16
IRC v G Angus & Co (1889) 23 QBD 579 .... 10.13
IRC v Maple & Co (Paris) Ltd [1908] AC 22 .... 10.6
IRC v Plummer [1980] AC 896, [1979] 3 WLR 689, [1979] STC 793 .... 10.45
Illingworth v Houdsworth *sub nom* Yorkshire Woolcombers Association, Re [1903] 2 Ch 284; *aff'd* [1904] AC 355 .... 4.29
Imperial Land Co of Marseilles, ex p Colborne, Re (1870-71) LR 11 Eq 478 .... 2.16
Indian Oil Corpn Ltd v Greenstone Shipping SA (Panama) (The Ypatianna) [1988] QB 345, [1987] 3 WLR 869, [1987] 3 All ER 893 .... 3.45
Ind's Case, Re *see* International Contract Co, Re (1871-72) LR 7 Ch App 485
Inglis v Usherwood (1801) 1 East 515, 102 ER 198 .... 5.51
International Contract Co, Re *sub nom* Ind's Case, Re (1871-72) LR 7 Ch App 485 ... 2.40

J

J Sainsbury plc v O'Connor (Inspector of Taxes) [1991] 1 WLR 963, [1991] STC 529, [1991] STC 318 .... 4.55
Jartray Developments, Re (1982) 22 BLR 134 .... 3.40
Jeavons, ex p Mackay, ex p (1872-73) LR 8 Ch App 643 .... 5.33
Jenkins (Inspector of Taxes) v Brown [1989] 1 WLR 1163, [1989] STC 577, 62 TC 226 .... 10.45
John F Hunt Demolition Ltd v ASME Engineering Ltd [2007] EWHC 1507 (TCC), [2008] Bus LR 558, [2008] 1 All ER 180 .... 6.22
Jones & Co v Coventry [1909] 2 KB 1029 .... 2.24

K

Kahler v Midland Bank Ltd [1950] AC 24, [1949] 2 All ER 621, 65 TLR 663 .... 3.10
Kayford Ltd (in liquidation), Re [1975] 1 WLR 279, [1975] 1 All ER 604, (1974) 118 SJ 752 .... 1.30; 3.17
Kelly v Cooper Associates [1993] AC 205, [1992] 3 WLR 936, [1994] 1 BCLC 395 .... 6.38, 6.41, 6.42, 6.43, 6.44, 6.53
Kelly v Rogers (Inspector of Taxes) [1935] 2 KB 446, 19 TC 692 .... 10.47
Kidson (Inspector of Taxes) v MacDonald [1974] Ch 339, [1974] 2 WLR 566, (1973) 49 TC 503 .... 10.45
Knight v Knight (184) 3 Beav 148, 49 ER 58 .... 3.27
Kwok Chi Leung Karl v Comr of Estate Duty [1988] 1 WLR 1035, [1988] STC 728, (1988) 85 (33) LSG 44 .... 5.51

L

Lang v Smyth (1831) 7 Bing 284, 131 ER 109 .... 2.21
Larussa-Chigi v CS First Boston Ltd [1998] CLC 277, [1997] All ER (D) 121 .... 7.142
Leeds City Brewery Ltd's Debenture Stock Trust Deed, Re *sub nom* Leeds City Brewery v Platts [1925] Ch 532 .... 6.10
Lehman Brothers International (Europe) (in administration), Re *sub nom* Lomas v Rab Market Cycles (Master) Fund Ltd [2009] EWHC 2545 (Ch) 3.29, 3.41, 3.48
Lehman Brothers International (Europe) (in administration), Re [2009] EWHC 3228 (Ch), [2010] BCLC 301 .... 7.86, 7.92, 7.102
Lehman Brothers International (Europe), Re [2009] EWCA Civ 1161, [2010] Bus LR 489, [2010] BCC 272 .... 3.48

Lehman Brothers International (Europe) (in administration), Re [2010] EWCA Civ
917, [2011] Bus LR 277, [2011] 2 BCLC 184 .... 7.86
Lehman Brothers International (Europe) (in administration), Re [2010] EWHC 2914
(Ch) 2.40; 3.28, 3.41
Lehman Brothers International (Europe) (in administration), Re [2011] EWCA Civ
1544, [2012] 2 BCLC 151 .... 3.28, 3.41
Lehman Brothers International (Europe) (in administration) & in the matter of
the Insolvency Act 1986 [2012] UKSC 6, [2012] Bus LR 667, [2012] 3 All
ER 1 .... 3.6; 7.85, 7.86, 7.159, 7.160
Lewis v Great Western Rly Co (1877) 3 QBD 195... 6.10
Libyan Arab Foreign Bank v Bankers Trust Co [1989] QB 728, [1989] 3 WLR 314,
[1988] 1 Lloyd's Rep 259 .... 2.16
Liggett v Kensington [1993] 1 NZLR 257.. 3.36
Linden Gardens Trust Ltd v Lenesta Sludge Disposal Ltd [1994] 1 AC 85, [1993]
3 WLR 408, [1993] 3 All ER 417 .... 4.45
Livingstone v Rawyards Coal Co (1880) 5 App Cas 25, (1880) 7 R (HL) 1 .... 6.21
Lomax (Inspector of Taxes) v Peter Dixon & Son Ltd [1943] KB 671, [1943] 2 All ER
255, 25 TC 353... 10.59
London & County Banking Co Ltd v London & River Plate Bank Ltd (1887) LR 20
QBD 232... 2.17, 2.24
London & South Western Rly Co v Gomm (1882) 20 Ch D 562................................. 10.13
London Wine Co (Shippers), Re [1986] PCC 121.............................. 3.27, 3.31, 3.33, 3.34
Lord Sudeley v A-G [1897] AC 11 .... 5.54

M

MacJordan Construction Ltd v Brookmount Erostin Ltd [1992] BCLC 350, [1994]
CLC 581, 56 BLR 1 .... 3.6, 3.40, 3.42
Macmillan Inc v Bishopsgate Investment Trust plc (No 3) [1995] 1 WLR 978, [1995]
3 All ER 747.. 5.25
Macmillan Inc v Bishopsgate Investment Trust plc (No 3) [1996] 1 WLR 387, [1996]
1 All ER 585, [1996] BCC 453... 5.26, 5.40, 5.41, 5.51, 5.52
Macmillan Inc v Bishopsgate Investment Trust plc (No 3) [1995] 1 WLR 978, [1995]
3 All ER 747.. 5.27
Marks & Spencer plc v Freshfields Bruckhaus Deringer [2004] EWHC 1337 (Ch),
[2004] 1 WLR 2331, [2004] 3 All ER 773 .... 6.48
Marquess of Northampton v Pollock (1890) 45 Ch D 190.. 4.55
Marshall (Inspector of Taxes) v Kerr [1995] 1 AC 148, [1994] 3 WLR 299, [1994]
3 All ER 106.. 5.54
Martin v Nadel [1906] 2 KB 26 .... 5.50, 5.68
Maudslay Sons & Field, Re [1900] 1 Ch 602.. 5.51
Micklefield v SAC Technology Ltd [1990] 1 WLR 1002, [1991] 1 All ER 275, [1990]
IRLR 218 .... 6.13
Midland Bank Trustee (Jersey) Ltd v Federated Pension Services [1996] Pens LR 179,
1995 Jer 352... 6.7, 6.9, 6.32
Miller v Race (1758) 1 Burr 452, 97 ER 398 .... 2.21, 2.25
Mills v Sportsdirect.com Retail Ltd (formerly Sports World International Ltd) [2010]
EWHC 1072 (Ch), [2010] 2 BCLC 143, [2010] 2 P & CR DG19 .... 3.40
Moody v Cox [1917] 2 Ch 71, [1916-17] All ER Rep 548.. 6.47

N

National Westminster Bank Ltd v Halesowen Presswork & Assemblies Ltd [1972] AC
785, [1972] 2 WLR 455, [1972] 1 All ER 641 .... 5.33
National Westminster Bank plc v Spectrum Plus Ltd (in creditors' voluntary liquida-
tion) see Spectrum Plus Ltd (in liquidation), Re [2005] UKHL 41, [2005] 2 AC
680, [2005] 3 WLR 58
Neste Oy v Lloyds Bank plc (The Tiiskeri, The Nestagas & The Enskeri) [1983]
2 Lloyd's Rep 658, [1983] Com LR 145, (1983) 133 NLJ 597 .... 3.15, 3.40
New York Life Insurance Co v Public Trustee [1924] 2 Ch 101 .... 5.51
Noakes v IRC (1900) 83 LT 714.. 10.20
Norris v Chambres (1861) 29 Beav 246, 54 ER 621 .... 5.51

O

Oakley Inc v Animal Ltd [2005] EWCA Civ 1191, [2006] Ch 337, [2006] 2 WLR 294..... 4.97

P

Parinv (Hatfield) v IRC [1996] STC 933; aff'd [1998] STC 305, (1999) 78 P & CR 169, [1998] BTC 8003 ..... 10.29
Parker v McKenna (1874-75) LR 10 Ch App 96 ..... 3.15
Pass v Dundas (1880) 43 LT 665 ..... 6.32
Photo Porduction Ltd v Securicor Transport Ltd [1980] AC 827, [1980] 2 WLR 283, [1980] 1 All ER 556 ..... 6.7
Pilcher v Rawlins (1871-72) LR 7 Ch App 259, (1872) 20 WR 281, (1872) 41 LJ Ch 485 ..... 4.45, 4.74
Portolana Compania Naviera Ltd v Vitol SA Inc (The Afrapearl) [2004] EWCA Civ 864, [2004] 1 WLR 3111, [2004] 2 All ER (Comm) 578 ..... 6.7

Q

QRS 1 ApS v Frandsen [1999] 1 WLR 2169, [1999] 3 All ER 289, [1999] STC 616.. 10.52
Queensland Mercantile & Agency Co, ex p Australian Investment Co, Re [1891] 1 Ch 536 ..... 5.40

R

R v Clowes (Peter) (No 2) [1994] 2 All ER 316 ..... 3.6
R v Williams [1942] AC 541 ..... 10.57
R (on the application of Cukorova Finance International Ltd) v HM Treasury [2008] EWHC 2567 (Admin), [2009] Eu LR 317 ..... 4.97
Raiffeisen Zentralbank Österreich AG v Five Star General Trading LLC (The Mount I) [2001] EWCA Civ 68, [2001] QB 825, [2001] 2 WLR 1344 ..... 5.26, 5.51
Rayack Construction v Lampeter Meat Co Ltd (1979) 12 BLR 30 ..... 3.40
Reed International v IRC [1976] AC 336, [1975] 3 WLR 413, [1975] 3 All ER 218 ... 10.31
Reid's Trustees v IRC (1929) 14 TC 512 ..... 10.47
Republica de Guatemala v Nunez [1927] 1 KB 669 ..... 5.40
Rossano v Manufacturers' Life Insurance Co [1963] 2 QB 352, [1962] 3 WLR 157, [1962] 2 All ER 214 ..... 10.52
Royal Brunei Airlines v Tan [1995] 2 AC 378, [1995] 3 WLR 64, [1995] 3 All ER 97 .. 6.67
Russell Cooke Trust Co v Elliot [2007] EWHC 1443 (Ch), [2007] 2 BCLC 637 ..... 4.29
Russell Cooke Trust Co v Prentis (No 1) [2002] EWHC 2227 (Ch), [2003] 2 All ER 478, [2003] WTLR 81 ..... 3.6, 3.55
Russian Bank for Foreign Trade, Re [1934] 1 Ch 720 ..... 5.51

S

Sarrio SA v Kuwait Investment Authority [1999] 1 AC 32, [1997] 3 WLR 1143, [1997] 4 All ER 929 ..... 5.14
Simmons v London Joint Stock Bank [1891] 1 Ch 270 ..... 2.16
Société Générale de Paris v Walker (1885) 11 App Cas 20 ..... 2.13
South Australian Insurance Co v Randell (1869) 16 ER 775, (1869-71) LR 3 PC 101 ... 3.3
Space Investments Ltd v Canadian Imperial Bank of Commerce Trust Co (Bahamas) Ltd [1986] 1 WLR 1072, [1986] 3 All ER 75, (1986) 2 BCC 99302 ..... 3.3, 3.6
Spectrum Plus Ltd (in liquidation), Re sub nom National Westminster Bank plc v Spectrum Plus Ltd (in creditors' voluntary liquidation) [2005] UKHL 41, [2005] 2 AC 680, [2005] 3 WLR 58 ..... 4.29, 4.50, 4.71
Speight v Gaunt (1883) 9 App Cas 1 ..... 6.30
Spence v Union Marine Insurance Co Ltd (1867-68) LR 3 CP 427 ..... 3.45
Speyer Bros v IRC [1908] AC 92 ..... 10.20
Spiliada Maritime Corpn v Cansulex Ltd (The Spiliada) [1987] AC 460, [1986] 3 WLR 972, [1986] 3 All ER 843 ..... 5.14
Spiro v Glencrown Properties [1991] Ch 537, [1991] 2 WLR 931, [1991] 1 All ER 600 ..... 10.13
Stapylton Fletcher Ltd (in administrative receivership), Re sub nom Ellis Son & Vidler Ltd (in administrative receivership), Re[1994] 1 WLR 1181, [1995] 1 All ER 192, [1994] BCC 532 ..... 3.27, 3.33, 3.34, 3.42

Stephenson (Inspector of Taxes) v Barclays Bank Trust Co Ltd [1975] 1 WLR 882, [1975] 1 All ER 625, 50 TC 374.. 10.45
Swain v Law Society [1982] 1 WLR 17, [1981] 3 All ER 797, (1981) 125 SJ 542...... 3.5
Swiss Bank Corpn v Lloyds Bank Ltd [1979] Ch 548, [1979] 3 WLR 201, [1979] 2 All ER 853; *rev'sd* [1982] AC 584, [1980] 3 WLR 457, [1980] 2 All ER 419; *aff'd* [1982] AC 584, [1981] 2 WLR 893, [1981] 2 All ER 449...................... 3.10, 3.40

T

Tai Hing Cotton Mill Ltd v Lui Chong Hing Bank Ltd (No 1) [1986] AC 80, [1985] 3 WLR 317, [1985] 2 All ER 947 .... 6.22, 6.38, 6.73
Target Holdings Ltd v Redferns [1996] AC 421, [1995] 3 WLR 352, [1995] 3 All ER 785... 6.25, 6.37, 6.44, 6.72
Texas Land & Cattle Co Ltd v IRC (1888) 16 R 69 .... 10.20
Trendtex Trading Corpn v Central Bank of Nigeria [1977] QB 529, [1977] 2 WLR 356, [1977] 1 All ER 881.. 5.14
Twinsectra Ltd v Yardley [2002] UKHL 12, [2002] 2 AC 164, [2002] 2 WLR 802.. 6.32, 6.67

V

Venables v Baring Bros & Co [1892] 3 Ch 527.. 2.16
Vickery, Re *sub nom* Vickery v Stephens [1931] 1 Ch 572, [1931] All ER Rep 562.... 6.10

W

Wait, Re [1927] 1 Ch 606 .... 3.27, 3.28
Walker v Stones [2001] QB 902, [2001] 2 WLR 623, [2000] 4 All ER 412................ 6.32
Waterman's Will Trusts, Re [1952] 2 All ER 1054, [1952] 2 TLR 877, [1952] WN 538... 6.31
Webb v Herne Bay Comrs (1869-70) LR 5 QB 642.. 2.16
Welsh Development Agency v Export Finance Co Ltd [1992] BCC 270, [1992] BCLC 148... 4.64
Westminster Bank Executor & Trustee Co (Channel Islands) Ltd v National Bank of Greece SA (1970) 46 TC 472; *aff'd* [1970] 1 QB 256, [1969] 3 WLR 468; *aff'd* [1971] AC 945, [1971] 2 WLR 105, [1971] 1 All ER 233.................................... 10.59
White v Jones [1995] 2 AC 207, [1995] 2 WLR 187, [1995] 1 All ER 691 .... 6.22
White v Shortall (2006) 9 ITELR 470 (New South Wales SC) 2.40; 3.28, 3.41, 3.42
Wigan Coal & Iron Co Ltd v IRC [1945] 1 All ER 392 .... 10.16
Wight v Olswang (No 1) (1998-99) 1 ITELR 783.. 6.7
Wilkins v Hogg (1861) 66 ER 346, 3 Giff 116.. 6.41, 6.44
Williams v Singer [1921] 1 AC 65... 10.47
Winans v A-G (No 2) [1910] AC 27 .... 10.57
Winkworth v Christie Manson & Woods Ltd [1980] Ch 496, [1980] 2 WLR 937, [1980] 1 All ER 1121.. 5.67

Y

Yorkshire Woolcombers Association Ltd, Re *see* Illingworth v Houdsworth [1903] 2 Ch 284
Young v Phillips 58 TC 232... 10.57

List of Abbreviations

1989 G30 Report	Group of 30 *Clearance and Settlement in the World's Securities Markets*, 1989
ADR	American depositary receipt
AIF	Alternative Investment Fund
AIFM	Alternative Investment Fund Manager
AIFMD	Directive 2011/61/EU on Alternative Investment Fund Managers
AIFMD Level 2 Regulation	draft EU Regulation implementing the AIFMD
AMA	Advanced Measurement Approach
Angell Report	Group of Experts on Payment Systems of the central banks of the Group of Ten countries, BIS *The Report on Netting Schemes*, 1989
ARM	approved reporting mechanism
Banking Winding Up Directive	Directive 2001/24/EC of the European Parliament and of the Council of 4 April 2001 on the reorganisation and winding up of credit institutions
Basel II	Basel Committee on Banking Supervision, International Convergence of Capital Measurement and Capital Standards: A Revised Framework (updated November 2005)
BCD	Banking Consolidation Directive (Directive 2006/48/EC of the European Parliament and the Council of 14 June 2006 relating to the taking up and pursuit of the business of credit institutions (recast))
Bernasconi Report	Christophe Bernasconi *The Law Applicable to Dispositions of Securities Held through Indirect Holding Systems*, Hague Conference on Private International Law
BIS	Bank for International Settlements
Brussels Convention	Brussels Convention on Jurisdiction and the Enforcement of Judgements
Brussels Regulation	Council Regulation 44/2001/EC on Jurisdiction and the Recognition and Enforcement of Judgments in Civil and Commercial Matters
CASS	FSA Client Assets sourcebook
CCAP	collateralised capped assured payment
CCP	central counterparty
CD	certificate of deposit

CDI	CREST dematerialised depository interest
CEBS	Committee of European Banking Supervisors
CEECSDA	Central and Eastern European Securities and Clearing Houses Association
CEO	Chief Executive Officer
CESAME	Clearing and Settlement Advisory and Monitoring Expert Group
CESR	Committee of European Securities Regulators
CESR-ECB Standards	CESR-ECB working group 'Standards for Securities Clearing and Settlement in the European Union', September 2004
CGO	Central Gilts Office
CHAPS	Clearing House Automated Payment System
Clearstream	Clearstream Banking, société anonyme
CMA	CREST cash memorandum account
CMAR	Client Money and Asset Return
CMO	Central Moneymarkets Office
CMR	FSA Client Money Rules (CASS Chapters 7 and 7A)
COBS	FSA Conduct of Business sourcebook
CREST (this is not an acronym)	The UK settlement system operated Euroclear UK & Ireland Limited
CREST Regulations	Uncertificated Securities Regulations 2001 (SI 2001/3755), as amended
CPSIPS	*Core Principles for Systemically Important Payment Systems*, January 2001
CPSS	Committee on Payment and Settlement Systems
CPSS/IOSCO Principles	CPSS/IOSCO *Principles for financial market infrastructures*, April 2012
CPSS/IOSCO Recommendations	CPSS/IOSCO Joint Task Force on Securities Settlement Systems *Recommendations for Securities Settlement Systems*, November 2001
CSD	Central Securities Depository
DBV	delivery by value
DMO	Debt Management Office (UK)
DR	depositary receipt
DTC	The Depository Trust Company
DTCC	The Depository Trust & Clearing Corporation
DTCC CCP White Paper	The Depository Trust & Clearing Corporation *Central Counterparties: Development, Cooperation and Consolidation – A White Paper to the Industry on the Future of CCPs*, October 2000
DVP	delivery versus payment
EACB	European Association of Co-operative Banks

EACH	European Association of Central Counterparty Clearing Houses
EBF	European Banking Federation
ECAG	Eurex Clearing AG
ECB	European Central Bank
ECOFIN	Council of European Finance Ministers
ECON	EU Parliament's Committee on Economic and Monetary Affairs
ECSA	European Credit Sector Association
ECSDA	European Central Securities Depositories Association
EDS	CREST eligible debt security
EEA	European Economic Area
EEA member state	At the time of writing, the EU member states and Norway, Iceland and Liechtenstein
EFTA	European Free Trade Area
EI	exposure indicator
EIB	European Investment Banks
EMIR or the European Market Infrastructure Regulation	Regulation (EU) No 648/2012 of the European Parliament and of the Council of 4 July 2012 on OTC derivatives, central counterparties and trade repositories
ESBG	European Savings Banks Group
ESCB	European System of Central Banks
ESES	Euroclear Settlement of Euronext-zone Securities
ESMA	European Securities and Markets Authority
ESF	European Securities Forum
ETF	exchange-traded fund
EU	European Union
EU member state	At the time of writing, Austria, Belgium, Bulgaria, Cyprus, Czech Republic, Denmark, Estonia, Finland, France, Germany, Greece, Hungary, Ireland, Italy, Latvia, Lithuania, Luxembourg, Malta, Netherlands, Poland, Portugal, Romania, Slovakia, Slovenia, Spain, Sweden, United Kingdom
EUI	Euroclear UK and Ireland Limited
Euroclear	Euroclear Bank, SA/NV
EUSD	Directive 2003/48/EC on the taxation of savings income in the form of interest payments
FATCA	acronym used to describe the 'Foreign Accounts Tax Compliance' provisions of the United States' Hiring Incentives to Restore Employment Act 2010
FCA	Financial Conduct Authority
FESE	Federation of European Securities Exchanges

xxxviii *List of Abbreviations*

FIBV	Fédération Internationale Des Bourses de Valeurs
Financial Collateral Directive	Directive 2002/47/EC of the European Parliament and of the Council of 6 June 2002 on financial collateral arrangements
Financial Collateral Regulations	Financial Collateral Arrangements (No 2) Regulations 2003 (SI 2003/3226)
Financial Services Action Plan	Communication of the Commission *Financial Services: Implementing the Framework for Financial Markets: Action Plan*, COM(1999) 232, 11 May 1999
FMI	financial market infrastructure
FSA	Financial Services Authority
FSB	Financial Stability Board
FSMA	Financial Services and Markets Act 2000
G30	The Group of Thirty, a private not-for-profit international body established in 1978
G30 Report	Group of Thirty Securities Clearance and Settlement Study, 1989
GDR	global depositary receipt
GEMM	gilt-edged market-maker
Giovannini 2001 Report	The Giovannini Group *Cross Border Clearing and Settlement in the European Union*, November 2001
Giovannini 2003 Report	The Giovannini Group *Second Report on EU Clearing and Settlement Arrangements*, April 2003
GSTPA	The Global Straight Through Processing Association
HMRC	Her Majesty's Revenue & Customs (in the UK)
ICSD	international central securities depository
IDO	international delivery order
IIO	international import order
IMF	International Monetary Fund
IMRO	Investment Management Regulatory Organisation Limited
Insolvency Regulation	Regulation 1346/2000/EC of 29 May 2000 on insolvency proceedings
Insurance Winding Up Directive	Directive 2001/17/EC on the reorganisation and winding up of insurance undertakings
IOSCO	International Organization of Securities Commissions
IRB Approach	Internal Ratings Based Approach
IRS	Internal Revenue Service (in the United States)
ISD	Council Directive 93/22/EEC of 10 May 1993 on investment services in the securities field
ISD Consultation Document	European Commission, Internal Market Directorate General *Overview of Proposed Adjustments to the Investment Services Directive*
ISDA	International Swaps and Derivatives Association, Inc

ISE	Irish Stock Exchange
ISIN	International Securities Identifying Number
ISSA	International Securities Services Association
Lamfalussy Netting Report	*Report of the Committee on Interbank Netting Schemes of the Central Banks of the Group of Ten Countries*, 1990
Lamfalussy Securities Markets Report	*Final Report of The Committee of Wise Men on The Regulation of European Securities Markets*, 15 February 2001
LCH	LCH.Clearnet Limited
Lugano Convention	Lugano Convention on Jurisdiction and the Enforcement of Judgments
MARD	Directive 2001/44/EC regarding Mutual Assistance Recovery
MiFID	Directive 2004/39/EC of the European Parliament and of the Council of 21 April 2004 on markets in financial instruments
MiFID2	the draft Directive to amend and replace MiFID
MiFID implementing Directive	Commission Directive 2006/73/EC of 10 August 2006 implementing Directive 2004/39/EC of the European Parliament and of the Council as regards organisational requirements and operating conditions for investment firms and defined terms for the purposes of that Directive
MiFID Regulation	Commission Regulation 1287/2006/EC of 10 August 2006 implementing Directive 2004/39/EC of the European Parliament and of the Council as regards recordkeeping obligations for investment firms, transaction reporting, market transparency, admission of financial instruments to trading, and defined terms for the purposes of that Directive
MTF	multilateral trading facility
Myners Report	Myners Report *Institutional Investment in the United Kingdom: A Review*, March 2001
NAPF	National Association of Pension Funds
NFFE	any Non-US Entity that is not a Foreign Financial Institution (for the purposes of the UK IGA)
NSCC	National Securities Clearing Corporation
OECD	Organisation for Economic Co-operation and Development
OEIC	open-ended investment company
OTC	over the counter
OTF	organised trading facility
PRA	Prudential Regulatory Authority
PRIMA	Place of the Relevant Intermediary Account
PVP	payment versus payment

List of Abbreviations

RCCP	*Recommendations for Central Counterparties*, November 2004
RCH	recognised clearing house
Regulated Activities Order	Financial Services and Markets Act 2000 (Regulated Activities) Order 2001 (SI 2001/544)
repo	repurchase agreement
Rome Convention 1980	Convention on the Law Applicable to Contractual Obligations opened for signature in Rome on 19 June 1980 (80/934/EEC)
Rome I Regulation	Regulation 593/2008/EC of the European Parliament and of the Council of 17 June 2008 on the law applicable to contractual obligations
RSSS	*Recommendations for Securities Settlement Systems*, November 2001
RTGS	real time gross settlement
Sandler Review	*Medium and Long-Term Retail Savings in the UK: A Review*, July 2002
SDRT	stamp duty reserve tax
SE	Council Regulation 2157/2001/EC of 8 October 2001 on the Statute for a European company
Securities Law Directive	the proposed European legislation to harmonise various rights in respect of securities held through intermediaries
SEMB	Stock Exchange Money Broker
Settlement Finality Directive	Directive 98/26/EC of the European Parliament and of the Council of 19 May 1998 on settlement finality in payment and securities settlement systems
SFA	Securities and Futures Authority Limited
SIB	Securities and Investments Board Limited
SIS	SIX SIS AG
SIX	SIX Swiss Exchange
SRO	self regulatory organisation
SSE	Euroclear Single Settlement Engine
SSS	securities settlement system
STP	straight through processing
SWIFT	Society for Worldwide Interbank Financial Telecommunication
SYSC	Senior Management Arrangements, Systems and Controls
TA 2000	Trustee Act 2000
TCF	Treating customers fairly (FSA term)
TFM	Transaction Flow Monitor
Third Money Laundering Directive	Directive 2005/60/EC of the European Parliament and of the Council of 26th October 2005 on the prevention

	of the use of the financial system for the purpose of money laundering and terrorist financing
UCC	Uniform Commercial Code (US)
UCITS	Undertaking for Collective Investment in Transferable Securities
UCITSIV	see UCITS Directive
UCITSV	the proposed Directive to amend and replace UCITSIV
UCITS Directive	Directive 2009/65/EC on the coordination of laws, regulations and administrative provisions relating to undertakings for collective investment in transferable securities (UCITS), as amended.
UCTA	Unfair Contract Terms Act 1977
UK	United Kingdom (England and Wales, Scotland and Northern Ireland, but not the Channel Islands or the Isle of Man)
UK IGA	Intergovernmental agreement dated 12 September 2012 signed by the United Kingdom and the United States to improve international tax compliance and to implement FATCA
UK RFI	Reporting United Kingdom Financial Institution (for the purposes of the UK IGA)
UNCITRAL	United Nations Commission on International Trade Law
UNIDROIT	*Institut International pour l'Unification du Droit Privé* (International Institute for the Unification of Private Law)
US TIN	United States tax payer identification number
Virgos Reports	M Virgos and E Schmit *Report on the Convention on Insolvency Proceedings*, 1996
x-clear	SIS x-clear AG

FSA Handbook

The FSA Handbook consists of various sections (known as sourcebooks or manuals) and guidance. At the time of writing the Handbook includes:

APER	Statements of Principle and Code of Practice for Approved Persons
BCOBS	Banking: Conduct of Business Sourcebook
BIPRU	Prudential Sourcebook for Banks, Building Societies and Investment Firms
BSOCS	Building Societies Sourcebook
BSOG	The Building Societies Regulatory Guide
CASS	Client Assets Sourcebook
COAF	Complaints against the FSA
COBS	Conduct of Business Sourcebook
COLL	Collective Investment Schemes Sourcebook
COLLG	The Collective Investment Scheme Information Guide
COMP	Compensation Sourcebook
COND	Threshold Conditions
CRAG	The Credit Rating Agencies Guide
CREDS	Credit Unions New Sourcebook
DEPP	Decision Procedure and Penalties Manual
DISP	Dispute resolution: Complaints
DTR	Disclosure Rules and Transparency Rules
EMPS	Energy Market Participants
FEES	Fees Manual
FINMAR	Financial Stability and Market Confidence Sourcebook
FIT	The Fit and Proper Test for Approved Persons
GEN	General Provisions
GENPRU	General Prudential Sourcebook
ICOBS	Insurance: New Conduct of Business
INSPRU	Prudential Sourcebook for Insurers
LR	Listing Rules
MAR	Market Conduct (including Code of Market Conduct, Stabilisation rules, Support of the Takeover Panel's Functions, Multilateral Trading Facilities, Systematic Internalisers and Disclosure regarding trades outside a regulated market or MTF)
MCOB	Mortgages and Home Finance: Conduct of Business
MIPRU	Prudential Sourcebook for Mortgage and Home Finance Firms, and Insurance Intermediaries

OMPS	Oil Market Participants
PERG	The Perimeter Guidance Manual
PR	Prospectus Rules
PRIN	Principles for Businesses
PROF	Professional Firms
RCB	Regulated Covered Bonds
REC	Recognised Investment Exchanges and Recognised Clearing Houses
RPPD	The Responsibilities of Providers and Distributors for the Fair Treatment of Customers
SERV	Service Companies
SUP	Supervision
SYSC	Senior Management Arrangements, Systems and Controls
TC	Training and Competence
TCF	Treating customers fairly
UNFCOG	The Unfair Contract Terms Regulatory Guide
UPRU	Prudential Sourcebook for UCITS Firms

CHAPTER 1

Introduction

OVERVIEW

1.1 Global custody[1] is a service whereby a financial institution assumes responsibility for the safekeeping and administration of its client's international portfolio of securities.

1   The term global custody was developed in the early 1990s. It may also be referred to as global securities services, or some other term, but the fundamental question is whether the entity providing the service is holding securities on behalf of its client.

International securities portfolios

1.2 A number of different types of institution invest in large international portfolios of investment securities. These include pension funds, charities, educational bodies such as universities, insurance companies, managed funds (both wholesale and retail), building societies, banks, and commercial companies acting through their corporate treasury operations. The size of these institutions' portfolios will inevitably grow over time, and become increasingly international, as opportunities for domestic investment fail to keep pace with demand[1].

1   See Chapter 5 for a discussion of other factors leading to increases in cross-border investment.

1.3 International investors need access to local facilities, so that they are able to liaise with the issuers of their securities in relation to corporate actions, and relevant tax authorities in relation to withholding tax (or information reporting). Such liaison is traditionally achieved through banks operating in the issuer's jurisdiction. In addition, where securities are bought and sold, the processing of such transactions frequently takes place through domestic and international electronic systems[1]. Direct access to these systems is often restricted[2].

1   These include clearing, settlement and straight through processing systems. See Chapter 8.
2   Whether on financial or operational criteria. Although this is intended to change – see CPSS/IOSCO Joint Task Force *Principles for financial market infrastructures*, April 2012, p 101, discussed in Chapter 8. (CPSS is the Committee on Payment and Settlement Systems set up in 1990 by the Governors of the central banks of the Group of Ten countries (the 'G10 Governors') to consider payment system issues, including cross-border and multicurrency interbank netting issues (the CPSS is one of the permanent central bank committees reporting to the G10 Governors); IOSCO is the International Organization of Securities Commissions, an international co-operative forum (originally set up in 1983) for securities regulatory agencies from around the world, whose aims include co-operation to promote high standards of regulation in order to maintain a just, efficient and sound market.)

Global custody

1.4 It is often impracticable and in some cases impossible for the investor itself to access all the facilities and systems necessary for the administration and settlement of its international portfolio. Rather than instruct each local bank and electronic system directly, the client appoints a global custodian to do so on its behalf, or in many cases acting through the global custodian's own local branches. The client's contractual relationship and dealings are with the custodian only, which keeps the global network behind the scenes. This offers the convenience of 'one stop shopping' to the client.

1.5 In theory, it might be possible for each local bank and electronic system to hold and/or process the assets in the client's name, dealing with the global custodian as agent. However, this is not generally the position. In most cases, the counterparty wishes to deal with the global custodian as principal, and not to take note of the identity of the ultimate clients. Reasons for this include desire to achieve administrative convenience and to limit levels of regulatory and civil law duty. Thus, the account with the local bank or electronic system is generally maintained in the name of the global custodian, usually with a general client designation. The individual entitlements of the global custodian's clients are recorded only on the records of the global custodian. Thus, the global custodian holds or controls title to the assets and, in addition to administration and settlement, the global custody service (as its name suggests) involves safekeeping.

The global custody industry

Background

1.6 Global custody was first developed in the US, in response to the regulatory needs of pension funds, including the obligation to have independent custodians. The service was developed in London in the 1980s, and today many of the leading global custodians operating in London are the UK branches of US banks. More recently, global custody has been developed on continental Europe, with several continental banks taking a leading position in the industry.

Challenges and opportunities

1.7 Since the mid-1990s, global custodians have been under pressure from a number of sources. Over-provision served to drive down fees, and increased regulatory compliance obligations have encouraged significant withdrawals from the industry. A number of mergers and business transfers have also served to reduce the number of global custodians. Establishing and maintaining the electronic systems required to provide a global custody service involves a very significant investment. Depressed market conditions reduce the enthusiasm of some global custodians for this. Meanwhile, enhancements to the post-trade infrastructure are reducing the inefficiencies to which global custody is the traditional solution[1].

1   See Chapter 8. Indeed, international settlement systems are enhancing their services so as to rival global custody, and increasing the focus on the need for harmonised regulation of settlement systems in the European Union. See for example the EU Parliament's Committee on Economic and Monetary Affairs (ECON) draft report of 13 July 2012 regarding the EU Commission proposal for a regulation on improving securities settlement in the EU and on central securities depositories.

1.8 Some smaller players remain in the field[1]. Institutional investors increasingly appoint multiple fund managers, and look for accurate measurements of their respective performances. As indicated below, global custodians are able to meet this need by presenting organised portfolio information, that enables clients to compare like with like. In an associated development, demand has grown for the performance-enhancing financial services that global custodians are able to offer, including cash management and securities lending. Another major trend is the outsourcing by fund managers of their middle and back office functions[2] to global custodians[3]. While not part of traditional global custody, outsourcing services may be provided by financial institutions from within the same business divisions as global custody services, which they may naturally complement[4]. With an ageing population across Europe, the institutional investment industry which forms the client base of global custodians is expected to grow very significantly. Legal and operational risk analysis associated with global custody is reaching new levels of sophistication and a number of new initiatives serve to enhance the operational standards in the industry[5]. A measure of the operational robustness of the major global custodians is provided by the aftermath of 11 September 2001. While the New York Stock Exchange was closed for a week, global custody operations in general continued business without significant disruption[6]. The consequences of the insolvency of a custodian are a different matter. The return of custody assets to clients of Lehman Brothers International (Europe) has taken a number of years, although this was prior to the creation of the Investment Bank Special Administration Regulations 2011[7] which have been used for the administration of entities such as MF Global Ltd respecting which the return of client assets has taken considerably less time[8].

1   Some industry commentators suggest that smaller global custodians serve the smaller institutional investors which are arguably less attractive to the major established global custodians, which may impose minimum account sizes on their client base.

2   These terms are used in the industry with a range of meanings: usually 'middle office' is taken to mean post-trade and pre-settlement functions, including matching, allocation and reporting, while 'back office' is taken to mean settlement and post-settlement functions.

3   With a view to improving efficiency and saving costs by concentrating on management, and in particular sharing development costs with the outsourcing service provider. The massive investment required by global custodians to meet the challenge of T+1 settlement, discussed in Chapter 8, is beyond the budget of many thinly capitalised fund managers. See Chapter 7 for regulatory issues surrounding outsourcing.

4   In some cases, fund managers will choose as their global custodian the institution which is able to provide outsourcing services for the middle office.

5   See Chapter 8.

6   Jonathan Brown 'Recovery wakes up to extreme risk' *Euromoney*, November 2001, 82 at 84–5.

7   See further comments on the Investment Bank Special Administration Regulations 2011 (SI 2011/245) in Chapter 3, para 3.13.

8   Although it would be simplistic to regard the difficulties with Lehman Brothers International (Europe) as resulting solely from the absence of applicable regulations. As discussed in many of the court cases arising from the administration of Lehman Brothers International (Europe), the complexity of an entity's business and failures to comply with existing regulatory requirements make the task of the insolvency officials considerably more difficult.

1.9   Over the last few years, custodians have had a large number of major developments to contend with, whether directly in terms of the impact of regulatory changes resulting from developments such as Basel III[1], or indirectly in the context of anticipating and the proposed amendments to MiFID[2], and the various initiatives requiring recovery and resolution plans ('living wills'), not to mention AIFMD[3], the proposals for UCITSV[4] and in the UK a host of FSA[5] regulatory and structural changes. There is also the need to adapt custody and settlement services provided to clients to reflect the increasing consolidation of settlement systems, the additional services provided by and new codes and standards introduced for settlement systems, and the changes in markets resulting from developments such as EMIR[6]. In addition, in the general context of disturbed markets, lack of liquidity and increased focus on risk limitation, custodians may be increasingly involved in collateral structures but equally subject to increasing competitive pressures.

1   Basel Committee on Banking Supervision, Basel III: A global regulatory framework for more resilient banks and banking systems (December 2012) (Revised June 2011).

2   Directive 2004/39/EC of the European Parliament and of the Council of 21 April 2004 on markets in financial instruments.

3   Directive 2011/61/EU of the European Parliament and of the Council of 8 June 2011 on alternative investment fund managers

4   The proposed Directive published 9 July 2012 which will amend Directive 2009/65/EC of the European Parliament and of the Council of 13 July 2009 on the coordination of laws, regulations and

4 *The Law of Global Custody*

administrative provisions relating to undertakings for collective investment in transferable securities (UCITS) (recast) (known as UCITS IV).

5   Financial Services Authority.

6   Regulation (EU) No 648/2012 of the European Parliament and of the Council of 4 July 2012 on OTC derivatives, central counterparties and trade repositories.

Development of the service

1.10   Traditional global custody comprises the core services of safekeeping and settlement[1]. Customarily associated with these are basic portfolio administration[2] together with foreign exchange services[3]. In addition, as global custodians compete to retain and expand their client base, value-added services are developed. Without these, global custodians may be unable to win new mandates. These include the cross-selling of financial products[4]; information and accounting services[5]; (crucially) collateral management[6]; tax advice[7]; reporting; and compliance monitoring and other supervisory services[8]. Global custodians have traditionally provided access to electronic settlement systems; as the post-trade infrastructure for securities develops, clients may also be provided with access to clearing[9] and straight through processing[10]. Thus, the larger global custodians are able to offer comprehensive investor services to their clients.

1   That is, the receipt and delivery of securities and cash to settle client trades, as discussed below and in Chapter 8.

2   That is, income and dividend collection and withholding tax reclamation, proxy voting, handling corporate actions and trade portfolio reporting.

3   For example, converting sale proceeds from one currency into another to finance a purchase.

4   These include cash management, cash lending, stock lending, repos (repurchase agreements), and derivatives. With contractual settlement, cash and (more rarely) securities are credited to the client's account on the date they should have been received, irrespective of the date of actual receipt.

5   Including consolidated and multi-currency record keeping, valuation and portfolio analysis including value at risk calculations and performance measurement.

6   Assisting the client in developing the potential of its portfolio to collateralise credit exposures and thereby raise finance, whether from third parties or from the global custodian, as discussed in Chapter 4.

7   In practice, global custodians may provide significant guidance and assistance to clients in relation to withholding tax (and information reporting). However, they may not wish to assume legal responsibility for giving tax advice. See Chapter 10 for a discussion of withholding tax.

8   For example, the custodian may agree to monitor a fund manager's compliance with a fund's investment powers, or (less commonly) assume express responsibility to a fund client for monitoring the compliance of the investment manager with investment powers and guidelines. It is crucial clearly to define the scope of any such duties: see the discussion in Chapter 7 and (in relation to straight through processing) Chapter 8.

9   Access to clearing would often be provided by a broker associated with the global custodian.

10 By global custodians acting as 'concentrators': see the discussion in Chapter 8.

Other custody functions

1.11   Financial institutions may hold securities and related assets for clients in contexts other than global custody. Very large sections of the securities markets involve repackaging, whereby new securities are issued on the economic basis of other underlying securities. Important examples include depositary receipts (in which a depositary holds legal title to underlying shares[1] on behalf of the holders of depositary receipts issued by it); and structured notes (in which a custodian holds underlying assets on behalf of a special purpose vehicle issuing notes)[2]. Safekeeping of securities portfolios may also arise in the context of investment funds and collateral structures[3].

1 Or debt securities. In some structures, the underlying assets may consist of securities and a guarantee or insurance policy, so that the instrument representing such assets has a better credit rating than the relevant securities.

2 Although this structure may also be in the form of a synthetic structure, where in place of underlying assets held in custody, credit derivatives and other derivatives are used to back the new notes.

3 See Chapter 4.

1.12 A very rudimentary analysis of the current service providers involved in the safekeeping of securities and related assets might divide the players into the (primarily) large bank entities (often providing a full global custody service); small custodians historically offering chiefly intra-group services[1]; and trustee entities used in the context of capital market issues. Thus, the introduction of custodial intermediaries serves a range of operational functions beyond the portfolio administration traditionally associated with global custody. In any case, it is important to note that such intermediation also fundamentally changes the nature of the client's asset, as discussed in Chapters 2 and 3.

1 Non-bank custodians also include brokers, and some fund managers who provide custody in-house for their clients. Smaller institutions may also offer global custody services.

THE LEGAL ANALYSIS

Electronic, intermediated, cross-border securities markets

1.13 As discussed in Chapters 2 and 3, global custodians and the systems which they use operate in an electronic, intermediated, and cross-border environment. A major source of legal risk here is legal anachronism. While banks have provided investment custody services for centuries, the traditional legal analysis of such arrangements is outdated. Many of the relevant cases date from an era when banker's custody meant promissory notes in strong boxes. The ideas judicially developed in those cases (relating to the ownership, safekeeping, transfer, and use as collateral, of such securities) rested on the assumption that paper documentation, and therefore physical possession, were involved.

1.14 Today, physical assets have been replaced by electronic records[1]. This alters the traditional analysis of the nature of the investor's asset, her relationship with the custodian, and the duties of the custodian to the client[2]. Moreover, '[c]ross-border holdings of securities often involve several layers of intermediaries acting as custodians'[3]. Thus, the asset in which the investor has an interest may generate credit entries in accounts maintained by a number of intermediaries. In turn, these intermediaries may operate in different jurisdictions. This multiplication of databases has raised questions concerning the true nature of the investor's asset, and where it is legally located. It is necessary to answer these questions in order to address legal risk in cross-border securities collateral arrangements[4]. Issues may also arise in connection with structures involving intermediated holdings of securities, including from a fiscal perspective[5].

1 See Chapter 2.

2 See Chapters 2, 3 and 6 respectively.

3 'In a direct holding system, each beneficial or direct owner of the security is known to the CSD or the issuer. In some countries, the use of direct holding systems is required by law. Alternatively, an indirect holding system employs a multi-tiered arrangement for the custody and transfer of ownership of securities (or the transfer of similar interests therein) in which investors are identified

6   The Law of Global Custody

only at the level of their custodian or intermediary. In either system, the shareholder list may be maintained by the issuer, CSD, securities registrar, or transfer agent.' CPSS/IOSCO *Principles for financial market infrastructures*, April 2012 ('CSD means Central Securities Depository').

4   See Chapter 5.

5   See discussion in Chapter 10 regarding *HSBC Holdings plc and The Bank of New York Mellon Corporation v HMRC* [2012] UKFTT 163 (TC).

Analytic and law reform context

1.15   The first edition of this book was written at a time[1] when the legal analysis of the above issues in this jurisdiction was limited, although in the US an important debate had surrounded the 1994 revision of Pt 8 of the Uniform Commercial Code[2]. Since that time, tremendous international and UK industry, public sector, and academic attention has turned to the subject, generating considerable literature, particularly in relation to settlement issues, and in recent years the insolvencies of a number of significant market players and the associated market disruptions have focused a great deal of attention on the safety of client assets held by third parties and the ability to recover such assets on insolvency. There have also been important law reform initiatives seeking to address insolvency risk and to clarify the applicable conflict of laws rules[3].

1   The first edition of this book was published in 1996 and was based on a PhD thesis, drawing on Dr Joanna Benjamin's experience in legal practice.

2   See, for example, C W Mooney *Beyond Negotiability* (1990) 12 Cardozo Law Review 2; J Rogers 'Policy Perspective on the Revised UCC Article 8' UCLALR, June 1996, 1413.

3   These are discussed in Chapters 4 and 5, and include Directive 2002/47/EC of the European Parliament and of the Council of 6 June 2002 on financial collateral arrangements (the Financial Collateral Directive). Other important developments include the UK Banking Act 2009, and similar legislation in other jurisdictions designed to improve the process for handling banks in financial difficulties, and special insolvency procedures such as the Investment Bank Special Administration Regulations 2011 (SI 2011/245) and Investment Bank Special Administration (England and Wales) Rules 2011 (SI 2011/1301). See also discussion of the proposed Securities Law Directive in Chapter 7.

Scope

1.16   For the purposes of the discussions in this book, for the most part it is assumed that the global custodian operates in London and that English law governs the global custody contract. The impact of the electronic environment on securities is considered in Chapter 2, and on the custody relationship in Chapter 3. Chapter 4 discusses the use of the custody portfolio as collateral. Chapter 5 considers cross-border issues, particularly in relation to collateral and sub-custodian insolvency. The custodian's duties at general law are discussed in Chapter 6, and under the regulatory regime established under the Financial Services and Markets Act 2000 (including the impact of MiFID[1]) in Chapter 7. Chapter 8 gives a brief overview of the post-trade infrastructure, while Chapter 9 considers CREST. Taxation (including the impact of FATCA) is discussed in Chapter 10; some concluding observations are set out in Chapter 11.

1   Directive 2004/39/EC of the European Parliament and of the Council of 21 April 2004 on markets in financial instruments.

Changes from the third edition

1.17   The third edition of *The Law of Global Custody* was published in 2009. As already indicated, there have been very significant legal and operational changes since that time, in response to which this work has been revised and updated. The first edition was written by Dr Joanna Benjamin alone, the second edition involved in addition Madeleine Yates (primarily responsible for Chapter 7 (regulation), Chapter 9 (settlement systems) and, jointly with Dr Benjamin, Chapter 6 (duties)) and Gerald Montagu (responsible for Chapter 10 (taxation)). Both the third and fourth editions were updated by Madeleine Yates, apart from Chapter 10 (taxation) which is the work of Gerald Montagu.

FUNDAMENTAL CONCEPTS

1.18 The legal analysis of international securities settlement, clearing, custody, and collateral is sometimes regarded as a highly technical specialised area, impenetrable to outsiders. This is not wholly true. Half the battle is mastering the jargon and, in order to assist the non-specialist reader, this section will consider the key operational and legal concepts that inform this area. As a brief introduction to these concepts, this section is necessarily simplistic. It will not assist the experienced reader, and does not do justice to the subtlety of many of the issues involved. However, it may prove useful to the beginner as a basis from which to go on to further reading, some of which is indicated in the footnotes.

1.19 This section will briefly consider the following: the nature of securities; securities trading, clearing and settlement; personal rights, property rights and insolvency; securities collateral; possession; and legal categories of assets.

The nature of securities[1]

1.20 The services, products and arrangements discussed in this book all concern securities; this discussion will therefore start with the nature of securities. Securities are a form of transferable financial asset, of which equities and bonds are the most common examples[2]. When a company, government agency or other institution wishes to raise capital, it may consider borrowing from a bank. However, bank lending is in general comparatively expensive and short term. An alternative is to raise capital by issuing securities. In this case, new assets in the form of intangible rights, known as securities, are issued (ie created) and delivered either to members of the public (in a public offer) or selected investors (in a private placement) in exchange for cash. The issuer obtains a large sum of capital in the form of the aggregate issue price of the securities.

1   For a more detailed discussion of the nature of securities and the securities markets, see: R Tennekoon *The Law and Regulation of International Finance* (2006, 3rd edn, Tottel Publishing); J Benjamin *Financial Law* (2007, Oxford University Press); C Bamford *Principles of International Law* (2011, Oxford University Press); D Adams *College of Law LPC: Banking and Capital Markets 2012* (2012, College of Law Publishing); and *Financial Markets and Exchanges Law* (edited by M Blair and G Walker, 2012, Oxford University Press).

2   For a note of the historic development of the meaning of the term 'securities', see J Benjamin *Interests in Securities* (2000, Oxford University Press).

Debt and equity

1.21 In terms of holders' rights, securities are divided into two broad categories, namely debt and equity[1]. In the case of debt securities, investors are owed a debt by the issuer, and the relationship between the holder and the issuer is that of creditor and debtor. The terms of issue of the securities characteristically entitle the holders to the repayment of the principal sum (usually at a specified maturity date) and also to regular interest payments. In addition, depending on the terms of issue of the debt securities, holders are usually entitled to other rights, including the right to vote at holders' meetings and to receive certain information from the issuer.

1   Certain types of securities have characteristics of both debt and equity. Examples of such 'hybrid' securities are preference shares, convertible bonds, and equity warrants.

1.22   Equity securities (also known as shares) may only be issued by companies. The holder of equities is an ordinary shareholder in the issuing company. Ordinary shareholders are entitled to a return of their capital only on the company's winding up, and are paid only after all creditors of the company have been paid first, and then only to the extent that sufficient assets are available. Shareholders do not have an automatic right to income, and are paid income in the form of dividends at the discretion of the directors of the company in accordance with company law, depending on the company's profitability. However, if the value of the company increases over time, this will be reflected in the value of the shares, so that shareholders may have the prospect of capital growth. Also, shareholders generally have voting rights, and other rights protected by company law[1]. From an issuer's perspective a significant difference between debt and equity funding is that a tax deduction may be available with respect to interest paid on a debt security, whereas dividends on equity are paid out of post-tax profits.

1   'A share is an item of intangible property. It is itself a "bundle of rights", giving the shareholder neither ownership of the company's assets nor ownership of the company as a "thing", but attracting to itself the protection of the law to a degree that warrants the label "property"': Sarah Worthington 'Shares and Shareholders: Property, Power and Entitlement, Part 1' (2001) Comp Law 22(9) at 258.

Bearer and registered securities

1.23   Securities are also categorised according to another basic distinction, namely that between bearer and registered securities. This distinction relates to the manner in which securities are traditionally evidenced and transferred. In the case of a security in bearer form, the issuer creates a physical instrument (ie a formal document), which in legal theory constitutes the security. The security is held by whoever holds the instrument from time to time, and the security is transferred simply by transferring possession of the instrument. In the case of registered securities, the issuer (or, more commonly, a registrar acting as its agent) maintains a database (known as a register) in which the names of the holders from time to time are recorded. In order to transfer registered securities, it is necessary for the register to be amended, so as to show the name of the transferee in the place of the name of the transferor in respect of the securities in question.

Computerisation

1.24   The practice of evidencing and transferring holdings of securities has been radically altered by the computerisation of the securities markets. Chapter 2 considers this development, and its implications for the legal nature of securities.

Securities trading, clearing and settlement

Trading

1.25   The issue of new securities is known as primary market activity. Of course, the first holder of securities may decide to hold them indefinitely or to maturity. However, in many cases, the holders of securities wish to realise their investment by sale. The securities are transferred to the third party, who becomes their holder in place of the original holder. In exchange for this, the third party pays the original holder a purchase price. The sale of securities from holder to holder is known as securities trading, and occurs in the secondary markets. Much secondary market activity takes place on organised and officially recognised markets known as stock exchanges. However, securities are also frequently bought and sold away from stock exchanges through electronic networks and multilateral trading facilities (MTFs).

Clearing

1.26 Clearing is a function that is now common in securities markets[1]. Where clearing is provided, it operates after trading and before delivery (or settlement, as discussed below). Broadly, clearing generally involves techniques designed to address the risk of counterparty default after trading and before settlement, primarily through the netting of obligations, and the use of a well-capitalised intermediary, known as a clearing house. The clearing house assumes the contractual obligations of each party (ie it is bound both as buyer to the seller, and seller to the buyer) to settle the trade. This means that even if one party defaults post-trade and pre-settlement, settlement will still go ahead. Clearing is discussed in Chapter 8.

1 Clearing has long been a feature of the derivatives markets, and a new regime requiring clearing in relation to standardised over-the-counter (OTC) derivatives contracts is imposed by Regulation (EU) No 648/2012 of the European Parliament and of the Council of 4 July 2012 on OTC derivatives, central counterparties and trade repositories (know as EMIR).

Settlement

1.27 Settlement means delivery (usually against payment). Once a trade has taken place, the buyer is contractually bound to deliver the securities to the seller, and the seller is contractually bound to pay the purchase price to the seller. It is then necessary to arrange for delivery and payment to take place, in order to discharge these contractual obligations. Whereas securities trades generally take place on markets, securities settlement generally takes place through electronic systems known as settlement systems, which are designed to avoid the delays and inconvenience of paper-based settlement, and to synchronise the payment and delivery side of each transaction ('delivery versus payment'). Settlement is discussed in Chapter 8.

Personal rights, property rights, and insolvency[1]

1.28 The following is an extremely brief discussion of a complex area of law, and is intended for elementary guidance only. Private legal rights are divided into two fundamental categories, namely personal rights and property rights. In the financial markets, the main practical importance of the difference between personal and property rights relates to insolvency.

1 For discussions of these issues, see R M Goode 'Ownership and Obligation in Commercial Transactions' (1987) 103 LQR 433 and *Legal Problems of Credit and Security* (2008, 4th edn, Sweet & Maxwell), and L Gullifer *Intermediated Securities: Legal Problems and Practical Issues* (2011, Hart Publishing). A huge theoretical literature exists in this area. Particularly recommended are K Gray 'Property in Thin Air' (1991) CLJ 252; and Wesley Newcomb Hohfeld *Fundamental Legal Conceptions* (2000, The Lawbook Exchange, Ltd) (first printed 1919). For a discussion of property rights in relation to securities and interests in securities, see J Benjamin *Interests in Securities* (2000, Oxford University Press).

Personal rights

1.29 A personal right, as its name suggests, is a right which is enforceable against a person (whether a natural person or a legal person such as an incorporated company).

An example of a personal right is a debt. In commercial practice, a personal right is only as good as one's ability successfully to enforce it against the person who owes it (known as the obligor)[1]. Crucially, if the obligor becomes insolvent, the value of a personal right in general[2] is reduced and may become worthless. The holder of the personal right (the obligee) may be paid late, only in part, or indeed not at all, depending on the outcome of the insolvency proceedings. The risk that personal rights may lose their value in the obligor's insolvency is known as credit risk.

1   Of course, the obligee may seek to sell its personal right to a third party, but the purchase price she is able to obtain will in practice reflect the prospects of successful enforcement.

2   However, rights of insolvency set-off may be available in some circumstances.

Property rights

1.30 In contrast, a property right is a right which is enforceable directly against an asset. An example of a property right is ownership; another example is a mortgage. In the financial markets, the great advantage of property rights is that they are not subject to credit risk, and are in general not affected by the insolvency of third parties. For example, if I *own* 100 bonds which you hold on my behalf, my rights to the bonds are proprietary[1], and should not be affected by your insolvency[2]. On the other hand, if you *owe* me 100 bonds (eg under an unsettled trade), my rights are merely personal, and may be defeated by your insolvency.

1   In this example, I have property rights against you in relation to the bonds. However, the issuer of the bonds owes only personal rights under their terms of issue: this is discussed further below and in Chapter 5.

2   Assets belonging to clients of an insolvent entity do not form part of the insolvent entity's estate, and are not available to creditors. See, for example, *Barclays Bank Ltd v Quistclose Investments Ltd* [1970] AC 567, [1968] 3 WLR 1097, [1968] 3 All ER 651; and *Re Kayford Ltd* [1975] 1 WLR 279, [1975] 1 All ER 604. In the case of a bankrupt individual, see Insolvency Act 1986, s 283(3)(a).

1.31 In the securities markets, two contexts in which the successful assertion of property rights is crucial are custody and settlement. The custody client is not willing to take the credit risk of the custodian in relation to its portfolio of securities. For this reason, it is important that, as against the custodian, the rights of the client are proprietary. This is discussed in detail in Chapter 3. In the context of settlement, it is important for the purchaser to be confident that the insolvency of the vendor will not affect her rights in the settled securities[1]. For this reason, it is crucial that, as against the vendor, the rights of the purchaser of securities are, upon settlement, proprietary[2].

1   Particularly if the price of those securities has risen since the trade was concluded, so that the trade is profitable for the purchaser.

2   See Chapter 8.

1.32 Another context in which property rights are of central important is securities collateral.

Securities collateral

1.33 Collateralisation is a technique which is designed to address credit risk. Where A owes B a personal obligation, B bears A's credit risk. B may address this by requiring A to deliver to B property rights in identified assets which serve as collateral. In the event that A becomes insolvent or otherwise defaults, B will be able to enforce her property rights against the assets, and thereby avoid suffering loss through A's default[1]. Thus collateralisation involves the use of property rights to support personal rights, and thereby address credit risk.

1   The position may also need to be analysed from the opposite perspective: if the collateral is provided by A to B, is there any risk to A in relation to the collateral if B is insolvent?

1.34 The question arises, what assets should serve as collateral? Securities are an important and increasingly popular form of collateral, provided they are of a type which is easy to value and highly liquid (ie easy to deliver). Securities collateral is discussed in detail in Chapter 4.

Possession

1.35 Possession is a legal concept[1] which is related to property, but distinct from it[2]. As indicated above, property comprises legal rights in relation to assets, such as rights of ownership. In contrast, possession is (broadly speaking) physical control of a tangible asset (ie an asset which one can touch). Whereas property is a question of law, possession is (in part) a question of fact. For example, if A lends B her watch, A remains the owner of the watch, but B has possession. If B places A's watch on her own wrist, B has physical control. Because A retains the right to call for the return of her watch at any time[3], she has the ability to recover possession. In legal terms, while B has *actual* possession, A has *constructive* possession. Another example of constructive possession is where goods are stored in a warehouse, and the warehouse keeper (who has actual possession) acknowledges[4] that she holds the goods for a client: in this case, the client has constructive possession[5].

1   For old but unsurpassed discussion of possession, see Sir Frederick Pollock *An Essay on Possession in the Common Law* (1888, Clarendon Press). Note that, notwithstanding the case of *Gray v G-T-P Group Ltd, Re F2G Realisations Ltd (in liquidation)* [2010] EWHC 1772 (Ch) and the concept of possession under the Financial Collateral Regulations 2003 (SI 2003/3226), the meaning of possession for the purposes of the Financial Collateral Regulations is in fact a question of European law (see further discussion in Chapter 4, paras 4.101–4.105).

2   For further discussion of the relationship between possession and property, see N Palmer 'Possessory Title' in Palmer and McKendrick *Interests in Goods* (1998, 2nd edn, LLP).

3   But not otherwise.

4   Such acknowledgment is known as attornment.

5   'A person has actual possession (*de facto* possession, possession in fact) of a thing when he exercises physical control over it ... A person has constructive possession ... when someone representing him has actual possession of the thing': *Jowitt's Dictionary of English Law* (1985, 2nd edn, Sweet & Maxwell) under 'Possession'.

1.36 As discussed in Chapter 3, the traditional legal analysis of custody was based on possession, as were many important securities delivery and collateral arrangements (particularly negotiation and pledge). However, as Chapters 2 and 3 will argue, the computerisation of the securities markets has in many cases replaced physical instruments (which may be subject to possession) with electronic records (which may not)[1]. This has very significantly reduced the importance of possession in these markets, and altered the legal nature of relationships between market participants and their assets. Failure to appreciate this is a source of legal risk.

1   The proposition that an intangible may not be subject to possession is developed in Chapter 3. See also comments in Chapter 4, para 4.103.

Legal categories of assets

1.37 Assets are divided into broad legal categories. Roughly speaking, *real assets* comprise freehold land and related assets[1], and *personal* assets comprise all other asset types. Personal assets are in turn sub-divided into tangible personal assets (known as goods, or 'choses in possession') and intangible personal assets (known as claims, or 'choses in action')[2]. The key point here is that the computerisation of the securities markets has converted clients' investment assets from (in the case of traditional bearer securities) choses in possession into choses in action.

1   Such as certain rights of way.

2   Tangible personal assets are called choses in possession because rights in them can be enforced by physically seizing the assets, or taking possession. Intangible personal assets are called choses in action, because the normal way to enforce them is to sue, or take legal action.

1.38   It is important to note that any type of asset may be the subject of property rights[1]. Some commentators have questioned whether claims may be subject to property rights. Of course, as against the obligor, a claim confers only personal rights. However, a wide variety of commercial structures involve intermediation, whereby claims are held through third parties. For example, an investor may hold her debt securities through a custodian. She does not take the credit risk of the custodian because, *as against it*, her rights are proprietary. This is developed in Chapter 3. Also, the investor may borrow money from a bank and collateralise that debt by granting a security interest in her bond portfolio. In her insolvency, the bank is able to enforce its rights against the portfolio because *as against the investor*, its rights are proprietary. This is developed in Chapter 4.

1   Things of value which may not be subject to property rights, such as human lives or clean air, are not assets.

CHAPTER 2

Securities in the electronic environment – how transfers occur

2.1 In the late twentieth century and the new millennium, securities and related assets have seen a growing trend towards computerisation. Paper instruments and certificates have been replaced by electronic records. Because these records are in general maintained by intermediaries and not by issuers, increased computerisation means increased intermediation.

2.2 The trend towards computerisation is driven by the ever increasing systems capacity of electronic technology[1]. However, it has far-reaching legal consequences. In the absence of clarifying legislation and case law, these consequences have not always been fully analysed[2].

1   A vivid example of the rapid and extensive developments in technology is the fact that Voyager 1, launched in 1977, has only about 68kb of computer memory (voyager.jpl.nasa.gov/faq).
2   An interesting sequence of analysis can be seen in J Benjamin 'Negotiability and Computerisation' (1995) 10 JIBFL 253–357; R M Goode 'The Nature and Transfer of Rights in Dematerialised and Immobilised Securities' (1996) 10 JIBFL 167; J Benjamin *Interests in Securities* (2000, Oxford University Press), chs 2 and 3; and S L Schwarcz 'Intermediary Risk in a Global Economy' (2001) 50 Duke LJ 1541; E Micheler 'Farewell Quasi-Negotiability? Legal Title and Transfer of Shares in a Paperless World' (2002) JBL 358; G Davies 'Using Intermediated Securities as Collateral: equitable interests with inequitable results' (2007) 2 JIBFL 70.

2.3 Two types of legal consequence are considered in this book. These are changes to the legal nature of the investors' assets (which are discussed in this chapter); and changes to the legal nature of the relationship between investors and their custodians (which are discussed in the following chapter).

2.4 Commercial arrangements relating to computerised securities often operate cross-border, and a legal analysis of them necessarily involves a consideration of private international law. However, the starting point of this analysis is the position under English domestic law, and the following discussion is made on the basis that English domestic law governs the commercial arrangements relating to computerised securities. While somewhat artificial, it is a necessary preliminary to a consideration of the position under English private international law, which will follow in Chapter 4.

IMMOBILISATION AND DEMATERIALISATION

2.5 The original cause of the computerisation of securities and related assets is the need for efficient settlement. As discussed in Chapter 8, the settlement of securities used to involve the physical movement of paper instruments[1], certificates[2], and transfer forms. By the late twentieth century the delays and other inefficiencies associated with paper-based settlement became intolerable to the developed securities markets, and the transition to electronic settlement gathered pace. The original terms of the debate concerning electronic settlement were set by a seminal report of the Group of 30 in 1989 entitled *Clearance and Settlement in the World's Securities Markets* (the '1989 G30 Report'). This identified two broad models of electronic settlement, namely immobilisation and dematerialisation[3]. A feature shared by both immobilisation and dematerialisation is book entry transfer.

1   As discussed below, instruments are the formal legal documents which constitute bearer securities in traditional form.

2   As discussed below, certificates are the documents which evidence, but do not constitute, registered securities in traditional form.

3   Chapter 8 considers this together with subsequent developments in the post trade infrastructure.

Book entry transfer

2.6   Book entry transfer involves an electronic system known as a settlement system. The settlement system maintains accounts in favour of market participants (and/or their nominees and custodians). When participant 1 wishes to transfer assets to participant 2, both participants send matching electronic instructions to the settlement system. Provided sufficient assets are available in the relevant accounts, the settlement system then debits the account of participant 1 and credits that of participant 2. Account entries are colloquially known as 'book entries', and because the legal effect of such debits and credits is to transfer property rights in relation to the assets from participant 1 to participant 2, this arrangement is known as book entry transfer.

Immobilisation

2.7   The 1989 G30 Report defined immobilisation as: 'The storage of securities certificates in a vault in order to eliminate physical movement of certificates/documents on transfer of ownership.' With immobilisation, paper instruments and/or certificates exist, but they no longer move from person to person in the secondary markets. Instead, they are retained by a depositary which is linked to a settlement system. Property rights in relation to the immobilised securities move between participants in the settlement system by book entry transfer.

2.8   The majority of immobilised securities are issued in global form. This means that a single paper instrument or certificate exists in respect of the entire issue of securities. Such 'globals' are distinguished from 'definitives', ie individual securities in traditional form.

2.9   The original reason for issuing globals instead of definitives was the desire to avoid adverse US taxation and regulatory consequences in the international securities markets. It used to be customary, in the case of *temporary* global securities, for definitives to be issued to the depositary at the end of a 40-day 'lock up' period, upon certification by the settlement system (in practice, Euroclear and/or Clearstream) that the participants for whom definitives were to be issued had in turn certified that the investments were not beneficially owned by US persons. Further, while definitives were security printed, globals were not. Because of the expense and delay involved in security printing, international debt securities are today generally issued in *permanent* global form. This means that, in the absence of issuer or settlement system default, definitives are never issued. A *temporary* global would be exchangeable wholly or in part at the request of the holder for definitives, and would be reduced in value pro rata by the value of definitives issued in exchange. Partial exchanges were endorsed on the global, which would be cancelled when it was exchanged in full. In contrast, a *permanent* global is generally only exchangeable for definitives upon default[1].

1   However, if the issuer fails to issue definitives on default, the following enforcement problem arises. Investors generally have no locus standi against the issuer, as they are not the holders of the securities which are held through intermediaries standing between them and the issuer. Their rights

under the global may be enforced through a trustee (in cases where a trustee is appointed). Where no trustee is appointed, the rights of investors under the global can only be enforced through the settlement system or its depositary. In practice such entities are unwilling to enforce on behalf of investors, as they do not consider this to be part of their role and the settlement system depositary does not have a direct relationship with the investors.

To overcome this problem, it is usually provided that, if the issuer fails to issue definitives within 30 days of default, the obligations of the issuer under the global will become void; in their place, new obligations on the issuer arise under a deed poll executed directly in favour of investors (ie participants in Euroclear and Clearstream having entitlements under the global credited to their accounts). The effect of such provision is sometimes referred to as 'the disappearing global'. Note that this describes the general approach for debt instruments. In different areas of the market, the approach may vary. For example, in relation to depositary receipts, while the general structure is similar in that depositary receipts are commonly issued in global form for settlement through a settlement system, the default and enforcement mechanism is not the same. Broadly, aside from settlement system failure, an investor's main method of recourse is to request cancellation of its depositary receipts and obtain the underlying securities represented by such receipts. (In a depositary structure, the depositary issuing the depositary receipts is essentially acting as a conduit only.)

Dematerialisation

2.10 Dematerialisation is defined as follows in the 1989 G30 Report:

'The elimination of physical certificates or documents of title which represent ownership of securities so that securities exist only as computer records.'

2.11 In the UK, examples of dematerialised registered securities are equities and gilts within CREST.

2.12 Securities may be held through a chain of intermediaries with a large number of links. For the sake of simplicity, the term 'investor' will be taken here to mean an investor whose interest is as direct as possible, ie the participant in the settlement system to whose account the assets are credited.

2.13 This chapter will seek to establish the effect of computerisation on the legal nature of investors' interests in securities. The issue falls naturally into two parts, as securities fall into two categories: bearer securities and registered securities. As indicated in Chapter 1, the difference between them may be summarised as relating to the procedure for their legal transfer. A bearer security promises on its face to pay the bearer (ie the holder) of the instrument, and the chose in action (ie the claim) against the issuer is considered at law to be locked up in the instrument. Because they consist of tangible instruments, bearer securities are categorised as choses in possession. In general, whoever possesses the instrument legally owns the bearer security, which is transferable by delivery of the instrument. In this sense, bearer instruments are like paper money. Examples of bearer securities are bearer bonds and certificates of deposit. In contrast, legal ownership of registered securities is determined prima facie by the register of holders maintained by or on behalf of the issuer[1]. In order legally to transfer a registered security, it is necessary for the register to be amended in favour of the transferee. Examples of registered securities are equities[2] and gilts[3]. Bearer securities will be considered briefly in paras **2.14–2.34** and registered securities in paras **2.35–2.36** below.

1 Société Générale de Paris v Walker (1885) 11 App Cas 20. While certificates may be issued, they are not documents of title, but merely documents evidencing title.
2 That is, ordinary shares of companies.
3 That is, registered debt securities issued by the government of the UK.

BEARER SECURITIES IN THE ELECTRONIC ENVIRONMENT

2.14 The most important example of bearer securities in the electronic environment is in the eurobond markets, where most securities are both immobilised and issued in global form. The major impact of computerisation on investors' interests in bearer securities appears to be the loss of negotiable status. In this discussion the term 'computerised bearer securities' will mean the assets of investors (being participants in a settlement system) which are derived from bearer securities[1] and bearer securities not in electronic form will be referred to as traditional bearer securities.

1 Derived because (in the case of immobilised securities) the underlying securities are in bearer form or (in the case of global securities) the definitive securities are, or would if issued be, in bearer form. As explained at paras **2.37–2.40** below, it is assumed for the purposes of this discussion that the arrangements are fungible, in the sense that there is no allocation between a particular participant and a particular underlying instrument. Non-fungible arrangements are less common today. An earlier example in the UK was the Central Moneymarkets Office ('CMO') in which physical instruments retained their negotiable status, whereas fungible computerised bearer securities in the CMO and (after the merger of the CMO into CREST in 2003) in CREST, it is argued, do not.

Negotiability

2.15 The secondary markets in bearer securities have traditionally benefited from the doctrine of negotiability. A negotiable instrument has two attractive features. First, it is transferable without formalities[1]. Second, honest acquisition confers good title (even if the transferor did not have good title)[2]. Thus, market transfers are informal and reliable. The holder in due course[3] takes the instrument free from prior equities or defects in the title of the transferor. The general view is that these benefits are *not* available to securities which are not negotiable instruments[4].

1 By physical delivery, or by endorsement and delivery in the case of certain instruments requiring endorsement, such as cheques.

2 Provided the instrument is negotiated (ie transferred) prior to maturity: see *Brown v Davies* (1789) 100 ER 466.

3 That is, broadly, the good faith purchaser. See Bills of Exchange Act 1882, s 29(1).

4 See, however, E Micheler 'Farewell Quasi-Negotiability? Legal Title and Transfer of Shares in a Paperless World' (2002) *Journal of Business Law* 358.

2.16 An instrument may acquire negotiable status either by statute or by commercial usage, as reflected in the law merchant. It is generally[1] established that traditional bearer securities in the secondary markets are negotiable instruments[2].

1 Certain provisions that have been incorporated in commercial paper have been considered adversely to affect their status as promissory notes negotiable under s 83 of the Bills of Exchange Act 1882. Such provisions include withholding tax grossing up provisions (having the result that the note is not a promise to pay a sum certain); restrictions (driven by US regulatory requirements) on negotiation of the instrument to nationals of certain countries (so that the note is not an unconditional promise to pay); and the enfacement of guarantees on the instrument. These provisions must be considered on a case-by-case basis.

2 Domestic corporate bonds: *Re General Estates* (1868) 3 Ch App 758; *Higgs v Northern Assam Tea Co Ltd* (1869) LR 4 Exch 387; *Re Imperial Land Co of Marseilles* (1870) LR 11 Eq 478; *Bechuanaland Exploration Co v London Trading Bank* [1898] 2 QB 658.

Foreign government and corporate bonds: *Gorgier v Mieville* (1824) 3 B & C 45; *Simmons v London Joint Stock Bank* [1891] 1 Ch 270; *Bentinck v London Joint Stock Bank* [1893] 2 Ch 120; *Venables v Baring* [1892] 3 Ch 527.

Scrip for bonds (ie certificates acknowledging the holder's entitlement to be issued with bonds): *Goodwin v Robarts* (1875) LR 10 Exch 337.

Secured bearer bonds: *Webb v Herne Bay* (1870) LR 5 QB 642.

The above references are quoted in J S Ewart 'Negotiability and Estoppel' (1900) 14 LQR 135 at 156. See also the following:

Bearer bonds, whether foreign or domestic, corporate or government: *Edelstein v Schuler* [1900-3] All ER Rep 884.

Certificates of deposit: *Customs and Excise Comrs v Guy Butler (International) Ltd* [1977] QB 377 at 382; *Libyan Arab Foreign Bank v Bankers Trust Co* [1988] 1 Lloyd's Rep 259 at 276.

The introduction of Euro-notes and Euro-commercial paper to the London secondary markets raised the question of whether these new forms of bearer security were negotiable in the absence of clear statutory or judicial authority. The general consensus in the legal community is that these physical instruments have become negotiable on the basis of commercial custom in London.

A new class of negotiable instrument?

2.17 In the UK there is no statutory basis for claiming negotiable status for bearer computerised securities. Therefore, to show that bearer computerised securities are negotiable, it would be necessary to argue that they have been recognised under the law merchant as a new class of negotiable instrument. There is ample authority that the law merchant is a dynamic branch of law, evolving to reflect changing commercial practice from time to time. Thus, in principle, the law merchant is capable of recognising bearer computerised securities as negotiable. The question is whether it has in fact done so.

Arguments against negotiability

Indirect

2.18 One obstacle to treating bearer computerised securities as negotiable is their indirect nature, in the following sense. The ability of the holder from time to time of an instrument to enforce it in her own name against its issuer has generally been taken to be an essential criterion of negotiability[1]. In general, an investor in computerised securities does not have directly enforceable rights against the issuer[2].

1 See *London and County Banking Co Ltd v London and River Plate Bank Ltd* (1887) 20 QBD 232 at 236. See also *Crouch v Crédit Foncier of England* (1873) LR 8 QB 374, per Blackburn J.

2 Any direct rights arising on default under 'disappearing global' arrangements (see para **2.9** n 1 above) are not rights under a negotiable instrument, because they arise under a deed poll.

2.19 However, an alternative view has been expressed. In the past the London legal community considered this question in relation to physical Eurodollar bonds constituted under a trust deed which imposed limitations on bondholders' rights to sue the issuer, so that generally only the trustee had rights of enforcement, and bondholders were able to sue the issuer only if the trustee failed in its duties on their behalf. One leading counsel argued that the instruments were not negotiable because on the face of the bonds the person holding them for the time being was prevented from suing on them in her own name. Another leading counsel argued that the instruments were negotiable, and that the requirement of negotiability was not that the holder should have an unrestricted right to sue, but that in circumstances where she is given such a right, she should not need to sue in the names of prior holders. For this reason, the absence of direct rights of enforcement under bearer computerised securities may not necessarily be incompatible with negotiable status.

Intangible

2.20 The stronger argument against bearer computerised securities being treated as negotiable is their intangibility. Bearer computerised securities comprise intangible assets on the following basis. In the case of dematerialised securities, no tangible asset exists to which the investor's property rights relate. In the case of immobilised securities, provided the underlying instrument is in global form, the investor's property rights do not attach to any particular definitive instruments, for none exist. Rather, the investor's rights relate to an unallocated share of the global. In the absence of attachment, the investor cannot be said to hold a tangible asset. Her co-proprietary rights form a distinct intangible asset which relates to the underlying global, but does not exhaust it. This argument is continued at paras **2.37–2.40** below[1].

1   Investors may have the right to call for underlying physical securities; however, if they do so, they convert their investment from computerised securities to physical securities.

2.21   The early negotiable instruments (bills of exchange and promissory notes) were recognised as negotiable because they were like paper money, and used by merchants as an alternative method of payment for goods[1]. Indeed, the test of negotiability has been held to be that the instrument should pass from hand to hand like money[2]. 'Money passes with good title because it is money; and notes because they are like money'[3].

1   'A Bill of exchange is a security, originally invented among merchants in different countries, for the more easy remittance of money from the one to the other, which since spread itself into almost all pecuniary transactions': Blackstone *Commentaries*, Book II, at 466.
2   See *Lang v Smyth* (1831) 7 Bing 284; *Miller v Race* (1758) 1 Burr 452 and *Friedlander v Texas* 130 US 416 (1889).
3   J S Ewart 'Negotiability and Estoppel' (1900) 14 LQR 135 at 152.

2.22   The general rule with paper money is that property passes with possession. Equally, 'For the purpose of rendering bills of exchange negotiable, the rights of property in them pass with the bills ... The property and the possession are inseparable'[1]. Thus property is with the holder, or the person having possession. For this reason, a negotiable instrument must be capable of possession. If it were incapable of possession, it could not confer upon its possessor (a holder) the status of holder in due course.

1   *Collins v Martin* (1797) 1 Bos & P 648 at 651, per Eyre CJ.

2.23   There is no clear authority for treating an intangible as a negotiable instrument, and it may be legally impossible to do so. To extend the concept of negotiability to intangibles would be a major departure from the existing law merchant, and perhaps only achievable by statute[1].

1   Section 8 of the Electronic Communications Act 2000 arguably provides an opportunity for extending negotiable status to computerised bearer securities. However, consultation among bankers and practitioners conducted by Hugh Pigott and Joanna Benjamin through The Centre for Law Reform on behalf of the Law Commission during 1999 and 2000 indicated that there was little appetite in London for such provision.

2.24   It is true that in the case of immobilised securities, there are tangible instruments (and directly enforceable rights) in the hands of an intermediary depositary[1]. This does not, however, render the interest of the investor a negotiable instrument, because all negotiable instruments 'are intended to be ambulatory'[2]. The physical securities underlying the immobilised securities are (as the term suggests) immobilised with depositaries acting for settlement systems such as Euroclear or Clearstream. Thus the indicia of negotiability are distributed between the asset held by the depositary and the investor. The physical instrument (expressed to be negotiable) and directly enforceable rights are held by the depositary, and the 'ambulatory' assets are held by the investors.

1   These underlying physical securities will also be expressed on their face to be negotiable; this is also a necessary (but not sufficient) criterion of negotiability: *London and County Banking Co v London and River Plate Bank Ltd* (1887) 20 QBD 232; *Jones & Co v Coventry* [1909] 2 KB 1029.

2   J S Ewart 'Negotiability and Estoppel' (1900) 14 LQR 135 at 155.

Conclusion

2.25   In the absence of authority to the contrary, the features of negotiability appear to remain first, that an instrument should be transferable, like cash, by delivery and second (subject to the comments at paras **2.18–2.19** above) that the instrument should be capable of being used upon by the holder from time to time[1].

1   'It may therefore be laid down as a safe rule that where an instrument is by the custom of trade transferable, like cash, by delivery, and is also capable of being used upon by the person holding it pro tempore, then it is entitled to the name of a *negotiable instrument*, and the property in it passes to a bona fide transferee for value, though the transfer may not have taken place in market overt. But that if either of the above requisites be wanting, ie, if it be either not accustomably transferable, or, though it be accustomably transferable, yet, if its nature be such as to render it incapable of being put in suit by the party holding it pro tempore, it is not a *negotiable instrument*, nor will delivery of it pass the property of it to a vendee, however bona fide, if the transferor himself have not a good title to it, and the transfer be made out of market overt', per Blackburn J in *Crouch v Crédit Foncier* (1873) LR 8 QB 374 at 381, quoting from the notes to *Miller v Race* (1758) 1 Burr 452.

2.26   Delivery is the transfer of possession. As an intangible, a computerised bearer security is incapable of possession and therefore of delivery in the technical legal sense of that term. It would therefore seem that computerised bearer securities cannot be negotiable instruments.

2.27   Nor would it be commercially helpful to seek to argue that, on the contrary, bearer computerised securities are negotiable instruments. This is because the existing law merchant assumes that negotiable instruments are capable of physical delivery, signature and endorsement. In the absence of legislation, the application of the law relating to such matters to intangible assets would be uncertain and unpredictable.

2.28   In crossing into the electronic era, the secondary markets in bearer securities have (it is argued) crossed an important legal boundary, and left the law merchant.

The benefits of negotiability

2.29   The chief benefits of negotiability are ease[1] and security[2] of transfer[3]. It is argued below that such benefits may also be enjoyed by bearer computerised securities, not under the law merchant, but by statute.

1   That is, no need for written transfers or notice to the issuer.

2   That is, the general inability of the trade to be reversed due to defects in the transferor's title.

3   For a full discussion of the benefits of negotiability, see Bank of England *The Future of Money Market Instruments*, November 1999, Appendix II.

Ease of transfer

2.30   At the time of writing the major international settlement systems for computerised bearer securities (Euroclear and Clearstream) are located on continental Europe. Book entry transfers within such systems are not governed by English law, but rather by local statutory regimes. However, the London-based settlement system, CREST, has many cross-border links as discussed in Chapter 9. Where book entry transfers of computerised bearer securities take place under English law, the position would be as follows.

2.31 Transfers of intangible assets are, at the time of writing, subject to statutory formalities under ss 136 and 53(1)(c) of the Law of Property Act 1925. There is legislative power to disapply such provisions under s 8 of the Electronic Communications Act 2000, and such general disapplications could be made in favour of electronic securities settlement. Moreover, a number of technical legal arguments are available that these statutory formalities do not apply to electronic securities settlement[1]. Nevertheless, the Uncertificated Securities Regulations 2001, as amended[2], which provide a statutory regime for book entry transfers through CREST, expressly disapply ss 136 and 53(1)(c)[3].

1   See ch 3, section C of J Benjamin *Interests in Securities* (2000, Oxford University Press).
2   SI 2001/3755.
3   Regulation 38(5). Note that this disapplication applies to transfers through CREST, not to transfers of interests in securities which a person has as a result of holding through a custodian or nominee which is a CREST member.

Security of transfer[1]

2.32 A transfer is secure if the good faith purchaser is able to retain the transferred assets free from adverse claims. It is arguable that, by removing negotiable status, the computerisation of securities has reduced security of transfer under the general principles of English law. However, CREST operates under a statutory regime. Opinion of leading counsel has been obtained to the general effect that reg 29 of the Uncertificated Securities Regulations 1995[2] (now incorporated in reg 35 of the Uncertificated Securities Regulations 2001) provides security of transfer comparable to that enjoyed by negotiable instruments.

1   This same concept is also called 'security of receipt'. See Peter Birks in P Birks (ed) *Overview: Tracing, Claiming and Defences, Laundering and Tracing* (1995, Clarendon).
2   SI 1995/3272.

2.33 In Luxembourg, art 7 of the Grand Ducal Decree of 17 February 1971 Modifying the Circulation of Securities has the effect of transferring the risk of adverse claims from the purchaser to Clearstream. The Belgian Royal Decree No 62 of 10 November 1967 has the effect of defeating unpublished adverse claims once securities have entered Euroclear.

Conclusion

2.34 In conclusion, because they are intangible, bearer computerised securities are not negotiable instruments. In the UK and elsewhere, the traditional benefits of negotiability (ease and security of transfer) therefore require must be replicated by statute.

REGISTERED COMPUTERISED SECURITIES[1]

2.35 Securities held through CREST are computerised registered securities[2], ie unlike traditional registered securities they are evidenced and transferred without paper certificates or instruments of transfer.

1   Registered securities in electronic form will be referred to as registered computerised securities, and registered securities not in electronic form as traditional registered securities.
2   They are known as uncertificated securities, as discussed in Chapter 9.

2.36 The impact of computerisation on the legal nature of registered securities is much less extensive than its impact on the legal nature of bearer securities. This is because traditional registered securities have never enjoyed negotiable status and (like computerised registered securities) are intangible assets[1].

1   A share is a chose in action: *Colonial Bank v Whinney* (1886) 11 App Cas 426. A registered share is not the same as a share certificate, which is not a document of title but a document evidencing title.

INTERESTS IN SECURITIES

2.37 This chapter has considered the consequences of computerisation for the legal nature of investors' interests in securities. It has shown that, for bearer securities, computerisation has cost negotiability. However, in practice the secondary markets should not be affected, as the benefits of negotiability are arguably provided by statute.

2.38 In contrast, because traditional registered securities have never enjoyed negotiable status, and are intangible, computerisation has not significantly altered the legal nature of investors' assets.

2.39 The preceding discussion has considered computerisation in the narrow sense of the replacement of paper instruments and certificates with the electronic records associated with electronic settlement. In practice, the introduction of electronic settlement has been accompanied by two other related developments. These are intermediation and commingling. Because direct participation in electronic settlement systems is not always possible and/or practicable for many clients, it is common for them to gain access to electronic settlement through custodians. Thus in many cases the custodian, and not the client, has a direct relationship with the settlement system, and the title of the client to the underlying assets is asserted through the custodian. As discussed in the following chapter, the natural legal characterisation of such a custody relationship is as a trust, so that the rights of the client are equitable and not legal. Moreover, it is customary for the custodian to commingle the like assets of its different custody clients, which are held together in a commingled pool. As also discussed in the following chapter, the combined effect of such intermediation and pooling is to render the interest of the client equitable and co-proprietary. In technical terms, this interest arises under an equitable tenancy in common.

2.40 Such equitable tenancies in common are called 'interests in securities' and are discussed in detail by Joanna Benjamin in her book of that title[1]. The key significance of the market participant's asset comprising interests in securities, as opposed to securities in their traditional form, relates to the legal requirements of creating effective cross-border collateral arrangements, as discussed in Chapter 5 of this work. Another consequence is as follows. Traditional bearer securities are physical, allocated assets, where the root of title is possession, and which are transferred by delivery. In contrast, traditional registered securities are intangible, unallocated assets[2], where the root of title is a register entry, and which are transferred by amending the register. On the basis that interests in securities are intangible, unallocated assets, where the root of title is an entry in the custodian's accounts, and which are transferred by amending those accounts, interests in securities are arguably a form of registered security. The key relevance of this analysis is in the conflict of laws, in attributing a situs or legal location to such assets, as discussed in Chapter 5. For ease of reference, this book will in general refer to the assets of custody clients as securities.

1   J Benjamin *Interests in Securities* (2000, Oxford University Press).

2   'There is no identity in stock': *Bank of England v Cutler* [1907] 1 KB 889 at 909, per Lawrence J. See also *Ind's Case* (1872) 7 Ch App 485 at 487, per Mellish LJ and, more recently, *Hunter v Moss* [1993] 1 WLR 934; affd [1994] 1 WLR 452, [1994] 3 All ER 215; *Re Harvard Securities Ltd (in liquidation)* [1997] 2 BCLC 369; *White v Shortall* 9 ITELR 470 (December 2006, Supreme Court of New South Wales); and *Re Lehman Brothers International (Europe) (in administration)* [2010] EWHC 2914.

CHAPTER 3

Custodian as trustee – the custody relationship in the electronic environment[1]

3.1 The impact of the electronic environment on the legal nature of investors' assets was considered in the previous chapter. Its effect on the legal nature of the custody relationship will now be assessed.

1 See also J Benjamin 'Custody: an English Law Analysis' (1994) 9 JIBFL 121 at 188; A O Austen-Peters *Custody of Investments* (2000, Oxford University Press), ch 2; and Joanna Benjamin *Interests in Securities* (2000, Oxford University Press), chs 2 and 10.

THE ACCOUNTS

3.2 The custodian maintains both cash accounts and securities accounts in the name of the client. The cash from time to time credited to the cash accounts may represent the proceeds of sale of custody assets and/or dividends and other income received in respect of them. The securities accounts record the securities held by or through the custodian for the client. The legal nature of the asset recorded in each type of account will be considered in turn.

CASH

The debtor/creditor principle

3.3 Custodians have traditionally been banks. It is a clear principle of banking law that the deposit of cash with a bank establishes the relationship of debtor and creditor between the bank and the depositor (the 'debtor/creditor principle')[1]. Depositors' money is not held by the bank by way of trust[2]. The bank is free to use the deposited money as it pleases[3], and so the money is available to the bank's creditors on its insolvency. The depositor's rights of repayment are contractual and not proprietary[4]. On the bank's insolvency, therefore, the depositor must prove as an unsecured creditor[5] (subject to any available deposit protection scheme)[6].

1 *Carr v Carr* (1811) 1 Mer 541n.
2 *Foley v Hill* (1848) 2 HL Cas 28.
3 *South Australian Insurance Co v Randell* (1869) 16 ER 775 at 759.
4 'True it is that in the case of money paid into the banker's account it is converted into a debt, while in the case of money placed in a special repository it remains in specie': *Re Halletts Estate, Knatchbull v Hallett* (1880) 13 Ch D 696 at 746, per Thesiger LJ.
5 *Space Investments Ltd v Canadian Imperial Bank of Commerce Trust Co (Bahamas) Ltd* [1986] 1 WLR 1072, [1986] 3 All ER 75.
6 This principle creates an exposure for the global custodian in respect of cash balances with correspondent banks, including foreign currency. Where, for example, the global custodian maintains a US dollar account in favour of the client with a balance of $10,000, the global custodian remains liable to pay that sum even if the New York correspondent bank with which the global custodian holds its dollar assets becomes insolvent. While in theory a global custodian might draft 'limited recourse' wording into its contract with the client to provide that its obligation to pay the client was dependent on the solvency of its New York correspondent, such a provision does not reflect normal

banking practice and may be unacceptable to clients (and would in the UK raise issues regarding the application of client money rules – see Chapter 7, paras **7.66–7.67**).

3.4 It has generally been assumed that the debtor/creditor principle applies to custodians in respect of clients' cash accounts[1]. Custodians generally conduct their business on the basis of that principle, using the money credited to the custody cash accounts for their own purposes, and not segregating it as trust money. While this approach is, in the authors' view, correct, two points arise. First, the debtor/creditor principle applies to money deposited with banks, and may not apply to non-bank custodians. Second, the credit balance of the custody cash accounts may not represent deposits.

1   Barings Brothers & Co Ltd acted as a global custodian. In March 1995, after the company went into administration and before the announcement of the agreement of ING Bank to buy the Barings group and take over its debts, it was generally assumed in the City of London that the balance of the cash accounts held by the company for pension fund custody clients was at risk. This cash amounted to some £100 million.

Trust over cash

3.5 The credit balances of the cash accounts may represent the proceeds of sale of custody assets or income derived from custody assets. Paragraphs **3.10–3.22** below will argue that, in a computerised environment, custody assets are in most cases held by the custodian for the client as trustee. The proceeds of sale of trust property[1] and income derived from trust property[2] are generally subject to the same trusts as the property to which they relate. This raises the risk for custodians of a duty to segregate cash.

1   See *Re Hallett's Estate, Knatchbull v Hallett* (1880) 13 Ch D 696.
2   *Swain v Law Society* [1981] 3 All ER 797 at 813, CA, per Oliver LJ.

3.6 The answer to this problem for the bank custodian is provided by *Space Investments*[1]. In this case it was held that, where a bank trustee lawfully deposits trust money with itself *as banker*, it becomes beneficially entitled to that money, and owes only a contractual duty of repayment. In order to be certain of benefiting from this rule, bank custodians should include express wording in their custody agreements, authorising them to deposit any monies credited to the cash accounts with themselves as banker[2].

1   *Space Investments Ltd v Canadian Imperial Bank of Commerce Trust Co (Bahamas) Ltd* [1986] 3 All ER 75.
2   Some of the case law regarding this area is not wholly helpful. *Mac-Jordan Construction Ltd v Brookmount Erostin Ltd* [1992] BCLC 350 (CA) and *Russell-Cooke Trust Company and another v Richard Prentis and Co Ltd* [2002] EWHC 2227 (Ch) indicate that appropriate allocation or segregation of cash is required for certainty when holding cash on trust. However, consider also the following: *R v Clowes and another (No 2)* [1994] 2 All ER 316, CA. Here, the view was expressed that 'a requirement to keep moneys separate is normally an indicator that they are impressed with a trust, and that the absence of such a requirement, if there are no other indicators of a trust, normally negatives it. The fact that a transaction contemplates the mingling of funds is, therefore, not necessarily fatal to a trust'. This is curious, as the specific question of certainty of subject matter for a valid trust is not considered, and generally this case, and other cases following it, seem to focus on whether an intention to create a trust has been demonstrated by a requirement to segregate, or actual segregation, of funds (thus giving certainty of subject matter), rather than whether a trust fails for lack of segregation and therefore certainty. Nevertheless, in this case it was concluded that there were terms in the relevant documents 'expressly committing Barlow Clowes to placing investors' funds in a separate, "designated", account and to treating the investors as beneficial owners, and hence Barlow Clowes as trustees, of such funds'. *ILG Travel Ltd (in administration)* [1995] 2 BCLC 128, Ch. In this case, the documentation expressly stated that the relevant funds were to be held on trust, but there was no obligation to segregate the funds in a separate account. It was concluded that there was no trust in favour of ILG as beneficial owner, but instead 'a trust under which ILG takes a charge in equity' over the relevant funds. Per (Jonathan Parker J): 'In some cases, and

Stephens is one of them, freedom to mix may not suffice to negate the existence of a bare trust. But that conclusion will necessarily depend upon the terms of the particular instrument which has to be construed.' And 'I accordingly conclude that the trust created by cl 19 is a trust under which ILG has a charge in equity over the pipeline moneys to secure payment of the agent's outstanding indebtedness to ILG under the 1990 agreement'. In *Re BA Peters plc (in administration)* [2008] EWHC 2205 (Ch), [2008] All ER (D) 392, it was accepted that certainty of subject matter was necessary for the existence of a trust, but the reasoning underlying the conclusions reached seems to be based on lack of intention to create a trust rather than a trust failing for lack of certainty of subject matter. In *Cooper v PRG Powerhouse Ltd (in creditors' voluntary liquidation)* [2008] EWHC 498 (Ch), [2008] BPIR 492, Ch, it was concluded there was a purpose trust, despite the commingling of funds with the recipient's own funds, and hence tracing remedies applied. Consider also *In the matter of Lehman Brothers International (Europe) (In Administration) and In the matter of the Insolvency Act 1986* [2012] UKSC 6, 29 February 2012, where the fact that cash subject to the client money trust was paid into a house account was not considered an obstacle to such cash being held on trust under the client money trust.

While the position is not perhaps wholly clear, and it would appear that lack of clarity as to the funds held on trust may not necessarily be fatal to a claim be the beneficial owner, in arrangements where the issue is important, relevant documentation should require that cash to be held on trust is held in a separate account, and the beneficial owner should seek appropriate confirmation that this has in fact been done, particularly where the entity holding the funds is a bank and hence may otherwise be holding as banker rather than on trust.

3.7 However, some clients do not wish to take the credit risk of their custodians as banker in respect of their cash balances. In order to avoid such credit risk, it is necessary to establish a trust over the cash in the hands of the custodian. As discussed in more detail later in this chapter, a valid trust requires certainty of subject matter. Therefore, it is necessary to identify a particular asset in the hands of the custodian, corresponding to the cash balance, which will be subject to the trust[1]. If the account is a sterling account, a particular sterling sum in the hands of the custodian must be segregated in order for the trust to take effect. In practice, this is achieved by the custodian placing a sterling sum on deposit with a third party bank, and declaring a trust over its rights of repayment from that bank. For commercial and operational reasons, custodian banks may be reluctant to place client cash with their rival banks. A pragmatic alternative is for the greater part of client cash balances to be regularly invested in 'near cash', ie highly liquid debt instruments such as CDs, or units in 'cash funds', ie collective investment schemes investing in near cash. Because they are highly liquid, these assets enable the custodian promptly to meet payment obligations arising on the client's account. Because they comprise securities (and not merely the payment obligation of the custodian to the client) they can be the subject of a trust in the hands of the custodian[2].

1   Of course, the cash account itself cannot serve as the trust asset, as it records the liability of the custodian to pay the client, and under English law a liability as opposed to an asset cannot be subject to a trust.

2   From the 1995 failure of Barings Brothers onwards, and even more after the commencement of insolvency proceedings in relation to Lehman Brothers International (Europe) on 15 September 2008, the appetite of UK clients for custodian credit risk is continuously reducing, and greater use has been made of such 'near cash' arrangements. (Similarly, where custodians provide securities lending services, typically cash collateral received on behalf of the client is invested at the direction of the client or its investment manager, arguably both to maximise investment returns and to minimise credit risk taken by the client in relation to the custodian.)

3.8 For custodians regulated by the Financial Services Authority under the Financial Services and Markets Act 2000, the Client Money Rules[1] ('CMR') generally apply (broadly) to money received or held from or on behalf of a client in the course of 'designated investment business' or 'MiFID business' as appropriate[2], which in practice will include custody services. The general effect of the CMR is to create a statutory trust over client money[3], thus protecting it from the insolvency of the custodian. However, an exemption is available for relevant banks[4], which will include most bank custodians. The bank exemption relates to money held by an appropriate bank in an account with itself. It requires that the bank gives written notice to the client, which (broadly) warns it that the money is held by it as banker and not as trustee, and will not be held in accordance with the CMR.

1   The CMR comprise Chapters 7 and 7A of the Financial Services Authority ('FSA') Client Assets sourcebook ('CASS') in relation to cash held in connection with both non-MiFID business and MiFID business (and also CASS Chapter 5 in relation to cash held in connection with insurance mediation activity). See further in Chapter 7, paras **7.58–7.82** below.

2   See the definitions in the FSA Handbook Glossary. (MiFID refers to Directive 2004/39/EC of the European Parliament and of the Council of 21 April 2004 on markets in financial instruments). Designated investment business includes safeguarding and administering investments for the purposes of art 40 of the Financial Services and Markets Act 2000 (Regulated Activities) Order 2001, as amended (SI 2001/544) (the 'Regulated Activities Order') provided (broadly) the assets include designated investments as defined in the Glossary. The definition of 'MiFID business' is quite complex, but very broadly, means investment services or activities regulated by MiFID. For further discussion, see Chapter 7.

3   CASS Chapter 7, section 7.7.

4   An 'approved bank' (CASS 7.1.11AR) or a 'BCD credit institution' (CASS 7.1.8R) for the purposes of CASS Chapter 7. See Chapter 7, para **7.62** for explanation of these terms.

3.9   Some firms offering custody in London are not banks, and are not authorised to carry on the business of accepting deposits in the UK[1]. Such custodians are generally not permitted to treat the credit balances of custody cash accounts as debts owed by them to their clients, but instead must hold such credit balances on trust for their clients, for a number of reasons. First, non-banks will not benefit from the debtor/creditor principle as a matter of general law. Second, it is prudent to assume that the operation of a custody cash account otherwise than on a trust basis would amount to accepting deposits. Third, where such firms receive or hold client money in the course of designated investment business or MiFID business, such custodians will generally be subject to the CMR[2]. However, they will not be exempt from the CMR as they are not banks (although custody clients who are either eligible counterparties[3] or professional clients[4] may opt out of client money protection in a non-MiFID context)[5]. In practice, such non-bank custodians usually maintain custody cash accounts as client money accounts with third party banks, and operate those accounts as trustees on their clients' behalf.

1   For the purposes of art 5 of the Regulated Activities Order.

2   CASS 7.1.1R.

3   See the definition in the FSA Handbook Glossary, and the discussion in Chapter 7 para **7.33**.

4   See the definition in the FSA Handbook Glossary, and the discussion in Chapter 7 para **7.33**.

5   CASS 7.1.7DR. There is no equivalent of this opt out in CASS Chapter 7 for client money held in the context of MiFID business.

INTERESTS IN SECURITIES, BAILMENT AND TRUST

3.10   Whereas custody clients are generally willing to take custodian credit risk in respect of their cash accounts, it is imperative to ensure that securities credited to client securities accounts are not at risk[1] in the custodian's insolvency[2], or otherwise available to its creditors[3]. The traditional characterisation of the custodian in respect of traditional bearer securities[4] (and other non-cash assets such as bullion[5]) is as the bailee of the client. This characterisation is based on physical possession[6].

1   But see para **3.13** below.

2   'Local laws and regulations should ensure that there is segregation of client assets from the principal assets of their custodian; and no possible claim on client assets in the event of custodian bankruptcy or a similar event': 1995 G30/ISSA Recommendations, recommendation 8. See the G30 website at www.group30.org. See also Commission Directive 2006/73/EC of 10 August 2006 implementing

Directive 2004/39/EC of the European Parliament and of the Council as regards organisational requirements and operating conditions for investment firms and defined terms for the purposes of that Directive (the 'MiFID implementing Directive'), Article 16(1)(d) which obliges Member States to require investment firms holding client assets to comply with the following: '(d) they must take the necessary steps to ensure that any client financial instruments deposited with a third party, in accordance with Article 17, are identifiable separately from the financial instruments belonging to the investment firm and from financial instruments belonging to that third party, by means of differently titled accounts on the books of the third party or other equivalent measures that achieve the same level of protection; (e) they must take the necessary steps to ensure that client funds deposited, in accordance with Article 18, in a central bank, a credit institution or a bank authorised in a third country or a qualifying money market fund are held in an account or accounts identified separately from any accounts used to hold funds belonging to the investment firm; (f) they must introduce adequate organisational arrangements to minimise the risk of the loss or diminution of client assets, or of rights in connection with those assets, as a result of misuse of the assets, fraud, poor administration, inadequate record-keeping or negligence.'

3   For example, following execution by a judgment creditor.

4   'These bonds are her bonds deposited with Mr Hallett according to the receipt, for safe custody, which would make him, no doubt, an ordinary bailee': *Re Hallett's Estates, Knatchbull v Hallett* (1880) 13 Ch D 696 at 708, per Jessell MR. See also *Kahler v Midland Bank* [1950] AC 24, [1949] 2 All ER 621, HL.

5   See *Dollfus Mieg v Bank of England* [1949] Ch 369, [1949] 1 All ER 946.

6   '"Custody" here clearly relates to the possession or control of the certificates as physical objects': *Swiss Bank Corpn v Lloyds Bank Ltd* [1980] 2 All ER 419 at 431, CA, per Buckley LJ.

3.11   The essence of bailment is the delivery of possession, or physical control (as opposed to the delivery of title, or ownership) by the bailor to the bailee[1]. Thus, the bailee custodian has possession of the physical custody securities, but they remain owned by the client and are unavailable to the creditors of the custodian upon its insolvency.

1   'a person who voluntarily takes another person's goods into his custody holds them as bailee of that person (the owner)': *KH Enterprise v Pioneer Container, The Pioneer Container* [1994] 2 AC 324. See also Palmer and McKendrick (eds) *Interests in Goods* (2nd edn, 1998, Lloyd's of London Press), Chapter 3 'Possessory Title' (N Palmer), p 88: 'certain rights of possession qualify their holders to sue in tort and confer on their holders the status of bailor'; and Chapter 19 'The Place of Bailment in the Modern Law of Obligations' (A Bell), p 461: 'In recent times ... a new definition has emerged that sees bailment as based on the bailee's voluntary assumption of possession of the bailor's goods, whether or not the bailor consents to it.' And see also the famous classification of bailments in the judgment of Holt CJ in *Coggs v Bernard* (1703) 2 Ld Raym 909.

3.12   This traditional view of the custody relationship is challenged by computerisation. Chapter 2 argued that, in the electronic environment, the assets in the hands of the custodian in general comprise, not physical instruments, but intangibles. It will be argued below that intangibles cannot be the subject of possession, nor therefore of bailment, and that for these reasons the natural characterisation of the contemporary custody relationship is as a trust.

3.13   A distinction should of course be made between the legal position, and what happens in practice. As has been seen with the administration procedures for Lehman Brothers International (Europe), it has taken an extremely long time for the administrators to redeliver client securities and client money (both held on trust) to clients. There is however now a special procedure for 'investment banks' (as defined in the Banking Act 2009)[1], namely the Investment Bank Special Administration Regulations 2011[2]. Under these Regulations, it is important to note that the focus is on return of client assets as the administrator has three main objectives, namely to ensure the return of client assets as soon as is reasonably practicable, to ensure timely engagement with market infrastructure bodies and the Bank of England, HM Treasury and the FSA, and to either rescue the investment bank as a going concern or wind it up in the best interests of the creditors. In particular, the administrator is entitled to deal with and return client assets in whatever order the administrator thinks best achieves the return of client assets as soon as is reasonably practicable[3]. In the context of these objectives, the administrator is given the power to set a bar date for submission of claims by clients of the custodian in relation to assets held by the clients with the custodian. Following the setting of a bar date, the administrator is required to return client assets to clients in accordance with the procedure set down by the Investment Bank Special Administration (England and Wales) Rules 2011. The possibility of the bar date is significant, because as a result of the terms of the Regulations and Rules, the existence of a bar date has the result that any client assets returned to a client who made a claim prior to the bar date cannot be recovered by the administrator or any other person, and any client who made a claim prior to the bar date to whom assets have been returned acquires good title to such assets as against a client who made a claim after the bar date. In addition, where claims by clients relate to client assets in an omnibus client account of the custodian, any shortfall of assets in that omnibus account which cannot be remedied will be borne pro rata by all such clients[4], but this is subject to the points in the preceding sentence, therefore any client which makes a claim after the bar date is more likely to suffer loss as a result of a shortfall in an omnibus account. In many respects this is quite a radical approach and treats the property rights of custody clients in much the same way as contractual claims, permitting loss or reduction of property rights by failure to comply with a bar date[5].

1   Broadly, entities incorporated in any part of the UK, including England, and providing custody or banking services. Thus the definition does not solely refer to banks.

2   SI 2011/245.

3   See Investment Bank Special Administration Regulations 2011, regs 10(1) and (2).

4   See Investment Bank Special Administration Regulations 2011, regs 11 and 12.

5   See also Chapter 7, para **7.160** regarding possible changes to recovery of client assets in insolvency situations.

Possession

3.14   The common law recognises both physical (or actual) and legal (or civil) possession. Legal possession has been described as the right to possess. However, the ultimate basis of possession is always fact rather than law because 'the existence of the *de facto* relation of control or apparent dominion [is] required as the foundation of the alleged right'[1]. The concept of constructive possession (discussed in Chapter 1) enables possession to arise without direct physical control[2]. However, constructive possession (like legal possession) is derived from actual possession, and therefore is unlikely to apply to intangible assets[3].

1   Sir Frederick Pollock *An Essay on Possession in the Common Law* (1888, Clarendon Press), p 10.

2   Relevant case law concerning constructive possession is mainly concerned with matters such as keys to rooms and boxes in which physical assets are contained.

3   'Most of the older definitions of bailment seem to require that an overt physical transfer ... be present': *Palmer on Bailment* (2010, 3rd edn, Sweet & Maxwell), p 23, para 1-023. But see generally Chapter 30 'Intangible Property' of the same work, which notes that 'the general law of bailment has developed in many directions' since the conclusion in the second edition of *Palmer on Bailment* that 'bailment is confined to tangible chattels' and 'has no application ... to intangible property'. Reference is made in Chapter 30 to 'the difficulty of translating the vocabulary of bailment into situations involving non-material things' but suggests that in principle bailment of intangibles may be a possibility, although 'whether courts are prepared to recognise intangibles as a proper subject of bailment may well depend on the context in which that issue arises'. Consider also *Re Lehman Brothers International (Europe) (in administration)* [2012] EWHC 2997 (Ch) in which 'It was common ground between counsel that rights properly classified in English law as a general lien were incapable of application to anything other than tangibles and old-fashioned certificated securities',

but Briggs J 'invited the parties to consider whether the time might have come for English law to take a broader view of the matter'. In this case counsel rejected such invitation, but the comments of Briggs J suggests that it is not certain that English courts would reject an argument that a lien (and possibly therefore also bailment) may apply to intangibles.

3.15 As indicated above, the bailor client retains ownership of the bailed assets, which are not available to the creditors of the bailee in its insolvency. If the computerisation of the securities markets precludes the characterisation of the custodian as bailee, it is necessary to identify another basis on which to protect the client from the credit risk of the custodian. Under English law, the only available alternative is trust. In relation to bailment, 'It is almost universally agreed that no one can become a bailee without possession of a tangible chattel'[1] and 'A bailment passes no general property in the subject chattel and cannot by itself make the bailee owner of the goods'[2], but in contrast trust property may be intangible since 'any property may be held in trust'[3]. The role of the custodian has evolved far beyond its traditional status as a bailee[4]. The question arises, has it taken the law relating to bailment with it, so that bailment may now relate to intangibles? Or has it left bailment behind so that now the custodian is a trustee? In the absence of direct judicial authority, it would be prudent to assume that the custodian, by moving into the electronic environment, has moved into a new legal category[5], and is a trustee[6].

1   But see para **3.14** n 3.
2   *Palmer on Bailment* (2010, 3rd edn, Sweet & Maxwell), para 1-131, p 134, and para 3-031, p 203.
3   *Snell's Equity* (2011, 32nd edn, Sweet & Maxwell), para 21-034. See also *Lewin On Trusts* (2011, 18th edn, with 2nd Supplement, Sweet & Maxwell); and *Underhill & Hayton: Law Relating to Trusts and Trustees* (2010, 18th edn, Butterworths).
4   Note that holding as 'agent' is not a further option under English law. Agency is the concept of one person exercising the rights and powers of another (notably, to create contractual relations) on behalf of such person. It is not a concept of holding assets on behalf of another. If an agent holds assets on behalf of its principal, it will hold as bailee or trustee, depending on the circumstances. An agent is a fiduciary relationship (see *Parker v McKenna* (1874) 10 Ch App 96) and if an agent holds assets for its principal, cases such as *Burdick v Garrick* (1870) 5 Ch App 233 and *Brown v IRC* [1965] AC 244 indicate the agent is regarded as holding the assets as trustee. Unless of course on the facts that arrangement agreed between agent and principal is different; for example, where (in relation to cash) the agent has a contractual obligation to repay but does not hold on trust (*Neste Oy v Lloyds Bank plc* [1983] 2 Lloyd's Rep 658). An interesting question, for which there currently seems to be no clear answer, is whether a custodian holds assets as trustee and carries out its other functions as agent, or the custodian is subject to the duties of a trustee in relation to all of its functions as custodian. Arguably the distinction may be of little significance provided that the custody terms clearly define the extent of the custodian's services, because the custodian is likely to be subject to a high duty of care whether holding assets, or providing services in connection with assets it holds.
5   For a supporting analysis, see A O Austen-Peters *Custody of Investments* (2000, Oxford University Press), ch 2. For a contrary view, see A Beaves 'Global Custody – A Tentative Analysis of Property and Contract', ch 6 in N Palmer and E McEndrick (eds) *Interests in Goods* (1998, 2nd edn, Lloyd's of London Press). See also David J Hayton and Charles Mitchell (eds) *Hayton and Marshall: Cases and Commentary on the Law of Trusts and Equitable Remedies* (2005, 12th edn, Sweet & Maxwell).

    The bailment analysis will still, of course, be available where the relevant assets are physical instruments and are directly held by the custodian.

    Interestingly, the bailment analysis was laid aside in the US in the preparation of the revised art 8 of the Uniform Commercial Code: 'Relatively early in the drafting process, the decision was reached to eschew the approach of trying to squeeze the analysis of the property interest of a person who holds securities through an intermediary into old legal concepts, such as bailment': J S Rogers *Policy Perspectives on Revised UCC Article 8,* UCLA Law Rev, June 1996, p 1431 at 1496.
6   Custodians who are trustees should not be confused with custodian trustees for the purposes of s 4(3) of the Public Trustee Act 1906. Statutory custodian trustees hold trust property while leaving the administration and management of the trust to managing trustees. Custodian trustees may be appointed in connection with a debenture issue.

Trust

3.16 A trust is a legal relationship in respect of assets (known as 'trust assets') between (i) one or more persons each known as a trustee and (ii) one or more persons each known as a beneficiary. The trustee holds the trust assets on trust for (ie for the benefit of) the beneficiary. While the trustee has technical or legal ownership of the trust assets, the beneficiary has the economic or beneficial ownership.

3.17 Trust assets are not available to the creditors of the trustee, and are thus protected from the credit risk in respect of the trustee[1]. This insolvency protection is the reason why it is necessary to characterise the custodian in the electronic environment as a trustee. However, trustee status has other legal consequences including, importantly, the following.

1   In the case of the bankruptcy of an individual, assets held by the individual on trust are excluded from her estate by s 283(3)(a) of the Insolvency Act 1986. In the case of a corporate insolvency, the authority for the exclusion of trust assets lies in the general principle that only assets owned by the company from part of its estate, as reflected in case law. See, for example, *Barclays Bank Ltd v Quistclose Investments Ltd* [1970] AC 567, [1968] 3 WLR 1097, [1968] 3 All ER 651; and *Re Kayford Ltd* [1975] 1 WLR 279, [1975] 1 All ER 604, as well as cases discussed in relation to the allocation question below. (It should of course be noted that, as a practical matter, even where there is no dispute that relevant securities were held by the trustee or custodian for a particular client, as demonstrated in the administration process for Lehman Brothers International (Europe), it may take some time for the insolvency official to identify and redeliver the securities to the client.)

3.18 First, under the general law the trustee is subject to a high level of implied fiduciary duties towards the beneficiary, and it follows that the custodian will wish carefully to limit the level of its fiduciary duties by contract[1].

1   For a discussion of contractual limitation of implied fiduciary duty, see Chapter 6.

3.19 Second, English law distinguishes between two types of property interest:

(1) Property interests recognised by the general body of English law (common law) are known as legal interests.

(2) Equitable interests are those interests recognised by the branch of English law known as Equity.

3.20 The law of trusts forms part of the law of equity, and the interests of beneficiaries under a trust in the trust assets are equitable and not legal. On this basis, the property rights in the custody portfolio of the client are equitable. This contrasts with the property rights of a bailor client, which are legal.

3.21 Equitable ownership is as effective as legal ownership in addressing the custodian's credit risk. However, where competing interests in the custody portfolio arise (in the event of fraud or double dealing), the priority of an equitable interest is in some circumstances weaker than that of a legal interest[1].

1   The general principle is that a person acquiring a legal interest in good faith, for value and without notice of a prior equitable interest, takes the disputed asset free from the prior equitable interest.

3.22 Third, a technical requirement arises concerning the establishment of a valid trust; this is discussed in the following paragraphs.

THE ALLOCATION QUESTION[1]

3.23 The allocation question is a technical issue associated with the customary practice among custodians of holding client securities on an unallocated or fungible basis.

1   There is now a large critical literature on this legal question. Particularly recommended are D Hayton 'Uncertainty of Subject-Matter of Trusts' (1994) 110 LQR 335; S Worthington 'Sorting out ownership interests in a Bulk: Gifts, Sales and Trusts' [1999] JBL 1; and P Birks 'Mixtures', Chapter 9 in Palmer and McKendrick (eds) *Interests in Goods* (1998, 2nd edn, Lloyd's of London Press). In relation to custody, see J Benjamin *Custody: an English Law Analysis* (1994) 9 JIBFL 188 and Joanna Benjamin *Interests in Securities* (2000, Oxford University Press), ch 2, section B.3, as well as A O Austen-Peters *Custody of Investments* (2000, Oxford University Press), ch 3.

Fungible custody and equivalent redelivery

3.24   Custodial arrangements in respect of securities are in most cases fungible, in the following sense. The custodian aggregates the holdings in securities of a particular issue which it holds for its various clients into one commingled holding ('client holding'). In the case of securities held through a sub-custodian, the client holding will usually be represented in the books of the sub-custodian by a designated client account in the name of the custodian. The client holding in securities held through a settlement system in which the custodian is a participant will usually also be held in a designated client account in the name of the custodian. In cases where a sub-custodian or settlement system is not employed, the client holding in registrable securities will be registered (with a client designation) in the name of the custodian or its nominee and physical bearer securities will be physically held (and earmarked for clients) by the custodian or its nominee. While the custodian's house position[1] in any security will be segregated from the client holding, there will in general be no record of any allocation between clients in the books of the relevant sub-custodian, settlement system, register or in the physical holding, as the case may be. The only note of the respective entitlements of the individual clients within the client holding will be in the books of the custodian. This arrangement is referred to in the following discussion as 'fungible custody'[2].

1   The house position is any holding by the custodian for its own account, beneficially owned by it.
2   Reasons for fungible custody include economies of scale, administrative convenience and accounting facility.

3.25   Thus, while it is possible at any time to determine how many of the individual securities comprised in the client holding are attributable to a particular client, it is not possible to determine which ones. A corollary of fungible custody is that the redelivery obligation owed by the custodian to each client is not an obligation to return the assets originally delivered in specie, but merely an obligation to return assets equivalent to those originally delivered.

3.26   During the 1990s a line of case law prompted a debate in the London legal community concerning the impact of fungible custody on the trust relationship between the client and the custodian, which debate is referred to in this chapter as 'the allocation question'. The allocation question concerns the possible legal difficulty in asserting proprietary rights over assets forming part of the commingled pool or bulk, in circumstances where one cannot identify which particular assets within the pool are subject to such purported proprietary rights.

The requirement for allocation

3.27   The allocation question concerns 'the law's insistence that proprietary rights cannot be acquired in fungibles forming an unidentified part of a bulk until they have been separated by some suitable act of appropriation'[1]. This requirement applies both at law and in equity. The common law rule is well established in case law concerning the sale of goods[2], and is given statutory force in s 16 of the Sale of Goods Act 1979[3]. The rule in equity is based on the principle that a trust cannot be validly established without certainty of subject matter[4]. As Lord Mustill stated in *Re Goldcorp Exchange*:

> 'It makes no difference what the parties intended if what they intend is impossible as is the case with an immediate transfer of [legal and equitable] title to goods whose identity is not yet known.'[5]

1   R M Goode 'Ownership and Obligation in Commercial Transactions' (1987) 103 LQR 433 at 436.

2   See, for example, *Healy v Howlett & Sons* [1917] 1 KB 337; *Re Wait* [1927] 1 Ch 606; *Carlos Federspiel & Co SA v Charles Twigg & Co Ltd* [1957] 1 Lloyd's Rep 240; *Re London Wine Co (Shippers) Ltd* [1986] PCC 121; *Re Goldcorp Exchange Ltd (in receivership)* [1995] 1 AC 74, [1994] 3 WLR 199, [1994] 2 All ER 806 and, more recently, *Glencore International AG v Metro Trading Inc* [2001] Lloyd's Rep 284; and *HM Customs and Excise v Everwine* [2003] All ER (D) 97 (a sale of goods case distinguishing *Re Stapylton Fletcher* (see paras **3.33–3.34** below) to conclude that the claim succeeded regarding the ascertained goods but failed in relation to the unascertained goods).

3   This provides as follows: 'Subject to section 20A below, where there is a contract for the sale of unascertained goods no property in the goods is transferred to the buyer unless and until the goods are ascertained.'

Section 20A (inserted by the Sale of Goods (Amendment) Act 1994, s 1(1) in response to Law Commission paper No 215) provides for title in ex-bulk goods to pass under a tenancy in common, where the purchase price has been paid.

This provision relates to goods, and securities are not goods but (generally) choses in action. Goods are defined in s 61(1) of the Sale of Goods Act 1979 to exclude things in action.

4   *Knight v Knight* (1840) 3 Beav 148.

5   [1994] 2 All ER 806 at 814.

3.28 Accordingly, a trust cannot be created by the legal owner of a commingled pool of goods who purports to transfer to another person equitable ownership of an unallocated amount of that pool[1].

1   See *Re Wait* [1927] 1 Ch 606. A trust of six of my cases of Château Lafite 1961 where I own 12 cases is void for uncertainty, while a trust of half of my cases of Château Lafite 1961 is valid. But compare *White v Shortall* 9 ITELR 470 (2006, NSWSC) where such an arrangement regarding shares was considered to be effective, following *Hunter v Moss* (see paras **3.37–3.41** below), and see also *Re Lehman Brothers International (Europe) (in administration); Pearson and others v Lehman Brothers Finance SA and other companies* [2010] EWHC 2914 (Ch) and *In the matter of Lehman Brothers International (Europe) (in administration)* [2011] EWCA Civ 1544.

3.29 Because, in fungible custody, the particular securities are not allocated to particular clients, some commentators have argued that the rights of clients may be confined (broadly) to a contractual right against the custodian, arising under the custody agreement, to call for redelivery of securities equivalent to those originally deposited[1]. If this were the position, the implications would be serious, both for the clients and for the custodian. The client's assets would be available to general creditors in the custodian's insolvency. Further, the value of the portfolio as collateral would be reduced[2]. Fortunately, in the light of recent case law, the general view is that fungible custody is compatible with the protection of clients' property rights in the custody portfolio under a trust relationship with the custodian, as discussed below[3]. It is noteworthy that in one of the court cases resulting from the administration of Lehman Brothers International (Europe)[4], the judge had no difficulty in concluding that assets held under custody terms (in that case as part of a prime brokerage arrangement) were held on trust, even though the term 'trust' was not used in the agreement. The question of certainty of subject matter of the trust was not even raised.

1   See Robert Ryan 'Taking Security Over Investment Portfolios held in Global Custody' [1990] 10 JIBL 404.

2   If the client has no proprietary rights in the custody assets, the value of such collateral to any third party will depend upon the credit risk of the custodian, as well as that of the issuer of the underlying securities.

3   But see discussion in the context of the proposed Securities Law Directive for an indication of the difficulties some have with the concept of omnibus holding of securities and fungibility (Chapter 7 para **7.189**).

4   *In Re Lehman Brothers International (Europe)* [2009] EWHC 2545 (Ch).

The cases

3.30   Debate about the allocation question has focused on the following line of cases.

Re London Wine (Shippers) Ltd[1]

3.31   This case concerned a wine importing company to which a receiver had been appointed pursuant to a floating charge in favour of a bank. The company held wine in various warehouses. Most of the wine had been sold to clients who left the wine in the possession of the company's warehouse agent. There was no segregation of any wine crates or cases in favour of clients generally or any particular client. The clients claimed that they had proprietary interests in the wine. The receiver argued that they had merely personal claims against the company for delivery of wine.

1   *Re London Wine (Shippers) Ltd* [1986] PCC 121.

3.32   Judgment was given in favour of the receiver. This was on the basis that there had been no allocation to the clients: proprietary rights could not pass at law for want of allocation or under a trust for want of certainty of subject matter.

Re Stapylton Fletcher Ltd[1]

3.33   The facts of this case were similar to those of *Re London Wine*[2], except that the wine intended for customers was segregated from the trading stock of the company. This difference was held to be crucial[3] and judgment was given in favour of the claimants from the liquidators: 'They will take as tenants in common'[4].

1   *Re Stapylton Fletcher Ltd; Re Ellis, Son & Vidler Ltd* [1994] 1 WLR 1181, [1995] 1 All ER 192.

2   *Re London Wine (Shippers) Ltd* [1986] PCC 121.

3   'I do not regard that decision [in *Re London Wine*] as inevitably governing the case before me. One obvious difference in the present case is the segregation of the wine purchased by the customers in a separate part of the warehouse and the careful maintenance of records within the company. Further as the London Wine Company was free to sell its stock and satisfy the customers from any other available source, there was no ascertainable bulk in that case': per Judge Paul Baker QC at [1994] 1 WLR 1181 at 1194.

4   [1994] 1 WLR 1181 at 1200.

3.34   As custodians segregate their house positions from client holdings, this case supports a robust approach to the allocation question. However, it would be prudent to note that, unlike *Re (London Wine), Stapylton Fletcher* related only to legal interests arising in the sale of goods and not to interests under a trust[1].

1   'As I have found for the first four claimants in the case relating to ESV on the basis of the passing of property at law, I do not have to consider the alternative lines of argument based on trusts, fiduciary relationships or other equitable principles in relation to these claims': [1994] 1 WLR 1181 at 1201.

Re Goldcorp Exchange Ltd (in receivership)[1]

3.35   Goldcorp, a dealer in precious metals, agreed with certain customers ('the unallocated customers') to sell gold to them and to hold it for them on an unallocated basis. It represented that it would set aside and hold a pool of gold sufficient to meet the claims of the unallocated customers, but did not do so. Goldcorp became insolvent and its stock of gold was insufficient to meet the claims of the unallocated customers. In a dispute between receivers appointed pursuant to a floating charge and unallocated customers, judgment was given in favour of the receivers. The claims of the unallocated customers were held to be merely contractual.

1   [1994] 2 All ER 806.

3.36   The judgment distinguishes between 'generic' goods (the source of which is not specified) and 'ex-bulk' goods (which must come from a specified source)[1]. The case for the claimants failed (both at law and in equity) because on the facts *Goldcorp* related to generic goods[2]. If it had been a question of ex-bulk goods, the position might have been different[3]. Thus, it could be argued that, because custodians segregate house position from client holdings, fungible custody falls outside the scope of the decision in *Goldcorp*. However, the judgment remains unclear on this point. Nowhere is it unequivocally stated that if client and house assets had been segregated, the interest of unallocated clients would have been proprietary. As Cooke P understated in the court below, 'it is a difficult area of law'[4].

1   [1994] 2 All ER 806 at 814.
2   [1994] 2 All ER 806 at 814.
3   [1994] 2 All ER 806 at 820.
4   *Liggett v Kensington* [1993] 1 NZLR 257 at 268.

Hunter v Moss[1]

3.37   The custody industry was therefore grateful for the decision in *Hunter v Moss*. The facts of this case were as follows. Moss was the registered holder of 950 shares in a company with 1,000 shares in issue. Moss made a declaration of trust over 5 per cent of the company's issued share capital in favour of Hunter. A valid trust was held by Colin Rimer QC, a deputy judge, to have arisen from the intention to create a trust over 50 of Moss's shares. Moss applied by motion for the judgment to be recalled to deal with the overlooked point that the trust failed for want of certainty of subject matter.

1   [1993] 1 WLR 934; affd [1994] 1 WLR 452, [1994] 3 All ER 215, CA.

3.38   However, Rimer QC held that, in a trust over intangibles, the requirement for certainty of subject matter does not apply.

> 'The defendant did not identify any particular 50 shares for the plaintiff because to do so was unnecessary and irrelevant. All 950 of his shares carried identical rights ... Any suggested uncertainty as to subject matter appears to me to be theoretical and conceptual rather than real and practical.'[1]

1   [1993] 1 WLR 934 at 946, per Colin Rimer QC (sitting as deputy High Court judge). But in these days of mass production, many tangibles are identical.

3.39   The Court of Appeal dismissed the appeal on the erroneous ground that, just as a person can by will give a specific number of her shares in a particular company, so equally she can declare herself a trustee of 50 of her shares in a particular company. However, on death the settlor is divested of all legal and beneficial ownership of her shares. In life she can only divest herself of the beneficial interest in shares when she has done everything necessary to identify those shares to which she has relinquished beneficial entitlement, namely when she has segregated 50 from those of which she retains beneficial ownership.

3.40 This decision has been treated with some caution in the legal community[1]. In particular, in the Court of Appeal, inter vivos transfers are not distinguished from testamentary transfers. On the particular facts of the case, it was clearly in the interests of justice that a valid trust should be found in the absence of a contractual entitlement. The judgment, which was pragmatic, focused more on the merits of the dispute before the court than the wider principles of equity. There is plenty of authority that certainty of subject matter is essential to a trust over a type of intangible asset, namely cash at bank, which is not adequately dealt with in this case[2].

1   See David Hayton 'Uncertainty of Subject-Matter of Trusts' (1994) 110 LQR 335.

2   See, for example, *Mac-Jordan Construction Ltd v Brookmount Erostin Ltd* [1992] BCLC 350. See also *Re Jartray Developments Ltd* (1982) 22 BLR 134; *Rayack Construction v Lampeter Meat Co Ltd* (1979) 12 BLR 30; *Neste Oy v Lloyds Bank plc* [1983] 2 Lloyd's Rep 658; *Concorde Construction Co Ltd v Colgan Ltd* (1984) 29 BLR 120; *Mills and others v Sportsdirect.com* [2010] EWHC 1072 (Ch). However, these cases may be distinguishable on the basis that they relate to generic and not ex bulk assets.

    A purported trust created for value over an unallocated part of a pool of intangibles may create a mere charge if by way of security for payment of a debt: *Swiss Bank v Lloyds Bank* [1979] Ch 548, [1979] 3 WLR 201, [1979] 2 All ER 853; revsd [1982] AC 584, [1980] 3 WLR 457, [1980] 2 All ER 419; affd [1982] AC 584, [1981] 2 WLR 893, [1981] 2 All ER 449. See also *ILG Travel Ltd (in administration)* [1995] 2 BCLC 128 (Ch).

3.41 However, in spite of these problems, *Hunter v Moss* has now been followed in *Re Harvard Securities*[1], the Hong Kong case of *CA Pacific*[2], and *White v Shortall*[3], and may appear to be good law. And more recently, see *Re Lehman Brothers International (Europe) (in administration); Pearson and others v Lehman Brothers Finance SA and other companies* [2010] EWHC 2914 (Ch), which followed *Hunter v Moss* and was not disagreed with in the Court of Appeal judgement (*In the matter of Lehman Brothers International (Europe) (in administration)* [2011] EWCA Civ 1544)[4].

1   *Re Harvard Securities (in liquidation)* [1997] 2 BCLC 369. Neither this case nor the Hong Kong case should be cited in court proceedings covered by *Hunter v Moss*: see *Practice Note* [2001] 2 All ER 510.

2   *Re CA Pacific Finance Ltd (in Liquidation)* [2000] 1 BCLC 494.

3   9 ITELR 470 (2006, NSWSC). Here Campbell J concluded that the trust declared over 220,000 shares of the total 1.5 million shares held was a declaration of trust over all the shares, deciding that, 'in substance ... 220,000 of the shares he held were on trust for the plaintiff, and the rest were on trust for himself', stating that the beneficiary was entitled to a proportion, and describing the trust as 'a trust of a fund ... for two different beneficiaries'. The judgment contains considerable emphasis on the nature of shares and the absence of a need to identify specific shares. Nevertheless, it is arguable that this case is not authority for arguing that certainty of subject matter is not necessary for a valid trust, but that on the facts the conclusion was reached that there was a trust over the commingled pool, with each beneficiary having a proportional entitlement (rather than that there was a valid trust over an unidentifiable part of a larger pool).

4   'Hunter v Moss has not been without its academic and judicial critics, but its conclusion that there is no objection on the grounds of uncertainty to a trust of part of a shareholding of the trustee has been generally followed, in this country in *Re Harvard Securities* [1997] 2 BCLC 369[1997] 2 BCLC 369, in Hong Kong in *Re CA Pacific Finance Ltd* [2000] 1 BCLC 494, and in Australia in *White v Shortall* [2006] NSW SC 1379. The difficulty with applying the Court of Appeal's judgment in *Hunter v Moss* to any case not on almost identical facts lies in the absence of any clearly expressed rationale as to how such a trust works in practice. There has not been unanimity among those courts which have followed *Hunter v Moss*, nor among the many academics who have commented upon it, as to the correct approach. The analysis which I have found the most persuasive is that such a trust works by creating a beneficial co-ownership share in the identified fund, rather than in the conceptually much more difficult notion of seeking to identify a particular part of that fund which the beneficiary owns outright. A principal academic advocate for the co-ownership approach is Professor Roy Goode: see for example "Are Intangible Assets Fungible?" [2003] LMCLQ 379. Among the judicial commentators I have found the analysis of Campbell J in *White v Shortall* (supra) at para 212 to be the most persuasive. My own preference for the co-ownership analysis may be observed in *LBIE v RAB Market Cycles* [2009] EWHC 2545 (Ch), at para 56. I propose to adopt it for the purposes of the analysis which follows.' *Re Lehman Brothers International (Europe) (in*

administration); Pearson and others v Lehman Brothers Finance SA and other companies [2010] EWHC 2914 (Ch), Briggs J, at paras 231, 232.

Equitable tenancy in common

3.42 In the authors' view, *Hunter v Moss*[1] may be (roughly) reconciled with *MacJordan*[2] and the other cases referred to above relating to trusts over cash accounts, by taking the current position to be as follows. In fungible custody arrangements, provided client assets are segregated from house assets, the requirement for certainty of subject matter is not inapplicable; however, it is automatically satisfied by an implied co-ownership arrangement, whereby the custodian holds the client holding under a single trust for all clients to whose accounts it has credited the relevant security, as equitable tenants in common. This analysis is consistent with the decision in *Re Stapylton Fletcher*[3], but not with that in *CA Pacific*[4]. It is submitted that the latter is unreliable. It is also submitted that it should not be assumed that clients enjoy property rights unless the client holding is segregated from the house position[5]. Thus, in collateral arrangements where the custodian is permitted to credit client securities to its house account[6], it should be assumed that the client's rights are merely contractual, so that she takes the credit risk of the custodian[7], unless the custodian holds on trust for both itself and its client(s)[8].

1   [1993] 1 WLR 934; affd [1994] 1 WLR 452, [1994] 3 All ER 215, CA.

2   *Mac-Jordan Construction Ltd v Brookmount Erostin Ltd* [1992] BCLC 350.

3   *Re Stapylton Fletcher Ltd; Re Ellis, Son & Vidler Ltd* [1994] 1 WLR 1181, [1995] 1 All ER 192.

4   *Re CA Pacific Finance Ltd (in Liquidation)* [2000] 1 BCLC 494.

5   Without such segregation, the assets would be generic and not ex bulk, and therefore outside the scope of *Re Stapylton Fletcher* and related cases.

6   For example, under prime brokerage arrangements.

7   See David J Hayton and Charles Mitchell (eds) *Hayton and Marshall: Cases and commentary on the law of Trusts and Equitable Remedies* (2005, 12th edn, Sweet & Maxwell).

8   As in *White v Shortall* 9 ITELR 470 (2006, NSWSC).

Two lines of cases

3.43 An advantage of the above 'tenancy in common' approach is that it reconciles the cases relating to the allocation question with another line of cases, relating to mixing.

3.44 The issue under consideration in the allocation cases discussed above was the acquisition, by the purchasers, of proprietary interests in assets forming part of a fungible pool. In all these cases the mixing of the whole *antedates* the possible ownership of part.

3.45 Another line of cases establishes the principle, based on Roman law, that where the goods of different owners are mixed together so that they cannot be separated, the owners will hold the commingled goods as tenants in common[1]. In these cases, the mixing of the whole *predates* the possible ownership of part. These cases concern the preservation of existing proprietary rights, as opposed to the creation of new ones.

1   See *Buckley v Gross* (1863) 3 B & S 566, 122 ER 213; *Spence v Union Marine Insurance Co Ltd* (1868) LR 3 CP 427; *Indian Oil Corpn Ltd v Greenstone Shipping SA, The Ypatianna* [1988] QB 345, [1987] 3 WLR 869, [1987] 3 All ER 893; and *Glencore International AG v Metro Trading Inc* [2001] 1 Lloyd's Rep 284.

3.46 In practice, the operational complexities of settlement are such that it may not be possible to determine which part of a client's custody portfolio is governed by which line of case law. It is therefore helpful to conclude that such determination is unnecessary, on the basis that the position will be the same in any event, and that the client enjoys property rights under an equitable tenancy in common.

Conclusions

3.47 In relation to the custody securities portfolio, it is necessary to protect the client from the credit risk of the custodian. The traditional legal technique for achieving this, by characterising the custodian as a bailee, is ineffective in an electronic environment. It is therefore necessary to establish a trust. With fungible custody, the lack of allocation between any particular client and particular underlying securities raises the allocation question: is there sufficient certainty of subject matter in order to establish a valid trust? As discussed above, the natural answer to the allocation problem is co-ownership. Rather than seek to identify a trust in favour of each client over their unallocated portion of the client securities, one may identify one global trust over all the client securities of a particular type in favour of all relevant clients as tenants in common[1].

1   A separate tenancy in common exists in relation to each type of security from time to time comprised in clients' portfolios. This is because, in practice, it will not be the case that each client's portfolio includes the same range of securities in the same proportions. A necessary feature of a tenancy in common is unity of possession. Charles Harpum, Stuart Bridge and Martin Dixon *Megarry and Wade The Law of Real Property* (2007, 7th edn, Sweet & Maxwell).

   This multiplication of tenancies in common should not create any administrative difficulty, because their existence is notional and automatic, and does not require any practical step to be taken.

3.48 Another requirement under English law for a valid trust is certainty of intention. Given that English law looks at the substance of the intention of the parties, rather than simply the title of the document, the absence of any reference to a trust in a custody agreement is not an obstacle to the custodian holding the custody assets on trust. This was made clear in a case arising out of the administration of Lehman Brothers International (Europe)[1] where the judge concluded there was a trust as a result of a clear intention in the agreement that the client retained ownership of the relevant securities[2].

1   In *Re Lehman Brothers International (Europe)* [2009] EWHC 2545 (Ch).

2   In this case, Briggs J stated that 'Where an entity ("A") transfers legal title to property to another ("B") pursuant to a detailed written agreement, the question whether A has retained some proprietary or beneficial interest in the property transferred depends upon the parties' deemed mutual intention, on the true interpretation of that agreement.' Based on 'the parties ... use of the words "custody" and "custodian", and by the phrases ... "belong to the Counterparty" and "do not belong to the Prime Broker"'. Briggs J concluded that the parties had 'used the clearest language to display their intention that securities held by the Prime Broker for the time being continue to belong beneficially to the Counterparty'. Moreover, even where securities were held in an omnibus account so that 'the proprietary interest of any particular Counterparty is to a rateable share in the fungible account rather than in particular securities in that account', he considered that 'there is no reason ... why that interest should not be recognised as proprietary, or that the obligations of the account holder (be it as custodian or sub-custodian) are those of a trustee.' Briggs J also stated that he regarded the wording quoted from the agreement and the provisions prohibiting the mixing of client securities with securities of the custodian or sub-custodian 'as powerful indicators in favour of the recognition of the creation of a trustee/beneficial relationship between the Prime Broker and Counterparty in relation to securities.' In addition, in Re Lehman Brothers International (Europe) [2009] EWCA Civ 1161, where the Court of Appeal refused to allow a scheme of arrangement which would vary the rights of beneficiaries under a trust, the trusts in question were established under prime broker agreements and custody agreements, and there was no suggestion that the rights of clients under such agreements to assets held for them by Lehmans were other than as beneficial interests under a trust.

3.49 In the interests of legal clarity, it may be prudent to include express wording in the custody documentation to confirm the existence of such equitable tenancies in common among the custody clients over the commingled client holdings.

SHORTFALLS

3.50 Even if a trust or similar arrangement is recognised in the insolvency of the custodian, the client will still suffer loss if there is a shortfall in the securities held for it by the custodian.

> 'Shortfalls in custodial holdings may develop for a number of reasons, including the failure of trades to settle as anticipated, poor accounting controls, or intentional fraud. The shortfalls may be temporary or long-standing. Allocation of the risk of loss from a shortfall will vary depending on the circumstances under which the shortfall arose. Of course, if the custodian is solvent, no real problems arise; it may either replace the missing securities, or pay damages, or both. However, if the custodian is insolvent, or the shortfall arises from fraud or insolvency on the part of a sub-custodian or CSD, the investor's risk of loss may be severe.'[1]

1   Bank for International Settlements *Cross-Border Securities Settlement* (May 1995, Basle), p 20.

Shortfalls and commingled accounts

3.51 A risk associated with commingled custody accounts is that shortfalls attributable to the business of one client may be borne by other clients sharing the account. Where client-specific segregation is not offered, therefore, clients may wish to know whether the custodian engages in practices which heighten the risk of shortfall.

3.52 One source of shortfall risk is presented by security interests in favour of intermediaries in the global custody chain, such as sub-custodians and settlement systems. For example, if a global custodian becomes insolvent, a sub-custodian may enforce a lien over the client assets it holds for the global custodian in respect of unpaid fees[1].

1   The possibility of this is now limited where the custodian is regulated by the FSA by the restriction of the grant of liens and similar interests of over client securities (see Chapter 7, paras **7.41–7.44**). The FSA Conduct of Business Rules ('COBS') still require a custodian to inform (but not agree in writing with) the client (for all categories of client) of 'the existence and terms of any security interest or lien which the firm has or may have over the client's designated investments or client money, or any right of set-off it holds in relation to the client's designated investments or client money' (COBS 6.1.7R(2)(a) and (4)) And that 'a depositary may have a security interest or lien over, or right of set-off in relation to those instruments or money'. See further Chapter 7, para **7.47**).

3.53 A further source of potential shortfall risk is the deduction of liquidator's costs. The case of *Berkeley Applegate (Investment Consultants) Ltd*[1] established the principle that, where the assets of the insolvent company are insufficient to meet the liquidator's costs in administering property held on trust by the company for its clients, the court has discretion to award those costs out of the trust assets[2]. This principle may pose a threat to the assets of custody clients where the custodian does not have substantial assets of its own, and where adequate records of the custody business have not been kept, so that significant work is required to clarify the entitlements of clients.

1   [1988] 3 All ER 71.
2   [1988] 3 All ER 71 at 76, 82. See also *Re Sports Betting Media Ltd* [2007] All ER (D) 123.

3.54 Shortfalls may arise as a result of contractual settlement, a service offered by some global custodians in relation to cash or (more rarely) securities. The custodian agrees that, where moneys or securities are due to be received under a trade, those assets will be credited to the client's account on the date agreed for settlement with the counterparty, whether or not they are actually received on that date by the custodian. The custodian reserves the right to reverse the credit entry if the assets do not arrive within a reasonable period[1]. Contractual settlement amounts to the lending of cash and/or securities[2]. Where contractual settlement is offered in connection with a commingled securities account, the following risk arises. If a purchase of bonds is contractually settled, the client is free to sell them to a third party. If such a sale leaves the client's holding at zero and the original trade fails, the custodian cannot reverse the credit entry without causing a shortfall. Further, as the contractual settlement of securities amounts to securities lending, the question arises, from whom is the client borrowing? It will only be borrowing from the custodian if the custodian transfers new securities into the commingled account to support the transaction. If the custodian does not do this, the client is borrowing securities from the other clients of the custodian, possibly without their consent or knowledge. Such arrangements may well be unlawful.

1 Custodians only offer contractual settlement in markets where they are confident of timely settlement.
2 This raises issues of authority to lend and borrow such assets, as well as taxation issues.

Allocation of shortfall

3.55 Where there is a shortfall in the pooled client securities account of an insolvent custodian, the question arises how the shortfall will be borne by the respective clients. Where the account has been very active, it seems likely that the loss would be borne pro rata among all the affected clients in order to 'apportion a common misfortune'[1]. However, the position would be less clear in the unlikely event that the account was inactive, so that as a matter evidence it was relatively easy to identify the transactions which had caused the shortfall. In such a case, the courts might apply the traditional tracing rules to attribute the 'missing' securities to a particular client or clients[2].

1 See *Barlow Clowes International v Vaughan* [1992] 4 All ER 22. See also *Russell-Cooke Trust Company and another v Richard Prentis and Co Ltd* [2002] EWHC 2227 (Ch) where the same principle was applied to some assets, but for assets considered to have been specifically allocated to specific and identified clients Lindsay J rejected the 'proposition that, wherever there is shared common misfortune, clearly discernible separate property rights are to be surrendered or overridden. Investors may, so to speak, be in the same boat but that, of itself, does not require anyone to give up the life jacket which he is already plainly wearing'.

Interestingly, the risk warnings required to be given to commingled clients by the FSA under the old rules applicable in a non-MiFID context assumed that shortfalls would be pro rated: see CASS 2.3.3G:

'When explaining the meaning of pooling to a retail client, firms are expected to advise the retail client that ... in the event of an unreconcilable shortfall after the failure [note – defined to mean insolvency situations] of a custodian [in context, meaning a subcustodian], clients may share in that shortfall in proportion to their original share of the assets in the pool.'

There is no equivalent of the above in the current CASS Chapter 7, although under COBS 6.1.7R(1)(b) a custodian must notify a retail client if client assets are held in an omnibus account with a third party and give 'a prominent warning of the resulting risks' (but no guidance is given as to the form or content of such warning).

2 In *Barlow Clowes*, the loss was pro rated because the accounts had been so active that the application of the traditional tracing rules would have been unduly complex.

CHAPTER 4

The use of the custody portfolio as collateral

4.1 This chapter will consider the use of the custody portfolio as collateral. This is commercially important for a number of reasons.

4.2 First, the provision of a global custodial service can involve significant credit exposures for the global custodian (particularly in the context of credit lines granted by a custodian to a client to facilitate settlement), which the global custodian will wish to collateralise as effectively as possible by use of the custody portfolio. This is particularly important for custodians who are banks or otherwise subject to the increasingly complex capital adequacy regime regarding risk-weightings for counterparties and collateral.

4.3 Second, as holder of assets for clients who wish to use such assets as collateral, custodians commonly provide collateral management services. As collateral manager, the global custodian either assists the client in offering the custody portfolio as collateral to third parties, or alternatively itself offers credit facilities to the client, collateralising these exposures against the custody portfolio. An important example of the latter type of arrangement is prime brokerage, discussed below, but similar issues may arise in any structure where one party holds a pool of assets on behalf of another (whether such service is termed custody, safekeeping, escrow or something else).

OVERVIEW

Nature of collateralisation

4.4 Collateralisation is a technique for managing credit risk. Chapter 2 discussed the difference between personal rights (which are enforceable against persons) and property rights (which are enforceable against assets). Because a personal right such as a debt is enforceable only against the person who owes it (the debtor), it may become valueless if for any reason the creditor's ability successfully to enforce is affected. In the financial markets, the most commercially significant reason why debts and other personal rights may become valueless is insolvency. When a debtor becomes insolvent, the debt generally cannot be successfully enforced in the normal way, and the debtor must prove in the insolvency proceedings as an unsecured creditor. Depending on the outcome of the insolvency proceedings, the debtor is likely to face delay in payment, and may receive only a fraction of the sum owed, or indeed nothing at all. This exposure to a counterparty's insolvency is called credit risk.

4.5 In order to manage credit risk, creditors and other persons who are owed a personal obligation[1] may require that their counterparties collateralise these exposures. Collateralisation involves the delivery from the debtor[2] to the creditor[3] of property rights in identified assets. If the collateral giver defaults, the collateral taker is able to satisfy its claims out of the collateral assets.

1 Such as, for example, a right to the redelivery of loaned securities under a securities lending agreement.

2   Or other obligor.

3   Or other obligee.

Financial institutions as collateral takers

4.6 Throughout the 1990s and into the new millennium and beyond, there has been a significant growth in the use of collateral by financial institutions. Whenever there are market difficulties, be it the market turbulence of 1998 or the market difficulties beginning in 2007/2008 involving 'a sharp decline in investors' appetite for credit risk'[1], attention focuses on the need carefully to manage credit exposures. Further, regulated institutions are subject to regulatory capital requirements in respect of their credit exposures, and such requirements are very significantly relieved by collateralisation. The need to demonstrate a good return on capital in an increasingly competitive environment encourages regulated institutions to seek ever greater capital efficiencies, by collateralising their credit exposures to the greatest possible extent.

1   'EBF's general policy overview on the Financial Crisis' (published by the European Banking Federation, April 2008), section entitled 'Background and causes of the global market crisis'.

4.7 A number of other developments in the securities markets are causing a significant increase in the use of collateral. These include the continuing development of the securities lending and repo markets; and the increasing use of central counterparties, and the use of central bank money, in securities settlement[1].

1   See Chapter 8.

4.8 Another factor which may increase the use of collateral by global custodians and other financial institutions is the particular regulatory or legislative regime applicable to a particular client. For example, when extending credit to insurance companies, it is important to be aware of the implementation of the Insurance Winding Up Directive[1]. Article 10 provides for the priority of insurance claims over the claims of other unsecured creditors[2]. Because the priority provisions serve to subordinate unsecured claims which do not arise under insurance contracts, the credit standing of insurance companies in the financial markets is arguably reduced, and the cost of credit for them should be adjusted accordingly[3]. Because these provisions significantly reduce the value of an unsecured debt or other personal claim against an insurance company, custodians may consider negotiating to secure exposures to insurance company clients.

1   Directive 2001/17/EC on the reorganisation and winding up of insurance undertakings. The Insurance Winding Up Directive applies to reorganisation measures and winding up proceedings. These terms are (widely) defined in arts 2(c) and (d) respectively. Insurance undertaking is defined in art 2(a) so as to include direct insurance business, but not reinsurance.

2   For this purpose, the term 'insurance claims' is defined in art 2(k) as 'any amount which is owed by an insurance undertaking to insured persons, policy holders, beneficiaries or to any injured party having a direct right of action against the insurance undertaking and which arises from an insurance contract ... in direct insurance business ...'. This clearly excludes reinsurance.

   Two options are available for the implementation of the priority of insurance claims. First, there may be absolute precedence of insurance claims with respect to insurers' assets representing technical provisions; alternatively, insurance claims may take precedence with respect to all the assets of the insurers, with the possible exception of certain preferential claims.

3   Also, financial counterparties may seek to restructure their credit arrangements so as to bring them within the definition of insurance claims, and therefore the priority provisions of this Directive.

4.9 However, it is also important to appreciate the limits of collateral. This remains an important lesson to be drawn from the near collapse in 1998 of the hedge fund, Long-Term Capital Management[1]. Collateralisation should complement, but should never substitute, effective credit control. Similarly, providers of collateral must consider the potential consequences of the arrangements, particularly in the context of the provision of title transfer collateral. For example, where there is a transfer to a counterparty of assets by way of title transfer collateral but the amount of such assets is very large compared with the obligations in respect of which the collateral is provided, the collateral-provider will have a large unsecured claim against the collateral-taker if the collateral-taker becomes insolvent.

1   'A related concern is whether the LTCM Fund's counterparties were lulled into a false sense of security based solely upon their collateral arrangements with the Fund. Counterparties' current credit exposures were in most cases covered by collateral. However, their potential future exposures were likely not adequately assessed, priced, or collateralised relative to the potential price shocks the markets were facing at the end of September 1998, and relative to the creditworthiness of the LTCM Fund at that time. Further, expectations about the ability to collect on collateral calls were probably unrealistic for an entity like the LTCM Fund, particularly in the market environment of last Fall. Thus, counterparties that were relying on variation margin to manage credit risk were left with the unsatisfactory prospect of liquidating collateral and closing out exposures in a declining market': *Hedge Funds, Leverage, and the Lessons of Long-Term Capital Management*, Report of the President's Working Group on Financial Markets, April 1999, p 15.

Financial assets as collateral

4.10   Any type of asset may in theory serve as collateral. However, it is important for the collateral taker that collateral assets should be capable of being readily valued and, upon enforcement of the collateral arrangement, readily sold. For these reasons, financial assets such as cash at bank (and in particular US dollars) and securities (and in particular US Treasuries) are highly sought after by collateral takers. As the demand for financial collateral increases, other forms of financial collateral, including corporate debt securities and, in some cases, equities[1], are increasingly used to collateralise financial exposures.

1   Equities have traditionally been regarded as unattractive collateral, primarily because of their volatility.

Collateral and the global custodian

4.11   As indicated above, the use of the custody portfolio as collateral is important for the global custodian, both to collateralise its own settlement exposures to the client, and also in the development of collateral management products, where the collateral taker is either the custodian itself or a third party.

The global custodian's settlement exposures

4.12   The provision of a settlement service to clients may involve the global custodian in significant and unpredictable exposures. Many global custodians extend credit to clients in order to facilitate settlement, not least because transfers of securities to the custodian for the benefit of the client may take place in one time zone whereas the transfer of cash takes place in a different time zone, thus necessitating that the global custodian settles a client's purchase instruction out of its own funds where the client has not pre-funded the transaction. As discussed in Chapter 3, many global custodians offer a service called 'contractual settlement', in relation to cash or (more rarely) securities accounts. It is agreed with the client that, where moneys or securities are due to be received on the settlement of a trade, those assets will be credited to the client's account[1] by the global custodian on the date agreed for settlement with the counterparty, whether or not they are actually received on that date by the global custodian. The global custodian reserves the right to reverse the credit entry if the assets do not arrive within a reasonable period. In practice, this service is only offered in markets where global custodians are generally confident of timely settlement. Contractual settlement amounts to the lending of cash and/or securities[2], and exposes the custodian to the credit risk of the client.

1   So that they are available to the client for delivery to third parties.

2   It is important to establish that the client has authority to borrow such assets, and to consider the taxation implications of the arrangements.

4.13   Possible credit and liquidity problems associated with the settlement systems[1] with which the global custodian deals present a further source of potential credit risk. The global custodian will customarily contract as principal with settlement systems. Under standard terms of participation, these counterparties take indemnities from the global custodian in respect of exposures associated with the global custodian's business. Suppose the client instructs the global custodian to settle a purchase of 1,000 ABC securities through a settlement system, and subsequently instructs the global custodian to settle a sale of the same securities, leaving the ABC client account at the settlement system at zero. The next day it transpires that the initial credit to the account reflected a bad delivery (perhaps under insolvency avoidance provisions affecting the vendor to the client), and the credit is reversed, so that the account has a negative balance. Under its terms of participation in the settlement system, the global custodian will be contractually required to deliver 1,000 ABC securities into the account, at its own expense if necessary. Clearly, under its own global custody agreement with the client, the global custodian will have a contractual right to recover the associated costs from the client under an indemnity. However, an indemnity confers only a personal right against the client, and hence involves credit risk. If the client is insolvent, the indemnity may be worthless.

1   Equivalent issues arise in relation to sub-custodians.

4.14   Standard global custody agreements contain provisions whereby the global custodian may use the custody portfolio to collateralise such exposures. Because such client settlement exposures may be very significant indeed, it is important to ensure that these provisions are robust. A number of sensitivities arise, as discussed at paras **4.33–4.78** below.

Collateral management products

IN FAVOUR OF THIRD PARTIES

4.15   In many cases, global custody clients incur credit exposures to third party financial institutions, and wish to offer assets within the custody portfolio as collateral to such third parties. One possibility is that the global custodian acts as agent of the custody client in entering into collateralised transactions with third parties, for example, under agency securities lending arrangements.

4.16   Another possibility is that the assets to be delivered by the client as collateral remain with the custodian, which (thereafter) holds them on behalf of the collateral taker. In this case, the collateral taker must satisfy itself that the custody arrangements, as well as the collateral arrangements, are legally robust. Bespoke collateral arrangements may be drafted to support particular credit facilities in favour of the client. Importantly, global custodians may develop collateral netting services in order to enable their clients to make the most efficient use of available collateral assets. These services may range from cross-product netting arrangements with particular counterparties of the custody client, to cross-market collateral netting services for central counterparties, as indicated in Chapter 8[1].

1 With the increased reliance on central counterparty arrangements in the securities markets (discussed in Chapter 8), there is significant commercial demand to achieve the greatest possible netting efficiencies in the collateralisation of such arrangements, so that surplus collateral available in relation to one market can be applied without delay to meet collateral needs arising in another market.

4.17 Under such arrangements, in addition to providing a custody service to the custody client, the global custodian provides services to the collateral taker, monitoring and administering the whole or part of the custody portfolio that comprises the collateral on its behalf. It is important to consider potential conflicts of interest that may arise between the global custody client and the collateral taker. As discussed in Chapter 6, the global custodian owes implied fiduciary duties of undivided loyalty, so that in general it must not allow its duties to one client to conflict with its duties to another client. Implied fiduciary duties may be effectively modified by contract, provided the contractual relieving provisions are sufficiently clear and detailed. Thus, it is important that in the documentation supporting these arrangements, potential conflicts are disclosed and permitted. Also, for commercial reasons, it is obviously important to clarify the rights and duties of the global custodian in the event of conflict between the custody client and the collateral taker, for example, upon default and enforcement.

IN FAVOUR OF THE GLOBAL CUSTODIAN — PRIME BROKERAGE

4.18 Another way in which global custodians can assist their clients to develop the potential of the custody portfolio as a collateral pool is through services such as prime brokerage, where the global custodian is both collateral manager and collateral taker.

4.19 Prime brokerage is a service which has been developed, somewhat controversially, by financial institutions (including global custodians) in favour of hedge fund clients. Hedge funds are a type of unregulated collective investment scheme offering a high risk/high reward investment to sophisticated investors[1]. A key characteristic of hedge funds is that they are often highly geared, ie their borrowings are extremely large relative to their net assets[2]. This enables hedge funds, which may raise a relatively small sum from investor's subscriptions, to gain a very large exposure to the financial markets. In turn, this permits spectacular profits when the portfolio management strategy is successful and, unfortunately, equally spectacular failures when it is not[3].

1 'The term "hedge fund" is commonly used to describe a variety of different types of investment vehicles that share some similar characteristics. Although it is not statutorily defined, the term encompasses any pooled investment vehicle that is privately organised, administered by professional investment managers, and not widely available to the public. The primary investors in hedge funds are wealthy individuals and institutional investors': Report of the President's Working Group on Financial Markets *Hedge Funds, Leverage, and the Lessons of Long-Term Capital Management*, April 1999, p 2 ('Report of the President's Working Group'). For a further discussion of legal aspects of prime brokerage and hedge funds, see Joanna Benjamin *Interests in Securities* (2000, Oxford University Press), ch 10, section B.

2 Leverage may be 30 times capital: see Report of the President's Working Group, p 5.

3 A major hedge fund, Long Term Capital Management, notoriously nearly failed in 1998, threatening the stability of the New York financial markets.

4.20 The prime broker enters into complex contractual arrangements with the client, which may include (in simplified form) the following provisions[1]. The prime broker purchases securities on behalf of the client, itself lending the purchase price. The prime broker then holds the purchased securities in custody for the client, subject to collateral arrangements in its favour. These collateral arrangements characteristically fall into two parts. First, the client grants a security interest to the prime broker over the securities. As a quid pro quo for permitting the client to pay a discounted rate of interest on the loan, the prime broker normally states in its terms that it has the power at any time to transfer securities out of the client's custody account and into its own account, subject to a contractual obligation to redeliver equivalent securities to the client (in effect, creating an outright title transfer collateral arrangement[2]). This enables the prime broker to use the securities in its own business with third parties, as collateral or as loaned securities, itself retaining associated profits.

1   This is a very brief summary of customary provisions; in practice, prime brokerage terms are complex and vary from case to case.

2   Note that this is not necessarily a right of use as applicable under the Financial Collateral Regulations – see paras **4.55, 4.74** and **4.79** et seq below.

4.21   Under these arrangements, it is important to consider a second type of potential conflict of interest. The previous section discussed potential conflicts between two clients of the global custodian. In contrast, it is necessary here to consider potential conflicts between the client as collateral giver and the global custodian as collateral taker. Because there is a general implied fiduciary duty of avoiding such conflicts (discussed in Chapter 6), clear and detailed provisions in the client documentation are necessary to relieve the custodian of fiduciary obligations which could otherwise prevent it from taking collateral.

4.22   These arrangements raise certain other legal sensitivities, discussed at paras **4.33–4.78** below.

LEGAL STRUCTURES OF COLLATERAL[1]

4.23   In order to understand the legal sensitivities surrounding collateral arrangements, it is necessary briefly to consider the different legal structures that are available. These fall into two broad categories, namely security interests (which are recognised in all systems of commercial law) and outright collateral transfers (which are in origin Anglo-Saxon structures, and historically less widely recognised in civil law jurisdictions). The difference between them relates to the nature of the property interest received by the collateral taker in the collateral assets prior to enforcement. As discussed below, the implementation of the Financial Collateral Directive[2] reduces the difference between the two structures.

1   The following is a very brief summary of a complex area of law. For more detail, see Joanna Benjamin *Interests in Securities* (2000, Oxford University Press), chs 4, 5 and 6.

2   Directive 2002/47/EC of the European Parliament and of the Council of 6 June 2002 on financial collateral arrangements.

Security interests

4.24   Under a security interest, the collateral giver delivers to the collateral taker a limited property right or interest. This limited interest (the security interest) confers certain rights on the collateral taker, including (crucially) the right upon the default of the collateral giver to sell the collateral assets and apply the proceeds of sale to discharge the collateralised obligation. Any surplus must be returned to the collateral giver (or, if it is insolvent, its insolvency official). Exceptionally, a lien does not generally confer a power of sale, but only a right of retention, as discussed below.

4.25   However, in the absence of default, the collateral taker is in general not free to deal with the collateral assets. This is because the non-defaulting collateral giver retains a residual property right in them, which is known as the equity of redemption. This is the right, upon the discharge of the secured obligation, to the return of the particular assets that were originally delivered as collateral. Because it is a property right, the equity of redemption is not at risk in the insolvency of the collateral taker. Thus, the collateral giver who discharges its collateralised debt can recover the collateral assets from the collateral taker's insolvency official. Where the value of the collateral assets exceeds the value of the debt by a significant margin, the equity of redemption has a correspondingly significant value to the collateral giver in managing its credit exposure to the collateral taker. (However, as discussed below, the implementation of the Financial Collateral Directive confers a right of use on the collateral taker in wholesale financial collateral arrangements, which cuts across the equity of redemption.)

4.26 Many systems of law have only one form of security interest, often known as a pledge. However:

> 'There are ... four kinds of consensual security known to English law: (i) pledge; (ii) contractual lien; (iii) equitable charge and (iv) mortgage. A pledge and a contractual lien both depend on the delivery of possession to the creditor as security. The difference between them is that in the case of a pledge the owner delivers possession to the creditor as security, whereas in the case of a lien the creditor retains possession of goods previously delivered to him for some other purpose. Neither a mortgage nor a charge depends on the delivery of possession.'[1]

1   *Re Cosslett (Contractors) Ltd* [1997] 4 All ER 115 at 125, per Millett LJ.

4.27 It was argued in Chapter 2 that custody assets are intangible and therefore cannot be subject to possession. On this basis, it is arguable that security interests in relation to the custody portfolio cannot take effect either as pledge or as lien[1].

1   This is notwithstanding the fact that traditional global custody agreements routinely refer to the security interest of the global custodian as a lien; see the discussion below. But see also para **4.72** n 2.

4.28 A mortgage may be either legal (where legal ownership is delivered by way of security, subject to the equity of redemption) or equitable (where equitable ownership is delivered by way of security, subject again to the equity of redemption). Chapter 3 argued that the custody relationship involves a trust, and therefore the asset of the client in the custody portfolio is equitable and not legal. On this basis, if the collateral assets remain in the hands of the global custodian, the interest of a third party[1] collateral taker in the client's custody assets can only take effect in equity[2]. Such a security interest could be characterised as an equitable mortgage, or alternatively as a charge.

1   It is arguable that a security interest in favour of the custodian (either as principal or as agent) may take effect as a legal mortgage, on the basis that the global custodian holds legal title to the assets. The counter argument (indicating an equitable mortgage or charge) is that the global custodian acquired legal title as trustee, and not as mortgagee; a legal mortgage involves the delivery of legal title *by way of security* (and not by way of custody).
2   It is not possible to acquire a legal interest in an equitable asset. This is because an equitable asset is an asset recognised by equity, but not by the common law. The law will not recognise a property right where the asset to which it relates is not also recognised by it.

4.29 A charge can only take effect in equity and not at law[1]. There are two types of charge, namely fixed charges and floating charges.

> 'The essence of a floating charge is that it is a charge, not on any particular asset, but on a fluctuating body of assets which remain under the management and control of the chargor, and which the chargor has the right to withdraw from the security despite the existence of the charge. The essence of a fixed charge is that the charge is on a particular asset or class of assets which the chargor cannot deal with free from the charge without the consent of the chargee.'[2]

1   The exception is a charge over land. See Roy Goode *Legal Problems of Credit and Security* (2003, 3rd edn, Sweet & Maxwell), paras 1–51, 1–52.

2   *Re Cosslett (Contractors) Ltd* [1997] 4 All ER 115 at 143, per Millett LJ. While the floating charge has never been judicially defined, the classic description of the floating charge is given by Romer J in *Re Yorkshire Woolcombers Association Ltd* [1903] 2 Ch 284 at 295: 'I certainly do not intend to attempt to give an exact definition of the term "floating charge," nor am I prepared to say that there will not be a floating charge within the meaning of the Act, which does not contain all the three characteristics that I am about to mention, but I certainly think that if a charge has the three characteristics I am about to mention it is a floating charge. (1) If it is a charge on a class of assets of a company present and future; (2) if that class is one which, in the ordinary course of the business of the company, would be changing from time to time; and (3) if you find that by the charge it is contemplated that, until some future step is taken by or on behalf of those interested in the charge, the company may carry on its business in the ordinary way as far as concerns the particular class of assets I am dealing with.' See also Lord Macnaghten in *Illingworth v Houldsworth* [1904] AC 355 at 358. A very interesting discussion of the floating charge is contained in the judgment of Millett LJ in *Agnew v IRC* [2001] UKPC 28, [2001] 2 AC 710, [2001] 3 WLR 454, and also in the later cases of *Re Brumark* [2001] 2 AC 710; *National Westminster Bank plc v Spectrum Plus Limited* [2005] UKHL 41; and *The Russell Cooke Trust Company Limited v Elliot* [2007] EWHC 1443 (Ch).

Outright collateral transfers

4.30   Whereas, under a security interest, the collateral giver retains residual property rights in the collateral assets, which it continues to enjoy concurrently with the security interest of the collateral taker, an outright collateral transfer (as its name suggests) involves the transfer of the entirety of the interest of the collateral giver to the collateral taker. This means that the collateral giver retains no property rights in the collateral assets. Obviously, the non-defaulting collateral giver expects to receive assets back upon the discharge of the collateralised obligation. However, these rights of redelivery are personal (enforceable against the collateral taker) and not proprietary (enforceable against the collateral assets). Moreover, these redelivery rights are fungible, in the following sense. Rather than being able to call for the return of the particular securities originally delivered as collateral, the collateral giver's right is to the redelivery of *equivalent* securities. This means that it is entitled to the return of the same number and type of securities as were originally delivered, but not the same ones.

4.31   It follows from this that the collateral taker is free, from the moment it receives the collateral securities, to deal with them as it pleases. Its only obligation is to meet its equivalent redelivery obligation; as a practical matter, this may involve getting in the relevant type of securities just in time. Because the financial institutions which receive collateral under certain transactions are also obliged to deliver collateral under other transactions, this right of use has great commercial value. Indeed, it is generally regarded as the chief advantage of an outright collateral transfer over a security interest. As discussed below, the implementation of the Financial Collateral Directive extends the right of use to security interests over financial assets in wholesale arrangements.

4.32   In the event that either party defaults, set off applies[1]. This means that collateralised obligation of the collateral giver to the collateral taker, and the redelivery obligation of the collateral taker to the collateral giver, are valued, automatically converted into debts to pay their respective values, and then set off one against the other, so that only a net sum is payable. Repos[2] and, in London, securities loans are structured as outright collateral transfers, as are the collateral arrangements supporting many swaps[3].

1   Such transactions are generally entered into as part of a programme involving many transactions under master agreements. The default provision of such master agreements provides for close out netting as a preliminary to set off. As discussed below, close out netting reduces all the outstanding

obligations of each party to a single net obligation. These net obligations of each party are then set off against each other. Article 2.1(n) of the Financial Collateral Directive defines a 'close-out netting provision' as follows: 'a provision of a financial collateral arrangement, or of an arrangement of which a financial collateral arrangement forms part, or, in the absence of any such provision, any statutory rule by which, on the occurrence of an enforcement event, whether through the operation of netting or set-off or otherwise: (i) the obligations of the parties are accelerated so as to be immediately due and expressed as an obligation to pay an amount representing their estimated current value, or are terminated and replaced by an obligation to pay such an amount; and/or (ii) an account is taken of what is due from each party to the other in respect of such obligations, and a net sum equal to the balance of the account is payable by the party from whom the larger amount is due to the other party.'

2   Chapter 10 in the second edition of this work included a short discussion of the taxation treatment of repos and of manufactured payments. In a consultation document, 'Proposed changes to tax rules on manufactured payments' (27 March 2012) HMRC proposed a root and branch reform of the taxation treatment of manufactured payments and it is expected that the necessary legislation will be enacted in the Finance Act 2013. It is also understood that the Government intends to introduce a new regime in the Finance Act 2013 to tax 'disguised interest' and that this new regime should replace (amongst other things) the existing income tax rules relating to repos and quasi-stock lending arrangements; see HMRC 'Possible changes to the income tax rules on interest: Summary of Responses' (October 2012), para 6.5. As a result of the extent and significance of these prospective changes, we have decided to omit discussion of repos, stock lending and manufactured payments from this third edition of this work. This complex area is discussed in much more depth in Chapter 12 of *Norfolk and Montagu on the Taxation of Interest and Debt Finance* (Looseleaf, Bloomsbury Professional) and it is proposed that, depending on the timing of the Finance Act 2013's progress through Parliament, issue 25 (to be published on 1 June 2013) or 26 (to be published on 1 December 2013) of that work should include a discussion of the new rules introduced by the Finance Act 2013.

3   See Joanna Benjamin *Interests in Securities* (2000, Oxford University Press), ch 6 for more details.

SENSITIVITIES

4.33 This section briefly considers some of the legal sensitivities for the collateral taker. Sensitivities associated with all types of collateral assets, and also sensitivities particularly associated with the use of a custody portfolio as collateral, will be considered in turn. It should be emphasised that this discussion gives an overview only of key sensitivities, and is not intended to address all relevant legal issues. Legal advice should be sought in relation to any particular proposed collateral arrangements.

4.34 A fundamental principle of insolvency law is that all creditors who have the misfortune to be owed money by the insolvent party should be treated equally[1]. This is known as the pari passu principle. Notwithstanding the pari passu principle, the effect of successful collateralisation is to remove the collateral taker from the ranks of unsecured creditors, ensuring that the collateral taker is paid before the unsecured creditors. This depletes the pool of assets available for unsecured creditors. In general, most systems of commercial law permit some form of collateralisation. However, because collateralisation cuts across the pari passu principle, the circumstances in which collateralisation is permitted to succeed in the insolvency of the collateral giver may be restricted. The sensitivities discussed below generally reflect such restrictions. Law reform initiatives such as the Financial Collateral Directive[2], the EU Insolvency Regulation[3] and the Banking Winding Up Directive[4], discussed briefly below, seek to address many of these sensitivities within the EU.

1   For an interesting contrary view, see R J Mokal 'Priority as Pathology: The Pari Passu Myth' (2001) 69(3) CLJ 581–621.

2   Directive 2002/47/EC of the European Parliament and of the Council of 6 June 2002 on financial collateral arrangements, as amended.

3   Council Regulation 1346/2000/EC of 29 May 2000 on insolvency proceedings.

4   Directive 2001/24/EC of the European Parliament and of the Council of 4 April 2001 on the reorganisation and winding up of credit institutions.

For all types of collateral assets

4.35 The following points arise irrespective of the nature of the collateral assets. Sensitivities associated with all collateral structures, with security interests, and with outright collateral transfers, will be considered in turn.

All collateral structures

4.36 This section will consider sensitivities that may arise irrespective of the collateral structure.

INSOLVENCY DISPLACEMENT

4.37 If the collateral giver is affected by insolvency at the time of the collateral transaction, or shortly thereafter, its insolvency official may be able to claim back the collateral assets, displacing the interest of the collateral taker. This reflects a concern of insolvency law that the assets available to general creditors should not be unfairly depleted. Insolvency displacement provisions are included in all systems of developed commercial law, and broadly speaking fall into two categories. First, the giving of collateral at a time when the collateral giver is insolvent is, in general, automatically void as a post-insolvency disposition[1]. (A further risk in some jurisdictions is presented by 'zero hour' rules, which may have the effect of moving the commencement of insolvency to the beginning of the 24-hour day.) Second, transactions concluded prior to insolvency but close enough to it to fall within the statutory 'suspect period'[2] may, at the option of the insolvency official, be avoided if they offend rules designed to protect general creditors against unfair prejudice, such as rules against preferences[3]. Collateral arrangements that are put in place in respect of pre-existing and originally unsecured debts may be particularly vulnerable[4].

1   Under English law, see s 127 of the Insolvency Act 1986. Note that the EU Insolvency Regulation provides that the validity of post insolvency dispositions of registered securities is governed by the law of the member state where the register is kept (art 14). In relation to the insolvency of banks, the equivalent provisions in the Banking Winding Up Directive are contained in art 31, and are drafted more widely. They relate to 'instruments or rights in such instruments the existence or transfer of which presupposes their being recorded in a register, an account or a centralised deposit system held or located in a Member State'. The provisions of art 14 of the EU Insolvency Regulation may not be sufficiently widely drafted to cover bonds or interests in bonds held through Clearstream or Euroclear.

2   Also known as the 'hardening period', because transactions made within it are 'soft', or potentially avoidable.

3   Under English law, in the Insolvency Act 1986, see s 238 (transactions at an undervalue), s 239 (preferences) and s 245 (avoidance of floating charges). Section 240 defines the hardening periods.

4   In the UK, in the Insolvency Act 1986, see the provisions for the avoidance of floating charges under s 245.

4.38 As a general principle, it is not possible to contract out of the mandatory provisions of insolvency law[1], and in order to address the risk of insolvency displacement, well advised collateral takers will always undertake counterparty credit assessment, and avoid doing business with an actually or potentially insolvent counterparty. However, unforeseen insolvency is a fact of commercial life. Therefore it is customary for collateral takers to seek legal opinions to the effect that, should the collateral giver be affected by insolvency, the transaction would not fall foul of insolvency displacement rules, as a preference or otherwise. Under English law, very broadly speaking, the risk of insolvency displacement is generally remote in the case of bona fide arm's length collateral arrangements with solvent counterparties for new money (ie where the collateralised exposure did not predate the delivery of the collateral).

1   In the UK, see *British Eagle International Airlines Ltd v Compagnie Nationale Air France* [1975] 1 WLR 758, [1975] 2 All ER 390.

4.39 With foreign counterparties, insolvency displacement risk should always be assessed under the law that would govern the counterparty's insolvency. The conflict of laws rules for cross-border insolvency are complex, as discussed in Chapter 5. As a broad generalisation[1], it is prudent for the collateral taker to consider the law under which the collateral giver is incorporated or otherwise established and, if different, the law of the branch through which it entered into the transaction. Recent EU measures have altered the position within Europe, as discussed in Chapter 5. Very broadly, the EU Insolvency Regulation applies to individuals and companies other than credit institutions, insurance companies, investment services firms and retail collective investment schemes. It provides in general that insolvency is handled by the courts and governed by the laws of the member state where the insolvent's centre of main interests is located; in the case of a company, the registered office is presumed to be the centre of main interests (unless proven otherwise). Although pre-existing property rights arising under foreign law collateral arrangements will be respected, they are subject to the insolvency displacement rules of the law of the centre of main interests. The cross-border insolvency of banks and insurance companies is governed by the Banking Winding Up Directive[2] and the Insurance Winding Up Directive[3] respectively. The position under these measures is in some respects similar to that under the EU Insolvency Regulation, except that the relevant jurisdiction is the home member state in which the bank or insurance company is authorised, rather than the centre of main interests, and the Directives do not permit other member states to allow secondary insolvency proceedings.

1   This is a very rough summary; see Chapter 5 for more detail.
2   Implemented in the UK by the Insurers (Reorganisation and Winding Up) Regulations 2004 (SI 2004/353).
3   Implemented in the UK for most purposes by the Insurers (Reorganisation and Winding Up) Regulations 2003 (SI 2003/1102), subsequently repealed and replaced by the Insurers (Reorganisation and Winding Up) Regulations 2004 (SI 2004/353).

MARGINING OR MARKING TO MARKET[1]

4.40 Many collateralised transactions are subject to margining, or marking to market. It is customary for the value of the collateral assets to exceed the value of the collateralised exposure by an agreed margin. The value of the financial assets serving as collateral, and in some cases also the collateralised exposure, may vary from time to time, either enlarging or reducing the margin from that originally agreed. In order to restore the agreed margin, cash and/or other collateral assets are delivered between the parties to eliminate collateral shortfalls and excesses that arise from time to time. Such margining or marking to market may take place several times a day, and is helpful in enabling the parties to manage their credit exposures. However, a number of sensitivities may arise. First, where collateral shortfalls are eliminated under marking to market arrangements, the result is that part of the collateral pool has been delivered at a later time than the original collateral delivery. As well as possible priority problems[2], this may raise the risk of insolvency displacement[3]. As discussed below, the Financial Collateral Directive offers protection in relation to wholesale financial collateral arrangements within the EU. A further possible risk relates to recharacterisation as a floating charge. As discussed in more detail below, floating charges suffer from a number of disadvantages, including the requirement for registration. If margining provisions are so drafted as to confer on the collateral giver an unqualified right to the release of particular types of collateral asset to eliminate a collateral excess, this might be interpreted as conferring on the collateral giver freedom to deal in the collateral assets. As discussed below, this is the hallmark of a floating charge. Care is taken in drafting margining provisions to minimise this risk, often by having the collateral taker and not the collateral giver select the asset type to be returned.

1   The near failure of LTCM in 1998 illustrated how margining can turn a liquidity problem into a credit problem. Many financial firms fail because of their inability to meet margin calls.

2   It is important to ensure that the new assets are treated as being subject to the original security interest, in order that the interest of the collateral taker should not be postponed to any security interests created after the original security interest but prior to the top up delivery.

3   This might be for various reasons. The later delivery (but not the original delivery) might amount to a post insolvency disposition, or fall within the hardening period. The later delivery might also be treated as the collateralisation of a pre-existing debt.

SUBSTITUTION

4.41   The general principle is that the collateral giver retains a position in the collateral assets, having the risks and rewards of ownership[1], and may therefore wish to actively manage these assets during the collateral transaction. For example, if the value of the collateral assets is falling, the collateral giver may wish to cut its losses by selling them; if it is rising, the collateral giver may wish to take the profits, again by selling them. For this reason, it is customary in collateralised transactions to provide for substitution, whereby original collateral assets are returned to the collateral giver upon the delivery of new assets of equal value.

1   This is because, in the absence of default, the collateral assets will be returned to the collateral giver. Even upon default, any excess in the value of the collateral over the debt will be returned to the collateral giver, who remains liable to the collateral taker in respect of any shortfall. Thus, increases in value of the collateral involve a capital gain for the collateral giver, and falls in value involve a capital loss.

4.42   This raises similar priority, insolvency displacement and recharacterisation sensitivities to margining, discussed above. The Financial Collateral Directive provides protection against insolvency displacement, and addresses the recharacterisation risk potentially associated with both rights of substitution and marking-to-market by stating that: 'Any right of substitution, right to withdraw excess financial collateral in favour of the collateral provider or, in the case of credit claims, right to collect the proceeds thereof until further notice, shall not prejudice the financial collateral having been provided to the collateral taker as mentioned in this Directive.'[1] Recharacterisation risk is often addressed by making substitution subject to the consent of the collateral taker.

1   Financial Collateral Directive, art 2(2).

PRIORITIES

4.43   Questions of priorities arise where third parties are able to assert property rights in the collateral assets, which compete with the property rights of the collateral taker. If the value of the collateral assets is insufficient to meet all the property claims that arise against them, it is crucial to determine the order in which these claims will be met. This is a question of priorities, and the collateral taker will wish to ensure that, in the event that it faces competing claims to the collateral assets, its claims have the highest possible priority. Such competing rights may arise for a range of reasons. The collateral giver may improperly deliver client assets to the collateral taker in respect of its own exposures, leaving the collateral taker vulnerable to competing claims from the defrauded clients[1]. The collateral giver may properly[2] or improperly engage in double dealing, and purport to deliver the same assets as collateral to more than one collateral taker.

1   It is customary for the collateral taker to require a warranty of beneficial ownership, but this does not eliminate the risk that client assets may be fraudulently delivered in breach of warranty.

2   The parties may have agreed that the collateral giver may grant successive security interests in the same collateral assets.

4.44 Many systems of commercial law have rules which generally favour good faith purchasers over holders of prior interests, in order to protect the smooth operation of commercial markets. Such rules may benefit the collateral taker where it is challenged by a holder of a prior competing interest, and disadvantage the collateral taker where it is challenged by the holder of a subsequent competing interest.

4.45 In the UK, the rules governing priorities are complex and their application highly sensitive to the facts of each particular case. However, the following principles generally apply:

(1) The general rule at common law is that the priority of competing interests in the same asset is determined by the order in which such interests were created. This means that, where two interests are granted in the same asset, the first in time prevails. This general rule is displaced in certain circumstances by the following special rules.

(2) The good faith purchaser[1] (or collateral taker) of a negotiable instrument generally has priority over earlier claims. Chapter 2 argued that the electronic nature of most assets currently held in global custody is incompatible with negotiable status.

(3) A subsequent legal interest will take priority over an earlier equitable interest, provided the subsequent interest holder is the bona fide purchaser of the legal interest for value without notice of the earlier claim, otherwise known as 'equity's darling'[2].

(4) Where the collateral asset comprises a debt or (by analogy) other intangible financial asset, priority depends, not on the order of creation of the competing interests, but the order in which they were notified in writing to the debtor or other obligor[3].

(5) A fixed charge in general takes priority over a prior floating charge, unless the prior floating charge included a negative pledge of which the fixed chargee had notice.

(6) Where the collateral assets comprises a debt or other contractual claim, but the assignment of such rights is prohibited by the relevant contract, assignment of such rights by way of security (or outright) will be ineffective to give the assignee rights against the person owing such rights[4].

1   Known as the holder in due course. See s 29(1) of the Bills of Exchange Act 1882.

2   *Pilcher v Rawlins* (1872) 7 Ch App 259. It was argued in Chapter 3 that the global custodial relationship is a trust, so that the asset of the custody client is equitable and not legal. This means that the equitable priority rules in (3) above may apply. Where, for example, a collateral taker receives securities collateral from a global custodian, which proves to have been delivered without the authority of the custody client, the collateral taker faces the risk of competing claims from the defrauded client. Because the defrauded client will be claiming back her equitable interest, the equitable rules of priority will apply. The outcome of the dispute will generally depend on the nature of the interest acquired by the collateral taker. If it acquired merely an equitable interest (such as a charge), the client will generally win, on the basis that her interest was prior in time. However, if the collateral taker acquired a legal interest (such as a legal mortgage) the collateral taker will generally win. This is on the basis that the collateral taker is equity's darling.

3   *Dearle v Hall* (1828) 3 Russ 1, [1824–34] All ER Rep 28. Where the collateral assets comprise securities held in global custody, the well-advised collateral taker will give immediate written notice of its interest to the global custodian.

4   *Linden Gardens Trust Ltd v Lenesta Sludge Disposal Ltd* [1993] 3 All ER 417. This will be important where the person owing the debt or other claim amount wishes to rely on set-off rights and therefore does not wish such rights to be disrupted by a third party's claims under a security interest or otherwise.

4.46 The law relating to priorities would have been significantly altered by the proposals of the Law Commission to reform the law relating to the registration of security interests[1].

1   Registration of Security Interests: Company Charges and Property other than Land, Consultation Paper No 164, 2002, followed by a more detailed Consultation Paper No 176, Company Security Interests, A consultative report, in August 2004, and a final report in August 2005, Law Commission Final Report No 296, Company Security Interests. A system of notice filing was proposed and, very broadly speaking, priority would be determined by the time of filing under a simplified electronic notice filing system (rather than the time of creation of the security interest). However, where the secured creditor advanced the purchase price of the collateral assets, their security interest (a 'purchase-money security interest') would take priority over an already filed non-purchase money security interest. The 21-day time limit would not apply, and failure to file would not avoid the security, but would potentially result in loss of priority. It was proposed that all charges should be registrable unless excluded. Exclusions were proposed for registered security interests over shares, and those involving delivery of certificates (The reference to certificates was of course somewhat anachronistic, given the widespread use of CREST.) While certain 'quasi-security' arrangements (such as retention of title clauses and hire purchase agreements) would be registrable, it was proposed that repos should be excluded. Interestingly, it was proposed to extend the regime to unincorporated businesses. Global custodians would therefore need to consider whether certain of their trustee and managed fund clients may be required to register the security interests they give to the global custodian. These proposals were not reflected in the new Companies Act 2006, but further amendments were proposed by the Department for Business Innovation & Skills ('BIS') in the Consultation Document 'Registration of Charges Created by Companies and Limited Liability Partnerships: Proposals to amend the current scheme and relating to specialist registrars', 12 March 2010, and a further Consultation Document from BIS 'Revised Scheme for Registration of Charges created by Companies and Limited Liability Partnerships: Proposed revision of Part 25, Companies Act 2006', August 2011. The latest development of these proposals is discussed in paras **4.50–4.54** below.

Security interests

4.47 The above sensitivities apply to any type of collateral structure. Additionally, the following sensitivities should be considered where the interest of the collateral taker consists of a security interest (as opposed to an outright collateral transfer).

PERFECTION

4.48 It is a general principle of commercial law that security interests are required to be perfected before they are enforceable against third parties such as unsecured creditors of the collateral giver. 'Perfected' for this purpose does not mean 'made perfect', because even a perfected security interest may be defective, for example, because it is weaker in priority than another perfected security interest. In this context, 'perfected' means potentially[1] enforceable against third parties. Perfection requirements often involve an act of publicity such as notarisation of the security agreement, or physical delivery of the collateral assets[2]. Perfection requirements vary from jurisdiction to jurisdiction and in relation to the types of security interest and/or underlying asset. At one extreme, an English law floating charge may be perfected merely by the execution of a valid agreement and identification of the pool of assets to which it relates. In contrast, civil law security interests may require notarisation of the security agreement and the inclusion of special forms of wording. In the case of financial collateral assets, it is necessary to consider carefully the type of account entries that are required to perfect a security interest.

1   Subject to priorities and any registration requirements.
2   The legal theory behind perfection is that, because property rights bind third parties, they should not become enforceable unless they are visible to third parties.

4.49 Within the EU and in relation to financial collateral, the position is intended to be simplified by the implementation of the Financial Collateral Directive, as discussed below.

REGISTRATION

4.50 In the case of security interests created by a company incorporated in England and Wales, only certain types of security interest are registrable currently[1]. Unless particulars of registrable charges so created are delivered to the Registrar of Companies within 21 days of the date of creation of the charge, the charge will be void as against the liquidator, administrator or any creditor of the company. In the international financial markets, two types of registrable charge regularly fall to be considered. These are floating charges (over any type of asset) and fixed charges over book debts[2]. Considerable legal effort is exerted in seeking to structure collateral arrangements so that such registrable charges are not created, in order to avoid the administrative burden and publicity involved in registration.

1   Under Part 25 (s 860 et seq) of the Companies Act 2006 (prior to 1 October 2009, s 395 et seq of the Companies Act 1985). Note that s 409 (registration of charges over property in England and Wales by an overseas company with an 'established place of business' in England and Wales) of the 1985 Act was not reproduced in the 2006 Act, although the Secretary of State was given power to make regulations regarding the registration of charges by overseas companies: see Companies Act 2006, s 1052. This resulted in the Overseas Companies (Execution of Documents and Registration of Charges) Regulations 2009 (SI 2009/1917), pursuant to which an overseas company granting a security interest over property situated in the UK on or after 1 October 2009 was only required to register the charge at Companies House in the UK if at the time of the creation of the security interest the company had delivered certain information to the registrar of companies under the Overseas Companies Regulations 2009 (SI 2009/1801) (which require delivery of such information when an overseas company opens an establishment (a branch or other place of business) in the UK). However, with effect from 1 October 2011, registered overseas companies are no longer required to register any security created by them with Companies House in the UK (see the Overseas Companies (Execution of Documents and Registration of Charges) (Amendment) Regulations 2011 (SI 2011/2194) which amends SI 2009/1917).
2   The law relating to fixed charges over book debts was clarified by *Agnew v IRC* [2001] UKPC 28, [2001] 2 AC 710, [2001] 3 WLR 454, and considered further in some detail in *Re Brumark* [2001] 2 AC 710 and *National Westminster Bank plc v Spectrum Plus Limited* [2005] UKHL 41.

4.51 Following the BIS August 2011 Consultation Document[1], draft text to replace Part 25 of the Companies Act 2006 was published by BIS in November 2011. This was followed by the publication of draft Regulations in August 2012 (and Regulations creating a similar registration regime for limited liability partnerships), with comments requested by 7 September 2012, on the basis that the changes would come into force in April 2013.

1   BIS, 'Revised Scheme for Registration of Charges created by Companies and Limited Partnerships: Proposed revision of Part 25, Companies Act 2006', August 2011.

4.52 A major effect of the changes to be made by the Regulations is that *all* charges created by companies incorporated in the UK will be registrable (subject only to certain exceptions[1]). This is a significant change to English law because it means that fixed charges, which in general do not require registration, will, once this amendment to the Companies Act 2006 is in force, require registration unless it is clear that the charge is within the scope of the Financial Collateral

Regulations[2] (see paras **4.95–4.106**). Conceptually this is a considerable change in approach under English law. Historically the underlying logic has generally been that certain types of charges (such as fixed charges) are obvious to third parties therefore do not need to be registered, whereas, for example, floating charges or charges over book debts are less obvious to third parties therefore a registration requirement is appropriate. The new approach is apparently that all charges should be disclosed to third parties by registration except where one of the limited exceptions applies.

1   Exceptions are: '(a) cash taken or held by a landlord as security for the due performance and observance of a tenant's obligations under a lease of land; (b) a charge created by a member of Lloyd's (within the meaning of the Lloyd's Act 1982) to secure its obligations in connection with its underwriting business at Lloyd's; (c) a pledge or lien of or over property; (d) a charge excluded from the application of this section by or under any other Act.' (Draft revised text of, the Companies Act 2006, s 859A(6).) Paragraph (d) prevents conflict with the Financial Collateral Regulations (see paras **4.79–4.111**). Paragraph (c) is odd because pledges or liens (being based on possession) have never been required to be registered under English law, although the August 2011 consultation document indicates that such wording is solely for the avoidance of doubt. (This does not of course help clarify the question of whether a lien together with a power of sale is registrable.)

2   This should be the case for a fixed charge; see discussion in paras **4.102–4.106** regarding the difficulties with determining the application of the Financial Collateral Regulations.

4.53   The requirements imposed by the amended provisions also include a mandatory requirement to set out details of any negative pledge when registering the charge (rather than such disclosure being optional as at present), and an obligation for any person enforcing their right under a security interest by appointing a receiver (or obtaining a court order to do so) to notify the registrar of companies within seven days (and non-compliance is an offence incurring a fine). Failure to register a charge is however no longer to be a criminal offence. One of the earlier proposals[1] was that any amendment of an existing charge to add further charged assets or increase the amount secured by the charge would be regarded as the creation of a further charge (and therefore would require a new registration). Such a requirement would be potentially onerous, but does not appear in the latest draft Regulations. However, if an existing charge is amended by adding or amending 'a term that (a) prohibits or restricts the creation of any fixed security or any other charge having priority over, or ranking pari passu with, the charge, or (b) varies, or otherwise regulates the order of, the ranking of the charge in relation to any fixed security or any other charge', the chargor or chargee 'may' (but is not obliged to, and there is no sanction for failure to do so) register a certified copy of the amending document and certain other information.

1   See BIS, 'Revised Scheme for Registration of Charges created by Companies and Limited Partnerships: Proposed revision of Part 25, Companies Act 2006', August 2011.

4.54   One of the main practical effects of the proposed amendments to the Companies Act 2006 is to enable electronic submission of documentation for registration. In particular, draft s 859A(3) only requires submission of a certified copy of the instrument creating the charge, and draft s 859G states that signatures are not required to be included in the certified copy. It is also intended that there should be one registration scheme for all companies incorporated in England and Wales, Northern Ireland or Scotland. These practical changes are to be welcomed, but the need for certain other changes is less clear. For example, BIS has expressed the wish to 'reduce uncertainty as to what charges must be registered'[1], but the proposed solution of making all charges registrable (subject to a few exceptions) seems a disproportionate solution since it disrupts a significant aspect of existing English law, and is likely to have a significant effect on the use of security interests by UK companies in future.

1   See explanatory notes accompanying the draft Regulations published by BIS in August 2012.

RIGHT OF USE

4.55 It was indicated above that the essential feature of a security interest, which distinguishes it from an outright collateral transfer, is that the collateral giver retains a residual property right in the collateral assets, known as the equity of redemption[1]. The equity of redemption entitles the collateral giver to the return of the original collateral assets upon the discharge of the secured obligation. Because the collateral giver retains a property right in the collateral assets, the collateral taker is in general not free to dispose of them in the absence of collateral giver default, but must hold the original collateral assets available for return upon the discharge of the secured obligation[2]. While certain techniques have been developed with a view to reconciling a right of use with the equity of redemption, they are rarely both legally robust and commercially appropriate in the international financial markets, and it is difficult to obtain clean legal opinions in relation to them.

1   It can be of considerable importance for taxation purposes that the giver of collateral should retain the ability to enjoy an asset as the 'owner' of that asset (see eg *J Sainsbury plc v O'Connor* [1991] STC 318 (CA)). If beneficial ownership were to pass to a collateral taker, the collateral giver could be treated as having disposed of the property and would realise a taxable gain or a loss for taxation purposes. Furthermore, in the context of withholding tax, an exemption from withholding tax could (depending on the terms of the exemption) cease to apply unless the collateral giver were to remain beneficially entitled to interest payments. Finally, if beneficial ownership were to pass, a charge to *ad valorem* stamp duty/SDRT could arise. (See also Chapter 10.)

2   The general rule is that a contractual provision which is incompatible with the equity of redemption may not be effectively included in the collateral contract. 'The principle invoked by the Plaintiff is summed up in the epigrammatic formula "once a mortgage always a mortgage". Whenever a transaction is in reality one of mortgage, equity regards the mortgaged property as security only for money, and will permit of no attempt to clog, fetter, or impede the borrower's right to redeem and to rescue what was, and still remains, in equity his own': *Marquess of Northampton v Pollock* (1890) 45 Ch D 190 at 215, per Bowen LJ. For a fuller discussion of this area of law, see Joanna Benjamin *Interests in Securities* (2000, Oxford University Press), ch 5, section C.

4.56 This creates a real tension in practice, for the following reason. It was indicated above (in the discussion of outright collateral transfers) that institutional collateral takers are under commercial pressure to use the assets they receive from collateral givers to collateralise their own obligations to third parties. It was also indicated that in such cases, the appropriate arrangement is for the assets to be received under an outright collateral transfer, which confers such a right of use. However, there are cases in which a collateral taker, who requires a right of use, is unable to take collateral under an outright transfer, and must receive it under a security interest. As discussed below, these include cases where the insolvency jurisdiction of the counterparty does not permit insolvency set off[1], and where recharacterisation risk is present[2]. Such cases should be carefully considered on a case by case basis. As discussed below, in wholesale transactions within the EU relating to financial collateral, the ability to agree a right of use is conferred by the implementation of the Financial Collateral Directive. This in many ways erodes the legal difference between outright collateral transfers and security interests, following the US model.

1   However, as discussed in Chapter 5, within the EU the EU Insolvency Regulation and the Banking Winding Up Directive protect insolvency set off which is permitted by the law governing the claim of the insolvent entity, even where the law of the insolvency jurisdiction does not permit it.

2   As discussed below, the Financial Collateral Directive is intended to provide protection against recharacterisation risk in wholesale transactions within the EU.

Outright collateral transfers

4.57 The previous section considered certain legal sensitivities potentially associated with security interests. This section will consider key legal sensitivities potentially associated with outright collateral transfers.

INSOLVENCY SET OFF AND NETTING

4.58 As indicated above, a security interest confers a property right in the collateral assets on the collateral taker. This protects the collateral taker in the insolvency of the collateral giver in the following way. Only assets belonging to the insolvent entity are available to the insolvency official to make available to general creditors. Because the collateral assets are impressed with the property rights of the collateral taker, they are not available to the insolvency official until the collateral taker has been paid off, and these rights are discharged. Thus, a perfected and enforceable security interest is protected from the collateral giver's insolvency under the most basic principle of insolvency law, namely the principle that third party assets are not available to general creditors.

4.59 In contrast, an outright collateral transfer protects the collateral taker in the insolvency of the collateral giver through insolvency set off. Under English law, insolvency set off of mutual debits and credits is mandatory[1]. However, it is crucial to note that the circumstances in which mandatory insolvency set off operates are strictly controlled[2]. In certain systems of law, insolvency set off is available only in narrowly defined circumstances, which may not include standard financial collateral arrangements. For these reasons, it is important to establish that the default arrangements of a proposed outright collateral transfer would be recognised under the system of law that would govern the insolvency of the counterparty. If it may not be, outright collateral transfer is not appropriate, and a security interest should be considered. Protection is provided by each of the Financial Collateral Directive[3], the EU Insolvency Regulation[4] and the Banking Winding Up Directive[5].

1   Under Insolvency Rules 1986 (SI 1986/1925), r 4.90.
2   Rule 4.90 requires, inter alia, that debits and credits should be mutual (ie owed by each party in the same capacity) in order to be set off. This raises potential sensitivities in relation to agency and trust transactions.
3   See para **4.79** onwards.
4   As discussed in Chapter 5, the EU Insolvency Regulation provides that, in general, the law of the forum will determine the availability of insolvency set off. However, even where the law of the forum does not permit set off, creditors may nevertheless set off their claims against the claims of the insolvent entity where the law governing the latter claims set off.
5   As with the EU Insolvency Regulation, the law of the forum will determine the availability of insolvency set off, but even where this does not permit set off, creditors may nevertheless set off their claims against the claims of the insolvent where the law governing the latter claims permits set off. See Chapter 5.

4.60 Many collateralised transactions are entered into (together with large numbers of like transactions) under the terms of master agreements. Such master agreements contain close out netting provisions. Close out netting is a procedure which takes place upon the default of either party, as a preliminary to set off. Very broadly speaking, close out netting may involve four stages:

(1) All outstanding transactions are accelerated so as to be 'closed'[1] immediately (ie the collateralised exposure becomes repayable, and equivalent collateral redeliverable, immediately).

(2) All non-cash obligations are converted into debts (so that the obligation to re-deliver equivalent collateral is converted into an obligation to pay its current market price).

(3) All debts in a currency other than the contractually specified base currency are converted into the base currency at an agreed rate of exchange.

(4) All debts are aggregated.

1   In *Drexel Burnham Lambert International v Mohamed El Nasr* [1986] 1 Lloyd's Rep 356 at 359, Staughton J refers to 'the process described as closing – or by those with a fondness for the unnecessary adverb, closing out'.

4.61   At this stage, the parties should each owe the other a single debt. As mutual debits and credits, these are candidates for insolvency set off.

4.62   Certain jurisdictions restrict the availability of close out netting. As a precondition to insolvency set off, it is important for the collateral taker to ensure that close out netting is available under the insolvency law of the collateral giver. Protection is provided by the Financial Collateral Directive (as discussed in para **4.79** onwards) and the Banking Winding Up Directive[1] (but unfortunately not the EU Insolvency Regulation).

1   Article 25: 'Netting agreements shall be governed solely by the law of the contract which governs such agreements.'

RECHARACTERISATION RISK

4.63   If the availability of insolvency set off is the first major precondition for robust outright collateral transfers, the second is the absence of recharacterisation risk. In general terms, recharacterisation risk is the risk that the courts may reject the characterisation that the parties have given to a transaction, for example, by declaring that a purported property licence is a lease, or that a purported fixed charge is a floating charge. Recharacterisation is generally based on the principle[1] that the courts look to the substance and not the form of a transaction. In relation to purported outright collateral transfers, the sensitivity is that the courts may declare the transaction to be a security interest. This is potentially undesirable for a number of reasons, including the danger that a security interest may be avoidable for want of registration[2].

1   Derived from the law of equity.
2   For a note of other disadvantages of such recharacterisation, see J Benjamin 'Recharacterisation and Conflict of Laws', in *Butterworths Journal of International Banking and Financial Law*, December 1997; see also discussion in Joanna Benjamin *Interests in Securities* (2000, Oxford University Press), ch 6.

4.64   English law is slow to recharacterise outright collateral transfers, and in general will only do so if the transaction is a sham, or contains provisions which are legally inconsistent with outright transfer[1]. Provided industry standard documentation is used in accordance with its terms, recharacterisation risk is likely to be absent, and standard form opinions to this effect have been prepared by leading trade associations. However, a number of commercially important jurisdictions would recharacterise purported outright collateral transfers. It is important to address recharacterisation risk, not only under the governing law of the agreement, but also under the insolvency jurisdiction of the counterparty as well as, ideally, under the law of the jurisdiction where the collateral assets are located[2].

1   See *Welsh Development Agency v Export Finance Co Ltd* [1992] BCLC 148.
2   Admittedly, this last step is not customary, except where very large values are involved. As discussed in Chapter 5, the Banking Winding Up Directive provides that repurchase agreements (which rely on outright transfer) are governed solely by their contractual governing law: art 26. However, it is not clear that this will address recharacterisation risk, as the latter is not purely a matter of contractual construction, but relates to the proprietary effect of a contract. Further protection is provided in EU wholesale transactions by the Financial Collateral Directive, as discussed below.

For collateral comprising securities held in custody

4.65 This section will consider sensitivities that arise where the custody portfolio is used as collateral, looking in turn at: points that may arise in all cases; at those that arise when the collateral taker is a custodian; and at those that arise when the collateral taker is a prime broker.

In all structures – intermediation and lex situs

4.66 As discussed in Chapter 1, global custody involves intermediation, in the sense that one or more custodian, sub-custodian, depositary or other intermediary may stand between the client and the issuer of underlying securities. An interesting legal question is posed by such intermediation. As indicated in Chapter 5, it is a general principle of private international law that property rights (including those enjoyed by collateral takers) are determined by the law of the place where the assets in question are legally located, or lex situs. Where, for example, interests in bonds are held by a London global custodian for its client, through (in turn) Euroclear (in Belgium) and a local depositary (in Italy), the question arises whether the client's assets are located in London, Belgium or Italy. Where the client seeks to deliver those assets as collateral to a bank, the bank has to determine the location of the assets as a precondition of establishing (if it has taken a security interest) that its interest is perfected and (if it has taken an outright collateral transfer) arguably, that recharacterisation risk is absent.

4.67 As discussed in Chapter 5, the better view is that such assets are located in the jurisdiction of the account to which they are credited, ie England in the case of assets credited to an account maintained by a London custodian. This approach simplifies tremendously the legal and operational aspects of cross-border financial collateral, and a number of law reform initiatives (considered in Chapter 5) are being developed in order to ensure that it applies. However, until that process of law reform is complete, cross-border collateral arrangements must be considered on a case-by-case basis.

In favour of global custodian

4.68 In addition to the issues discussed above, the following sensitivities should be considered where the global custodian seeks to use its client's custody assets as collateral for the global custodian's exposures to the client. Some types of client present legal sensitivities related to their institutional nature. For example, local authorities are restricted from creating charges by s 47(7) of the Local Government and Housing Act 1989), and there is a debate as to whether charges created by trustees over trust assets should be registered against the trustee or the beneficial owner[1]. However, such issues are beyond the scope of this discussion.

1   But see Law Commission Consultation Papers Nos 164 and 176.

CLIENT'S FREEDOM TO DEAL

4.69 One of the major services performed by the global custodian for its clients is to settle its client's transactions, including of course the delivery of assets out of the custody portfolio when the client or its agent so instructs. At an operational level, the custodian's systems may provide for 'straight through processing', as discussed in Chapter 8, whereby client instructions are implemented automatically, without human intervention. At a commercial level, the client may expect all such transactions to be promptly settled, and will be unwilling for the global custodian to restrict its asset management strategy in any way. However, there may be good commercial and legal reasons for the custodian to restrict the automatic settlement of all client instructions[1].

1   See Chapter 8 for a more developed discussion.

CREDIT LIMITS

4.70   The following is a commercial rather than a legal point. A global custodian's credit policy may require that uncollateralised exposures to the client above a certain limit should be assessed by senior staff before they are incurred. The commercial effect of settling a transaction may be very significantly to reduce the value of the collateral relative to the exposure (either because it depletes the portfolio, or because it increases the exposure). Prior credit assessment will not be possible if implementation of settlement instructions is automatic. This may be an argument for limiting the circumstances in which client instructions are implemented 'straight through'.

FLOATING CHARGE

4.71   As discussed above, it is the hallmark of a floating charge that the collateral giver is free to remove assets from the collateral pool without the consent of the collateral taker. The legal risk therefore arises that the collateral interest of the global custodian is a floating charge, notwithstanding the terminology used in the relevant documentation, unless the client is willing to make the settlement of transactions that deplete the collateral pool subject to the consent of the global custodian. In practice, most custodians do not seek to impose such terms. However, because of the disadvantages associated with floating charges[1], custodians may seek to negotiate appropriate settlement restrictions where very major credit exposures are involved[2].

1   These include registrability (unless within the scope of the Financial Collateral Regulations – see below), low priority (note in particular the priority of administration expenses (unless within the scope of the Financial Collateral Regulations) which are potentially much wider than just administrator fees) and potential insolvency avoidance.
2   Arguably, since decisions such as *Agnew v IRC* [2001] UKPC 28, [2001] 2 AC 710, [2001] 3 WLR 454 and *National Westminster Bank plc v Spectrum Plus Limited* [2005] UKHL 41, it would be necessary also to restrict the client's freedom to withdraw proceeds of sale from custody cash accounts in order to avoid the danger of recharacterisation as a floating charge.

NOT LIEN

4.72   Traditional custody documentation often describes the interest of the custodian as a lien. However, this does not remove the very real risk that such an interest will be recharacterised by the courts as a floating charge, because the courts look to the substance and not the form of transactions. In most cases the substance of the transaction will not suggest a lien. The first reason for this is that, broadly speaking, a contractual lien is a possession-based security interest, and arguably cannot relate to intangible assets such as those generally making up the custody portfolio. Second, standard drafting grants the custodian a power of sale on the default of the client. A contractual lien confers a right to retain possession, but not a right of sale[1]. A security interest over intangibles which confers a right of sale on the collateral taker and a right of withdrawal on the collateral giver is arguably likely to be characterised as a floating charge, although a contrary view is not impossible[2].

1   A banker's lien confers a right of sale. However, the custodian's lien is not a banker's lien (even if the custodian happens to be a bank) because it holds the assets as custodian, and not as a banker (eg

for the purpose of presenting instruments for payment): *Brandao v Barnett* (1846) 12 Cl & Fin 787, 3 CB 519, HL, per Lord Campbell.

2   The case of *Re Hamlet International plc (in administration), Trident International Ltd v Barlow and others* [1999] 2 BCLC 506, CA held a purported lien with a contractual power of sale could take effect in accordance with its terms. However, it is debateable whether this case assists a custodian, as it related to tangible goods, so that the security interest with a power of sale could in any event take effect as a pledge (pledges are not registrable as they involve dispossession of the collateral giver, which is visible to third parties; the chief purpose of registration is rendering security interests registrable). This case was unfortunately not considered in *Re Lehman Brothers International (Europe) (in administration)* [2012] EWHC 2997 (Ch). In that case, Briggs J was apparently willing to consider the possibility of a lien applying to intangible assets: 'Bearing in mind the apparent desire of the draftsman of the MCA to confer upon the custodian a general lien over Property ... consisting mainly or almost exclusively of intangibles, I invited the parties to consider whether the time might have come for English law to take a broader view of the matter' (*Re Lehman Brothers International (Europe) (in administration)* [2012] EWHC 2997 (Ch), at para 34) but the point was not argued since counsel on both sides had agreed 'that rights properly classified in English law as a general lien were incapable of application to anything other than tangibles and old-fashioned certificated securities'. As a result, Briggs J concluded that the arrangement described as a 'general lien' did not in fact 'create a general lien in the strict sense' on the basis that he considered it 'highly improbable and therefore most unreasonable to attribute to commercial parties an intention to create security rights of a type incapable of applying to the overwhelming bulk of the property' (*Re Lehman Brothers International (Europe) (in administration)* [2012] EWHC 2997 (Ch), at para 38).

In favour of prime broker

4.73   The economic basis for the low rates of interest charged by the prime broker to its hedge fund clients is the prime broker's ability to use the client assets for its own account. Thus, as indicated above, the prime broker is permitted to remove assets from the client's account (eg in order to deliver them to a third party under a repo transaction), subject to a contractual obligation to return equivalent assets to the client's account. Because the client assets also serve as collateral for the prime broker's exposure to its client, the following points arise.

RIGHT OF USE

4.74   Characteristically, the prime broker's collateral interest in the client assets arises under a security interest. In some cases, it is provided in the terms and conditions of business that, should the prime broker elect to remove assets from the client account, this security interest will be automatically converted into an outright collateral transfer. Under English law, prior to the implementation of the Financial Collateral Directive[1], or if the arrangements are outside the scope of the Financial Collateral Directive, such provision may be contractually invalid under the rules discussed above which protect the equity of redemption. The implications for the collateral interest of the prime broker must be assessed[2]. Also, on the prime broker's insolvency, the hedge fund client may be exposed. This is because the value of its assets held by the prime broker may exceed the value of its borrowings from the prime broker by a significant margin. It may be unable to recover this margin from the insolvent prime broker if the assets have been delivered out to a third party collateral taker. This raises the prospect of the third party collateral taker facing a tracing action from the hedge fund client. However, such an action may be unlikely to succeed where the third party is a good faith purchaser of the legal interest in the disputed securities, for value and without notice of the client's equity of redemption[3].

1   Directive 2002/47/EC of the European Parliament and of the Council of 6 June 2002 on financial collateral arrangements.

2   It might be argued that there can be no continuing security interest, because the removal of the original assets from the prime broker's hands extinguishes the original security interest. Further, the

receipt by the prime broker of equivalent collateral at a time after the delivery of original collateral may raise priority problems, and insolvency displacement risk. However, the Financial Collateral Directive may provide protection against the latter, see paras **4.79** onwards below.

3   Under the rule in *Pilcher v Rawlins* (1872) 7 Ch App 259.

FLOATING CHARGE

4.75   The collateral pool held by the prime broker is likely to change from time to time, for two reasons. First, the hedge fund client will continue to manage the portfolio in the normal course, disposing of old assets and acquiring new assets. As discussed above, an unfettered right on the part of the client to remove assets from the collateral pool may cause the collateral interest to be recharacterised as a floating charge. Therefore the prime broker may wish to reserve the right to decline to settle instructions that deplete the collateral pool. Second, the prime broker will from time to time remove securities from the pool for its own use, replacing them with a contractual redelivery obligation, and in due course returning equivalent securities. However, this latter point should not raise recharacterisation risk, as the hallmark of a floating charge is the collateral *giver*'s freedom to deal in the assets, and the prime broker is the collateral *taker*.

REGULATORY RESTRICTIONS

4.76   As discussed in Chapter 7 (see paras **7.41, 7.42**), there are significant regulatory restrictions on the ability of an FSA-authorised custodian to grant lien or set-off rights (and probably security interests) over client custody assets in favour of sub-custodians, settlement systems or other third parties. This may cause problems, depending on the nature of the relevant structure involving the custodians.

4.77   If the party holding assets in custody is an FSA-authorised prime broker, and takes a security interest over the custody assets together with a right of use, there are additional compliance requirements (see Chapter 7, paras **7.154–7.158**).

4.78   There are already restrictions on the use of title transfer collateral arrangements by FSA-authorised entities (see Chapter 7, paras **7.70–7.73**), but receipt of collateral by way of title transfer from retail clients will be prohibited altogether if MiFID2 takes effect in the form currently proposed (see Chapter 7, para **7.14**).

THE FINANCIAL COLLATERAL DIRECTIVE[1]

4.79   In the last decade, significant industry and public sector effort has been devoted to addressing legal risk in the use of financial assets as collateral, and this has led to a number of collateral related law reform initiatives. This section will consider the Financial Collateral Directive (the 'Directive') and its implementation into English law by the Financial Collateral Arrangements (No 2) Regulations 2003, as amended[2] (the 'Financial Collateral Regulations'). Other key initiatives concerned primarily with insolvency and the conflict of laws, but highly relevant to collateral, are discussed in Chapter 5.

1   Directive 2002/47/EC of the European Parliament and of the Council of 6 June 2002 on financial collateral arrangements.

2   SI 2003/3226 (these Regulations replace the Financial Collateral Arrangements Regulations 2003 (SI 2003/3112) which were defective), subsequently amended by SI 2010/2993.

Progress

4.80 In its 1999 Financial Services Action Plan[1], the European Commission emphasised the importance of addressing legal risk in cross-border financial collateral arrangements[2], and identified the introduction of the Directive as a 'priority 1' action[3]. The Directive was required to be implemented in member states by the end of 2003[4].

1 Financial Services: Implementing the Framework for Financial Markets: Action Plan, Communication of the Commission, Com (1999) 232, 11 May 1999.

2 'Work on the implementation of the Settlement ... Finality Directive shows the importance of common rules for collateral pledged to payment and securities systems. Priority should be given to further progress in the field of collateral beyond this field. The mutual acceptance and enforceability of cross-border collateral is indispensable for the stability of the EU financial system and for a cost-effective and integrated securities settlement structure. At present, these conditions are not fulfilled: there is a higher risk of invalidation of cross-border collateral arrangements and uncertainty as regards enforceability should the collateral provider become insolvent. If such difficulties are not resolved, cross-border securities transactions will be subject to higher costs and risks' (p 8).

3 In relation to priority 1 actions the Commission indicates: 'There is broad consensus that these actions call for immediate attention. These measure are crucial to realisation of the full benefits of the euro and to ensuring the competitiveness of the Union's financial services sector and industry whilst safeguarding consumer interests' (p 21).

4 At the time of writing, this Directive has been implemented into local law in Austria, Belgium, Bulgaria, Cyprus, the Czech Republic, Denmark, Estonia, Finland, France, Germany, Greece, Hungary, Ireland, Italy, Latvia, Lithuania, Luxembourg, Malta, the Netherlands, Poland, Portugal, Romania, Slovakia, Slovenia, Spain, Sweden, and the UK. The Directive has also been incorporated into local law in Iceland and Norway, and equivalent provisions exist under Swiss law. However, note comments below regarding potential issues with differences in implementation by different jurisdictions.

Overview

4.81 The Directive complements the Settlement Finality Directive[1] and the insolvency related directives discussed in Chapter 5. It addresses the legal risk associated with financial collateral, particularly that associated with the differing provisions of national insolvency laws within the EU[2]. The Directive seeks to facilitate the use of collateral[3] in the form of cash, securities and credit claims[4] in the wholesale financial markets[5] through a number of measures. These, inter alia, disapply certain provisions of insolvency law. Their overall effect is to protect the position of the collateral taker. The recitals state the objective of establishing 'A Community regime ... for the provision of securities and cash as collateral under both security interest and title transfer structures including repurchase agreements (repos). This will contribute to the integration and cost-efficiency of the financial markets as well as to the stability of the financial system in the Community ...'[6]. The Directive is thus intended to facilitate the implementation of the common monetary policy[7].

1 Directive 98/26/EC of the European Parliament and of the Council of 19 May 1998 on settlement finality in payment and securities settlement systems, as amended. See Chapter 8.

2 See European Parliament *Recommendation for Second Reading*, 24 April 2002, p 6.

3 Article 1(4)(a). Under art 1(4)(b), member states may exclude collateral consisting of the shares of the collateral giver and comparable arrangements. Such assets are excludable as they are directly linked to the means of production of the collateral provider.

4 Art 2(1)(o): '"credit claims" means pecuniary claims arising out of an agreement whereby a credit institution, as defined in Article 4(1) of Directive 2006/48/EC, including the institutions listed in Article 2 of that Directive, grants credit in the form of a loan.'

5 Retail transactions are excluded by the criteria set out in art 1(2), discussed below.

6   Recital 3.
7   Recital 12. See also *Communication from the Commission to the European Parliament*, March 2002, SEC (2002) 278 final, p 2: 'The proposed directive seeks to resolve the main problems affecting cross-border use of collateral in wholesale financial markets. It therefore promotes integration of the European financial market and secures the full benefits of the single currency.'

4.82 The Directive seeks to achieve these aims by removing formal requirements[1]; providing insolvency protection for collateral arrangements, close out netting, margining and substitution[2]; confirming that the law applicable to questions of property rights and enforcement is the law of the place where the account to which they are credited is maintained[3]; facilitating enforcement[4]; permitting the use of collateral by the collateral taker[5]; and addressing recharacterisation risk for outright collateral transfers[6]. These provisions are considered in turn below.

1   Article 3.
2   Articles 7 and 8.
3   Article 9.
4   Article 4.
5   Article 5.
6   Article 6.

4.83 The benefits of the Directive apply to any arrangement which is a 'financial collateral arrangement', defined to mean 'a title transfer financial collateral arrangement or a security financial collateral arrangement whether or not these are covered by a master agreement or general terms and conditions'[1]. A 'title transfer financial collateral arrangement' is defined to mean 'an arrangement, including repurchase agreements, under which a collateral provider transfers full ownership of, or full entitlement to, financial collateral to a collateral taker for the purpose of securing or otherwise covering the performance of relevant financial obligations'[2]. A 'security financial collateral arrangement' is defined to mean 'an arrangement under which a collateral provider provides financial collateral by way of security to or in favour of, a collateral taker, and where the full or qualified ownership of, or full entitlement to, the financial collateral remains with the collateral provider when the security right is established'[3]. The UK Financial Collateral Regulations use the same definition of 'financial collateral arrangement' but contain an extended definition of 'title transfer financial collateral arrangement' and 'security financial collateral arrangement' in order to incorporate reference to the fact that such arrangements must be evidenced in writing, that neither the collateral provider nor the collateral taker may be a natural person and (in the case of a security financial collateral arrangement) that the collateral taker has appropriate possession or control[4]. Certain aspects of these definitions are discussed below.

1   Article 2(1)(a).
2   Article 2(1)(b).
3   Article 2(1)(c).
4   Financial Collateral Regulations, reg 3.

Removing formal requirements

4.84 Article 3 removes the requirement for formalities (such as execution of a deed, notarisation, advertisement etc)[1] for the creation, validity, perfection, enforceability or admissibility in evidence of collateral arrangements[2]. However, in order to address fraud risk[3], the Directive does require in effect that the collateral taker (or its agent) should have possession or control of the collateral assets[4]. Moreover, the Directive applies only to 'financial collateral' once it has been provided and if that provision can be evidenced in writing[5], and only to 'financial collateral arrangements' if the arrangement can be evidence in writing or in a legally equivalent manner[6]. Such evidencing must (broadly) identify the collateral assets; identification of the credit of the collateral to a relevant account is sufficient for this purpose[7]. On this basis, where interests in securities[8] are delivered as collateral, no formalities beyond book entry transfers are required[9].

1   Article 4 of the original Proposal gave a non-exhaustive list of such formalities; this now appears in Recital 10.
2   Article 3(1).
3   See Recital 10.
4   Article 2(2).
5   Article 1(5), first sentence, and Article 3(2).
6   Article 1(5), final sentence, and Article 3(2). 'In this respect it should be noted that the common position aims at providing a balance between market efficiency, which is the reason behind the exclusion of formal acts, and the safety of the parties to the arrangement and third parties, thereby avoiding inter alia the risk of fraud': *Statement of the Council's Reasons*, 5 March 2002, 5530/3/02 REV 3 ADD 1, p 8. An example of evidencing which is legally equivalent to writing is the taping of telephone conversations: ibid, p 6.
7   Article 1(5). See, however, *Statement of the Council's Reasons*, 5 March 2002, 5530/3/02 REV 3 ADD 1, p 6: 'The financial collateral arrangement must be evidenced in writing or in any other legally enforceable manner provided for by the law applicable to the financial collateral arrangement, eg taped telephone conversations.'
8   'For the purposes of this Directive, acts required under the law of a Member State as conditions for transferring or creating a security interest on financial instruments other than book entry securities, such as an endorsement in the case of instruments to order, or recording on the issuer's register in the case of registered instruments, are not considered as formal acts': *Statement of the Council's Reasons*, 5 March 2002, 5530/3/02 REV 3 ADD 1, p 8.
9   The text of the Directive suggests that it will be sufficient to credit the assets to the account of the collateral taker, or to a special account of the collateral giver (where they are not subject to the collateral giver's control, such as escrow accounts in CREST), or where the assets are held by a third party custodian to ensure that the relevant assets are appropriately designated in the records of the custodian and that only the collateral taker may instruct the custodian regarding those assets: see art 2(2). However, the text of implementing legislation should be carefully examined to determine whether this remains the position once the Directive is implemented.

4.85 In the UK, the Financial Collateral Regulations disapply various formalities, including the need to register certain types of charge which would otherwise be void for lack of registration[1].

1   Regulations 4–7: see in particular reg 4(4) regarding disapplication of ss 860ff of the Companies Act 2006.

Insolvency protection

4.86 Article 7 provides for the recognition of close-out netting provisions, ensuring that they can take effect in accordance with their terms, notwithstanding the winding-up or reorganisation of either party[1] or interveners[2], and without formalities[3].

1   Article 7(1)(a).
2   Article 7(1)(b). This provides that close out netting provisions will take effect in accordance with their terms notwithstanding (inter alia) any purported assignment. While helpful to collateral takers, this may be unhelpful to some securitisations, which may rely on silent assignments.
3   Other than those agreed by the parties, such as notice: art 7(2).

4.87 Article 8 protects collateral arrangements[1] from insolvency displacement on the basis of zero hour rules[2]; hardening periods[3]; and (broadly) where the relevant insolvency event has taken place on the same day as the collateral arrangement, collateralised obligation or collateral delivery, where the collateral taker did not have actual or constructive notice of it[4]. Margining or mark to market and substitution provisions are protected from displacement on the basis of hardening periods, zero hour rules[5] and the absence of new money[6]. However, by virtue of art 8(4), these provisions leave 'unaffected the general rules of national insolvency law in relation to the voidance of transactions entered into during the prescribed period'[7].

1   Improving on the drafting of the original Proposal, art 8 serves to protect both the collateral contract and the delivery of assets pursuant to it.
2   Article 8(1)(a).
3   Article 8(1)(b).
4   Article 8(2).
5   Article 8(3)(i).
6   Article 8(3)(ii).
7   The period 'referred to in paragraph 1(b) and in paragraph 3(i)' of art 8. This is essentially intended to deal with rules regarding fraud or similar in the relevant period.

4.88   The UK Financial Collateral Regulations provide that close-out netting provisions within the scope of the Regulations will take effect in accordance with their terms despite the insolvency of one or other of the parties, unless, broadly, one party was aware of the insolvency of the other party at the time of entering into the arrangement. In addition, the terms of the arrangement replace the mandatory insolvency rules regarding mutual credit and set-off[1].

1   Regulation 12.

Enforcement

4.89   Article 4 provides for the collateral taker, upon the occurrence of an enforcement event[1], to realise securities collateral by sale, appropriation[2] or set off[3] and to realise cash collateral by set off[4].

1   Note that the enforcement provisions in the Directive are not reciprocal, even though the standard close out netting provisions in outright collateral transfer arrangements are reciprocal, ie apply equally to collateral giver and collateral taker.
2   Appropriation is only possible if it has been agreed to by the parties, and valuation has been agreed upon: art 4(2). Member states not permitting appropriation on the date on which the Directive comes into force are not obliged to permit it pursuant to the Directive: art 4(3). However, no member states have made use of this article (see *Report From The Commission To The European Parliament And The Council 'Evaluation report on the Financial Collateral Arrangements Directive (2002/47/EC)'*, 20 December 2006) and therefore the amendments in 2009 to the Financial Collateral Directive included deletion of art 4(3) (see Directive 2009/44/EC of the European Parliament and of the Council of 6 May 2009 amending Directive 98/26/EC on settlement finality in payment and securities settlement systems and Directive 2002/47/EC on financial collateral arrangements as regards linked systems and credit claims).
3   Article 4(1)(a).
4   Article 4(1)(b). Interestingly, the different drafting for cash and securities collateral suggests that the Directive favours *Re Charge Card Services Ltd* [1987] 1 Ch 150, [1986] 3 WLR 697, [1986] 3 All ER 289 over *Re BCCI (No 8)* [1995] Ch 46, [1994] 3 WLR 911, [1994] 3 All ER 565. See the discussion on charge backs in Joanna Benjamin *Interests in Securities* (2000, Oxford University Press), pp 109, 110.

4.90   Regulation 17 of the Financial Collateral Regulations permits a collateral taker to appropriate collateral 'in accordance with the terms of the security financial collateral arrangement' without needing to obtain a court order, and reg 18 contains certain requirements regarding valuation of collateral on appropriation, reflecting the relevant provisions of art 4. In particular, reg 18(1) requires that financial collateral must be valued 'in a commercially reasonable manner'[1].

1   Although note that the Directive does not actually require this, but simply states that art 4 (and arts 5, 6 and 7) 'shall be without prejudice to any requirements under national law to the effect that the realisation or valuation of financial collateral and the calculation of the relevant financial obligations must be conducted in a commercially reasonable manner' (art 4(6)).

Right of use[1]

4.91 Article 5 in effect protects provisions in collateral agreements conferring a right of use, even where the collateral assets have been provided under a security interest[2]. Where the collateral taker exercises this right of use, it incurs a contractual obligation (broadly) to replace the original assets with equivalent assets[3], which upon default is set off against the collateralised obligation[4]. The collateral taker's interest in such redelivered assets is protected generally[5], and from priority and insolvency displacement problems that might otherwise arise due to such assets not having formed part of the original collateral delivery[6].

1   These provisions do not alter the position that the right of use involves a credit exposure for the collateral giver, as discussed earlier.
2   Article 5(1). It improves on the drafting of the original Proposal (art 6), which discussed the right of use but did not confer it. Note that the right of re-use is not automatic, but must be agreed by the parties in the terms in place between them.
3   Article 5(2). Alternatively, the collateral arrangements may provide for automatic valuation of the collateral and set off (even in the absence of default): art 5(2), second para.
4   Article 5(5).
5   The drafting of art 5(4) appears obscure to the authors. However, the above interpretation accords with the comments in *Statement of the Council's Reasons*, 5 March 2002, 5530/3/02 REV 3 ADD 1, p 10. The *Communication from the Commission to the European Parliament* March 2002 SEC (2002) 278 final, pp 7, 8 comments that: 'The new paragraph 4 in Article 5 in the Common Position makes it clear that the use of collateral does not invalidate the collateral arrangement vis-à-vis third parties for the reason that the collateral is not in the possession or under the control of the collateral [taker] as required in Articles 1(5) and 2(2).'
6   Article 5(3). Equivalent collateral is treated as subject to the same security interest as the original collateral, and (importantly for the purpose of hardening periods) as provided at the same time.

4.92 Regulation 16 of the Financial Collateral Regulations reflects the terms of art 5 of the Directive, although makes it clear that the alternative of set off in circumstances other than on default only applies if the terms of the collateral arrangement so provide[1].

1   Regulation 16(2).

Recharacterisation risk

4.93 Article 6 requires Member States to ensure that outright collateral transfer arrangements can take effect in accordance with their terms[1], subject to default close out netting[2]. This serves to address the risk that such arrangements might be recharacterised as security interests.

1   Article 6(1). This is an improvement on the drafting of the equivalent provision in the original Proposal (art 7), which in effect provided that such arrangements *would* take effect in accordance with their terms, thus appearing to prevent recharacterisation even where the arrangement was a sham, or contains provisions which are inconsistent with outright transfer. By providing that such arrangements *can* take effect in accordance with their terms, art 6 of the Directive is compatible with existing English case law, which recognises transfer of title *provided* contractual provisions reflect the genuine intention of parties and nothing in the arrangement is inconsistent with outright transfer.
2   Article 6(2).

4.94 Since English law generally[1] regards transfer of title arrangements as effective, there is no specific further amendment of English law in the Financial Collateral Regulations to reflect art 6.

1 See comment at para **4.93** n 1 above regarding the approach of English case law.

Criteria[1]

4.95 In order for a financial collateral arrangement to benefit from the Directive, each of the parties must be[2]:

- a public authority[3];

- a public bank, ie a central bank, the European Central Bank ('ECB'), the Bank for International Settlements ('BIS'), a multilateral development bank, the International Monetary Fund ('IMF') or the European Investment Bank ('EIB')[4];

- a financial institution subject to prudential supervision[5];

- an infrastructure service provider, ie a central counterparty ('CCP'), settlement agent or clearing house[6];

- trustees acting for bondholders or for any of the above[7]; or

- a counterparty (other than a natural person)[8] to any of the above[9].

1 The policy reasoning behind the threshold criteria may have been as follows. The proposals significantly enhance the position of collateral takers relative to unsecured creditors, and in this respect represent an erosion of the pari passu principle. They could therefore not be justified if their application were general, and in particular should not apply to retail arrangements. However, between major financial institutions, the systemic benefits of addressing legal risk in collateralisation may outweigh the policy objections to eroding the pari passu principle.

2 Article 1(2). The original Proposal included a threshold criterion of a capital base of €100 million or gross assets of €1,000 million (art 2.4(c)); this does not appear in the Directive.

3 Article 1(2)(a).

4 Article 1(2)(b).

5 Article 1(2)(c). Unlike the original Proposal, the Directive gives a non-exhaustive list of financial institutions subject to prudential supervision including (i) credit institutions, (ii) investment firms, (iii) financial institutions, (iv) insurance undertakings, (v) Undertakings for Collective Investment in Transferable Securities ('UCITS') and (vi) UCITS management companies.

6 Article 1(2)(d).

7 Article 1(2)(d).

8 Many fund and SPV structures are constituted as trusts and partnerships. An individual acting as trustee or a group of individuals (not being a partnership or an unincorporated firm) would not satisfy this requirement.

9 Article 1(2)(e). Member states may opt out of this provision: art 1(3).

4.96 The last criterion (counterparty to any of the above) was not included in the original Proposals. This raised concerns that many economically important collateral arrangements were excluded, including the collateralisation of securities lending from pension funds[1] and collateralised swaps with special purpose vehicles in structured finance arrangements. However, the inclusion of the counterparty criterion significantly extends the scope of the Directive, in effect requiring only one institutional party, whereas the original Proposal required two. The opt out possible under art 1(3) means that the scope of application of the Directive, as implemented into local law, varies in different jurisdictions, which may have significant implications for a collateral arrangement, depending on the nature of the parties involved[2].

1 It is not clear that a pension fund is a financial institution subject to prudential regulation for the purposes of the threshold criteria.

2   According to the 2006 evaluation report, in Austria both parties to a collateral arrangement were required to be within the relevant list excluding a counterparty described in art 1(2)(e), and in the Czech Republic, France, Germany, Slovenia and Sweden, there were additional criteria for counterparties within the art 1(2)(e) category. However, as noted above, the UK (and also Belgium, Denmark, Estonia, Finland, France, Germany, Italy, Luxembourg and Spain) has in its implementing legislation extended the scope to persons not mentioned by the Directive. (See *Report From The Commission To The European Parliament And The Council 'Evaluation report on the Financial Collateral Arrangements Directive (2002/47/EC)'*, 20 December 2006, section 4.2).

4.97 In the UK, the criteria for a financial collateral arrangement to be within the scope of the Regulations include the requirement that both collateral provider and collateral taker are 'non-natural persons'[1]. However, there is no specific requirement that either or both parties should be within the other categories stated in art 1(2) of the Directive. In this respect, the Financial Collateral Regulations extend the scope of the financial collateral concept beyond what is contemplated by the Directive. The Regulations might therefore be argued to be invalid to the extent that the types of parties involved in collateral arrangements are not within the categories specified by the Directive because the Directive does not give power to extend the relevant categories[2].

1   '[a]ny corporate body, unincorporated firm, partnership or body with legal personality except an individual, including any such entity constituted under the law of a country or territory outside the United Kingdom or any such entity constituted under international law': Financial Collateral Regulations, reg 3.

2   In the UK the principle has been considered by the Court of Appeal (not in relation to the Financial Collateral Regulations but regarding a similar issue) which concluded that the implementation powers of the Secretary of State under s 2(2) of the European Communities Act 1972 allowed a broad approach to 'the bringing into force of Community obligations arising from the Treaty' and did not require 'a line by line approach to the Directive': *Oakley Inc v Animal Ltd and others* [2005] EWCA Civ 1191, per Waller LJ. However, it is worth noting the following comment from Jacob LJ: 'One test as to whether or not a Directive is properly implemented by a statutory instrument is to compare the Directive with the purportedly implementing statutory instrument. If there is nothing in the latter which is not explicitly contemplated in the Directive (whether as an option or not) then it is a case falling within s 2(2)(a). In such a case the statutory instrument is made solely for the purpose and solely for enabling implementation. This is such a case.' Arguably there is a distinction between taking steps to implement an option permitted by a Directive (even if the details for such steps are not prescribed by the Directive) and extending particular categories beyond those specified in a Directive, therefore it is possible that, notwithstanding *Oakley v Animal,* the scope of the UK Financial Collateral Regulations might be open to challenge, although an attempt to challenge by judicial review was rejected in *R v HM Treasury ex p. Cukurova* [2008] EWHC 2567.

4.98 In the Financial Collateral Regulations, a security financial collateral arrangement means an arrangement which satisfies the listed requirements, including the requirement that 'the purpose of the agreement or arrangement is to secure the relevant financial obligations owed to the collateral-taker'[1]. Is it always the case that the secured obligation are obligations owed to the collateral-taker? It is not an uncommon structure that a security interest is granted to a person acting as security agent where the secured obligations include, or consist solely of, obligations owed by the collateral-giver to third parties. On a strict construction of this regulation, it could be argued that a security interest granted to a security agent would not fall within the scope of the Financial Collateral Regulations. However, in *Re Lehman Brothers International (Europe) (in administration)* [2012] EWHC 2997 (Ch), Briggs J concluded that a security interest granted to secure obligations owed to persons other than the collateral taker would not for that reason be regarded as outside the scope of the scope of the Financial Collateral Regulations.

1   Financial Collateral Regulations, reg 3(1) (Interpretation).

Floating charges

4.99 As discussed above, the collateral interest of the global custodian over the client's portfolio will in many cases be characterisable as a floating charge, because of the client's freedom to remove assets from the portfolio. A floating charge is not a concept recognised in all jurisdictions, and it might be argued that the Directive does not apply to floating charges, on the basis that: no reference is made to them; art 2(2) in effect requires dispossession (or the transfer of control of the collateral to the collateral taker)[1]; and the defining characteristic of a floating charge is that the collateral taker retains some measure of control over the collateral assets, as discussed above.

1   'References in this Directive to financial collateral being "provided", or to the "provision" of financial collateral, are to the financial collateral being delivered, transferred, held, registered or otherwise designated so as to be in the possession or under the control of the collateral taker or of a person acting on the collateral taker's behalf': Financial Collateral Directive, art 2(2). The words 'or otherwise designated' do not remove the requirement for the collateral taker to have possession or control, but are subject to that requirement.

4.100 However, in the UK the Financial Collateral Regulations specifically contemplate that floating charges are within the scope of the Regulations. In reg 3, a 'security financial collateral arrangement' is defined to mean an arrangement where, inter alia, 'the collateral provider creates or there arises a security interest in financial collateral to secure those obligations', and 'security interest' is defined as 'any legal or equitable interest or any right in security, other than a title transfer financial collateral arrangement, created or otherwise arising by way of security including ... a charge created as a floating charge where the financial collateral charged is delivered, transferred, held, registered or otherwise designated so as to be in the possession or under the control of the collateral-taker or a person acting on its behalf'. The main question is therefore what constitutes 'possession' or 'control' for the purposes of a floating charge within the scope of the Regulations. This cannot be the same concept of control which applies when deciding whether a charge is a fixed or floating charge for English law purposes (see paras **4.29** and **4.75** above), since a collateral taker with control under this test would have a fixed charge rather than floating charge, hence a floating charge would automatically be outside the scope of the Regulations. Similarly, 'possession' must be a concept capable of applying to 'book entry securities collateral'[1].

1   See in particular reg 19(4)(b).

4.101 Where a custodian holds securities for a client and the client has granted a floating charge in favour of the custodian over such assets, the custodian does have possession in the sense in which the term possession is normally understood, and therefore arguably has satisfied this aspect of the requirements of the definition, without the need to consider further what constitutes control for this purpose. This approach could be rationalised on the basis that whatever the terms in place between the custodian and the client, the client can never withdraw securities from the custody account without the involvement of the custodian. Furthermore, where a floating charge is created over securities in an account, the fundamental point of such a charge is that it is over the securities in such account from time to time, and does not attach to securities once transferred out of the account, therefore arguably a custodian will always have possession and/or control over the subject of the charge, namely the securities held in the relevant account, even if it cannot control when securities move into or out of that account. (The commercial question of whether this charge will be useful upon enforcement if there are no securities in the account at that time is a separate point.) However, care should be taken with this approach, since if, for example, a custody client has the ability to access the securities held with a custodian at any time by way of 'straight-through-processing' instructions with no means of intervention by the custodian, this might be regarded as creating a situation where the client has some form of constructive possession.

4.102 An opportunity to clarify the interpretation of the Financial Collateral Regulations was provided by the case of *Gray v G-T-P Group Ltd Re F2G Realisations Ltd (in liquidation)*[1]. Unfortunately this case has created considerably uncertainty rather than clarifying the situation. Somewhat bizarrely, when analysing the effect of the Financial Collateral Regulations, rather than considering what 'possession' should mean for the purposes of the Financial Collateral Directive, the judge concluded that possession was a difficult concept and declined to consider it in the context of a charge over intangible securities, stating that 'possession has no meaning in English law as regards intangible property'[2]. The judge focused on the meaning of the term 'control', but in an equally strange approach, effectively construed the term by reference to the usual English law tests for determining the difference between a fixed charge and a floating charge. From the judge's conclusion, it appears to be the case that under English law a security interest is only certainly within the scope of the Financial Collateral Regulations if it is a fixed charge. This does not make much sense given that the definition of 'security interest' in the Financial Collateral Regulations specifically includes a floating charge. The reasoning in the *Gray* case has been much criticised, and was considered further in *Re Lehman Brothers International (Europe) (in administration)*[3].

1 [2010] EWHC 1772 (Ch).
2 [2010] EWHC 1772 (Ch), para 54.
3 [2012] EWHC 2997 (Ch).

4.103 In reality, the main decision in *Re Lehman Brothers International (Europe) (in administration)*[1] was that the Financial Collateral Regulations could not apply to charges created before such Regulations came into force and for this reason the charge under consideration could not fall within the scope of the Financial Collateral Regulations. However, the judge reached various conclusions which are of interest, in the absence of other case law, as indicative of current judicial thinking following the *Gray* case discussed above. In particular, the judge concluded that it was not impossible to have 'possession' of intangible assets for the purpose of the Financial Collateral Regulations, but then went on to observe that 'both "possession" and "control" mean something more than mere custody'[2]. The discussion which follows this comment is curious because it seems to confound the two concepts of possession and control, effectively imposing on an entity who might otherwise be regarded as having collateral in its possession an additional requirement of some level of control over the relevant collateral.

1 [2012] EWHC 2997 (Ch).
2 [2012] EWHC 2997 (Ch), at para 131.

4.104 Following the *Gray* case, and considerable lobbying of the Treasury by concerned industry bodies, the Financial Collateral Regulations were amended with effect from 6 April 2011[1], and the amendments include the insertion of the following as new reg 3(2): 'For the purposes of these Regulations "possession" of financial collateral in the form of cash or financial instruments includes the case where financial collateral has been credited to an account in the name of the collateral-taker or a person acting on his behalf (whether or not the collateral-taker, or person acting on his behalf, has credited the financial collateral to an account in the name of the collateral-provider on his, or that person's, books) provided that any rights the collateral-provider may have in relation to that financial collateral are limited to the right to substitute financial collateral of the same or greater value or to withdraw excess financial collateral.'

1   By the Financial Markets and Insolvency (Settlement Finality and Financial Collateral Arrangements) (Amendment) Regulations 2010 (SI 2010/2993).

4.105 This attempt at guidance on the meaning of possession is helpful in some respects, as it evidently rejects the idea that 'possession' has no relevance in relation to collateral securities held through intermediaries, but it is not an exhaustive definition, and is not wholly successful in providing clarity. For example, the definition of security financial collateral arrangements in the Financial Collateral Regulations refers to financial collateral 'in the possession *or* under the control of the collateral-taker' (emphasis added). However, the purported clarification of the concept of possession appears to confound the two concepts of possession and control. The wording refers not just to the person holding the collateral (who, as argued in para **4.101** above, should be regarded as having possession by doing so) but also to the rights of the collateral provider over the collateral, requiring that such rights should consist only of 'the right to substitute financial collateral of the same or greater value or to withdraw excess financial collateral'. The new wording therefore includes in the concept of possession ideas which are typically considered in the analysis of whether a person has control over assets, and appears to conclude that a collateral-taker can only have possession of collateral if the collateral-giver does not have control except to the limited extent mentioned. This seems an odd conclusion, given that possession and control are apparently intended to be alternatives.

4.106 The new wording also raises other issues. For example, the rights which a chargor may have without preventing the collateral-taker having possession are substitution 'or' withdrawal of excess collateral. Does this mean there is a potential issue if the chargor has both such rights? Moreover, what fact pattern is contemplated by the situation 'where financial collateral has been credited to an account in the name of the collateral-taker or a person acting on his behalf (whether or not the collateral-taker, or person acting on his behalf, has credited the financial collateral to an account in the name of the collateral-provider on his, or that person's, books)'? Arguably a custodian who holds securities for a client, and is granted a security interest by such client over the custody securities, is an example of this situation. However, a custodian would typically not restrict the rights of a custody client to the extent required by the explanation of possession. Can collateral-takers place any reliance on the fact that the explanation of possession only states that it "includes" the scenario it describes? Perhaps so, but this leaves a collateral-taker without clear guidance on what else may constitute possession for the purposes of the Financial Collateral Regulations, and therefore gives little certainty as to whether or not the Financial Collateral Regulations apply. This is a particular problem given the proposed widening of the requirements for registration of charges (see paras **4.50–4.54**), and appears to leave collateral-takers in the undesirable position of having to choose between a fixed charge or title transfer collateral if they require certainty as to the effect of the collateral arrangements. The case discussed in para **4.103** does not assist since it takes a similar approach of blurring the distinction between possession and control, apparently concluding that possession for the purposes of the Financial Collateral Regulations does not have its usual meaning but imports a requirement for dispossession of the collateral giver's rights of control by giving the collateral taker the legal right to refuse to transfer at the collateral giver's request.

Policy issues

4.107 The original proposal for the Directive was controversial, as it enhances the position of the collateral taker at the expense of that of the collateral giver and its general creditors. Some commentators argued that it represented the assertion of Anglo-Saxon (and particularly New York) legal concepts and business practices that are in many respects at odds with continental European law and practice[1]. There are indications that the drafting of the final form of the Directive has sought in some measure to respond to such concerns[2].

1   In particular, the proposal to confer a right of use on the collateral taker reflects the provisions of art 9 of the US Uniform Commercial Code, but cuts across established principles of some systems of continental civil law, which protect the residual rights of the collateral giver in the collateral assets.

2   In relation to the right of use, Recital 19 provides that: 'This reuse however should be without prejudice to national legislation about separation of assets and unfair treatment of creditors.' This tends to suggest that member states may require that the equity of redemption be protected by the segregation of collateral, so that it is not available for use by the collateral taker. However, this theme is not picked up in the body of the Directive. In the UK, the FSA client asset rules in effect relieve collateral takers of the usual duty to segregate collateral where there is a right of use. The FSA Client Assets sourcebook ('CASS') Chapter 3 (as did the earlier forms of the rules in this chapter) disapplies the client asset rules in relation to securities transferred by one party to another where 'legal title and associated rights' are transferred 'subject only to an obligation to return', but not where the transfer of securities is only for the purpose of giving 'a bare security interest (without rights to hypothecate)' (CASS 3.1.3R, 3.1.5G). The same approach is taken in Recital 27 of the Directive 2004/39/EC of the European Parliament and of the Council of 21 April 2004 on markets in financial instruments (MiFID) ('Where a client ... transfers full ownership of financial instruments or funds to an investment firm for the purpose of securing or otherwise covering present or future, actual or contingent or prospective obligations, such financial instruments or funds should likewise no longer be regarded as belonging to the client'), as implemented by CASS 6.1.6R and 7.2.3R. (Note that CASS 7.2.5G clarifies that the disapplication of the client money rules for a security arrangement including rights of re-use only applies when the right of re-use is exercised, and it is submitted that a similar approach would be taken in relation to securities.)

The original proposal provided that enforcement must be subject to any national legal requirements for commercial reasonableness in collateral realisation or valuation (art 5(4)). In the final form of the Directive, this provision is extended to include also commercial reasonableness in the calculation of collateralised obligations, and applies not only to enforcement, but also to the right of use, and the recognition of outright transfer arrangements and close out netting (art 4(6)). See also Recital 17.

Further, in relation to the types of collateral asset covered by the Directive, in art 1(4): 'Subparagraph (b) has been introduced to make sure that Member States may exclude from scope certain financial collateral which, although it might fall under the definition of financial instruments, is directly linked to the means of production of the collateral provider' (*Statement of the Council's Reasons*, 5 March 2002, 5530/3/02 REV 3 ADD 1, p 5).

Governing law

4.108 As mentioned in para **4.66** above, where a party holding securities in an account with a custodian wishes to create a security interest over those securities, questions may arise as to the correct jurisdiction or jurisdictions to consider when determining the legal requirements for matters such as creating a valid security interest and perfection, and there is the risk that the position under the laws of the relevant jurisdictions (for example, the laws of the jurisdiction which govern the agreement creating the security interest, or the jurisdiction in which the chargor is incorporated, or the jurisdiction in which the custodian provides its services) may conflict. The Financial Collateral Directive is intended to simplify the position by stating that in relation to book entry securities collateral (defined to mean 'financial collateral provided under a financial collateral arrangement which consists of financial instruments, title to which is evidenced by entries in a register or account maintained by or on behalf of an intermediary'[1]), certain specific issues 'shall be governed by the law of the country in which the relevant account is maintained'[2]. These issues include 'the legal nature and proprietary effects of book entry securities collateral', and 'the requirements for perfecting a financial collateral arrangement relating to book entry securities collateral and the provision of book entry securities collateral under such an arrangement, and more generally the completion of the steps necessary to render such an arrangement and provision effective against third parties'[3]. The 'relevant account' for these purposes means 'the register or account – which may be maintained by the collateral taker – in which the entries are made by which that book entry securities collateral is provided to the collateral taker'[4].

1   Article 2(g).
2   Article 9(1).
3   Article 9(2)(a) and (b).
4   Article 2(h).

4.109 The result of this should be that where, for example, a collateral provider in France creates a security interest in favour of a collateral taker in Spain over securities held by the collateral provider with a UK custodian who holds the securities in an account with a settlement system in Euroclear, only one jurisdiction will determine the 'legal nature and proprietary effects' and certain other aspects of the book entry securities collateral (ie the collateral provider's rights against the UK custodian), and each of the EU jurisdictions will agree on this and not seek to apply their own laws to these issues[1]. Problems will arise if the relevant jurisdictions have a different view of (a) what constitutes the 'relevant account' in this context, and (b) the country in which such account is maintained. The Directive definition of 'relevant account' should mean that implementing jurisdictions take a similar view on this point, but the question of where an account is maintained may not be easy to resolve. There are various points which may be regarded as indicative. The location of the branch of the custodian with which the client has its day to day relationship and against which the client would usually seek to enforce its claim, seems an obvious choice, but other factors might point to a different jurisdiction, such as the place from which account statements originate, where the relationship contact for the client is based, where the computer(s) through which the account is operated is/are situated, where a call centre (if relevant) is located, and the location of any entity to which the custodian has outsourced the services, or other factors specific to the relevant arrangements, for example, specific agreement or indication in documentation regarding the place where the account is maintained.

1   The Directive will not of course be of relevance to a jurisdiction which has not implemented it, and if, for example, the securities were issued under the law of such a jurisdiction, the collateral taker may well wish to consider whether there is any risk that the validity of the security arrangements could be challenged under the laws of that jurisdiction, and whether as a practical matter the collateral taker will ever be in a situation where it needs to take steps to enforce its security rights in such jurisdiction.

4.110 Regulation 19 of the UK Financial Collateral Regulations is in much the same terms as art 9 of the Directive, although the definition of 'relevant account' is slightly different because it seeks to incorporate the Directive clarification of what is meant by financial collateral being provided. As a result, the definition in the Regulations refers not to the account entries 'by which that book entry securities collateral is provided to the collateral taker' but to the account entries 'by which that book entry securities collateral is transferred or designated so as to be in the possession or under the control of the collateral taker or a person acting on its behalf'[1].

1   Regulation 3. See also paras **4.104–4.106**.

General comments

4.111 Where the Financial Collateral Directive (as implemented into relevant local legislation) applies to a collateral arrangement, it ought to be helpful in relieving the parties from formalities (such as registration) which would otherwise apply, disapplying some mandatory insolvency rules, and providing clarity and certainty regarding the law which applies to the creation of the collateral arrangement. However, careful consideration of the position under the law of other jurisdictions is still necessary if, for example, the jurisdiction of incorporation of the collateral giver, the jurisdiction of incorporation of the collateral taker and the jurisdiction of the place where the relevant collateral account are maintained are three different jurisdictions. One or more of these jurisdictions may be a non-EU state which has insolvency or other rules which conflict with the approach of the Financial Collateral Directive. Even if all three jurisdictions are EU member states which have implemented the Financial Collateral Directive, the detail of the implementation will not necessarily be the same. For example, different jurisdictions may have a different view of the country in which the relevant account is maintained, or may have a different approach to the categories of person who must be party to a collateral arrangement in order for it to fall within the scope of this Directive as implemented in the relevant jurisdiction. In particular, the situation under English law is currently very difficult, because of the uncertainty as to when a collateral-taker has sufficient control or possession to enable it to fall within the scope of the Financial Collateral Regulations except where the collateral is subject to a fixed charge.

4.112 The Alternative Investment Fund Managers Directive ('AIFMD') is discussed in more detail in Chapter 7, paras **7.164–7.176**, but it is worth noting that it has an impact on the collateral arrangements for funds which are Alternative Investment Funds ('AIFs'). An AIF is only permitted to hold financial instruments registered in its own name, or through its depositary (and it is not permitted to have more than one depositary). As a result, if collateral is transferred by the AIF to a third party other than by way of title transfer, the AIFMD regime will require that the third party must hold as delegate of the AIF's depositary for this purpose, and such third party will be subject to the relevant requirements of the AIFMD and Level 2 measures in this context (see Chapter 7, para **7.175**).

CHAPTER 5

Cross-border questions

5.1

'The expanding volume of cross-border securities transactions in recent years can be attributed to several factors. In a global context, these factors include technological advancement, the growth in size of financial markets as international capital movements have been liberalised and as financial deregulation has resulted in a wider range of financial products and services. In an EU-specific context, cross-border securities transactions have been further stimulated by the introduction of the euro ...'[1]

1   The Giovannini Group Cross-Border Clearing and Settlement Arrangements in the European Union, Brussels, November 2001, p 7.

5.2 The greater part of the legal complexity associated with global securities investment and collateral arrangements relates to their cross-border nature. Market participants need to know which system of law will determine a number of important legal questions, including the following:

- Will the client assets be at risk in the sub-custodian's insolvency?
- Does the collateral taker have a good interest in the collateral securities?

5.3 The treatment of these questions in cross-border situations will be considered at paras **5.30–5.36** and **5.37–5.73** below respectively. Paragraphs **5.5–5.29** below will provide a very brief introduction to the branch of law governing cross-border questions, known as the conflict of laws. The focus of the following discussion is the English conflict of laws rules.

5.4 The conflict of laws is a complex area, and important conflict of laws questions are far from settled. The discussion in this chapter is highly simplified and generalised. It is intended as an elementary introduction only, which suggests an initial approach to cross-border questions; for more precise analysis, readers are referred to the excellent textbooks which are available, and in particular to *Dicey and Morris*[1].

1   L Collins et al (eds) *Dicey, Morris and Collins: The Conflict of Laws* (2012, 15th edn, Sweet & Maxwell).

THE CONFLICT OF LAWS

5.5 The areas of law that are important to global securities investment and collateral arrangements (including the law of property and insolvency law) differ from country to country[1]. For example, French insolvency law is fundamentally different from New York insolvency law. Financial arrangements may span countries whose systems of law provide different answers to key legal questions. Where the answer to a legal question depends upon which of several potentially relevant systems of law applies, it is clearly important to identify the applicable law. This is the role of conflict of laws rules.

1   Or, to be precise, from jurisdiction to jurisdiction. 'Jurisdiction' in this context means law system, for example, France, England and Wales, and New York. 'Jurisdiction' also means the power of a court to hear cases. Because of this dual meaning and in order to avoid confusion in the discussion of the jurisdiction of the courts below, the term 'country' is used to indicate 'law system'. Of course, 'country' is an inexact equivalent of 'law system': for example, New York is the latter but not the former.

78 The Law of Global Custody

5.6 Conflict of laws rules, also known as private international law, form part of the law of each country. Thus, where an English court hears a matter involving cross-border questions, it applies the English conflict of laws rules.

Jurisdiction

Overview

5.7 Where a cross-border matter requires litigation, the first issue to be determined is which court or courts have jurisdiction to hear it. The courts of a number of different countries may potentially have jurisdiction. Because their treatment of the questions in issue may differ, choice of forum[1] is often decisively important. This is a complex area of law, and jurisdiction clauses in global custody and collateral agreements should always be professionally drafted.

1   That is, the choice of which country's courts will hear the matter.

5.8 The rules of jurisdiction differ depending on whether or not the matter relates to insolvency.

Jurisdiction – non-insolvency

5.9 In non-insolvency matters, the position is currently somewhat fragmented.

(1) Where the defendant is domiciled in an EU member state, the position is now governed by the Brussels Regulation[1].

(2) Where the defendant is domiciled in EFTA[2] the position is governed by the Lugano Convention[3].

(3) Broadly, if the defendant is domiciled elsewhere, the rules of common law jurisdiction apply.

1   Council Regulation 44/2001/EC on Jurisdiction and the Recognition and Enforcement of Judgments in Civil and Commercial Matters. This came into force (except in relation to Denmark: see art 1(3)) on 1 March 2002, and became applicable to Denmark pursuant to the agreement between Denmark and the European Community of 19 October 2005.

2   The European Free Trade Area (Switzerland, Iceland, Norway and Liechtenstein, although the latter is excluded for this purpose).

3   The Lugano Convention on Jurisdiction and the Enforcement of Judgments of 30 October 2007, as implemented in the UK by the Civil Jurisdiction and Judgments Act 1982.

5.10 The rules under the Brussels and Lugano Conventions are broadly similar (although not identical) to those under the more recent Brussels Regulation. For the sake of simplicity, only the Brussels Regulation and the common law rules(s) will be discussed below.

BRUSSELS REGULATION[1]

5.11 The Regulation generally applies to civil and commercial matters[2] (but not insolvency-related matters or arbitration)[3]. The rules determining jurisdiction under the Regulation are primarily based on the domicile of the defendant[4]. The general rule is that a defendant shall be sued in the member state where it is domiciled[5], and may be sued in another member state only in accordance with special rules of jurisdiction[6]. Different rules (designed to protect the weaker party)[7] apply in matters relating to insurance[8]; consumer contracts[9]; and individual contracts of employment[10]. In proceedings concerning any rem rights in immovable property[11], exclusive jurisdiction is conferred on the contracting state where the property is situated[12]. However, there is no such general provision for moveable property. The Regulation generally gives support to exclusive jurisdiction clauses[13].

1   For a general discussion, see W Kennett 'The Brussels I Regulation' (2001) ICLQ 725.

2   Article 1.

3   Article 1(2)(b) and (d).

4   A company or other legal person or association is domiciled where it has its statutory seat, or central administration, or principal place of business: art 60(1). In the UK, 'statutory seat' means registered office or, if none, place of incorporation or, if none, place under the law of which formation took place: see art 60(2).

5   Article 2(1).

6   Article 3(1).

7   See Recital 13.

8   Articles 8–14.

9   Articles 15–17. Provision in art 16 that a consumer may sue the contractual counterparty in either the counterparty's or its own domicile were resisted by those seeking to promote E-Commerce in the EU.

10 Articles 18–21).

11 Whereas, in the domestic law of property, a distinction is made between real (ie land related) and personal property, in private international law the distinction is between immovable and movable property.

12 Article 22(1). Other cases where the Regulation confers exclusive jurisdiction include (broadly) proceedings concerning the constitution of companies; entries in public registers; parents, trademarks and designs; and the enforcement of judgments: art 22.

13 Article 23. In many cases, UK global custodians and collateral takers provide for the English courts to have non-exclusive jurisdiction, so that they have the option (but are not obliged) to litigate any dispute locally.

COMMON LAW REGIME[1]

5.12   The common law rules of jurisdiction apply where the European regime is inapplicable. Whereas the European regime discussed above is based on *domicile*, the common law regime discussed below is based on *presence*[2]. An English court has jurisdiction if the defendant is present (at the time of service of process, even fleetingly) in England, or submits to the jurisdiction of the court[3]. It would seem that this is the case even where the action relates to movable property which is situated in another country[4].

1   A broadly similar picture emerged in the discussions of the proposed Hague Convention on International Jurisdiction and Foreign Judgements in Civil and Commercial Matters. See the 'Preliminary Documents' section relating to this Convention at www.hcch.net.

   The draft Convention provides for the general enforceability of exclusive jurisdiction clauses (art 4). It contained no express provision relating to disputes concerning rights in rem in personal property (although there was a proposal to prohibit the assertion of jurisdiction on the grounds of the presence in the jurisdiction of property belonging to the defendant, except where the dispute was directly related to that property (art 18(2)). However, there was no consensus on this issue. The proposed art 12(1) provided (broadly) that in proceedings concerning rights in rem in immovable property, the court of the contracting state where the property was situated had exclusive jurisdiction. 'A general view very soon emerged to the effect that it must be possible for all actions relating to immovable property rights (challenging the title of property, for example) to be brought before the court of the place where the immovable property is situated. This is in fact a universally recognised jurisdiction ...': Synthesis of the Work of the Special Commission of June 1997 on International Jurisdiction and the Effects of Foreign Judgments in Civil and Commercial Matters, drawn up by Catherine Kassedjian, November 1997, para 35. Insolvency proceedings were excluded from the scope of the Convention: art 2(e).

Ultimately, the proposed Convention was reconsidered because 'it became clear that no consensus could be reached on a text covering all sorts of jurisdictional bases, ranging from contract to tort, a general defendant's forum and other bases' (Hague Conference 'The Hague Convention of 30 June 2005 on Choice of Court Agreements – Outline of the Convention'). The Convention finally adopted by the Hague Conference in June 2005 (the Convention on Choice of Court Agreements of 30 June 2005) is more limited in scope as it concerns only 'exclusive choice of court agreements concluded in civil or commercial matters' when in the context of 'international cases' (art 1), although there is an option for contracting states to extend the requirement for recognition and enforcement of judgments to judgments given in a state specified in a non-exclusive jurisdiction clause. The Convention is not yet in force, and at the time of writing has been signed but not ratified by the USA and the European Union (pursuant to Art 30, all member states will therefore become Contracting States when ratified and when the Convention takes effect), and acceded to by Mexico. The Convention will come into force on the first day of the month following the expiration of three months after ratification, acceptance, approval or accession by at least two States.

2   The rules of jurisdiction are in effect based on the ability to serve process; a claimant can serve as of right if a defendant is in England (even fleetingly); a claimant can only serve out of the jurisdiction with the permission of the court, which will only be granted if the case falls within one of those listed in the Civil Procedure Rules (SI 1998/3132) (see para **5.13** n 1 below).

3   A well-drafted English jurisdiction clause (appointing an English process agent) will bring a defendant within the jurisdiction of the English court.

4   However, as indicated below, the practical value of a court order obtained in such an action may depend on its enforceability against the foreign assets.

5.13 The circumstances in which process may be served on a defendant abroad are set out in the Civil Procedure Rules[1].

1   Part 6 III (Special Provisions about Service Out of the Jurisdiction). The Civil Procedure Rules are available on www.justice.gov.uk. See also L Collins et al (eds) *Dicey, Morris and Collins: The Conflict of Laws* (2012, 15th edn, Sweet & Maxwell).

5.14 The English court may lose or, as a matter of discretion, decline jurisdiction which it prima facie has in accordance with certain rules[1].

1   Including the following:

- The rule of sovereign immunity (codified in the State Immunity Act 1978, implementing the European Convention of State Immunity 1972) provides that a foreign state is generally immune from the jurisdiction of the English courts, subject to important exceptions (including an exception in relation to commercial transactions: see s 3(1) of the Act, according with the earlier common law rule reflected in *Trendtex v Central Bank of Nigeria* [1977] QB 529, [1977] 2 WLR 356, [1977] 1 All ER 881, CA).

- In accordance with the doctrine of forum non conveniens the English courts may, inter alia, stay or strike out an action when this is necessary to prevent injustice. This doctrine is based on the view that some other forum is more appropriate, and may be invoked to prevent forum shopping. See *Spiliada Maritime Corpn v Cansulex* [1987] AC 460, [1986] 3 WLR 972, [1986] 3 All ER 843; *Re Harrods (Buenos Aires) Ltd* [1992] Ch 72, [1991] 3 WLR 397, [1991] 4 All ER 334.

- The related doctrine of lis alibi pendens applies when simultaneous actions are pending in different contracting states involving the same parties and the same or related matters. In the case of simultaneous actions in England and (broadly) EC or EFTA countries, the Conventions require proceedings in the second jurisdiction to be stayed, and jurisdiction to be declined, in certain circumstances. A broad commonsense approach should be taken to determining whether two matters are 'related' for this purpose: see *Sarrio v Kuwait Investment Authority* [1999] 1 AC 32 at 41, per Lord Saville.

- The English court also has no jurisdiction in matters such as those concerning the validity of entries in public registers maintained in a contracting state other than the UK, where the Conventions confer exclusive jurisdiction on the court of that other contracting state.

Jurisdiction – insolvency[1]

5.15 Different rules of jurisdiction apply in insolvency. Clearly, these will be relevant in the insolvency of a UK sub-custodian. Also, in practice, legal disputes concerning collateral arrangements are most likely to arise in the context of insolvency[2]. (However, as discussed below, legal actions in which collateral arrangements are tested may or may not form part of insolvency proceedings.)

1   The rules of insolvency jurisdiction (and choice of law) are complex, and the following general comments are intended to be indicative only. For more detail, see I F Fletcher *Insolvency in Private International Law* (2005, 2nd edn, Oxford University Press, as supplemented in 2007) and R Sheldon *Cross-Border Insolvency* (2012, 3rd edn, Bloomsbury Professional).

2   This is because (broadly speaking) the purpose of collateral is to protect the collateral taker from the insolvency of the collateral giver by removing it from the ranks of unsecured creditors. Thus, it is in the insolvency of the collateral giver that the collateral taker is most interested in enforcing its rights in relation to the collateral (by legal action if necessary). Because effective collateralisation depletes the pool of assets available to general creditors, the insolvency official of the collateral giver may have an interest (and indeed a legal duty) to challenge the legal effectiveness of collateral arrangements. For these reasons, insolvency provides the richest source of collateral-related litigation.

5.16 In the theory of the private international law of insolvency, two conflicting sets of principles determine the varying approaches of different courts to insolvency jurisdiction. Under the principles of universality and unity, one set of insolvency proceedings governs the insolvent's assets worldwide[1]. Under the principles of plurality and territoriality, each forum deals with assets located within its territory[2].

1   See Recital 16 of the Banking Winding Up Directive (2001/24/EC).

2   In practice, a compromise between the two is usually reached.

EUROPEAN INSOLVENCY REGULATION

5.17 Within the EU, the position is governed by the EU Insolvency Regulation[1]. The EU Insolvency Regulation confers international insolvency jurisdiction on the courts of the member state within the territory in which the centre of a debtor's main interests is situated ('main proceedings'). In the case of a company or other legal person, its registered office is presumed to be its centre of main interests[2]. Recital 13 provides that the centre of main interests 'should correspond to the place where the debtor conducts the administration of his interests on a regular basis and is therefore ascertainable by third parties.' This should probably be taken to refer to management and not to the location of assets.

1   Council Regulation 1346/2000/EC of 29 May 2000 on insolvency proceedings, which came into force on 31 May 2002 (except in Denmark – see Recital 33). But this Regulation does *not* apply to credit institutions, or investment undertakings holding funds or securities for third parties (into one of which categories most custodians are likely to fall), or insurance undertakings or collective investment undertakings.

2   Article 3(1).

5.18 In addition, the courts of another member state where the debtor has an establishment[1] may open insolvency proceedings ('local proceedings'). Such local proceedings are restricted to assets of the debtor situated in that member state[2].

1   Article 2(h): ' "establishment" shall mean any place of operations where the debtor carries out a non-transitory economic activity with human means and goods.' In the absence of local operations, the presence in the jurisdiction of local creditors and assets in insufficient.

2   Article 3(2). See also art 27.

RECOGNITION OF PROCEEDINGS

5.19 Main or local proceedings will be automatically recognised in all other member states[1]. If main proceedings have already been opened, local proceedings will proceed as secondary insolvency proceedings[2]. Main proceedings take automatic effect in all member states, provided local proceedings have not been opened[3]. Local proceedings are effective to restrict creditors' rights only in relation to local assets, or with the consent of creditors[4]. Provided no other insolvency proceedings have been opened, the liquidator in the main proceedings may exercise his or her powers in, and remove assets from, another member state. However, this is subject to third party rights in rem (including collateral interests) and reservation of title arrangements[5]. Judgments relating to either the main or local proceedings are automatically recognised in other member states, and must be enforced by them[6].

1   Article 16(1).

2   Article 16(2). Article 33 provides a procedure whereby the liquidator in the main proceedings may request the stay of secondary proceedings.

3   Article 17(1).

4   Article 17(2).

5   Article 18(1), subject to arts 5 and 7. Of course reservation of title arrangements involve third party rights in rem. The better view is that art 5 (together with art 2(g)) does not create a new rule of conflict of laws whereby rights in rem in receivables are governed by lex situs as opposed to governing law. See art 95 of the Virgos Report (M Virgos and E Schmit *Report on the Convention on Insolvency Proceedings* (1996)). Clearly, this is a key concern in securitisations and related structures.

6   Article 25. A member state may refuse to recognise proceedings or enforce judgments relating to it on grounds of public policy: art 26.

5.20 The EU Insolvency Regulation applies to collective insolvency proceedings which entail the partial or total divestment of a debtor and the appointment of a liquidator[1]. Under UK law, this includes administration and members' voluntary winding up, but does not include administrative receivership[2].

1   Article 1(1).

2   The types of proceedings covered by the EU Insolvency Regulation are listed in Annex A to such Regulation. See art 2(a).

BANKING WINDING UP DIRECTIVE

5.21 As noted above, the EU Insolvency Regulation does not in general apply to insolvency proceedings concerning financial institutions[1]. In the reorganisation or winding up of credit institutions[2], the position is governed by the Banking Winding Up Directive[3], which was implemented into English law in May 2004[4]. Under the Banking Winding Up Directive, as also discussed in Chapter 4, authorities of the home member state where the credit institution is authorised are responsible for its reorganisation[5] and winding up[6], including that of offices in other member states[7].

1   Article 1(2): 'This Regulation shall not apply to insolvency proceedings concerning insurance undertakings, credit institutions, investment undertakings which provide services involving the holding of funds or securities for third parties, or to collective investment undertakings.' Pure reinsurance companies seem to be covered, however.

2   Under art 1(1) the Banking Winding Up Directive applies to EU credit institutions having their head office and branches in different member states. Certain of its provisions also apply to non-EU credit institutions having their head office outside the EU, but branches in at least two member states: art 1(2).

3   Directive 2001/24/EC of 4 April 2001 on the reorganisation and winding up of credit institutions.

4   Credit Institutions (Reorganisation and Winding Up) Regulations 2004 (SI 2004/1045), in force from 5 May 2004.

5   Article 3(1).

6   Article 9(1).

7   Generally, the English insolvency procedures for UK credit institutions are the same as for any other corporate, but note the existence of special powers for HM Treasury in relation to insolvency situations affecting UK deposit takers under the Banking Act 2009.

JURISDICTION OF ENGLISH COURTS

5.22 The English courts' jurisdiction to wind up a company depends on whether the company is English registered and, if it is not, whether there is a sufficient connection with England and Wales. The English courts have discretionary jurisdiction to wind up any company registered in England and Wales[1]. An unregistered company is a company not registered under the Companies Acts[2]. The English courts have jurisdiction to wind up an unregistered company if, broadly, the company has ceased business, is unable to pay its debts, or if it is just and equitable to do so[3]. In practice the English courts take a liberal approach to this provision, and may assume jurisdiction to wind up a foreign company if either the company at the time a petition is presented has assets in England, or at any time has carried on business in England either directly or through an agent, and in both cases where there is a reasonable possibility of benefit accruing to English creditors[4].

1   Insolvency Act 1986, s 117.
2   Insolvency Act 1986, s 220. 'Company' for this purpose is widely defined.
3   Insolvency Act 1986, s 221.
4   But not of course if jurisdiction is given to the courts of another state by the EU Insolvency Regulation or the Banking Winding Up Directive (or the Insurance Winding Up Directive (Directive No 2001/17/EC on the reorganisation and winding up of insurance undertakings), implemented in the UK by SI 2004/353). In practice it may also be necessary to show that there are no home state proceedings or that the home state liquidator agrees to the institution of an English liquidator, or alternatively that the foreign proceedings are prejudicial to English creditors. See the discussion of the relevant case law in I F Fletcher *Insolvency in Private International Law* (2005, 2nd edn, Oxford University Press, as supplemented in 2007).

5.23 In principle, English insolvency relates to the assets of the insolvent irrespective of where they are located[1]. However, in practice, this universal approach may be limited by pragmatic difficulties of enforcement. The co-operation of foreign courts is required for enforcement of any order against foreign assets, and where insolvency proceedings are taken out in other countries, the English courts will in general seek to co-operate. The English courts do not necessarily limit their own jurisdiction over English assets of foreign companies in accordance with the same universal approach[2].

1   Insolvency Act 1986, s 144.
2   As indicated above, the English courts may assume jurisdiction over the liquidation of a foreign company in certain circumstances. Where a court does so, its jurisdiction is not limited to an English branch of the company or its English assets, but in principle may extend to the whole of the company (although, if there is also a home state proceeding an English court is likely to order that the English liquidation be ancillary, ie territorial). Contrast this 'universal approach' to the 'ring-fence' approach of Germany (where it is understood that local proceedings for a foreign company are confined to the local branch and local assets) and the 'no local proceedings' approach of Belgium (where it is understood that no local proceedings are held for a foreign company, but where there is recognition of home state liquidation).

5.24 Consideration must also be given to the Cross-Border Insolvency Regulations 2006[1] which implement in the UK the Model Law on cross-border insolvency as adopted by the United Nations Commission on International Trade Law[2] on 30 May 1997. Broadly, the effect of these Regulations is to require recognition by English courts of insolvency proceedings taking place in the centre of main interests of the insolvent entity, or where such entity has an establishment. However, these Regulations do not apply in certain circumstances, including where the relevant entity is a bank, or an insurer, or if the EU Insolvency Regulation applies, or if the result would conflict with the application of certain other applicable legislation, in particular the Financial Collateral Arrangements (No 2) Regulations 2003[3], the Financial Markets and Insolvency (Settlement Finality) Regulations 1999[4], and Part VII of the Companies Act 1989[5].

1   SI 2006/1030, which came into force from 4 April 2006.

2   UNCITRAL. A body established by the United Nations General Assembly in 1966, aiming to develop the international legal framework 'in pursuance of its mandate to further the progressive harmonization and modernization of the law of international trade'. Its members are UN member states, and currently comprise around 60 of such states.

3   SI 2003/3226, implementing the Financial Collateral Directive (Directive 2002/47/EC of the European Parliament and of the Council of 6 June 2002 on financial collateral arrangements). See Chapter 4, paras **4.79** onwards.

4   SI 1999/2979, implementing the Settlement Finality Directive (Directive 98/26/EC of the European Parliament and of the Council of 19 May 1998 on settlement finality in payment and securities settlement systems). See Chapter 8.

5   See Chapter 9, para **9.23** n 3.

Choice of law

5.25 Where an English court has assumed jurisdiction to hear a case, it is then necessary to determine which system of law will apply to each cross-border question it considers. An English court will apply foreign law to cross-border questions, where the English rules of private international law so require[1]. The court will hear evidence on the provisions of foreign law from expert witnesses such as foreign law academics or practitioners[2]. Of course, a single case may involve a number of different cross-border questions, and a different system of law may apply to each of these[3].

1   In commercial matters, foreign law means foreign domestic law, and not foreign private international law. The problem of 'renvoi' arises when a reference to foreign law is taken to mean foreign private international law, which in turn refers the matter to a third jurisdiction (or indeed back to England, creating a hall of mirrors). See L. Collins et al (eds) *Dicey, Morris and Collins: The Conflict of Laws* (2012, 15th edn, Sweet & Maxwell), vol I, p 79, para 4-006 et seq. Renvoi has long enchanted academics. It originated in nineteenth-century cases concerning the formal validity of wills. It is excluded by the Rome Convention (Convention On The Law Applicable To Contractual Obligations opened for signature in Rome on 19 June 1980 (80/934/EEC)), art 15, and by art 20 of Rome I (see n 3 below). English case law provides some argument that renvoi is inapplicable to commercial matters: see *Macmillan Inc v Bishopsgate Investment Trust plc (No 3)* [1995] 3 All ER 747 at 766, 777, per Millet J.

2   Foreign law must be proved by the parties as a question of fact. See L Collins et al (eds) *Dicey, Morris and Collins: The Conflict of Laws* (2012, 15th edn, Sweet & Maxwell), vol I, p 318, para 9-002. See also *Baker v Archer-Shee* [1927] AC 844 at 874, HL, per Lord Blanesburgh.

3   For contractual matters, the Rome Convention (Convention On The Law Applicable To Contractual Obligations opened for signature in Rome on 19 June 1980 (80/934/EEC)) was implemented into English law by the Contracts (Applicable Law) Act 1990 and, very broadly, takes the approach of allowing the parties to a contract to choose the governing law of the contract, subject to certain special rules for areas such as employment or consumer arrangements. The Rome Convention is now, for all contracts made on or after 17 December 2009, replaced by the new EU Regulation 'Rome I' (Regulation 593/2008/EC of the European Parliament and of the Council of 17 June 2008 on the law applicable to contractual obligations ('Rome I Regulation')) which came into force on that date. There were concerns about the way the Rome I Regulation was prepared, and some issues may still arise since the Regulation is not identical in approach to the Convention. Nevertheless, although the UK exercised its right not to be bound by the new Regulation, after a lengthy negotiation process the broad approach of the Regulation is similar to the Convention, and the UK therefore opted in at the same time as other member states (according to a press release dated 28 July 2008 from the UK Ministry of Justice, the public consultation exercise between April and June 2008 produced an 'overwhelming response' recommending that the UK should opt in to the Rome I Regulation. Of additional interest is Regulation 864/2007/EC of July 2007 on the law applicable to non-contractual obligations. This took effect as part of English law as from 11 January 2009 (no implementing

legislation was required). Previously under English law, the basic rule was that the law applicable to a tort was the law of the country in which the events constituting the tort occurred. In broad terms, the Regulation allows parties to an agreement freely negotiated in a commercial context to choose the law which governs a tort (subject to certain exceptions), but aside from this, the basic rule is that the governing law will be the law of the jurisdiction in which the damage occurs.

5.26 In general, the methodology of the English courts to choice of law questions involves a two-stage process as follows[1]. First, each cross-border question is placed into a private international law category. English law as the law of the forum determines categorisation. Thus, where a custodian wrongly delivers client securities to a third party as collateral for the custodian's own borrowings, the English courts may categorise the ensuing dispute between the defrauded client and the third party as a matter of priorities.

1 'Both parties accept that, at common law, the identification of the appropriate law may be viewed as involving a three-stage process: (1) characterisation of the relevant issue; (2) selection of the rule of conflict of laws which lays down a connecting factor for that issue; and (3) identification of the system of law which is tied by that connecting factor to that issue: see *Macmillan Inc v Bishopsgate Investment Trust plc (No 3)* [1996] 1 WLR 387 at 391–2 per Staughton LJ. The process falls to be undertaken in a broad internationalist spirit in accordance with the principles of conflict of laws of the forum, here England': *Raiffeisen Zentralbank Österreich AG v Five Star Trading LLC* [2001] EWCA Civ 68, [2001] QB 825 at 840, per Mance LJ.

5.27 Second, the courts refer to the rules of private international law to identify the factor linking questions within the relevant category to a particular system of law. For example, the connecting factor for priorities disputes[1] is the law of the place where the disputed assets are legally located, or lex situs[2].

1 Of the above type, ie between defrauded clients and third party good faith purchasers.

2 *Macmillan v Bishopsgate Investment Trust plc (No 3)* [1995] 1 WLR 978 at 989. Another example is that the formal validity of a marriage is determined by the place where it is celebrated.

5.28 In insolvency proceedings, courts will generally apply local insolvency law[1]. Within the EU, under the EU Insolvency Regulation, main proceedings[2] and local proceedings[3] are generally governed by the law of the forum[4]. For credit institutions, under the Banking Winding Up Directive reorganisation[5] and winding up proceedings[6], they are generally governed by the law of the home member state (ie the member state where the credit institution is authorised). However, there are important exceptions to this general rule. The English courts may apply foreign law at the request of certain foreign courts[7]. Within the EU, both the EU Insolvency Regulation and the Banking Winding Up Directive create special rules in relation to the availability of set off[8]; and post-insolvency dispositions of (under the EU Insolvency Regulation) registered securities and (under the Winding Up Directive) book entry instruments[9]. The EU Insolvency Regulation creates special rules in relation to rights of and obligations to payment systems, settlement systems and financial markets[10]. The Banking Winding Up Directive creates special rules in relation to property rights in registered or book entry instruments[11]; netting agreements[12]; repurchase agreements[13]; and transactions carried out on regulated markets[14].

1 See I F Fletcher *Insolvency in Private International Law* (2005, 2nd edn, Oxford University Press, as supplemented in 2007).

2 Article 4(1).

3 Articles 4(1) and 28.

4 Although the Regulation does not apply in the UK to the extent it is irreconcilable with insolvency law obligations arising from arrangements with the Commonwealth: art 44(3)(b). This ties in with s 426 of the Insolvency Act 1986.

5 Article 3(2).

6 Article 10(1).

7 Under Insolvency Act 1986, s 426
8 See the discussion of set off below.
9 See the discussion in Chapter 4.
10 See Chapter 8.
11 See Chapter 4.
12 Under art 25 these are governed solely by the contractual governing law.
13 Under art 26 these are governed solely by the contractual governing law. However, it is not clear whether this addresses recharacterisation risk, in relation to which the Financial Collateral Directive may assist. See Chapter 4.
14 Under art 27 these are governed solely by the contractual governing law. See Chapter 8.

Enforcement

5.29 The well-advised custody client and collateral taker will consider, not only jurisdiction and choice of law, but also the practicalities of enforcement. It will identify the courts that are in a position to deliver the disputed assets, or alternatively to withhold them. This will often be the courts in the country where the assets are located. When assessing the legal robustness of custody or collateral arrangements, the opinion of lawyers in the country where the assets are located is therefore crucial[1].

1 This is the case whether those courts are being asked to enforce their own order, or the order of a foreign court. A large body of law has been developed to determine the circumstances in which courts will recognise and enforce foreign judgments. Where, for example, judgment is obtained in England concerning assets held abroad, local recognition and enforcement of that judgment remains a key issue, and the enforcement of competing local or foreign judgments against the assets cannot be excluded.

SUB-CUSTODIAN INSOLVENCY ISSUES[1]

5.30 As discussed in Chapter 1, the global custodian is unlikely to have branches in each country in which its clients wish to hold assets, and in practice relies on a network of sub-custodians. These sub-custodians may be companies in the same group as the global custodian or independent institutions. However, in each case they are separate legal entities, appointed by the global custodian to hold client assets on its behalf under the terms of a sub-custody agreement. Clearly, both the global custodian and its clients will be concerned to ensure that, in the event of a sub-custodian's insolvency, the assets will not be at risk[2]. This is sometimes referred to as establishing an 'insolvency ring-fence'. Chapter 3 discussed the position under English law. It explained that the traditional method of establishing an insolvency ring-fence for custody assets is under a bailment, but that in the electronic environment an insolvency ring-fence is established under a trust.

1 See Chapter 7 for a note of the regulatory requirements relating to sub-custodian risk.
2 To be more accurate, the concern is to establish that the client assets will not be available to the creditors of the sub-custodian, in its insolvency or otherwise. For example, an unpaid creditor of a solvent sub-custodian may obtain judgment against it, and seek to enforce this against the client assets. However, in practice, insolvency is the chief concern.

Trust and bailment

5.31 The trust is an Anglo-Saxon concept, and not generally recognised as part of the domestic law of civil law countries[1].

1 The full equitable trust as recognised in common law systems does not form part of the domestic law of civil law jurisdictions, and in the past the perception arose that the trust was alien to civil

law, involving as it does the separation of legal and beneficial ownership. 'Is [the trust] not rooted in the duality between law and equity, ie in the separation in English history of two jurisdictions, namely equity in the Court of Chancery, and law in the common law courts, which finds no parallel in continental legal history?': D J Hayton, S C J J Kortmann and H L E Verhagen (eds) *Principles of European Trust Law* (1999, Kluwer), p 3. However, 'The truth is rather different. The elements of the law of trusts are and always have been present in the Roman-based systems and are to be found in the library of the Roman law itself. The question is only as to the extent to which those foundations are used and built upon' (ibid). 'It is also evident that ends achieved by the trust in the common law have also been achieved by other civil law jurisdictions by way of functionally equivalent, but doctrinally different institutions': ibid, p 4.

However, an English law trust may be recognised if a country is bound by the Hague Convention on the Law Applicable to Trusts and on their Recognition of 1 July 1985, in force from 1 January 1992. The Convention was implemented in the UK by the Recognition of Trusts Act 1987. It has also been implemented by Australia, Bermuda, British Virgin Islands, Canada (except for Ontario and Quebec), Gibraltar, Guernsey, Hong Kong, Isle of Man, Italy, Jersey, Liechtenstein, Luxembourg, Malta, Monaco, the Netherlands, Switzerland and the Turks and Caicos islands. 'The Convention *does not* introduce the trust concept into the domestic law of countries lacking the concept ("non-trust countries") ... The Convention *does* make non-trust countries, like trust countries, recognise trusts of property as a matter of private international law (subject to significant safeguards)': J Glasson *International Trust Laws* (1992, Penguin), cls 5 and 6.

The Convention provides as follows:

> 'Such recognition shall imply, as a minimum, that the trust property constitutes a separate fund ... In so far as the law applicable to a trust requires or *provides*, such recognition shall imply, in particular –
>
> (a) that personal creditors of the trustee shall have no recourse against the trust assets;
>
> (b) that the trust assets shall not form part of the trustee's estate upon his insolvency or bankruptcy ...' (art 11).

5.32 The concept of bailment may not be available under civil law in cases where client assets are held on an unallocated basis. In countries where neither trust nor bailment is available, an alternative basis for an insolvency ring-fence must be established. For this reason, the major international settlements systems have legislative backing that provides for an insolvency ring-fence[1].

1 In the case of Euroclear, the Royal Decree No 62 of 10 November 1967, as amended, and in the case of Clearstream, the Law of 1 August 2001. See also the Luxembourg Fiduciary Contracts Law of 18 July 1983.

In New York, art 8 of the Uniform Commercial Code creates an insolvency ring-fence in favour of purchasers of interests in securities (known as securities entitlements) held by financial intermediaries on an unallocated basis: art 8-313(1)(d)(ii) and (iii), and 8-313(2). Of course, New York is not a civil law jurisdiction.

Risks of sub-custodian insolvency

5.33 It is crucial to appreciate that terms of the sub-custody agreement providing for an insolvency ring-fence will not necessarily be reliable. This is because, when a foreign sub-custodian becomes insolvent, the mandatory provisions of applicable insolvency law will determine the fate of the disputed assets. Where these conflict with contractual provisions, the latter will generally be disregarded[1].

1 Under English law, see *British Eagle International Airlines Ltd v Compagnie Nationale Air France* [1975] 1 WLR 758, [1975] 2 All ER 390; *National Westminster Bank Ltd v Halesowen Presswork and Assemblies Ltd* [1972] AC 785, [1972] 2 WLR 455, [1972] 1 All ER 641, HL; Ex p Mackay (1873) 8 Ch App 643.

5.34 In assessing the risk of sub-custodian insolvency, it is necessary to consider, first, which courts are likely to assert jurisdiction over the insolvent sub-custodian and, second, which system of insolvency law those courts are likely to apply. In the light of the rules discussed at paras **5.5–5.29** above, where the sub-custodian is an

EU bank, with effect from 2004, the law of the member state where it is authorised should be considered. Outside the EU, it should be very broadly assumed that the courts of the country of incorporation will take jurisdiction. In addition, where the sub-custodian operates through a branch in a second country, the courts of that country may also assert jurisdiction, particularly where local assets are available to meet the claims of local creditors.

Local ring-fence opinions

5.35 As indicated at paras **5.5–5.29** above, courts having insolvency jurisdiction often apply their local law to insolvency questions. For this reason, global custodians seek the opinions of lawyers practising in the sub-custodian's country, to the effect that the client assets are protected by an insolvency ring-fence under local law ('local ring-fence opinions')[1].

[1] Standard opinions obtained pursuant to Rule 17f-5 of the US Investment Companies Act 1940 include answers to the following question: 'If the Bank becomes insolvent, are there (in addition to the period necessary for the liquidator on insolvency to sort out the affairs and assets of the bank) restrictions under the laws of England on the ability of the client or the client's customers to recover securities or cash assets held directly by the Bank?'

5.36 The risk may arise that client assets are not ring-fenced where special structures are introduced in order to hide the identity of investors and thereby to avoid aspects of the regime of the issuer country. For example, securities may be placed in 'street names', ie the names of local brokers, in order to escape local restrictions on foreign holdings of securities in a number of far eastern countries. Also, intermediaries may be introduced in countries having a double taxation treaty with the issuer country. In each case, it would appear to the authorities in the issuer country that the intermediary is the beneficial owner. The legality and effect of such arrangements should be carefully considered. Moreover, in the insolvency of the intermediary, the beneficial owner or the global custodian acting on its behalf will probably require the co-operation of the courts in the issuer country to recover the assets. In the circumstances, the local courts may be unsympathetic to their claims.

Other risks

5.37 Of course, an insolvency ring-fence will only be effective to protect assets which remain in the hands of the insolvent sub-custodian. It addresses the risk of insolvency, but not the further risk that assets may be missing from the sub-custodian's client holding. Such a shortfall may arise for a wide range of reasons[1], including sub-custodian negligence and fraud. The pressures faced by a sub-custodian shortly before insolvency may sometimes make negligence and fraud more likely[2]. In practice, therefore, in addition to obtaining local ring-fence opinions, global custodians and their clients require regular due diligence to be undertaken to establish that the sub-custodian's systems and procedures are adequate, and that the global custodian's and the sub-custodian's accounts are regularly reconciled[3].

[1] Where contractual settlement (discussed in Chapter 4) is offered in relation to securities, it is important to ensure that the custodian is not in effect using the securities of one client to lend to another client who has suffered a delay in settlement. If this is the case, this may be an additional source of shortfalls in the client securities accounts.

[2] London Business School *Custodianship and the Protection of Client Property*, July 1994. This study of the London markets has shown that losses of client securities in the hands of intermediaries have not been caused by fraud alone (presumably because a fraudulent but solvent intermediary would be compelled to return the missing assets), but by the combination of fraud and insolvency (p 3).

[3] See Chapter 7 for a discussion of regulatory requirements.

CROSS-BORDER COLLATERAL ISSUES

Overview

5.38 Chapter 4 discussed the importance of securities in financial collateral arrangements. Such collateral arrangements often operate cross-border. Indeed, a bank in one country may take collateral from a debtor in a second country, consisting of securities issued from a third country, and held through an intermediary in a fourth. This raises a number of interesting conflict of laws questions.

Conflict of laws analysis of collateral arrangements

5.39 Chapter 4 provides a detailed discussion of the use of the custody portfolio as collateral. As discussed there, the essential achievement of successful collateral arrangements is to confer on the collateral taker property rights in the collateral assets, thereby addressing the risk of the collateral giver's default. The greater part of this section therefore considers the conflict of laws analysis of property rights. However, the collateral taker must address a number of other issues, including the following. It must address issues of power (or capacity)[1] and authority[2] (under the law of the collateral giver's constitution)[3]. It must establish that the collateral arrangement is entered into with essential[4] validity (under the governing law of the contract)[5] and formal validity[6] (under either the governing law or the law of the place where it was concluded)[7], and also that is has been duly executed (generally under the law of the collateral giver's constitution). The collateral giver may be subject to registration requirements[8] and regulatory requirements[9] (under the law of incorporation or of any branch through which it operates), and these must be satisfied.

1   That is, that the constitution of the collateral giver, being an institution, permits such business.
2   That is, that the individual who executed the agreement on behalf of the collateral giver had authority to bind the collateral giver.
3   *Carl Zeiss Stifftung v Rayner & Keeler (No 2)* [1967] 1 AC 853 at 972E and 919G.
4   That is, that nothing in its essential nature invalidates it, such as (under English law) the absence of consideration.
5   Article 8 of the Rome Convention 1980 (Convention on the Law Applicable to Contractual Obligations opened for signature in Rome on 19 June 1980 (80/934/EEC)); Art 10 of the Rome I Regulation (Regulation (EC) No 593/2008). See para **5.25** n 3 above.
6   That is, that any formal requirements are satisfied, such as the agreement being in writing, in the form of a deed, signed or notarised.
7   Article 9 of the Rome Convention 1980; Art 11 of the Rome I Regulation (Regulation (EC) No 593/2008). See **5.25** n 3 above.
8   For example, for companies incorporated in England and Wales, the registration requirements of Companies Act 2006, s 860. See also proposals for reform, discussed in Chapter 4.
9   That is, regulatory requirements affecting its business.

5.40 As indicated in Chapter 4, the acquisition of property rights in the collateral assets breaks down into several issues. The collateral assets in question must generally be identified in a process known as attachment[1]; property rights must generally be rendered enforceable against third parties by a process known as perfection[2]; and where more than one property interest is perfected in the same assets, the priorities between them must be determined[3]. Arguably, because they relate to property rights, all these issues are determined by the law of the place where the assets are located, or lex situs[4].

1   Although English law recognises floating charges, which do not attach to particular assets, but relate to a changing class of assets: see Chapter 4. Attachment in this sense should not be confused with attachment in the sense of enforcement against assets.

2   Perfection often involves a process of publicity, eg registration or notarisation.

3   That is, it must be determined which interest will be met first: this is crucial where the value of the assets is insufficient to meet all the interests in full.

4   The choice of law rules for priorities disputes are discussed by Millett J in *Macmillan v Bishopsgate Investment Trust plc (No 3)* [1996] 1 WLR 387 at 758. He indicates that, where a fiduciary wrongly disposes of client assets to a third party, in a priorities dispute between the client and the third party, lex situs applies. In contrast, where a priorities dispute arises due to successive dealings in the same asset, Millett J argued that the law of the forum applies, ie English law in the English courts. However, the case law on this latter point is complex. Some cases support the lex fori rule (eg *Bankers Trust International Ltd v Todd Shipyards Corpn, The Halcyon Isle* [1981] AC 221 at 230–231). Others suggest governing law of the contract constituting the disputed asset (eg *Republica de Guatemala v Nunez* [1927] 1 KB 669; and others lex situs (eg *Re Queensland Mercantile and Agency Co* [1891] 1 Ch 536.

5.41   As a practical matter, the collateral taker must identify the steps required to enforce its interest and remit the proceeds[1] (generally under lex situs)[2]. Finally, the collateral taker must assess the risk that, after enforcement, its collateral interest might be displaced if the collateral giver is affected by insolvency[3] (under the insolvency law of the country of incorporation or any branch)[4], or if the collateral assets beneficially belonged to clients of the collateral taker, and were delivered in breach of duty[5] (arguably, under lex situs)[6].

1   That is, it must ascertain whether there are any exchange controls in place.

2   Because, as a practical matter, enforcement by exercising a power of sale and remittance of proceeds of sale take place in and from the jurisdiction where the assets are located. (Of course, legal location (lex situs) and geographical location do not always coincide.)

3   Under preference rules or other rules of insolvency displacement.

4   Or, within the EU, under the detailed rules of jurisdiction and choice of law discussed in Chapter 4.

5   The risk for the collateral taker here is that the defrauded beneficial owners will bring an action for the return of their assets.

6   See *Macmillan v Bishopsgate Investment Trust plc (No 3)* [1996] 1 WLR 387.

Property rights

5.42   The fundamental premise on which collateralisation relies is that the collateral taker is not merely a creditor with personal rights against the insolvent debtor, but also enjoys property rights in the collateral assets. This enables it to jump the queue of unsecured creditors in insolvency by removing the collateral assets from the insolvent's estate, and applying them to satisfy its claims. In cross-border arrangements, therefore, it is crucial to establish that the collateral taker's property rights will stand up under the relevant system or systems of law, and hence the intense commercial interest in these conflict of laws issues.

Property rights in intangible assets

5.43   The collateral taker's rights are proprietary, notwithstanding that the assets in question are intangible assets such as registered securities. As indicated in Chapter 1, this proposition has to be considered both as against the issuer and as against the insolvent collateral giver.

5.44   It might be objected that an intangible asset is merely an obligation (in the case of debt securities, broadly the right to be paid by the issuer). Obligations or claims are personal and not proprietary by nature and (it might be argued) cannot therefore be subject to property rights. Thus, *as against the issuer*, the holder of unsecured debt securities has only personal rights, which may become valueless in the issuer's insolvency.

5.45 However, as several (common law) commentators have pointed out, obligations may be subject to property rights *as against third parties* such as collateral givers. If the collateral giver becomes insolvent, but the issuer remains solvent, the lender who took debt securities as collateral expects to be paid, because, *as against the collateral taker* its rights in relation to the securities are proprietary.

Jurisdiction

5.46 Legal proceedings that test the validity of collateral arrangements may originate in different ways. The collateral taker may seek to enforce its interest by suing the collateral giver (whether directly or through its insolvency official). Alternatively, the insolvency official may itself commence the hearing by seeking directions from the court as part of the insolvency proceedings. Although the procedural conflict of laws analysis of these many alternatives differ, it will be argued that the result is the same.

5.47 As discussed above, proceedings commenced by the collateral taker may often be brought in the country where the assets are located, because of the practicalities of enforcement. Insolvency proceedings may be most likely to take place in the country of incorporation of the insolvent collateral giver, although they may be brought in a branch country, or even a third country where there are significant local assets. Within the EU, see the detailed rules discussed in Chapter 4.

Choice of law – the lex situs rule

5.48 In non-insolvency proceedings, the general rule is that property rights are determined in accordance with lex situs or the law of the place where the assets in question are located[1]. The courts will therefore apply lex situs to determine whether the collateral taker enjoys property rights in the collateral assets, which are effective to protect its interest in the insolvency of the collateral giver.

1   *Cammell v Sewell* (1858) 3 H & N 617: 'If personal property is disposed of in a manner binding according to the law of the country where it is, that disposition is binding everywhere': per Pollock CB at 624. The Rome Convention on the Law Applicable to Contractual Obligations (implemented by the Contracts (Applicable Law) Act 1990) does not apply to property rights: see p 10 of the *Guiliano and Lagarde Report on the Rome Convention*.

5.49 The same approach should also be adopted in insolvency proceedings. It was indicated above that, as a general rule, insolvency proceedings are governed by the law of the country in which they are conducted. However, this general rule relates to the substantive law of insolvency (including such matters as insolvency displacement). The impact of insolvency law on collateral arrangements is subject to an important principle concerning the recognition of pre-existing property rights. Property rights arising under foreign law prior to the onset of insolvency should be recognised in insolvency proceedings[1], providing of course that the transactions giving rise to such rights are not avoidable under preference rules or other mandatory provisions of insolvency law[2]. If such mandatory provisions are satisfied, the courts governing the insolvency of the collateral taker should respect the interest of the collateral taker, provided such interest amounted to a property interest under lex situs[3], prior to the onset of insolvency. However, the risk may remain that the insolvency courts of certain countries outside the scope of the EU measures would be tempted to disregard legal principle, and refuse to recognise foreign law property rights that would not have been recognised under domestic law, if this would serve to increase the assets available to local creditors[4]. It is therefore customary for collateral takers to assess their property rights under the law of the insolvency country, as well as lex situs[5].

1 See art 5 of the European Insolvency Regulation: 'The opening of insolvency proceedings shall not affect the rights in rem of creditors or third parties in respect of tangible or intangible, movable or immovable assets – both specific assets and collections of indefinite assets as a whole which change from time to time – belonging to the debtor which are situated within the territory of another member state at the time of the opening of the proceedings.' Article 21 of the Banking Winding Up Directive, which applies to credit institutions is in like terms.

2 See art 5(4) of the EU Insolvency Regulation and art 21(4) of the Banking Winding Up Directive.

3 See Recital 25 and art 5 of the EU Insolvency Regulation, and art 21 of the Banking Winding Up Directive.

4 The Hague Convention on securities held with an intermediary discussed in paras **5.59–5.61** below includes provision to prevent such action by insolvency courts (see art 8).

5 As a practical matter, if the assets are located in country A, which recognises the interest of the collateral taker, but the insolvency jurisdiction is country B, which does not, the collateral taker may seek to enforce its interest in A (assuming it is able to ignore any penalties B may seek to impose).

5.50 Within the EU, the impact of the EU Insolvency Regulation on the lex situs rule must be assessed. Article 5(1) provides that the opening of insolvency proceedings shall not affect the rights in rem[1] of creditors or third parties in respect of assets belonging to the debtor and situated in a third party state. This must be read together with art 2(g), which provides broadly that for this purpose publicly registered assets are situated in the member state under the authority of which the register is kept, and that claims are situated in the member state where the obligor has the centre of his or her main interests. In the case of a company, this is presumed to be the place of its registered office[2]. These rules equate broadly but not exactly[3] to the rules of English law for determining the situs of such assets. However, it does not appear that the EU Insolvency Regulation is intended to alter the lex situs rule. The provisions of art 5(1) merely serve to limit the impact of insolvency proceedings for pre-existing property rights; they do not provide for such rights to be acquired.

1 This term was deliberately left undefined: see para 100 of M Virgos and E Schmit Report on the Convention on Insolvency Proceedings, 1996 (the 'Virgos Report').

2 Article 3(1).

3 For example, under arts 2(g) and 3(1), bank debts payable at a particular branch would be treated as located at the member state in which the bank has its registered office. This contrasts with the position under English law, whereby such a bank debt would be located with the relevant branch: *Martin v Nadel* [1906] 2 KB 26 at 31.

Applicability to intangibles

5.51 The lex situs rule undoubtedly applies to land[1] and to chattels[2]. There has been a debate as to whether the rule applies also to intangible assets[3]. One school of thought has argued that, because intangibles are creatures of contract, their transfer is determined by the governing law of the contracts that constitute them[4]. However, on the basis outlined earlier that intangibles may be subject to property rights as against third parties, it is argued that lex situs remains the correct connecting factor[5], and this is now supported by case law[6]. The situs of intangibles is generally the place where they are in the ordinary course enforceable[7] so that, for example, a simple debt is located with the debtor[8].

1 *Norris v Chambres* (1861) 29 Beav 246.

2 *Inglis v Usherwood* (1801) 1 East 515.

3 This debate has of course become very important with the development of the weightless economy, in which the more significant part of economic activity relates to intangibles.

4 See P J Rogerson 'The Situs of Debts in the conflict of Laws – Illogical, Unnecessary and Misleading' [1990] CLJ 441.

5   This choice of connecting factor is supported by *Re Maudslay* [1900] 1 Ch 602; *New York Life Insurance Co v Public Trustee* [1924] 2 Ch 101; and *Jabbour v Custodian* [1954] 1 All ER 145.

6   *Macmillan v Bishopsgate (No 3)* [1996] 1 WLR 387 at 404, 405, per Staughton LJ; at 410, 411, 412, per Auld LJ; at 423, 424, per Auldous LJ. For a contrary view in the context of an assignment of an insurance assignment, however, see *Raiffeisen Zentralbank Österreich AG v Five Star Trading LLC* [2001] EWCA Civ 68, [2001] QB 825.

7   *Alloway v Phillips* [1980] 1 WLR 888 at 894, per Waller LJ; *Re Russian Bank for Foreign Trade* [1934] 1 Ch 720 at 767, per Maugham J.

8   See, for example, *Kwok Chi Leung Karl v Comr Estate Duty* [1988] 1 WLR 1035 at 1040, per Lord Oliver; and *Comr of Stamps v Hope* [1891] AC 476 at 481, per Lord Field.

5.52 The traditional rules for determining property rights in securities might be very broadly summarised as follows[1]. Registered shares are located with the register[2], which usually[3] coincides with the place of incorporation, and bearer securities, as tangible assets, are located with the instrument constituting them from time to time[4]. The challenge is how to adapt these traditional rules in an electronic environment.

1   This is a complex area of law. For a more detailed discussion, see R Potok (ed) *Cross Border Collateral: Legal Risk and the Conflict of Laws* (2002, Butterworths), ch 10.

2   *Macmillan v Bishopsgate (No 3)* [1996] 1 WLR 387 at 411, per Auld LJ. However, different views were also expressed in this complex judgment. See also art 2(g), second indent, of the EU Insolvency Regulation.

3   But not always. See *Brassard v Smith* [1925] AC 371 at 376, per Lord Dunedin.

4   *Alcock v Smith* [1892] 1 Ch 238.

5.53 They need to be adapted for two reasons. First, paper instruments have receded in favour of electronic databases. Second, these databases have proliferated through the use of intermediaries. As discussed in Chapter 1, it is customary for investors to hold their securities through custodians and other intermediaries which participate in wholesale electronic delivery systems. In cross-border investment arrangements, several intermediaries are likely to stand between the investor or collateral taker and the issuer of the underlying assets. Each intermediary maintains its own database as a record of its clients' entitlements. If an investor's holding in securities generates credit entries in the accounts of three intermediaries, each standing between it and the issuer, and if each intermediary is located in a different country, the question then arises, where are the investor's assets located?

PRIMA[1]

5.54 It is argued that, under the existing principles of English private international law, the assets are located with the intermediary with whom the investor has a direct relationship and against whom he or she has a directly enforceable claim. This conclusion follows from a number of points. First, intangibles are legally located where they are in the normal course enforceable[2], and a client's interests in securities are normally enforceable against the custodian which maintains a securities account in the client's name. Second, it was argued in Chapter 3 that the custody client's interest is an unallocated[3] interest arising under a trust: existing case law indicates that such interests are legally located with the trustee (ie in this case, the custodian)[4]. Third, this approach is helpful in simplifying the legal analysis of cross-border collateral arrangements, because it enables the collateral taker to refer to a single system of law (that of the intermediary's country) as lex situs[5]. Where the collateral asset consists of a portfolio comprising interests in securities issued from a number of underlying countries, this approach avoids the need to refer to each of them[6].

1   Richard Potok of Potok & Co takes credit for promoting this concept and also this happy acronym (Place of the Relevant Intermediary Account – 'PRIMA'). See, inter alia, *Cross Border Collateral:*

Legal Risk and the Conflict of Laws (2002, Butterworths). The first edition of this book (and an earlier article by J Benjamin 'Custody – An English Law Analysis' (1994) 9 JIBFL 121 at 188) used the term 'Intermediary Jurisdiction Approach' in place of PRIMA. For an early advocation of PRIMA (although not by that name) see Randall Guynn in *Modernising Securities Ownership, Transfer and Pledging Laws* (1996, IBA).

2 See L Collins et al (eds) *Dicey, Morris and Collins: The Conflict of Laws* (2012, 15th edn, Sweet & Maxwell), vol II, ch 22.

3 As discussed in Chapter 3, it is customary for the holdings of different clients to be commingled in the hands of custodians and other intermediaries, and this serves to break the direct property link between the investor and the underlying issuer.

4 See, for example, *Lord Sudeley v Attorney-General* [1897] AC 11; *Baker v Archer-Shee* [1927] AC 844; and *Marshall v Kerr* [1995] 1 AC 148, [1994] 3 WLR 299, [1994] 3 All ER 106. See also *Re Cigala's Settlement Trusts* (1878) 7 Ch D 351; *Attorney-General v Johnson* [1907] 2 KB 885; *Favorke v Steinkopf* [1922] 1 Ch 174; and *Stamp Duty Comr (Queensland) v Hugh Duncan Livingston* [1965] AC 694, [1964] 3 WLR 963, [1964] 3 All ER 692. A different rule applies to allocated trust interests: see *Attorney-General for Hong Kong v Reid* [1994] 1 AC 324, [1993] 3 WLR 1143, [1994] 1 All ER 1.

5 Commercial convenience is an important factor shaping the rules of private international law.

6 The authors are grateful to Lee Mitchell for raising the following interesting question relating to priorities. Where interests in securities are held for a client through a chain of intermediaries, if each of the client and the intermediaries grants a security interest, which takes priority? The position is understood to be as follows. If an underlying intermediary gives a security interest over client assets for its own borrowings *with the consent of its client*, this interest in general takes priority over a security interest granted by the client. This is on the basis that the client's asset derives from the asset held by the intermediary, and is therefore subject to any encumbrances on the latter.

If the above happens *without the consent of the client, ie in breach of duty*, the above proposition would be subject to the rules of equitable tracing and following. Thus (broadly) the collateral taker from the intermediary could only take the security interest in priority if it could show that it was the good faith purchaser of the legal estate for value without notice of the breach of duty. Importantly, it would not be in this position if its interest was a charge (ie equitable only). However, this is a complex area of law, on which the authors are not aware of any direct authority.

5.55 These arguments are now reflected in *Dicey and Morris*[1]. The approach broadly accords with the US rules for securities entitlements, which under the US Uniform Commercial Code ('UCC') are generally located with the intermediary providing services directly to the client[2].

1 L Collins et al (eds) *Dicey, Morris and Collins: The Conflict of Laws* (2012, 15th edn, Sweet & Maxwell), vol II, para 22–042.

2 Article 8.110. 'Because [the client's] property is "located" at Custodian, it is clear, as a matter of general principle, that the only proper subject of legal process by [the client's] creditors would be Custodian': S J Rogers *Policy Perspectives on Revised UCC, Article 8*, (1996) UCLA Law Rev, June, 431 at 1457.

5.56 Internationally, this approach has gained widespread acceptance under the term 'Place of the Relevant Intermediary Account' or 'PRIMA'. PRIMA is being adopted in a range of legislative measures discussed below and the authors would argue that this development is wholly welcome. However, PRIMA is not universally accepted, and a measure of legal risk will remain as long as the courts of countries which do not accept PRIMA may assume jurisdiction[1].

1 In such countries, local courts may be less likely to decline jurisdiction in matters affecting locally issued securities. For this reason, the forum of a dispute is a key issue. Indeed, once an action concerning foreign securities has been commenced in the country of the issuer, the English courts may be most unlikely to entertain an action on the same issue.

A measure of pragmatism is called for. Collateral takers will often have to tolerate some measure of legal risk, and should focus upon practical issues relating to enforcement. Control of the assets is of primary importance. Will the intermediary settlement system or custodian co-operate in enforcing the collateral interest sufficiently rapidly, so that challenge at issuer level may come too late? Does the settlement system have more than one depositary in the relevant jurisdiction, so that a third party claiming the assets would be unable to identify and therefore attach the assets through the local courts? Finally, and subject to the need to avoid illegality, does the collateral taker have any assets of its own in the issuer jurisdiction against which adverse claims or penalties might be enforced?

Settlement Finality Directive

5.57 The Settlement Finality Directive is discussed further in Chapter 8 (paras **8.108–8.109**) and in Chapter 9 in relation to CREST (Chapter 9, paras **9.28** and **9.53–9.56**). Article 9(2) supports PRIMA in relation to collateral delivered through designated settlement systems[1]. Unfortunately, in the implementation of the Directive in the UK under the Financial Markets and Insolvency (Settlement Finality) Regulations 1999, as amended[2], art 9(2) is interpreted narrowly[3]. It does not benefit, for example, collateral provided by one commercial participant to another.[4]

1 It provides as follows.

   'Where securities (including rights in securities) are provided as collateral security to participants and/or central banks of the Member States or the future European central bank ... and their right (or that of any nominee, agent or third party acting on their behalf) with respect to the securities is legally recorded on a register, account or centralised deposit system located in a Member State, the determination of the rights of such entities as holders of collateral security in relation to those securities shall be governed by the law of that Member State.'

2 SI 1999/2979.

3 In reg 23, which reads as follows: 'Where (a) securities (including rights in securities) are provided as collateral security to a participant, a system operator or a central bank (including any nominee, agent or third party acting on behalf of the participant, the system operator or the central bank), and (b) a register, account or centralised deposit system located in an EEA State legally records the entitlement of that person to the collateral security, the rights of that person as a holder of collateral security in relation to those securities shall be governed by the law of the EEA State or, where appropriate, the law of the part of the EEA State, where the register, account, or centralised deposit system is located.'

   'Both "collateral security" and "participant" are defined terms in reg 2, as follows: collateral security is defined to mean "any realisable assets provided under a charge or a repurchase or similar agreement, or otherwise (including credit claims and money provided under a charge): (a) for the purpose of securing rights and obligations potentially arising in connection with a system ("collateral security in connection with participation in a system"); or (b) to a central bank for the purpose of securing rights and obligations in connection with its operations in carrying out its functions as a central bank ("collateral security in connection with the functions of a central bank"); and participant is defined to means "(a) an institution; (aa) a system operator; (b) a body corporate or unincorporated association which carries out any combination of the functions of a central counterparty, a settlement agent or a clearing house, with respect to a system; or (c)an indirect participant which is treated as a participant, or is a member of a class of indirect participants which are treated as participants, in accordance with regulation 9".

   As a result of these definitions, reg 23 implements art 9(2) of the EU Settlement Finality Directive in a "narrow" sense, with the result that, broadly, a collateral taker is covered only if it is (i) a central bank, (ii) the European Central Bank or (iii) a regulated financial institution or public authority acting as a central counterparty, settlement agent, clearing house or provider of liquidity to an EU settlement system designated under the EU Settlement Finality Directive'.

4 In 2001 the Treasury published a consultation document (HM Treasury *Domestic and International Initiatives Concerning Conflict of Law Issues Relating to Securities: Consultation Document*, July 2001) proposing to widen the interpretation of art 9(2) so that PRIMA would benefit all securities collateral arrangements where 'a register, account or centralised deposit system legally records the entitlement of the collateral taker' (proposed amended reg 23) so that the class of collateral takers to which PRIMA applies would not be limited, nor would PRIMA be restricted to designated settlement systems. However, such amendment has not been made to date. Rather bizarrely, although the consultation resulted in new regulations (the Financial Markets and Insolvency (Settlement Finality) (Amendment) Regulations 2001 (SI 2001/997)) being laid before Parliament on 15 March 2001, expected to come into force on 5 April 2001 (which would have had the effect that the rights of a person to securities recorded in a register, account or centralised deposit system would be governed by the law of the country in which the register, account or system was located), the new regulations were then revoked (by SI 2001/1349 taking effect on 5 April 2001) because (despite the earlier consultation) concerns were raised regarding the effect of the new regulations on contractual terms in bond issues.

Other EU measures

5.58 Provisions supporting PRIMA are also contained in the EU Insolvency Regulation[1], the Banking Winding Up Directive[2], and the Financial Collateral Directive[3].

1   Article 14.
2   Articles 24 and 31.
3   See the discussion of the Financial Collateral Directive in Chapter 4.

Hague Convention on Securities held with an Intermediary[1]

5.59 The Hague Conference on Private International Law worked for a number of years on a project on securities held with an intermediary, and developed the Convention on the Law Applicable to Certain Rights in Respect of Securities held with an Intermediary, which was adopted by the Hague Conference in December 2002. For some years, because of concerns regarding the way in which the Convention's choice of law rules differ from those in the Settlement Finality Directive and the Financial Collateral Directive, the Convention was not signed by any member state[2]. However, it was signed by Switzerland and the US in 2006 and by Mauritius in 2008, and ratified by Switzerland and Mauritius in September 2009 and October 2009 respectively. The Convention is now referred to formally as the Convention of 5 July 2006 on the Law Applicable to Certain Rights in Respect of Securities held with an Intermediary but will not enter into force until 'the first day of the month following the expiration of three months after the deposit of the third instrument of ratification, acceptance, approval or accession'[3]. At the time of writing, no other member states have signed the Convention[4].

1   For a detailed background discussion, see Christophe Bernasconi *The Law Applicable to Dispositions of Securities Held through Indirect Holding Systems*, Hague Conference on Private International Law, to the working group of January 2001 on securities collateral (the 'Bernasconi Report'). See also Roy Goode, Hideki Kanda and Karl Kreuzer *Explanatory Report on the 2006 Hague Securities Convention* (2005, Koninklijke Brill NV).

2   For an analysis of possible issues and the overall benefits of the Convention, see the Financial Markets Law Committee paper 'Hague Convention of the Law Applicable to Certain Rights in respect of Securities held with an Intermediary – Legal assessment of the arguments relating to the signing of the Hague Securities Convention – the need for, and benefits of, the Hague Securities Convention', November 2005.

3   Article 19(1).

4   The European Commission called upon all EU member states to sign the Convention in the interests of improving certainty in relation to securities arrangements and facilitating creation of a 'fully integrated single securities market' (European Commission press release 'Securities markets: Commission calls upon member states to sign Hague Securities Convention', 5 July 2006), but later adopted the opposite view (in March 2009, see information regarding the Hague Convention on the EU website (ec.europa.eu)). This change of approach is understood to have been prompted by disagreement among member states regarding the benefits of this Convention.

5.60 Whereas the PRIMA provisions in the Settlement Finality Directive and Financial Collateral Directive relate only to collateral arrangements, the Hague Convention extends to all dealings in intermediated securities, whether by way of collateral or otherwise[1]. This is welcome, as a fragmented approach depending on the purpose of the transfer is conceptually and practically unsatisfactory.

1   See art 2.

5.61 The primary choice of law rule in the Convention is contained in art 4. In an interesting departure from the EU measures discussed above[1], rules for determining applicable law are influenced by the agreement of the parties, and do not simply follow the place where the account is maintained. (The difficulties of agreeing objective rules for the latter in an electronic environment were extensively debated during the drafting of the Convention[2].) Under art 4, the law applicable to the specified issues[3] is the law agreed by the parties to govern the account agreement (or another law if the parties expressly agree such law applies to the relevant issues), provided that (broadly) the intermediary has an office in the state whose law has been selected and operates securities accounts from that office (although notably, is not required to operate the securities accounts maintained under the relevant account agreement from such office). If the selected law cannot apply because the office test is not satisfied, art 5 contains successive fallback rules, looking first to the law of the jurisdiction in which the intermediary's office is located if the account agreement clearly identifies the intermediary as entering into the agreement through that office and, second, to the law of the jurisdiction in which the intermediary is incorporated or otherwise organised at the time of entry into the account agreement[4].

1   And perhaps reflecting a US commitment to party autonomy.

2   See art 6.

3   Specified in art 2(1), including the legal nature and effects against the intermediary and third parties of the rights resulting from a credit of securities to a securities account, requirements for perfection of a disposition of securities held with an intermediary, and whether a person's interest in securities held with an intermediary extinguishes or has priority over another person's interest.

4   The qualifying test referring to the location of a relevant office was introduced because of the concern that an unqualified right to choose the applicable law could result in arbitrary selection of a law with no connection at all to the arrangements (although in practice this seems unlikely given that it is not in the interests of the intermediary or the client to select a law with which they are unfamiliar or has little relevance to the arrangements).

UNIDROIT[1]

5.62 UNIDROIT has considered the issues arising in relation to securities held through intermediaries over some years, working on the basis that maximum harmonisation of substantive rules would be beneficial, rather than relying on rules (whether the PRIMA concept or the Hague Convention rules discussed at paras **5.59–5.61** above) which only identify the jurisdiction whose laws apply. It can be argued that the UNIDROIT approach resolves, or at least minimises, problems arising from potential conflicts between, for example, the Financial Collateral Directive and the Hague Convention, since in principle it should be less of a concern to identify the relevant law if the position under the different possible laws is the same[2]. (There will of course still be the need to identify which laws apply for technical reasons, and there may still be issues arising from different implementation, interpretation or application in different jurisdictions.) However, implementation of this type of Convention could have quite radical implications for jurisdictions which already have a well-developed concept of the rights arising in connection with holding through an intermediary. As has been discussed elsewhere in this work, English law has a complex system of common law, case law, statute and regulation concerning trusts and custodians, and the rights of persons holding assets with such entities. A Convention requiring the introduction into English law of detailed rules regarding the responsibilities of intermediaries and the rights of their clients could have significant implications for not only custodians but also for any of the many arrangements where an intermediary holds securities for a client (eg bond trustees, security trustees, unit trusts, depositary receipts, nominee arrangements and private trusts under wills or similar).

1   UNIDROIT is the *Institut International pour l'Unification du Droit Privé* (the International Institute for the Unification of Private Law), a body established by a multilateral agreement (the UNIDROIT statute) in 1940, whose members are the 61 member states who currently have acceded to the

UNIDROIT statute. It is funded by contributions from its member states. UNIDROIT is intended to function as an independent intergovernmental body which can focus on harmonising the private commercial laws of states, in particular aiming to unify substantive law rules regarding new technical or commercial areas which are of common concern by producing international Conventions.

2   For further discussion of the benefits of UNIDROIT creating a uniform approach, see K Devonport and D Turing 'Reducing risk and costs in cross-border transactions: Are Hague and UNIDROIT missing pieces in the puzzle?' (2007) 1 *Journal of Securities Operations & Custody* 1, July.

5.63   After considerable discussion and negotiation of several drafts of the proposed 'Convention on Substantive Rules regarding Intermediated Securities', a final version was adopted by the Diplomatic Conference in Geneva on 9 October 2009, ie the 'UNIDROIT Convention on Substantive Rules for Intermediated Securities'[1]. This Convention is now known as the Geneva Securities Convention, and will come into force on the first day of the month following the expiration of six months after ratification, acceptance, approval or accession by three jurisdictions. At the time of writing, the Convention has been signed (but not ratified) by Bangladesh only. It seems probable that the reason for no other jurisdiction signing so far is a consequence of concerns regarding overlap or conflicts with existing law.

1   See Conventions section of www.unidroit.org.

5.64   A detailed analysis of the Geneva Securities Convention and its potential implications if implemented in the UK in its current form would be sufficient material for a book in itself, but for the purposes of this discussion the following points of interest are noted:

(1)   The meaning or scope of some of the definitions is not entirely clear. For example, 'intermediated securities' is defined to mean 'securities credited to a securities account *or* rights or interests in securities resulting from the credit of securities to a securities account'[1] (emphasis added). The first part of this definition suggests the intermediated securities may be the actual securities themselves, rather than the rights which the intermediary's client has in respect of the securities held by the intermediary. This seems somewhat circular, preserving the confusion of ownership at several levels which the Convention is intended to minimise.

The definitions of 'securities account' and 'intermediary' are quite wide, referring, respectively, to 'an account maintained by an intermediary to which securities may be credited or debited' and 'a person (including a central securities depository) who in the course of a business or other regular activity maintains securities accounts for others or both for others and for its own account and is acting in that capacity'[2]. These definitions do not focus on who holds securities for another, but who maintains accounts. In principle this suggests that a registrar or similar function[3] may be within the scope of the Convention, but that a person who holds securities for another but does not maintain accounts will be outside its scope. Admittedly in most circumstances a custodian or similar service provider would be expected to maintain accounts recording the securities it holds, but it raises the question of the position where there is a failure to maintain accounts, or a genuine division of functions so that one entity holds assets and another entity maintains the relevant records or accounts.

An 'account holder' is 'a person in whose name an intermediary maintains a securities account, whether that person is acting for its own account or for others (including in the capacity of intermediary)'[4]. It is not clear how this would apply in a situation where a custodian holds for a client but has agreed that the name on the account will be the client's customer rather than the name of the client itself. In such case, the client should still be regarded as the account holder, ie the person for whom the custodian holds the securities, even if the client in turn holds the securities for its customer.

(2) Article 9(1)(a) states the following: 'The credit of securities to a securities account confers on the account holder: (a) the right to receive and exercise any rights attached to the securities, including dividends, other distributions and voting rights: (i) if the account holder is not an intermediary or is an intermediary acting for its own account; and (ii) in any other case, if provided by the non-Convention [ie other local] law.'

Rather than stating a result which local law should achieve, this apparently requires that a credit to a securities account creates a right of itself, regardless of any rules of existing law. In an English law context, this raises the question of what rights a custody client has to securities which a custodian receives on the client's behalf but before such securities are recorded in the relevant client securities account[5].

If an account holder is not within 9(1)(a)(i) (ie it is an intermediary holding on behalf of its own client), it is not wholly clear why the account holder only has rights if so provided by relevant local law.

Article 9(2)(b) goes on to state that 'the rights referred to in paragraph 1(a) may be exercised against the relevant intermediary or the issuer of the securities, or both, in accordance with this Convention, the terms of the securities and the applicable law'. It is unclear which law is meant by reference to the 'applicable law', or in practice how the relevant rights could effectively be exercised against the issuer, unless there is special provision in local law which allows this, since otherwise there is the risk of confusion from both the intermediary (assuming it is legal owner of the relevant securities) and its client being entitled to exercise such rights.

(3) Article 12 contains provisions intended to clarify how a holder of securities through an intermediary can grant a security interest (or other interest) in favour of a third party, broadly by creating an appropriate control agreement or designation of the account. However, there are also specific terms allowing contracting states to implement these provisions in a number of different ways, so this will not necessarily create a uniform result, nor is it clear how these rules would affect or be affected by the Financial Collateral Directive where implemented into local law.

(4) Under Article 15(1)(a), an intermediary is only permitted to make a debit of securities from a securities account if authorised to do so by the account holder, and only permitted to make or remove a designation for the purposes of granting a security interest if authorised to do so by the account holder or (where removing the designation) the person in whose favour the designation is made. It seems a little odd to require the recipient of a security interest to authorise an intermediary with whom it otherwise has no relationship to make the relevant designation in connection with the grant of a security interest by the intermediary's client. However, perhaps the more significant point is the status of a debit in the absence of authority. If it is invalid, the securities will still belong to the intermediary's client (and/or remain subject to a charge in favour of the person granted an interest in such securities), unless the securities have been transferred to a third party who is protected by art 18. However, it is left to local law (and, if such local law permits, the terms of the agreement or settlement system rules) to decide the consequences of unauthorised debits, unauthorised removal of designations, unauthorised designations or other unauthorised dispositions.

Article 18 will apply to protect from liability a person acquiring securities without knowledge (this includes a form of constructive knowledge) of the competing rights or interest provided that the acquisition was not as a result of a 'gift or otherwise gratuitously'. This is interesting since it seems to be trying to create a statutory equivalent of the concept of a bona fide purchaser discussed in Chapter 2 (paras **2.15–2.34**) in the context of negotiability.

(5) Article 19 is curious, because although it states that in principle interests created by an account holder in favour of the intermediary and third parties rank in priority in order of the time at which they are created or notified to the intermediary, an intermediary's interest will rank behind a third party's interest even if created later in time unless the intermediary and that third party expressly agree otherwise. This seems to create a difficult position for the intermediary who will in this manner be involved in the negotiation of terms even though in principle the relevant arrangements between the account holder and the third party are not the concern of the intermediary.

(6) Article 22 is intended to prohibit of upper-tier attachment, so that if a client holds securities with a custodian which in turn holds with a sub-custodian which in turn holds with a settlement system, the client (or its liquidator or creditors) should not be able to make claims against the relevant sub-custodian or settlement system. However, it is not clear that the proposed wording achieves this. Article 19(1) prohibits specifically 'attachment of intermediated securities of an account holder'. In the example given, it is not clear whether this would prevent a claim against the sub-custodian or settlement system since, in principle, this would involve attachment of intermediated securities of the custodian or sub-custodian, as applicable, rather than intermediated securities of the account holder. Furthermore, Article 22(3) permits a contracting state to 'declare that … an attachment of intermediated securities of an account holder made against or so as to affect a person other than the relevant intermediary has effect also against the relevant intermediary'. It is not clear in what circumstances this would be considered necessary, but to the extent this causes further complexity in the context of attachment, and results in different processes in different jurisdictions, it is difficult to see how this assists simplify or harmonise this aspect of holding through intermediaries.

(7) Article 26: arts 24 and 25 contain provisions requiring, broadly, the intermediary to hold for, and allocate to, its clients an amount of securities equal to the amount records in the accounts on its books. This is not entirely consistent with the idea of intermediated securities being acquired by a credit to an account, since by definition this acknowledges the existence of a security underlying the record of the security. Article 26 sets out rules for allocation of shortfalls, such that, unless securities 'have been allocated to a single account' then account holders shall bear the shortfall 'in proportion to the respective number or amount of securities of that description credited to their securities accounts'. While this may well be the position under English law where there is no clear indication of the persons bearing the loss, this would constitute a significant change in situations where, although securities are held in an omnibus account, it is nonetheless possible to show how the shortfall arose and which particular clients should bear it.

(8) Chapter V, arts 31–38, contain provisions relating to title transfer or security arrangements respecting intermediated securities which seem to be intended to follow a similar approach to that of the Financial Collateral Directive, clarifying that such arrangements are valid and enforceable (including on insolvency), and that a right of use applies to a security arrangement if the parties so agree. However, the definition of 'security collateral agreement' is considerably wider than under the Financial Collateral Directive, since the provision of collateral is not required to involve giving possession or control by transfer or designation (although possibly the assumption is that collateral arrangements respecting intermediated securities will only be entered into as contemplated by art 12, see above), and there is no restriction on the types of person or arrangement to

which these provisions may apply (although art 38 permits contracting states to disapply Chapter VI altogether or to limit its scope). It is unclear therefore how this Chapter is to apply in jurisdictions which have implemented the Financial Collateral Directive.

1   Geneva Securities Convention, art 1(b).
2   Geneva Securities Convention, art 1(c) and (d).
3   But Article 6 of the Convention states that 'This Convention does not apply to the functions of creation, recording or reconciliation of securities, vis-a-vis the issuer of those securities, by a person such as a central securities depository, central bank, transfer agent or registrar.' This is useful to avoid application to central systems such as CREST which maintain a central register of title, as well as other registrars. Somewhat confusingly, Article 7 allows a contracting state to 'declare that ... a person other than the relevant intermediary is responsible for the performance of a function or functions (but not all functions) of the relevant intermediary'. It is not clear what the purpose of this wording *is*.
4   Geneva Securities Convention, art 1(e).
5   Similar issues arise in connection with art 11(1), which states that 'intermediated securities are acquired by an account holder by the credit of securities to that account holder's securities account'.

5.65 In principle, although the aims of the Geneva Securities Convention are reasonable, it seems likely that the implementation of the Convention as currently drafted could cause much more confusion than it resolves. But see also the Law Commission paper of May 2008 'The UNIDROIT Convention on Substantive Rules regarding International Securities – Further Updated Advice to HM Treasury' which was largely supportive of the Convention. It remains to be seen whether this Convention will receive the necessary signatures and ratifications to enable it to take effect and have a real effect on issues relating to intermediated securities.

Conceptual issues

5.66 Although it is gaining widespread commercial support, PRIMA has its critics and much of this criticism is conceptual. Critics have argued that the root of title of the securities in relation to which investors and collateral takers have property interests, and therefore the location of their assets, is with the underlying paper (in the case of bearer instruments) or with the underlying issuer register (in the case of registered securities). This is called the 'look through' approach[1]. Market participants have generally resisted the look through approach for pragmatic reasons. As indicated above, where the collateral portfolio comprises interests in securities issued from 20 underlying countries, the look through approach would involve the expense and administrative burden of 20 legal opinions (some of which may be unfavourable)[2].

1   On the basis that it involves 'looking', from the point of view of the investor or collateral taker, 'through' the intermediaries to the underlying issuer.
2   The difficulty is compounded where actively traded, so that the issuer jurisdictions involved change from time to time.

5.67 Of course, it is not a sufficient answer to the look through approach to state that it is inconvenient[1]. It is necessary also to develop the substantive law analysis on which PRIMA rests[2]. The investor or collateral taker holds its interest through one or more intermediary. The investor's asset is not at risk in the insolvency of the intermediary and therefore economically, and also for balance sheet, taxation and regulatory purposes, the asset is indistinguishable from the underlying securities. However, as was argued in Chapter 3, it is legally distinct. The commingling of the assets of different clients in the hands of the intermediary prevents the claims of any client from attaching to particular underlying securities, so that the client's rights are not allocated, but in the nature of co-ownership. Moreover, in the normal course the client has no direct rights of enforcement except through the intermediary. Thus, such intermediation is a form of legal repackaging, and the client's assets consist of indirect co-ownership rights, which the authors have called interests in securities, and which the UCC terms securities entitlements. Lawyers in the area of English common law have long been familiar with structures like the unit trust, where investors hold units conferring indirect co-ownership rights in an underlying portfolio. We intuitively distinguish the unit from the underlying assets to which they are legally and economically related. With the intermediation that computerisation has brought to the financial markets, it is argued that this old common law conception now has a new use, as it simplifies the cross-border aspects of property rights in the electronic securities markets[3].

1   Although it is part of an answer. The reason regularly given for the lex situs rule in early judgments is the importance of enabling purchasers conveniently to establish title. See, for example, *Cammell v Sewell* (1860) 5 H & N 728 at 1374, per Crompton J. More recently, see *Winkworth v Christie* [1980] 1 Ch 496 at 512, per Slade J.

2   This was the purpose of Joanna Benjamin *Interests in Securities* (2000, Oxford University Press).

3   See Joanna Benjamin *Interests in Securities* (2000, Oxford University Press) for a fuller discussion.

Interests in securities and cash

5.68   PRIMA has been advocated in relation to interests in securities. Of course, global custody clients also hold multi-currency cash balances, and may wish to deliver these to third parties as collateral. However, the analysis here is different. In the case of interests in securities, the clients enjoy property rights in relation to the underlying securities, and hence the debate as to whether PRIMA or look through is the correct approach. In the case of cash balances, the client does not enjoy property rights in any underlying foreign currency balance[1], but is merely a debtor of the global custodian[2]. As a bank debt, the client's assets are located with the global custodian[3], and no question of the look through approach arises.

1   Because of the structure of the international banking settlement system, currency is generally held in the country in which it is legal tender. See the discussion of Eurodollars by Terrence Prime in *International Bonds and Certificates of Deposit* (1990, Butterworths) pp 4, 5. Thus, where a London global custodian (being a UK bank) maintains a credit balance of US$10,000 for a custody client, it will not of course keep a large pile of dollar bills in its vaults in London to match that credit balance. The asset of the global custodian corresponding to the credit balance will be a further credit balance of, say, US$1,000,000 in favour of the global custodian in the books of its correspondent bank in New York. Where US dollar income or proceeds of sale of custody securities are paid to the global custodian on behalf of clients, they are likely to be credited directly to the account of the New York correspondent bank. This account in New York may be said to constitute dollars, and that in favour of the custody client in the books of the London global custodian may be said to constitute Eurodollars. Because of the use of correspondent banks, it might be thought that the global custodian is holding the client's non-sterling cash overseas. However, this is not the case. The asset of the client is not the dollars in New York, but the Eurodollars in London. Thus the client's asset comprises a debt owed by the global custodian to pay $10,000. The debt of the New York correspondent bank to pay US$1,000,000 is owed, not to the client, but to the global custodian, and the client enjoys no rights in it.

2   See Chapter 3 for a discussion of this principle.

3   Or, if the sums credited to the account are payable at a particular branch of the global custodian, at that branch: *Martin v Nadel* [1906] 2 KB 26 at 31.

Securities Law Directive

5.69   The approach taken by the Financial Collateral Directive to the choice of law to govern certain issues relating to collateral is discussed in Chapter 4. The draft wording for the Securities Law Directive follows much the same approach. The draft Securities Law Directive is in fact a list of draft Principles set out in the European

Commission consultation document published in November 2010 which is intended to form the draft text for a new Directive. The intention is to increase harmonisation of the applicable law in EU member states, aiming to set out the results to be achieved rather than requiring particular legal arrangements, and thus to avoid difficulties arising due to the different legal systems in different jurisdictions. In particular, Principle 14 seeks to determine the sole national law which applies to certain issues. It states that 'the national law of the country where the relevant securities account is maintained by the account provider' will govern various matters, including 'the legal nature of account-held securities', 'the legal nature and the requirements of an acquisition or disposition of account-held securities as well as its effects between the parties and against third parties', 'the effectiveness of an acquisition or disposition and whether it can be invalidated, reversed or otherwise undone', and 'whether a person's interest in account-held securities extinguishes or has priority over another person's interest'[1].

1 European Commission, Legislation on Legal Certainty of Securities Holding and Dispositions (November 2010), p 23.

5.70 Principle 14 uses the concept of the laws of the place where an account is 'maintained'. As may be seen from the text quoted above, the issues to be governed by this law are similar, but not identical, to the issues which in the Financial Collateral Directive are covered by the law of the place where the 'relevant account' is maintained (see Chapter 4, para **4.108**). This causes the potential problem of conflicting approaches. If a particular situation is within the scope of both Directives, the different approaches could mean that different laws govern the same aspects.

5.71 The current drafting for Principle 14 is arguably preferable to the approach in the Financial Collateral Directive, since it sets out a clearer test for identifying the jurisdiction in which an account is maintained. Principle 14 states that: 'Where an account provider has branches located in jurisdictions different from the head offices' jurisdiction, the account is maintained by the branch which handles the relationship with the account holder in relation to the securities account, otherwise by the head office'.

5.72 There are of course a number of issues which still require careful consideration. For example, it may not always be clear which branch handles the relevant relationship. Moreover, particular difficulties arise where there is a transfer of securities from a securities account maintained in one jurisdiction to a securities account maintained in another jurisdiction. In such a case, under the Principle 14 test, the law applicable to each account may well be different, and each such law may have a different view of what is 'the legal nature of account-held securities', or 'whether a person's interest in account-held securities extinguishes or has priority over another person's interest', or 'the effectiveness of an acquisition or disposition and whether it can be invalidated, reversed or otherwise undone'.

Set off

5.73 Rights of set off are widely relied on by banks and other financial institutions to manage their credit exposures to clients. As discussed in Chapter 4, outright collateral transfer arrangements depend for their effectiveness on the availability of insolvency set off. It is therefore crucial for the collateral taker to confirm that set off would be available in the insolvency of the collateral giver[1]. Both the EU Insolvency Regulation and the Banking Winding Up Directive provide that, in general, the law of the main insolvency forum will determine the availability of insolvency set off[2]. However, even where the law of the forum does not permit set off, creditors may nevertheless set off their claims against the claims of the insolvent where the law governing the latter claims set off[3]. (This is subject to the normal rules against preferences etc[4].)

[1] In the case of *Bank of Credit and Commerce International SA (No 11)* [1997] Ch 213, [1997] 2 WLR 172, [1996] 4 All ER 796, the English courts applied English insolvency set off in ancillary proceedings, even through insolvency set off was not available under Luxembourg law, which governed the main proceedings. This decision has been widely criticised. See I F Fletcher *Insolvency Private International Law: National and international approaches* (2005, 2nd edn, Oxford University Press, supplemented in 2007). See also I F Fletcher 'International Insolvency: Recent Cases' (1997) JBL 471.

[2] Article 4(2)(d) of the EU Insolvency Regulation and art 10(2)(c) of the Winding Up Directive.

[3] Article 6(1) of the EU Insolvency Regulation and art 23(1) of the Winding Up Directive. This in effect permits the parties contractually to choose the insolvency laws that will apply to set off. Thus, under the Winding Up Directive, in Greek law insolvency proceedings against a Greek bank, an English bank could set off an English law overdrawn account against an account in credit, even if Greek insolvency law did not permit such set off.

[4] Article 6(2) of the EU Insolvency Regulation and art 23(2) of the Winding Up Directive.

Thus for example in the Greek insolvency of a company which owed a debt governed by English law to X, art 6 permits X to set off that debt pursuant to English law insolvency set off rules, notwithstanding that such insolvency set off would not be permitted by Greek insolvency law. This allows financial institutions by contract to avoid the impact of debtor-friendly jurisdictions' restrictions on insolvency set off. In the light of these provisions, financial institutions may wish to review the governing law clauses of the financial agreements which rely on insolvency set off to ensure they take advantage where appropriate of these provisions. However, it is important to note that art 6(1) relates to the governing law of the claim which it is sought to set off, and not the governing law of any master agreement or netting agreement, if different.

Conversely, in English law insolvency proceedings, insolvency set off would not be disturbed by the insolvent's claim being governed by Greek law, because art 6(1) is drafted in permissive and not mandatory terms, so that the position remains governed by art 4(2)(d). See Recital 26 and para 109 of the Virgos Report.

Unlike the Banking Winding Up Directive, the EU Insolvency Regulation does not make similar provisions for netting. Therefore these appear not to be protected in debtor friendly jurisdictions.

CHAPTER 6

The global custodian's duties

6.1 The global custodian owes legal duties arising from a number of different sources. This chapter will consider duties under general English law. Duties under the regulatory regime established under the Financial Services and Markets Act 2000 are considered in Chapter 7. The question of criminal liability is beyond the scope of this book.

OVERVIEW

6.2 Operational failures in the holding, settlement and administration of a portfolio of securities can cause significant losses to clients. Where such losses occur, global custodians may choose to cover the client's losses make them good irrespective of legal liability, in order to preserve the client relationship. However, losses may be so great that liability would have severe consequences for the global custodian, so that the question of the extent of legal liability arises. Very broadly, under general English law the custodian will not be liable unless client losses have been caused[1] by the custodian's breach of duty[2]. Duty is the measure of potential liability. Control of levels of legal duty is therefore a part of risk management for the global custodian.

1 The question of causation is extremely complex, particularly in the electronic securities markets, where a loss may be overdetermined (ie attributable to more than one cause). See the discussion of intervening cause in the context of breach of contract in Andrew Burrows (ed) *English Private Law* (2008, 2nd edn, Oxford University Press), para 21.40. See also the interesting discussion of causation in the context of tortious liability in *Bristol and West Building Society v Mothew* [1998] Ch 1, [1997] 2 WLR 436, [1996] 4 All ER 698. A detailed discussion of legal causation is beyond the scope of this chapter.

2 Breach of duty is a necessary condition for the client to establish liability for contractual, tortious, equitable or fiduciary liability, but is not the only condition. As discussed below (except in the case of breach of fiduciary duty), it may also be necessary to satisfy requirements of causation and remoteness of damage.

6.3 The chief method of controlling levels of duty is the inclusion in the global custody contract of duty defining clauses and limitation of liability clauses. To the extent possible, the global custody contract should contain an exhaustive list of the services that will be provided, and comprehensive operational detail[1]. Also, the level of care to be taken by the global custodian in providing these services should be specified. These duty defining clauses define the extent of the contractual duties of the global custodian to the client. While duty defining clauses specify what the client is entitled to expect, limitation clauses serve to limit the client's recourse in circumstances where the client does not receive the service it expects.

1 It is customary to specify detailed provisions in a service level agreement or service annex, which is incorporated by reference in the global custody agreement.

6.4 The emphasis of the following sections is on the duties and liabilities of the global custodian associated with its trustee status. In relation to contractual and tortious duties and liabilities, there is only a very brief discussion of some of the fundamental principles.

LIMITATION CLAUSES

Generally

6.5 Limitation of liability is arguably the chief commercial benefit for the global custodian of putting a global custody contract[1] in place. These clauses are highly effective in protecting the global custodian from liability where it has been in breach of its duties to the client. Conversely, the practice of offering undocumented global custodian services exposes the global custodian to the risk of unmodified general law duties, which may result in commercially unacceptable levels of potential liability.

1   Of course, custodians are likely to be required by a relevant regulatory regime to put in place client documentation (see discussion in Chapter 7 regarding the regulatory position for custodians subject to the UK regulatory regime). Also, where trustees appoint a custodian under Trustee Act 2000, s 17 (discussed below), the appointment must be in or evidenced in writing: s 17(3).

6.6 However, the use of limitation clauses is subject to a number of restrictions. Statutory restrictions are discussed below in this section. In addition, special restrictions apply to clauses which seek to limit liability for breach of trustee's duties; these are discussed in paras **6.24–6.55** below. Further, UK-regulated custodians are not permitted to seek to exclude liability for breach of a regulatory duty[1].

1   See the Financial Services Authority ('FSA') Conduct of Business sourcebook, Rule 2.1.2R.

6.7 Any limitation clause will be restrictively construed by the court and any doubt or ambiguity resolved against the global custodian seeking to rely on it[1]. It is advisable to draw clients' attention to limitation clauses prior to the execution of the custody agreement, but there is no need to suggest that clients should take independent legal advice on such clauses[2].

1   *Photo Production Ltd v Securicor Ltd* [1980] AC 827, [1980] 2 WLR 283, [1980] 1 All ER 556; *Midland Bank Trust Co (Jersey) Ltd v Federated Pension Services* [1995] JLR 352 at 391; *Wight v Olswang* (1999) 1 ITELR 783, CA; *Portolana Compania Naviera Ltd v Vitol SA Inc and another* [2004] EWCA Civ 864.

2   This is important on the basis that the global custodian is a trustee (see Chapter 3). See David Hayton 'The Irreducible Core of Trusteeship' [1996] JTCP, p 3: '[t]here needs to be full frank disclosure ... so that a fully informed consent can be given, because a fiduciary relationship exists even before the trust instrument is finally executed.' See *Bogg v Raper* (1998) 1 ITELR 267, CA, and *Bonham and another v Fishwick and another* [2007] EWHC 1859 (Ch).

6.8 It is customary for global custodians operating in London to accept liability for their own negligence and wilful default (and fraud since such liability cannot be excluded). UK-regulated global custodians are not required to accept any specific level of liability[1]. However, other global custodians (particularly those based in the US) may seek to exclude liability for anything other than fraud, wilful default and gross negligence. The legal meaning of these terms is discussed below.

1   Although this was the case at one time. Prior to 1 November 2007, any custodian authorised and regulated by the FSA was prohibited from disclaiming responsibility for losses arising directly from the fraud, wilful default or negligence of the custodian, and between 1 November 2007 and 31 December 2008, this prohibition applied to any custodian providing custody in a non-MiFID context (see further discussion of the concepts of MiFID and non-MiFID context in Chapter 7, para **7.13**). But consider the potential effect of the AIFMD (see Chapter 7, paras **7.164–7.176**).

Negligence and gross negligence

6.9 The difference between negligence and gross negligence is discussed in *Midland Bank Trust Company (Jersey) Ltd v Federated Pension Services*[1]. In this case, the trustee's conduct 'was not mere negligence consisting of a departure from the normal standards of conduct of a paid professional trustee, but a serious, unusual and marked departure from that standard which amounted to 'gross negligence'[2]. However, gross negligence does not connote bad faith[3]. It has been argued that the difference between negligence and gross negligence is not fundamental in English law[4].

1   [1995] JLR 352.

2   [1995] JLR 352.

3   It is different from recklessness, as pointed out by the Court of Appeal in *Armitage v Nurse* [1998] Ch 241 at 252, per Millett LJ. And not the same as fraud: Rix LJ warns against 'watering down this ingredient [here, dishonesty] into something akin to negligence, however gross': *AIC Ltd v ITS Testing Services (UK) Ltd – The Kriti Palm* [2006] EWCA Civ 1601, [2007] 1 All ER (Comm) 667 at 726. See also Flax J's reference to 'the importance of not confusing fraud with incompetence, even if it amounts to gross negligence'; *Grosvenor Casinos Ltd v National Bank of Abu Dhabi* [2008] EWHC 511 (Comm), [2008] 2 All ER (Comm) 112 at 138.

4   'It would be very surprising if our law drew the line between liability for ordinary negligence and liability for gross negligence. In this respect English law differs from civil law systems, for it has always drawn a sharp distinction between negligence, however gross, on the one hand and fraud, bad faith and wilful misconduct on the other. The doctrine of the common law is that: "Gross negligence may be evidence of mala fides, but is not the same thing". (See *Goodman v Harvey* (1836) 4 Ad & El 870 at 876, All ER 1011 at 1013 per Lord Denman CJ.) But while we regard the difference between fraud on the one hand and mere negligence, however gross, on the other as a difference in kind, we regard the difference between negligence and gross negligence as merely one of degree. English lawyers have always had a healthy disrespect for the latter distinction. In *Hinton v Dibbin* (1842) 2 QB 646, 114 ER 253 Lord Denman CJ doubted whether any intelligible distinction exists; while in *Grill v General Iron Screw Collier Co* (1866) 35 LJCP 321 at 330 Willes J famously observed that gross negligence is ordinary negligence with a vituperative epithet. But civilian systems draw the line in a different place. The doctrine is *culpa lata dolo aequiparetur*; and although the maxim itself is not Roman the principle is classical. There is no room for the maxim in the common law; it is not mentioned in Broom *Selection of Legal Maxims Classified and Illustrated* (10th edn, 1939)': *Armitage v Nurse* [1998] Ch 241 at 254, per Millett LJ. However, the court did not have cited to it bailment cases revealing that gross negligence is required before gratuitous bailees (as opposed to bailees for reward) can be liable. See the Trust Law Committee Consultative Paper on Trustee Exemption Clauses (15 April 1999), currently accessible at www.umds.ac.uk/schools/law/research/tlc, listed under Consultation Papers.

Wilful default

6.10   The meaning of the term 'wilful default' has been the subject of much judicial and scholarly discussion[1]. In the context of a limitation clause, wilful default probably means deliberate or reckless breach of duty[2], which (as indicated below) cannot be excluded at general law.

1   Much of this discussion has been in the context of Trustee Act 1925, s 30(1); this has been repealed by the Trustee Act 2000

2   '[T]he expression "wilful default" is used in the cases in two senses. A trustee is said to be accountable on the footing of wilful default when he is accountable not only for money which he has in fact received but also for money which he could with reasonable diligence have received. It is sufficient that the trustee has been guilty of a want of ordinary prudence (see eg *Re Chapman, Cocks v Chapman* [1896] 2 Ch 763). In the context of a trustee exclusion clause, however, such as s 30 of the Trustee Act 1925, it means a deliberate breach of trust (*Re Vickery, Vickery v Stephens* [1931] 1 Ch 572, [1931] All ER Rep 562). The decision has been criticised, but it is in line with earlier authority (see *Lewis v Great Western Rly Co* (1877) 3 QBD 195; *Re Trusts of Leeds City Brewery Ltd's Debenture Stock Trust Deed, Leeds City Brewery Ltd v Platts* [1925] Ch 532 and *Re City Equitable Fire Insurance Co Ltd* [1925] Ch 407, [1924] All ER Rep 485). Nothing less than conscious and wilful misconduct is sufficient': *Armitage v Nurse* [1998] Ch 241 at 252, per Millett LJ.

Statutory restrictions

Unfair Contract Terms Act 1977 ('UCTA')

6.11   In accordance with s 3 of UCTA, exclusion clauses relating to liability of businesses for breach of contract contained in one party's written standard terms of business are subject to a test of reasonableness.

6.12   An exemption may be available as follows. Paragraph 1 of Sch 1 to UCTA provides that:

> 'Sections 2 to 4 of this Act do not extend to ... any contract so far as it relates to the creation or transfer of securities or of any right or interest in securities.'

6.13   This exclusion was designed primarily to assist brokers and not custodians. It is not wholly clear that it exempts the terms of the global custody agreement, as of course this relates to the holding and administration of securities as well as their transfer. However, this exemption may protect the settlement side of the global custody service[1].

1   The view that UCTA applies to a limitation clause in some circumstances and not others may be supported by the case of *Micklefield v SAC Technology* [1990] 1 WLR 1002, [1991] 1 All ER 275, [1990] IRLR 218. In this case the court emphasised that the exception applies to '*any* contract *so far as* it relates to the creation or transfer of securities' (at 281, emphasis in original).

6.14   To the extent that the exemption is not available, the custodian's limitation clauses are subject to a statutory reasonableness test[1]. It might be argued that this test is satisfied in cases where the terms in question are in market standard form.

1   Section 2(2). This is defined in s 11 as the requirement 'that the term shall have been a fair and reasonable one to be included having regard to the circumstances which were, or ought reasonably to have been, known to or in the contemplation of the parties when the contract was made'.

Unfair Terms in Consumer Contracts Regulations 1999[1]

6.15   These regulations impose requirements of fairness and plain English, and apply (in addition to UCTA) to terms which have not been individually negotiated, in contracts for the supply of goods or services by businesses to consumers. For this purpose, a consumer is a natural person (ie not a company or, probably, in a partnership or unincorporated association) who is acting for purposes which are 'outside his trade, business or profession'[2]. Thus, terms in standard form global custody contracts with high net worth individuals who are not involved in investment business may prima facie be caught[3].

1   SI 1999/2083 (as amended). These implement the EC Directive on Unfair Terms in Consumer Contracts (93/13/EEC).
2   SI 1999/2083, reg 3(1), definition of 'consumer'.
3   There are of course various other regulations and legislation to be considered when providing services to consumers, particularly in the context of consumer credit.

Contractual duties[1]

6.16

> 'The general aim of damages for breach of contract is to put the claimant into as good a position as if the contract had been performed.'[2]

1   See generally Hugh Beale (ed) *Chitty on Contracts* (2012, 31st edn, Sweet & Maxwell).
2   Andrew Burrows (ed) *English Private Law* (2008, 2nd edn, Oxford University Press), para 21.17.

6.17 In other words, the approach is prospective (in contrast with the retrospective approach for assessing tortious damages: see para **6.21** below).

> '[A] defendant will not be liable for loss suffered by the claimant that is too remote from the breach of contract.'[1]

1   Andrew Burrows (ed) *English Private Law* (2008, 2nd edn, Oxford University Press), para 21.27. 'Where two parties have made a contract which one of them has broken, the damages which the other party ought to receive in respect of such breach of contract, should be such as may fairly and reasonably be considered, as either arising naturally, ie according to the usual course of things, from such breach of contract itself, or such as may reasonably be supposed to have been in the contemplation of both parties at the time they made the contract as the probable result of the breach of it': *Hadley v Baxendale* (1854) 9 Exch 341 at 354, per Alderson B.

6.18 This may be a significant restriction in the context of securities market operations, where a default may produce complex chains of consequential defaults (see the discussion of systemic risk in Chapter 8).

> '[A] claimant must take all reasonable steps to minimize its loss so that it cannot recover for any loss which it could reasonably have avoided but has failed to avoid.'[1]

1   Andrew Burrows (ed) *English Private Law* (2008, 2nd edn, Oxford University Press), para 21.42.

6.19 Under the Contracts (Rights of Third Parties) Act 1999 a person who is not a party to a contract (a 'third party') may enforce a term of the contract if either the contract expressly so provides or the term purports to confer a benefit on the third party[1] (unless, in the latter case, on a proper construction of the contract it appears that the parties did not intend the term to be enforceable by the third party[2]). Global custodians may consider it prudent expressly to exclude the right of third party beneficial owners in their own right to enforce the terms of the contract where the custodian enters into the contract with an entity such as a fund or other client holding on behalf of its own clients.

1   Contracts (Rights of Third Parties) Act 1999, s 1(1).
2   Contracts (Rights of Third Parties) Act 1999, s 1(2).

TORTIOUS DUTY OF CARE[1]

6.20

> 'The boundaries of liability for the tort of negligence are drawn by the three principle elements of the tort, a duty of care, breach of that duty, and damage caused by that breach.'[2]

1   See generally W Rogers *Winfield and Jolowicz on Tort* (2010, 18th edn, Sweet & Maxwell).
2   Andrew Burrows (ed) *English Private Law* (2008, 2nd edn, Oxford University Press), para 17.25.

6.21 The measure of damages for negligence or other torts is the award which is necessary to put the claimant back into the position it would have been in had the tort never occurred (ie it is retrospective)[1]. As with contractual liability, the claimant is under a duty to mitigate losses, and tortious liability does not extend to damages which are too remote. Further, there are limits to the ability to recover damages for pure economic loss in negligence[2].

1   See *Livingstone v Rawyards Coal Co* (1880) 5 App Cas 25 at 39, per Lord Blackburn:

> 'The basic principle for the measure of damages in tort ... is that there should be *restitutio in integrum*. Apart from the special cases we have considered, where any injury is to be compensated by damages, in settling the sum of money to be given for reparation of damages you should as nearly as possible get at that sum of money which will put the party who has been injured, or who has suffered, in the same position as he would have been in if he had not sustained the wrong for which he is now getting his compensation or reparation.'

2   See *Hedley Byrne v Heller* [1964] AC 465, [1963] 3 WLR 101, [1963] 2 All ER 575. A huge amount has been written on this topic.

6.22 Contractual and tortious liability can be concurrent[1]. However, the courts are reluctant to find tortious liability where the parties' relationship is contractual[2].

1   See *Henderson v Merrett* [1995] 2 AC 145, [1994] 3 WLR 761, [1994] 3 All ER 506 and *White v Jones* [1995] 2 AC 207, [1995] 2 WLR 187, [1995] 1 All ER 691 at 730; and *John F Hunt Demolition Ltd v ASME Engineering Ltd* [2007] EWHC 1507 (TCC).

2   *Tai Hing Cotton Mill Ltd v Liu Chong Hing Bank Ltd* [1986] AC 80 at 956, per Lord Scarman:

'Their Lordships do not believe that there is anything to the advantage of the law's development in searching for a liability in tort where the parties are in a contractual relationship. This is particularly so in a commercial relationship ... their Lordships believe it to be correct in principle and necessary for the avoidance of confusion in the law to adhere to the contractual analysis: on principle because it is a relationship in which the parties have, subject to a few exceptions, the right to determine their obligations to each other, and for the avoidance of confusion because different consequences do follow according to whether liability arises from contract or tort, eg in the limitation of action ... Their Lordships do not, therefore, embark on an investigation whether in the relationship of banker and customer it is possible to identify tort as well as contract as a source of the obligations owed by the one to the other. Their Lordships do not, however, accept that the parties' mutual obligations in tort can be any greater than those to be found expressly or by necessary implication in their contract.'

6.23 The relationship between negligence and breach of a fiduciary's duty of care is discussed by Lord Browne-Wilkinson in *Henderson v Merrett*[1]: 'A fiduciary's liability in negligence is derived from equitable duties of care. The two heads of liability cannot be claimed as alternatives, for the tortious and equitable duties of care are in essence the same. In either case, a contractual relationship between the parties determines the extent and nature of the duty of care'[2].

1   [1995] 2 AC 145 at 205.
2   [1995] 2 AC 145 at 206.

TRUSTEE'S DUTIES

6.24 The traditional legal characterisation of the custodian of securities is as bailee of the client[1]. However, Chapter 3 argued that the global custodian is not a bailee but a trustee.

1   The bailee's duty of care at common law is as follows. 'A bailee's duty of care extends beyond simply avoiding causing damage to the goods. He must take care to protect the goods from third parties who might damage or steal them' and a bailee should 'take as much care as a prudent man would take of his own goods': A Bell 'The Place of Bailment in the Modern Law of Obligations', Chapter 19 in Palmer and McKendrick (eds) *Interests in Goods* (1998, Lloyd's of London Press), pp 474, 475.

6.25 The courts are likely to seek to take a commercial approach to the application of trust law to the global custodian, particularly where non-private clients are involved[1]. However, the principle remains that a custodian incurs liability to the client where it is in breach of trust and this breach results in loss to the client. The measure of this liability is to make good such loss[2]. Remote or unforeseeable damages are arguably not excluded[3], and the claimant is not obliged to mitigate its losses[4], but there must be some causal connection between the breach of duty and the loss to establish liability[5]. Liability is subject to contractual or statutory relieving provisions.

1   *Target Holdings Ltd v Redferns* [1996] AC 421 at 435, per Lord Browne-Wilkinson:

'But in my judgment it is important, if the trust is not to be rendered commercially useless, to distinguish between the basic principles of trust law and those specialist rules developed in relation to traditional trusts which are applicable only to such trusts and the rationale of which has no application to trusts of quite a different kind.'

2   This is essentially akin to the position at common law. See *Target Holdings v Redferns* [1996] AC 421 at 432, per Lord Browne-Wilkinson:

> 'At common law there are two principles fundamental to the award of damages. First, that the defendant's wrongful act must cause the damage complained of. Second, that the plaintiff is to be put "in the same position as he would have been in if he had not sustained the wrong for which he is now getting his compensation or reparation" ... Although, as will appear, in many ways equity approaches liability for making good a breach of trust from a different starting point, in my judgment those two principles are applicable as much in equity as at common law.'

3   See the discussion of *Bristol and West Building Society v Mothew* [1998] Ch 1, [1997] 2 WLR 436, [1996] 4 All ER 698 below.

4   See *Target Holdings v Redferns* [1996] AC 421 at 799, quoting from the judgment of Hoffmann LJ in *Bishopsgate Investment Management Ltd (in liquidation) v Maxwell (No 1)* [1994] 1 All ER 261: '[i]t is sound law that a plaintiff is not required to engage in hazardous litigation in order to mitigate his loss.'

5   See *Target Holdings v Redferns* [1996] AC 421 at 434, per Lord Browne-Wilkinson:

> 'Even if the immediate cause of the loss is the dishonesty or failure of a third party, the trustee is liable to make good that loss to the trust estate if, but for the breach, such loss would not have occurred ... Thus the common law rules of remoteness of damages and causation do not apply. However, there does have to be some causal connection between the breach of trust and the loss to the trust estate for which compensation is recoverable, viz the fact that the loss would not have occurred but for the breach.'

In *Target* the issue was breach of an equitable duty of care and not breach of core fiduciary duty. This latter issue is considered in the following cases.

The insistence on some causal connection alters the earlier rule that loss flowing from nondisclosure by a fiduciary attracts strict liability (*Brickenden v London Loan & Savings Co* [1934] 3 DLR 465 at 469). However, in respect of active misrepresentations, liability remains strict: *Bristol and West Building Society v Mothew* [1998] Ch 1, [1997] 2 WLR 436, [1996] 4 All ER 698.

6.26   Statutory relief is in theory available under s 61 of the Trustee Act 1925, where the custodian has acted honestly and reasonably and ought fairly to be excused[1]. However, it is considered unlikely that such relief would be granted to a professional trustee such as a global custodian[2].

1   'If it appears to the court that a trustee, whether appointed by the court or otherwise, is or may be personally liable for any breach of trust, whether the transaction alleged to be a breach of trust occurred before or after the commencement of this Act, but has acted honestly and reasonably, and ought fairly to be excused for the breach of trust and for omitting to obtain the directions from the court in the matter in which he committed such breach, then the courts may relieve him either wholly or partly from personal liability for the same.'

Similar provisions in relation to company directors are contained in s 1157 of the Companies Act 2006.

2   'Although there is no doubt about the court's jurisdiction to grant relief under section 61 to a trustee who is remunerated, there appears from the cases to be a marked reluctance to do so': Law Commission Report No 236 *Fiduciary Duties and Regulatory Rules*, December 1995, p 95.

The 23rd Report of the Law Reform Committee looked at the whole question of the powers and duties of trustees and considered the issue of whether it was desirable to incorporate the distinction between professional and voluntary trustees into statute. It concluded that this was not necessary, stating that s 61 of the Trustee Act 1925 was an adequate statutory provision to allow this difference to be recognised. The courts would be far more likely to give relief to a voluntary trustee under s 61 than to a professional trustee.

6.27   The duties of the global custodian as trustee will be considered in two parts, namely the trustee's duty of care, and fiduciary duties.

Trustee's duty of care

6.28   The trustee's duty of care is as follows.

Trustee Act 2000

6.29 The Trustee Act 2000 ('TA 2000') provides[1] for a statutory duty of care, which applies in certain circumstances[2], including the exercise and review of investment powers[3], and the appointment and review of agents, nominees and custodians (including sub-custodians)[4]. The statutory duty of care may be expressly excluded[5]. Where it applies, the trustee must:

> '...exercise such care and skill as is reasonable in the circumstances, having regard in particular –
>
> (a) to any special knowledge or experience that he has or holds himself out as having, and
>
> (b) if he acts as trustee in the course of a business or profession, to any special knowledge or experience that it is reasonable to expect of a person acting in the course of that kind of business or profession.'[6]

1 TA 2000, s 1.
2 These are specified in Sch 1. See TA 2000, s 2.
3 TA 2000, Sch 1, para 1. A global custodian is unlikely to have general powers of investment, but may have specific powers of investment, for example under cash management or securities lending arrangements, although arguably in such cases the relevant entity would be acting as investment manager not as trustee or custodian.
4 TA 2000, Sch 1, para 3.
5 TA 2000, Sch 1, para 7.
6 TA 2000, s 1(1).

Case law

6.30 Where the statutory duty of care does not apply, the duty of care of the trustee is defined by case law in broadly similar terms[1].

1 They are similar in the case of professional trustees. The general law test for a non-professional trustee is the level of care with which an ordinary prudent man of business would conduct his own affairs: *Speight v Gaunt* (1883) 9 App Cas 1 at 19, per Lord Blackburn:

> '...as a general rule the trustee sufficiently discharges his duty if he takes in the managing of trust affairs all those precautions which an ordinary prudent man of business would take in managing similar affairs of his own.'

6.31 The rule in *Re Waterman's Will Trusts*[1] provides that the trustee holding itself out as possessing special skills and which is paid for its services must observe a higher standard of diligence and knowledge than an unpaid trustee; and will be expected to exercise a greater degree of care. This rule was expanded in the case of *Bartlett v Barclays Bank*[2] in which Brightman J set the test as 'the special skill and care which [the professional trustee] professes to have'[3].

1 [1952] 2 All ER 1054 at 1055 per Harman J:

> 'I do not forget that a professional trustee is expected to exercise a higher standard of diligence and knowledge than an unpaid trustee and that a bank which advertises itself largely in the public press as taking charge of administrations is under a special duty.'

2 [1980] Ch 515.
3 [1980] Ch 515 at 534.

Limitation clauses

6.32 Limitation clauses are highly effective in limiting the liability of trustees for breach of their duty of care[1]. Old authority indicates that liability for gross negligence and wilful default[2] is inexcludable. However, it is now clear that a properly drafted exemption clause may relieve a fiduciary from liability for loss caused by its own gross negligence, provided the exclusion is clearly brought to the attention of the client[3], but such a clause cannot relieve liability for actual fraud, ie dishonesty[4].

> 'In my judgment cl 15 exempts the trustee from liability for loss or damage to the trust property no matter how indolent, imprudent, lacking in diligence, negligent or wilful he may have been, so long as he has not acted dishonestly.'[5]

1 See the unreported High Court judgment of Harman J in *Galmerrow Securities Ltd v National Westminster Bank* [2002] WTLR 125, in which a trust deed is considered which contained relieving provisions limiting trustee liability to losses resulting from its fraud and negligence:

> 'However high a standard of skill and care is imposed by the general law, and I would wish to impose the highest standard on Trustee departments of major clearing banks, the duty has still to be defined by reference to the actual trust deed in the case before the Court. In *Bartlett*'s case (supra) no terms like those in the Trust Deed constituting the 22nd PAUT existed.' (p 35).

This view was endorsed by the Law Commission in its Report No 236, December 1995, Cm 3049, *Fiduciary Duties and Regulatory Rules*, p 11:

> 'We stated in the consultation paper that a fiduciary could not exclude liability for fraud, deliberate breach of duty and, possibly, gross negligence. Beyond that, our provisional view was that, in general, no restriction operated as a matter of fiduciary law to prevent a fiduciary from contracting out of or modifying his fiduciary duties, particularly where no prior fiduciary relationship existed and the contract sought to define the duties of the parties.'

2 In the case of *Pass v Dundas* (1880) 43 LT 665 Bacon VC held that the effect of the decision in *Wilkins v Hogg* (1861) 66 ER 346 was that an appropriate exemption clause 'does protect a trustee from loss that may have been sustained in the course of administering the trust estate, unless you can impute to him gross negligence or personal misconduct'.

3 In *Midland Bank Trust (Jersey) Ltd v Federated Pension Services* [1995] JLR 352 the Jersey Court of Appeal held that liability for gross negligence may be excluded unless prohibited by statute.

In *Walker v Stones* [2001] QB 902, the same line of reasoning was followed, it being accepted that the exclusion clause could effectively restrict liability to cases of 'wilful fraud or dishonesty', although it was stated that the 'test of honesty may vary from case to case, depending on, among other things, the role and calling of the trustee' (per Slade LJ at 939). (In *Walker*, it was considered that a solicitor-trustee would be dishonest even if it met the subjective test in *Armitage v Nurse* [1998] Ch 241 in that it honestly believed that it was acting in the interests of the beneficiaries, if 'by any objective standard, no reasonable solicitor-trustee could have thought that what he did or agreed to do was for the benefit of the beneficiaries' (per Slade LJ at 939). This is clearly important in the context of a professional custodian where a limitation clause may successfully exclude liability for gross negligence, but under the high level of care expected of a custodian, a decision of a custodian may be regarded as dishonest and therefore incurring liability for fraud if it is a decision which in the context would not be expected from a 'reasonable' professional custodian. See also *Twinsectra v Yardley* [2002] UKHL 12, [2002] 2 AC 164, [2002] 2 WLR 802, in which the test of dishonesty for the purpose of dishonest assistance was held to have a mixed subjective and objective element. Consider also the application of regulatory obligations, see Chapter 7.

4 See *Armitage v Nurse* [1998] Ch 241. In this judgment Millett LJ considered a limitation clause in the following terms: 'No Trustee shall be liable for any loss or damage which may happen to [the beneficiary's] fund or any part thereof or the income thereof at any time or from any cause whatsoever unless such loss or damage shall be caused by his own actual fraud …' He held that: 'In my judgment, therefore, cl 15 is apt to exclude liability for breach of trust in the absence of a dishonest intention on the part of the trustee whose conduct is impugned' (at 250).

5 *Armitage v Nurse* [1998] Ch 241 at 251.

6.33 Dishonesty for this purpose does not necessarily involve personal gain[1]. There is an irreducible core of fiduciary obligation, but it relates to honesty and does not involve any level of care[2].

> 'The duty to act in good faith (ie honestly and consciously) in respect of any trust matter cannot, of course, be excluded. To do so would make a nonsense of the trust relationship as an obligation of confidence.'[3]

1   *Armitage v Nurse* [1998] Ch 241 at 710:

> 'It is the duty of a trustee to manage the trust property and deal with it in the interests of the beneficiaries. If he acts in a way which he does not honestly believe is in their interests then he is acting dishonestly. It does not matter whether he stands or thinks he stands to gain personally from his actions. A trustee who acts with the intention of benefiting persons who are not the objects of the trust is not the less dishonest because he does not intend to benefit himself.'

2   *Armitage v Nurse* [1998] Ch 241 at 712:

> 'I accept ... that there is an irreducible core of obligations owed by the trustee to the beneficiaries and enforceable by them which is fundamental to the concept of a trust. If the beneficiaries have no rights enforceable against the trustees there are no trusts. But I do not accept the further submission that these core obligations include the duties of skill or care, prudence and diligence. The duty of the trustees to perform the trusts honestly and in good faith for the benefit of the beneficiaries is the minimum necessary to give substance to the trusts, but in my opinion it is sufficient.'

> And see also Kitchen J's comment in *Barnes and others v Tomlinson and others* [2006] EWHC 3115 (Ch), [2006] All ER (D) 95, referring to *Armitage v Nurse*: 'It has been long established that the test of honesty in the context of an express trustee is whether the trustee is conscious that he is committing a breach of duty or is recklessly careless whether he is committing a breach of duty or not.'

3   David Hayton 'The Irreducible Core Content of Trusteeship' [1996] JTCP, p 3.

6.34   Also, limitation clauses are effective retrospectively but not prospectively, as:

> '...a trustee who relied on the presence of a trustee exemption clause to justify what he proposed to do would thereby lose its protection: he would be acting recklessly in the proper sense of the term.'[1]

1   *Armitage v Nurse* [1998] Ch 241 at 254, per Millett LJ.

6.35   Trustee exemption clauses attracted specific interest in Law Commission Consultation Paper No 171 entitled 'Trustee Exemption Clauses' in January 2003. This paper expressed concern about the use of exemption clauses by trustee[1], but the 2006 report[2] on the feedback received regarding the consultation paper concluded that while no statutory restriction was desirable (largely on grounds of lack of certainty, the risk of increased litigation and creating disincentives for trustees to take action) a non-statutory 'rule of practice requiring trustees to disclose trustee exemption provisions'[3] would be beneficial[4]. The report proposed that 'Compliance with the rule would be a matter of professional conduct for the trustee' and 'The consequence of non-compliance in respect of a particular clause would not be to invalidate or in any way affect reliance on that clause' but 'would ... render the trustee open to professional disciplinary measures' and the 'decision whether to invoke disciplinary sanctions would be in the hands of the relevant regulatory body'[5]. This of course assumes that trustees are regulated by a particular regulatory body[6]. However, at the time of writing it is not clear that there is any proposal by the relevant supervisory authorities to monitor compliance with the suggested rule of practice. In principle, it might be expected that in the course of any normal commercial negotiation of documentation terms, the exemption clause would be the subject of discussion, and that to minimise the risk of issues arising from UCTA[7] or general contractual principles[8], the relevant provision would be drawn to the attention of the counterparty. In any event, to the extent that this rule may be regarded as an example of good practice, for a custodian regulated by the FSA the cautious approach may be to consider this rule when entering into client agreements to minimise the scope for argument based on this rule that there has been a failure to treat the client fairly[9], although inevitably this will depend on the circumstances of the particular arrangements.

1   Although the reasons for such concern were not wholly clear.

2   Law Commission Report No 301, 'Trustee Exemption Clauses', July 2006.

3   Law Commission Report No 301, Part 6, section 6.48.

4   The suggested rule of practice is as follows: 'Any paid trustee who causes a settlor to include a clause in a trust instrument which has the effect of excluding or limiting liability for negligence must before the creation of the trust take such steps as are reasonable to ensure that the settlor is aware of the meaning and effect of the clause.'

5   Law Commission Report No 301, Part 6, sections 6.43 and 6.44.

6   For example, the FSA, or, pursuant to the Money Laundering Regulations 2007 (SI 2007/2157, implementing the Third Money Laundering Directive, Directive 2005/60/EC of the European Parliament and of the Council of 26th October 2005 on the prevention of the use of the financial system for the purpose of money laundering and terrorist financing), HMRC if not subject to another designated supervisory authority.

7   See paras **6.11–6.14** above.

8   See paras **6.32–6.34** and **6.5–6.8** above.

9   See further discussion of this concept in Chapter 7, paras **7.23–7.29**.

Fiduciary duty[1]

6.36

'To describe some one as a fiduciary, without more, is meaningless.'[2]

1   The acknowledged expert on fiduciary duty is P D Finn. See *Fiduciary Obligations* (1977, Law Book Co, Sydney) (described by Millett LJ as his 'classic work' in *Bristol and West Building Society v Mothew* [1998] Ch 1 at 18) and T G Youdan (ed) *The Fiduciary Principle, Equity, Fiduciaries and Trusts* (1989, Carswell).

   The interrelation of fiduciary duties and regulatory rules has been much discussed. Debate was stimulated by a May 1992 Law Commission Consultative Paper *Fiduciary Duties and Regulatory Rules* and a subsequent report having the same title and published in December 1995 (No 236, Cm 3049). Dr Black expressed the view that the tension between fiduciary duty and regulatory rules provided one of the original motives for the Financial Services Act 1986 (the predecessor of the Financial Services and Markets Act 2000): see Julia Black *Rules and Regulators* (1997, Oxford University Press Inc). See also discussion of the duties of care imposed by regulators on custodians in Chapter 7.

2   *Re Goldcorp Exchange Ltd (in receivership)* [1995] 1 AC 74 at 98, per Lord Mustill.

6.37 There may be considerable tactical advantages to the claimant in establishing breach of fiduciary duty. Unlike breach of contract and negligence, breach of fiduciary duty may provide the basis of a proprietary claim (and therefore be effective against an insolvent defendant); it is not subject to common law rules of causation and remoteness[1]; and the claimant is not obliged to mitigate its losses by litigation[2]. However, for this purpose, breach of fiduciary duty is narrowly[3] defined to connote disloyalty or infidelity[4]. It should not be confused with the wider category of breach of trust[5], or with breach of the trustee's duty of care[6]. Liability for the latter two is (arguably) subject to rules on causation and remoteness[7].

1   See *Bristol and West Building Society v Mothew* [1998] Ch 1 at 8, per Millett LJ:

   'It was common ground below that no damages would be recoverable at common law for breach of contract or tort unless the society could show that it would not have proceeded with the transaction if it had been informed of the facts. The society, however, submitted that the position was different in equity. It alleged that the defendant had committed a breach of trust or fiduciary duty, and submitted that common law principles of causation and remoteness of damage have no application in such a case so that it was not necessary for the society to show that it would not have proceeded with the transaction if it had been informed of the facts.'

2   See *Bishopsgate Investment Management Ltd (in liquidation) v Maxwell (No 1)* [1994] 1 All ER 261, quoted in *Target Holdings v Redferns* [1996] AC 421 at 440.

3   See *Bristol and West Building Society v Mothew* [1998] Ch 1 at 16, per Millett LJ:

   'The expression "fiduciary duty" is properly confined to those duties which are peculiar to fiduciaries … it is obvious that not every breach of duty by a fiduciary is a breach of fiduciary duty.'

4   See *Bristol and West Building Society v Mothew* [1998] Ch 1 at 18, per Millett LJ:

   'Breach of fiduciary obligation, therefore, connotes disloyalty or infidelity. Mere incompetence is not enough. A servant who loyally does his incompetent best for his master is not unfaithful and is not guilty of breach of fiduciary duty.'

   The no profit and no conflict rules are proscriptive, as opposed to the trustee's duty of care, and specific trust duties, which are prescriptive.

5   See *Armitage v Nurse* [1998] Ch 241 at 251, per Millett LJ:

   'Breaches of trust are of many different kinds. A breach of trust may be deliberate or inadvertent; it may consist of an actual misappropriation or misapplication of the trust property or merely of an investment or other dealing which is outside the trustee's powers; it may consist of a failure to carry out a positive obligation of the trustees or merely of a want of skill and care on their part in the management of the trust property;'

6   See *Bristol and West Building Society v Mothew* [1998] Ch 1 at 16 per Millett LJ:

   '... there can be no justification for treating an unconscious failure as demonstrating want of fidelity ... It is similarly inappropriate to apply the expression to the obligation of a trustee or other fiduciary to use proper skill and care in the discharge of his duties.'

7   See *Bristol and West Building Society v Mothew* [1998] Ch 1 at 17 per Millett LJ:

   'Equitable compensation for breach of the duty of skill and care resembles common law damages in that it is awarded by way of compensation to the plaintiff for his loss. These is no reason in principle why the common law rules of causation, remoteness of damage and measure of damage should not be applied by analogy in such a case. It should not be confused with equitable compensation for breach of fiduciary duty ...'

THE NATURE OF FIDUCIARY DUTY

6.38   While fiduciary duty is a very uncertain area of law, it is possible to make the following generalisations. Fiduciary relationships are relationships of special trust, so that the fiduciary is required to put the client's interests above her own interests[1]: 'The "fiduciary" standard for its part enjoins one party to act in the interests of another – to act selflessly and with undivided loyalty'[2]. The significance of fiduciary status here is that fiduciaries owe special implied[3] duties to their beneficiaries[4]. Fiduciary duties are summarised in four basic rules:

- the no conflict rule,
- the no profit rule,
- the undivided loyalty rule, and
- the duty of confidentiality[5].

1   See *Bristol and West Building Society v Mothew* [1998] Ch 1 at 18, per Millett LJ:

   'A fiduciary is someone who has undertaken to act for or on behalf of another in a particular matter in circumstances which give rise to a relationship of trust or confidence. The distinguishing obligation of a fiduciary is the obligation of loyalty. The principal is entitled to the single-minded loyalty of his fiduciary. This core liability has several facets. A fiduciary must act in good faith; he must not make a profit out of his trust; he must not place himself in a position where his duty and his interest may conflict; he may not act for his own benefit or the benefit of a third person without the informed consent of his principal. This is not intended to be an exhaustive list, but it is sufficient to indicate the nature of fiduciary obligations. They are the defining characteristics of the fiduciary.'

   Law Commission Report No 236, pp 1, 11:

   'Broadly speaking, a fiduciary relationship is one in which a person undertakes to act on behalf of or for the benefit of another, often as an intermediary with a discretion or power which affects the interests of the other who depends on the fiduciary for information and advice ... in determining whether a relationship was fiduciary, and if so, the extent of the fiduciary duties, a court would look at the substance of a relationship and not merely its description in the contract.'

2   P D Finn The Fiduciary Principle, Equity, Fiduciaries and Trusts (1989, Youdan (ed), Carswell), p4.

3   Arguably, fiduciary duties are imposed and not implied. See the discussion of tortious duties in *Tai Hing Cotton Mill Ltd v Liu Chong Hing Bank Ltd* [1986] AC 80, per Lord Scarman at 104:

   '... the test of implication is necessity ... Implication is the way in which necessary incidents come to the recognised in the absence of express agreement in a contractual relationship. Imposition is apt to describe a duty arising in tort, but inept to describe the necessary incident arising from a contractual relationship.'

4   More generally, in certain common law jurisdictions including England, 'to designate someone a fiduciary is to expose that person to the full rigour of equity both in method [for example, in reversal of the onus of proof, in presumptions of wrongdoing and in disregard of notions such as causation, foreseeability and remoteness] and in remedy [from avoidance through damages and the account of profits to the constructive trust] ...' P D Finn The Fiduciary Principle, p 2.

   Arguably, it would be more correct to refer to these as imposed duties rather than implied duties. See *Tai Hing Cotton Mill Ltd v Liu Chong Hing Bank Ltd* [1986] AC 80, in which Lord Scarman discusses (at 104) non-contractual (tortious) duties; the same analysis may apply to fiduciary duties.

5   Law Commission Report No 236, pp 1, 2:

   'The exact scope of the fiduciary's obligations and the consequences of breach vary according to the particular circumstances but the duties may conveniently be summarised in the following basic rules:

   (i)   The "no conflict" rule A fiduciary must not place himself in a position where his own interest conflicts with that of his customer, the beneficiary. There must be a "real sensible possibility of conflict";

   (ii) The "no profit" rule A fiduciary must not profit from his position at the expense of his customer, the beneficiary;

   (iii) The "undivided loyalty" rule A fiduciary owes undivided loyalty to his customer, the beneficiary, not to place himself in a position where his duty towards one customer conflicts with a duty that he owes to another customer. A consequence of this is that a fiduciary must make available to a customer all the information that is relevant to the customer's affairs;

   (iv) The "duty of confidentiality" A fiduciary must only use information obtained in confidence from his customer, the beneficiary, for the benefit of the customer and must not use it for his own advantage, or for the benefit of any other person.'

   These are default rules that can be ousted by contractual provision, or provision in the trust deed. See *Kelly v Cooper Associates* [1993] AC 205.

6.39 Beyond these rules (which are derived from the general duty to act in the interests of the beneficiary) fiduciary status does not prescribe positive duties. Thus, the particular services that a global custodian must render are determined by its agreement with its client, and not by implied fiduciary status. Fiduciary status does not determine the content of the relationship between the parties; rather it is (in essence) merely a judicial remedy for want of loyalty where loyalty is owed[1].

1   See P D Finn The Fiduciary Principle, Equity, Fiduciaries and Trusts (1989, Youdan (ed), Carswell), p 28.

THE GLOBAL CUSTODIAN AS FIDUCIARY

6.40 The argument that a global custodian is not a fiduciary is considered to be untenable. Because of its safekeeping role, the custodian is either a trustee or (in the rare cases where client assets comprise physical securities in the hands of the custodian) a bailee[1]. A trustee is always a fiduciary[2]. Whether or not a bailee is a fiduciary will depend on all the circumstances and the terms of the bailment[3]. However, because the custodian role actively combines safekeeping with administration and settlement on behalf of the client, it would be prudent to assume that the global custodian is a fiduciary[4].

1   See Chapter 3.

2   Law Commission Report No 236, pp 27, 28:

118   The Law of Global Custody

'... it is possible to divide fiduciaries into two categories, status-based fiduciaries and fact-based fiduciaries ... [The latter] include people who, by virtue of their involvement in certain relationships are considered, without further inquiry, to be fiduciaries. Such relationships include those between trustee-beneficiary, solicitor-client, agent-principal, director-company, and partner-partner.'

3   *Re Andrabell Ltd (in liquidation), Airborne Accessories Ltd* [1984] 3 All ER 407, per Peter Gibson J.

4   *Reading v A-G* [1949] 2 KB 232, [1949] 2 All ER 68:

'... a "fiduciary relation" exists ... wherever the plaintiff entrusts to the defendant property ... and relies on the defendant to deal with such property for the benefit of the plaintiff or for purposes authorised by him, and not otherwise ...'

Thus, the argument that the global custodian is a fiduciary is strengthened in cases where, for example, the global custodian operates a discretionary securities lending programme on the client's behalf.

See also *Re Brooke Bond & Co Ltd's Trust Deed* [1963] Ch 357, [1967] 2 WLR 320, [1963] 1 All ER 454, in which a custodian trustee is held to be subject to the fiduciary 'no profit' rule. See also P D Finn *The Fiduciary Principle, Equity, Fiduciaries and Trusts* (1989, Youdan (ed), Carswell), p 35:

'In many instances property is a subject of a legal relationship with one party having custodial or other rights in or to that property. To the extent that party has limited or indeed no rights to its beneficial use and enjoyment, that person's position is incipiently fiduciary.'

In a writ issued on 5 June 1992 by MGN Pension Trustees Limited against Bank of America National Trust and Savings Association and Crédit Suisse, the trustees of the Maxwell pension fund sued Bank of America as custodians of the pension fund assets, asserting that they should not have settled instructions from the managers whereby the pension fund assets were lost. The writ asserted that Bank of America was a fiduciary:

'In the premises, and by reason of the [custody] Agreement and by reason of its position as custodian of assets of the [pension fund], BA owed fiduciary duties to the Trustee and the [pension fund]' (p 25).

LIMITATION CLAUSES[1]

6.41   There is longstanding authority that the terms of a fiduciary's appointment may limit its duties[2]. Moreover, the position of the global custodian seeking to rely on contractual limitation of their fiduciary duties was enormously strengthened by the case of *Kelly v Cooper Associates*[3]. In this case it was stated[4] that a fiduciary relationship arising in the context of a contractual deal should not alter the nature of the deal. Lord Browne-Wilkinson quoted[5] an earlier case[6] as follows:

'That contractual and fiduciary relationships may co-exist between the same parties has never been doubted. Indeed, the existence of a basic contractual relationship has in many situations provided a foundation for the erection of a fiduciary relationship. In these situations, it is the contractual foundation which is all important because it is the contract that regulates the basic rights and liabilities of the parties. The fiduciary relationship, if it is to exist at all, must accommodate itself to the terms of the contract so that it is consistent with, and conforms to them. The fiduciary relationship cannot be superimposed upon the contract in such a way as to alter the operation which the contract was intended to have according to its true construction.'

1   Limitation clauses cannot remove the fiduciary status of the global custodian; however, they are effective to modify its fiduciary duties, subject to the core fiduciary duty of loyalty as discussed below.

2   See *Wilkins v Hogg* (1861) 66 ER 346.

3   [1993] AC 205. This was a Privy Council decision, on appeal from the Court of Appeal of Bermuda. The case concerned the practices of an estate agent and its failure to notify one vendor client that it also acted for a vendor of an adjoining property.

4   Obiter, by Lord Browne-Wilkinson.

5   [1993] AC 205 at 215.

6   Mason J in the case of *Hospital Products International Pty Ltd v United States Surgical Corpn* (1984) 156 CLR 41.

6.42   The Law Commission discusses *Kelly* in the following terms:

'It confirmed that where a fiduciary relationship arises out of a contract, a clearly worded duty defining or exclusion clause will circumscribe the extent of the fiduciary duties owed to the other party.'[1]

1   Law Commission Report No 236, p. 4.

6.43   The report summarises the conditions that must be satisfied before the principle in *Kelly* may be relied upon[1] and draws attention to its limits[2].

1   Law Commission Report No 236, pp 85, 86:

'*Kelly* will provide a solution where the following conditions are satisfied. First, the duty defining and exclusion clause must clearly cover the transaction in question: it will have to do so unambiguously since it will be subject to the *contra proferentum* rule of interpretation. Secondly, in those situations where the relationship between the firm and client has altered over time, this altered relationship will also have to be caught by the clause. And thirdly, it must be the substance of the relationship between the client and the firm that is covered by the clause and not what the parties call it. If these three conditions are satisfied, then *Kelly* provides a way of solving the problems that arise from any mismatch between fiduciary rules, regulatory rules and market structure.'

2   Law Commission Report No 236, p 24 in relation to conflicts of interest:

'However, there are three situations of conflict in which, despite *Kelly*, it will be necessary either to make appropriate provision in the contract or obtain the informed consent of the customer in order to avoid breaching a fiduciary duty. The first is where the firm is acting for two customers in the same transaction. The second is where there is a conflict between the firm's own interest and the duty which it owes to a customer and that conflict is more acute than that which arose in *Kelly* ... The conflict would be more acute if, for example, (i) a firm has a direct beneficial interest in a transaction with a customer, such as where it sells its own property to a customer ... The third situation is where there has been "iniquity".'

6.44   This approach was endorsed in the case of *Clark Boyce v Mouat*[1]. 'A fiduciary duty ... cannot be prayed in aid to enlarge the scope of contractual duties.'[2] There is much judicial authority to the effect that implied fiduciary duty cannot distort a commercial contractual relationship[3]. However, while fiduciary duties must conform with the contract, they are not entirely subsumed within it, for 'the essence of a fiduciary relationship is that it creates obligations of a different character from those deriving from the contract itself'.[4]

1   [1994] 1 AC 428, [1993] 3 WLR 1021, [1993] 4 All ER 268. This was another Privy Council decision, on appeal from the Court of Appeal of New Zealand. The case concerned a claim against a solicitor; the plaintiff mortgaged her house to secure a loan to her son, and the solicitor acted for both of them.

2   Per Lord Jauncey of Tullichettle, at 437.

3   In addition to the judgments in *Kelly* and *Clarke Boyce* see, for example, *Target Holdings Ltd v Redferns* [1996] AC 421, [1995] 3 WLR 352, [1995] 3 All ER 785.

4   *Re Goldcorp Exchange Ltd* [1995] 1 AC 74 at 98. See also *Henderson v Merrett* [1995] 2 AC 145 at 206, per Lord Browne-Wilkinson.

6.45   It is also clear from case law that fiduciaries have a core minimum duty of loyalty that cannot be excluded by any relieving provisions[1].

1   *Wilkins v Hogg* (1861) 66 ER 346 at 348.

6.46   It is customary for global custodians (and indeed fund managers, brokers and other financial institutions who may be characterised as fiduciaries) to include in their contracts provisions designed to modify implied fiduciary duties. These permit conflicts of interest to arise (both between the client and the global custodian and between the client and other clients of the global custodian); disclose profits that the global custodian may derive from the relationship with the client and permit the global custodian to retain them; and relax the implied duty of confidentiality by permitting the global custodian to disclose client information to associates or other third parties.

CONFLICTS OF INTEREST

6.47 As briefly indicated above, the fiduciary must avoid two types of potential conflict of interest. First, it must not allow its own interests to conflict with those of its customer (the 'no conflicts rule')[1]. Second, it must not allow its duties to one customer to conflict with its duties to another customer (the 'undivided loyalty rule')[2].

1   Bray v Ford [1896] AC 44.

2   See Bristol and West Building Society v Mothew [1998] Ch 1 at 18, per Millett LJ:

> 'A fiduciary who acts for two principals with potentially conflicting interests without the informed consent of both is in breach of the obligation of undivided loyalty; he puts himself in a position where his duty to one principal *may* conflict with his duty to the other: see Clark Boyce v Mouat [1993] 3 WLR 1021, [1994] 1 AC 428, [1993] 4 All ER 268, and the cases there cited. This is sometimes described as "the double employment rule". Breach of the rule automatically constitutes a breach of fiduciary duty.'

> And at 19, per Millett LJ:

> 'Even if a fiduciary is properly acting for two principals with potentially conflicting interests he must act in good faith in the interests of each and must not act with the intention of furthering the interests of one principal to the prejudice of those of the other ... I shall call this "the duty of good faith". But it goes further than this. He must not allow the performance of his obligations to one principal to be influenced by his relationship with the other. He must serve each as faithfully and loyally as if he were his only principal. Conduct which is in breach of this duty need not be dishonest but it must be intentional. An unconscious omission which happens to benefit one principal at the expense of the other does not constitute a breach of fiduciary duty, though it may constitute a breach of the duty of skill and care ... Finally, the fiduciary must take care not to find himself in a position where there is an *actual* conflict of duty so that he cannot fulfil his obligations to one principal without failing in his obligations to the other: see Moody v Cox [1917] 2 Ch 71, [1916–17] All ER Rep 548 and Commonwealth Bank of Australia v Smith (1991) 102 ALR 453. If he does, he may have no alternative but to cease to act for at least one and preferably both. That fact that he cannot fulfil his obligations to one principal without being in breach of his obligations to the other will not absolve him from liability. I shall call this "the actual conflict rule".'

6.48 Many of the entities acting as global custodians are multi-function financial institutions, whose divisions may include fund management, brokerage and corporate finance. Therefore, conflicts of interest routinely arise, and must be managed by the informed consent of the client[1].

1   An ad hoc Chinese Wall may not be effective in addressing a conflict of interest. See Prince Jefri Bolkiah v KPMG [1999] 2 AC 222, [1999] 2 WLR 215, [1999] 1 All ER 517. And consider also Marks and Spencer plc v Freshfields Bruckhaus Deringer [2004] 3 All ER 144 regarding the limitations of Chinese Wall arrangements.

6.49 As discussed in Chapter 4, an important and growing function of custody securities is collateral. For reasons of administrative convenience[1] custodians are often asked to act in two capacities, both as custodian for their clients and as collateral trustee for their client's secured creditors[2]. The arrangement may be documented by one tri-party contract[3]. Clearly, acting for the parties on both sides of a collateral arrangement involves a potential conflict of interests. Very careful drafting is required to manage this conflict. Indeed, where the custodian has any discretionary powers in relation to the management or enforcement of collateral on behalf of the collateral taker, its position may be untenable.

1   And because the transfer of securities can involve delay, expense and tax.

2   In other words, the client both places its securities with the custodian, and charges them to the creditor, and the creditor appoints the custodian to act on its behalf in relation to the administration and enforcement of the charge.

3   To which the client, the secured creditor and the custodian are parties.

6.50   Where a trustee appoints a custodian under s 17 of TA 2000, it is not permitted to allow the custodian to restrict its liability or act in circumstances capable of giving rise to a conflict of interest, unless it is reasonably necessary to do so[1]. As such terms are standard in global custody contracts[2], and no major global custodian is likely to be willing to act without them, trustee clients are likely to find that their inclusion is reasonably necessary for the purposes of TA 2000.

1   TA 2000, s 20(2), (3). The same restriction is placed by these subsections on terms permitting the sub-custodian to appoint a substitute.

2   Where the global custodian is a multi-function financial institution, conflicts of interest will regularly arise.

SECRET PROFITS

6.51   It was indicated above that, as a fiduciary, the global custodian is generally not permitted to profit from its position at the expense of the client[1]. An aspect of the rule is that in general the global custodian can retain no profits indirectly derived from its service to the client. While this rule can be modified by the informed consent of the client, any 'secret profits'[2] must be accounted for to the client[3].

1   Prior to TA 2000, the custodian could not be remunerated unless fees were expressly agreed with the client. Under TA 2000, in the absence of express provision (s 29(5)) the custodian is entitled to receive reasonable remuneration for its services (s 29(1) and (3)). Also, the custodian is entitled to be reimbursed for expenses properly incurred by it (s 31(1)) and may remunerate and reimburse the expenses of agents, nominees and [sub]-custodians (s 32).

2   That is, profits to which the client has not given informed consent.

3   See *Re Brooke Bond Trust Deed* [1963] Ch 357, [1963] 2 WLR 320, [1963] 1 All ER 454.

6.52   Competitive pressure has reduced custodian fees to minimal levels, and the profits associated with global custody are no longer fee-based, but derived from the 'cross selling' of the financial services which the bank custodian is able to offer. The global custodian may undertake discretionary securities lending of the clients' portfolios, and provide foreign exchange and derivative services, retaining significant profits in each case. These profits are not always expressly disclosed.

6.53   Many custodians take a middle course, and include provision in the global custody contract giving general advance disclosures relating to cross selling and associated profits[1]. In its report[2] the Law Commission argued that *Kelly v Cooper Associates*[3] permits firms to rely on advance disclosures[4].

1   Note that for custodians regulated under MiFID (Directive 2004/39/EC of the European Parliament and of the Council of 21 April 2004 on markets in financial instruments amending Council Directives 85/611/EEC and 93/6/EEC and Directive 2000/12/EC of the European Parliament and of the Council and repealing Council Directive 93/22/EEC), there are specific disclosure obligations regarding provision or receipt of any fee or commission, or non-monetary benefit, in relation to the provision of investment or ancillary services to the client (see Art 26 of the MiFID implementing Directive (Commission Directive 2006/73/EC of 10 August 2006 implementing Directive 2004/39/EC of the European Parliament and of the Council as regards organisational requirements and operating conditions for investment firms and defined terms for the purposes of that Directive) and FSA Conduct of Business sourcebook, Rule 2.3.1R).

2   December 1995.

3   [1993] AC 205, [1992] 3 WLR 936.

4   Law Commission Report No 236 (1995), p 47:

> 'We now believe that a sufficiently precise general advanced disclosure made in a contract will be effective provided that the contract clearly delimits the fiduciary duties owed to the customer and displaces the obligation to make full disclosure of all material facts, and the customer has not been misled as to the nature of the relationship between the parties.'

6.54   However, some clients who are trustees may fear that general advance consent may involve them in breach of trust to their beneficiaries[1]. Further, a note of caution is sounded by the case of *Glynwill Investments NV v Thomson McKinnon Futures Ltd*[2], where a foreign exchange dealer was held liable for breach of fiduciary duty, and was not able to rely on contractual provision which did not accord with the commercial realities of its client business[3].

1   See Hayton 'Developing the Law of Trusts for the Twenty-First Century' (1990) 106 LQR 87 at 89.

2   (Unreported), 13 February 1992, Tuckey QC.

3   Law Commission Report No 236, pp 29, 30:

> 'This case also considered the extent to which the contract can determine the scope of fiduciary duties. The defendant firm was a foreign exchange dealer. It acted for the plaintiff in currency transaction, charging a commission and also, in some cases, taking a mark-up on the price at which it had bought in the market. It did not disclose the mark-up to the plaintiff. The plaintiff contended that the defendant was acting as its agent and was therefore liable to account for the mark-up. The defendant claimed that it was acting, as the contract between it and the plaintiff specified, as principal. However, the deputy judge concluded that in the light of the other evidence, including the agreement of commission and the market order method used by the plaintiffs, the trading relationship was one of principal and agent. The plaintiff was therefore entitled to recover the amount of the mark-up from the defendant.'

6.55   The prudent approach would be to assume that profits from cross selling may only be retained if expressly detailed in the global custody agreement.

LIABILITY FOR THIRD PARTIES[1]

6.56   The global custodian is at the centre of a communications and service network. When losses occur to a client's portfolio, they will often be attributable, not to the global custodian itself, but to a third party. For this reason, global custody contracts often seek to exclude liability for the defaults of third parties, including brokers[2]. This section will consider two topical issues, namely the liability of the global custodian in respect of sub-custodian default[3], and fraudulent instructions from managers.

1   See the discussion of outsourcing in Chapter 7.

2   Exclusion of liability for the defaults of brokers may be unnecessary: as brokers are not appointed or supervised by the global custodian, it is unlikely that the global custodian owes any general duty to the client in respect of the actions of brokers.

3   See also discussion of implications of AIFMD in Chapter 7, paras **7.171–7.176**.

Liability for sub-custodians

6.57   One of the most commercially sensitive issues facing the global custodian is the extent to which it should stand behind its sub-custodians.

6.58   Some clients mistakenly believe that the law imposes strict liability upon custodians for the defaults of their delegates, but this is far from true. Where the sub-custodian is a nominee or close associate of the global custodian, it may be unrealistic for the global custodian to expect to escape liability. However, for independent sub-custodians, liability is much more limited.

6.59 Technically, the legal position depends upon whether the sub-custodian was appointed under s 17 of TA 2000 or under an express term of the global custody agreement[1]. In the former case, the global custodian is obliged to comply with the statutory duty of care[2] when entering into the sub-custody arrangements[3]. Also, it must keep the sub-custody arrangements under review[4] and (broadly) where appropriate, exercise their powers of intervention[5], again complying with the statutory duty of care. Provided it complies with these requirements, the global custodian is not liable for any act or default of the sub-custodian.

1 It is advisable for any global custody agreement to include an express power to appoint sub-custodians. If a global custodian wished to bring its power of appointment under s 17, and so benefit from the exclusion of liability in s 23(1) discussed below, it could provide in the global custody agreement that the power of appointment arises pursuant to TA 2000, s 17.

2 That is, as discussed above, to exercise the care and skill which is reasonable in the circumstances (having regard to any special knowledge or experience that the custodian has or holds him or herself out as having, and, if acting as a trustee in the course of a business or profession, any special knowledge or experience that it is reasonable to expect of a person acting in the course of that kind of business or profession). As indicated earlier, the duty of care may be expressly disapplied: TA 2000, Sch 1, para 7.

3 TA 2000, s 23(1)

4 TA 2000, s 22(1)(a).

5 TA 2000, s 22(1)(b). Of course, the Act does not compel the global custodian to exercise powers of intervention which it does not have under the terms of the sub-custody agreement.

6.60 Where the sub-custodian is not appointed under s 17 of TA 2000, it is possible that a similar position arises under case law, so that provided a global custodian exercises reasonable care in the appointment and supervision of its global custodial network, it should escape liability for their defaults[1]. On this basis, to avoid liability under this section for third party losses, the global custodian must show ordinary prudence in the appointment and supervision of its global custodial network.

1 This was the position under Trustee Act 1925, s 30(1), now repealed; it reflected the earlier equitable position prior to codification in its legislative predecessors.

6.61 Global custodians should take care in the initial choice of the members of their network, and in reviewing that choice from time to time. Criteria should include all matters affecting the safety of client assets, including local custodial and administrative arrangements and staff controls. These should be considered in the light of local law and market practice. In particular, the global custodian should consider the impact of local insolvency law on its ability to recover client assets in the event of the third party's insolvency[1].

1 See Chapter 7 discussion of regulatory requirements, and in particular the duties imposed regarding appointment and periodic review of sub-custodians.

6.62 It should be noted that since there is now a statutory power to appoint agents, custodians and nominees in TA 2000, the omission of the power of delegation from a custody agreement will no longer result in a custodian incurring strict liability for its delegates because it made the delegation in breach of trust[1].

1 TA 2000, s 17. This in effect disapplies the general rule of English law that *delegatus non potest delegare*, which would otherwise mean that the custodian must act personally, on the basis that the client is deemed to have chosen the custodian personally to carry out its duties, without delegation or sub-delegation, unless expressly permitted to delegate by the custody agreement.

6.63 Global custodians sometimes take indemnities from sub-custodians. However, the usefulness of any such indemnity might be limited for the following reasons. The major risk associated with sub-custodians may be their credit risk; their insolvency would clearly affect the value of an indemnity issued by them. Moreover, if the global custodian's exposure is due to its breach of duty, an indemnity in respect of it may be unenforceable, as discussed below.

Fraudulent instructions

6.64 An important potential exposure to the custodian is the arrangement, customary in pensions business, where instructions come not from the client, but from a fund manager[1].

[1] For the position relating to the liability of custodian trustees (as opposed to managing trustees) see the Public Trustee Act 1906, s 4(2).

6.65 Following the Maxwell scandal, the pension trustees sued Bank America as custodian for implementing the manager's instructions to make the free deliveries that led to the loss of the pension assets. Bank America settled the claim. It was not disputed that the instructions were technically valid[1]. The basis for the claim was that the custodian's suspicions should have been raised and, as a fiduciary, it should have reviewed the instructions and enquired into the circumstances surrounding them. This claim raises the suggestion that the custodian's duties may extend to oversight of the manager, or even co-management[2]. As the claim was settled out of court, these issues have not been judicially clarified.

[1] Although it may be argued that fraudulent instructions cannot be valid instructions under a custody contract.

[2] The writ alleged that a number of terms were implied into the custody agreement, including the following (p 27):

'(5) that BA would immediately inform the Trustees and if necessary each of the directors thereof of any instructions that it received in relation to the funds, which might involve risks to the assets under their management or alter the nature of their rights and duties and/or their performance thereof or which were abnormal, suspicious or otherwise out of the ordinary.

(6) that BA would not deal with the funds and securities that it held in any way which put them at risk or allowed them to be stolen or used for improper purposes or lost to the MGPS ...'

6.66 The suggestion that the custodian is obliged to vet manager's instructions is worrying for the custodian. First, it is contractually obliged to implement instructions, so that any obligation to decline to implement certain instructions might put it in breach of contract[1]. Second, in view of the high level of automation that is now customary in settlement operations, any duty to review or subjectively appraise particular instructions may be impractical to discharge. In any case, the staff involved in settlement may be trained for administrative duties, and not in a position to exercise judgments as to the propriety of instructions.

[1] As delayed settlement may put the manager into default and also prevent it from taking advantage of investment opportunities, damages may be significant.

6.67 There are strong arguments that the custodian is not under a general duty to review manager's instructions[1]. The case of *Galmerrow Securities Ltd v National Westminster Bank plc*[2] considered the position of the trustee of an unauthorised[3] unit trust scheme. Mr Justice Harman noted that the trust deed conferred exclusive power of and responsibility for management on the managers: 'Plainly these terms are inconsistent with NatWest as Trustee exercising a general supervision over the choice of property.'[4] On this basis, the trustee was held not to be liable for losses attributable to bad management[5].

[1] Although it can be liable for dishonest assistance in breach of fiduciary duty: *Royal Brunei Airlines v Tan* [1995] 2 AC 378, [1995] 3 WLR 64, [1995] 3 All ER 97; *Twinsectra v Yardley* [2002] UKHL 12, [2002] 2 AC 164, [2002] 2 WLR 802, [2002] 2 All ER 377; *Barlow Clowes International v Eurotrust International* [2006] UKPC 37, [2006] 1 WLR 1476.

The global custodian's duties

2 [2002] WTLR 125.

3 Of course, the trustee of an authorised unit trust scheme has certain regulatory monitoring functions; see the FSA's Collective Investment Schemes sourcebook, Chapter 6 regarding operating duties and responsibilities, in particular 6.6.4R. Similarly, under AIFMD a depositary has significant monitoring functions, see Chapter 7, para **7.168**.

4 *Galmerrow Securities Ltd v National Westminster Bank* [2002] WTLR 125.

5 The Goode Report also provides some support for this position. During September 1993 the Pension Law Review Committee, chaired by Professor Roy Goode, published its report on pension law reform (*Pension Law Reform – The Report of the Pension Law Review Committee*). There is a section discussing the custody of pension assets and the desirability of using a custodian independent of the sponsor and the manager. The report concludes as follows:

'...whilst recognising the value of custodianship services, we do not consider that it would be right to require trustees ... to place pension funds assets with independent custodians' (p 369).

Part of the basis for this conclusion is:

'...the fact that the custodian exercises ministerial rather than managerial functions and has no duty to investigate the propriety of instructions given to it, which appear to be in order, unless it has specifically undertaken a monitoring function' (p 367).

'The custodian will wish to see the provisions of the trust deed relating to the trustees' investment powers. When dealing with a fund manager the custodian should also verify the authority given to the fund manager, and, where that authority does not come direct from the trustees as a whole but from individual trustees or from a third party, the source of their power to confer that authority. But when these steps have been taken, the custodian is free to act on its instructions in the absence of circumstances putting it on enquiry that something may be amiss' (p 368).

'The use of custodians may well give the semblance of protection without the reality' (p 369).

In contrast, the Myners Report *Institutional Investment in the United Kingdom: A Review*, 2001 (see para **6.84** below) recommended that there should be a statutory requirement for pension funds to have an independent custodian on the basis that 'Protection for pension scheme members from the risk of fraud could be improved by making custody independent of the employer a mandatory requirement for pension funds' and 'This would make it more difficult for improper use to be made of a pension fund's assets'. This point was noted in the Pickering Report in July 2002, *A simpler way to better pensions; An independent report by Alan Pickering*, but was not the subject of any further recommendations, nor was it mentioned at all in the Sandler Review (*Medium and Long-Term Retail Savings in the UK: A Review*) also in July 2002, or reflected in the Pensions Act 2004. To date, the original Myners Report comment does not seem to have been followed up by any attempt to impose additional duties on custodians. Arguably such an approach would be incorrect, since the intention to distance pension fund assets from an employer's control is reasonable, but it would be a concern if custodians were expected to undertake monitoring functions.

6.68 Contractual provisions should be included in the global custody agreement confirming the ability to assume that technically valid instructions are in order[1] and that there is no duty of oversight of the manager. However, it would be prudent for global custodians to assume there may be some risk that they may not escape liability for acting on evidently fraudulent instructions, and for this reason may consider implementing controls that alert them to free deliveries or possibly unusually large transfers[2]. Timely transaction reports to clients may also reduce risk.

1 It should be provided that the custodian is entitled to act in accordance with instructions unless it has actual knowledge that the instructions are fraudulent or in breach of the instructor's duties.

2 Because the contractual provision may not be wholly enforceable, care should be taken to ensure that 'partial invalidity' boilerplate is also included (ie provision that, if any part of the agreement is invalid, the remainder will remain in effect).

Nexus

6.69 Where a custody client suffers loss due to the default of a sub-custodian, its ability to recover damages for breach of duty at civil law will often depend on its ability to demonstrate that it is in a direct relationship with the defendant[1]. Of course, such relationships can be established between the client and the global custodian. However, unless the global custodian was in breach of its duty of care in appointing or supervising the sub-custodian, fault does not arise at this level. There may be fault at sub-custodian level, but no liability, because there was no relationship on which to establish duty owed to the client[2]. In an intermediated service such as global custody, the client has no direct nexus with the sub-delegates responsible for losses: therefore duty and fault may be unlikely to coincide in the same person, and the client is more exposed than in a service where there is no sub-delegation.

1   Because, under English law, fiduciary duties only arise where there is a relationship of special trust, and negligence can only be established where duties of care are owed. However, as discussed above, the Contracts (Rights of Third Parties) Act 1999 permits third parties to enforce contractual rights in certain circumstances.

2   Any agency between the global custodian and sub-custodians is usually avoided, in order to prevent a direct contractual relationship between the third parties and the global custody clients, which might in turn undermine the commercial position of the global custodian.

PARTICULAR CLAUSES

6.70 Certain additional exclusions are customary in global custody agreements. Precisely what is included depends on the concerns and negotiating strength of the parties. The matters discussed in paras **6.71–6.75** below are important examples[1].

1   Other specific limitations that are commonly included in global custody contracts include limitation or exclusion of liability for receipt of invalid or forged securities; reversals of credits to an account; delays while the custodian seeks clarification of ambiguous instructions; and the investment risks of assets held by the custodian.

Force majeure

6.71 The global custodian's ability to discharge its duties may be particularly vulnerable to computer failure. Force majeure clauses (excusing performance where it is rendered impossible or impracticable) are very important[1]. However, they can be no substitute for practical measures such as disaster recovery systems and insurance. Immediately following the events of 11 September 2001, industry attention focused on disaster recovery, and in particular the importance of a geographical spread of data processing back-up systems. Global custodians are also aware of the need to clarify the adequacy of their clients' back-up systems[2].

1   See generally Hugh Beale (ed) *Chitty on Contracts* (2012, 31st edn, Sweet & Maxwell).

2   J Brown 'Recovery Wakes up to Extreme Risk' (November 2001) *Euromoney* 82 at 84–5.

Consequential damages

6.72 In view of the judgment in *Target Holdings Ltd v Redferns*[1] it is important for global custodians contractually to exclude liability for consequential damages[2]; such provision must, however, be brought clearly to the attention of clients.

1   [1996] AC 421 at 434, per Lord Browne-Wilkinson:

   '... the common law rules of remoteness of damages and causation do not apply ... The plaintiff's actual loss as a consequence of the breach is to be assessed with the full benefit of hindsight. Foreseeability is not a concern in assessing compensation ...'

2   And equally important to be clear what 'consequential loss' means. See *Hadley v Baxendale* (1854) 9 Ex 341, and *BHP Petroleum v British Steel* [1999] 2 Lloyd's Rep 583, analysis by Rix J subsequently approved by the Court of Appeal in *Hotel Services v Hilton International Hotels* [2000] All ER (D) 331.

Erroneous instructions

6.73 It is common practice among global custodians to provide in the global custody agreement that customers must examine the periodic statements provided by the global custodian, and notify it of any error within a stated period, and further that in the absence of such notification the customer may not challenge the statement. In a banking context, such provision was held to be ineffective in *Tai Hing Cotton Mill Ltd v Liu Chong Hing Bank Ltd*[1] because it was not sufficiently clear and unambiguous to bring home to the customer the burden of examining the statements and the consequences of its failing to so do[2]. It is likely that many such clauses that are included in standard global custody agreements would fail the test in *Tai Hing*[3].

1   [1986] AC 80, [1985] 3 WLR 317, [1985] 2 All ER 947. Tai Hing was a Hong Kong textile manufacturer. It was defrauded by its clerk, which, inter alia, forged the managing director's signature on cheques drawn on the company's banks. The cheques were paid and the sums debited from the company's accounts. The banks' terms of business provided that its bank periodic account statements would be deemed to be confirmed by the company if no errors were notified to the bank within a stated period. However, the company's internal control systems were inadequate, the clerk was almost unsupervised and the fraud was not discovered for many years. The company sought a declaration in the Hong Kong High Court that the sums had been wrongly debited. It was held that the company was estopped by its implied representation (by its silence) that the accounts were correct, and that the banks had relied on this to their detriment. An appeal to the Hong Kong Court of Appeal was dismissed on the basis that the company was estopped by its negligence from disputing the correctness of the statements. On appeal to the Privy Council, judgment was given for the company. If a bank wished to oblige the customer to examine bank statements and to estop the customer from challenging those statements after a certain period, the effect of this must be very clearly brought to the customer's attention. At general law, the duty of the customer in relation to forged cheques was only to refrain from drawing a cheque in such a manner as may facilitate fraud or forgery (and not to take care in the operation of its business as a whole), and to inform the bank as soon as it became aware of any fraud or forgery.

2   *Tai Hing Cotton Mill Ltd v Liu Chong Hing Bank Ltd* [1986] AC 80 at 985, per Lord Scarman:

'If banks wish to impose on their customers an express obligation to examine their monthly statements and to make those statements, in the absence of query, unchallengeable by the customer after expiry of a time limit, the burden of the obligation and of the sanction imposed must be brought home to the customer. In their Lordships' view the provisions which they have set out above do not meet this undoubtedly rigorous test ... Clear and unambiguous provision is needed if the banks are to introduce into the contract a binding obligation on the customer who does not query his bank statement to accept the statement as accurately setting out the debit items in the accounts.'

3   The three different provisions which were treated as failing the test were as follows: 'A monthly statement for each account will be sent by the Bank to the depositor by post or messenger and the balance shown therein may be deemed to be correct by the Bank if the depositor does not notify the Bank in writing of any error therein within ten days after the sending of such statement ...' (at 957). 'The Bank's statement of my/our account will be confirmed by me/us without delay. In the case of absence of such confirmation within a fortnight, the bank may take the said statement as approved by me/us' (at 957). 'A statement of the customer's account will be rendered once a month. Customers are desired: (1) to examine all entries in the statement of account and to report at once to the bank any error found therein. (2) to return the confirmation slip duly signed. In the absence of any objection to the statement within seven days after its receipt by the customer, the account shall be deemed to have been confirmed' (at 958).

The impact of the Unfair Contract Terms Act 1977 should also be considered (see paras **6.11–6.14** above).

Information

6.74 The global custody service may involve the global custodian in receiving information provided by third parties and forwarding it to the client[1]. Clearly, errors and omissions in the information may cause loss to the client. It is important to establish whether or not the global custodian will be liable for such losses. This of course turns on whether or not the duties of the global custodian include examining such information. In the absence of express provision, the global custody contract may be construed as including such a duty within the general duty of care. Therefore, where the global custodian will not in practice examine third party information, this should be made clear by stating that no such service will be provided, and that no liability will be accepted[2].

1   See the discussion of corporate actions below.
2   Such clear provision is preferable to a bare limitation of liability. In other words, the point should be addressed both in the duty defining and in the limitation of liability provisions of the global custody contract.

Indemnities for breach of duty

6.75 Where a manager wishes the global custodian to act in breach of its duties to its client (eg by appointing a sub-custodian in a jurisdiction where it cannot prudently do so) the manager may offer the global custodian an indemnity in respect of the global custodian's exposure for that breach. The global custodian should treat this with caution, as such an indemnity may be unenforceable[1].

1   See Hugh Beale (ed) *Chitty on Contracts* (2012, 31st edn, Sweet & Maxwell).

CORPORATE ACTIONS

6.76 In the light of the preceding discussion of the nature of a custodian's duties it may be useful to consider a particular example of a situation where a custodian may be required to take action in relation to the assets it holds. As indicated in Chapter 3, unless a custodian is holding physical assets (eg bearer securities), a custodian is most likely to be regarded as a trustee by English law. As a trustee, the custodian has the legal title[1] to the securities but holds the entire beneficial interest for the benefit of the custody client[2]. This means that in principle any matter affecting the securities, whether rights arising in connection with the securities, or benefits accruing to a holder of the securities[3], must be passed on by the custodian to the client, so that the client is effectively in the same position as if it were the direct holder of the securities. While this is the basic position, it will be subject to the express terms of the custody contract[4].

1   The custodian may in practice delegate the holding of legal title to a nominee, a sub-custodian or a settlement system, but the principle remains the same as between the custodian and its client.
2   Subject to the terms of the custody agreement, such as rights of set off or lien, whether phrased as such or in the form of permission to deduct fees or expenses from cash held for the custody client.
3   In theory, the liabilities relating to the relevant assets should also be passed on; however, technically any liabilities under relevant securities would be the liability of the holder of such securities but would be passed to the underlying client of the holder as a result of the holder claiming under the indemnity in its agreement with the client (or pursuant to TA 2000, s 31 which (broadly) entitles a trustee to reimbursement of expenses properly incurred by him or her).
4   However, to the extent relevant attributes of the ownership of the securities are not dealt with in the contract, the general law will apply. It is for this reason that the content of a custody contract is of great importance to both custodian and client, and in particular in relation to corporate actions.

What do we mean by 'corporate action'?

6.77 In its widest sense, 'corporate action' is the term used to refer to any event involving the issuer of the securities which arises in relation to securities, and which has an affect on, or requires action by, the holder of the securities. The custodian must determine how the impact of such events can be passed to the client. For convenience, we may regard corporate actions as falling into three main categories:

(1) 'mandatory' events, where the event occurs without intervention from the holder of the securities, and the holder of securities has no choice as to what happens, but is required to accept the relevant resulting asset (such events would include a decision by a company to make a stock-split by replacing each share of a particular class with a number of shares of reduced nominal value);

(2) 'discretionary' events, where the event occurs and a holder of securities has an option whether to take action in connection with such event, for example, to exercise voting rights or to participate in a rights issue; and

(3) 'voluntary' events, where the event is triggered if the holder of the securities exercises a right available to it at its option, for example, the exercise of rights to requisition an extraordinary meeting[1] or other rights which may be granted to shareholders of that specific class[2].

1   Under the Companies Act 2006, s 303, a requisition to convene an extraordinary general meeting may be made by holders of not less than 5 per cent of the paid up shares carrying voting rights.

2   Other examples may be a 'right' or 'benefit' which does not arise from the nature of the asset itself, but results from the actions of third parties: for example, a class action proposed by third parties who invite other shareholders to participate.

Generally

6.78 Unless the custodian has specifically agreed with the custody client that it will not assist with the exercise of the relevant rights, or has limited its duties in such areas to the matters set out in the agreement, the custodian would arguably be obliged to take steps to enable the relevant rights to be exercised by or on behalf of the client, since the custodian would otherwise be depriving the client of part of the benefits held on trust for the client and would be in breach of trust.

6.79 A custody agreement would normally contain provisions relating to the processing of 'mandatory' corporate actions, because in practice neither the custodian nor the client has any choice whether such events occur. Such provisions would, in broad terms, deal with the passing on by the custodian to the client of benefits requiring no positive actions by the holder of the securities[1]. Where there are 'discretionary' corporate actions, decisions need to be taken by the holder of the securities, and therefore in such cases the custodian would normally agree to seek instructions from the client. It is usual to include specific provisions relating to the exercise of voting rights. Such provisions may simply agree that voting rights will not be exercised, or may set out detailed procedures whereby the custodian will pass to the client any notices received from the relevant company regarding matters to be voted upon, following which the client will instruct the custodian regarding the manner in which votes should be exercised, and the custodian will arrange the exercise of proxy votes in accordance with such instructions. In general, provisions relating to other types of 'discretionary' or 'voluntary' corporate actions are less commonly included because of the difficulty of predicting, and creating appropriate provisions dealing with, the possible voluntary corporate action events, but given the residual fiduciary obligations of the custodian which apply as discussed above, the prudent approach would be to include some form of wording, even if inevitably not setting out the position in exhaustive detail, in order to reduce the potential risk.

1   This would include the receipt and remittance of dividends or non-cash distributions, although such matters are usually covered separately rather than included in provisions respecting corporate actions.

Issues for the client

6.80 The custody client's attitude to corporate actions may vary, depending on the underlying reasons for holding the relevant securities. For example, the custody client may not be concerned to exercise voting rights, although in principle would probably wish to ensure that rights issues offered on favourable terms were accepted. In contrast, a custody client may regard as a high priority the ability to attend and vote at meetings[1]. A blanket refusal by the custodian to deal with any corporate action events would potentially mean the loss of a significant part of the value of the holding of the securities for the client in the same way as a blanket refusal to pass on any benefits in the form of income arising on assets held (and would in practice be unusual). The level of corporate action service provided by the custodian will depend on which issues are important to the client and of course the question of what steps the custodian is able to take in practice.

1   Whether a client can be permitted to attend at shareholder or bondholder meetings will depend on whether the custodian is willing to appoint the client as its representative (whether a proxy or otherwise) or to transfer the relevant securities into the name of the client for the purposes of the relevant meeting.

6.81 If a client is concerned to have the facility to decide in each case whether to exercise rights or take up opportunities, whether or not it is in a position to do so will depend on the ability of the custodian to forward in good time all information received from the relevant company (or other relevant sources). Whether the client requires that all information of any description relating to the assets held is forwarded, or is just concerned about notification of voting rights or rights issues, timing will be a key issue. For example, if the custodian is delayed in passing to the client information regarding the existence of an issue on which the client may wish to vote, or a rights issue which the client may wish to accept, there may be very little time for the client to come to a decision regarding its preferred course of action, and there is a risk that by the time instructions are given to the custodian by the client, the deadline for exercising the relevant rights will have passed. A custodian may be able to offer systems specifically designed to facilitate communication in relation to these types of issue, but the custody client will need to consider whether this in practice provides the service required. (Such systems may range from dedicated electronic communication services between custodian and client to provision for straight-through-processing, where client instructions which are to be forwarded by the custodian can simply be sent via the custodian's systems to the relevant destination.)

6.82 In principle, where a client is concerned to receive the benefit of any rights or opportunities arising in connection with its assets, ideally the custody agreement should set out clearly what steps the custodian would take in each envisaged situation. However, in practice, because of the problem of covering all possible scenarios, it is more likely that the relevant agreement would deal with the main issues of concern in detail, and attempt to cover any other eventualities with appropriate general wording. The challenge would of course be to provide a general approach which satisfied the client that there was a mechanism for passing on all benefits, but which was not too vague to be helpful or too onerous for a custodian to accept.

6.83 Under the Companies Act 2006, ss 145–153, the position has changed slightly in favour of holders of shares in UK companies[1]. Section 145 allow a company to amend its articles of association to allow a shareholder to nominate another person (or persons) to exercise or have the benefit of certain shareholder rights instead of that shareholder (including the rights to receive a proposed written resolution, to require directors to call a general meeting or to appoint a proxy to attend a company meeting). It is not clear how many companies have amended their articles for this purpose, but it seems likely that, where companies do so, custodians may come under pressure to make such nominations in relation to their clients (or perhaps their clients' customers). Pursuant to s 146, even if the articles of a company have not been changed, a shareholder is permitted to nominate another person to receive (in addition to the shareholder) information from the company which would otherwise only be sent to shareholders (or shareholders of the same member class as the nominating shareholder). It should be noted that in both cases, it is only the shareholder, not the nominated person, who can enforce these rights against the company. Where relevant shares are registered in the name of a custodian (or its nominee), custody clients may request the custodian to make the appropriate nomination (or procure that its nominee does so) to enable the clients to obtain information regarding matters such as corporate events more quickly[2].

1   Consider also the possible developments proposed under the Securities Law Directive, see Chapter 7, paras **7.177–7.193**, which would be significant if implemented in such form.

2   Another new development may also result in the rights of shareholders being protected, albeit in a slightly different way. The Civil Justice Council (an advisory public body established under the Civil Procedure Act 1997 with responsibility for overseeing and co-ordinating the modernisation of the civil justice system; see further www.civiljusticecouncil.gov.uk) published a paper on 5 August 2008 entitled 'Improving Access to Justice through Collective Actions'. This paper contains various recommendations to the Lord Chancellor regarding changes to the law to permit a 'generic collective action' (ie class action claims) in England and Wales. Broadly, the recommendations consider the possibility of more effective access to justice for small entities and consumers, and the benefits of efficiency and economy, from a collective claims procedure, as well as the need to balance against the concerns of potential defendants (unmeritorious class actions could be made simply to cause problems for a company) by requiring a court to certify whether a collective claim may proceed. In July 2009, the UK government's response did not favour the creation of a generic right of collective action but instead a sector-based approach. The Financial Services Act 2010 amends the Financial Services and Markets Act 2000 to give the FSA power to create a consumer redress scheme, but does not contain provisions allowing a representative claimant to bring proceedings on behalf of a class of customers or other claimants, as was proposed in an early draft Bill. However, the government also published in July 2009 a White Paper entitled 'A Better Deal for Consumers: Delivering Real Help Now and Change for the Future' which announced the appointment of a Consumer Advocate in 2010, and the UK Department for Business Innovation & Skills published a consultation paper on the powers of the proposed Consumer Advocate ('Consultation on the role and powers of the Consumer Advocate', 2 December 2009), indicating the Consumer Advocate would be authorised to being collective actions on behalf of consumers. There seems to have been little progress since then, possibly because the question of class actions has been raised in other areas. On 4 February 2011, the European Commission published a consultation paper 'Towards a Coherent European Approach to Collective Redress', which among other things raised the question of whether such a regime was necessary. In addition, in April 2012, the UK Department for Business Innovation & Skills published a consultation paper entitled 'Private Actions in Competition Law: A Consultation on Options for Reform' the proposals in which include the possibility of class actions in relation to breaches of competition law.

6.84   As regards the expectations of clients regarding the exercise of voting rights[1] by custodians, it should be noted that the Myners Report[2] included the observation that fund managers did not make enough effort to exercise rights arising from shares and should intervene more actively where this would increase the value of the shares. This was intended to prompt more focus on 'discretionary' and 'voluntary' corporate actions, which, inter alia, would make fund managers more demanding of custodians in this respect. However, other views were expressed in the wake of the Myners Report. For example, the Association of British Insurers expressed the concern that legislation requiring particular action by shareholders and pension fund trustees was likely to increase efforts to narrow the particular situations where action would be required, in order to restrict the exposure to liability, rather than causing the relevant parties to focus on involvement in the companies in which shares are held[3]. Nevertheless, the Myners Report resulted in a set of principles which pension fund trustees were expected to adopt on a voluntary basis. In particular, in relation to shareholder activism, the trustees were expected to require investment managers to have an appropriate explicit strategy for exercising shareholder rights as part of the management process, including active monitoring and communication in relation to the issuers of the shares. A review by HM Treasury in 2004[4] concluded that the principles were not being complied with to the extent intended, and this review was followed in 2007 by a report by the National Association of Pension Funds ('NAPF')[5] and a consultation paper from HM Treasury in March 2008[6]. Generally the report and consultation paper acknowledge that the market context in which pension funds are now operating has changed considerably[7], and recommend various revisions to the original principles. The NAPF Report states in relation to shareholder activism that it is 'The generally held view ... that behaviour had changed in the way envisaged by the Principle' regarding this issue, and that the Institutional Shareholders' Committee[8] Statement of Principles entitled 'The Responsibilities of Institutional Shareholders and Agents' is 'generally incorporated into managers' contracts by way of a side letter or in the scheme's SIP[9,10]. The HM Treasury Report recommended updating the shareholder activism principle by including a specific requirement to adopt the Institutional Shareholders' Committee Statement of Principles referred to above, and to ensure appropriate disclosure by investment managers of their strategy in this respect. This makes it even more likely that custodians can expect particular focus on the services provided in relation to exercise of voting rights.

1   There have been various Myners Reports on 'Impediments to Voting UK Shares' in, respectively, January 2004, March 2005, November 2005 and July 2007. The 2007 report concluded that, although some changes to the Combined Code (now the UK Corporate Governance Code published by the Financial Reporting Council on 28 May 2010) and the Companies Act 2006 reflected recommendations to improve transparency and efficiency of proxy voting arrangements, there were certain areas which still required further work, in particular the encouragement of voting agents and custodians not to set deadlines for receipt of voting instructions from clients which were significantly less than 10 working days or two weeks in advance of the issuer's deadline. There are of course obvious practical issues with this point, since a custodian would wish to have a reasonable period of time in which to receive and process instructions, as well as allowing sufficient time to seek clarification or correction of incomplete or unclear voting instructions. This is a particular concern where there is a lengthy chain of intermediaries between the ultimate beneficial owner of shares and the holder of legal title to shares ('The decline in the role of the individual shareholder has been paralleled by an explosion of intermediation.', Professor John Kay 'The Kay Review of UK Equity Markets and Long-Term Decision Making', Final Report, July 2012 (the 'Kay Report'), a review commissioned by the Secretary of State for Business Innovation and Skills.) The UK Corporate Governance Code includes an expectation that institutional shareholders should 'enter into a dialogue with companies based on the mutual understanding of objectives' (Principle 1, Main Principle, UK Corporate Governance Code, p 36). Somewhat oddly a footnote to this Principle states that where institutional shareholders appoint agents (such as investment managers, or voting services, the Principles 'should accordingly be read as applying where appropriate to the agents of institutional shareholders'. This cannot be appropriate in the case of custodians, since custodians do not exercise any discretion but act on the instructions of their clients (see Chapter 7, paras **7.125** and **7.126** regarding the importance of custodians not have any discretion regarding the exercise of voting rights).

2   *Institutional Investment in the United Kingdom: A Review*, prepared by Paul Myners, published 4 March 2001.

3   See ABI News Release, 7 May 2002.

4   HM Treasury Report *Myners principles for institutional investment decision-making: review of progress*, December 2004.

5   NAPF Report *Institutional Investment in the UK: six years on. Report and recommendations*, November 2007.

6   HM Treasury Consultation Paper *Updating the Myners principles: a consultation*, March 2008.

7   The NAPF Report makes particular reference to the 'Scheme funding crisis: In 2001 around half of all schemes were in surplus. By the middle of 2007, scheme deficits for FTSE 100 companies stood at £21 billion. Watson Wyatt Pension Deficit Indices' (p 8).

8   A forum intended to enable UK institutional shareholders to 'exchange views and, on occasion, coordinate their activities in support of the interests of UK investors', the constituent members of which are the Association of British Insurers, the Association of Investment Companies, the Investment Management Association and the National Association of Pension Funds (see http:"institutionalshareholderscommittee.org.uk).

9   Statement of Investment Principles.

10 NAPF Report, pp 25 and 26

6.85 Revised Myners Principles were published by HM Treasury in October 2008, and included an expectation that trustees should adopt, or ensure that investment managers adopt, the Institutional Shareholders' Committee Statement on the responsibilities of shareholders and agents, and should both include a statement of the scheme's policy on responsible ownership in the Statement of Investment Principles, and report periodically to members on the discharge of such responsibilities. Subsequently, the Walker Report[1] noted that 'In a developed stock market such as that in the UK, the link between the ultimate beneficial owner and an investee company can be complex and may involve a transition in which the focus of behaviour shifts from that of ownership, with an emphasis on creating longer-term value, to that of an investor, with the fund manager under more or less pressure to produce short-term returns with performance calibrated against a peer group or benchmark index.'[2] It is also noted that increased shareholder engagement encounters problems such as 'impediments to voting shares' which include 'custodian practices' and 'difficulty in ascertaining the beneficial ownership of shares held in nominee accounts or other aggregated forms of holding'.[3] Among other things, it was concluded that it is best practice if fund managers 'and other institutional investors' should disclose their voting record. It is unclear whether this is expected to apply to a custodian or indeed how a custodian could make such disclosure without the authority of each client for whom it holds shares, and arguably such a requirement should only apply to persons who direct the exercise of voting rights, rather than simply acting on instructions. Following the Walker Report in 2009, and the publication of the UK Corporate Governance Code (see above, para **6.84** n 1), early in 2011 the Pensions Investment Research Consultants Limited ('PIRC') published their Shareholder Voting Guidelines 2011 in which PIRC expressed the view that any entity offering nominee services in relation to shares should as a starting point offer all clients both information and voting rights in relation to shares held as nominee. In practice, it seems likely that when a custodian holds shares for a client, the extent of the services which the custodian agrees to provide in respect of voting and information will depend on the importance of such services to the client, the system's capacity of the custodian, and the amount the client is willing to pay for the relevant services.

1   'A review of corporate governance in UK banks and other financial industry entities – Final recommendations', 26 November 2009.

2   Walker Report, para 5.3, p 69.

3   Walker Report, para 5.16, p 74.

Issues for the custodian

6.86 The main issue for the custodian is to determine the types of corporate actions where it is prepared to provide assistance. Accordingly it will need to decide what limitations of the scope of its services are appropriate in the custody contract so that the client is clear what services are being provided. It is also important to consider how the custodian can best carry out the agreed functions, taking into account matters such as the timing issues when forwarding information and receiving instructions.

6.87 If a corporate action is not processed properly, and the contractual documentation does not cover the circumstances in which this happened (eg specifically limiting or excluding liability if there is a delay in transmitting information), the potential loss to the client may be large. This means there is the risk of large claims by the client against the custodian. The consequences for the client of being unable to exercise voting rights or accept a rights issue may be considerable.

There may also be added complexity in valuing the client's claim, since it may be unclear what the consequences would have been if the relevant voting rights had been exercised, or it may be difficult to value the securities which the client had wanted to subscribe for in the rights issue. It may not be possible to compensate the client directly (by replacing the assets) if there is illiquidity in the relevant securities following the corporate action so that it is not possible to obtain such securities in the open market. If the amount of damages due is then calculated, the normal contractual measure of damages is to put the client in the position it would have been in had the contract been performed. However, in these situations it is difficult to define the extent of the loss, because the market price of the securities might have been different if the client had exercised the relevant rights. Because of the different types of corporate action and the potentially broad range of events causing problems, this is a complicated matter to cover comprehensively in documentation and it is likely that there will be areas where the liability of the parties and values involved can only be determined with difficulty. It is at least helpful if a custodian includes in its custody terms clear contractual terms defining the extent of liabilities, for example setting a cap on liability of the market value of the securities as at the date of the breach of duty.

6.88 There is the further question of how a failure to arrange for the exercise of rights in relation to 'discretionary' or 'voluntary' corporate actions would be treated in the context of the general level of liability accepted by the custodian. While most custodians would accept liability for their own negligence (or possibly gross negligence: see discussion in paras **6.8–6.9** and **6.32–6.35** above), it may be debatable (depending on the terms of the contract, the facts of the matter, or market practice generally) whether the events which have occurred involved negligence on the part of the custodian or not.

6.89 As discussed above, while the timing of instructions is a major concern for the client, it is also an issue for the custodian. Where the sequence of events is that information is passed from the custodian to the client, instructions are given by the client to the custodian, and then action is taken by the custodian, there are various stages at which the transmission of information may be delayed, lost or corrupted. The custodian will need to ensure that it has made clear to the client the nature of the service being offered, and also what the limits of the service being offered are, making, as necessary, appropriate disclosures and disclaimers in the agreement with the client.

6.90 In theory a custodian might wish to try to circumvent the timing issues for seeking instructions by simply agreeing to deal with the corporate actions on behalf of the client without the need to seek instructions. In order to do so, the custodian would need authority from the client to exercise its discretion in the exercise of rights arising in relation to the securities held for the client. However, this is undesirable for a number of reasons. In principle, it is preferable for the client if the client takes this type of decision itself, rather than delegating it to an entity with less in-depth knowledge of the client's business and investment strategy. From the custodian's perspective, such a service could be seen as an investment management function, thus importing additional regulatory considerations, and could result in disclosure obligations for the custodian under Chapter 5 of the FSA's Disclosure and Transparency Rules sourcebook and Part XII of the Financial Services and Markets Act 2000[1]. In addition, as a fiduciary the custodian would in principle be under a high level of care when making decisions regarding the exercise of the corporate actions and would therefore be exposed to a further risk of claims for breach of fiduciary duty from the client if the client were to dispute the decisions made.

1   See Chapter 7, paras **7.123–7.126**.

CHAPTER 7

Regulatory duties

7.1 In order to give a better idea of the regulatory context in which a custodian operates in the UK, this section gives an overview of the main UK regulatory requirements affecting custody and deposit taking in the UK at the time of writing, with a particular focus on rules applicable to the holding of securities. Starting first with a brief summary of the old regulatory structure (up to 30 November 2001), this section will then turn to the arrangements under the Financial Services and Markets 2000 ('FSMA') and MiFID[1], and the possible effects of MiFID2[2].

1   Directive 2004/39/EC of the European Parliament and of the Council of 21 April 2004 on markets in financial instruments amending Council Directives 85/611/EEC and 93/6/EEC and Directive 2000/12/EC of the European Parliament and of the Council and repealing Council Directive 93/22/EEC.

2   The Directive to update and replace MiFID, a provisional version of which was published by the European Commission on 20 October 2011, commencing the process of negotiation by the Council of Ministers and the European Parliament. To date, a considerable number of drafts have been produced, and at the time of writing the most recent draft is the compromise proposal draft published by the Cyprus EU Council Presidency on 20 November 2012. It was intended that final text should be agreed by the end of 2012, but in practice this seems likely to slip to early 2013.

CUSTODY AS A REGULATED ACTIVITY

Regulation of custody

7.2 Custody has not always been a regulated form of business. Following an amendment to the Financial Services Act 1986[1], with effect from 1 June 1997 custody became one of the specified forms of investment business[2], although the term 'custody' was not itself used in the operative wording of the Act (despite the relevant heading of 'Custody of Investments'). As a result of this amendment to the Act, any custodian operating in the UK had to ensure that it complied with the requirements of the Act if its activities involved it in providing the services caught by the relevant provisions of the Act and, if no relevant exemption[3] applied, non-authorised custodians had to become authorised persons. Custodians with existing authorisation in respect of other investment business had to ensure that their scope of business as authorised persons was wide enough to cover this area of activity. In practice, most custodians fell into the latter category.

1   The Financial Services Act 1986 (Extension of Scope of Act) Order 1996 (SI 1996/2958), made 25 November 1996, arts 1 and 2 in force 6 January 1997, remainder in force 1 June 1997.

2   Financial Services Act 1986, Sch 1, para 13A.

3   For example, the Bank of England was an exempted person, as were any entities fulfilling the requirements of SIB (the Securities and Investments Board Limited, now the Financial Services Authority, the 'FSA') in order to be a recognised investment exchange or recognised clearing house, and similar exemptions apply under the current legislation.

7.3 FSMA came into force on 30 November 2001 and, inter alia, replaced the previous regulatory regime under the Financial Services Act 1986 and the Banking Act 1987[1]. The basic structure of FSMA is much the same as the Financial Services Act 1986, namely that a person cannot carry on a 'regulated activity' in the UK, or purport to do so, unless they are an 'authorised person' or an 'exempt person'[2]. However, the regulated activities in question are not limited to the old investment business activities under the Financial Services Act 1986, but cover both functions formerly regulated as investment business and a wide range of other activities, including deposit-taking business[3]. Most of the detail of whether a particular activity is regulated under FSMA is contained in subsidiary legislation rather than in FSMA itself[4]. The implementation of MiFID with effect from 1 November 2007 was another major development (see paras **7.10–7.13** below), and further changes will result from the amendment of FSMA changing the relevant regulatory authority in the UK (see paras **7.6–7.9** below) and the replacement of MiFID by MiFID2 (see para **7.14**).

1   Both Acts were repealed by SI 2001/3649, arts 3(1)(c) and (d) respectively, with effect from 1 December 2001, and replaced by FSMA which came fully into force at midnight on 30 November 2001.
2   FSMA, s 19(1).
3   FSMA also covers activities such as insurance business (including in the context of Lloyds) and the activities of building societies and friendly societies.
4   In particular, the Financial Services and Markets Act 2000 (Regulated Activities) Order 2001 (SI 2001/544), as amended, discussed in paras **7.15–7.16** below.

7.4   As discussed in Chapter 1 the term 'custody' itself may be interpreted as meaning a range of activities, from the simple holding of a safe-deposit box, to the provision of a global securities handling and settlement service in numerous different jurisdictions, together with cash management, stocklending and other services. Consequently, for the purposes of FSMA (originally the Financial Services Act 1986), it is necessary to clarify the particular area of activity concerned. The text of the current legislation[1] refers to 'safeguarding of assets belonging to another' and 'the administration of those assets, or arranging for one or more other persons to carry on that activity', or agreeing to do the foregoing. It is important to note the conjunctive way in which this is worded, because the provision of either one of the elements of safeguarding (eg just providing a safe-deposit box) or administering (eg giving instructions in relation to assets held by a third party) on its own would not constitute investment business. Both elements have to be conducted together, and conducted in relation to the same investments[2].

1   See art 40 and art 64 of the Financial Services and Markets Act 2000 (Regulated Activities) Order 2001 (SI 2001/544) (the 'Regulated Activities Order').
2   A useful discussion of the regulators' approach to the meaning of 'safeguarding' and 'administration' was set out in the Guidance Release produced by the Securities and Investments Board Limited ('SIB', now the Financial Services Authority, the 'FSA') in June 1997 (SIB Guidance Release 5/97), although the list of functions set out in this Guidance is not exhaustive. This Guidance is old but still helpful in the context of current regulatory requirements: see further discussion below. See also art 43 of the Regulated Activities Order for the statement of what does not constitute the administration of assets for the purposes of art 40 (although as discussed in para **7.18** below, there are difficulties with this).

UK REGULATORY AUTHORITIES

Financial Services Authority

7.5   Under the regulatory structure under FSMA, the sole regulatory body is currently the Financial Services Authority (the 'FSA')[1], although this is in the process of changing (see paras **7.6–7.9** below). All relevant entities conducting regulated activities in the UK[2] therefore at present have to become authorised by the FSA (unless falling within a relevant exemption), and must comply with the relevant FSA Rules set out in the FSA Handbook. The Handbook consists of various sections (known as sourcebooks or manuals), different parts of which apply to the relevant regulated entities[3], depending on the type of activities carried out by such entities in the UK.

Certain sections apply to all regulated entities, such as the High Level Standards, and others have specific application, such as the Interim Prudential Sourcebook for Banks. At the time of writing the Handbook includes:

- High Level Standards: Principles for Businesses (PRIN); Senior Management Arrangements, Systems and Controls (SYSC); Threshold Conditions (COND); Statements of Principle and Code of Practice for Approved Persons (APER); The Fit and Proper Test for Approved Persons (FIT); Financial Stability and Market Confidence Sourcebook (FINMAR); Training and Competence (TC); General Provisions (GEN); and Fees Manual (FEES).

- Prudential Standards, including: General Prudential Sourcebook (GENPRU); Prudential Sourcebook for Banks, Building Societies and Investment Firms (BIPRU); Prudential Sourcebook for Insurers (INSPRU); Prudential Sourcebook for Mortgage and Home Finance Firms, and Insurance Intermediaries (MIPRU); Prudential Sourcebook for UCITS Firms (UPRU).

- Business Standards, including: Conduct of Business Sourcebook (COBS); Insurance: New Conduct of Business (ICOBS); Mortgages and Home Finance: Conduct of Business (MCOB); Banking: Conduct of Business Sourcebook (BCOBS); Client Assets (CASS); Market Conduct (MAR) (including Code of Market Conduct, Stabilisation rules, Support of the Takeover Panel's Functions, Multilateral Trading Facilities, Systematic Internalisers and Disclosure regarding trades outside a regulated market or MTF).

- Regulatory Processes: Supervision (SUP); and Decision Procedure and Penalties Manual (DEPP).

- Redress: Dispute resolution: Complaints (DISP); Compensation (COMP); and Complaints against the FSA (COAF).

- Specialist Sourcebooks: Building Societies sourcebook (BSOCS); Collective Investment Schemes (COLL); Credit Unions New sourcebook (CREDS); Professional Firms (PROF); Regulated Covered Bonds (RCB); and Recognised Investment Exchanges and Recognised Clearing Houses (REC).

- Listing, Prospectus and Disclosure: Listing Rules (LR); Prospectus Rules (PR); Disclosure and Transparency Rules (DTR).

- Various Handbook Guides for particular types of FSA regulated entities, including: Energy Market Participants (EMPS); Oil Market Participants (OMPS); and Service Companies (SERV).

- Regulatory Guides for particular subjects, including: The Building Societies Regulatory Guide (BSOG); The Collective Investment Scheme Information Guide (COLLG); The Credit Rating Agencies Guide (CRAG); The Perimeter Guidance Manual (PERG); The Responsibilities of Providers and Distributors for the Fair Treatment of Customers (RPPD); and the Unfair Contract Terms Regulatory Guide (UNFCOG).

1   This was not a wholly new entity created in December 2001, as the SIB existed under the earlier regime, but it changed its name, and was given much wider powers under FSMA, as well as replacing the functions of entities such as IMRO and the SFA. The FSA took over the control of the SFA and IMRO, and such entities legally ceased to exist on 1 December 2001.

2   Unless operating under an appropriate passport. See discussion in paras **7.145–7.150** below.

3   And some sections are of wider application, for example: the Market Conduct sourcebook giving guidance on what may be market abuse for the purposes of s 118 of FSMA; Chapter 5 of the Disclosure and Transparency Rules which is applicable to, broadly, any person holding voting rights in an issuers whose financial instruments are admitted to trading on a regulated market where the home state of the issuer for these purposes is the UK; the Listing Rules; and the Prospectus Rules.

Financial Conduct Authority and Prudential Regulatory Authority

7.6 In a major restructuring of the current regulatory regime, in 2013 relevant legislation[1] will effect the replacement of the FSA by two new regulatory bodies, namely the Prudential Regulatory Authority (the 'PRA') and the Financial Conduct Authority (the 'FCA'). The PRA will be a subsidiary of the Bank of England and will be responsible for prudential regulation of entities regarded as 'managing significant risks on their balance sheets' and requiring 'a sophisticated level of prudential regulation'[2] (broadly, deposit takers, insurance firms and some investment firms). The FCA will be an independent statutory body and will be responsible for 'ensuring that the relevant markets function well' and will have 'operational objectives focused on market integrity, consumer protection and effective competition'[3]. The FCA will therefore have responsibility for regulating the conduct of business of firms which are subject to the prudential regulation of the PRA, as well as responsibility for both the prudential regulation and the conduct of business of all other investments firms, exchanges and financial services providers. The FCA's functions will include certain functions currently performed by the FSA, such as acting as the UK Listing Authority and regulation of market abuse, as well new functions such as regulation of consumer credit arrangements. It is intended that a memorandum of understanding between the PRA and the FCA will set out a high level framework for coordination of the respective functions of the two regulators.

1   The Financial Services Bill sets out the relevant legislative changes, amending the Bank of England Act 1998, FSMA and the Banking Act 2009. The Bill was introduced into the House of Commons on 26 January 2012, received its second reading on 6 February 2012, and at the time of writing has gone through the report stage and third reading and is at the Committee stage in the House of Lords, and is currently expected to receive assent by the end of 2012 and to take effect in April 2013.

2   See Explanatory Notes prepared by HM Treasury in relation to the Financial Services Bill introduced in the House of Commons on 26 January 2012.

3   See n 2.

7.7 The Financial Policy Committee, a committee of the Bank of England, will have responsibility for prudential regulation at a high level, overseeing the stability and resilience of the UK financial system as a whole, and will have certain powers to direct and make recommendations to both the PRA and the FCA. The Bank of England itself will be responsible for prudential regulation of systemic infrastructure, namely clearing, payment and settlement systems.

7.8 In preparation for the new structure, the FSA introduced on 2 April 2012 a new regulatory approach involving a separate prudential supervisory team and conduct of business supervisory team so that firms who will in future be subject to regulation by both the FCA and the PRA could start the process of dealing with two regulatory teams (although firms who will be regulated only by the FCA deal only with the conduct of business supervisory team).

7.9 Although in many respects the FCA will have similar responsibilities to the FSA at present, current indications are that the FCA aims to take a much more rigorous approach to protection of consumers, particularly in review and approval of potential consumer products[1]. There will be new rulebooks for each of the PRA and the FCA; these are expected to be released in draft form in early 2013.

1   See the FSA Business Plan 2012/2013, in which the section entitled 'Regulatory reform' explains that under the dual regime introduced in April 2012, the supervisory approach of the conduct of business supervisory team (the precursor of the FCA) will change 'with a more focused approach to prudential and conduct issues and bolder, earlier intervention to tackle potential risk to consumers and market integrity'. See also www.fsa.gov.uk/about/what/reg_reform/fac-journey/faqs which

includes the comment that: 'It's clear that the FCA is being set up with an expectation that it will act sooner, and it will be more focused on how things affect consumers" and "regulation is going to be more intrusive overall'.

UK REGULATORY FRAMEWORK

MiFID and MiFID2

MiFID

7.10 MiFID[1] is the Directive which replaced the earlier Council Directive 93/22/EEC of 10 May 1993 on investment services in the securities field (the 'ISD')[2]. MiFID, and the 'Level 2' legislation (namely the MiFID implementing Directive[3] and the MiFID Regulation[4]), were required to be implemented into the local law of each European Economic Area ('EEA') member state with effect from 1 November 2007. The ISD, as its name suggests, related to investment services and was intended to harmonise to some extent the provision of such services, to make it easier for firms providing such services to do so in different member states within Europe. The scope of MiFID is much wider than the ISD in various respects; MiFID and the Level 2 legislation together contain considerably more detail than the ISD[5], therefore moving closer towards the result of achieving similar regulatory regimes for investment services in the EEA member states.

1   Directive 2004/39/EC of the European Parliament and of the Council of 21 April 2004 on markets in financial instruments. The ISD was amended several times before being replaced by MiFID.

2   MiFID is the ISD successor, hence in earlier literature on the subject MiFID is referred to as 'ISD2'.

3   Commission Directive 2006/73/EC of 10 August 2006 implementing Directive 2004/39/EC of the European Parliament and of the Council as regards organisational requirements and operating conditions for investment firms and defined terms for the purposes of that Directive (the 'MiFID implementing Directive').

4   Commission Regulation 1287/2006/EC of 10 August 2006 implementing Directive 2004/39/EC of the European Parliament and of the Council as regards recordkeeping obligations for investment firms, transaction reporting, market transparency, admission of financial instruments to trading, and defined terms for the purposes of that Directive (the 'MiFID Regulation'), adopted by the Commission in September 2006.

5   By way of example of the extension of scope: the categories of financial instruments to which MiFID applies include certain derivative contracts relating to commodities and concepts such as climatic variables and emission allowances; the giving of investment advice is a service within Section A (the equivalent of a core service under the ISD, whereas it was not a core service under the ISD); and MiFID requires regulatory regimes for multilateral trading facilities ('MTFs') and systematic internalisers. There are still certain categories of entity which are outside the scope of MiFID (including 'persons which provide investment services exclusively for their parent undertakings, for their subsidiaries or for other subsidiaries of their parent undertakings' (MiFID, art 2(1)(b)) and 'collective investment undertakings and pension funds whether coordinated at Community level or not and the depositaries and managers of such undertakings' (MiFID, art 2(1)(h)).

7.11 MiFID itself does not contain detailed requirements regarding the regulation of custody activities, simply requiring that EEA member states should require: (a) investment firms holding financial instruments for clients to 'make adequate arrangements so as to safeguard clients' ownership rights, especially in the event of the investment firm's insolvency, and to prevent the use of a client's instruments on own account except with the client's express consent'[1]; and (b) investment firms holding cash for clients to 'make adequate arrangements to safeguard the clients' rights and, except in the case of credit institutions, prevent the use of client funds for its own account'[2].

1   MiFID, art 13(7)

2   MiFID, art 13(8).

7.12 The MiFID implementing Directive contains more details regarding the obligations which EEA member states are required to impose on investment firms holding financial instruments and funds for clients. These detailed requirements are in the UK reflected in the relevant FSA rules (see paras **7.34–7.57** below) and relate to matters such as record-keeping, appointment and review of delegates, and certain disclosures and risk warnings[1].

1   See MiFID implementing Directive, arts 16 to 19, 32 and 43.

7.13 It is important to note that custody services are not always within the scope of the MiFID regime. Under MiFID, the safekeeping and administration of financial instruments is an ancillary service, and MiFID only applies to 'investment firms', meaning persons 'whose regular occupation or business is the provision of one more investment services to third parties and/or the performance of one or more investment activities on a professional basis'[1]. Investment services and activities are listed in Section A of Annex I of MiFID and do not include ancillary activities, therefore an entity providing custody services but no Section A services or activities is not within the scope of MiFID. Similarly, an entity which safeguards and administers assets which are not financial instruments would not be subject to MiFID requirements regarding custody (although given the broad definition of financial instruments[2] this is perhaps unlikely, unless holding, for example, only bullion or other metals, or real estate). In addition, a custodian is outside the scope of MiFID in certain other circumstances, notably if providing investment services exclusively to its parent, subsidiaries, or other subsidiaries of the same parent[3]. The question of whether a custodian's activities are subject to MiFID or not is important for the purposes of certain FSA rules applicable to custodians (see para **7.22** below).

1   MiFID, art 4(1)(1).
2   MiFID, Annex I, Section C.
3   MiFID, art 2(1)(b).

MiFID2

7.14 On 20 October 2011, the European Commission published the proposed draft of a new Directive intended to repeal MiFID and replace it with an updated form (generally referred to as MiFID2). At the time of writing, the text of MiFID2 is still under discussion; it is intended that the final form will be agreed by the end of 2012, but this seems more likely to occur sometime in the first half of 2013. To date the proposed drafts of MiFID2 contain the same general requirements regarding 'adequate arrangements' for the safeguarding of clients' rights to financial instruments and cash as in MiFID[1], and it is not clear that any amendments are proposed to the MiFID implementing Directive. However, a significant issue for custodians is the fact that under MiFID2 safekeeping and administration of financial instruments for clients is apparently intended to be changed from an ancillary service to a service within Section A of Annex I[2]. Arguably this goes beyond the overall purpose of this Directive since MiFID (and the ISD) were only intended to regulate activities relating to trading and transactions, not post-trade services such as custody and settlement. However, it is evident that making safekeeping and administration a core service is now regarded as an important aspect of investor protection. It could be said that the change is not significant on the basis that most jurisdictions already regulate custody activities in some way, and that this change will simply achieve consistency and encourage more harmonisation of custody regulation in Europe. Nevertheless, this is a major concern for any entity currently providing no Section A services, since such an entity is not currently within the scope of the MiFID regime but as a result of this change will become subject to the MiFID2 regime. This will result in such an entity being subject to all regulatory requirements implementing MiFID2 and the MiFID implementing Directive. This will also affect any exemptions from regulatory requirements currently available to custodians not within the scope of MiFID (see paras **7.20**, and **7.127–7.129** below).

1   But in addition a new provision will prohibit firms regulated under MiFID2 from taking collateral by way of title transfer from any retail client. This will affect custodians (and other firms) who provide services to retail clients.

2   Although the proposals are not entirely clear. The Cyprus EU Council Presidency text published on 5 November 2012 still includes custody as a core service (as is consistent with most of the preceding drafts) but the text adopted by the European Parliament on 26 October 2012 lists custody as an ancillary service.

Regulated activities

7.15 An activity is a regulated activity for the purposes of FSMA if it is 'an activity of a specified kind', is carried on by way of business, and either 'relates to an investment of a specified kind' or is an activity specified as regulated in relation to 'property of any kind'[1]. In order to determine whether an activity falls within the category of regulated activity, it is necessary to look at the relevant subsidiary legislation which (i) specifies the relevant kinds of activity and investment, namely the Financial Services and Markets Act 2000 (Regulated Activities) Order 2001, as amended (the 'Regulated Activities Order')[2], and (ii) determines whether the relevant activity is carried on by way of business, namely the Financial Services and Markets Act 2000 (Carrying on Regulated Activities by Way of Business) Order 2001, as amended[3]. The activities specified in the Regulated Activities Order include accepting deposits[4], effecting and carrying out contracts of insurance, dealing in investments as principal or agent, arranging deals in investments, managing investments, assisting in the administration and performance of a contract of insurance, establishing or operating a collective investment scheme, advising on investments, activities relating to Lloyd's syndicates, providing funeral plan contracts, entering into regulated mortgage contracts as lender, and entering into a regulated home reversion plan as plan provider, as well as safeguarding and administering investments. The term 'investment' is not defined, but the types of investment which are relevant for the purposes of the Regulated Activities Order are listed in arts 74–89 of that Order (although not all types are relevant for each specified activity).

1   FSMA, s 22.
2   SI 2001/544.
3   SI 2001/1177.
4   Subject to certain exemptions, in the Regulated Activities Order 'deposit' means 'a sum of money ... paid on terms (a) under which it will be repaid, with or without interest or premium, and either on demand or at a time or in circumstances agreed by or on behalf of the person making the payment and the person receiving it; and (b) which are not referable to the provision of property (other than currency) or services or the giving of security.' (art 5(2))

7.16 Pursuant to the Financial Services and Markets Act 2000 (Carrying on Regulated Activities by Way of Business) Order 2001, a person carries on the specified activity of accepting deposits 'by way of business' if he or she holds him or herself out as accepting deposits on a day-to-day basis, and the deposits are not 'accepted only on particular occasions'. For example, in relation to the specified activity of safeguarding and administering investments, as well as for dealing in investments as principal or agent, arranging deals (subject to certain exceptions[1]), managing investments, safeguarding and administering investments, sending dematerialised instructions, establishing or operating a collective investment scheme, establishing or operating a stakeholder pension scheme, advising on investments, or agreeing to provide any of these services, a person is not to be regarded as carrying on such activities by way of business 'unless he carries on the business of engaging in one or more such activities'. It should be noted that in this case it is not required that the person performing a particular specified activity should be engaging in *that* particular activity by way of business, nor is it necessary that the relevant activity which is engaged in by way of business should be carried out in the UK. In practice, in most cases it is likely to be difficult to rely on the argument that an activity is not carried out by way of business if such activity falls within in the Regulated Activities Order.

1   Broadly, in relation to Lloyds' syndicate capacity and syndicate membership.

Specified activities

7.17   Under the Regulated Activities Order the form of regulated activity which is informally called custody involves carrying out both safeguarding of assets belonging to another, and administration of such assets. Therefore carrying out only safeguarding or only administration will not of itself be subject to regulation. It is also a specified activity to arrange for such services to be provided, or to agree to do so. However, the action of *offering* to provide safeguarding and administering services is not an activity attracting regulation (it was prior to the FSMA regime, but the omission was arguably uncontentious in that it was never clear how relevant regulation would apply to the 'offering' on its own, other than by requiring any such offers to be made subject to the relevant rules regarding the issuance of investment advertisements or the making of unsolicited calls.)

Meaning of 'safeguarding' and 'administration'

7.18   The guidance regarding the meaning of 'safeguarding' and 'administration' as set out in the Guidance Release produced by the SIB (now the FSA) in June 1997[1] is still helpful in its discussion of the probable interpretation of such words[2]. For example, 'administration' is said to include 'any one or more of ... (a) maintaining accounts with clearing houses; (b) settling transactions in investments; (c) operating through depositories or sub-custodians in the United Kingdom or elsewhere; (d) operating nominee accounts, including pooled accounts, which identify each customer's assets in a ledger; (e) cash processing associated with customers' assets; (f) collecting and dealing with dividends and other income associated with the assets; (g) carrying out corporate actions such as proxy voting (including exercising rights conferred by an investment on behalf of the beneficial owner)'. It is also worth noting that the Regulated Activities Order itself (like the Financial Services Act 1986 previously) specifies certain actions which would *not* be regarded as administration, namely providing information on the number or value of assets held, converting currency or receiving documents in relation to assets held simply in order to forward such documents as instructed. However, this should be considered carefully in view of the fact that, as noted, the 1997 Guidance Release indicates that, for example, 'cash processing' or 'collecting and dealing with dividends' would be regarded as administration. In principle, it is difficult to see how an entity could hold assets and provide a currency conversion service, without also being regarded as providing a service involving 'cash processing' or 'collecting and dealing with dividends'. In practice, therefore, careful consideration should be given to the facts before relying on the argument that either safeguarding, or administration, is being provided, but not both.

1   Guidance Release 5/97 'Custody of Investments under the Financial Services Act 1986'.

2   See also the FSA's Perimeter Guidance Manual (PERG), 2.7.9G and 2.7.10G.

7.19 It is also important to note that the safeguarding and administration of assets cannot fall within art 40 of the Regulated Activities Order if the assets do not 'consist of or include any investment which is a security or contractually based investment'. For this purpose, 'security' means an investment within arts 76 to 82 of the Regulated Activities Order (or art 89 of the Regulated Activities Order if referring to investments within arts 76 to 82), broadly, shares, debt instruments, warrants, depositary receipts, fund units, or any right or interest in such assets, and 'contractually based investment' means, broadly, rights under insurance contracts which are not reinsurance contracts, options, futures, contracts for differences and funeral plan contracts, or any right or interest in such assets. As a result, custody of, for example, precious metals or of share certificates for shares which are not bearer shares, are not within the scope of art 40[1]. Moreover, although the Regulated Activities Order contemplates custody of items such as options, futures and contracts for differences, in practice it is unlikely that an entity providing custody services would wish to 'hold' such items as custodian, since these are contractual arrangements and the custodian would therefore have to enter into the relevant contract itself in order to hold the benefit of the contractual obligations, which would be unusual.

1   Note that PERG 2.7.9G is slightly confusing in this respect. It states, inter alia, that 'Safeguarding is acting as custodian of the property, for example, holding any documents evidencing the investments such as the share certificate'. The holding of a share certificate indeed constitutes the safeguarding of such share certificate, but in the common situation where the legal owner of the shares is the person whose name is entered on the share register as the holder of the shares, holding a share certificate does not constitute the safeguarding of the shares to which the share certificate refers. (The situation could of course be different if the shares were bearer shares.)

Nominees

7.20 In this context, consider also the position of a nominee. Usually, this would be little more than a shelf company with the bare minimum of assets and officials in order to be properly constituted as a company, but nevertheless being a separate legal entity in whose name registrable assets may be registered. Custodians usually use a nominee for the registration of assets held by the custodian for clients where a custodian wishes to provide added protection to its clients by registering registrable securities in a name separate from that of the custodian[1]. Although the nominee is not a substantial entity, it is legally holding the assets on behalf of another (normally the custodian, which in turn holds for the client). As a result, if it provides such service in the UK, the nominee would be regarded as providing to the custodian both safeguarding and administering services (since it both holds legal title and would legally be the entity responsible for operations such as receiving and forwarding dividends or exercising any voting rights). Consequently, such a nominee must, unless a relevant exemption applies, be authorised for regulatory purposes. Because such an authorisation requirement could be quite onerous for an insubstantial entity, the Regulated Activities Order (as also the Financial Services Act 1986 previously) provides an exception from the authorisation requirement which may apply to nominees. The exception[2] applies where a third party regulated for the provision of custody in the UK[3], with respect to the owner of the assets accepts responsibility for the activity of the nominee[4] which is no less onerous than the third party would have if it were safeguarding and administering the assets itself. It should be noted that for this exception to apply, the entity taking responsibility must be authorised to carry out safeguarding and administration functions within art 40 in the UK; the exception would not apply if a third party accepted liability but such third party was not authorised to carry out safeguarding and administration functions within art 40 in the UK.

1   See also the FSA Client Assets sourcebook (CASS) 6.2.3R which only permits a custodian to register client securities in the name of an entity other than the client or a nominee where the securities

144 *The Law of Global Custody*

are 'subject to the law or market practice of a jurisdiction outside the United Kingdom', therefore effectively necessitating the use of a nominee when holding securities issued by a UK company if registration in the name of the client is not possible.

2   SI 2001/544, art 41.

3   Authorised under FSMA or operating under passport arrangements (see paras **7.145–7.150** below).

4   Or other entity. The exception is not restricted to nominees, but this is the most likely situation in which it would apply, as a custodian would not normally wish to accept this level of liability for a third party with functions other than limited nominee functions.

Relevant rules

7.21   The relevant rules in relation to the conduct of custody business are set out in the FSA Client Assets sourcebook ('CASS') as well as certain sections of the FSA Conduct of Business sourcebook (the 'Conduct of Business Rules' or 'COBS'). CASS contains sections on collateral, custody of securities, client money, mandates (ie where an entity controls but does not hold client assets) and prime brokerage, and specific rules for insurance entities in relation to holding cash[1], and from 1 October 2012 the requirement regarding a CASS resolution pack[2]. COBS includes general provisions regarding client categorisation, information for clients and financial promotions which apply to custodians as well as other regulated entities. COBS also contains specific sections applicable to persons holding client securities or cash, covering matters such as risk warnings and statements.

1   CASS, Chapter 5, which applies to 'a firm that receives or holds money in the course of or in connection with its insurance mediation activity' (CASS 5.1.1R(1)).

2   See paras **7.121–7.122** below.

Context – MiFID business or non-MiFID business

7.22   From 1 November 2007 to 31 December 2008[1], there were two parallel sets of CASS rules, the application of which depended on, broadly, whether the regulated entity was holding client securities or cash in the context of MiFID business or holding such assets in the context of investment activities regulated under FSMA but not constituting MiFID business[2]. The approach in the two sets of rules was slightly different, as in general the rules implementing MiFID are less prescriptive but (arguably) less clear as a result. As from 1 January 2009, the MiFID and non-MiFID CASS chapters were combined, and for most purposes the same rules (based on the rules created to implement MiFID) now apply in both cases, but there are still some important differences. In particular, for both client securities and client money, in the context of non-MiFID business, assets held for affiliates must not be held subject to the rules which apply to holdings for other clients unless the affiliate holds the assets for its own client or the affiliate is treated as an arm's length client, whereas in the context of MiFID business client securities and client money held for affiliates must be subject to the same rules as for other clients. In relation to client money, it is not possible to agree an opt out of the FSA's Client Money Rules ('Client Money Rules' or 'CMR')[3] in the context of MiFID business, but firms holding client money in a non-MiFID context for a professional client are still permitted to agree with the client that the client money rules do not apply[4].

1   FSA Consultation Paper 08/6 'Review of the Client Assets sourcebook (CASS)' was published in March 2008, and followed by FSA Policy Statement 08/10 'Client Assets sourcebook (Common platform provisions) Instrument 2008' containing the final form of the amendments to the CASS rules to take effect as from 1 January 2009. The FSA intention was to simplify the CASS rules by deleting the specific non-MiFID chapters, and requiring all holders of client securities or client money to comply with the rules implementing MiFID.

2   The non-MiFID rules were essentially the FSA rules which applied to all FSA regulated custodians prior to the implementation of MiFID taking effect on 1 November 2007.

3   For the purposes of this chapter, CASS Chapters 7 and 7A.

4   See further discussion of client money rules at paras **7.58–7.116** below.

General principles and 'treating customers fairly'

7.23 General principles apply directly to all persons regulated by the FSA, and these affect the way in which a custodian provides its services. The FSA can impose sanctions if a firm is in breach of such Principles. The FSA Principles are part of the High Level Standards, and are very similar to the old SIB Principles made under the Financial Services Act 1986 regime, with the exception of the addition of the requirement (Principle 6) to 'pay due regard to the interests of customers and treat them fairly'. Arguably this new Principle goes beyond the idea of avoiding conflicts between the interests of clients, and introduces a more wide-ranging (and nebulous) concept of 'fairness', which may involve consideration of what is appropriate or suitable for customers, the need to avoid preferential treatment of one client in contrast with other clients and additional concepts.

7.24 It is also important to be aware that the FSA rules are subject to 'purposive interpretation'[1], meaning in principle that compliance with the letter of rules may not be sufficient if the relevant purpose has not also been considered.

1   GEN 2.2.1R: 'Every provision in the Handbook must be interpreted in the light of its purpose.' Note also GEN 2.2.2G: 'guidance may assist the reader in assessing the purpose of the provision, but it should not be taken as a complete or definitive explanation of a provision's purpose.'

7.25 Treating customers fairly ('TCF') is a major concern for the FSA, and is regarded by the FSA as 'central to our retail strategy'[1]. An initial discussion paper was published in 2001[2], followed by various further publications resulting in the FSA paper published in July 2006 entitled 'Treating customers fairly – towards fair outcomes for consumers' which set out 'six improved outcomes for retail consumers'[3] and stated that the FSA expected firms 'to make TCF an integral part of their business culture' and specifically to implement strategies to achieve the six outcomes by the end of March 2007. Not all firms providing services to retail clients were able to meet the March 2007 deadline, therefore, this was extended to December 2008.

1   'FSA update on the Treating Customers Fairly initiative and the December deadline', November 2008.

2   FSA Discussion Paper 7 'Treating customers fairly after the point of sale'.

3   Outcome 1: Consumers can be confident that they are dealing with firms where the fair treatment of customers is central to the corporate culture; Outcome 2: Products and services marketed and sold in the retail market are designed to meet the needs of identified consumer groups and are targeted accordingly; Outcome 3: Consumers are provided with clear information and are kept appropriately informed before, during and after the point of sale; Outcome 4: Where consumers receive advice, the advice is suitable and takes account of their circumstances; Outcome 5: Consumers are provided with products that perform as firms have led them to expect, and the associated service is both of an acceptable standard and as they have been led to expect; Outcome 6: Consumers do not face unreasonable post-sale barriers imposed by firms to change product, switch provider, submit a claim or make a complaint.

7.26 While Principle 6 applies to all clients of an FSA regulated firm, the focus of the TCF initiative is on services provided to retail clients. The FSA produced a new guidance section of the FSA Handbook in July 2007 entitled *The Responsibilities of Providers and Distributors for the Fair Treatment of Customers* ('RPPD') which 'is intended to be relevant to all regulated firms involved in the supply of products or services to consumers'[1] and states that reference to 'the 'customer' in this Guide' is 'a convenient name for the end-customer in the retail supply chain (which may include potential customers)'[2].

1 RPPD 1.7.
2 RPPD 1.11.

7.27 The status of the TCF outcomes and guidance is not immediately obvious, because although it is evidently of considerable importance to the FSA, there are no specific FSA rules requiring compliance with TCF rules. The FSA website[1] refers to Principle 6[2] as the key principle for TCF purposes, but also refers to Principles 2, 3, 7 and 9[3]. The FSA website also expresses the view that 'It is only through establishing the right culture that senior management can convert their good intentions into actual fair outcomes for consumers and ensure that delivery of those outcomes is sustainable.'[4] The FSA expects firms 'to be able to demonstrate that they are consistently treating customers fairly' by collecting management information, namely information to evidence and monitor how customers are treated[5]. In practice it seems that failure by a firm to reflect the TCF issues in its general approach to compliance (eg in the context of information provided to clients, training of staff who deal with clients, and follow-up with the client if client or market circumstances change) will be relevant when the FSA is considering whether a complaint against the firm should result in disciplinary action by the FSA[6].

1 See www.fsa.gov.uk/doing/regulated/tcf/who.
2 'A firm must pay due regard to the interests of its customers and treat them fairly.'
3 Principle 2: 'A firm must conduct its business with due skill, care and diligence.' Principle 3: 'A firm must take reasonable care to organise and control its affairs responsibly and effectively, with adequate risk management systems.' Principle 7: 'A firm must pay due regard to the information needs of its clients, and communicate information to them in a way which is clear, fair and not misleading.' Principle 9: 'A firm must take reasonable care to ensure the suitability of its advice and discretionary decisions for any customer who is entitled to rely upon its judgment.'
4 See www.fsa.gov.uk/doing/regulated/tcf/culture.
5 FSA publication 'Treating customers fairly – guide to management information', July 2007.
6 Consider, for example, the FSA announcement on 28 July 2008 that Hastings Insurance Services Ltd was fined £735,000 for failing to treat its customers fairly in relation to cancelling around 4,550 incorrectly priced car insurance policies. Although the firm had the legal right to cancel the relevant policies, and apparently gave some consideration to how to deal with the issue, the FSA considered that 'the way in which the policies were cancelled and the service that the firm gave to its customers following the cancellation showed the firm focussed on the financial cost to itself and did not properly consider the alternatives or the detrimental effect on customers' (FSA Press Release, 28 July 2008 (FSA/PN/080/2008)).

7.28 In this context, it is also important to be aware of the FSA's Unfair Contract Terms Regulatory Guide ('UNFCOG'). This provides guidance which 'explains the FSA's policy on how it will use its powers under the Unfair Terms Regulations'[1], since 'The FSA has powers as a qualifying body under the Regulations'[2]. The Unfair Terms Regulations apply 'with certain exceptions, to terms in contracts concluded between a seller or supplier and a consumer[3] which have not been individually negotiated'[4]. The FSA has powers under the Unfair Terms Regulations to consider the fairness of a contract if a consumer complains, or on the FSA's own initiative, and can request a firm to stop using unfair terms and, if necessary, seek an injunction to enforce this. UNFCOG 1.3.1G refers to the fact that under the Unfair Terms Regulations, terms cannot be regarded as unfair if they reflect '(a) mandatory statutory or regulatory provisions; or (b) the provisions or principles of international conventions to which the EEA States or the EU as a whole are party'[5]. Also, terms will not be regarded as unfair if 'written in plain, intelligible language' and relating to 'the definition of the main subject matter of the contract; or the adequacy of the price or remuneration, as against the goods or services supplied in exchange'[6]. The guidance specifically states that the FSA does 'not consider that it is enough that a lawyer could understand the term for it to be excluded from such a review. The term must be plain and intelligible to the consumer'[7]. UNFCOG Annex 1 gives FSA's views on the specific issue of when a unilateral variation clause would be fair. This guidance also explains that the FSA does not have the power under the Unfair Terms Regulations to compensate consumers, but consumers can complain to the relevant firm and seek redress, and can complain to the Financial Ombudsman Service if not satisfied with the firm's response. The FSA can exercise its usual powers if a term is unfair term and this constitutes breach of the FSA Rules[8].

1   UNFCOG 1.1.1G. The 'Unfair Terms Regulations' are the Unfair Terms in Consumer Contracts Regulations 1999 (SI 1999/2083), as amended by SI 2001/1186 and SI 2001/3649.
2   UNFCOG 1.2.3G.
3   For this purpose 'any natural person acting for purposes outside his trade, business or profession' (see FSA Glossary).
4   UNFCOG 1.3.1G(1).
5   UNFCOG 1.3.1G(2).
6   UNFCOG 1.3.1G(3).
7   UNFCOG 1.3.1G(3).
8   The FSA has indicated (although not in formal guidance) that unfair terms in a firm's consumer contracts will be treated as clear evidence that the firm is not treating customers fairly. By way of example of the FSA's approach to wording in consumer contracts, in a general statement published on 5 August 2008 (see www.fsa.gov.uk/pubs/other, 'Statement on using the words "consequential loss" in general insurance contracts'), the FSA expressed the view that the use of the term 'consequential loss' in general insurance contracts for consumers was not 'plain and intelligible' and therefore a provision using this term 'may be unfair under Regulation 5' of the Unfair Terms Regulations. See also the FSA Finalised Guidance 'Unfair contract terms: improving standards in consumer contracts', January 2012. This is guidance, not Handbook text, and is not an exhaustive list of unfair terms, but draws attention to terms which the FSA is likely to regard as unfair, including the right to vary a contract unilaterally, a discretion in the exercise of powers under a contract, and terms that are not in plain and intelligible language (giving as examples 'indemnify', 'tort', 'lien', 'consequential loss', 'force majeure' and 'time is of the essence' (para 3.35, p 11)).

7.29 Another very broad general requirement under the FSA rules which will apply to custodians as well as other regulated entities is the requirement to 'act honestly, fairly and professionally in accordance with the best interests of its clients'[1]. This applies specifically to all investment business for retail clients (see explanation of client classification in para **7.33** below), and to all categories of client in the context of MiFID business[2]. In addition, a regulated firm is prohibited from seeking to exclude or restrict any regulatory duty or liability to a client[3], and should not have, or rely on, any exclusion or limitation of liability in relation to a retail client unless 'honest, fair and professional' to do so[4].

1   COBS 2.1.1R(1).
2   COBS 2.1.1R(2).
3   COBS 2.1.2R.
4   COBS 2.1.3G.

Protection of client assets

7.30 The FSA Principle of particular relevance to custodians[1] is the Principle concerning client assets[2]. Under the old SIB Principles, the general requirement was to arrange 'proper' protection for client assets over which a regulated firm has control, whether by segregation and identification or otherwise 'in accordance with the responsibility it has accepted'. Under the FSA Principle, a firm is required to arrange 'adequate protection' where it is responsible for client assets. Despite the change in wording, it seems likely that both the old and new Principle are aimed at similar circumstances, namely where an entity regulated by the FSA is holding client assets as custodian, or is arranging for a third party to hold the client's assets, or has authority to give instructions to the client's custodian.

1   Although as noted above, Principle 6 is of increasing concern.

2   Principle 10, Clients' assets: 'A firm must arrange adequate protection for clients' assets when it is responsible for them'. (PRIN 2.1.1R)

7.31   In the context of significant market upheavals, including the aftermath of the liquidation of Bernard L Madoff Investment Securities, the lengthy insolvency proceedings for Lehmans Brothers International (Europe) and related entities, and the consequent increased perception of the risk of insolvency and the consequences thereof, there has been intense concern regarding the safety of client assets. The FSA has focused much effort on examination of the compliance by firms holding client assets with the current rules, imposing some very large fines for non-compliance and creating a number of new rules both for custodians and their auditors[1]. The FSA has also promised a 'comprehensive review' of client asset rules once the court cases analysing the application of client money rules are concluded, and indicated that such review may result in 'fundamental changes'[2].

1   Consider, for example: the general letter dated 20 March 2009 from the FSA to all Compliance Officers to remind them of the responsibility under Principle 10; the general letter dated 19 January 2010 from the FSA to all CEOs, drawing attention to the need for compliance with client asset requirements because the FSA was concerned that 'firms are not always achieving an adequate level of protection'; the FSA 'Client Money & Asset report', January 2010, which concluded that more must be done to ensure CASS compliance; the launch by the FSA in June 2010 of the Client Asset Sector, a specialist unit to increase focus on regulation of client assets (see FSA Policy Statement PS 10/16: 'Client Assets Sourcebook (Enhancements) Instrument 2010', October 2010); the restriction with effect from 1 December 2010 of the taking of title transfer collateral from retail clients (see FSA Consultation Paper 10/15 'Quarterly consultation (No. 25)', July 2010, and FSA Handbook Notice 104, November 2010); the introduction of the new controlled function of CASS operational oversight responsibility from 1 January 2011 (see FSA Policy Statement PS 10/16: 'Client Assets Sourcebook (Enhancements) Instrument 2010', October 2010); the limitation with effect from 1 June 2011 of the holding of client money with an entity in the same group to a maximum of 20 per cent (see FSA Consultation Paper 10/9 'Enhancing the Client Assets Sourcebook', March 2010, and FSA Policy Statement PS 10/16: 'Client Assets Sourcebook (Enhancements) Instrument 2010', October 2010); the new requirement as from 1 June 2011 for a Client Money and Assets Return ('CMAR') to the FSA (see FSA Policy Statement PS 10/16: 'Client Assets Sourcebook (Enhancements) Instrument 2010', October 2010, and FSA Policy Statement PS 11/6 'The Client Money and Asset Return (CMAR): Operational Implementation', May 2011); the new audit requirements from 1 June 2011 intended to improve auditors' client assets compliance reports (see FSA Policy Statement PS 11/5 'Auditor's client assets report', March 2011); restriction on the granting of lien and set-off rights over clients assets (from 1 April 2012 for all new agreements, and from 1 October 2012 for all agreements executed before 1 April 2012) (see FSA Consultation Paper CP 11/15 'Client assets sourcebook: (1) Custody liens (2) Title transfer collateral arrangements', July 2011, and FSA Policy Statement PS 10/16: 'Client Assets Sourcebook (Enhancements) Instrument 2010', October 2010, and FSA Policy Statement PS 12/2 'Client assets sourcebook: Custody liens', January 2012); the new requirements from October 2012 regarding 'Recovery and Resolution Plans' for all banks and 'significant investment firms', as well as *all* custodians, resulting in the new rules requiring certain information from custodians within 48 hours (see FSA Consultation Paper CP 11/16 'Recovery and Resolution Plans', August 2011, and FSA Policy Statement PS 12/6 'The CASS Resolution Pack', March 2012); and FSA Consultation Paper CP 12/22 'Client assets regime: EMIR, multiple pools and the wider review', September 2012, which among other things proposes certain changes to the pooling arrangements affecting client money on the insolvency of a firm (see paras **7.109–7.116**), as well as raising the possibility of future changes to the CASS rules generally, followed by FSA Policy Statement PS 12/23 'Client assets regime: changes following EMIR', December 2012 which sets out the changes to CASS to take effect from 1 January 2013.

2   See FSA Policy Statement PS 10/16: 'Client Assets Sourcebook (Enhancements) Instrument 2010', October 2010, and the FSA Business Plan 2012/2013 published March 2012. See also paras **7.159–7.161** below.

General provisions

7.32 In addition to the particular CASS and COBS rules and Principles which relate specifically to custody, a custodian will also need to bear in mind the other FSA sourcebooks which will be relevant, such as general COBS rules which apply to most firms regulated by the FSA, as well as the other areas of the Handbook which apply to specific aspects of business operations, such as senior management responsibilities or money laundering controls.

Client classification

7.33 Under COBS Chapter 3, a custodian, like any FSA regulated entity which is subject to the COBS rules, must categorise its custody client as a retail client[1], a professional client[2] or an eligible counterparty[3] (as such terms are defined in MiFID and incorporated in the FSA rules). Apart from a few exceptions[4], the CASS rules apply in much the same way whether a client is a retail client, a professional client or an eligible counterparty. However, in certain sections of the COBS rules, for example, the rules concerning risk warnings to custody clients, the requirements regarding retail clients are significantly more extensive[5].

1   A client which is neither a professional client nor an eligible counterparty.

2   There are detailed criteria which determine when a client may be categorised as a professional client ('per se' professional clients) as well as certain conditions permitting a client to be treated as a professional client if it does not otherwise qualify (broadly, persons with sufficient assets and/or expertise). In general, 'per se' professional clients include credit institutions, investment firms, insurance companies, collective investment schemes pension funds, commodity or commodity derivatives dealers, national or regional governments, central banks, and international or supranational institutions, as well as entities meeting certain conditions as to size (broadly, in terms of balance sheet and turnover).

3   In general (subject to the conditions permitting a professional client to be treated as an eligible counterparty if it does not otherwise qualify, broadly where persons have sufficient assets and/or expertise), this means investment firms, credit institutions, insurance companies, collective investment schemes authorised under the UCITS Directive, pension funds, national governments, central banks, and supranational organisations. Under the FSA COBS rules, an eligible counterparty is a type of professional client which for the purposes of certain rules has the benefit of the eligible counterparty exemptions, but for the purposes of CASS, an eligible counterparty is treated in the same way as any other professional client (this is rather different from the position prior to 1 November 2007, where there was a concept of 'market counterparty' for which certain FSA custody rules were disapplied). As a result, if a custody client is an eligible counterparty, the CASS rules will apply in the same way as for other professional clients, but certain parts of the COBS rules are disapplied (see COBS 1, Annex 1, Part 1, Section 1) in relation to custody services to the extent such services are directly related to dealing or the execution, receipt or transmission of orders, for example, rules requiring 'appropriate information' about the services to be provided to the client (COBS 2.2.1R), disclosure regarding fees and commissions (COBS 2.3.1R), record-keeping (COBS 8.1.4R), certain risk warnings (COBS 6.1.7R) and statements to clients (COBS 16.4.1R).

4   Although some exceptions can be quite significant, for example, the requirement to seek 'prior written consent' from retail clients, rather than simply notifying professional clients, where securities are to be registered in the name of the custodian (CASS 6.2.3R(4)(b), see further at paras **7.49–7.56** below).

5   See COBS 6.1.7R.

Custody services

7.34 As noted in paras **7.21–7.22** above, the main FSA rules applicable to custodians are set out in the CASS sourcebook (as well as certain sections of the COBS sourcebook). Particular aspects are considered in the following paragraphs.

Sub-custodians

7.35 In CASS Chapter 6, section 6.3, there is a generic reference to the holding of client securities with a 'third party'. This term is not defined and while in principle the types of sub-custodian, nominee or settlement system which may be used are not restricted, there are additional requirements which apply, in particular the following:

(1) A custodian may hold client securities with a third party 'only if it exercises all due skill, care and diligence in the selection, appointment and periodic review of the third party and of the arrangements for the holding and safekeeping of those safe custody assets'[1]. Prior to MiFID implementation[2], a client could instruct the custodian to hold client securities other than as required by the relevant CASS rules and in such case the custodian was required to notify the client that 'the consequences of doing so are at the client's own risk, unless the firm has agreed otherwise'[3]. It is not uncommon to find that wording reflecting the old CASS rule has been retained in custody terms, but there is no equivalent under CASS Chapter 6, therefore, in principle, regardless of what the custodian and client may intend, the CASS rules do not permit the client to instruct the custodian to hold assets other than in accordance with the CASS rules. As a result, the custodian will remain responsible for selecting, appointing and reviewing the relevant sub-custodian with all due skill, care and diligence in all cases. It should also be noted that this requirement applies to *all* types of third party appointed to hold client assets, whether such a third party is a nominee, a settlement system or another custodian entity. Thus, even if a custodian agrees in its custody terms different levels of liability for different types of delegate, as a regulatory matter, this rule will apply equally in such cases, subject to what may be considered to be an appropriate level of care constituting 'due skill, care and diligence' in each such case.

(2) A custodian can only deposit client assets with a third party if: (a) the deposit is with the third party in a jurisdiction 'which specifically regulates and supervises the safekeeping of safe custody assets for the account of another person' and the third party is 'subject to such regulation'[4]; or (b) where the deposit is with a third party 'in a country that is not an EEA State ... and which does not regulate the holding and safekeeping of safe custody assets for the account of another person', if the nature of the client securities or of 'the investment services connected with' such securities 'requires' that the securities are deposited with such third party, or the client is a professional client (see further discussion of client classification in para **7.33** above) and the client requests the custodian in writing to hold the securities with such third party[5]. This constitutes a restriction on the types of sub-custodian, nominee, settlement system or other third party through which a custodian may hold client assets. A custodian may in practice generally use regulated entities as its delegates, but in some cases the extent of the restrictions may not be altogether clear. For example, in relation to (a), can we argue that a custodian should not be prevented from using a delegate in a jurisdiction which regulates custody where the delegate is exempt from such regulation (arguably such entity is 'subject to' the relevant regulation although not itself a regulated entity)? Also, it is debateable in what circumstances the nature of securities or connected investment services (query by or to whom such services should be provided) 'require' use of a particular entity in an unregulated jurisdiction. In certain structures, it may be the case that the securities simply cannot be held in any other way, but in other cases it may be possible to hold in another way but it may be very expensive or administratively complex to do so. It is not clear whether both such scenarios would be regarded as a situation where the securities are *required* to be held in this way, although at least in the case of professional clients any uncertainty can be resolved if the client makes a written request.

(3) A custodian is only permitted to grant lien and set-off rights over client assets in favour of third parties in very limited circumstances (see paras **7.41–7.44** below).

1   CASS 6.3.1R(1).

2   And under CASS Chapter 2 prior to 1 January 2009, see para **7.22** above.

3   CASS 2.3.11R (deleted with effect from 1 January 2009).

4   CASS 6.3.4R(1).

5   CASS 6.3.4R(2). Note that CASS 6.3.4R(1) and (2), respectively, follow the wording used in art 17(2) and (3) of the MiFID implementing Directive (Commission Directive 2006/73/EC, see further para **7.10** n 3 above), where (2) refers to 'safekeeping' and (3) refers to 'holding and safekeeping', but it is not apparent that this different terminology is intended to have any particular consequences.

Content of custody agreements

7.36 As regards the custody terms in place between a custodian and client, under the old CASS Chapter 2 for non-MiFID custody, the basic requirement was that a custodian 'must notify the client as to the appropriate terms and conditions which apply to this service, including, where applicable', a list of certain specified provisions[1].

1   CASS 2.3.2R (deleted with effect from 1 January 2009).

7.37 CASS Chapter 6 takes a different approach, as there is no specific requirement to have a custody agreement containing a list of particular terms. However, under the COBS rules, there are requirements to 'provide appropriate information in a comprehensible form to a client about' various matters, including 'the firm and its services' and 'designated investments and proposed investment strategies; including appropriate guidance on and warnings of the risks associated with investments in those designated investments or in respect of particular investment strategies ... so that the client is reasonably able to understand the nature and risks of the service and of the specific type of designated investment that is being offered and, consequently, to take investment decisions on an informed basis'[1]. In addition, a retail client must be provided with an agreement 'setting out the essential rights and obligations of the firm and the client', either before or immediately after the client is bound by the agreement[2], and a firm is also required to 'provide a client with a general description of the nature and risks of designated investments, taking into account, in particular, the client's categorisation as a retail client or professional client'[3]. Certain general information must be provided to retail clients[4], and also specific risk warnings for custody clients[5]. This approach is less prescriptive but also gives less guidance regarding the nature of the terms which as a regulatory matter should be included in the custody terms. In practice, global custody agreements have not changed radically in content, since the terms included are generally those which are appropriate to set out the scope of the services to be provided, and are expected by clients in this market. However, in specialised structured arrangements where a custody service forms part of a wider complex of documentation, the greater flexibility of terms is of some assistance in creating terms which are better tailored to the nature of the particular structure (except of course in situations where documentation is simply duplicated from earlier deals without regard to the regulatory context). Nonetheless, because of the broader rules which now apply, there remains the potential risk that in the event of a dispute by a client, it would be open to the FSA to conclude that on the facts the relevant terms were not 'appropriate', particularly in the context of a retail client, and to raise questions as to whether the clients were treated fairly (see paras **7.23–7.28** above).

1   COBS 2.2.1R(1), although this does not apply where the client is an eligible counterparty.
2   COBS 8.1.2R.
3   COBS Chapter 14, Section 14.3. Note this does not apply where the client is an eligible counterparty.
4   COBS 6.1.4R, 6.1.9R.
5   COBS 6.1.7R, although only certain of the specific warnings are required for professional clients and no such warnings are required for eligible counterparties.

Protection of client assets

7.38   In CASS Chapter 6 (rules relating to securities), a custodian is required to 'make adequate arrangements so as to safeguard clients' ownership rights, especially in the event of the firm's insolvency, and to prevent the use of safe custody assets belonging to a client on the firm's own account except with the client's express consent'[1]. Also, a custodian 'must introduce adequate organisational arrangements to minimise the risk of the loss or diminution of clients' safe custody assets, or the rights in connection with those safe custody assets, as a result of the misuse of the safe custody assets, fraud, poor administration, inadequate record-keeping or negligence'[2]. These provisions simply copy out the corresponding wording in MiFID[3], and the MiFID implementing Directive[4], respectively, but the effect of such rules in this form is not entirely clear. There would seem little point for such rules if they can be satisfied by simply complying with the other rules regarding, for example, segregation of client assets, use of client assets and record-keeping, but it is hard to see what additional steps are required for the purposes of compliance. In principle, there is a risk that even if a custodian has acted in accordance with other applicable FSA rules, and taken relevant steps in accordance with appropriate market practice at the time, an event such as loss of client assets in the insolvency of the custodian, or as a result of fraud or inadequate record-keeping (not necessarily that of the custodian), could of itself be regarded as a breach of these rules.

1   CASS 6.2.1R.
2   CASS 6.2.2R.
3   MiFID, art 13(7).
4   MiFID implementing Directive, art 16(1)(f).

Stock lending

7.39   CASS also contains rules regarding use of client assets and stock lending. In CASS Chapter 6[1], the use of client assets for 'securities financing transactions' (a wide definition covering both stock lending and repos) 'or otherwise' requires 'express prior consent' from the client, which is required to be obtained from *all* categories of client (although only in relation to retail clients is it specified that such consent must involve providing a signature or 'equivalent alternative mechanism'). Similarly, where client securities are held on a pooled basis, any client, regardless of categorisation, whose assets are held in the pool must give express prior consent to use of such securities for securities financing transactions or otherwise, unless 'the firm has in place systems and controls which ensure that only financial instruments belonging to clients who have given express prior consent … are used'[2].

1   CASS Chapter 6, Section 6.4. See MiFID implementing Directive, art 19.
2   CASS 6.4.1R(2).

7.40   It is important to note that such rules are relevant not just where the custodian and its client have clearly agreed to transactions described as securities lending or repos. Similar issues would arise where the parties are entering into arrangements which achieve the same result. The most obvious example of this is what is known as contractual settlement, where a custodian holding assets or cash for a client agrees to credit the client's securities account or cash account with the relevant securities or cash on the date such assets are due to be received by the client, whether or not such assets are actually received[1]. In relation to cash, this arrangement is in effect allowing the client to borrow the relevant cash from the custodian by making credit available to such circumstances. Where securities are made available, a loan of securities by the custodian to the client is taking place, presumably to be reversed once the relevant securities are received by the custodian for the account of the client. (A similar situation arises if the client has granted the custodian a security interest over the cash and/or securities, together with a right of use[2], and the custodian then exercises such right of use to remove the relevant cash or securities from the client account.) The question to be asked in relation to the loan of securities is where the securities for the loan are provided from, since they may be the custodian's own securities, or may be provided from the pooled securities of the relevant type held by the custodian for other clients. If the second scenario is true, the custodian must ensure that the other clients entitled to such assets have been notified, or have given consent, as appropriate.

1   See also Chapter 4 for a discussion of contractual settlement. The contractual settlement of securities is less common than in relation to cash.

2   Under English law, only possible if the security is a security financial collateral arrangement for the purposes of the Financial Collateral Regulations (see Chapter 4, paras **4.55–4.56** and paras **4.91–4.92**).

Lien and set-off rights

7.41   Under the rules in CASS 6.3.5R to 6.3.9R (effective from 1 April 2012 for all new agreements, and from 1 October 2012 for all existing agreements), a custodian cannot grant 'a lien, or a right of retention or sale' over client securities or 'a right of set-off over any client money derived from' client securities, in favour of any third party unless a relevant exception applies (CASS 6.3.5R). There are three exceptions, namely:

(1) if the lien or right of retention or sale is over securities in one account with the third party and covers only 'properly incurred charges and liabilities arising from the provision of custody services in respect of safe custody assets held in that account.' (CASS 6.3.6R(1)); *OR*

(2) if the lien or right of retention or sale 'arises under the operating terms of a securities depository, securities settlement system or central counterparty in whose account safe custody assets are recorded or held, and provided that it does so for the purpose only of facilitating the settlement of trades involving the assets held in that account' (CASS 6.3.6R(2)); *OR*

(3) if the lien or right of retention or sale 'arises in relation to those safe custody assets held in a jurisdiction outside the United Kingdom' and is 'a result of local applicable law in that jurisdiction or is necessary for that firm to gain access to the local market in that jurisdiction', and the firm has 'taken reasonable steps to determine that holding those assets subject to that lien or right is in the best interests of that client' (or the client is a professional client who has instructed the firm to hold assets in the relevant jurisdiction 'notwithstanding the existence of that lien or right') (CASS 6.3.6R(3)).

7.42   These rules are curious in several respects. They are not derived from any provision of MiFID or the MiFID implementing Directive, except to the extent they may be regarded as resulting from the general requirement under MiFID[1] to maintain adequate arrangements for the safeguarding of clients' rights to custody assets. Moreover, in principle, the existence of any such rights over client assets is already covered by the requirement in COBS 6.1.7R(2) to disclose to the client the existence of the any security interest or lien, or right of set-off, of the firm or a depositary over the client's securities or client money (this rule applies to retail clients but is also extended to professional clients by COBS 6.1.7R(4) as required by the MiFID implementing Directive[2]).

1   MiFID, arts 13(7) and 13(8).
2   MiFID implementing Directive, arts 29(3) and 32(6).

7.43   As may be seen, these rules refer to liens, rights of retention or sale, and set-off, but not to security interests. However, the cautious approach is to assume that the restriction applies to security interest in the same way. The result is that if a particular structure requires rights to be granted over client assets to a third party, and no relevant exemption applies, the rights will need to be granted by the client itself. This may raise issues with the structuring and documentation for the relevant transaction, since the client can only grant rights over the assets to which it has rights (namely the interest[1] in the assets held by the custodian), rather than over the assets to which the custodian has rights (the rights against the third party).

1   Under English law probably a beneficial interest under a trust, see Chapter 3.

7.44   Technically the restrictions do not apply to set-off rights granted in respect of all client money, but only to client money derived from a safe custody assets subject to these rules. This presents difficulties, because a custodian is unlikely to record cash derived from custody assets (such as dividends or other income, or proceeds of sale) in a separate account holding only those amounts, therefore in practice the restriction would apply to all client money held for a client, unless the custodians' (and third party's) systems are capable of indentifying client money derived from client securities as distinct from other client money. (This issue does not of course arise where the custodian is bank holding cash for the client in an account with itself, because although the restriction on granting liens, rights of retention (and, as noted above, security interests) will apply, the custodian does not hold client money[1].)

1   See para **7.62**.

Maintenance of records

7.45   CASS Chapter 8 contains specific rules relating to the situation where a regulated firm does not hold assets (ie the relevant securities are not recorded in the name of the firm or its delegate), but is authorised to give instructions to the holder of the assets (ie the client's custodian) under a suitable mandate from the client. A typical situation would be where an investment manager is authorised by the client to act as agent of the client and in such capacity to give instructions to the client's custodian. The provisions of CASS Chapter 8 essentially focus on the maintenance of adequate records, and include a specific requirement to safeguard any documents of the client held by the regulated firm in connection with the mandate. Although the scope of Chapter 8 seems relatively straightforward, there has apparently been some uncertainty regarding the circumstances to which it applies. The FSA has therefore concluded that amendments to clarify the scope of this chapter are appropriate[1], but do not intend that the new rules will change the effect of this chapter, but simply make it clearer when such chapter applies.

1   New rules in force as from 1 January 2012, see FSA Consultation Paper CP 12/15 'Client Assets: Firm Classification, Oversight, Reporting and the Mandate Rules', July 2012.

Risk warnings

7.46 CASS 6.2.3R requires notice to be given to clients where client securities are registered in the name of the custodian or a third party (see further discussion of registration of title in paras **7.49–7.56** below), and prior written consent must be obtained from retail clients (but not professional clients or eligible counterparties) to registration in the name of the custodian itself, but there is no provision contemplating clients instructing the custodian to register the securities in a manner not required by the rules and at the client's own risk[1]. Other risk warning requirements are now set out in the relevant section of COBS, in particular COBS 6.1.7R, the terms of which follow the relevant articles in the MiFID implementing Directive[2]. The requirements of COBS 6.1.7R do not apply where a client is an eligible counterparty, and do not require notification to any client that a sub-custodian may be an entity in the same group as the custodian, or to a professional client that client securities are held in an omnibus account (although it is prudent (and not uncommon) to do so for the reasons discussed in relation to risk disclosure in Chapter 6).

1   CASS 6.2.3R(3), (4). Unlike under the old CASS 2.3.11R (deleted with effect from 1 January 2009).
2   Commission Directive 2006/73/EC, arts 29(3), 30(1)(g) and 32.

7.47 The notifications required to professional clients are minimal, namely warning that accounts containing client assets are subject to the laws of non-EEA states and that the rights of the client in relation to such assets 'may differ accordingly'[1], and notifying of any security interest, lien or set-off rights which the custodian or 'a depositary' may have over the client assets[2].

1   COBS 6.1.7R(1)(d); 6.1.7R(4).
2   COBS 6.1.7R(2); 6.1.7R(4). Note that this refers to set-off rights as well as liens or security interests. In practice, a custodian is likely to wish to set out the scope of its own lien, security interest and set off rights in detail for the purposes of contractual clarity, and should also ensure that it has authority to grant such rights (subject to the restrictions discussed in paras **7.41–7.44** above) to any third party holding the client assets as delegate of the custodian otherwise the client may claim that the grant of such rights is outside the custodian's authority and a breach of the custody agreement (in such a case, the custodian would have strict liability for any loss to the client resulting from the existence of such rights). (Note also that the reference in COBS 6.1.7R(2)(b) is to disclosure of the rights which a 'depositary' may have, which reflects the use of the term 'depositary' in the MiFID implementing Directive, art 32(6). This term is not defined in the Directive, and is probably an error, since the term 'depositary' was used in earlier drafts in each case where the term 'third party' is now used (eg when imposing the obligation to select with due skill, care and diligence). Although technically beyond the requirement of COBS 6.1.7R(2)(b), a custodian would be well advised to make the relevant disclosure in relation to all third parties, not just depositaries, who have relevant rights over client assets for the reasons discussed in this footnote.)

7.48 The warnings to retail clients are extensive, and potentially of considerably wider scope than the warnings under the old non-MiFID CASS rules. For example, COBS 6.1.7R(1)(a) requires a custodian to notify a retail client 'if applicable, (i) that the designated investments or client money of that client may be held by a third party on behalf of the firm; (ii) the responsibility of the firm under the applicable national law for any acts or omissions of the third party; and (iii) the consequences for the client of the insolvency of the third party'. This could be interpreted as requiring notification to the client of the liability (if any) which the custodian accepts for the sub-custodian, but in (ii) it is not clear whether 'applicable national law' means the relevant law applicable to the firm or to the third party. Similarly, (iii) may mean that the custodian should clearly state what liability it accepts in the insolvency of sub-custodians, or could be interpreted as requiring the custodian to explain to the client the effects of insolvency procedures in another jurisdiction which would be an onerous obligation. Another example is COBS 6.1.7R(1)(e), which requires a custodian to give the retail client 'a summary description of the steps which it takes to ensure the protection of any designated investments belonging to the client or client money it holds, including summary details of any relevant investor compensation or deposit guarantee scheme which applies to the firm by virtue of its activities in an EEA State'. The provision of a summary regarding deposit protection schemes is relatively straightforward, but it is not clear what is required by way of protection summary, whether this requires a summary of security processes, disaster recovery arrangements, control arrangements with delegates, or something else.

Registration of title

7.49 The pre-MiFID CASS rules contained specific rules regarding the way in which a custodian was required to register client securities[1] in the relevant record of title (note that this means the register or other record which gives the named person legal title, rather than an account entry on the books of the custodian or its delegates). These rules appear in CASS Chapter 6 in substantially the same form[2], even though there is no corresponding requirement in MiFID or the MiFID implementing Directive. Some aspects of these rules are slightly odd; therefore it is worth considering them further.

1   CASS 2.2.10R (deleted with effect from 1 January 2009).
2   Substantially similar but not identical. CASS 6.2.3R.

7.50 In both the pre-MiFID CASS rules and the current CASS rules, there are four permitted options for registration. Under the current rules, very broadly, securities must be registered in the name of (a) the client; or (b) a nominee company (a company whose only business is to act as nominee); or (c) any third party[1]; or (d) the custodian itself. This requirement only applies 'to the extent practicable', but since the underlying reason for such rule is evidently to protect the client's assets from being confused with other assets, it is not clear in what circumstances a custodian would be able to rely on an argument that registration as required was not 'practicable' in order to disapply this rule.

1   Note that there is no requirement in CASS 6.2.3R(3) that this must be an entity to which the custodian has delegated the holding of securities, ie the third party in whose name the securities are registered could be the regulated firm's sub-custodian, or an entity appointed by such sub-custodian, or its sub-delegate.

7.51 Since securities are frequently held through delegates, situations where it is possible for securities to be registered in the name of the client are not usual.

7.52 Registration in the name of a nominee is common, but the particular requirements of the CASS rules should be noted carefully. The nominee must be a 'nominee company' as explained in para **7.50** above, and must be controlled by the custodian itself, or by one of its affiliated companies, or by a recognised investment or designated investment exchange, or by a third party appointed by the custodian to hold client assets. In some senses, it is hard to see the logic of the reference to recognised or designated investment exchanges, since it is not clear in what circumstances such exchanges would control nominee companies; the exchanges are systems for entering into trades not for settlement or holding of the relevant securities. Also, where registered securities are held by a custodian through a settlement system, such that the securities are ultimately registered on the record of title in the name of a nominee company controlled by the settlement system or by a depositary holding on behalf of the settlement system, it may not be clear whether the nominee is within the definition of 'nominee company'. Even if it is, it may not be obvious that such securities are registered in accordance with the requirement regarding nominee companies. It is also important to note that if the custodian relies on the ability to register securities in the name of a nominee controlled by a 'third party', that third party must have been appointed by the custodian as a delegate[1].

1   CASS 6.2.3R(2)(d).

7.53   A custodian is only permitted to register a security in the name of 'any other third party'[1], or in the name of the custodian itself, if such security is 'subject to the law or market practice of a jurisdiction outside the United Kingdom and the firm has taken reasonable steps to determine that it is in the client's best interest to register or record it in that way, or it is not feasible to do otherwise, because of the nature of the applicable law or market practice'[2]. The reference to 'any other third party' without a requirement for the custodian to have appointed such entity is helpful, because where securities are held through a chain of intermediaries, the third party in whose name the securities are registered may not necessarily have been appointed by the custodian. A point which is not so clear is the fact that to be registered in this manner a security must be 'subject to the law or market practice of a jurisdiction outside the United Kingdom'. This could be interpreted as meaning securities which are issued under the law of a jurisdiction outside the UK, but it is not clear that such an interpretation would be correct. For example, if securities issued by a company incorporated under the laws of England and Wales are held through a non-UK settlement system, arguably such securities have become subject to the law or practice of the jurisdiction where the settlement is located. This approach reflects the realities of the situation, because in such case it will not be possible for the custodian to control the name in which the settlement system arranges for the securities to be registered. Arguably the same approach should apply where a custodian uses a non-UK sub-custodian for the same reasons. However, even if such requirements of the rules can be regarded as satisfied, a custodian will still need to consider carefully whether it is in the client's best interest to register or record in this way, or not feasible to do otherwise, and how the custodian can demonstrate that it has taken reasonable steps to determine this.

1   Note that there is no requirement that this third party must be an entity to which the custodian itself has delegated the holding of securities, ie the entity could be appointed by a delegate or sub-delegate of the custodian.
2   CASS 6.2.3R(3), (4).

7.54   The custodian must also notify the client in writing where securities may be registered in the name of a third party or the custodian.

7.55   Where registration is in the name of the custodian, the custodian must obtain prior written consent from retail clients, and an additional risk warning (a 'prominent warning of the resulting risks') must be given (to retail clients only) if 'it is not possible under national law for designated investments belonging to a client held with a third party to be separately identifiable from the proprietary designated investments of that third party or of the firm'[1].

1   COBS 6.1.7R(1)(c).

7.56   The pre-MiFID rules contained an additional provision, permitting registration of client securities in the name of 'any other person, in accordance with the client's specific written instruction' provided that the custodian had warned the client that (unless otherwise agreed) this was at the client's own risk, and provided that such other person was not an associate of the custodian[1]. There is no equivalent of this provision in the current CASS rules.

1   CASS 2.2.10R(5); CASS 2.3.11R (deleted with effect from 1 January 2009).

Affiliates

7.57 Although CASS Chapter 6 applies for most purposes to custody provided in the context of both MiFID business and non-MiFID business, there are still some differences in approach, in particular in relation to services provided to affiliates. In the context of non-MiFID business, where a custodian holds securities on behalf of an affiliated company, CASS Chapter 6 does not apply unless the custodian has been notified that the securities belong to clients of the affiliated company, or the affiliated company is an arm's length client[1]. In contrast, for custody services provided in the context of MiFID business, the fact that a client is an affiliated company does not make any difference to the application of the custody rules[2]. A similar approach is taken in the client money rules (CASS Chapter 7), where the rules do not apply to client money held for affiliated companies (subject to certain similar exceptions) in the context of non-MiFID business[3], whereas in the context of MiFID business there is no such disapplication and a guidance note states that where client money is held for affiliated companies, the firm 'must treat the affiliated company as any other client'[4]. It is understood that the reason for the pre-MIFID approach was to limit the custody client's exposure to risks which arise in connection with members of the same group as the custodian. For example, if the custodian is insolvent and client assets (including assets of an affiliate of the custodian) are held by the custodian in an omnibus account, a shortfall may arise because settlement of the affiliate's transaction has been reversed but the affiliate is also now insolvent (not unlikely if the whole group is in financial difficulties) and cannot provide replacement assets. However, neither MiFID nor the MiFID implementing Directive provides for disapplication or variation of custody protections for affiliates, therefore the FSA has no authority to take the pre-MiFID approach in relation to MiFID business[5]. Arguably therefore this is an example of a situation where the MiFID regime weakens the protections of the rules which previously applied. It is certainly more onerous for entities who only hold securities or client money for companies within the same group in the context of MiFID business and who as a result of this change in approach have become subject to both the client money rules and the custody rules[6].

1   CASS 6.1.10AG.
2   CASS 6.1.10G.
3   CASS 7.1.12AR.
4   CASS 7.1.12G.
5   The FSA proposed in CP 08/6 to remove the non-MiFID approach for affiliates, but there was apparently considerable feedback objecting to this, hence the revisions to the CASS rules in PS 08/10 retained the relevant provisions for both client money rules and the custody rules in a non-MiFID context.
6   Unless of course such entities are within the scope of the exemption applicable under MiFID to persons providing investment services exclusively to group entities.

Client money[1]

7.58 The MiFID rules respecting client money (CASS Chapter 7) were created in much the same form as the pre-MiFID client money rules (CASS Chapter 4)[2], unsurprisingly, since MiFID and the MiFID implementing Directive do not contain much detail regarding the holding of client money. The essence of the protection for clients under the client money rules[3] is that client money will be held by the regulated entity in an account with an appropriate bank[4] and that such money will be held by the regulated entity on trust[5]. The client money account must also be segregated from money belonging to the firm, in that the client money account can only be used to hold client money (apart from certain exceptions)[6]. This means that the client money is protected in the insolvency of the regulated entity, although the client is still exposed to the credit risk of the relevant bank with which the regulated entity holds the cash[7].

1   See the discussion of custody cash accounts in Chapter 3.
2   The pre-MiFID client money rules were developed from the earlier client money rules of SIB.
3   For the purposes of this discussion, the focus is on CASS Chapter 7, rather than CASS Chapter 5 (client money in the context of insurance mediation activity).
4   A central bank, a BCD credit institution ('a credit institution that has its registered office (or, if it has no registered office, its head office) in an EEA State, excluding an institution to which the BCD [Directive 2006/48/EC of the European Parliament and the Council of 14 June 2006 relating to the taking up and pursuit of the business of credit institutions] does not apply under article 2 of the BCD'), or a bank authorised in a third country. (CASS 7.4.1R). Note that firms are also permitted to hold client money in a 'qualifying money market fund' but in that case the firm will hold units in the relevant fund subject to the custody rules, rather than holding cash subject to the client money rules (see CASS 7.4.3G).
5   As explained in Chapter 3, cash on deposit with a bank constitutes a debt owed by the bank to the depositor. Thus, under the client money trust, the trust asset is the debt owed by the bank to the firm, which the firm in turn holds as trustee for clients, and the trust terms are as set out in the client money rules: see in particular CASS 7.7.2R.
6   Such as a minimum amount necessary to keep the account open, or a payment comprising amounts due to both the firm and its client which is required to be paid into the client account in the first instance, but while in such account will be treated as client money. Consider also the rules regarding the 'normal approach' and 'alternative approach' relating to the account to which client money should be credited on receipt (CASS 7.4.14G – 7.4.29G). See paras **7.90** and **7.94** below.
7   But note also the terms of the client money trust: broadly, on the insolvency of the regulated entity, cash in all client money accounts (and any client money temporarily or incorrectly held in a house account – see discussion in paras **7.85–7.98** below) is aggregated and divided pro rata among the clients for whom the entity was holding client money (subject to deduction of distribution costs as permitted by the client money rules), thus the entitlement of each client may be reduced as a result of any unallocated shortfall (see discussion of similar issues in relation to securities in Chapter 3, paras **3.50–3.55**).

7.59 The client money rules specify the terms of the trust on which the cash is held. Broadly, the firm holds the client money for the client (but subject to payment of proper costs if the firm becomes insolvent), and thereafter for the firm itself (which is useful where for example a firm has had to put its own money into a client money account to keep the account open). The client money rules require the regulated entity to obtain from the bank holding the client money for the firm an acknowledgement that the money is held by the firm as trustee, and that the bank has no right to set off against the client money any amounts owed by the firm in respect of any other accounts maintained with that bank (CASS 7.8.1R). (Note also the further limits on set-off which may arise as a result of CASS 6.3.5R – 6.3.9R, see paras **7.41–7.44** above.)

7.60 There are some differences between the application of the client money rules to MiFID business and non-MiFID business, the most significant of which is the fact that in the context of non-MIFID business it is possible for the firm to agree with a professional client that the client money rules do not apply, in which case the trust arrangement does not apply and the client is simply an unsecured creditor of the firm in relation to the cash[1]. The other difference which is of interest is the situation regarding affiliated companies as discussed in para **7.57** above.

1   CASS 7.1.7DR. CASS 7.1.7BR specifies that this does not apply to MiFID business.

Application of rules

7.61 The client money rules apply where a firm 'receives money from or holds money for, or on behalf of, a client in the course of, or in connection with ... its

MIFID business', or 'its designated investment business' (broadly, the activities specified in the Regulated Activities Order) other than MiFID business[1].

1   CASS 7.1.1R.

Disapplication of rules

7.62 The client money rules do not apply if the firm holding or receiving client money is a bank of the appropriate type[1] and holds the money 'in an account with itself'[2]. Many custodians are banks and are therefore able to take advantage of this provision, but it is important to note that this disapplication only applies where the money is an account with, and therefore where the client takes the credit risk of, the bank. If the custodian opens a bank account in the name of the client with a third party[3] and agrees that the client takes the credit risk of such third party itself, it is clear that the relevant cash is not held in an account with the custodian itself: therefore, even if the custodian is an appropriate bank, the disapplication will not apply and the custodian will be required to comply with the client money rules in relation to such cash (unless of course in such case the client, not the custodian, is the client of the third party bank).

1   Either: a BCD credit institution (a credit institution that has its registered office (or, if it has no registered office, its head office) in an EEA State, unless it is a credit institution to which the BCD (the Banking Consolidation Directive, namely the Directive of the European Parliament and the Council of 14 June 2006 relating to the taking up and pursuit of the business of credit institutions (No 2006/48/EC)) does not apply) (CASS 7.1.8R); or an 'approved bank' which is not a BCD credit institution (CASS 7.1.11AR) (at the time of writing, 'approved bank' is defined in the FSA Glossary as a bank which is '(a) if the account is opened at a branch in the United Kingdom: (i) the Bank of England; or (ii) the central bank of a member state of the OECD; or (iii) a bank [as defined in the FSA Glossary]; or (iv) a building society [as defined in the FSA Glossary]; or (v) a bank which is supervised by the central bank or other banking regulator of a member state of the OECD; or (b) if the account is opened elsewhere: (i) a bank in (a); or (ii) a credit institution established in an EEA State other than the United Kingdom and duly authorised by the relevant Home State regulator ; or (iii) a bank which is regulated in the Isle of Man or the Channel Islands; or (c) a bank supervised by the South African Reserve Bank; or (d) any other bank that: (i) is subject to regulation by a national banking regulator; (ii) is required to provide audited accounts; (iii) has minimum net assets of £5 million (or its equivalent in any other currency at the relevant time) and has a surplus revenue over expenditure for the last two financial years; and (iv) has an annual audit report which is not materially qualified.'

2   CASS 7.1.8R, 7.1.9G (in relation to BCD credit institutions); and CASS 7.1.11AR (in relation to approved banks).

3   For example, a correspondent bank, or perhaps in circumstances where the local law in the jurisdiction where a sub-custodian is appointed requires that a cash account is maintained by the sub-custodian in the name of the ultimate client.

7.63 If cash is held by a custodian as client money subject to the client money rules, such rules specify certain circumstances when the cash will cease to be client money, namely if it is paid: '(1) to the client , or a duly authorised representative of the client ; or (2) to a third party on the instruction of the client , unless it is transferred to a third party in the course of effecting a transaction, in accordance with CASS 7.5.2R (Transfer of client money to a third party); or (3) into a bank account of the client (not being an account which is also in the name of the firm); or (4) to the firm itself, when it is due and payable to the firm (see CASS 7.2.9R (Money due and payable to the firm)); or (5) to the firm itself, when it is an excess in the client bank account (see CASS 7.6.13R(2) (Reconciliation discrepancies)).'[1].

1   CASS 7.2.15R.

7.64 The reference to CASS 7.5.2R contemplates the situation where cash is transferred by the firm to an entity such as an exchange, a clearing house or intermediate broker, and that entity holds the cash for the firm, so that, in a manner similar to the firm holding client money with an appropriate bank, the cash is held by the firm as client money.

7.65 In relation to the question of when cash is 'due and payable' to the firm, CASS 7.2.10G gives the example of a firm paying for securities on behalf of the client in advance of receiving the purchase money from the client, but also states that the circumstances in which it is due and payable 'will depend on the contractual arrangement between the firm and the client.' It is therefore important that a custodian wishing to be able to rely to transfer amounts from a client's money held in a client money account to reimburse the custodian for amounts due from the client ensures that the documentation in place with the client states clearly when such amounts are due and payable from the client[1].

1   See also discussion in paras **7.102–7.108**.

Holding of cash by custodian

7.66 The issues arising in connection with the holding of cash by a custodian can perhaps be most easily understood by considering three possible scenarios for the manner in which cash may be 'held' by a custodian which is a bank.

(A) Client cash is held by the custodian bank 'in an account with itself', such that the account record on the books of the custodian bank shows the debt owed by the bank to the client from time to time, and the account record is marked up or down accordingly when cash is received or paid out by the custodian bank's correspondent banks or sub-custodians. The debt owed by the custodian bank to the client is separate from, although it corresponds to the amounts of, the debts owed to the custodian from time to time by the correspondent banks and sub-custodians. If a correspondent bank or sub-custodian becomes insolvent and cannot in practice make payment to the custodian, the custodian is still subject to its debt obligation to its client. In effect, the custodian bank does not delegate the holding of cash in the same way that it delegates the holding of securities, because the 'holding' of cash is in reality the creation of a debt to the client. The client bears the credit risk of the custodian but not that of the correspondent banks or sub-custodians.

(B) The custodian holds cash received from the sale of, or income paid in respect of, client assets in a cash account with a third party bank (eg a sub-custodian which is a bank). The cash account is in the name of the custodian and the custodian will maintain a corresponding cash account in its own books in the name of the client. However, the custodian has agreed with the client that in the event of the insolvency or other failure to pay by the third party bank, the custodian's obligation to pay the client is conditional upon the custodian being paid in turn by the third party bank, or is a limited recourse obligation whereby the custodian's obligation is limited to the amount which the custodian recovers from the third party bank, so that the client bears the credit risk of the third party bank. (In such cases, the custodian may agree that it holds the benefit of the third party account on trust, which will at least protect the client in the insolvency of the custodian, or may not, in which case the client is exposed to the credit and insolvency risk of both the custodian and the third party bank.)

(C) The custodian bank, on behalf of its client, opens a cash account with a third party bank in the name of the client, and the third party bank owes the amount recorded in such account to the client rather than to the custodian. The custodian does not itself hold that cash or owe it to the client, although it will probably have authorisation from the client to operate that account. In relation to the cash in this account, the client bears the credit risk of the third party bank but not the credit risk of the custodian.

7.67 In summary:

In scenario (C), the client money rules do not apply at all because the cash is held for the client by the third party not by the custodian, whereas in scenario (A) the client's cash is held for the client by the custodian subject to what is arguably a normal banking relationship (the client money rules are disapplied to the extent that the bank exemption applies, as discussed above). Scenario (B) is more difficult because the client has a cash account with the custodian, but it is difficult to view the cash in the third party account as held by the custodian in an account with itself, because the client is bearing the credit risk of the third party bank and (probably) also the credit risk of the custodian. Consequently, it is arguable that in this case the custodian should be complying with the client money rules in relation to the cash held with the third party bank (this is significant because it will limit the type of entities with which the client money can be held). In this context, it is important for a custodian bank to consider carefully the terms agreed with clients regarding the holding of cash because, if there is any lack of clarity regarding the proposed arrangements, a custodian may risk being in the position of needing to comply with the client money rules but may not be aware of this.

Scenario	Entity maintaining bank account	Bank account in name of	Client bears credit risk of custodian bank	Client bears credit risk of third party bank	Client Money Rules apply to custodian bank
A	Custodian bank	Client	✓	✗	✗
B	Third party bank	Custodian	Probably	✓	Arguably
C	Third party bank	Client	✗	✓	✗[1]

1   CASS Chapter 7 does not apply, but CASS Chapter 8 applies if the custodian is given authority to control the client's bank account.

Opting out

7.68 As noted above, an entity[1] subject to the client money rules in the context of non-MiFID business can, where the client is a professional client, opt out of the client money rules. However, it cannot opt out in relation to a retail client.

1   Other than a sole trader (CASS 7.1.7DR).

7.69 Where cash is held in the context of MiFID business and subject to the client money rules, no opt out is available. However, if a client transfers 'full ownership' of cash to the regulated entity 'for the purpose of securing or otherwise covering present or future, actual or contingent or prospective obligations', the cash is not subject to the client money rules[1]. This is not really an exception to the client money rules, because it is simply a situation where the regulated entity is not holding cash for the client but will be holding the cash for its own account. Depending on the nature of the services provided to the client, it may be possible (if the client agrees) to structure the arrangements so that 'full ownership' of cash is transferred in order to collateralise relevant obligations and therefore the client money rules do not apply. This would not be usual in a normal global custody context, although may be appropriate in the context of more complex structured finance arrangements.

1   CASS 7.2.3R(1)

Regulatory duties 163

7.70 There are however restrictions on the use of title transfer collateral arrangements. CASS 7.2.6G draws attention to the general requirement under COBS 2.1.1R (see para **7.29** above) to act 'honestly, fairly and professionally in accordance with the best interests of its client'.

7.71 In relation to retail clients, there are additional concerns. COBS 7.2.7G states that in relation to title transfer by a retail client, a firm should ensure there is a 'reasonable link between the timing and amount' of collateral transferred and the obligation collateralised, and that collateral should be transferred back to the client when 'no longer necessary'. This suggests that arrangements could be open to criticism[1] by the FSA if the amount of collateral was significantly larger than the obligation collateralised (although in principle it is hard to see that normal margin arrangements would cause issues), or if the collateral was transferred a long time in advance of relevant obligation arising. As a result, in practice, any title transfer collateral arrangements should be considered carefully in each case.

1   It seems not unlikely that such requirements could be applied by the FSA to arrangements with professional clients too, given the broad obligation to act in the best interests of clients (see COBS 2.2.1R).

7.72 In addition, there is a specific prohibition on title transfer of money belonging to a retail client where the purpose of such transfer 'is to secure or otherwise cover that client's present or future, actual, contingent or prospective obligations under a contract for differences or a rolling spot forex contract that is a future, and in either case where that contract is entered into with a firm acting as market maker'[1].

1   CASS 7.2.3R(2).

7.73 The existence of a prohibition in certain circumstances, and guidance on the nature of title transfer arrangements with retail clients, might be regarded as indicating that, subject to such prohibition and guidance, there is no particular difficulty with receiving title transfer collateral from retail clients. However, the FSA has indicated[1] that transfer of full title to assets by way of collateral is unlikely ever to be appropriate for retail clients. Moreover, the position seems likely to become even more restrictive for firms providing services to retail clients because the latest draft of MiFID2[2] contains a specific prohibition on receipt of title transfer collateral from a retail client for any purpose.[3]

1   See FSA Consultation Paper CP 11/15 'Client assets sourcebook: (1) Custody liens; (2) Title transfer collateral arrangements', July 2011, p 16, para 3.13.
2   See para **7.14** above.
3   See Article 16(10) of the MiFID2 draft published as a Presidency compromise on 31 August 2012. This is unlikely to be a concern for most custodians, but could create problems for entities which are not authorised or regulated for the provision of custody services and therefore receive all assets from or for the account of clients as title transfer collateral.

Trustee firms

7.74 Provided that a trustee firm (a firm which is acting as a trustee or personal representative but not a trustee for an occupational person scheme)[1] is holding money other than in connection with MiFID business, only specific parts of CASS Chapter 7 will apply to it. This of course assumes that a trustee is conducting investment business subject to the FSA regulatory requirements, rather than operating under an applicable exemption available in the Regulated Activities Order[2]. A trustee firm is required by the CASS rules to hold client money separately from its own money at all times and subject to the limited client money rules specified to be applicable to a trustee[3]. In particular, a trustee is required to hold client money on the terms set out in the relevant trust deed, and subject to this, to hold client money on the terms of trust set out in the client money rules[4]. This will of course depend on whether the trustee is holding the relevant cash on trust[5].

1   Note that the client money rules do not apply to a depositary (broadly, the entity holding the assets of a fund, such as the trustee of a unit trust) (see CASS 1.4.6R) or to an investment company with variable capital incorporated under the Open-Ended Investment Companies Regulations 2001 (SI 2001/1228) or to an operator, trustee or depositary of a UCITS (see CASS 1.2.3R(1)).
2   See paras **7.127–7.129** below.
3   CASS 7.1.15ER, 7.1.15FR.
4   CASS 7.7.3R.
5   See discussion in Chapter 3 regarding the status of the custodian as trustee in relation to the holding of securities but not (usually) cash.

7.75   There is no exemption or special regime for a trustee firm holding client money in the context of MiFID business, therefore in such case CASS Chapter 7 applies in full.

Use of a non-approved bank

7.76   In the pre-MIFID context, although generally client money was required to be held in a client bank account with an 'approved bank'[1], the FSA Rules in certain limited circumstances allowed a regulated entity (but not a trustee firm) to use a bank which was not an approved bank. Under CASS Chapter 7, there is no ability to use a bank other than a central bank, a BCD credit institution, a bank authorised in a third country or a qualifying money market fund, regardless of whether the client money is held in the context of MiFID business or non-MiFID business. However, since these categories are very wide, arguably an equivalent of the old rule applicable in the non-MiFID context is unnecessary.

1   See para **7.62, n 1** above for definition of this term.

Prior written notice

7.77   Somewhat curiously, whereas under the pre-MiFID rules an FSA firm holding client money outside the UK was required to give prior written notice that this was the case, there is no equivalent requirement in CASS Chapter 7. However, whether a firm holds client money in the context of MiFID business or non-MiFID business, there is a specific duty to 'exercise all due skill, care and diligence in the selection, appointment and periodic review' of the relevant bank holding the money and of 'the arrangements for the holding of this money'[1]. Also, under the COBS rules, the firm must notify clients if the client money 'will be subject to the law of a jurisdiction other than that of a EEA State' and 'that the rights of the client relating to' such client money 'may differ accordingly', and notify of any set-off rights which the firm or any 'depositary'[2] may have in relation to the client money[3]. There are also additional warnings required to be given to retail clients, in particular informing the client of '(i) [the fact] that the … client money of that client may be held by a third party on behalf of the firm; (ii) the responsibility of the firm under the applicable national law for any acts or omissions of the third party; and (iii) the consequences for the client of the insolvency of the third party'[4].

1   CASS 7.4.7R.
2   See comments at para **7.47** n 2 above regarding the interpretation of this term.
3   COBS 6.1.7R(1)(d), (2) and (4).
4   COBS 6.1.7R(1)(a). See comments at para **7.48** above regarding these requirements.

Unclaimed funds

7.78 The client money rules contain provisions which allow firms to cease to treat unclaimed money as client money in certain circumstances which may be of particular interest to custodians[1].

1   CASS 7.2.19R.

7.79 As a practical matter, it is not uncommon for custodians holding assets for clients to find that there are funds in the client account which for some reason have over time not been claimed by clients and where it is now not possible to trace the clients entitled to such funds[1]. Since this is client money, the custodian remains subject to all relevant requirements under the FSA rules, including the obligation to provide statements to the client, although in practice it will be unable to do so if the relevant client cannot be identified. Similarly, the custodian will be unable to terminate the arrangement with the client if it does not know to whom a termination notice should be given. Unless the arrangement is terminated, then in principle the firm must continue to hold the client money in accordance with the client money rules, since it is unable to vary the terms on which it holds such money (because it cannot agree this with an unidentified client)[2].

1   See further discussion regarding unclaimed securities as well as cash at para **7.144** below.
2   It is risky for the custodian simply to decide to treat the client money as its own money, because the unidentified client still has a claim to the relevant amount, and therefore any such step by the custodian could leave the custodian open to claims for unjust enrichment, conversion or, in extreme cases, theft.

7.80 The relevant CASS rules are intended to allow a firm to cease to treat money as client money where it has not been claimed, but only if the firm 'can demonstrate that it has taken reasonable steps to trace the client concerned and to return the balance'[1]. The 'reasonable steps' required might, for example, include advertising in appropriate publications, such as the London *Gazette*. However, the relevant rules also specify particular steps which should be included in the reasonable steps taken by a firm to trace a client. These steps[2] consist of:

(a) having a written agreement with the client that if after six years there has been no movement on the client money balance, the money held may cease to be treated as client money;

(b) checking that there has been no movement on the client's balance in the last six years;

(c) writing to the client at the last known address warning that money will cease to be treated as client money and giving the client 28 days to claim;

(d) keeping records of all balances which cease to be treated as client money; and

(e) giving an undertaking to make good any valid claim against money no longer treated as client money (such undertaking to be legally enforceable by persons with a valid claim).

These steps are not stated to be requirements of the FSA in a binding CASS rule, but are evidential provisions therefore failure to perform any of the specified steps may be regarded by the FSA as indicating that a firm has not taken reasonable steps as required.

1   CASS 7.2.19R.
2   CASS 7.2.20E.

7.81 As may be seen, in practice these specified steps are quite onerous because, if the relevant cash is unclaimed and it is unclear to whom it belongs, it will be difficult to enter into the written agreement mentioned in (a) or to write to the client as mentioned in (c). While the equivalent result to (c) could probably be achieved by suitable advertisements, it is likely that the need for written agreement can only be satisfied if standard client terms include such a provision, and it is clear that, even if the particular client cannot be identified, such client must have become a client of the custodian by becoming party to an agreement incorporating such a provision. It will depend on the facts whether it is possible to achieve this result, but in practice custodians should consider including such a provision in standard client agreements. However, a custodian entity may not wish to create legally enforceable undertakings in favour of unknown third parties as suggested by the guidance term described in (e) above, and may consider that the burden of maintaining client money procedures in relation to unclaimed client money does not outweigh the burden created by this type of undertaking. Nevertheless, if the main concern for a custodian is to end unnecessary compliance with the client money rules, this new Rule does at least provide a basis for discussion with the FSA[1].

1   There is no equivalent regulatory provision regarding unclaimed assets, the situation regarding which is considered further at para **7.144** below.

7.82   For banks, the position regarding unclaimed assets is now simplified[1] by the Dormant Bank and Building Society Accounts Act 2008[2]. Broadly, where an account has been dormant for 15 years (in that there have been no movements on the account on the instructions of the account holder during that time), the cash in such account should be transferred from the relevant bank account to the 'reclaim fund', and the bank account will be closed so that if the unknown client were to reappear such person would have no claim against the relevant bank. However, the client will have the right to claim against the reclaim fund for the full amount of the claim which the client would have had against the relevant bank[3].

1   Although this will not assist in connection with unclaimed client money, since in normal circumstances the client money rules do not apply to banks, see further at para **7.62** above.

2   This Act received Royal Assent on 26 November 2008 and came into force on 12 March 2009 pursuant to the Dormant Bank and Building Society Accounts Act 2008 (Commencement and Transitional Provisions) Order 2009.

3   The claim against the reclaim fund is an unsecured claim for payment. The funds held by the reclaim fund are to be used for charitable purposes, therefore in theory there is no guarantee that sufficient funds will be available to meet the claims of a former bank account holder.

BCOBS and set-off

7.83   In this context, it is also worth noting the application of the FSA's Banking: Conduct of Business sourcebook ('BCOBS') to the existence and exercise of set-off rights. The requirements of BCOBS only apply to a firm accepting deposits from banking customers from an establishment maintained by the firm in the UK[1]. For these purposes, a banking customer means a consumer (broadly, any natural person acting for purposes outside his trade, business or profession), a micro-enterprise (broadly, a business, in whatever form, with under 10 employees and a turnover or annual balance sheet that does not exceed EUR 2 million), or a charity with annual income of less than GBP 1 million. Consequently, in broad terms, BCOBS will not apply except to a bank providing services to a retail client falling within the definition of banking customer.

1   BCOBS 1.1.1R.

7.84   Under BCOBS 4.1.1R a firm 'must provide or make available to a banking customer appropriate information about a retail banking service and any deposit made in relation to that retail banking service: (1) in good time; (2) in an appropriate medium; and (3) in easily understandable language and in a clear and comprehensible form; so that the banking customer can make decisions on an informed basis.' (BCOBS 4.1.1R). In connection with this rule, the guidance in BCOBS 4.1.4AG indicates that where a bank has set-off rights in respect of the client, the bank is expected to provide to its client 'an explanation of the nature and extent of the firm's set-off rights in good time before the consumer is bound by the relevant contract, and to notify the client within a reasonable period (considered by the FSA to be at least 14 days) before exercise of set-off rights. Compliance with this requirement is also likely to be material if the FSA is considering whether or not a bank has treated a client fairly[1].

1   See further discussion in paras **7.23** to **7.28**.

Client money and case law

7.85   For many years there has been little case law regarding the interpretation and application of the FSA client money rules, but in the context of the market upheavals over the last five years or so, there have been a large number of court proceedings examining this subject, in most if not all cases arising from the insolvency of entities holding client securities, client money, or both[1].

1   For example, *Re Global Trader Europe Ltd* [2009] EWHC 602 (Ch); and the progress through the courts of one of the matters arising from the administration of Lehman Brothers International (Europe) Limited ('LBIE') culminating in the Supreme Court judgment in February 2012: *In the matter of Lehman Brothers International (Europe) (In Administration) and In the matter of the Insolvency Act 1986* [2012] UKSC 6, 29 February 2012.

7.86   Of particular interest are the following three judgments: (a) *In the matter of Lehman Brothers International (Europe) (in administration)* [2009] EWHC 3228 (Ch); (b) *In the matter of Lehman Brothers International (Europe) (In Administration) and In the matter of the Insolvency Act 1986* [2010] EWCA Civ 917 (CA); and (c) *In the matter of Lehman Brothers International (Europe) (In Administration) and In the matter of the Insolvency Act 1986* [2012] UKSC 6, 29 February 2012. It should be noted that these cases consider the application of the CASS client money rules which applied to MiFID business prior to 1 January 2009, but the differences from the CASS client money rules after such date are not material.

When client money trust applies

7.87   The main conclusion of the Supreme Court judgement was that any money received by a firm which falls within the definition of client money (broadly, money which is received and held by the firm for a client[1]) is held by the firm on trust (the client money trust) from the time of receipt of such money. The other conclusions arguably follow logically from this, namely that (i) when a primary pooling event, such as the commencement of administration, occurs in relation to a firm, all client money held by the firm at that time must be pooled for distribution to clients, whether such client money was at the time held in designated client money accounts or still remained in the firm's house accounts; and (ii) the client money pool must be distributed among all clients on whose behalf the firm received and held money, whether or not it is the case that the money in the relevant client money account (and house accounts) is money received or segregated for those particular clients[2].

1   See further discussion in paras **7.58–7.77** above.

2   Note that this conclusion refers to distribution among all clients for whom client money was received by the firm, not all client to whom the firm owed money.

7.88 In many respects these conclusions seem reasonable, not least because if client money is not subject to the trust from the time of receipt but only from the time of credit to the client money account, the client has only a contractual claim rather than a beneficial interest under a trust, and will not know that this is the case. The argument was raised by dissenting judges that the allocation of the client money pool among not only clients whose money was paid into segregated client money accounts, but also clients whose money should have been segregated in this manner but was not, was inconsistent with trust law and in effect changed the terms of the trust upon the occurrence of the insolvency event. This reasoning seems odd, since it is the terms of the trust (the client money rules as terms of the client money trust) which provide for this pooling. It might seem reasonable that in an insolvency situation, cash held on trust for a particular client or clients should be returned to the particular client or clients only, but this is not the approach taken by the client money rules, and may be argued to be a sensible balance between the interests of the clients who have suffered a common misfortune and the time and complexity of identifying into which account was paid money of which client (particularly where client money is held in omnibus client accounts)[1]. Nevertheless, this conclusions to raise additional issues for consideration.

1   See similar pooling approach under general law in relation to client securities as discussed in Chapter 3, paras **3.50–3.55**.

7.89 Since the trust applies to client money when received by a firm, this means that the point at which cash is actually received by a firm is extremely important. This begs the question of how it can be shown that cash has been received, and will depend very much on the accuracy of the firm's systems and accessibility of relevant data.

7.90 It should be noted that, although the judgment is concerned with the alternative approach where client money can be paid into the firm's house account, even under the normal approach a firm is required to pay client money 'promptly, and in any event no later than the next business day after receipt' into a client bank account. Consequently, even under the normal approach there is a time during which client money has been received but not paid into a client bank account.

7.91 Since client money is subject to the client money trust upon receipt, it is logical that all client money, even if held in a house account, should be included in the client money pool to be distributed to clients in accordance with the client money rules. However, this does raise various questions.

Adequate arrangements and set-off rights

7.92 CASS 7.3.1R requires that 'A firm must, when holding client money, make adequate arrangements to safeguard the client's rights and prevent the use of client money for its own account.' If 'client money' now includes money received from or on behalf of clients and paid into a house account, this suggests that firms may need to take additional steps to demonstrate 'adequate arrangements' to safeguard the rights of clients to money in the house account and prevent use of such money for its own account. It is unclear what such arrangements might be. Briggs J suggested that such arrangements might include a firm ensuring that the relevant account always contained a minimum amount, or that an additional 'buffer' amount should be held in the account to minimise the risk of the account being in overdraft, and that a firm should not grant any security interest over a house account in which client money might be held, although also stated quite clearly that it was 'not for the court to specify the precise method' by which a firm should make 'adequate arrangements'[1].

1   *In the matter of Lehman Brothers International (Europe) (in administration)* [2009] EWHC 3228 (Ch).

7.93 As is noted in the judgement, there is no requirement in the client money rules that a firm should obtain from banks with which the firm holds its own money an acknowledgement that the house account may contain client money and that the bank must limit its set-off rights accordingly. It might however be argued that the meaning given to 'client money' and the requirement to make 'adequate arrangements' to safeguard client money mean this would be advisable.

7.94 It seems likely that the holding of trust monies in a house account with a bank will affect the rights of set-off and/or security interests which such bank may have in respect of amounts due to it from the firm. This is a major concern for any bank which relies on set-off rights and/or a security interest in respect of a client's house account in order to recover amounts due to the bank from the client. In a situation where the bank's client is regulated by the FSA and holds money for clients subject to the client money rules, the bank will have no way of checking whether such house account may contain client money (whether the bank's client uses the normal approach or the alternative approach). Although the bank would undoubtedly take usual representations and warranties regarding the client's authority to grant set-off rights or a security interest, and the absence of third party rights over the relevant cash, this is unlikely to assist if in fact client money has been received into the relevant account and the bank's client is insolvent.

Commingling

7.95 In the first instance judgment it was not disputed that client money accounts include client transaction accounts (broadly, accounts with an exchange, clearing house or intermediate broker, in which client money is held in the circumstances permitted by the client money rules (CASS 7.5). Arguably there is now a risk that the account with an exchange, clearing house or intermediate broker containing a firm's own money might in some circumstances contain client money if it can be shown that client money was paid into that account (even if this conflicts with the firm's obligations to the relevant exchange, clearing house or intermediate broker).

7.96 As was noted in several judgements, general trust law is relevant to the application of the client money trust. Although the pooling of client money is arguably not inconsistent with normal trust law, since the terms of the trust itself provide for pooling, there are puzzling questions regarding, for example, the extent to which trust money commingled with non-trust money in a house account can be identified for the purposes of certainty of the subject matter of the trust[1].

1   See Chapter 3.

7.97 While commingling trust monies with own funds in a house account is not necessarily inconsistent with the existence of a trust, it is difficult to see how money can be shown to be held subject to the client money trust if it is not possible to identify which money is subject to the trust (ie in this context, which of the money paid into the house account was money received on behalf of or for the account of a client). In an insolvency situation, it seems likely that a complex forensic accounting analysis will be necessary in order for the insolvency officials to identify the extent of the money in house accounts which should be regarded as client money.

Relevance of MiFID

7.98 In reaching the final conclusions, considerable weight was given in the various judgements to the fact that CASS Chapter 7 was created to implement MiFID and the MiFID implementing Directive, and therefore various determinations were made on the basis of what the draughtsman must have had in mind when drafting the relevant text. In practice, the text of CASS Chapter 7 before 1 January 2009 was very similar to what was at the time the non-MiFID CASS Chapter 4, both of which were substantially similar to the client money rules in existence before the amendment of the FSA rule to implement MiFID. The judges in their decisions in the Supreme Court evidently concluded there was considerable freedom to override or ignore the text of the client money rules to the extent incompatible with the overall purpose of compliance with the aims of MiFID. As a result, it is debateable whether, if similar issues were to arise in relation to the application of the CMR in the context of non-MiFID business, a different result would be reached, or whether it is safe to conclude that the similarity of the client money rules would mean the same reasoning would apply. This would seem not unreasonable for the purposes of consistency, although strictly speaking would be an odd result: it would mean that text which was, in reality, substantially drafted long before MiFID, as interpreted (and where considered necessary amended) as if drafted for the purposes of MiFID compliance, is then applied to rules never intended to apply in a MiFID context.

7.99 There are also other important points which were noted in the various judgements.

Reconciliations

7.100 In the Court of Appeal, it was concluded that it is the duty of the insolvency officials to carry out a final reconciliation in relation to client money as at the time of the commencement of the insolvency, and that pursuant to CASS 7.9.9R (now CASS 7A.2.7R), the client money entitlement of each client is to be calculated as at the time of the commencement of the insolvency. This seems only reasonable. In the lower courts it had been argued that the calculation of the client money pool and the allocation to each client should be determined based on the last reconciliation of client money held and the entitlement of each client carried out by LBIE prior to the commencement of administration, but it is hard to see the logic of proceeding on the basis of figures which would not take into account what had been received as client money since that date (or paid out on instructions of clients). It was also noted that there is no requirement under the client money rules that a firm has an obligation to make good a shortfall in client money.

Reliability of Client Money Rules

7.101 From all three judgements it is clear that there are ambiguities and errors in the existing client money rules. For example, CASS 7.9.8G (now CASS 7A.2.6G) was shown to be not completely correct. This Guidance states 'A client's main claim is for the return of client money held in a client bank account . A client may be able to claim for any shortfall against money held in a firm's own account. For that claim, the client will be an unsecured creditor of the firm.' However, the judgment has shown that to the extent that client money is held in a firm's own account, such money will be included in the pooling and allocation under the CMR. It is expected that the FSA will be amending the client money rules to reflect the conclusions in relevant case-law, as well as making any other changes considered appropriate[1].

1   See also paras **7.159–7.161**.

Deductions from client money

7.102 Of considerable interest is the question of the extent to which a firm is able to deduct from the client money it holds for a client amounts due to the firm from the client. In principle of course, it is always open to the client in the terms of its agreement with the firm to grant the firm the right to make deductions from the client money held by the firm for the client, and/or to grant a security interest to the firm over the client's beneficial interest under the client money trust. The question then arises as to what happens in the event of the insolvency of the firm. Even if the insolvency rules governing the firm's insolvency provide for mandatory set-off of amounts due from the firm to a client against amounts due from the client to the firm, set-off will not be applicable in relation to client money held by the firm for the client because the client money is an amount held on trust rather than an amount owed to the client[1]. A valid security interest will be enforceable by the firm, but only over the client's rights under the client money trust, in practice the amount of cash to which the client is entitled after the pooling and allocation under the client money distribution rules. The next question is then the amount of the client's entitlement following such distribution calculation, and the extent to which the terms of the trust themselves (the client money rules) permit deductions from the amount held on trust for the client.

1 See comments of Briggs J, *In the matter of Lehman Brothers International (Europe) (in administration)* [2009] EWHC 3228 (Ch), para 331.

7.103 CASS 7.2.9R and 7.2.15R are terms of the client money trust, and allow deductions of amounts due and payable to the firm. As drafted, CASS 7.2.9R suggests that client money automatically ceases to be client money when it is due and payable by the client to the firm, whereas CASS 7.2.15R indicates that client money only ceases to be client money when transferred from the client money pool to the firm (to an account of the firm or to its order). It could be argued that a firm is entitled either to deduct amounts due and payable to the firm when calculating a client's client money entitlement (see, for example, the reference in para 12(2) of Annex 1 to CASS Chapter 7), or having calculated such entitlement to deduct amounts due and payable to the firm.

7.104 This issue was considered in the judgement of Briggs J, and there are also relevant references in the Court of Appeal judgement although nothing of specific relevance in the Supreme Court judgement. In particular, in the initial discussion of the CASS rules by Briggs J, he concluded that CASS 7.2.15R overrides CASS 7.2.9R, so that amounts due and payable from the client money account only cease to be client money when actually paid out (para 93). Moreover, responding to specific questions from the Administrators, he stated that any money which was due to LBIE and which at the time of the commencement of the administration LBIE would have been entitled to withdraw from the client money pool, and which would in the normal course of events have been transferred into LBIE's house account, should be included in the client money pool. On this basis, amounts due and payable to an insolvent firm remain client money until actually paid out (para 362, 363). In addition, in para 408, Briggs J stated that the individual client balance is that defined at para 6(1)(a) of Annex 1 to CASS Chapter 7, and is not subject to para 12(2) of Annex 1 (which allows deduction of amounts due and payable when calculating client money requirement).

7.105 The Court of Appeal judgement did not consider this issue specifically, but included the following indicative points.

7.106 In the discussion of the regulatory regime (see para 21), reference was made to CASS 7.2.15R, and it was noted that this should be read with CASS 7.2.9R, and states that 'Client money which becomes properly due and payable to the firm ceases to be client money.' Could this be argued to mean that the Court of Appeal favoured the 'automatic' approach? However, in a later comment (para 126), in the context of an analysis of whether it was necessary to pool all client money, whether in client accounts or house accounts, it was observed that CASS 7.9.6R(2) envisages distribution of pooled client money in accordance with each client's 'client money entitlement', and that CASS 7.9.7R 'stipulates for set off in order to identify the amount of an entitlement for a client where claims go in opposite directions.' This apparently means that in order to calculate the amount of a client's client money entitlement, set off of amounts due from client to firm in respect of the client's client equity balance (ie amount due from client to firm on close out of margined transactions) is permitted. When considering the merits of the claims v contribution basis of sharing in the client money pool, it was stated (para 155) to be necessary to refer to Annex 1 to ascertain the meaning of individual client balances and equity balances. Nevertheless, when analysing the similar question of when money owed to client by firm becomes client money (para 171), it was concluded that money in a firm's house account is not client money solely because the firm owes an amount to the client but only when an amount is set aside for the client.

7.107 Similarly, although the Supreme Court judgement did not make specific reference to the point, it may be noted that it was commented (para 61, Lord Walker) that 'In the case of satisfaction of a monetary obligation of the firm to a client ... it is now common ground that the trust arises on the appropriation of funds in satisfaction of the obligation, normally by a payment into a segregated client account.' and that (para 111, Lord Clarke) notes 'By CASS 7.2.15 ... money ceases to be client money in certain specific circumstances, notably when it is paid away on the instructions of the client. Until then, the money remains client money ...'.

7.108 The conclusions and comments referenced above seem broadly to favour an argument that, if LBIE has not in fact transferred amounts due and payable to it from clients out of client money accounts at the time of commencement of administration, all the money in such accounts (bearing in mind this includes any client money in house accounts) is client money subject to the pooling rules, and must be allocated and distributed accordingly. However, arguably certain questions remain, such as: the extent to which as a practical matter there may be difficulties in proving the time at which a transfer was made out of a client money account, particularly where the relevant client money was in the house account at the time; the conclusion regarding amounts owed by the firm to client (that the existence of a debt obligation of firm to client does not mean that an amount equal to the debt in the firm's house account becomes client money until actually segregated) inevitably means that the same reasoning applies to amounts owed by clients to the firm, so that client money does not cease to be client money until paid out of the client money account; and whether, Briggs J's conclusions notwithstanding, a firm could argue that in order to determine a client's client money entitlement, it must follow the analysis in Annex 1, and that this should involve deduction of amounts due and payable to the firm.

Further client money developments

7.109 Further developments regarding the CASS rules appear in the FSA Consultation Paper CP 12/22 'Client assets regime: EMIR, multiple pools and the wider review' published in September 2012. This Consultation Paper sets out certain specific changes proposed for compliance with Regulation (EU) No 648/2012 of the European Parliament and of the Council of 4 July 2012 on OTC derivatives, central counterparties and trade repositories (generally known as the European Market Infrastructure Regulation or 'EMIR'), and also indicates possible future developments. The purposes of CP 12/22 are stated to be: (i) to set out the changes required to CASS Chapters 7 and 7A to comply with EMIR; (ii) to propose additional changes to the client money rules for the benefit of clients; and (iii) to raise the possibility of certain other amendments to CASS intended to achieve 'a better result in the context of client assets in a firm's insolvency'.[1]

1   FSA Consultation Paper CP 12/22 'Client assets regime: EMIR, multiple pools and the wider review', September 2012, section 1.2.

7.110   The effect of the changes to reflect EMIR is to facilitate the transfer of clients of an insolvent clearing member of a central counterparty ('CCPs') to another clearing member. If a client's transactions are to be transferred from one clearing member to another, the associated margin must also be transferred, but this will not be possible if such margin is subject to the client money pooling process which applies on the insolvency of an FSA-regulated clearing member[1]. The client money rules therefore need to be amended so that client money held by a firm with a CCP will not be subject to the general pooling requirement. The intention is that, pursuant to its obligations under EMIR, if another clearing member is willing to accept the transfer of the client, the relevant CCP will procure the transfer of margin together with transactions where the margin was held by the insolvent clearing member as client money with the CCP.

1   See para **7.58** n 7.

7.111   It should be noted that EMIR requires clearing members to offer each client either 'individual client segregation' (where the client's transactions and margin are recorded in a separate account at the CCP relating to that client only) or 'omnibus client segregation' (where the transactions and margin of a number of clients are recorded in the same account at the CCP). Where there is individual client segregation, any excess margin from the client must be held by the clearing firm with the CCP (whereas currently under the client money rules, firms are not permitted to hold excess margin with a CCP – see CASS 7.5.3G). This is not the case with omnibus client segregation, where any client money held by the firm outside the CCP will be pooled and allocated in the usual way under the client money distribution rules. Interestingly, the amendments to CASS 7.5.3G in the FSA Policy Statement following CP 12/22[1] suggest that the FSA will permit excess margin to be held in an omnibus client account with the CCP too.

1   FSA Policy Statement PS 12/23 'Client assets regime: changes following EMIR', December 2012.

7.112   Arguably it is reasonable that money provided by a client for a particular purpose, namely as margin in connection with transactions cleared through a specific CCP, should be excluded from general pooling on the insolvency of the clearing member and continue to be used for the required purpose of supporting the transactions transferred to another clearing member. On this basis, it might seem logical that all client money held in connection with transactions cleared through a CCP, whether within or outside the CCP, should be ring-fenced on insolvency of the clearing firm, but at present the FSA is not minded to proceed this far[1]. Additional records and processes will of course be necessary to support the new arrangements, and the details will need to be considered carefully.

1   See in particular discussion on pp 21–23 of PS 12/23.

7.113   The FSA proposals are not perhaps wholly straightforward, largely as a result of the requirement of EMIR. In particular, the FSA notes that if a firm receives margin from clients by way of title transfer, rather than holding cash with CCPs as client money, the firm is still required to offering to clients individual client segregation or omnibus client segregation. This is odd, given that the cash held in the CCP is the firm's own cash, and the result is that, pursuant to the EMIR requirements, cash repaid by the CCP on the firm's insolvency must (although it is the firm's own cash, albeit that the firm owes an equivalent amount to the client under the title transfer arrangement) be repaid to the relevant clients in priority to other unsecured clients of the firm. Moreover, firms using only title transfer arrangements will be subject to the same EMIR requirements (but not the client money rules), therefore arguably the FSA needs separate new rules outside the client money rules to regulate compliance by such firms with EMIR for this purpose. As noted by the FSA, money returned by a CCP to a clearing member on its insolvency which is the firm's own money is 'not client money for the purposes of CASS, but in accordance with EMIR must be held by the firm for the account of its clients', which is a fairly radical change to priorities of unsecured creditors on insolvency under English law.

7.114 CP 12/22 also proposes that firms should be allowed (or possibly required) to provide for certain other purposes separate pools of client money which will not be part of general pooling on insolvency. This seems an attractive option for clients who currently require individual designated client bank accounts in order to minimise the risk of problems arising from issues with payment flows for other clients of the firm, and would resolve the odd situation that such clients are for most purposes not exposed to other clients of the firm prior to the firm's insolvency but are exposed to such risk after the firm's insolvency. Nevertheless, the proposals may raise their own problems.

7.115 Although separate client money pools are likely to benefit clients, it seems unarguable that it will result in increased expense and operational complexity for firms. Clients receiving a more complex service will undoubtedly have to pay for this, but it is not easy to calculate the extent to which the new arrangement will improve the recovery of client money on insolvency. For example, the suggested draft rules state that a client only has a claim in respect of a pool in which it has an interest. It is therefore unclear what happens if cash has been credited to the wrong account for the wrong pool (or to a house account). (The risk of credit of cash to the wrong account seems particularly likely given that the draft rules contemplate mixed amounts going first into one client pool before payment of the relevant amount into the other client pool(s).)

7.116 The proposal for dealing with surpluses on client money accounts where there are both separate client money pools and a general client money pool is very odd. The current suggestion is that a surplus in a separate client pool should be transferred to the general pool, and a surplus in the general pool should be used to meet shortfalls in the separate pools. The reasoning underlying this is unclear. There seems no particular reason why this should be the case, unless there is clear evidence that cash has been wrongly credited to a particular account, given that the purpose of maintaining separate pools is to avoid confusion of different cash entitlements.

Collateral

7.117 Under the CASS rules the collateral chapter[1] only applies if a firm 'receives or holds assets in connection with an arrangement to secure the obligation of a client in the course of, or in connection with, its designated investment business, including MiFID business'[2]. The terms of this chapter state that if the firm has a right to use the collateral asset[3], and treats the collateral 'as if' all legal title and associated rights are transferred to the firm, then subject to an obligation to return equivalent assets, the only requirement is to maintain 'adequate records' to enable the firm to meet its further obligations, including delivery obligations'[4]. This is arguably a somewhat strange approach, given that the only rules applying to 'collateral' under this section are designed to apply to assets which are not collateral in the sense of being subject to a security interest, since they are transferred outright to the firm (eg as in the case of collateral provided in an English law repo or stock loan)[5]. Since the firm receives full title to the relevant assets and is not holding on behalf of the client, the firm is entitled to do what it likes with its own assets, and would as a matter of practice maintain records of its contractual obligations to return securities. It is difficult to see what these requirements add to the relevant rules relating to stock lending discussed earlier.

1   CASS Chapter 3.

2   CASS 3.1.1R.

3   See Chapter 4 for a discussion of collateral takers' rights to use collateral assets.

4   CASS 3.1.5G and 3.2.2R.

5   Or when exercising the right of re-use under the Financial Collateral Arrangements (No 2) Regulations 2003 (SI 2003/3226) ('Financial Collateral Regulations') where collateral is provided under a security interest, see Chapter 4. Note that in CASS 7.2.5G, the FSA observes that client money has been transferred outright, and is therefore no longer subject to the client money rules, only when the right of use is exercised. Prior to this transfer, the money remains in a client money account and is held subject to the client money rules. Following CASS 3.1.7G, there seems no reason to suppose that the same reasoning would not be applied to a charge over securities where there is also a right of re-use.

7.118 The important point to note is that FSA regulated entities must comply with the custody and client money rules in relation to assets received by such entity by way of security where a security interest but *not* outright title, or a security interest with a right of use which has not been exercised, is granted to such entity[1]. This may be particularly important where a security interest is granted over assets in favour of an FSA regulated entity and the assets are transferred to such entity by way of security, but the entity's scope of business as approved by the FSA does not include the provision of custody services in the UK, since in such case, unless a relevant exemption applies, the entity will be acting outside its scope of business.

1   CASS 3.1.3R.

Compliance

7.119 If the firm has *only* a security interest over assets held by it (with no right of use), it *must* comply with custody rules or client money rules, as applicable. This seems logical because in principle, if a firm has a security interest in the assets, rather than full legal and beneficial title, the remainder of the interest in the assets (the equity of redemption, as discussed in Chapter 4) must remain with the person granting the security interest (because there is no one else who holds such remainder). As a result, that remainder interest in the assets is held by the custodian for the client and should arguably be held subject to the protections set out in the custody rules or client money rules (depending on the nature of the assets held).

Extension of Rules

7.120 Where then does this leave the old argument that a delivery of assets by way of security is not subject to custody regulation? In principle, if an entity is not an authorised person regulated by the FSA, and the only reason that such entity could be regarded as requiring authorisation by the FSA is because it receives assets over which it takes security, it would still be possible to argue that the entity taking the security interest is *not* providing custody. As noted above, it would be extremely important in such case for the collateral taker to (a) maintain appropriate records of such arrangement, (b) avoid any indication that it regarded the assets as held in custody (whether in its records or by other actions), and (c) (ideally) clear such approach with the regulatory authority in advance[1]. In contrast, if the entity taking security is regulated by the FSA[2], it is subject to the CASS rules. CASS 3.1.3R is clear that a firm with a security interest must hold the assets subject to the relevant CASS rules. Consequently, 3.1.3R results in the CASS rules applying, even though in a non-MiFID context the custody rules only apply to the activity which is the regulated activity of safeguarding and administration of investments[3] and, as discussed above, holding assets by way of security may technically not fall within the scope of such activity. The position is arguably clearer in the MiFID context since the relevant rules apply where a relevant firm 'holds financial instruments belonging to a client'[4]. Nevertheless, this may be seen as an example of a situation where the rules applicable to an authorised person extend to activities which are not necessarily activities for which authorisation would be necessary.

1   This is particularly important where the question of whether or not the entity is providing custody determines whether or not the entity should be authorised for the purposes of FSMA. If the FSA took the view that holding assets as security would in the relevant case constitute a regulated activity, the entity could face criminal penalties for carrying on a regulated activity in breach of FSMA. When receiving assets by way of security, the holder has a security interest but does not have full title to the assets; the assets are held subject to the chargor's interest. The holder must therefore keep the assets safe but cannot use the assets for its own purpose. The manner of holding is difficult, because the chargee does not have legal title in the same sense that a custodian does, but has a title more akin to that of a mortgagee. In principle, therefore, the assets received by way of security should probably be recorded in a separate house account, and clearly designated and blocked to avoid any transfer or use of such assets until either enforcement of the security interest or transfer back to the chargor. In this context, see also Chapter 4.
2   As would be the case with most custodian entities in practice.
3   CASS 2.1.1R.
4   CASS 6.1.1R(1A).

CASS Resolution Pack

7.121   The requirements relating to the new CASS Resolution Pack (CASS Chapter 10) apply as from 1 October 2012[1]. The main purpose of these requirements is that firms must have certain specified information regarding client assets available for retrieval within 48 hours of the appointment of an insolvency official or on request from the FSA. Notably, the new guidance specifically states that the 48-hour period is for retrieval, not the time in which 'to start producing these documents'. This is to 'ensure that a firm maintains and is able to retrieve information that would, in the event of its insolvency, assist an insolvency practitioner in achieving a timely return of client money and safe custody assets held by the firm to that firm's assets.' (CASS 10.1.2.G) This is of course a worthy aim, and undoubtedly inspired by the criticism of the extremely long time taken to return client assets to clients of Lehman Brothers International (Europe) Limited following the commencement of its administration in September 2008. The major question is of course whether firms will be able to comply with the new rules in practice, and whether in any event compliance with such rules will speed up distribution of client assets in an insolvency situation.

1   See FSA Policy Statement PS12/6 'The CASS Resolution Pack', 26 March 2012.

7.122   CASS Chapter 10 only applies a firm which holds client securities or client money (CASS 10.1.1R(1)), therefore will apply to custodians and any other entity which holds client securities or client money but this will apply to any entity holding client money, as well as custodians. The new requirements will not apply where a firm arranges for client assets to be held by a third party but does not itself hold client assets for the client (CASS 10.1.1R(2)) or, presumably, where a firm controls, but does not hold, client assets. Similarly, a firm which includes custody in its scope of permitted business but does not actually hold client assets would only be subject to these requirements when it begins holding client assets. The challenges for firms are likely to be the form in which it is possible for such records to be maintained, and the speed with which they can be produced in a comprehensive form to constitute the Resolution Pack, which will depend very much on the complexity of the firm's business and the systems available to it for storage and retrieval of the relevant types of information. From the current text of CASS Chapter 10, there are certain areas of particular concern.

- The 48-hour period does not mean 48 hours within a business day (although this is stated in the Policy Statement but not in the Guidance). Firms therefore face the challenge of capacity to provide information at short notice out of business hours, and must consider setting up arrangements to ensure that appropriate staff and facilities are available in each location which may host relevant information in order to enable production of the necessary details in the required timeframe.

- Certain documents and records must be retrievable 'immediately' (CASS 10.1.9E(1)), such as the document identifying all institutions the firm has appointed to hold client money or client securities, acknowledgements from banks that cash is held by the firm on trust and set-off rights are limited, notifications to clearing houses and similar entities in relation to client money held in a client transaction account, and the most recent internal and external reconciliations regarding client money and client securities. This is an Evidential Provision, not a Rule, but failure to comply 'may be relied upon as tending to establish contravention of' the Rule requiring retrieval of the Resolution Pack within 48 hours (CASS 10.1.9E(3)).

- Firms are required to 'ensure' that services from service/system providers continue so the records are retrievable (CASS 10.1.9E(2)) (this is an Evidential Provision rather than a Rule). This suggests that firms will need to ensure that relevant service provider contracts do not contain insolvency termination provisions, but aside from this, it is unclear how a firm can compel a service provider to continue the provision of services in an insolvency situation, unless there is legislative support for this[1].

- CASS 10.1.5G(2) indicates that the Resolution Pack should be updated to reflect daily reconciliations, but confusingly new CASS 10.1.11R(2) requires correction of inaccuracies to be made 'no more than 5 business days' after the relevant change of circumstances which caused the information required for the Resolution Pack to be inaccurate. Arguably this could be read to mean that the new Rules permit a Resolution Pack retrieved in the required 48 hours to be inaccurate. This would be odd and is presumably not the intention, which therefore means there is an implicit requirement to update information immediately when a Resolution Pack is requested by the relevant insolvency practitioner or the FSA.

- The CASS Resolution Pack (the documents and records specified in CASS 10.2 and 10.3) must include a document identifying appointed representatives, tied agents, field representatives or other 'agents' of the firm which receive client money or client assets in the capacity of the firm's 'agent' (CASS 10.2.1R(3)). It is unclear what is contemplated here, since the CASS Rules only envisage a firm holding client money through a relevant credit institution, or client securities through a nominee or sub-custodian.

- As well as identifying institutions with which the firm holds client securities or client money, the firm is required to produce copies of 'each executed agreement' with the relevant institution (CASS 10.2.1R(5)). It would be unusual for a custodian to have written agreements with its nominees, but this rule indicates that such agreements will be necessary in future.

- Under CASS 10.2.1R(6)(a), a firm must produce a document which identifies each group member and third party involved in 'operational functions related to any obligations imposed on the firm by CASS 6 or CASS 7'. It is unclear what 'operational functions' means here, or to what extent functions must be linked to the relevant CASS obligations in order to be regarded as 'related' to such obligations. For example, while reference to subcustodians, settlement systems and payment systems is presumably intended, the FSA surely cannot want details of couriers and power suppliers.

- CASS 10.2.1R(8) requires that, in relation to third parties which the firm uses for the performance of 'operational functions' related to CASS 6 or 7, a firm must document how to 'gain access to relevant information held by that third party' (CASS 10.2.1R(8)(a)), and how to 'effect a transfer of any of the client money or safe custody assets held by the firm but controlled by that third party' (CASS 10.2.1R(8)(b)). This may be aimed at arrangements with registrars, or possibly settlement systems and subcustodians, but it is not clear. It would probably also catch arrangements with CREST sponsors ie the person sending dematerialised instructions on behalf of the firm.

1   See, for example, the Investment Bank Special Administration Regulations 2011 (SI 2011/245), reg 14, which prohibits a supplier of certain types of services from terminating that supply after the commencement of special administration

Control and custodians

7.123 Another area which may be of potential concern for custodians is the section of FSMA (Pt XII, ss 178–192) which requires notification to the FSA by any person in advance of taking steps to acquire or increase control over a UK authorised person. The FSA has 60 days in which to consider such notification (unless extended by no more than 20 days (or 30 days for certain non-EU entities) pursuant to a request by the FSA for further information[1]). It is an offence for a person to carry out the proposed action before the expiry of the assessment period if the FSA has not granted approval[2].

1   FSMA, s 190.
2   FSMA, s 191F

7.124 A person will acquire control for the purposes of this part of FSMA when it obtains 10 per cent or more of the shares or voting power in a UK authorised person or its parent undertaking, or is able to exercise 'significant influence' over the management of such person as a result of his or her shareholding (or voting power) in such person or its parent undertaking[1]. Similar provisions apply regarding the increase (or reduction) of control in an authorised person[2].

1   FSMA, s 181(1) and (2).
2   FSMA, ss 182, 183.

7.125 Certain shares are disregarded for the purposes of these requirements. In particular, shares held by a custodian or its nominee are disregarded, provided that the custodian or nominee is only able to exercise 'voting power represented by the shares' in accordance with instructions given in writing[1]. As a result, a custodian is not required to give notice to the FSA in respect of an acquisition of shares which it holds for its client (although the client will be subject to the notification requirement if its shareholding is of a sufficient size). This is logical, since a custodian might otherwise be subject to the notification requirement as a result of holding the same type of shares for a number of clients, even though not itself the beneficial owner of the shares or controlling the total voting rights. Without the exception, this would be a particular problem for custodians in a volatile market where many clients might wish to acquire the same stock if, because of the notification requirement, the custodian could not agree to accept delivery of the relevant stock into the name of the custodian or its delegate until the time limit imposed by the FSA had been followed. This would be a significant delay on business.

1   FSMA, s 184(3).

7.126 A similar situation exists under the FSA's Disclosure and Transparency Rules ('DTRs'). Chapter 5 of the DTRs requires monitoring and disclosure of voting rights held in relation to shares admitted to trading on a regulated market where the issuer's home state for these purposes is the UK. This could cause problems for a custodian holding shares of a particular type for various different clients and therefore in aggregate holding a large number of such shares. However, provided that the custodian has no discretion in the exercise of the relevant voting rights but can only exercise such rights 'under instructions given in writing or by electronic means', the relevant voting rights are to be disregarded when the custodian calculates its notification obligations under the DTRs[1].

1   DTR 5.1.3R(2).

Trustees and custody

7.127 We have discussed earlier (see Chapter 3) the idea that as a matter of English law it is probably most realistic to regard a custodian as a trustee, and in the above sections of this chapter we have considered some of the regulatory requirements which apply to custodians as a result of FSMA and certain sections of the FSA Handbook. However, in the context of identifying activities which may constitute regulated activities (see para **7.15** above), it is interesting to note that the Regulated Activities Order provides certain exemptions for trustees[1]. As a result, if a person which is a trustee carries out an activity specified in the Order and would otherwise need to be authorised by the FSA to carry on such activity in the UK, it may avoid the need for authorisation if it carries out the activity within the parameters of the relevant exemption. In relation to custody specifically, a person will not be regarded as performing the relevant activity[2] if it is done when 'acting as trustee or personal representative' *unless* 'he holds himself out as providing a service comprising' the relevant activity, or 'is remunerated for what he does in addition to any remuneration he receives as trustee or personal representative'[3].

1   Article 66 and 66A specifically relate to custody (although art 67 may also assist, together with certain other general exemptions). Note that although various exemptions in the Regulated Activities Order are subject to the narrower exemptions under MiFID, art 66 is subject only to art 4(4A) which only concerns persons carrying on insurance activities.

2   Article 40(1): '... both (a) the safeguarding of assets belonging to another, and (b) the administration of those assets, or arranging for one or more other persons to carry on that activity'.

3   Article 66(4) and (7). Note also Article 66(4A) which provides an exemption for arranging custody; in such case, there is no requirement that there should be no holding out or separate remuneration, but the person which the trustee arranges will provide custody must be a person who is authorised or exempt for the purposes of providing custody in the UK (or alternatively the custody must be arranged by such a person as well as the trustee).

7.128 On the basis that a custodian is a form of trustee, it is worth considering how the regulated activity of custody and the trustee exemption interrelate. At one extreme, it could be argued that apart from the case where a custodian is clearly a bailee of physical assets, a custodian will invariably be a trustee and fall within the trustee exemption and would therefore not need to become authorised for custody activities alone. At the other end of the spectrum, there is the argument that the exemptions in art 66 are essentially aimed at activities carried out ancillary to trustee functions, that the holding of assets is a core function of a trustee and so can never be ancillary, and that therefore a trustee which holds assets is always required to be authorised. While there is perhaps no clear answer to this, both these extreme arguments would seem to make something of a nonsense of the legislation. One way of approaching this is to go back to the analysis of a custodian as a particular type of trustee which has by agreement restricted its functions and liabilities. On this basis, the requirement of authorisation and regulatory compliance may be regarded as additional client protection which is advisable where the 'trustee' is in fact a custodian, whereas such additional protection is in principle not necessary where the trustee is subject to all usual trust obligations. Clearly, such analysis is not perfect, given that trustees in certain structures would aim to clarify and restrict the scope of their functions to the extent appropriate, but it does at least draw some form of distinction between a service described as a custody service and a service described as a trustee service. This is consistent with the requirements of the exemption that there should be no holding out of the provision of custody services separately, or separate remuneration for custody services. After all, if a client thinks that they are paying for a custody service, or has appointed the relevant entity because it has made claims about the nature of its custody services, it does not seem unreasonable to require the service provider to comply with the usual requirements that apply to custodians. In particular, it seems doubtful that a service which for most purposes appears to be a normal custody service would be within the scope of the trustee exemption merely because the arrangement is labelled a trust rather than custody. It is useful to note that art 66(7) states that 'a person is not to be regarded as receiving additional remuneration merely because his remuneration is calculated by reference to time spent'. In principle, therefore, a trustee is not prevented from charging for the time spent on aspects of the trustee function which in practice relate to safeguarding and administering assets, but, in contrast, it would be difficult to argue that the trustee was not 'receiving additional remuneration' if, for example, the agreed terms allocated the trustee a separate fee for custody services.

7.129 As suggested in the discussion above, for the purposes of the trustee exemption, the position where custody services are involved is perhaps not as clear as it might be[1]. It is a particular concern where entities wish to rely on the trustee exemption so that authorisation under the FSMA regime is not required, and in such cases great care should be taken to weigh up all the factors involved including the risks, since the consequences of conducting without authorisation an activity where authorisation is required are potentially significant.

1 There remains the question of whether an entity providing a custody service would need to be authorised if effectively selling the service as a trustee service rather than custody. It seems likely that the regulatory authorities would have little sympathy for an entity clearly trying to escape the regulatory regime by disguising its service, but it is conceivable that there could be situations where the answer is less clear cut.

Outsourcing

7.130 An additional potential area of concern for custodians may arise not from CASS or COBS but from the section of the High Level Standards relating to 'Senior Management Arrangements, Systems and Controls' ('SYSC').

7.131 A firm is required to 'take reasonable care to establish and maintain such systems and controls as are appropriate to its business' and to 'take reasonable care to establish and maintain effective systems and controls for compliance with applicable requirements and standards under the regulatory system and for countering the risk that the firm might be used to further financial crime'[1]. There is also the obligation under Principle 3 of the FSA's Principles to 'take reasonable care to organise and control its affairs responsibly and effectively, with adequate risk management systems'.

1   SYSC 3.1.1R and 3.2.6R.

7.132   The increased focus on operational risk is an issue for all regulated entities including custodians, but the aspect which may be of particular interest to persons using or providing custody services is the regulation of outsourcing. This may be relevant if a custodian's use of sub-custodians or other delegates is regarded as outsourcing, or the appointment of the custodian itself is regarded as an outsourcing by the custodian's client.

7.133   Certain regulatory obligations have existed for some time in relation to outsourcing, namely the requirement in the FSA Supervision sourcebook ('SUP') for a firm to notify the FSA when entering into (or significantly changing) a 'material outsourcing' and to enable the FSA to obtain information about a 'material outsourcing'[1], and the guidance regarding delegation and outsourcing in SYSC 3.2.4G[2]. Prior to 1 January 2007, and under the FSA Glossary for the purposes of some FSA rules and guidance (including SYSC 3.2.4G but importantly not SYSC Chapter 8), the term 'outsourcing' has the following meaning: 'the use of a person to provide customised services to a firm other than: (a) a member of the firm's governing body acting in his capacity as such; or (b) an individual employed by a firm under a contract of service.' From this definition it could be argued that use of a custodian or sub-custodian is a standard service provided on standard terms rather than a 'customised service'[3] and hence not an outsourcing for these purposes. This was in fact the approach taken in the outsourcing section of the old Interim Prudential Sourcebook for Banks (now replaced by BIPRU), Chapter OS[4] of which stated specifically that 'purchase of a standardised service from, for example, Bloombergs or Reuters and the provision of custody arrangements fall outside of the definition of material outsourcing'. As a result, although a regulated entity appointing a custodian or sub-custodian would need to consider appropriate arrangements for the appointment and use of such delegate (in the same way as would be appropriate when appointing any third party to provide services) in order to comply with the requirements discussed above to establish and maintain appropriate and effective systems and controls, for the purposes of these rules it is difficult to see why use of custody services in the normal course should be regarded as material outsourcing[5]. Moreover, any regulated custodian holding client assets with a sub-custodian is subject to various obligations under the CASS rules regarding the terms of the sub-custodian agreement[6], therefore it is not clear why an additional layer of regulation should be necessary.

1   SUP15.3.1R and 15.3.8G(1)(e), and SUP Chapter 2, section 2.3. A 'material outsourcing' means 'outsourcing services of such importance that weakness, or failure, of the services would cast serious doubt upon the firm's continuing satisfaction of the threshold conditions or compliance with the Principles' (FSA Glossary).

2   The guidance in SYSC 3.2.3G relating to how a firm is expected to comply with SYSC 3.1.1R refers in particular to the need for 'appropriate safeguards' when delegating functions, including assessing 'whether the recipient is suitable to carry out the delegated function or task', clarification of the 'extent and limits of any delegation ... to those concerned', and making 'arrangements to supervise delegation, and to monitor the discharge of delegates functions or tasks' (SYSC 3.2.3G(2), (3) and (4)). In addition, SYSC 3.2.4G states that 'guidance relevant to delegation within the firm is also relevant to external delegation ('outsourcing')' and that a firm 'should take steps to obtain sufficient information from its contractor to enable it to assess the impact of outsourcing on its systems and controls'.

3   This term is not defined in the FSA Glossary.

4   IPRU (Bank), Chapter OS, section 1.1(3)(b)(b). Although this particular rulebook applied to banks and insurance companies, it was generally considered helpful for other entities as an indication of the FSA's

general approach to outsourcing in relation to investment business. It is interesting to note that the earlier draft wording for the Integrated Prudential Sourcebook (CP97, published June 2001) (although this particular sourcebook no longer exists) contained a section relating to outsourcing which included the statement that 'The provision of custody services does not constitute material outsourcing'.

5   Although it is possible that this could be the case, depending on the circumstances. For example, if custody services were customised, rather than provided on a standard basis, or arguably if a global custodian delegates all operations to a global sub-custodian.

6   See CASS 6.3.1R–6.3.9R.

7.134 Under SYSC Chapter 8[1] which implements certain specific requirements of MiFID and the MiFID implementing Directive, there are additional rules relating to outsourcing which apply to any firm which is a 'common platform firm' (the definition of this is quite complex, but very broadly, means any building society, bank or investment firm subject to the FSA prudential requirements in the BIPRU sourcebook). These rules are somewhat curious as an example of the way in which MiFID provisions are reflected in the MiFID implementing Directive, and the provisions of both such Directives are implemented in the FSA rules.

1   For these purposes, the focus is on section 8.1 of this Chapter, since sections 8.2 and 8.3 concern the outsourcing of portfolio management for retail clients.

7.135 MiFID requires that investment firms should 'when relying on a third party for the performance of operational functions which are critical for the provision of continuous and satisfactory service to clients and the performance of investment activities on a continuous and satisfactory basis', ensure that they take 'reasonable steps to avoid undue additional operational risk'. Furthermore, firms should not outsource 'important operational functions ... in such a way as to impair materially the quality of ... internal control and the ability of the supervisor to monitor the firm's compliance with all obligations', and 'An investment firm shall have sound administrative and accounting procedures, internal control mechanisms, effective procedures for risk assessment, and effective control and safeguard arrangements for information processing systems'[1]. The concern in these provisions is apparently with delegation of 'critical' operational functions relevant to 'service to clients' and 'investment activities' or 'important' operational functions affecting internal controls and monitoring. The MiFID implementing Directive expands the scope further by defining the meaning of critical and important operational functions by reference to its effect on 'compliance of an investment firm with the conditions and obligations of its authorisation or its other obligations under' MiFID 'or its financial performance, or the soundness or the continuity of its investment services and activities', and listing various conditions to be complied with when outsourcing not only 'critical or important operational functions' but also 'any investment services or activities'[2]. However, the MiFID implementing Directive also states that certain functions 'shall not be considered as critical or important' for these purposes, including 'the purchase of standardised services'[3].

1   MiFID, art 13(5).
2   MiFID implementing Directive, arts 13 and 14.
3   MiFID implementing Directive, art 13(2)(b).

7.136 It is important to note here that under MiFID, 'investment services and activities' means the services and activities listed in Section A of Annex I to MiFID, but not ancillary services listed in Section B (which include custody services). As a result, under both MiFID and the MiFID implementing Directive, outsourcing the provision of custody services is currently outside the scope of these Directives[1] unless the custody services are seen as a 'critical or important operational function' which affects compliance with authorisation conditions and obligations or MiFID, financial performance or the provision of other investment services or activities.

Thus, if the only services that the delegated custody services could affect are not 'investment services and activities' (eg custody services or non-investment services), and failure or defects in the delegated custody services would not 'materially impair' compliance with authorisation conditions and obligations or MiFID, or financial performance, the delegated custody services should not be within the scope of outsourcing regulation. Even if the delegating entity provides investment services or conducts investment activities within Section A, or once custody becomes a core service, arguably it is unlikely that the delegation will be within scope if the services outsourced to the relevant custodian or sub-custodian are fairly standard therefore a replacement could be appointed without major difficulty, or the custodian or sub-custodian is one of a number of delegates hence termination of arrangements with such entity would not 'materially impair' the relevant services or activities.

1   Although at present it appears this will not be the case under MiFID2, see para **7.14**.

7.137   SYSC Chapter 8 implements the Directives but expands the scope of the rules even further. Operational functions are critical or important if a defect or failure in them would materially impair not only the matters described in the MiFID implementing Directive, but also compliance with any obligations under the FSMA regime, and the soundness or continuity of any ancillary services (as listed in MiFID Annex I, Section B) and any activities set out in the Regulated Activities which are not within the scope of MiFID. Similarly, the additional compliance conditions apply not just to outsourcing critical or operational functions, or investment services and activities (as listed in MiFID Annex I, Section A), but also to outsourcing any ancillary services (as listed in MiFID Annex I, Section B) and any activities set out in the Regulated Activities which are not within the scope of MiFID. For this purpose, the definition in the FSA Glossary of 'outsourcing' is potentially very wide, being 'an arrangement of any form between a firm and a service provider by which that service provider performs a process, a service or an activity which would otherwise be undertaken by the firm itself.' As a result, it is difficult to see why custody services would not be within the scope of SYSC Chapter 8, unless it is possible to argue in the relevant circumstances that the services would not otherwise be undertaken by the firm itself, or that the custody services are 'standardised services'[1]. Equally it is difficult to see the justification for applying the rules to custody services for the reasons discussed in the above paragraph, particularly since there are already regulatory controls under the CASS rules which apply to firms providing or delegating custody services.

1   See SYSC 8.1.5R, which reflects art 13(2) of the MiFID implementing Directive.

7.138   From the opposite perspective, custodians and other service providers will also need to bear in mind the regulatory context when providing services to FSA members if the custody service or any ancillary services[1] are of a nature or extent such that delegation could be regarded as an outsourcing or material outsourcing. In such cases, the entity outsourcing the services will undoubtedly be concerned to impose as many controls on the delegates as it can in order to protect its regulatory position.

1   For example, 'middle office' functions such as trade matching, allocation and reporting which may be delegated to custodians along with custody business.

RELATED ISSUES

Clients' right of action

7.139   Having considered the nature of the regulatory obligations which apply to the provision of custody services for clients, it may also be useful to consider whether breach of such obligations will give rise to a direct claim by the client against the custodian. This is in addition to any claim for breach of contract, in tort, or for breach of fiduciary duty, as discussed in Chapter 6.

7.140 The regulated entity may be subject to fines or other disciplinary action by the FSA if it breaches applicable requirements under FSMA such as the CASS rules. However, there are essentially two situations where the FSA requirements may give rise to claims by the custodian's client.

Breach of FSA rules

7.141 Under FSMA, s 150 a 'private person'[1] is entitled to bring a claim against a firm authorised by the FSA for breach of FSA rules. This is treated as a claim for breach of statutory duty and is therefore subject to any defences which the FSA member would have for such a claim.

1 See the Financial Services and Markets Act 2000 (Rights of Action) Regulations 2001 (SI 2001/2256), reg 3:

'(1) In these Regulations, "private person" means – (a) any individual, unless he suffers the loss in question in the course of carrying on – (i) any regulated activity; or (ii) any activity which would be a regulated activity apart from any exclusion made by article 72 (overseas persons) or 72A (information society services) of the Regulated Activities Order; and (b) any person who is not an individual, unless he suffers the loss in question in the course of carrying on business of any kind;

but does not include a government, a local authority (in the United Kingdom or elsewhere) or an international organisation.

(2) For the purposes of paragraph (1)(a), an individual who suffers loss in the course of effecting or carrying out contracts of insurance (within the meaning of article 10 of the Regulated Activities Order) written at Lloyds's is not to be taken to suffer loss in the course of carrying on a regulated activity.'

Breach of regulatory requirements

7.142 A client will have a claim against the custodian under the terms of the custody agreement (and therefore subject to any relevant limitations in such agreement) for breach of regulatory requirements if the regulatory requirements have been incorporated into the agreement as contractual terms. While it seems unlikely in normal circumstances that a custodian would wish to agree to this, case law[1] has shown that there may be a risk of inadvertently incorporating terms by reference when intending to make references for other purposes: therefore care should be taken when drafting cross-references to the terms of regulatory requirements (or other relevant wording, eg standard settlement system or stock exchange rules). Of course, a custody client might argue (somewhat disingenuously) that a custodian should intend to, and is required to, comply with its regulatory obligations anyway, therefore should have no difficulty in stating in its agreement that it will do so. However, it is not necessarily the case that a custodian would wish to give a person who is not a private person for the purposes of FSMA a direct contractual right of claim which it would not otherwise have, particularly where the relevant rules are drafted widely on a purposive basis rather than as clear contract terms.

1 *Chigi v CS First Boston Ltd* [1997] All ER (D) 121, QBD, Commercial Court. In this case, the wording causing particular problems was the following: 'All transactions in Securities shall be subject to the rules and customs of the exchange or market and/or any clearing house through which the transactions are executed (if any), the rules and regulations of the Securities and Investments Board, The Securities and Futures Authority Limited and the Bank of England so far as they are applicable and to applicable law so that: (a) if there is any conflict between: (i) these Terms and Conditions and (ii) any such rules, customs and applicable law, the latter shall prevail.' The client argued that this wording made the transactions subject to the London Code of Conduct (being

applicable regulations of the Bank of England) which prevailed over the brokers' standard terms and conditions. The broker argued that the wording 'was intended to ensure that if there was any conflict between the general terms of business and any regulatory provision' it would 'be entitled to comply with that regulatory provision'. The judge concluded that notwithstanding the intended limited effect of this wording, 'it did not naturally read in that way' and therefore it was correct that 'the transactions were made subject to the applicable regulations of The Bank of England, namely the London Code of Conduct' and as a result 'although no claim based upon a paragraph of the London Code gives rise to any statutory duty' the broker was nonetheless 'under the duties imposed by that code as a matter of contract'.

7.143 There is also a further argument that even if regulatory requirements have not been incorporated in the relevant agreement by reference, and the client is not a private person, any regulatory requirements which implement the requirements of MiFID or the MiFID implementing Directive are in fact requirements of relevant legislation therefore any breach of such requirements is breach of statutory duty under English law. However this approach has not to date been confirmed in any relevant proceedings.

Unclaimed assets

7.144 As noted above in the context of unclaimed money, the issue of unclaimed assets can be a considerable problem for custodians[1]. In such cases, the custodian is required by the regulatory regime to provide all appropriate protections for the client securities or cash but, because the client is unknown, may simply be unable to comply with certain requirements, such as reviewing the client classification for the client or providing regular statements to the client. Similarly, unless the custodian has always used the same form of custody terms, it may be impossible to identify what contractual terms were entered into by the custodian and the unknown clients and the custodian cannot amend or replace such terms since it cannot obtain the agreement of the client to do so. Are any methods of resolution open to the custodian, apart from the limited assistance which may be available under the Client Money Rules and new regulations for dormant accounts (see paras **7.78–7.82** above)? In practice, the situation is very difficult because there is no principle of law which extinguishes rights to unclaimed securities or cash, merely because such assets are unclaimed; therefore any attempt by a custodian to simply treat the assets as its own assets would risk the possibility of a claimant appearing at a later date and claiming for breach of contract (assuming it is a former client), conversion or unjust enrichment or, in extreme circumstances, alleging theft has occurred. In such a case, the custodian would also be in breach of trust and in breach of its regulatory obligations under the CASS rules not to combine client assets with its own assets. While there might be circumstances in which a custodian could become comfortable with the risks of treating the assets as its own, for example, after examining the effect of any relevant limitation periods and making provisions for possible claims, it seems unlikely that the regulators would be happy with this approach. Also, it is crucial to avoid any question of dishonesty, by giving clients adequate details of the proposed action. In practice, the best way to be relieved of the unwanted burden of unclaimed client assets is probably to go through the process of paying into court[2].

1 A possible source of unclaimed assets may be third party administrative error. Assets may be 'unclaimed' for a variety of reasons and through no fault of the custodian, for example, due to late delivery of cash or noncash distributions to the custodian in respect of assets which were held by the custodian for a client but are no longer. If the delivery identifies the assets to which they relate, the custodian should be able to determine which former client is entitled to the assets, but if the relevant person declines responsibility for the assets, the custodian is left with the assets. Similarly, confusion might arise if a client sells securities, then a late distribution is made, but neither client nor purchaser claims the distribution.

2 Under the Trustee Act 1925.

EEA passport arrangements

7.145 MiFID provides an EEA passport for the investment services and activities listed in Annex I, Section A, of MiFID (including 'Execution of orders on behalf of clients', 'Dealing on own account', 'Portfolio management' and 'Investment advice')[1]. Broadly, the passport allows an investment firm established and authorised in one EEA member state to conduct these investment services or activities regulated by its home state in other EEA member states without needing additional authorisation in such states. A similar passport was available under the ISD[2], whereby, in general, an entity operating in another EEA member state pursuant to the passport did not require authorisation in the host state and remained subject to the home state's prudential regulation (regarding capital requirements and holding of client assets), but was subject to the host state's conduct of business rules. Under the MiFID passport arrangements, an entity operating in another EEA member state pursuant to the passport is not subject to any of the host state rules, subject to the branch rule discussed below.

1   Note that under the ISD, giving investment advice was not a passportable service.

2   Council Directive 93/22/EEC of 10 May 1993 on investment services in the securities field, replaced by MiFID (see para **7.10** above).

7.146 Annex I, Section B of MiFID lists certain 'Ancillary services', including 'Safekeeping and administration of financial instruments for the account of clients, including custodianship and related services such as cash/collateral management'. Ancillary services are within the scope of MiFID for regulatory purposes, but cannot be passported unless provided together with a service or activity within Section A of Annex I. As a result, an investment firm cannot apply for a MiFID passport for custody services alone, but can apply for the passport if providing custody services together with, for example, portfolio management. Assuming that the final text of MiFID2 (see para **7.14** above) classifies safekeeping and administration as a service within Section A of Annex I, the situation will change so that the passport process can be used for custody services alone.

7.147 Even if an entity regulated under MiFID is conducting relevant activities or services in another EEA member state under the MiFID passport, if it conducts such activities or services through a branch in that state, the host state regulator 'shall assume responsibility for ensuring that the services provided by the branch within its territory comply with the obligations laid down in Articles 19, 21, 22, 25, 27 and 28 and in measures adopted pursuant thereto'[1]. The articles referenced are broadly conduct of business requirements, therefore this rule does not apply to custody services which will remain subject to home state regulation, except for certain aspects which fall within the conduct of business compliance regime (in particular, record-keeping and risk warnings).

1   MiFID, art 32(7). Note that this raises certain additional issues, such as which regulatory requirements apply where a branch within a host state provides services outside that territory.

7.148 Where an investment firm wishes to perform investment services or activities (and related ancillary services) in another EEA member state, it must notify its home state regulator of the other state in which it intends to perform such services and activities and the nature of such services and activities. The home state regulator must within one month of receiving such information notify the relevant regulator in the intended host state, after which notification the investment firm may begin performing the relevant services and activities in the host state[1].

1   MiFID, art 31(2), (3).

7.149 Where a custodian is a bank and wishes to perform relevant services in other EU member states, it will make use of the passport available under the Banking Consolidation Directive (the 'BCD')[1] for entities which are credit institutions[2]. In order to conduct activities on a cross-border basis in the UK pursuant to the BCD passport, a credit institution must notify its home state authority of the activities listed in Annex I[3] of the BCD which it intends to conduct in the UK[4]. Once a credit institution has given the required notice to its regulator in its home state, pursuant to the relevant provisions of FSMA the credit institution qualifies for authorisation in the UK, and has permission to carry on the services specified in the notice on a cross-border basis into the UK. The home state regulator is required by the BCD to send a copy of the credit institution's notification to the proposed host state within one month of receiving such notification from the credit institution. The host state must then within two months from the day on which it receives the copy of the notification prepare for supervision of the credit institution and notify the credit institution of the host state rules which the credit institution is required to comply with (if any) when performing its cross-border activities.

1   Directive 2006/48/EC of the European Parliament and the Council of 14 June 2006 relating to the taking up and pursuit of the business of credit institutions (recast). Article 28 sets out the main terms enabling a credit institution to 'exercise the freedom to provide services by carrying on its activities within the territory of another Member State'.

2   Defined in BCD, art 4(1) as '(a) an undertaking whose business is to receive deposits or other repayable funds from the public and to grant credits for its own account; or (b) an electronic money institution within the meaning of Directive 2006/46/EC'.

3   Such activities include: 'Acceptance of deposits and other repayable funds'; 'Trading for own account or for account of customers in: (a) money market instruments (cheques, bills, certificates of deposits, etc.); (b) foreign exchange; (c) financial futures and options; (d) exchange and interest-rate instruments; or (e) transferable securities'; 'Portfolio management and advice'; 'Safekeeping and administration of securities'; and 'Safe custody services'.

4   Note that, unlike under the MiFID passport, the credit institution is permitted to carry out the relevant cross-border services in the UK at this stage, although as a practical matter such credit institution will not be able to refer to the FSA register as evidence of authorisation until the FSA has received and acted upon notification from the credit institutions home state regulator.

7.150 If a credit institution or investment firm is carrying on activities or providing services in a host state for which a passport is not available, such entity will require authorisation and regulation by the host state regulator in the normal way. Similarly, if an entity uses the passport for certain services but is also providing services in the host state which are regulated in that state but for which no passport is available, the entity will require what is known as 'top-up permission' from the local regulator. This means that the entity is for passported services authorised and regulated by its home state (subject, where applicable, to the particular rules relating to branches as noted above), but for the additional services which are not covered by the passport, the entity will be regulated by the host state regulator.

Rights of indirect holders?

7.151 The question of the extent to which rights of custody clients should be extended to the customers of custody clients, or to which custody clients should be given direct rights against the custodian's delegates, is a perennial topic. The proposed Directive which attempts to tackle this is discussed in paras **7.177–7.193** below, but it is of some interest that the FSA has focused on this particular point in the context of platform operators and nominee companies. In a situation where investors acquire units in authorised funds (broadly, funds regulated by the FSA under Collective Investment Schemes sourcebook ('COLL')) which can be sold to retail investors) through platforms and hold such units through a nominee company rather

188 The Law of Global Custody

than directly, the FSA is concerned that important information (such as reports and accounts, and notification of changes affecting the relevant fund) are not forwarded by the nominee companies to the end investors[1].

1   See discussion in FSA Policy Statement PS11/9 'Platforms: Delivering the RDR and other issues for platforms and nominee-related services', August 2011, and also the FSA Consultation Paper which preceded this: CP10/29 'Platforms: Delivering the RDR and other issues for platforms and nominee-related services', November 2010.

7.152   As a result, the FSA proposed a new section of the Conduct of Business sourcebook (COBS 14.4[1]) imposing specific obligations on the 'intermediate unitholder'. This term is defined to mean, broadly, a nominee holder but excluding investment managers or fund depositaries, but would also include a custodian holding fund units for its clients in its own name. The obligations are to notify the beneficial owners of the fund units of the availability of, and to provide, certain information free of charge upon request (including the 'short report' referred to in COLL 4.5.13R), any information required by COLL to be sent by an authorised fund manager or depositary to a unitholder, and certain information about voting rights). These requirements are odd in some respects, not least because a nominee which is operating outside the FSA regime as a result of the exemption under Article 41 of the Regulated Activities Order (see para **7.20** above) will not be subject to the FSA COBS rules. Also, the new rules do not define the term 'beneficial owner' so it is arguable that the result may be to oblige the nominee to provide information not to the person for whom it holds the fund units but the ultimate beneficial owner (which may be difficult to determine).

1   See Appendix 1 to PS11/9 (the text of FSA Retail Distribution Review (Platforms) Instrument 2011, made 28 July 2011 and in force 31 December 2012), Annex B.

7.153   Further to PS11/9, evidently the FSA received a substantial number of further queries and comments regarding the application of the new rules in different operational contexts. As a result, the FSA proposed the deferral of the new rules until 31 December 2013, although it is not clear what further steps are intended, since the FSA specifically stated 'We will leave the existing rules in place because we are not intending to alter their basic structure'.[1]

1   FSA Consultation Paper CP12/11 'Quarterly Consultation Paper (No. 33)', June 2012.

Prime brokerage

7.154   Although the basic custody service does not include a brokerage aspect, it is appropriate to mention for completeness CASS Chapter 9 which came into force on 1 March 2011. The provisions of this chapter relate to prime brokerage services, defined quite widely as 'a package of services provided under a prime brokerage agreement which gives a prime brokerage firm a right to use safe custody assets for its own account and which comprises each of the following: (a) custody or arranging safeguarding and administration of assets ; (b) clearing services; and (c) financing, the provision of which includes one or more of the following: (i) capital introduction; (ii) margin financing; (iii) stock lending ; (iv) stock borrowing; (v) entering into repurchase or reverse repurchase transactions; and which, in addition, may comprise consolidated reporting and other operational support'.[1] As a result, an entity provides prime brokerage services as defined where such services include both dealing services and custody services.

1   FSA Glossary.

7.155   As a matter of general market practice, an entity acting as a prime broker will acquire securities for the client, and either: (a) hold such securities as custodian for the client, take a security interest over such securities, and have a right of use over such securities so that the broker can transfer the securities to itself from time to time (following which the client will have only a contractual claim for redelivery of such securities); or (b) receive such securities from the client by way of title transfer collateral to collateralise the client's obligations to the broker from time to time. In the relevant consultation paper, the FSA expressed concern regarding the lack of understanding by clients, even sophisticated clients, regarding the effect of the terms of prime brokerage agreements. It might be argued somewhat cynically that in an insolvency situation it is in a client's interests to argue that the it did not understand the relevant terms, on the basis that this may improve its chance of recovery, and that clients who accept particular terms on the basis of a lower service fee should be aware that there is a reason for the lower fee and should in any event familiarise themselves with the details of the agreement they have signed. Nevertheless, the FSA decided to create additional requirements designed to clarify the terms on which prime brokerage services are provided, and in particular to draw attention to any exercise of a right of use granted under the relevant security interest terms[1].

1   See FSA Consultation Paper CP10/9 'Enhancing the Client Assets Sourcebook', March 2010, in particular Chapter 2: 'Increasing re-hypothecation disclosure and transparency in the prime brokerage community', and FSA Policy Statement PS10/16: 'Client Assets Sourcebook (Enhancements) Instrument 2010', October 2010, in particular Chapter 3: 'Increased re-hypothecation disclosure and transparency in the prime brokerage community'.

7.156   In broad terms, the rules in CASS Chapter 9 require a firm providing prime brokerage services to provide a daily statement[1] to each clients containing detailed information about various matters, including the value of assets held for the client, total secured obligations of the client against the firm, total collateral held by the firm, disclosure of the firms' exercise of a right of use in respect of the collateral, and the 'location of all of a client's safe custody assets, including assets held with a sub-custodian'[2]. In addition, a firm must include in the agreement relating to the provision of prime brokerage services an annex which summarises the key provisions of the agreement which permit the use of the client's assets, including contractual limits on such use, relevant definitions, reference to the relevant provisions in the agreement, and a statement of key risks[3].

1   CASS 9.2.1R.
2   CASS 9.2.1R(3)(d). Query what exactly is meant by 'location' for this purpose. See discussion in Chapter 5.
3   CASS 9.3.1R.

7.157   Although the underlying purpose seems reasonable, there are some curiosities about the resulting rules. For example, because of the very broad definition of prime brokerage services, there is a potential risk that other types of services which involve a number of different aspects may be caught. The FSA indicated that it will be giving consideration to 'whether the proposals ... should be applied more broadly to other market participants who enter into rights of use arrangements to ensure there is a level playing field in the market.'[1] However, the FSA evidently currently considers that 'the made rules have been clarified to ensure they do not apply to pure wealth management business, as this is outside the definition of prime brokerage services.'[2]

1   See FSA Consultation Paper CP10/9 'Enhancing the Client Assets Sourcebook', March 2010, page 11, para 2.2, and FSA Policy Statement PS10/16: 'Client Assets Sourcebook (Enhancements) Instrument 2010', October 2010, page 15, para 3.3.
2   FSA Policy Statement PS10/16: 'Client Assets Sourcebook (Enhancements) Instrument 2010', October 2010, page 15, para 3.3.

7.158 The additional requirements for prime brokers are not a MiFID requirement and do not apply to EEA firms providing such services in the UK pursuant to a MiFID (or BCD) passport, but will apply to firms subject regulation by the FSA when providing its services from the UK. Arguably this hinders, rather than helps, create a level playing field between UK prime brokers and entities regulated in other EEA jurisdictions providing the same services. Moreover, although the summary annex is intended to draw attention to and clarify the terms regarding use of client assets by the prime broker, it is not intended to be legally binding[1], therefore a client wishing to understand the relevant terms would need to consider the terms of the agreement itself, not merely the summary. Also, if a client is unwilling to take the time to read the terms of the agreement, it is perhaps doubtful where such client would pay more attention to a summary non-binding annex. Nevertheless, it can be argued that these additional requirements at least encourage both prime broker and client to focus more attention on the relevant terms, and the statement of key risks in particular may prompt the client to consider more carefully the balance of fees payable and risks incurred in relation to the relevant service.

1   See FSA Consultation Paper CP10/9 'Enhancing the Client Assets Sourcebook', March 2010, page 7, para 1.14.

Further amendments to CASS?

7.159 In the wake of the Supreme Court judgment in February 2012[1], the FSA has announced a 'fundamental review of the client money and custody assets regime'[2]. The aims of such review are to 'improve the speed of return of client assets following the insolvency of an investment firm', to 'reduce the market impact of an insolvency of an investment firm that holds client assets' and to 'achieve a greater return of client assets to clients following the insolvency of an investment firm'[3]. On this basis, the FSA makes various suggestions for further amendment of both the client money rules and CASS rules relating to holding securities, and asks firms to consider specific questions, with a view to publishing a consultation on improvements to CASS in the first half of 2013.

1   *In the matter of Lehman Brothers International (Europe) (in Administration) and in the matter of the Insolvency Act 1986* [2012] UKSC 6, 29 February 2012.

2   FSA Consultation Paper CP 12/22 'Client assets regime: EMIR, multiple pools and the wider review', September 2012, para 4.1.

3   FSA Consultation Paper CP 12/22 'Client assets regime: EMIR, multiple pools and the wider review', September 2012, para 4.2.

7.160 It is an attractive argument that amendments to the client assets rules which would speed up the return of client assets in the event of a firm's insolvency would benefit all market participants. However, even with further amendment, it is difficult to see how the situation can be materially simplified where a firm has a complex business model. Moreover, it is significant that, as the FSA notes, insolvency officials will be very reluctant to return client assets except where 'title is established to a high degree of certainty because of their personal liability'[1]. In particular, some of the FSA proposals seem likely to cause more problems than they resolve, some examples of which are as follows.

- The FSA notes that retail clients and wholesale clients may have a different view on the priorities of speed of return and accuracy of return, and seems to be contemplating that different levels of client asset protection and distribution should apply to, respectively, retail clients and wholesale clients. The idea that the rights to return of assets should be dependent on the FSA's assumptions regarding the concerns of different types of clients about priority is surprising.

- It is proposed that client asset statements should be much more frequent (the current requirement is admittedly not very onerous, requiring only an annual statement[2]). It is not wholly clear why this requirement should be necessary, since clients may request or agree with custodians to receive statements more frequently, and there is no benefit in providing clients with statements they do not wish to receive. Also, in terms of maintenance of records, relevant information will be maintained regarding client assets pursuant to the requirements imposed by the CASS Resolution Pack rules[3].

- The relevant Supreme Court judgement[4] concluded that client money entitlements depend on the amounts which a firm should have segregated, rather than the amounts which were actually segregated. However, the FSA is apparently considering 'more emphasis on actual segregation and firms' record'[5]. While this might simplify the process for an insolvency official, this can hardly be said to benefit a client whose entitlement has, in error, not been segregated and/or recorded in the relevant records.

- The FSA refers to the fact that insolvency practitioners 'in other jurisdictions may liquidate all assets and all share in the shortfall (both client money and custody assets) equally', and says this is 'quicker and less expensive' for the insolvency official and 'can be seen as more equitable as all clients share equally in the event of a firm's failure'. A proposal to convert a client's securities, which it owns, into a cash amount for which it has claim for payment, is an extremely radical proposal. Not only does this seem to demonstrate fundamental confusion of claims for money amounts (albeit under a trust) and securities, it is difficult to see how removing property rights and giving instead a pro rata share in a cash amount which is exposed to losses incurred by other clients is 'more equitable', or how such an approach achieves 'greater return' for clients.

- Certain other fairly radical suggestions are: to require firms to set aside an amount of cash (to be held as client money) to meet the costs of distributing client assets in the firm's insolvency (thus effectively causing unsecured creditors to pay for the distribution of client assets); to require firms to hold in client bank accounts an amount equal to the money 'at risk' in house accounts under the alternative approach (it is not clear if the FSA assuming that client money is at risk as a result of being held in a house account or are contemplating the risk of the balance of such account falling below the amount of client money held in it); and to 'prioritise one set of clients over another, potentially leading to any shortfalls to be borne by those categories of clients lower down the prioritisation' (this is extremely odd, because although the FSA has powers to amend the client money trust, it is not clear on what basis the FSA could purport to change normal trust law in relation to the holding of securities, and effectively use the assets of one client for the benefit of another).

1 CP 12/22, para 4.18.

2 COBS 16.4.1R: (1) A firm that holds client designated investments or client money for a client must send that client at least once a year a statement in a durable medium of those designated investments or that client money unless such a statement has been provided in a periodic statement.

3 New CASS Chapter 10, applicable from 1 October 2012.

4 *In the matter of Lehman Brothers International (Europe) (in Administration) and in the matter of the Insolvency Act 1986* [2012] UKSC 6, 29 February 2012.

5 CP 12/22, para 4.28, Box 2.

7.161 It seems evident that the FSA is sensitive to the criticisms of the client assets rules in the various court cases, and wishes to be seen to be taking action to remedy the situation. However, given that there were particular difficulties[1] which complicated the administration proceedings for Lehman Brothers International

(Europe), it is not clear that a case has been made for the need for radical change to the CASS rules.

1   FSA Consultation Paper CP 12/22 'Client assets regime: EMIR, multiple pools and the wider review', September 2012, para 4.14 states such difficulties 'included insufficient and inadequate record-keeping, inadequate trust letters, excessive use of group banks to hold client money, failure to segregate for affiliates and insufficient importance placed on client assets issues by senior firm management.'

INTERNATIONAL REGULATORY DEVELOPMENTS

7.162   It is of course also important to consider the international regulatory context in which a custodian is providing services. This section considers some of international regulatory developments affecting custodians. In addition, the importance of custodians, settlement systems and central counterparties to the financial markets has received considerable industry and public sector attention, resulting in a number of initiatives proposed in relation to their regulation[1].

1   The collaboration project between the Committee of European Securities Regulators ('CESR') and the European System of Central Banks ('ESCB') in relation to securities clearing and settlement was announced in October 2001, with a view to developing standards for the post-trade infrastructure. Since then there have been various developments, as discussed in Chapter 8.

7.163   The regulatory requirements arising from MiFID and MiFID2 are discussed earlier in this chapter (see paras **7.10–7.14**), and the Financial Collateral Directive is considered in Chapter 4. The following are also of interest.

AIFMD

7.164   The AIFMD[1] is perhaps not obviously relevant to custodians since it is intended to regulate the activities of, broadly, funds other than UCITS ('AIFs'), the managers of such funds and the depositaries holding assets for such funds. However, the AIFMD is likely to have a major impact on custodians and general practice in the custody market for a number of reasons.

1   Directive 2011/61/EU of the European Parliament and of the Council of 8 June 2011 on Alternative Investment Fund Managers.

Depositary's liability for loss

7.165   The AIFMD imposes an extremely high level of liability on the depositary of an AIF in relation to the loss of financial instruments[1]. In particular: 'The depositary shall be liable to the AIF or to the investors of the AIF, for the loss by the depositary or a third party to whom the custody of financial instruments[2]. MiFID, Annex I, Section C, lists a very broad range of securities, including transferable securities[3], money-market instruments, units in collective investment undertakings, derivative instruments for the transfer of credit risk, financial contracts for the transfer of credit risk, and options, futures, swaps, forward rate agreements and any other derivative contracts relating to securities, currencies, interest rates or yields, or other derivatives instruments, financial indices or financial measures which may be settled physically or in case, derivatives relating to commodities that must or may be settled in cash, physically settled derivatives relating to commodities that are traded on a regulated market or MTF] held in custody in accordance with point (a) of paragraph 8 has been delegated. In the case of such a loss of a financial instrument held in custody, the depositary shall return a financial instrument of identical type or the corresponding amount to the AIF or the AIFM acting on behalf of the AIF without undue delay. The depositary shall not be liable if it can prove that the loss has arisen as a result of an

Regulatory duties

external event beyond its reasonable control, the consequences of which would have been unavoidable despite all reasonable efforts to the contrary.'[4] As a result, where there has been a loss of the AIF's financial instruments, the depositary can only avoid liability in limited circumstances, and that liability will require the return of financial instruments which the depositary may well not hold or be unable to obtain. It is not clear what the obligation to 'return ... the corresponding amount' means.

1 There is a considerable amount of political background to this. Briefly, the liquidation of Bernard L. Madoff Investment Securities drew attention to the fact that the provisions of Directive 2009/65/EC of 13 July 2009 on the coordination of laws, regulations and administrative provisions relating to undertakings for collective investment in transferable securities (commonly referred to as 'UCITS IV') regarding the liability of a depositary of a UCITS fund for loss of fund assets had been implemented in different ways in different EU jurisdictions. Notwithstanding the reference in UCITS IV to a UCITS depositary's liability for 'unjustifiable failure to perform its obligations or its improper performance of them', certain EU member states interpret the statement that a depositary's liability is not affected by use of delegates to mean that a depositary has strict liability for loss of fund assets by a delegate (regardless of the depositary's fault). Such EU member states were extremely critical of any approach other than strict liability, and used significant political pressure to influence the final form of the liability provisions of the AIFMD accordingly. Unsurprisingly, there is considerable overlap between the EU member states which advocated the strict liability approach, and EU member states which have little understanding of the concept of successive interests in securities under a trust and in whose jurisdictions delegation of the holding of securities is rare.

2 AIFMD, art 4(1)(n). 'financial instrument' is defined to mean 'an instrument as specified in Section C of Annex I to Directive 2004/39/EC[MiFID]'.

3 Defined as 'those classes of securities which are negotiable on the capital market, with the exception of instruments of payment, such as: (a) shares in companies and other securities equivalent to shares in companies, partnerships or other entities, and depositary receipts in respect of shares; (b) bonds or other forms of securitised debt, including depositary receipts in respect of such securities; (c) any other securities giving the right to acquire or sell any such transferable securities or giving rise to a cash settlement determined by reference to transferable securities, currencies, interest rates or yields, commodities or other indices or measures'. MiFID, art 4(1), (18).

4 AIFMD, art 21(12).

7.166 As regards what constitutes a 'loss of financial instruments' for the purposes of AIFMD, art 21(12), the current draft Level 2 measure[1] is very onerous. Draft Article 100 states the following: '1. A loss of a financial instrument held in custody within the meaning of Article 21(12) of Directive 2011/61/EU shall be deemed to have taken place when, in relation to a financial instrument held in custody by the depositary or by a third party to whom the custody of financial instruments held in custody has been delegated, any of the following conditions is met: (a) a stated right of ownership of the AIF is demonstrated not to be valid because it either ceased to exist or never existed; (b) the AIF has been definitively deprived of its right of ownership over the financial instrument; (c) the AIF is definitively unable to directly or indirectly dispose of the financial instrument.' However, draft Article 100(3) also states 'A financial instrument held in custody shall not be deemed to be lost within the meaning of Article 21(12) of Directive 2011/61/EU where an AIF is definitively deprived of its right of ownership in respect of a particular instrument, but this instrument is substituted by or converted into another financial instrument or instruments.' This draft text is surprising in various respects, not least in that it is unclear how a depositary could or should be responsible for an ownership right which never existed at all, and if an AIF is unable to dispose of a financial instrument, this may present problems but is not itself a loss.

1 At the time of writing, the informal draft of the proposed Level 2 Regulation released on 5 October 2012.

7.167 The question of when there is an external event beyond the reasonable control of the depositary also raises considerable concerns. Not only is the depositary required to 'prove' this, but also the text of draft Article 101 of the Level

2 measure means it would be extremely difficult for a depositary to fall within the exception.

7.168 Draft Article 101 of the Level 2 measure states that: '1. A depositary's liability under the second subparagraph of Article 21(12) of Directive 2011/61/EU shall not be triggered provided the depositary can prove that all the following conditions are met: (a) the event which led to the loss is not the result of any act or omission of the depositary or of a third party to whom the custody of financial instruments held in custody in accordance with point (a) of Article 21(8) of Directive 2011/61/EU has been delegated; (b) the depositary could not have reasonably prevented the occurrence of the event which led to the loss despite adopting all precautions incumbent on a diligent depositary as reflected in common industry practice; (c) despite rigorous and comprehensive due diligence, the depositary could not have prevented the loss. This condition may be deemed to be fulfilled when the depositary has ensured that the depositary and the third party to whom the custody of financial instruments held in custody in accordance with point (a) of Article 21(8) of Directive 2011/61/EU has been delegated have taken all of the following actions: (i) establishing, implementing, applying and maintaining structures and procedures and insuring expertise that are adequate and proportionate to the nature and complexity of the assets of the AIF in order to identify in a timely manner and monitor on an ongoing basis external events which may result in a loss of a financial instrument held in custody; (ii) assessing on an ongoing basis whether any of the events identified under the first indent presents a significant risk of loss of a financial instrument held in custody; –(iii) informing the AIFM of the significant risks identified and taking appropriate actions, if any, to prevent or mitigate the loss of financial instruments held in custody, where actual or potential external events have been identified which are believed to present a significant risk of loss of a financial instrument held in custody. 2. The requirements referred to in points (a) and (b) of paragraph 1 may be deemed to be fulfilled in the following circumstances: (a) natural events beyond human control or influence; (b) the adoption of any law, decree, regulation, decision or order by any government or governmental body, including any court or tribunal which impacts the financial instruments held in custody; (c) war, riots or other major upheavals. 3. The requirements referred to in points (a) and (b) of paragraph 1 shall not be deemed to be fulfilled in cases such as an accounting error, operational failure, fraud, failure to apply the segregation requirements at the level of the depositary or a third party to whom the custody of financial instruments held in custody in accordance with point (a) of Article 21(8) of Directive 2011/61/EU has been delegated. 4. This Article shall apply mutatis mutandis to the delegate when the depositary has contractually transferred its liability in accordance with Article 21(13) and (14) of Directive 2011/61/EU.'

7.169 As currently drafted, Article 101 has the result that the 'external event' exception can _never_ apply where the loss of financial instruments results from the act or omission of the depositary or a delegate, or an accounting error, operational failure, fraud, or failure to apply the segregation requirements at the level of the depositary or delegate, regardless of the reason for such act, omission or other event. This is also significant in that a depositary is made liable for the fraud of its delegate, even if it had no knowledge of, and could not prevent, such fraud. It is helpful that under AIFMD, art 21(11), final paragraph, a settlement system is not regarded as a delegate, but the effect of such provision is not entirely clear. Does the exclusion of settlement systems from the meaning of delegate mean that loss by a settlement system will be regarded as loss by a depositary, because the settlement system is not a delegate? Or does it mean that where financial instruments are held with a settlement system, the lower level of liability applies, and/or the depositary can limit or exclude liability for loss of financial instruments held by a settlement system.

7.170 Arguably some comfort is provided by the fact that the main loss liability provision in AIFMD, art 21(12) imposes the high level of liability in respect of loss 'by' the depositary or a third party to whom the custody of financial instruments is delegated, and, despite the wording of draft Article 100 of the Level 2 measure, the Level 2 measure cannot impose greater liability than AIFMD. Thus in principle normal questions of causation should apply, although it is not wholly clear how this is modified by the exception requiring proof that the loss arose as a result of an external event. For loss other than loss of financial instruments (for example, loss of assets which are not financial instruments, or loss resulting from delay or other default), the level of liability is less onerous, stating that the depositary will be liable for losses suffered by the AIF or investors in the AIF 'as a result of the depositary's negligent or intentional failure to properly fulfil its obligations pursuant to this Directive'[1]. Of course, this does not result in an insignificant level of liability, since under English law at least, an entity in the position of a depositary is likely to have to comply with a high level of care in order to avoid being regarded as negligent.

1   AIFMD, art 21(12), final paragraph.

Implications for Depositary's delegates

7.171 A depositary will in most cases need to hold the assets it holds for the AIF through a sub-custodian, nominee or settlement. Inevitably, where a an entity providing a service is subject to a very high level of liability, it will seek to impose a similar level of liability on its delegates, so that it is not at risk to the extent there is a mismatch between the liability it takes to its clients and the liability accepted by its delegates. Moreover, there are various aspects of AIFMD and the draft Level 2 measure which appear to apply automatically to any delegate of a depositary providing service to an AIF. As a result, not only will custodians providing services to an AIF depositary come under pressure from the depositary to include additional terms in the relevant custody agreement, but such custodian are likely to be subject to the relevant obligations automatically, regardless of the terms of the custody agreement. Examples are as follows.

7.172 The draft text of Article 98 of the Level 2 measure imposes on the depositary various due diligence obligations in relation to the appointment of a delegate holding financial instruments, and in addition states that these requirements 'shall apply mutatis mutandis'[1] where the delegate sub-delegates any of the functions delegated to it by the depositary. This seems to mean that the delegate must comply with similar due diligence requirements in relation to its sub-delegate. Similarly, draft Article 99 of the Level 2 measure imposes various obligations on a depositary for the purpose of segregation of AIF financial instruments in the hands of the depositary's custodian, and in particular requires the depositary to verify that the custodian: '(a) keeps such records and accounts as are necessary to enable it at any time and without delay to distinguish assets of the depositary's AIF clients from its own assets, assets of its other clients, assets held by the depositary for its own account and assets held for clients of the depositary which are not AIFs.'[2] Such requirements 'shall apply mutatis mutandis'[3] where the custodian sub-delegates the holding of the financial instruments. It is not entirely clear what 'mutatis mutandis' means in this respect, and could mean that the custodian is required to impose on its sub-delegates a very detailed level of segregation of accounts.

1   Level 2, draft Article 98(4).

2   Level 2, draft Article 99(1)(a).

3   Level 2, draft Article 99, final paragraph.

7.173 AIFMD, art 21(11) states that if a custodian appointed by the depositary sub-delegates the functions delegated to it by the depositary, 'paragraph 13[1] shall apply mutatis mutandis to the relevant parties'. AIFMD Art 21(13) states that the depositary's liability 'shall not be affected by any delegation referred to in paragraph 11', except where the narrow exception applies (broadly, if the depositary is able to transfer its liability to the delegate). It is not wholly clear what is intended by the application of paragraph 13 'mutatis mutandis to the relevant parties', or who the relevant parties would be. In principle, it would appear that, as a result of Article 21(11), paragraph 13 will apply to a custodian for a depositary so that the custodian's liability cannot be affected by any sub-delegation, except where the custodian is able to transfer its liability for loss to that sub-delegate. It is less clear what level of liability for loss the delegate is expected to accept and therefore transfer to its sub-delegates (in particular, it is not clear that a depositary's delegate is required by AIFMD or Level 2 to accept liability to the depositary for loss of financial instruments which is the same level of liability as AIFMD and Level 2 imposes on the depositary).

1   Of AIFMD, art 21.

7.174 In addition, there are certain provisions which the depositary is required, or will have a significant incentive, to impose on a custodian. In particular:

7.175 AIFMD, art 21(11) only permits a depositary to delegate the holding of financial instruments to a custodian if certain conditions are satisfied, such as the compliance by the depositary with its due diligence obligations under this Article, and includes the requirement that the depositary must ensure that the custodian meets certain conditions, such as having appropriate structures and expertise to hold the financial instruments, and is subject to effective regulation and supervision. A further condition is that the depositary must ensure that the custodian complies with the 'general obligations and prohibitions set out in paragraphs 8 and 10' of Article 21 (these are the general obligations imposed on the depositary to hold financial instruments and to verify ownership by the fund of other assets[1], and to act 'honestly, fairly, professionally, independently and in the interests of the AIF and the investors of the AIF', not to carry out activities resulting in conflicts of interest between the AIF, investors in the AIF, the AIFM and itself, and not to re-use AIF assets without the prior consent of the AIF or the AIFM[2]. The depositary is therefore likely to require that provisions reflecting these requirements are included in the custody agreement with the custodian.

1   AIFMD, art 21(8)(a) and (b). The effect of these provisions appears to be that the depositary must hold for the fund all financial instruments belonging to the fund (other than financial instruments registered in the name of the fund itself), but that any assets belonging to the fund other than financial instruments may be held for the fund either by the depositary or by a third party and the depositary's obligations in relation to such other assets are only the verification obligations.
2   AIFMD, art 21(10).

7.176 As noted above, AIFMD, art 21(13) only allows a depositary to limit or exclude its liability for loss of financial instruments held by a delegate if the depositary satisfies certain conditions, including the transfer of the relevant liability to the third party. It seems likely therefore that custodians will come under considerable pressure from depositaries for AIFs to agree to accept such transfer of liability, but the result would be to impose on the custodian the extremely high level of liability to which the depositary would otherwise be subject. One aspect of interest is that, as noted in para **7.169**, a CSD is not a delegate for the purposes of the AIFMD. As a result, there may be a benefit for a custodian which is able to do so in becoming a CSD (assuming of course that it is able to comply with applicable legislation and regulation for this purpose).

SECURITIES LAW DIRECTIVE

7.177 Another proposed Directive which would have considerable impact on custodians is the 'Securities Law Directive', currently in a very preliminary stage in the form of Principles[1]. The underlying aim of clarifying and protecting, on a harmonised basis, the rights of person holding securities through intermediaries is laudable, but arguably the approach adopted, involving detailed requirements, is unlikely to be workable in its current form given the different approaches to use of intermediaries in different jurisdiction which in turn are based on fundamental issues such as insolvency rules which would be extremely hard to harmonise or amend. The following sections considers some of the issues raised by the draft Principles. For these purposes it is assumed that a custodian will be an 'account provider' and therefore subject to the Directive, although the wording of the draft definition of 'account provider' seems likely to raise various questions as to potential scope[2].

1 Set out in the European Commission Consultation Document published in November 2010 entitled 'Legislation on Legal Certainty of Securities Holding and Dispositions' (see also discussion of choice of law under these Principles in Chapter 5).

2 See 'Legislation on Legal Certainty of Securities Holding and Dispositions', European Commission, November 2010, p 34: '"account provider" means a person who: maintains securities accounts for account holders and is authorised in accordance with Article 5 of Directive 2004/39/EC to provide services listed in Annex I Section A indent (9) of Directive 2004/39/EC or is a Central Securities Depository as defined in […] and, in either case, is acting in that capacity; [in relation to Principles 3 to 13, if not subject to a national law, in the course of a business or other regular activity maintains securities accounts for others or both for others and for its own account and is acting in that capacity;]'. In particular, it appears that the definition of 'account provider' may not include a custodian who is not regulated under MiFID (or MiFID2), although the reason for this is unclear.

Rights granted to persons other than legal owner

7.178 Principle 3[1]: 'The national law should clarify that securities standing to the credit of a securities account confer upon the account holder at least the following rights: (a) the right to exercise and receive the rights attached to the securities if the account holder is the ultimate account holder or if, in any other case, the applicable law confers the right to that account holder; (b) the right to effect a disposition under one of the harmonised methods (cf below); (c) the right to instruct the account provider to arrange for holding the securities with another account provider or otherwise than with an account provider, as far as permitted under the applicable law, the terms of the securities and, to the extent permitted by the national law, the account agreement and the rules of a securities settlement system.'

1 'Legislation on Legal Certainty of Securities Holding and Dispositions', European Commission, November 2010, p 6.

7.179 Pursuant to the wording of Principle 3, it appears that the grant of such rights by custodians to their clients will be mandatory, without any possibility of variation by contractual agreement. This could cause problems for any custody arrangement, particularly where the custody services are provided in the context of a wider structure where the custody client does not wish, or is not permitted, to have or exercise the relevant rights.

7.180 Similar issues arise under Principle 17[1]: '1. The national law should require that the account provider of the ultimate account holder should be bound to facilitate the determination of the exercise of rights attached to securities by the ultimate account holder against the issuer or a third party as requested by the ultimate account holder. 2. Such facilitation must at least consist in the account provider of the ultimate account holder (a) arranging for the ultimate account holder or a third person nominated by the ultimate account holder being the representative of the legal holder with respect to the exercise of the relevant rights, if the account provider or a third person is the legal holder of securities, in which case Article 11 of the Shareholders' Rights Directive applies correspondingly; or, (b) exercising the rights attached to the securities upon authorisation and instruction and for the benefit of the ultimate account holder, if the account provider or a third person is the legal holder of the securities; or, (c) providing the ultimate account holder, regardless of whether it is the legal holder of the securities or not, with evidence confirming its holdings and it being enabled to exercise the rights attached to the securities against the issuer or a third party, under a general framework guaranteeing the integrity of the number of available rights and the position of the legal holder of the securities in respect of lit. (c) of paragraph 2. The content and form of the evidence to be provided should be specified and standard forms should be developed, in particular to define under which conditions issuers should recognise such evidence for purposes of exercising rights attached to securities. 3. The extent to which the obligations following paragraphs 1 and 2 can be made subject to a contractual agreement between the ultimate account holder and its account provider as well as the formal requirements to be met by such agreement should be subject to restrictions for purposes of client protection.'

1 'Legislation on Legal Certainty of Securities Holding and Dispositions', European Commission, November 2010, pp 28, 29.

7.181 In practice, it may not be possible for a custodian to 'facilitate the determination of the exercise of rights attached to securities by the ultimate account holder against the issuer or a third party as requested by the ultimate account holder' if the law governing the issue of the relevant securities does not permit this. It is helpful that paragraph (3) of this Principle seems to permit variation by contractual agreement, this could interpreted as allowing agreement on the way rights will be facilitated but not agreement that no such services will be provided.

Loss of securities

7.182 Principle 4[1] is of particular significance since it concerns liability for loss:

'1. The national law should provide for acquisitions and dispositions of account-held securities and limited interests therein to be effected by crediting an account and debiting an account respectively. 2. The national law should provide that an account provider may credit the accounts of its account holders, for each description of securities, only if it holds a corresponding number of securities of the same description by (a) having available account-held securities in a securities account maintained for the account provider by another account provider; (b) arranging for securities to be held on the register of the issuer in the name, or for the account, of its account holders; (c) holding securities as the registered holder on the register of the issuer; (d) possessing relevant securities certificates or other documents of title; or (e) creating the initial electronic record of securities for the issuer in accordance with the applicable law, and that an account provider continuously holds that corresponding number. 3. If the applicable law allows crediting and debiting to be made conditional it should also define the extent to which such conditional crediting or debiting is taken into account in determining the number of securities referred to in the preceding paragraphs. Credits to a securities account the effectiveness of which is subject to a condition must be identifiable as such in the account. 4. If a corresponding number (paragraph 2) is not held, the account provider should promptly apply either or both of the following mechanisms in order to re-establish compliance: (a) reverse erroneous credits; (b) provide additional securities of the relevant description, to be held by one of the methods provided for in paragraph 2. The sharing of any cost entailed by the provision of additional securities pursuant to subparagraph (b) can be subject to a contractual agreement between the account provider and those account holders holding securities of the relevant description at the time of the occurrence of the loss in non-segregated accounts only in cases where the account provider held securities of the relevant description with another account provider pursuant to Article 17(3) subparagraphs (a) and (b) of the MiFID. 5. The applicable national law may in addition allow for acquisitions and dispositions being effected under one or more of the following methods: (a) earmarking account-held securities in an account, or earmarking a securities account, and the removing of such earmarking; (b) concluding a control agreement; or (c) concluding an agreement with and in favour of an account provider.'

1 'Legislation on Legal Certainty of Securities Holding and Dispositions', European Commission, November 2010, pp 9, 10.

7.183 As may be seen, Principle 4 requires that a custodian must not credit client accounts in its own books with securities unless the custodian holds a corresponding number of such securities (either directly or through a delegate), and if this is not the case must either 'reverse erroneous credits' or to 'provide additional securities of the relevant description'. In principle the idea that a custodian's records must match what it actually holds sounds perfectly reasonable, but there are difficulties with the requirements of Principle 4, particularly given the related requirements of other Principles.

7.184 Under Principles 7 and 8[1], the situations in which reversals of erroneous credits can be made are fairly narrow. Under Principle 7, reversals are dependent on consent from the client or the fact that the original entry was not authorised by the client, and under Principle 8, the national law of Member States must 'ensure' that an account holder is protected against reversal of crediting (and a person with the benefit of an earmarking of securities in the account is protected against its reversal) unless such person knew or ought to have known that the relevant credit or earmarking should not have been made. Notably, there is no exception for reversals required by insolvency rules or where there has been fraud. Principle 8 also appears to override the statement in Principle 7 that conditions for reversal 'should be, to the extent permitted by the applicable law, subject to any rule of a securities settlement system'. As drafted, the consequence would appear to be that reversals of account entries may be difficult in which case the custodian will be obliged to rectify the discrepancy by providing additional securities at its own expense even if it is not at fault. Moreover, the ability to pass this cost on to the client appears to be limited by Principle 4.

1 'Legislation on Legal Certainty of Securities Holding and Dispositions', European Commission, November 2010, pp 15–18

Non-discrimination regarding securities rights

7.185 Principle 15[1]: '1. the national law governing a securities issue as well as the national law governing the holding of securities should not discriminate against the exercise of rights attached to securities held in another jurisdiction on the sole grounds that the relevant securities are held in a specific manner, in particular – through one or more account providers, – through an account provider acting in its own name but for the account of its account holders, – through accounts in which securities of two or more account holders are held in an indistinguishable manner. 2. The national law should remain free to prescribe which holding methods account providers should offer to their account holders.'

1 'Legislation on Legal Certainty of Securities Holding and Dispositions', European Commission, November 2010, p 26.

7.186 The fundamental question is how the aim of 'non-discrimination' can be achieved in practice. Is the requirement that there must be no difference in the process for the exercise of rights by persons holding interests in securities directly, and persons holding interest in securities through an intermediary? It is not clear how a custodian could resolve this problem, given that the main issues arise from local requirements regarding the person entitled to rights arising under securities, normally only the person with legal title to the securities or in whose name they are credited in a particular securities depository. Principle 18[1] raises a similar point since it requires fees charged in respect of cross-border holdings of securities to be 'the same' as charges in relation to 'comparable domestic holdings'. How can this be achieved unless the processes and systems are the same for both types of holding?

1   'Legislation on Legal Certainty of Securities Holding and Dispositions', European Commission, November 2010, p 31.

Further developments

7.187 As a general point, a great deal of further analysis would be required in relation to the impact and draft of the proposed Securities Law Directive as outlined in the Principles before most of the requirement could be workable. If any attempt was made to progress a Directive based on the current wording[1], a large number of practical difficulties would arise, as well as conflicts with other legal requirements. Nevertheless, there are some useful aspects of the proposals. The proposal to clarify the law governing certain issues relating to securities by reference to the jurisdiction where the securities account is maintained is to be welcomed (see further Chapter 5, paras **5.69–5.73**), as is Principle 12[2] if it is effective to confirm that creditors of an account holder cannot seek to claim against anyone other than the account provider in respect of the account holder's assets (thus removing the concern regarding the risk of such creditors seeking to claim the assets from the account provider's delegate). Similarly, the proposal in Principle 13[3] is useful, since it aims to ensure that creditors of an account provider cannot attach securities held by such account provider with a third party where such securities are identified as client securities.

1   There have not been any significant developments regarding the concepts discussed in the European Commission's November 2010 'Legislation on Legal Certainty of Securities Holding and Dispositions' since its publication (although see new issues raised in October 2012 in para **7.188** onwards), although it has resulted in a large number of commentaries and discussion papers in response. In particular, an interesting discussion of the various issues arising may be found in the paper published by the European Parliament's Economic and Monetary Affairs Council (ECON) in May 2011 entitled 'Cross-border issues of securities law: European efforts to support securities markets with a coherent legal framework'. This paper notes that the purpose of the Securities Law Directive is that of 'comprehensively removing legal fragmentation in this area in order to allow for certainty of securities movements across Europe and for improved investor rights' in the context of a situation where 'The law governing various aspects of securities holding and disposition was, and still widely is, purely national law' (see pp 7 and 8 of the report). More recently, the European Commission 'Info-Letter on Post-Trading', Issue 4, August 2012, contains a short discussion entitled 'The Key Challenge in Securities Law – Who owns what?', which states that 'Clarifying ownership rights to securities has never been more vital, especially in a cross-border context', and 'If we can resolve these key challenges using our Securities Law Legislation, we will have taken a major step forward to a safer, more efficient Single Market for Financial Services that works to the benefit of us all.'

2   'Legislation on Legal Certainty of Securities Holding and Dispositions', European Commission, November 2010, pp 21, 22.

3   'Legislation on Legal Certainty of Securities Holding and Dispositions', European Commission, November 2010, p 22.

7.188 On 16 October 2012, the European Commission produced a further Discussion Paper entitled 'Legislation on Legal Certainty of Securities Holding and Dispositions' for discussion by the Member States Technical Expert Working Group.

This Discussion certainly indicates an intention to progress the production of some form of Securities Law Directive or other European legislation, and it is thought that new draft legislation may be published in earlier 2013, possibly in the form of a Directive and a Regulation.

Nature of ownership

7.189 However, the focus of the October 2012 Discussion Paper is somewhat alarming, because it does not build on the general principles discussed in earlier papers, but effectively concludes that a radically different approach is required because the earlier 'initiatives were based on a legal perspective developed before the crisis in 2008' and that there are 'fundamental issues' which mean that the proposals for legislation 'may require substantially different treatment if any proposed legislation is to be capable of providing viable solutions' (p 3). Of particular concern is the fact that the Discussion Paper indicates confusion of the nature of interests in securities, taking a simplistic view that in arrangements where investors hold securities entitlements rather than legal title to securities, such arrangements 'treat securities like money', and that such approach creates 'complex inter-relationships'. There is of course a fundamental difference between a contractual (personal) claim for money, and a property right in the form of an interest in securities, even if the underlying securities are fungible so that the investor does not have a right to specific securities[1]. Moreover, it seems unarguable that the holding of securities through a chain of intermediaries creates 'complex inter-relationships', but modern markets cannot operate without this. The Discussion Paper asks 'Do Member States' experts consider that securities should be treated as "property" and not as "claims" akin to money', which is deeply worrying if it indicates an intention that the proposed Directive should, contrary to the earlier proposals to focus on outcomes not methods of achieving such outcomes, attempt to change the nature of property rights in securities in each EU member state since such a radical change would cause major disruption to all relationships involving securities.

1 Unfortunately, this seems to demonstrate the same lack of comprehension of and weighting in favour of the views of EU member states whose legal systems do not include the concept of trusts and intermediary chains, as influenced the drafting of the AIFMD (see para **7.165** n 1).

Rights of use

7.190 Further confusion of ideas is demonstrated in the Discussion Paper's consideration of rights of use. Provision of collateral under a title transfer arrangement seems to be regarded as presenting the same issues as a right of use under a security arrangement. This is of course incorrect, since in a title transfer arrangement the recipient of collateral receives full title with only a contractual obligation to redeliver equivalent assets, whereas under a security arrangement with a right of use, the collateral provider remains the owner of the securities (subject to the security interest of the collateral taker) until the right of use is exercised. Some suggestions are sensible, namely that clients should be clearly informed of the extent of the collateral-taker's right of use, and should be notified when such right is exercised, and the exercise of a right of use should be reflected in account records by no longer recording that the asset 'used' is held for the client. However, it somewhat startling that one of the proposals is the amendment of the Financial Collateral Directive to remove the possibility of a right of use; the Directive does not grant such a right, but simply allows collateral givers and collateral takers to agree on the existence of such a right, therefore it would be odd to prohibit parties from agreeing such arrangements simply to 'remove legal uncertainties'. Other suggestions are a mandatory cap, or obligation to agree a cap, on the amount of collateral which may be subject to the right of use, and a limit on the duration of rehypothecation. While such suggestions might seem sensible as useful mechanisms to limit the exposure of the collateral giver to the risks of a right of use, the imposition of such requirements is likely to raise additional practical and legal problems. For example, in a situation where the exposure of the collateral-taker to the collateral-giver changes on a daily basis and intraday, would it be possible in practice for the collateral-taker to ensure that the value of the collateral in respect of which a right of use is exercised is within the cap set by reference to the value of the collateral-giver's obligations? And what is the result of a breach of the cap – does this affect the ability of the collateral-taker exercising its right of use to transfer good title to collateral to a third party?

Omnibus accounts

7.191 The Discussion Paper also raises other issues of concern, notably stating that the 'main obstacle' to 'promoting the book-entry in an account … as the definitive proof of rights' is not only 'the different concepts of ownership across the EU' but also 'the pooling of securities in omnibus accounts' which have the result that 'the holding chain is complex and opaque' and 'rights of account holders are unclear and may even be exercised more than once over the same security'. Such reasoning is, at best, misconceived. There is no difficulty with a book-entry in an account giving definitive proof of rights, even where there are a number of intermediary accounts; the point is simply that the rights in each case will be slightly different, and will relate to the person maintaining the relevant account in each such case. Notably, the examples of ownership interests arising where securities are held in different CSDs focus solely on domestic systems in Germany, France, Finland, Greece and the UK, and do not consider the important examples of Euroclear and Clearstream. It is difficult to see how any sensible analysis of intermediary structures is possible if not taking into account two settlement systems of major importance to the European securities markets.

The future?

7.192 Rather startlingly, the final question in the Discussion Paper asks 'What are Member States experts' views on harmonising the concept of ownership for account-held securities across Europe so that there is only one owner?' Given the fundamental differences between legal systems based on civil law and those which are not, it is very difficult to see that any such harmonisation is possible, and the earlier Securities Law Directive proposals did not even suggest this.

7.193 While it is evident that the Discussion Paper issues are prompted by grave concern for clarity regarding securities ownership and the wish to minimise scope for conflicting rights to securities, arguably a panic reaction to market difficulties (such as led to the creation of much of the AIFMD structure) is not the best way to produce legislative changes which do not themselves cause further disruption to markets. While some of the proposals in the Discussion Paper regarding transparency seem sensible, many of the ideas focusing on removing or changing deep-rooted concepts and structures such as rights of use, omnibus accounts and the legal nature of ownership rights would arguably result in more problems and lack of clarity than those which they seek to remedy.

CHAPTER 8

Overview of post-trade infrastructure

8.1 This chapter considers the clearing and settlement functions that constitute the post-trading infrastructure of the securities markets. This area continues to attract a large amount of attention from the securities industry and the public sector. Inefficiencies in the post-trading infrastructure have for some time been the focus of much concern as a significant source of risk and cost, and this focus has been increased by the various market and financial difficulties. Various reforms of clearing and settlement have been and will continue to be proposed, both at a national level and a European level, with a view to achieving operational efficiencies and managing risk, as well as to address the ongoing concerns regarding preventing or limiting the effects of further financial crisis affecting the European and global markets. The need for such reforms is important because, even with the present market difficulties, the volumes of domestic and cross-border securities transactions are expected to continue to increase in the years ahead, and more than ever there is a need to increase confidence in markets and systems. Although many reforming initiatives relate to the wider financial markets, including the markets in cash and derivatives transactions, the focus of this chapter will be the clearing and settlement of securities transactions in the European markets.

BACKGROUND

8.2 This section will briefly consider the background to the reform of the post-trading infrastructure. The following sections will consider in turn: risk management issues; the process of consolidation; and underlying legal principles.

OVERVIEW

8.3 Chapter 1 briefly explained the differences between trading, settlement and clearing. After a trade for the purchase or sale of securities has taken place, the next step is to ensure that the terms of the trade are agreed. This is achieved by a process called confirmation[1]. After this, the parties to the trade (or their agents) must arrange for the securities to be delivered from the seller to the buyer (or their agents). They must also arrange for the purchase price to be paid by the buyer to the seller (or their agents). This process of delivery, with associated payments, is called settlement. Although settlement is becoming quicker, in many markets a number of business days still elapse between trading and settlement (the 'settlement interval'). As discussed below, a number of risks arise for the parties during the settlement interval. Clearing is a process which takes place in order to manage such risks. Other issues arise as a result of settlement inefficiencies existing where there are numerous different systems and practices involved in the settlement process. This was the focus of the second Giovannini Report[2].

1 The existence of a separate operational stage to establish agreement upon the terms of a contract may perplex legal theorists who regard a contract as expressing the agreement of the parties. See The Giovannini Group *Cross Border Clearing and Settlement in the European Union*, November 2001 ('Giovannini 2001 Report'), p 5:

'OTC transactions are typically confirmed directly between the buyer and seller by electronic means, by telefax, or by specialised messaging service. Some trading systems provide automatic confirmation, while other securities exchanges or clearing agents produce confirmations based on data submitted by counterparties.'

For a discussion of confirmation, see also CPSS/IOSCO Joint Task Force on Securities Settlement Systems *Recommendations for Securities Settlement Systems*, November 2001, pp 9, 38 ('CPSS/IOSCO Recommendations'). (CPSS is the Committee on Payment and Settlement Systems set up in 1990 by the Governors of the central banks of the Group of Ten countries (the 'G10 Governors') to consider payment system issues, including cross-border and multicurrency interbank netting issues (the CPSS is one of the permanent central bank committees reporting to the G10 Governors); IOSCO is the International Organization of Securities Commissions, an international co-operative forum (originally set up in 1983) for securities regulatory agencies from around the world, whose aims include co-operation to promote high standards of regulation in order to maintain a just, efficient and sound market.) An alternative to confirmation and affirmation is automatic execution matching: see DTCC *T+1 White Paper*, 2002, p 13. The CPSS/IOSCO Recommendations were replaced in April 2012 by the CPSS/IOSCO *Principles for financial market infrastructures* ('CPSS/IOSCO Principles') which are intended to 'harmonise and, where appropriate, strengthen the existing international standards' and apply to all systemically important payment systems, central securities depositories, securities settlement systems, central counterparties, as well as to provide 'additional guidance for over-the-counter (OTC) derivatives CCPs and trade repositories'. However, it should be noted that the 'Recommendations for securities settlement systems' published in November 2002 have not been replaced in full: 'full reconsideration of the marketwide recommendations from the RSSS was not undertaken as part of this review. Those recommendations remain in effect. Specifically, RSSS Recommendation 2 on trade confirmation, RSSS Recommendation 3 on settlement cycles, RSSS Recommendation 4 on central counterparties, RSSS Recommendation 5 on securities lending, RSSS Recommendation 6 on central securities depositories, and RSSS Recommendation 12 on protection of customers' securities remain in effect. These recommendations are provided in Annex C for reference.' (CPSS/IOSCO Principles, pp 6, 7)

In September 2004 standards similar to the 2001 CPSS/IOSCO Recommendations were proposed by the Committee of European Securities Regulators and European System of Central Banks ('CESR-ECB') working group, the 'Standards for Securities Clearing and Settlement in the European Union' (the 'CESR-ECB Standards'). CESR-ECB followed this with the publication in May 2009 of the 'Recommendations for Securities Settlement Systems and Recommendations for Central Counterparties in the European Union'.

CESR was established under the terms of the European Commission Decision of 6 June 2001 (2001/527/EC), and its functions include improving co-operation and co-ordination among regulators in the EU and advising the EU Commission in relation to the implementation of European Directives (see www.cesr-eu.org). The ESCB comprises the European Central Bank ('ECB') and the central banks of all EU member states. The ECB is the central bank for the Euro established in 1998.

2   The Giovannini Group *Second Report on EU Clearing and Settlement Arrangements*, April 2003 ('Giovannini 2003 Report'). See further discussion in paras **8.60–8.63** below.

Nature of settlement

8.4   Although in terms of the sequence of events a trade is cleared before it is settled, it is conceptually easier to consider the nature of settlement before considering the nature of clearing.

Delivery and payment

8.5   As indicated above, settlement involves the delivery of securities (or, to be more accurate, legal rights in relation to them) from A to B. Delivery usually takes place against payment from B to A[1]. However, some deliveries are 'free', ie made without a corresponding payment. Examples would be the delivery of securities collateral against a loan of securities, and a delivery made pursuant to a margin call[2].

1   This would be the case in a purchase of securities, or a collateralised loan.

2   As discussed in Chapter 4, a margin call is a call for additional collateral to be delivered to eliminate a collateral shortfall pursuant to marking to market arrangements.

Book entry transfer

8.6 Chapter 2 briefly discussed the transition from paper based settlement to electronic book entry transfer. Historically, settlement involved the movement of pieces of paper. Bearer securities were transferred by the delivery of paper instruments; registered securities were transferred by the delivery of paper certificates and transfer forms, followed by reregistration; and payment was made by cheque. Paper-based settlement is risky, expensive, error-prone and slow. With rising transaction volumes, paper-based settlement was unable to keep pace with trading volumes. In the 1970s (in the US) and the 1980s (in the UK), the securities markets experienced what has become known as 'the paper crunch', as backlogs of unsettled trades threatened the integrity of the securities markets.

8.7 The answer to the paper crunch was electronic settlement, involving a technique called book entry transfer. This involves the use of an electronic settlement system, in which market participants (or their agents) maintain accounts which record their entitlements to securities and cash. When participant A wishes to settle a sale of securities to participant B, A and B give matching instructions to the settlement system. In response to these instructions[1], the settlement system debits the securities account of A and credits that of B. At the same time, it debits the cash account of B and credits that of A. Thus, delivery and payment are made promptly and synchronously.

1   Provided that sufficient assets are available in the parties' accounts.

8.8 In 1989 the Group of Thirty ('G30')[1] published its report *Clearance and Settlement Systems in the World's Securities Markets* (the '1989 G30 Report'). This tremendously influential report put the need for book entry transfer beyond doubt. It identified two models of book entry transfer, namely immobilisation and dematerialisation.

1   The Group of Thirty, established in 1978, is a private, nonprofit, international body composed of very senior representatives of the private and public sectors and academia. It aims to deepen understanding of international economic and financial issues ...': see the G30 website at www.group30.org.

8.9 As explained in Chapter 2, immobilisation involves the use of a depositary, which is electronically linked to a settlement system. Paper instruments and/or certificates are held by the depositary on behalf of a settlement system or its participants. The entitlements of participants in respect of the securities are recorded in electronic securities accounts maintained by the settlement system, and transferred by debiting and crediting those accounts. Thus, with immobilisation, paper securities exist, but they do not move in the course of settlement. In contrast, in the case of dematerialisation, securities are issued in electronic form 'straight onto the screen'. The terms of issue of dematerialised securities provide that such securities will be constituted by the electronic records of the settlement system. In the historic transition from paper-based to electronic practice in the securities markets, immobilisation often serves as a transitional phase prior to dematerialisation.

8.10 The 1989 G30 Report's call for book entry transfer has been widely heeded. 'In 1989, depositories and book entry settlement were used in only a minority of markets. Today, almost all markets use such systems.'[1] Important international electronic settlement systems[2] include, (in New York) the DTC[3]; (in Brussels) Euroclear and (in Luxembourg) Clearstream. The UK settlement system is CREST[4].

1   1995 G30/ISSA Recommendations reviewing the G30 1989 Recommendations, p 10. Indeed, in some jurisdictions book entry transfer is not merely available, but mandatory. (ISSA is the International Securities Services Association.) Consider also the proposed new requirements for dematerialisation in settlement systems in the EU (para **8.83** below).

2   Referred to in the industry as international central securities depositories, or 'ICSDs'.

3   The Depository Trust Company of New York. Both DTC and National Securities Clearing Corporation ('NSCC') are operating subsidiaries of The Depository Trust & Clearing Corporation ('DTCC').

4   Although strictly speaking CREST is not a depository since it does not hold securities. See further Chapter 9.

Nature of clearing

8.11   The term 'clearing' is used in different senses. In its narrower sense, the term is used to mean the calculation of the mutual post-trade obligations of market participants, usually on a net basis[1]. In its wider sense (which will be used in this discussion) the term 'clearing' involves the management of post-trading, pre-settlement credit exposures, to ensure that trades are settled in accordance with market rules, even if a buyer or seller becomes insolvent prior to settlement.

1   See the Giovannini 2001 Report, p 5.

Central counterparty

8.12   Clearing generally involves the use of a well capitalised financial institution known as a central counterparty ('CCP'). In the markets in which a CCP provides a clearing service, it becomes a party to every trade, acting as buyer to market participant sellers, and seller to market participant buyers[1]. In respect of unsettled trades, market participants therefore bear the credit risk of the CCP, and not that of each other. 'A CCP thus provides a standard credit risk to replace the variable, bilateral risk that firms take on each other in a decentralised market.'[2]

1   In many cases this is contractually achieved by novation, ie by replacing an original contract between two market participants with two new contracts, one between the CCP as seller and the market participant buyer, and one between the CCP as buyer and the market participant seller. In other cases (eg where LCH.Clearnet Limited ('LCH') clears UK equities and over the counter ('OTC') swap and repo trades) there is no initial market participant to market participant contract, and each trade is originally entered into with the CCP.

2   DTCC *Central Counterparties: Development, Cooperation and Consolidation – A White Paper to the Industry on the Future of CCPs*, October 2000 ('DTCC CPP White Paper'), p 16.

Netting

8.13   Another important clearing function is netting. Since each market participant has only one counterparty to its trades (the CCP) it can net its daily purchases and sales in like securities. Netting is widely identified as the key benefit offered by the use of a CCP. In particular, 'CCPs have the potential to reduce significantly risks to participants through the multilateral netting of trades and by imposing more-effective risk controls on all participants'[1].

1   CPSS/IOSCO Principles, p 9.

8.14   Netting can operate at two different levels[1]. First, trade or obligation netting may take effect contractually, so as to reduce the unsettled contractual obligations of the CCP to each market participant from gross to net. This significantly reduces the credit risk of the market participant to the CCP, and therefore related margin and regulatory capital requirement applicable to the market participant for its cleared trades, as discussed below.

1   See CPSS/IOSCO Principles, p 24.

8.15 Second, even where contractual netting is not available, as an operational matter settlement netting[1] permits settlement instructions to be given on a net and not gross basis, very significantly reducing the volume of settlements. Reduced settlement volumes in turn reduce costs and liquidity pressures.

1   Which is offered by LCH.Clearnet Limited for its equity trades, even though contractual netting is not offered, at least initially. See also reference to netting in the context of the central sponsor arrangements in CREST (Chapter 9, paras **9.95–9.105**).

Challenges

8.16 There has historically been a widespread perception among market participants, industry bodies and regulatory authorities that the post-trade infrastructure of the securities markets faces challenges in the form of increased trade volumes and increased cross-border activity.

8.17 The concern regarding the volume of securities trades[1] was that volumes would increase beyond the capacity of the existing infrastructure, creating an urgent need for reform. For this reason, settlement netting in particular was identified by the European Securities Forum ('ESF')[2] as a crucial development[3].

1   See DTCC *T+1 White Paper*, p 2.

2   See ESF Submission to the Basel Committee on Banking Supervision, *The New Basel Capital Accord*, 2001 ('ESF Submission on Basel'):

   'The European Securities Forum (ESF) is an organisation established by the major users of Europe's clearing and settlement infrastructure. ESF was established in response to rationalisation initiatives within the industry, to act as a neutral and objective facilitator of a rapid progression towards a powerful, efficient European capital market infrastructure. For more information on ESF and its activities, see our website at http:www.eurosf.com/' (p 1).

3   See the ESF Submission to DG MARKT in Response to the European Communication on Upgrading the Investment Services Directive 2000 ('ESF Submission on ISD'), p 10.

8.18 A further expected challenge was the increase in the proportion of cross-border trades. Where the buyer, the seller and/or the assets are located in different jurisdictions, clearing and settlement must often be provided on a cross-border basis. As discussed below, this involves special risks both operationally (due to variations in systems, procedures and operating hours) and legally (due to the conflict of laws issues). The issue of settlement of cross-border trades was the focus of the G30 Report 2003[1], and has been the subject of considerable attention at a European and global level, in particular as regards the question of creating a more efficient, cost-effective, harmonised approach by reducing the fragmentation of operational systems and legal structures (see paras **8.56–8.98** below).

1   G30 Steering & Working Committees of Global Clearing & Settlements Study Group: *Global Clearing and Settlements: A Plan of Action*, January 2003.

8.19 These developments coincide with rising levels of commercial and regulatory risk awareness. Competitive pressures within the securities industry, together with a growing perception of the importance of a robust infrastructure, have generated a high level of commitment to meet these challenges. A series of important studies and reports have and continue to generate new benchmarks, industry reforms and regulatory initiatives devoted to improving the post-trade infrastructure. In addition, the financial crisis has demonstrated the significant difficulties which arise where there is a massive loss of confidence in existing systems and procedures, resulting in parties seeking additional assurance in relation to matters which were historically accepted as part of the nature of trading, clearing and settlement. A huge number of regulatory and legislative developments have resulted from the efforts of governments and regulators at every level seeking to demonstrate their ability to respond to the crisis and to address fears regarding reliability and transparency in markets, systems and market participants. Certain of the studies, benchmarks and developments are briefly considered below.

RISK MANAGEMENT

8.20 This section will consider the key risks in the post-trade infrastructure; the basic risk management techniques that have been developed in relation to them; together with the leading studies and reports on such risks and their management.

Key risks in post-trade infrastructure

8.21 The securities industry has developed a sophisticated risk analysis in relation to the post-trade infrastructure. The following brief discussion involves a simplification of these risks, in order to provide a clear basis for the legal analysis developed in this chapter. Industry attention has focused on the following types of risk to which participants in the securities markets are exposed after trading and prior to the completion of settlement[1].

1   The Giovannini 2001 Report also identified cash deposit risk, custody risk and foreign exchange risk: see p 18.

Credit risk – principal risk

8.22 If a party to a securities trade delivers assets by way of settlement prior to receiving corresponding assets from the counterparty, it faces the risk that the counterparty will default without discharging its settlement obligations. This raises a form of credit risk known as principal risk, that is 'the risk that a counterparty will lose the full value involved in a transaction, for example, the risk that a seller of a financial asset will irrevocably deliver the asset but not receive payment.'[1]. In the foreign exchange markets, principal risk was so vividly illustrated by the 1974 failure of Bank Herstatt that it is often called 'Herstatt risk'[2]. The technique for addressing principal risk is the synchronisation of settlement of both sides of the transaction. In the securities markets, this is called delivery versus payment, or 'DVP'[3]. While conceptually simple, the achievement of true DVP is a complex and difficult matter for operational and legal reasons, as discussed later in this chapter.

1   CPSS/IOSCO Principles, p 19.

2   The bank became insolvent after having received payment under a foreign exchange transaction, but before making payment under the same transaction. The consequent disruption threatened the operation of wholesale dollar deliveries. See the discussion in BIS *Settlement Risk in Foreign Exchange Transaction*, 1996.

3   The concept of DVP is derived from that of payment versus payment ('PVP'), which was developed in the foreign exchange markets to address Herstatt risk. DVP is required by Standard 7 of the CESR-ECB Standards.

Credit risk – replacement cost risk

8.23 A second type of credit risk known as replacement cost risk is best illustrated by example. Suppose that on day 1 A agrees to sell to B 1,000 XYZ shares for £100,000. On day 2, this trade remains unsettled, and the market price of 1,000 XYZ shares has fallen to £50,000. If the trade is settled on day 3, A will make a profit, and such settlement will involve a corresponding loss for B. A's trade is said to be 'in the money' and B's trade 'out of the money'. If B defaults prior to settlement, A will lose the profit associated with the trade. On any day, the extent of A's potential loss is measured by the price A would need to pay to a third party in the market to induce them to enter into a like transaction on that day, so as to replace the defaulted transaction with B. For this reason, A's risk is called replacement cost risk, that is 'the risk of loss of unrealised gains on unsettled transactions with a counterparty (for example, the unsettled transactions of a CCP). The resulting exposure is the cost of replacing the original transaction at current market prices.'[1]. Because replacement cost risk arises prior to the settlement of the transaction, it is present even in a DVP environment.

1 CPSS/IOSCO Principles, p 41.

8.24 Replacement cost risk is addressed by two techniques. First, by ensuring that settlement occurs as early as possible after a trade serves to reduce the interval of time during which replacement cost risk arises. This explains the pressure to achieve shorter settlement cycles[1]. Second, even during short settlement cycles, the risk of counterparty default is reduced by the use of central counterparties, as discussed later in this chapter.

1 The benefit of shorter settlement cycles is also analysed as addressing market risk. See DTCC *T+1 White Paper*, p 24. The Giovannini 2003 Report specifically identified the existence of different settlement cycles as a barrier to settlement efficiency, noting that a move to T+2 would have benefits but would not be beneficial if this meant the European settlement process was different from the US, and CESR-ECB Standard 3 calls for rolling settlement in all markets, on the basis of no later than T+3.

Liquidity risk

8.25 The precise nature of liquidity is a matter of extensive debate[1]. However, one may state in general terms that a liquid securities market is one in which securities may be bought and sold without delay at a fair price. Illiquidity arises when market participants wishing to deal are unable promptly to find counterparties willing to deal with them at a fair price. Illiquidity may arise because markets are underdeveloped or fragmented. Illiquidity may also arise because of operational problems, where failure promptly to process existing trades delays the implementation of future trades. Failure of market confidence may also cause illiquidity, where participants withdraw from trading due to fears concerning the credit of market counterparties[2].

1 See the discussion in Ruben Lee *What is an Exchange? The Automation, Management, and Regulation of the Financial Markets* (1998, Oxford University Press), p 283:

'Other characteristics of a market have also been associated with liquidity by the SEC, including immediacy, depth, and continuity ... The SEC has expressly avoided equating liquidity with trading volume, stating that the two are not equivalent.'

2 A very vivid illustration of this was provided by the near failure of Long Term Capital Management in September 1998, and considerably more recently by the effect of the sub-prime mortgage lending problems on financial institutions globally and the general erosion of market confidence.

8.26 A number of techniques which are desirable in themselves also serve to improve liquidity, including infrastructure consolidation and the effective management of credit and operational risks. In addition, securities lending is a technique which serves directly to address illiquidity[1]. Because of the potential seriousness of liquidity problems[2], many settlement systems offer automatic securities lending facilities.

1 Controversially, short selling serves the same purpose.
2 See CPSS/IOSCO Principles, p 19:

'Liquidity problems have the potential to create systemic problems, particularly if they occur when markets are closed or illiquid or when asset prices are changing rapidly, or if they create concerns about solvency. Liquidity risk can also arise from other sources, such as the failure or the inability of settlement banks, nostro agents, custodian banks, liquidity providers, and linked FMIs [financial market infrastructures] to perform as expected.'

Operational risk – generally

8.27 Operational risk was defined in the Basel Capital Accord[1] as 'the risk of loss resulting from inadequate or failed internal processes, people or systems or from external events'. This is interpreted to include 'legal risk'[2]. Operational risk is particularly important in the post-trading infrastructure. 'In addition to the credit, liquidity, and other related risks that it faces from its payment, clearing, and settlement activities, an FMI also faces general business and operational risks.'[3] Both the automation and the consolidation[4] of clearing and settlement serve potentially to increase operational risk. In recent years it has attracted new levels of industry and regulatory attention. Importantly, the new Basel Capital Accord introduces a capital weighting for operational risk.

1   Basel Committee on Banking Supervision *International Convergence of Capital Measurement and Capital Standards: A Revised Framework* (updated November 2005), Part 2, Chapter V. Compare the definition in the CPSS/IOSCO Principles:

   'operational risk ... is the risk that deficiencies in information systems or internal processes, human errors, management failures, or disruptions from external events will result in the reduction, deterioration, or breakdown of services provided by an FMI [financial market infrastructure].' (p 20)

2   Basel Committee on Banking Supervision *International Convergence of Capital Measurement and Capital Standards: A Revised Framework* (updated November 2005), Part 2, Chapter V: 'Legal risk includes, but is not limited to, exposure to fines, penalties, or punitive damages resulting from supervisory actions, as well as private settlements.'

3   CPSS/IOSCO Principles, p 88. The Giovannini 2003 Report focuses on the incompatibility of systems and technology as a significant barrier to settlement efficiency.

4   Interestingly, the CPSS/IOSCO Principles identify various types of operational risk (see p 95), but do not mention consolidation, and are generally in favour of automation; contrast CPSS/IOSCO Recommendations, p 18, and see also Bob Hills et al 'Central Counterparty Clearing Houses and Financial Stability' (June 1999) *Bank of England Financial Stability Review* 124 at 131–2 ('Hills et al').

Operational risk – legal risk

8.28 Legal risk might be defined as the risk that the legal effect of a transaction or arrangement differs from that intended by one or more of the parties to it[1]. As discussed below, the operation of the post-trade infrastructure relies importantly on a number of legal techniques. Some measure of legal risk may be a fact of financial life. However, several factors raise the level of legal risk currently associated with the post-trade infrastructure to an unhelpful level. These include, in particular, the cross-border nature of the infrastructure; the relative novelty of some aspects of the automation of securities administration; and (in some jurisdictions) policy concerns relating to the protection of general creditors in insolvency. A number of key legal risk issues are discussed later in this chapter, together with law reform initiatives designed to address them[2].

1   And see also para **8.27** n 2 above.

2   The Giovannini 2003 Report identified as particular barriers to settlement efficiency three specific areas of legal uncertainty, namely the lack of an EU framework for the way ownership of securities is treated, the differences between local laws in the way netting is viewed, and different local laws in relation to dealing with the conflict of laws. The Legal Certainty Group *Second Advice of the Legal Certainty Group – Solutions to Legal Barriers related to Post trading within the EU*, August 2008, contains interesting proposals for resolving certain legal issues, see further discussion at para **8.78** below.

Systemic risk

8.29 Systemic risk is 'The risk that the inability of one or more participants to perform as expected will cause other participants to be unable to meet their obligations when due.'[1] Both clearing systems[2] and settlement systems[3] are potential sources of systemic risk, and they may transmit systemic risk to payment systems to which they are linked[4]. A further factor is the consolidation of the financial markets[5]. 'Increased integration of securities markets entails more interconnection between financial intermediaries on a cross-border basis, increasing their exposure to common shocks.'[6]

1   CPSS/IOSCO Principles, p 178.

2   As discussed later in this chapter, clearing serves to concentrate risk in CCPs. This may have the effect of reducing risk overall if the clearing house is financially stable, but of increasing it if it is not. 'As a result of their potential to reduce risks to participants, CCPs also can reduce systemic risk in the markets they serve. The effectiveness of a CCP's risk controls and the adequacy of its financial resources are critical to achieving these risk-reduction benefits.' See CPSS/IOSCO Principles, p 9.

3   'Poorly designed and operated FMIs can contribute to and exacerbate systemic crises if the risks of these systems are not adequately managed, and as a result, financial shocks could be passed from one participant or FMI to others.' CPSS/IOSCO Principles, p 11.

4   See DTCC *T+1 White Paper*, p 1 and CPSS/IOSCO Principles, p 18.

5   Communication of the Commission *Financial Services: Implementing the Framework for Financial Markets: Action Plan*, COM(1999) 232, 11 May 1999 ('The Financial Services Action Plan'), p 13:

    'The heightened tempo of consolidation in the industry, and the intensification of links between financial markets because of the euro call for careful consideration of structures for containing and supervising institutional and systemic risk.'

6   *Final Report of The Committee of Wise Men on The Regulation of European Securities Markets*, Brussels, 15 February 2001 (the 'Lamfalussy Securities Markets Report'), p 17. Unfortunately the market difficulties in recent years and ongoing consequences rather prove the truth of this.

Risk in cross-border trades

8.30 A cross-border trade is one where the seller, the buyer and/or the assets are located in different jurisdictions[1]. In practice, the types of risk discussed above may be particularly acute in relation to the clearing and settlement of cross-border trades, for operational reasons[2]. Also, the conflict of laws may introduce legal risk, as discussed below.

1   Further, agents through which the parties act and/or intermediaries through which the assets are held may be in different jurisdictions.

2   See CPSS/IOSCO Principles, pp 18, 48, 110, 119 and the Giovannini 2001 Report, p 10: '[c]ross-border clearing and settlement almost always involves intermediaries in the transaction chain, implying a significantly greater degree of complexity in the process.' This report identifies nine separate steps in the instruction flow for processing a cross border equity transaction, involving 11 intermediaries and 14 instructions between parties: see pp 12 and 15. The Giovannini 2003 Report identifies the absence of harmonised rules regarding ownership of securities as a barrier to settlement efficiency

Basic risk management techniques

8.31 The following discussion deals with the key techniques that have been developed to manage risk in the post-trade securities infrastructure.

DVP

8.32 As discussed above, principal risk is addressed by DVP[1]. However, DVP does not address several important risks, including replacement cost risk[2] and custody risk[3]. In assessing DVP within any system, it is important to consider the model of DVP; the quality of delivery and payment; and also the question of finality.

1   See CPSS/IOSCO Principles, p 76, and CESR-ECB Standard 7.

2   See paras **8.23–8.24** above.

3   CPSS/IOSCO Recommendations, p 14:

> 'DVP eliminates principal risk between direct participants in an SSS. However, settlement arrangements are typically tiered, with only a subset of market participants and intermediaries having direct access to the SSS. Achievement of DVP for direct participants in the SSS does not eliminate principal risk exposures between direct participants and their customers.'

> The CPSS/IOSCO Principles consider such relationships from the perspective of the impact of 'material dependencies between direct and indirect participants that can affect the FMI' (p 106).

> For a discussion of managing the risk of custodian insolvency, see Chapter 3.

MODELS

8.33   In its important 1992 study of DVP[1], the Bank for International Settlements ('BIS') identified three models. The key to understanding the different models is to distinguish between (on the one hand) the operational debiting and crediting of cash and securities accounts within the settlement system (which happens throughout the business day) and (on the other hand) the legal transfer of assets pursuant to such book entries. Model 1 DVP is the ideal. Here, the book entries have the immediate effect of achieving delivery and payment, so that both cash and securities are transferred on a gross basis throughout the business day (real-time gross settlement and payment). The least desirable is model 3, in which both payment and delivery is deferred until the end of the business day, and made on a net basis (end of day net settlement and payment). Model 2 involves real time gross settlement but end of day net payment[2].

1   Bank for International Settlements Delivery Versus Payment in Securities Settlement Systems, Basel, 1992.

2   Originally, CREST operated on a model 2 basis for all securities settlement. See Chapter 9.

8.34   Risks associated with end of day net settlement and payment have been discussed in detail, both in the BIS DVP Report and elsewhere[1]. However, the benefits of settlement netting in reducing volumes to manageable levels are also widely acknowledged, and 'it is important to ensure that credit risk reductions should not be at the expense of operational performance'[2]. The CPSS/IOSCO Principles do not call for model 1 DVP in all cases, but note the different DVP models and their advantages and disadvantages[3]. As an alternative to real time gross settlement, the G30/ISSA recommendations called for legally robust netting[4].

1   See CPSS/IOSCO Recommendations, p 14.

2   1995 G30/ISSA Recommendations, p 21.

3   CPSS/IOSCO Principles, pp 153, 154.

4   1995 G30/ISSA Recommendations, Recommendation 4. Note also that the Giovannini 2001 Report and 2003 Report focus on the different approaches to netting in different jurisdictions as a barrier to settlement efficiency.

QUALITIES

8.35   In assessing the quality of DVP, one must also consider the nature of the assets which are transferred synchronously. In relation to securities, the best quality of delivery is immediate legal title. In simple terms, this generally involves ensuring that the securities accounts of the settlement system determine legal title to the settled assets. 'If a CSD is also the registrar, it can eliminate any delay between settlement and registration.'[1] In CREST, the delivery event which is synchronised with the payment event was originally (and still is for non-UK securities) the transfer of equitable interest in securities, with legal title following within two hours. However,

Overview of post-trade infrastructure 213

for UK securities this was upgraded to immediate legal title in November 2001, as discussed in Chapter 9.

1   CPSS/IOSCO Recommendations, p 14.

8.36   In securities settlement (and indeed in the financial markets generally) payment is made by crediting a cash account[1]. The quality of payment depends on the credit standing of the bank which maintains this account. 'To conduct ... money settlements, an FMI can use central bank money or commercial bank money.'[2] The best quality of payment is in central bank money, and a number of European settlement systems have introduced, or propose to introduce it[3]. However, '[u]se of the central bank of issue as the single settlement bank may not ... always be practicable'[4]. There may also be arguments that it is not desirable. Securities settlement can involve very significant credit exposures, and it is not clear that these should be automatically borne by central banks. The use of commercial bank money in securities settlement would leave central banks with the regulatory choice of whether or not to bear the credit exposures associated with securities settlement, by acting as lender of last resort to a commercial settlement bank in financial difficulties. It is interesting to note that the CPSS/IOSCO Recommendations do not require the use of central bank money in all cases, but where central bank money is not used, require credit and liquidity risk to be effectively managed[5].

1   The bank may be the settlement system itself, as in the case of Euroclear and Clearstream, or a third party bank to which the settlement system is linked, as with CREST.

2   Note – CPSS/IOSCO Recommendations, p 17:

   'When multiple settlement banks are involved, any resulting interbank obligations between these commercial settlement banks are settled through an interbank payment system, typically a central bank payment system.'

3   In the UK, a modified form of access to central bank money is available, as discussed in Chapter 9.

4   CPSS/IOSCO Recommendations, p 17.

5   CPSS/IOSCO Principle 9: 'An FMI should conduct its money settlements in central bank money where practical and available. If central bank money is not used, an FMI should minimise and strictly control the credit and liquidity risk arising from the use of commercial bank money.'

FINALITY

8.37

'If an FMI settles transactions that involve the settlement of two linked obligations (for example, securities or foreign exchange transactions), it should eliminate principal risk by conditioning the final settlement of one obligation upon the final settlement of the other.'[1]

1   CPSS/IOSCO Principle 12.

8.38   It must be established as an operational matter at what point the transfer cannot be revoked by the party making payment or delivery, or by the operator of the settlement system[1]. Ideally it should also be established as a legal matter that a transfer cannot be reversed by the courts. Most systems of law provide for certain transfers to be reversible in certain circumstances if the transferor is affected by insolvency at the time of the transfer or shortly thereafter, and also in the case of fraud. As discussed below, certain legislative provisions address insolvency displacement, particularly in relation to key infrastructure systems[2]. However, to date it is not clear that any existing or proposed initiative addresses fraud risk[3], although if implemented the UNIDROIT Convention[5] would make some progress on this point by its proposal which effectively seeks to reproduce the benefits of negotiability for intermediated securities.

214 *The Law of Global Custody*

1   See CPSS/IOSCO Principle 8, Key Considerations, p 64.
2   Although the benefit of Financial Collateral Directive is not limited to major systems, as discussed in Chapter 4.
3   The concept of negotiability was developed in the medieval period to provide for finality of delivery to the holder in due course (broadly, the good faith purchaser of a negotiable instrument) even where a transferor acts fraudulently. However, as discussed in Chapter 2, intangible interests in securities recorded electronically do not benefit from negotiable status.
4   *Institut International pour l'Unification du Droit Privé* (the International Institute for the Unification of Private Law).
5   See further Chapter 5, paras **5.62–5.65**.

Shorter settlement cycles

8.39   As discussed above, one simple technique for addressing replacement cost risk is the introduction of shorter settlement cycles[1]. Batch settlement, in which all trades during a settlement account period remain unsettled until a specified date, has been widely rejected in favour of rolling settlement, in which settlement occurs on every business day, a fixed number of days after each trade[2]. The length of the settlement interval is customarily indicated by the number of business days between trade date ('T') and settlement, so that 'T+3' indicates settlement on the third business day after trade date. Like the 1989 G30 Report[3], the CPSS/IOSCO Principles retain 'T+3 settlement as a minimum standard'[4]. 'However, T+3 is often no longer regarded as best practice. In many markets, government securities already settle on T+1 or even T+0, and some equity markets are currently considering a T+1 settlement cycle'[5], although at the time of writing T+1 is not a short-term prospect in the US equity markets. Also, there is a call for unified settlement cycles for all instrument types. 'The variation in settlement periods between the international deposit and lending markets, corporate debt, government debt, equity securities and traded derivatives is inefficient and costly.'[6] Interestingly, the Giovannini 2003 Report refers to the need to harmonise settlement periods, rather than reduce them, in order to improve settlement efficiency, and although notes that T+2 would 'have the benefit of bringing the equity markets into line with the foreign exchange spot market', also points out that it would be unwise to move to a settlement period which would be inconsistent with other areas of the world, for example, the US.

1   See CPSS/IOSCO Principles, p 143 and FIBV Clearing and Settlement Best Practices Report 1999, p 5. However, unduly short settlement cycles may increase settlement failures. See *Joint work of the European System of Central Banks and the Committee of European Securities Regulators in the field of clearing and settlement, a call for contributions from interested parties*, March 2002, p 4.
2   CPSS/IOSCO Recommendation 3 (CPSS/IOSCO Principles, Annex C, p 142), CESR-ECB Standard 3.
3   Recommendation 7.
4   CPSS/IOSCO Recommendation 3 (CPSS/IOSCO Principles, Annex C, p 142).
5   CPSS/IOSCO Recommendation 3 (CPSS/IOSCO Principles, Annex C, p 142).
6   See also the European Securities Forum *Contribution on the Joint CESR/ECB Consultation on Clearing and Settlement*, 2002, ESF comment on consultation question 2.7:

   'There are benefits to ensuring that the settlement cycles of different securities are harmonised given the increasing frequency of complex trades.'

T+1

8.40   T+1 settlement has been set as the target for the developed international securities markets[1]. This is undoubtedly a considerable challenge, particularly in relation to cross-border trades[2], which will require very considerable operational improvements in the post-trade infrastructure. In July 2000 the DTCC published *The T+1 White Paper*[3], which 'details DTCC's best thinking on the changes that we as an industry – and our depository and clearing subsidiaries – need to make to provide for straight-through processing and, ultimately, T+1 settlement'[4]. However, as noted above, this issue is not considered in much detail in the Giovannini 2003 Report or later discussions of settlement, nor has the general target of T+3 been changed in the April 2012 CPSS/IOSCO Principles.

1   See 1995 G30/ISSA Recommendations, p 22.

2   See CPSS/IOSCO Recommendation 3 (CPSS/IOSCO Principles, Annex C, p 142) and DTCC *T+1 White Paper*, p 2.

3   DTCC: *Straight-Through Processing: A White Paper to the Industry on T+1* (June 2000).

4   *T+1 White Paper*, p 1.

STP

8.41   An important operational development which has been identified as a precondition of T+1 settlement is straight through processing, or 'STP'. STP involves the automation of the post-trade processing of securities[1] transactions, so as to avoid the re-entry of trade data by the different parties involved[2]. The need for STP is clear in the light of the levels of manual intervention, repetition[3], fragmentation[4], redundancy[5], error[6] and delay[7] currently involved in post-trade processing. To be simplistic, there are two problems with the pre-STP environment, namely multiple operational stages and data re-entry. First, as the Giovannini 2001 Report clearly illustrated, transaction processing involves multiple intermediaries and operational stages. This report identifies nine separate steps in the instruction flow for processing a cross-border equity transaction, involving 11 intermediaries and 14 instructions between parties. The heavily intermediated nature of the contemporary securities, cash and derivatives markets arises for a number of reasons, including restrictions on direct access to large value delivery systems, and the development of cross-border links. In the managed funds industry, the chain of intermediaries is lengthened further by the involvement of brokers and fund managers, and here the potential benefits of STP are particularly clear. For example, a broker may communicate its bids and offers to a fund manager by fax, and an agreement for a block trade between the broker and fund manager may be concluded by telephone. Then the fund manager may make a telephone call to the broker indicating how the block trade is to be allocated among its various clients. Trade confirmation may well be automated, but regulatory trade reporting may not be. The broker may then send a telex or SWIFT message to the lead custodian giving settlement instructions. If settlement involves a sub-custodian, the global custodian may send a fax to it in respect of the same trade. Finally the global custodian or sub-custodian will need to instruct that system. A separate intervention is required to progress each stage, and a delay in any of these stages serves to delay the transaction as a whole. A related point is that each stage requires the intermediary not only to act, but also to input trade data, but unsurprisingly, the chief cause of delay in transaction processing is erroneous data entry. Without STP, the same trade details are recorded again and again, sometimes incorrectly. The impact of the current lack of automation is made worse as cross-border investing and complex investment strategies increase. STP is needed, not merely to deliver shorter settlement cycles, but also to accommodate rapidly growing trade volumes[8].

1   Similar initiatives are taking place in the cash and derivatives markets.

2   See CPSS/IOSCO Principles, pp 141, 142.

3   DTCC *T+1 White Paper*, p 11:

216   The Law of Global Custody

'Today, institutional trades are primed for settlement through a series of sequential and repetitive steps, using process developed when the volume of trades was far lower than it is today and settlement occurred on T+5.'

See also p 14.

4   See DTCC *T+1 White Paper*, p 14.
5   See DTCC *T+1 White Paper*, p 13.
6   See DTCC *T+1 White Paper*, p 14.
7   See DTCC *T+1 White Paper*, p 14.
8   Although trade volumes declined in 2001.

8.42   The Giovannini 2003 Report does not refer to STP specifically, although does discuss steps to remove certain barriers, such as harmonisation of operating hours and settlement deadlines, and creation of standard protocols to remove problems with incompatibility of technology and interfaces, the implementation of which would assist STP. Further to this, the Giovannini Group asked SWIFT to define a common communication protocol for the European clearing and settlement market which resulted in SWIFT, after consultation, recommending a final protocol intended to remove Giovannini Barrier 1[1].

1   See SWIFT Consultation Paper 'The Proposal for the Removal of Barrier 1 of the Giovannini Report', January 2005; and SWIFT *Elimination of Giovannini Barrier One – Final Protocol recommendation*, March 2006. The 2006 paper notes in particular: 'Where relevant to other EU initiatives, such as MiFID, support for these standards should be implemented to ensure STP from pre-trade to asset servicing.'

8.43   The intention of STP types of system is to permit T+1 by automating the progress of a transaction from one operational stage to the next. Thus, provided the conditions for progressing the transaction are present, they will automatically proceed. Intervention will be required, not to progress the transaction, but to halt its progress.

8.44   The need for data re-entry is avoided by the use of a central record, to which all parties involved in the transaction have access, and which is updated as the transaction progresses.

8.45   However, STP is not without cost. Its development involves a significant investment, and it may benefit the larger players more than smaller institutions. Trades which will be processed straight through, without the possibility of manual intervention, will include bad trades, ie those which are input in error or unlawful. 'As settlement cycles shorten, the room for error and subsequent correction diminishes ...'[1]

1   DTCC *CCP White Paper*, p 9. For a discussion of the possible legal implication of the straight through processing of unlawful trades, see J Benjamin *Interests in Securities* (2000, Oxford University Press), pp 242–4.

Central counterparty

8.46   A further technique for managing replacement cost risk is the use of a central counterparty ('CCP'). The role of the CCP was discussed briefly above. The CCP serves to 'redistribute credit and market risk to those that are best able to bear them'[1].

1   DTCC CCP White Paper, p 2.

8.47   This section will consider those aspects of the role of the CCP that are most relevant to the reform of the post-trade infrastructure[1].

1   See also discussion in Chapter 9 regarding CCP links with CREST.

Collateralisation

8.48 In order to manage the risks that it assumes, it is customary for the CCP to take collateral from the market participants to which it provides clearing services. Collateral comprises a range of financial assets and is actively marked to market[1]. Demand for high quality financial collateral assets exceeds supply. As discussed below, a major factor in the drive towards consolidation of the European post-trading infrastructure is the need to achieve netting efficiencies in the collateralisation of clearing exposures, so that collateral surpluses in certain markets can offset collateral shortfalls in others.

1   See Hills et al, para **8.27** n 4 above, at 127. Marking to market is discussed in Chapter 4.

Default provisions

8.49 Even when a market participant member firm fails, the CCP settles that firm's trades as central counterparty. In order to manage the potential cost of such settlements without prejudicing the CCP's own solvency, detailed default provisions are put in place. These concern 'what happens when a market participant is unable to meet a margin call and defaults, leaving the central counterparty with uncollateralised losses. It will usually attempt to crystallise the loss immediately by closing out the defaulting member's proprietary positions and closing out or transferring any customer positions to other market participants. Central counterparties can then have various ways of allocating losses'[1]. While different CCPs have different approaches, by way of example, the order of recourse of the DTCC was outlined in 2000 as follows:

- '– margin cover of the defaulting member;
- – any additional default/participant fund2 contributions of the defaulting member (this and the preceding source of funds are used to ensure that defaulting members bear a significant cost first, protecting other members);
- – excess assets held by the defaulting member at other CCPs linked through cross-guarantee arrangements;
- – other members' participant fund contributions and the CCP's assessment rights (mutualising the risk);
- – insurance cover (laying off the risk);
- – reserves of the CCP; and
- – capital of the CCP (as a final line of defence before there are assessments against remaining members, with the risk that losses become systemic and require the intervention of the authorities).'[3]

1   Hills et al, para **8.27** n 4 above, at 127.
2   See also CPSS/IOSCO Principles, p 9 and 157.
3   DTCC *CCP White Paper*, pp 5, 6.

8.50 It is important to note that some of the default techniques relied on by CCPs may not accord with the general principles of insolvency law, for example because they may involve multi-lateral netting, or post-insolvency dispositions. Legal support may therefore be required, through special legislative protections. It is crucial to establish that such support is effective to permit the default provisions to withstand participant insolvency[1]. In cross-border arrangements, where more than one system of insolvency law is involved, this may involve a considerable challenge, as discussed below. Within the EU, a number of measures serve to protect default provisions from the general principles of insolvency law, as discussed briefly below and in Chapter 5.

1   See ESF EuroCCP; ESF's blueprint for a Single Pan-European Central Counterparty, 2000 ('ESF Blueprint'), pp 15, 16.

Benefits of clearing for market participants

8.51   Clearing offers important benefits to market participants[1]. These are, primarily, the reduction and standardisation of counterparty credit exposures[2]; related collateral and regulatory capital efficiencies[3]; and operational efficiencies[4]. Netting assists liquidity, both in normal market conditions and during market disturbances[5]. Additionally, the use of a central counterparty may offer post-trade anonymity[6]. The unrivalled access enjoyed by a CCP to market data is an important regulatory tool[7] in the management of macro risks (as well as a commercial sensitivity)[8].

1   Although these may vary from market to market. See Hills et al, para **8.27** n 4 above, at 125.
2   See Hills et al, at 126.
3   With trade netting, these are calculated in relation to net and not gross credit exposures.
4   With settlement netting, the volume of settlements is reduced. Margin deliveries may also benefit from netting.
5   See Hills et al, at 130.
6   See Hills et al, at 125, 126.
7   Hills et al, at 133.
8   See DTCC *CCP White Paper*, p 9.

8.52   However, because of the costs involved, 'Not all markets are necessarily suitable for central counterparty clearing'[1]. Moreover, the use of a CCP may introduce moral hazard. A series of financial crises historically associated with clearing houses were discussed by the Bank of England[2]. 'Previous failures (though rare) provide some cautionary tales.'[3]

1   See Hills et al, para **8.27** n 4 above, at 124.
2   In Hills et al, at 129.
3   Hills et al, at 133.

The development of clearing

8.53   In Europe, a number of clearing systems offer services in a range of markets[1]. While clearing in the US is relatively integrated, a number of distinct systems still operate[2]. In the development of clearing, two trends in particular are apparent.

1   See the discussions in the DTCC *T+1 White Paper*, p 7 and The Giovannini 2001 Report, pp 21–30. The DTCC *CCP White Paper*, p 7:

   'A group of the larger market participants in Europe have recently banded together to form the European Securities Forum (ESF), which, amongst several initiatives in trading, clearing, settlement and custody, is making the case for creating a single CCP supporting equity markets in Europe.'
2   See DTCC *CCP White Paper*, p 6.

DERIVATIVES TO CASH SECURITIES

8.54   Clearing originated in the derivatives markets, where the need to manage post-trade, pre-settlement risk was perceived early due to the long settlement periods associated with derivatives. More recently, with greater emphasis on risk management and capital efficiency, clearing is being introduced into the cash securities markets.

MARKET SPECIFIC TO MULTI-MARKET AND REMOTE CLEARING

8.55 'Until very recently, most CCPs have confined their operations to supporting a single market in a single country.'[1] This arrangement is described as a 'vertical silo'. However, the ESF explains that, in the US, the case for moving away from this model became clear in the 1960s and 1970s[2]. More recently, the multi-market model of clearing has developed across the financial sector, so that 'the CCP can, for example, use the correlations between, say, derivatives and equities to offset exposures ...'[3]. Multi-market clearing is often associated with the provisions of cross-border clearing services, known as remote clearing[4]. However, the 'horizontal' model is not universally accepted.

1   DTCC CCP White Paper, p 4.

2   See ESF Blueprint, pp 3, 4.

3   DTCC CCP White Paper, p 8. See also Hills et al, para **8.27** n 4 above, at 125:

'Where a clearing house acts as central counterparty to several markets which are subject to identical or highly correlated risks, the benefit of exposure netting may extend to market risk. This creates the possibility of margin offsets where firms are long in one market and short in another (for instance, margin against a long position in a bond futures contract might be offset against margin against a matching short position in repo).'

4   See ESF Submission on ISD, p 2.

Leading studies and reports

8.56 As indicated above, a series of important studies and reports address risk and propose reform in the post-trading infrastructure. The 1989 G30 Report broke new ground with nine recommendations relating respectively to:

- trade comparison;
- trade confirmation/affirmation;
- central securities depositories;
- trade netting;
- DVP;
- same day funds;
- T+3 settlement;
- securities lending; and
- common message standards.

8.57 '[T]he 1989 G30 recommendations remain the only standards that have achieved widespread support and official endorsement.'[1] However, the G30 1989 report is now out of date[2], and must be read together with subsequent works that built on its seminal insights. The 1992 report of the BIS on DVP, discussed above, importantly refined the industry's understanding of delivery versus payment. Its different DVP models are widely cited although, as indicated above, model 1 DVP is not universally accepted as a standard. In 1995 ISSA reviewed the 1989 G30 Report, and produced the nine *1995 G30/ISSA Recommendations*, which updated the original recommendations in the light of market changes. Also in 1995 the BIS produced a report on *Cross-Border Securities Settlement*, which contained important insights including the problem of 'the leap of faith': market participants or their agents are routinely required to give instructions for the transfer of securities or cash before confirmation that corresponding value will be received on the due date.

1   DTCC *T+1 White Paper*, p 1.
2   See DTCC *T + 1 White Paper*, p 1.

8.58   In 1997, the BIS and IOSCO published a *Disclosure Framework for Securities Settlement Systems* in order to facilitate the assessment of risk management in key settlement systems. This is a standard form questionnaire, to which settlement systems have published answers[1]. In 1998, ECSDA[2] published standards with which a European national settlement system must comply in order to participate in a series of bilateral settlement links. The initial purpose of this was to facilitate the cross-border delivery of collateral to central banks providing Euro liquidity through TARGET[3].

1   Some more informative than others.
2   The European Central Securities Depository Association.
3   See Standards for the use of EU securities settlement systems in ESCB credit operations, 1998.

8.59   In 2000, ISSA published eight revised recommendations. The following year the CPSS-IOSCO Joint Task Force on Securities Settlement Systems published 18 recommendations[1] (the CPSS/IOSCO Recommendations[2]) which set best practice standards for settlement. It identifies in 18 headline recommendations both the minimum requirements and best practice for securities settlement systems. The CPSS/IOSCO Recommendations relate to legal risk (recommendation 1, on the legal framework); pre-settlement risk (recommendations 2–5, on trade confirmations, settlement cycles, central counterparties and securities lending respectively); settlement risk (recommendations 6–10 on central securities depositories (CSDs), DVP, timing of settlement finality, CSD risk controls to address participant defaults, and cash settlement of assets respectively); operational risk (recommendation 11 on operational reliability); custody risk (recommendation 12 on protection of customers' securities); and other issues (recommendations 13–18 on governance, access, efficiency, communication procedures and standards, transparency and regulation and oversight respectively). In October 2000, the DTCC published *Central Counterparties: Development, Cooperation and Consolidation*, October 2000 ('DTCC CPP White Paper').

1   Recommendations for Securities Settlement Systems. See also Joint work of the European System of Central Banks and the Committee of European Securities Regulators in the field of clearing and Settlement, a call for contributions from interested parties March 2002, p 2:

    'It was recognised from the outset that the CPSS/IOSCO recommendations represent an obvious starting point for any work to be undertaken on the issue of setting standards for securities clearing and settlement.'

2   Available on www.bis.org and www.iosco.org.

8.60   In 2001 the Giovannini Group[1] published its first report on *Cross-Border Clearing and Settlement Arrangements in the European Union* (the 'Giovannini 2001 Report'), identifying the sources of inefficiency that currently exist. In 2002, the European Commission issued its consultative *Communication on clearing and settlement in the European Union; Main policy issues and future challenges*[2], in which it set out Commission policy. It identified the twin objectives in achieving an integrated post-trade infrastructure by removing barriers to finalising individual cross-border transactions, and removing competitive distortions in the EU post-trading environment[3]. Options on which it sought responses include the development of a harmonised EU regulatory environment for clearing and settlement entities[4].

Overview of post-trade infrastructure 221

1   'The Giovannini Group was formed in 1996 to advise the Commission on issues relating to EU financial integration and the efficiency of euro-denominated financial markets' (Giovannini 2001 Report, p 1).

2   COM(2002) 257.

3   European Commission *Communication on clearing and settlement in the European Union; Main policy issues and future challenges*, p 9.

4   See the further discussion in Chapter 7.

8.61   In January 2003, G30 published its report Global Clearing and Settlements: A Plan of Action – Twenty recommendations that constitute a plan of action for global clearing and settlement, following its review of the state of the post-trade infrastructure worldwide, analysing existing standards and principles, and considering governance and ownership issues.

8.62   Also in 2003, the Giovannini Group published *The Giovannini Group Second Report on EU Clearing and Settlement Arrangements*, April 2003. The Giovannini 2001 Report concluded that the markets were fragmented and inefficient in the EU, and identified 15 main areas causing such inefficiency (the 15 'barriers'). The 2003 Report considers how steps could be taken to remove the barriers identified, noting the need not only to remove the barriers but also to have an appropriate regulatory structure since there would limited benefits if 'multiple regulatory, fiscal and legal regimes', and emphasising that the order in which barriers are removed is important, since, in particular, removing rules which only allow certain settlement services in specific jurisdictions is important, such rules should not be removed until issues such as interoperability and legal certainty have been resolved, since otherwise wider access could increase operational and legal risk. The 2003 Report also notes that consolidation of systems is a common way in which entities seek to make settlement more efficient and that this can lead to a reduction in market competition, although it concludes (somewhat curiously) both that 'a consolidation of clearing and settlement infrastructure does not necessarily imply a reduction in competition' and that operational and legal risk could increase if clearing and settlement end up concentrated in a small number of service providers.

8.63   The following is a very brief summary of the barriers identified by the Giovannini 2001 Report and the remedies proposed by the Giovannini 2003 Report in the order set out in such Report: Barrier 7 (difficulties with incompatible operating hours and deadlines), to be resolved by harmonising operating hours and settlement deadlines; Barrier 1 (incompatibility of information technology and interfaces), to be resolved by standardising relevant protocols[1]; Barrier 4 (lack of intra-day final irrevocable delivery across borders), to be resolved by intra-day settlement finality for all links between settlement systems; Barrier 6 (national differences in settlement periods for EU equities), to be resolved by harmonising (possibly at T+3); Barrier 3 (national differences in rules regarding corporate actions and timing), to be resolved by harmonising such rules; Barrier 8 (national differences in securities issuance practice eg allocation of International Securities Identifying Numbers ('ISINs'), to be resolved by creating standard practices; Barrier 11 (domestic withholding tax regulations, allowing withholding tax agency services to be provided only by intermediaries established in the relevant jurisdiction), to be resolved by changing the local law to allow non-domestic agents to provide such services; Barrier 12 (collection of taxes only by local settlement system), to be resolved by changing local law to allow use of any settlement system for such purpose; Barriers 13, 14 and 15 (absence of EU framework for treatment of ownership of securities, differences in local law treatment of netting, differences in local rules regarding conflicts of laws), to be resolved by changing relevant laws[2]; Barriers 2 and 9 (national restrictions on location of clearing and settlement, and location of securities), to be resolved by changes of law to remove such restrictions[3]; Barrier 5 (problems with remote access to local clearing and settlement systems), to be resolved by changing any laws or regulations conflicting with this, and access criteria must be the same for resident and non-resident entities in the relevant jurisdiction[4]; Barrier 10 (local restrictions requiring dealers to establish local operations and use local systems), to be resolved by changes in the relevant law or regulation to removed such restrictions.

1   See para **8.42** n 1 above regarding the SWIFT protocol.

2   The Giovannini 2003 Report notes that the Financial Collateral Directive assists in relation to the issues with netting and conflicts of laws, as well as improving legal certainty in relation to use of book entry securities collateral, but also notes the difference between the test for identifying applicable law in such Directive and in the relevant Hague Convention (see Chapter 5, paras **5.59–5.61**) and that this will need to be resolved. Certainty regarding legal ownership of securities held with an intermediary is acknowledged in the Report to be a much more difficult area, but it is concluded that 'the objective is that the legal nature of ownership of securities would be the same across the EU, under each and every legal system'. This is of course a considerable challenge, given that it means dealing with a group of sovereign states whose laws may have developed in significantly ways, and developments which affect sensitive areas (such as control of fiscal policies or deeply rooted attitudes to what constitutes a fair approach in insolvency situations) may well meet resistance. This is at least one reason why it is perhaps over-simplistic to argue that settlement fragmentation and inefficiency can be overcome in the same way in the EU as in the US. But see also discussion of proposed UNIDROIT Convention in Chapter 5.

3   There have of course been developments in this respect as a result of Directive 2004/39/EC of the European Parliament and of the Council of 21 April 2004 on markets in financial instruments ('MiFID'). MiFID requires member states to ensure that investment firms from other members states do have 'the right of access to central counterparty, clearing and settlement systems in their territory', and such access rights must 'be subject to the same non-discriminatory, transparent and objective criteria as apply to local participants' (art 34(1)). Furthermore, member states are prohibited from requiring that central counterparty, clearing and settlement systems can only be used in connection with regulated markets or MTFs (multilateral trading facilities regulated under MiFID), and must require that regulated markets 'offer all their members or participants the right to designate' the settlement system they wish to use for settlement of trades on that market, although this second point is specifically subject to whatever arrangements are in place between the relevant market and settlement system 'as are necessary to ensure the efficient and economic settlement of the transaction in question' and the relevant regulator's approval of the "technical conditions for settlement" as being appropriate 'to allow the smooth and orderly functioning of financial markets' (art 34(2)).

4   See n 3.

8.64   In July 2004, the EU Commission established a Clearing and Settlement Advisory and Monitoring Expert Group ('CESAME') to monitor and advise regarding the steps taken to integrate securities clearing and settlement systems within the EU, with the intention of liaising with the G30 Group and other bodies concerned in this area.

8.65   The European Central Bank ('ECB')[1] and the Committee of European Securities Regulators ('CESR')[2] established a joint working group on clearing and settlement[3], with a view to adopting common European standards (based on the CPSS/IOSCO Recommendations), resulting in the CESR-ECB Report, *Standards For Securities Clearing And Settlement In The European Union*, approved in September 2004 (and published in October 2004), listing the 19 standards.

1   The central bank for the euro area, established in 1998, see further www.ecb.int.

2   The Committee of European Securities Regulators ('CESR') was established under Commission Decision 2001/527/EC of 6 June 2001 establishing the Committee of European Securities Regulators, with functions including improving cooperation and coordination among regulators in the EU and advising the European Commission in relation to the implementation of European directives. With effect from 1 January 2011, CESR was replaced by the European Securities and Markets Authority ('ESMA'), to continue the same work as CESR, but with additional powers. ESMA forms part of the European System of Financial Supervision ('ESFS'), and is an independent EU authority with powers including drafting technical standards that are legally binding in EU member states, resolving disputes between national authorities of EU member states, and monitoring systemic risks (in contrast, CESR was an advisory committee).

3   'Common standards will contribute to creating a level playing-field for the providers of securities clearing and settlement services and to overcoming the significant heterogeneity within the legislative frameworks of European countries': ECB/CESR press release, 25 October 2001.

8.66 The CESR-ECB working group reviewed the recommendations of CPSS-IOSCO Task Force on Securities Settlement Systems[1] with a view to creating equivalent standards of particular relevance to settlement systems in the EU, and took into account the high level standards produced in February 2001 by EACH[2], the first discussion paper produced by UNIDROIT[3] in 2002 in relation to securities held with an intermediary[4] and the G30[5] recommendations to improve clearing and settlement in 2003[6]. As a result, in addition to the 'worldwide' recommendations of the CPSS-IOSCO Task Force, CESR-ECB produced in its September 2004 Report Standards for Securities Clearing and Settlement in the European Union. These recommendations include adoption of rolling settlement in all securities markets (with final settlement no later than T+3), immobilisation or dematerialisation of securities and book entry transfer 'to the greatest extent possible', delivery versus payment to eliminate principal risk and 'Entities holding securities in custody should employ accounting practices and safe-keeping procedures that fully protect customers' securities. It is essential that customers' securities be protected against the claims of creditors of all entities involved in the custody chain'[7].

1   CPSS-IOSCO Recommendations for securities settlement systems produced November 2001; CPSS-IOSCO Recommendations for Central Counterparties produced in November 2004. Both sets of recommendations have no legal force, but are intended to indicate minimum standards for all relevant systems worldwide, and expected to be taken into account by relevant supervisors and regulators when considering appropriate standards of behaviour.

2   European Association of Central Counterparty Clearing Houses.

3   UNIDROIT is the International Institute for the Unification of Private Law, an 'independent intergovernmental Organisation' whose 'purpose is to study needs and methods for modernising, harmonising and co-ordinating private and in particular commercial law as between States and groups of States'. It is funded by contributions from its members (broadly, sovereign states, at the time of writing comprising: Argentina, Australia, Austria, Belgium, Bolivia, Brazil, Bulgaria, Canada, Chile, China, Colombia, Croatia, Cuba, Cyprus, Czech Republic, Denmark, Egypt, Estonia, Finland, France, Germany, Greece, Holy See, Hungary, India, Iran, Iraq, Ireland, Israel, Italy, Japan, Latvia, Lithuania, Luxembourg, Malta, Mexico, The Netherlands, Nicaragua, Nigeria, Norway, Pakistan, Paraguay, Poland, Portugal, Republic of Korea, Republic of Serbia, Romania, Russian Federation, San Marino, Slovakia, Slovenia, South Africa, Spain, Sweden, Switzerland, Tunisia, Turkey, the UK, the US, Uruguay and Venezuela).

4   'Harmonised Substantive Rules for the Use of Securities Held with Intermediaries as Collateral', June 2002.

5   G30 – The Group of Thirty, a private not-for-profit international body established in 1978. It is made up of senior persons from academia and the public and private sectors, and analyses international economic and financial issues relevant to market practitioners and policymakers.

6   'Global Clearing and Settlements: A Plan of Action', January 2003.

7   CESR-ECB Standards for Securities Clearing and Settlement in the European Union, September 2004 Report, List of the Standards, 'Standard 12: Protection of customers' securities'.

8.67 In January 2005, following a request by the Giovannini Group, SWIFT produced its Consultation Paper entitled 'The Proposal for the Removal of Barrier 1 of the Giovannini Report'.

8.68 A draft report was produced by Theresa Villiers, EU Parliament Rapporteur for clearing and settlement, in February 2005, expressing the view that additional regulation for clearing and settlement was not necessary and could cause further issues rather than helping remove Giovannini barriers, but in the same month the EU Commission announced the creation of a Legal Certainty Group which would consider the issues of legal uncertainty which were hindering integration of securities clearing and settlement systems in the EU.

8.69 April 2005 saw the publication by ECSDA of ten standards, the implementation of which was intended to enable for removal of Giovannini Barriers 4 and 7[1]. These standard set out steps such as required opening times and target dates for achieving relevant steps.

1 ECSDA The European Central Securities Depositories Association's First Annual Status Report Relating to its Standards for the Removal of Giovannini Barriers 4 and 7, 29 April 2005.

8.70 ESCB-CESR published a discussion paper on 16 July 2005 regarding the methods of applying proposed settlement system standards to custodians, and in particular considering the types of custodian to which such standards should apply. In August 2005, a Joint Working Group of the ESCB and CESR published a statement[1] reviewing the next steps regarding the proposed standards published in October 2004, including the development of an assessment methodology (similar to the CPSS-IOSCO assessment methodology) in relation to such standards, and proposing that these standards should apply to certain custodians as well, and suggesting ways of identifying the relevant types of custodians to which the standards should apply. Unsurprisingly, industry bodies were not slow to reply, and the comments included the fact that a detailed response was not possible until a detailed proposal was presented, that any proposal should 'clearly articulate the risks that ESCB-CESR perceives as posed by included intermediaries and described the shortcomings of existing regulation and supervision in respect of those risks', and stressed that extensive regulation already applies to custodians and that it was not clear that an applicability test based on size would be the appropriate test[2]. There was also criticism of the possibility of the duplication of bank regulation and an approach selecting 'significant custodians' only in contrast with 'the general banking regulation approach, which defines a regulatory objective applicable to all banks while ensuring proportionality and flexibility'[3], and lack of evidence regarding 'the existence of potential risks in the clearing and settlement activities of custodian banks that are not already covered by banking regulation and supervision'[4]. As a general point, it is true that both custodians and settlement systems hold securities on behalf of another, and a custodian can settle transfers of securities between two of its clients across its own books if such clients so wish. However, it is a considerable leap of logic to conclude that settlement system standards should therefore be applied to custodians. To do so would duplicate the regulatory requirements applicable to custodians, and would result in settlement standards applying at several levels of a chain of intermediaries which could result in confusion from overlapping or conflicting requirements.

1 CESR/ECB Public Statement Ref 05-502 'Follow-up work by ESCB/CESR Joint Working Group', 1 August 2005.

2 Response from the Association of Global Custodians, 13 September 2005.

3 Response from the Federation Bancaire de l'Union Europeenne, 12 October 2005.

4 Comments by the European Savings Banks Group in response to the ESCB–CESR Public Statement on Follow-Up Work by the ESCB/CESR Joint Working Group, 22 September 2005.

8.71 Also in August 2005 the European Savings Banks Group ('ESBG'), European Banking Federation and European Association of Cooperative Banks published a recommendation to remove Barrier 3 (the national differences in rules regarding corporate actions, beneficial ownership and custody).

8.72 In response to the CESR-ECB proposed standards produced in 2004, in September 2005 the ESBG published a statement[1] to the ESCB-CESR working group giving various views on follow-up work respecting the proposed standards, but also stating that the standards should not apply to custodians. This view was reiterated in the October 2005 statement from the EBF to ESCB-CESR[2] which, in addition to comments on further steps required in connection with the standards, queried whether it was appropriate to single out 'significant custodians' as a specific type of custodian to whom the standards should apply.

1   'Comments by the European Savings Banks Group in response to the ESCB-CESR Public Statement on Follow-up Work by the ESCB-CESR Joint Working Group', 22 September 2005.

2   'EBF Response to CESR-ECB Public Statement of 1 August 2005', 12 October 2005.

8.73   In 7 March 2006 the EU Commission evidently decided that insufficient progress was being made to improve settlement arrangements in Europe statement, and therefore published a statement[1] to the effect that unless the relevant market players progressed with improving the clearing and settlement arrangements in the EU, the European Commission would consider making appropriate rules to achieve this, noting that: 'The securities industry needs to accelerate work on removing a number of barriers significantly, and provide a firm timetable for change.'

1   EU Commission Press Release 'Clearing and Settlement', 7 March 2006.

8.74   Following this, in March 2006 SWIFT produced *Elimination of Giovannini Barrier One – Final Protocol Recommendation*, and in May 2006 G30 published *Global Clearing and Settlement: Final Monitoring Report*, reviewing clearing and settlement developments since the G30 January 2003 report, concluding that much had been achieved but there was much more to do to ensure efficient global clearing and settlement.

8.75   In July 2006 ECSDA published its second annual status report regarding the removal of Barriers 4 and 7, reporting a high level of entities meeting the standards, and noting that a larger number of CSDs intending to accept these standards as a result of ECSDA and the Central and Eastern European Securities and Clearing Houses Association ('CEECSDA') having merged in January 2006.

8.76   However, in November 2006 the EU Commission published a European Code of Conduct for Clearing and Settlement. This was intended to constitute a voluntary code, compliance with which would increase transparency and improve access rights and interoperability by clarifying the pricing of services provided, removing restrictions regarding system access by market participants, and increasing interoperability between different systems. At the same time, the Federation of European Securities Exchanges ('FESE'), the European Association of Central Counterparty Clearing Houses ('EACH') and the European Central Securities Depositories Association ('ECSDA') produced a statement confirming that their members would comply with the Code on a voluntary basis. The conclusions of the Council of European Finance Ministers ('ECOFIN') meeting on 28 November 2006 called for implementation of EU Commission Code of Conduct, and of the Economic and Financial Affairs Council meeting on 9 October 2007 specifically approved the Code sections regarding price transparency and access and interoperability, and also encouraged finalisation of the CESR-ECB Standards. It should be noted that the introduction to the Code stated that 'the Commission is considering proposing ... the further extension of the Code once it has entered into force' and 'the extension of the self-regulatory approach to other asset classes and service providers, as well as any differing provisions of the Code which may apply to such asset classes and service providers'. This is somewhat puzzling language, because this is a voluntary code, not legislation which will enter into force, and suggests the possibility that it might be applied to custodians in future. However, it is not clear that the Code is relevant to custodians as well as settlement systems (given the references to matters such as general access and interoperability), and to date therefore does not appear o be any intention to extend the Code to apply it to custodians.

8.77 The EU Commission Code of Conduct was considered further by the European Credit Sector Associations ('ECSAs')[1], as in March 2008 the EBF published a report of feedback received from the ECSAs[2] which, broadly, expressed the view that market infrastructures were making good progress in implementing the Code in relation to price transparency, but that access and interoperability were still presenting problems. However, in the May 2008 EU Commission report on the views of the Monitoring Group regarding the Code of Conduct relating to clearing and settlement[3], the Monitoring Group noted positive steps such as 'LCH.Clearnet's decision to agree interoperability with SIS x-clear' and the Frankfurt Stock Exchange efforts to develop requirements for third party clearing and settlement provider access. Further to this, the EU Council published the conclusions on clearing and settlement from the ECOFIN meeting on 3 June 2008 regarding progress with implementation of the Code of Conduct and removal of Giovannini barriers. In particular, the meeting considered that further work was needed on unbundling services, and encouraged ESCB-CESR to finalise draft Standards as 'non-binding Recommendations solely addressed to public authorities' the scope of which 'should include ICSDs, and exclude custodians – whilst CEBS [Committee of European Banking Supervisors] is invited to further review, in cooperation with CESR, the coverage of risks borne by custodians … so as to ensure a level playing field while avoiding inconsistencies in the treatment of custodians and double regulation by end 2008'. Similarly, in the June 2008 *EBF Newsletter*[4], there was reference to the CESR-ECB Standards, noting that pricing transparency had improved, but that access and interoperability between different systems was still encountering difficulties. (It was also stated that: 'There is a strong case for custodian banks active in this market not to be effectively double regulated by having to comply with existing prudential regulations as well as additional CESR-ESCB requirements.') Moreover, there was a meeting of the European Economic and Financial Affairs Council on 3 June 2008, following which the EU Council published the 'Council Conclusions of clearing and settlement'. The recommendations to ESCB/CESR in such Conclusions included finalising the CESR-ECB Standards as 'non-binding Recommendations solely addressed to public authorities', and proposed that the scope 'should include ICSDs, and exclude custodians'. It should however be noted that CEBS was 'invited to further review, in cooperation with CESR, the coverage of risks borne by custodians, taking into account that some CSDs/ICSDs/CCPs are also subject to the CRD, so as to ensure a level playing field while avoiding inconsistencies in the treatment of custodians and double regulation by end 2008'. Nevertheless, on 17 April 2009 CEBS published a report on the 'materiality of custodian banks 'internalising settlement activities or carrying out of Central Counterparty (CCP)-like activities'.[5] The report concluded that 'it does not appear that the level of internalisation amongst the custodian bank community would justify any intervention at European level' and it would be 'overly burdensome to impose or issue guidance applicable to the industry as a whole regarding this activity'.[6] Arguably this is the correct conclusion, given the extensive regulatory requirements which already apply to custodians. CEBS also concluded that there was no evidence 'that custodian banks commonly engage in CCP-like activity other than in their role as GCMs'[7].

1   The European Banking Federation ('EBF'), the European Savings Banks Group ('ESBG') and the European Association of Co-operative Banks ('EACB').

2   'ECSA Feedback in Response to the Implementation of the Pan-European Code of Conduct for Clearing and Settlement by Market Infrastructures', 7 March 2008.

3   European Commission: 'Code of Conduct on Clearing and Settlement – Sixth meeting of the Monitoring Group', 9 April 2008.

4   Issue 17.

5   CEBS Report, 17 April 2009, p 1.

6   CEBS Report, 17 April 2009, p 6.

7   CEBS Report, 17 April 2009, p 6.

8.78 In the EU Commission Legal Certainty Group's *Second Advice of the Legal Certainty Group – Solutions to Legal Barriers related to post-trading within the EU*, published in August 2008, there were various recommendations for dealing with Barrier 13, Barrier 3 and Barrier 9 which are to be considered by the EU Commission. The recommendations cover three main areas, first, concerning the legal effect of book entry records of securities held through intermediaries; second, how the processing of corporate actions may be made more efficient; and, third, the removal of any requirements that particular securities should be issued or held subject to a particular law. The implications of this final point could be quite significant, in particular for shares and the effect on wider company law issues, if the way forward is not simply to facilitate and clarify holding of shares through intermediaries but to allow shares to be issued under the laws of a jurisdiction other than the jurisdiction in which a company is incorporated.

8.79 In May 2009, CESR–ECB published its Recommendations for Securities Settlement Systems and Recommendations for Central Counterparties in the European Union in final form. These Recommendations were not binding[1] and were not intended to overlap with the European Code of Conduct for Clearing and Settlement, which would apply to account providers, although were intended to cover all aspects of clearing and settlement. These Recommendations were in the form of broad directions, rather than detailed requirements, for example, stating that settlement systems and central counterparties should have 'links between them or interoperable systems', that securities 'should be immobilised or dematerialised and transferred by book entry in CSDs to the greatest possible extent', and that systems should have 'objective and publicly disclosed criteria for participation that permit fair and open access'.

1   Public authorities in the EU were expected to 'promote and monitor the application of the Recommendations within their jurisdictions' and to 'integrate the Recommendations into their respective assessment frameworks and/or practices with which they assess the safety, soundness and efficiency of their respective CSDs and CCPs'.

8.80 The majority of the CPSS/IOSCO Recommendations were replaced in April 2012 by the CPSS/IOSCO Principles for financial market infrastructures ('CPSS/IOSCO Principles') which are intended to 'harmonise and, where appropriate, strengthen the existing international standards for' and apply to all systemically important payment systems, central securities depositories, securities settlement systems, central counterparties, as well as to provide 'additional guidance for over-the-counter (OTC) derivatives CCPs and trade repositories'. These Principles are apparently based on 'a comprehensive review' by the CPSS and the Technical Committee of IOSCO of: the Core Principles for Systemically Important Payment Systems ('CPSIPS') published in January 2001 'which provided 10 principles for the safe and efficient design and operation of systemically important payment systems'; the Recommendations for Securities Settlement Systems ('RSSS'), published in November 2001, which 'identified 19 recommendations for promoting the safety and efficiency of' securities settlement systems; and the Recommendations for Central Counterparties ('RCCP') published in November 2004, which 'provided 15 recommendations that addressed the major types of risks faced by CCPs'. This review began in February 2010 and was carried out 'in support of the FSB's broader efforts to strengthen core financial infrastructures and markets by ensuring that gaps in international standards are identified and addressed', and intended to 'harmonise and, where appropriate, strengthen the three sets of standards' as well as reflecting 'The lessons from the recent financial crisis, the experience of using the existing international standards, and recent policy and analytical work by the CPSS, the Technical Committee of IOSCO, the Basel Committee on Banking Supervision ('BCBS'), and others'. However, 'A full reconsideration of the marketwide recommendations from the RSSS was not undertaken as part of this review. Those recommendations remain in effect. Specifically, RSSS Recommendation 2 on trade confirmation, RSSS Recommendation 3 on settlement cycles, RSSS Recommendation 4 on central counterparties, RSSS Recommendation 5 on securities lending, RSSS Recommendation 6 on central securities depositories, and RSSS Recommendation 12 on protection of customers' securities remain in effect. These recommendations are provided in Annex C for reference. In addition to keeping RSSS Recommendations 6 and 12, this report contains focused principles on the risk management of CSDs (see Principle 11) and on the segregation and portability of assets and positions held by a CCP (see Principle 14). The CPSS and Technical Committee of IOSCO may conduct a full review of the marketwide standards in the future.'[1]

1   CPSS-IOSCO Principles, p 6.

8.81   The CPSS-IOSCO Principles are not legally binding but are intended to 'provide guidance for addressing risks and efficiency in FMIs' although in general 'do not prescribe a specific tool or arrangement to achieve their requirements and allow for different means to satisfy a particular principle'. The main point is that where systems are 'determined by national authorities to be systemically important', they are 'expected to observe these principles.'[1] National regulators are therefore expected to look to the Principles to decide what is best practice, and the Principles will therefore influence national regulatory requirements for relevant market infrastructures.

1   CPSS-IOSCO Principles, p 6.

8.82   Of some interest in this context is the publication in March 2011 by OICU-IOSCO of its 'Survey of Regimes for the Protection, Distribution and/or Transfer of Client Assets: Final Report'[1]. The survey responses on client assets protection are set out in Appendix B to the report and provide a fascinating view of the situation in the different jurisdictions covered (Australia, Brazil, Canada, China, France, Germany, Hong Kong, India, Italy, Japan, Mexico, Singapore, Spain, Switzerland, the United Kingdom, as well as specific responses from the CFTC[2] and the SEC[3] in the United States). The main purpose of the report is to provide information to regulators so that they are 'adequately informed' about the ways in which client assets are protected in different jurisdictions, and to 'enhance transparency and the ability of regulators and market participants to understand the methods (and positive and negative aspects of such methods) by which the responding Regimes protect Clients, both before and after the insolvency of an Investment Firm.'[4] An in depth review of this report is beyond the scope of this book, but a comparative analysis would provide an indication of the challenges presented by the different approaches in different jurisdictions.

1   The report can be accessed at www.iosco.org.
2   The Commodity Futures Trading Commission ('CFTC') is an independent agency of the United States government which is responsible for regulation of the futures and option markets in the United States.
3   The United States Securities and Exchange Commission is the federal agency which is responsible for enforcement of the federal securities laws and regulation of the United States securities industry.
4   OICU-IOSCO of its 'Survey of Regimes for the Protection, Distribution and/or Transfer of Client Assets: Final Report', pp 3 and 21.

8.83   On 13 July 2012, the EU Parliament's Committee on Economic and Monetary Affairs ('ECON') published a draft report on the EU Commission's proposal, published on 7 March 2012, for a regulation on improving securities settlement in the EU and on central securities depositories. In broad terms, the Regulation is intended to require increased dematerialisation of securities, to harmonise settlement processes, settlement discipline, conduct of business rules and prudential requirements, and to increase the choice and flexibility in settlement by requiring cross-participation by central securities depositories in each other. Arguably such aims were the reasons for the various Codes and Principles relating to settlement systems and financial market infrastructures, but apparently it has been concluded that a Regulation is now required to enforce such issues (although the draft Regulation itself acknowledges that it should follow the relevant Recommendations and Principles of CPSS-IOSCO). A significant point is the fact that, the CPSS-IOSCO Principles notwithstanding, the settlement period for all securities traded on regulated markets, MTFs and OTFs[1] must be T+2. Given that many markets operate on the basis of T+3, this is likely to provide a major operational challenge.

1   Multilateral Trading Facilities and Organised Trading Facilities, respectively.

8.84 In the general context of the many responses to the financial crisis, much recent focus[1] has been on the way in which banks and other entities of importance to the markets can be wound up without major disruption to the markets, requiring the creation of the so-called 'living wills' or 'resolution and recovery plans'.[2] In relation to financial market infrastructures, this is also a concern[3], therefore on 31 July 2012 IOSCO (the International Organisation of Securities Commissions) and CPSS (the Committee on Payment and Settlement Systems) published a consultative report on the recovery and resolution of financial market infrastructures. This builds on the CPSS-IOSCO Principles, indicating how the different types of financial market infrastructures should create recovery plans and resolution regimes in accordance with the CPSS-IOSCO Principles, as well as the Financial Stability Board's 'Key Attributes of Effective Resolution Regimes for Financial Institutions' which were published in 2011.

1   For further reading on some earlier background discussions, see also the 1989 report of the Fédération Internationale Des Bourses de Valeurs ('FIBV') on *Improving International Settlement*; IOSCO's 1990 *Report of the Technical Committee on Clearing and Settlement*; ISSA's 1992 *Report on Cross-Border Settlement and Custody*; Morgan Guaranty Trust Company of New York, Brussels Office's 1993 report *Cross-border Clearance, Settlement and Custody: Beyond the G30 Recommendations*; the BIS 1993 *Report on Central Bank Payment and Settlement Services with respect to Cross-Border and Multi-Currency Transactions*; the 1996 FIBV Clearing and Settlement Best Practices; the 1996 IOSCO *Report on Client Asset Protection*; the G30/ISSA Status Reviews of 1997, 1998 and 1999; the 2001 CPSS/BIS Core Principles for Systemically Important Payment Systems; and the 2001 Standards prepared by the European Association of Central Counterparty Clearinghouses ('EACH').

2   For example, in the UK the Financial Services Act 2010 gave the FSA powers to require UK banks to have living wills, and similar initiatives are in progress in many other jurisdictions.

3   'Financial market infrastructures (FMIs) play an essential role in the global financial system. The disorderly failure of an FMI can lead to severe systemic disruption if it causes markets to cease to operate effectively. Accordingly, all types of FMIs should generally be subject to regimes and strategies for recovery and resolution.' CPSS-IOSCO Press Release, 31 July 2012.

CONSOLIDATION

8.85 'The recent creation of the euro and longer-standing demographic and technological trends have stimulated demand from issuers and investors alike for integration of European capital markets.'[1] The major challenge which has been identified for the years ahead is the consolidation of the post-trade infrastructure[2].

1   DTCC CPP White Paper, p 7.
2   See the 1995 G30/ISSA Recommendations, pp 25, 26.

Current fragmentation of post-trade infrastructure

8.86 The European Commission's 1999 Financial Services Action Plan set the objective of an integrated European capital market by 2005[1]. However, the process of market integration, particularly in the securities markets, is hindered by a fragmented post-trading infrastructure[2]. 'It is perhaps no exaggeration to conclude ... that inefficiencies in clearing and settlement represent the most primitive and thus the most important barrier to integrated financial markets in Europe.'[3] The Lamfalussy Securities Market Report[4] discusses 'the excessive costs of cross-border clearing and settlement in the EU compared to the US, due to fragmentation'[5], and identifies potential annual savings of up to a billion Euros[6]. The DTCC has added its voice to this debate, emphasising the need for an integrated post-trading infrastructure, and (like the ESF) highlighting clearing in particular[7]. The ESF emphasises the cost of numerous different European settlement systems[8], requiring separate IT links and resulting in high transaction costs[9]. The Giovannini 2001 Report identifies three types of cost associated with fragmentation[10], namely direct costs in the form of higher fees; indirect costs in the form of additional back office expenses; and opportunity costs associated with inefficient use of collateral, failed trades and trades foregone. It also identified three types of barrier to efficient cross-border clearing and settlement[11]. These are: barriers relating to national differences in technical requirements/market practice[12]; barriers relating to national differences in tax procedures; and barriers relating to issues of legal certainty[13]. The European Commission suggests that perverse incentives may also bear some of the blame[14]. It is widely argued that the consolidation of clearing is the most urgent priority. 'A large part of the benefits to market participants that might accrue from fully integrating clearing and settlement across markets is realised by integrating CCPs alone.'[15]

1 The FSAP discusses current market fragmentation: 'Yet, the Union's financial markets remain segmented and business and consumers continue to be deprived of direct access to cross-border financial institutions' (p 3).

2 Giovannini 2001 Report, p 20:

'The existing infrastructure for the provision of clearing and settlement services in the European Union is the product of a fragmented securities market. Historically, the pattern of European securities trading has followed national lines, a pattern that was reinforced by the existence of different currencies (for a long time accompanied by exchange controls) and relatively basic technology.'

3 Giovannini 2001 Report, Foreword. See also p 20:

'The extent of fragmentation in the EU clearing and settlement infrastructure has been exposed by the increased demand for cross-border trading that is an inevitable consequence of financial integration ... the additional cost and risk associated with this fragmentation represents a significant limitation on the scope for cross-border securities trading in the European Union. By extension, it also represents an important limitation on exploiting the economic benefits of the Internal market and the euro.'

4 The report comments dryly that 'Market infrastructure (exchanges and clearing and settlement systems) is not as efficient as it might be and the chances of delivering the FSAP on time are close to zero' (p 12) and 'The Committee is convinced that further restructuring of clearing and settlement is necessary in the European Union' (p 16).

5 Lamfalussy Securities Markets Report, p 16. See also p 82:

'Managing the full web of bilateral linkages (which could amount to up to 650 bilateral links between the 26 existing settlement systems in the EU) is generally regarded as extremely cumbersome and a source of operational, some have said even systemic risk in itself.'

6 Lamfalussy Securities Markets Report, p 82.

7 See DTCC CPP White Paper, p 4.

8 The Giovannini 2001 Report laments, notwithstanding existing consolidation, 19 CSDs and two ICSDs remain.

9 ESF Submission on ISD, p 10.

10 See section 4.

11 See section 5.

12   These comprise: national differences in information technology and interfaces; national clearing and settlement restrictions that require the use of multiple systems; differences in national rules relating to corporate actions, beneficial ownership and custody; absence of intra-day settlement finality; practical impediments to remote access to national clearing and settlement systems; national differences in settlement periods; national differences in operating hours/settlement deadlines; national differences in securities issuance practice; national restrictions on the location of (underlying) securities; and national restrictions on the activity of primary dealers and market makers.

13   Three in particular are identified as follows: the absence of an EU-wide framework for the treatment of interests in securities; national differences in the legal treatment of bilateral netting for financial transactions; and uneven application of national conflict of laws rules.

14   Commission Communication *Clearing and settlement in the European Union, main policy issues and future challenges*, COM(2002) 257:

'However, the lack of progress may also be put down to perverse incentives among infrastructure owners, management and users. These arise either because the parties involved derive profit in some way from the current fragmented environment, or because those who would bear the costs of technical developments are not the ones who stand to gain the most from them.'

15   DTCC CPP White Paper, p 2.

8.87 The final shape that an integrated infrastructure will assume remains unclear[1], in particular in view of the somewhat perplexing comment in the Giovannini 2003 Report that 'a consolidation of clearing and settlement infrastructure does not necessarily imply a reduction in competition' contrasted with the BIS/CPSS concern regarding the risks of system interdependencies[2].

1   The Lamfalussy Securities Markets Report, p 82:

'Submissions to the Committee have highlighted the widespread differences as regards the optimal configuration of European clearing and settlement facilities.'

See also Joint work of the European System of Central Banks and the Committee of European Securities Regulators in the field of clearing and settlement, a call for contributions from interested parties, March 2002, p 4:

'The structure of the securities clearing and settlement industry in Europe has been hotly debated recently. An integrated market can be achieved via a number of routes, with concentration, interoperability and open access being the most obvious alternatives.'

2   Bank for International Settlements ('BIS') Committee on Payments and Settlement Systems ('CPSS') report The interdependencies of payment and settlement systems (June 2008). This report concluded that increased system links improve efficiency but increase risk of problems affecting others, therefore recommended further development of risk management strategies.

Consolidation of settlement[1]

8.88 The cross-border settlement of fixed income securities was consolidated by the early establishment of the international settlement systems (known as international central securities depositories or 'ICSDs'), Euroclear and Clearstream (formerly Cedel). Equity settlement remains fragmented[2]. Cross-border settlements in Europe are increasing not only because of the growth of cross-border trades, but also because of rights issues and other corporate actions in the context of cross-border takeovers. The CPSS/IOSCO Recommendations discuss channels of settlement for cross-border trades, and identify five:

- direct membership of the local CSD;
- use of local agent;
- use of global custodian;
- ICSDs; and
- links between CSDs[3].

1   In September 2002 CREST became part of the Euroclear group. See further Chapter 9.
2   Giovannini 2001 Report, pp 20, 21:

> 'The capacity of the ICSDs to provide international clearance and settlement services for the bond markets has been helped by the comparative homogeneity in fixed-income securities and the extent to which they have been commoditised. Equities are more heterogeneous instruments and more complex to manage particularly with respect to corporate actions and insofar as they require continuous communication between the company that has issued the equity and its holder. In consequence, cross-border ... settlement of equities ... is particularly challenging.'

3   CPSS/IOSCO Recommendations, pp 44, 45.

8.89 The last option has been the focus of considerable industry activity in recent years. Important strategic alliances have been formed between existing systems[1]. The final goal is 'one-stop shopping', whereby membership of one settlement system permits the settlement of securities transactions in any European jurisdictions. However: 'The jury is still out as to whether full integration of Central Securities Depositories (CSDs) is required or whether technical linkages between existing entities will be sufficient.'[2] As for links between existing systems, two competing models for this are offered. By developing links to the national systems, the ICSDs (notably Euroclear) promote the 'hub and spoke' model. In the model, the ICSD serves as the hub of a notional wheel, of which the spokes are the national settlement systems. ECSDA has advocated an alternative model, known colloquially as the 'spider's web'. Instead of a central hub, this involves a series of bilateral links between national systems, together with a series of linked local hubs (also known as 'relayed links'). Whichever model emerges, it seems clear that the development of one-stop shopping remains a medium to long term project[3].

1   Examples include the merger of Cedel and Deutsche Börse Clearing to form Clearstream, and the alliance between Euroclear and Sicovam to form Euroclear France. See further the discussion of the Euroclear group structure and proposals for a single platform structure in Chapter 9, paras **9.125–9.134**.
2   Lamfalussy Securities Markets Report, p 82.
3   In the US, 'DTCC will develop plans for a combined, single settlement system to replace the two separate systems now in place at DTC and NSCC' (DTCC *T+1 White Paper*, p 4).

Consolidation of clearing and/or CCP services[1]

8.90 As indicated earlier, greater industry attention has recently focused on the integration of clearing than on that of settlement, because of the clear benefits offered by the consolidation of CCP services. To a greater extent than fragmented settlement, fragmented CCP services increase credit exposures and therefore tie up market participants' capital[2]. Beyond this, consolidation among CCPs offers commercial risk management and operational efficiencies[3]. Also, such consolidation makes 'the functioning of the market more resilient during a crisis, when replacement cost risk may increase sharply'[4]. The DTC has described the consolidation of CCP services as 'one of the most important developments shaping the global investment servicing industry over the next five to ten years'[5]. Notwithstanding the conflicting concerns regarding encouragement of competition in the market and choice for participants, it appears that it is now generally accepted that the case for consolidation in Europe has been made. However, the commercial, operational and legal challenges cannot be underestimated, and the progress of consolidation has been disappointingly slow.

1   In July 2002 the entities then known as virt-x (now SWX Europe Limited), LCH (LCH.Clearnet Limited) and x-clear (SIS x-clear AG) announced a pan-European central counterparty.
2   See Lamfalussy Securities Markets Report, p 82.
3   DTCC CCP White Paper, p 2.

4   DTCC CCP White Paper, p 9.
5   DTCC CCP White Paper, p 3.

8.91 As with the consolidation of settlement, a number of alternative models for European consolidation are under discussion. The ESF was clear in its advocacy of a single EuroCCP[1], initially for equities and later for fixed income securities and derivatives. DTCC discussed the alternatives of the integrated clearer model (ie a CCP among CCPs); a joint venture model; and the use of common technology[2]. It comments that 'If the forces against consolidation are stronger than the forces for, many of the benefits may still be realised through cooperation'[3]. As an interim step, cross-margining agreements between CCPs may offer collateral netting efficiencies[4]. Moreover, from the proposed new EU legislation relating to settlement systems, the preference seems to be to require cross-participation by different systems (see para **8.83**).

1   See ESF Blueprint, pp 23, 24.
2   DTCC CCP White Paper.
3   DTCC CCP White Paper, p 11.
4   See CPSS/IOSCO Principles, pp 54, 55.

8.92 Regulation (EU) No 648/2012 on OTC derivative transactions, central counterparties and trade repositories (known as 'EMIR') was published in the Official Journal on 27 July 2012. This is an example of specific legislation driven by concerns about market risk and the cumulative effect on the markets of the exposure of counterparties to derivative transactions. Chapter 7 considers the impact of EMIR on client money requirements, but the main purpose of EMIR is to impose mandatory clearing through central counterparties for certain types of OTC derivative contract, as well as to require certain risk mitigation techniques for all uncleared OTC derivatives, increase reporting obligations in relation to all derivatives, and specify further regulation of central counterparties and trade repositories. As with much of the new regulatory controls and procedures intended to improve security and safety of the markets, these new requirements will not apply without a considerable cost in terms of development of operational systems and the increased need for collateral. It might therefore be argued that the new requirements are in effect a sophisticated way of mutualising exposures which would otherwise arise and impact market participants in a different way. There is also the question of how the increased level of legislation in Europe affects trade with entities outside Europe. In some respects, the main to increase protections for trades within Europe comes at the price of considerably increasing the complexity of trading which involves parties outside Europe.

8.93 At least one obvious effect of EMIR is to give rise to a large amount of related analysis and legislation. The following are some examples.

8.94 On 18 November 2011, the European Central Bank issued 'Standards for the Use of Central Counterparties in Eurosystem Foreign Reserve Management Operations'. These standards are intended to 'ensure that the selection of providers of clearing services meet three objectives: (i) ensuring safe and efficient use of infrastructure by the Eurosystem; (ii) ensuring consistency with the Eurosystem's broader objectives and statutory tasks in the field of clearing and settlement; and (iii) ensuring neutrality vis-a-vis the clearing industry'. It should be noted that these standards are not intended to duplicate existing standards for 'the oversight or supervision of CCPs'[1].

1   'Standards for the Use of Central Counterparties in Eurosystem Foreign Reserve Management Operations', European Central Bank, 18 November 2011, p 5.

8.95 In March 2012, the Bank for International Settlements ('BIS') published BIS Working Paper No 373 'Collateral Requirements for mandatory central clearing of over-the-counter derivatives', examining the amount of collateral that central counterparties should require from clearing members. Interestingly, notwithstanding the widespread concerns regarding the risks of concentrating counterparty exposure in one entity (ie a central counterparty) by requiring central clearing in most cases, and the increase in collateral requirements as a result of mandatory clearing, the Working Paper concludes that although clearing OTC derivatives through a central counterparty concentrates the position for derivative counterparties, this does not undermine the robustness of central clearing, is beneficial because it reduces collateral requirements through netting, and the greater use of central counterparties will not lead to a significant increase in collateral requirements of market participants.

8.96 On 25 June 2012, the European Securities and Markets Authority launched a consultation on its technical standards under EMIR. The consultation paper contains draft Regulatory Technical Standards and Implementing Technical Standards which are intended to reduce counterparty risks, make central counterparties safer and more resilient, and increase transparency[1].

1   ESMA Press Release, 25 June 2012.

8.97 In July 2012, BCBS (the Basel Committee on Banking Supervision) and IOSCO (the International Organization of Securities Commissions) published a Consultative Document: 'Margin Requirements For Non-Centrally-Cleared Derivatives'. The proposals in such document are apparently intended to reduce the counterparty risk exposure of the parties to derivatives which are not subject to clearing through a central counterparty. The intention is that all parties to this type of derivative transaction (other than non-systemically important corporates (ie not financial firms), sovereigns and central banks) should be required to provide initial margin on a two-way basis, as well as variation margin, and that the margin collateral by each party must remain segregated and that re-hypothecation of collateral should not be permitted. Such requirements would obviously significantly affect the way in which derivatives not subject to central clearing would operate, and greatly increase the amount of collateral required by the parties to such transactions. ISDA (International Swaps and Derivatives Association, Inc) has expressed its concerns about this, stating that these proposals if implemented would 'decrease systemic resiliency by introducing healthy amounts of liquidity risk (caused by the shortage of collateral) and economic risk (caused either by the shortage of liquidity and/or by all the economic risks that are likely to remain unhedged).'[1]

1   'No margin for error', 2 October 2012, see www.isda.org.

8.98 On 26 September 2012, the European Banking Authority adopted the draft technical standards on capital requirements for central counterparties under EMIR. As the title suggests, these standards specify the minimum capital to be held by central counterparties at all times. The draft standards have been sent to the European Commission for adoption, and once endorsed by the European Commission, the standards will have the legal form of a regulation and will be directly applicable across the EU.

UNDERLYING LEGAL PRINCIPLES

8.99 The need for a legally robust basis for the post-trade infrastructure is beyond doubt. Challenges in achieving this include: the legal nature of property rights; the impact of insolvency; and the conflict of laws. The chief legal instrument of private sector arrangements (including clearing and settlement systems) is contract.

However, a common feature of property rights, insolvency and the conflict of laws is that contractual provision is often ineffective to modify them. Therefore creating a legally robust post-trade infrastructure is largely dependent on national and international legislation. Very significant progress is being made by a number of law reform initiatives, discussed briefly below. Both the challenges and the initiatives that are designed to address them are discussed in turn below.

Property rights

8.100 It was indicated above that settlement involves the delivery of securities. To be more accurate, settlement involves the delivery of property rights in relation to securities. Property rights were very briefly considered in Chapter 1. While the legal nature of property rights is a matter of extensive academic debate, one essential feature of them is that they are enforceable against third parties[1]. There is a general principle that property rights should be public, as it would be unfair for third parties to be bound by rights, the existence of which they had no way of knowing. This general principle arguably explains a number of special rules which apply to property rights, including the requirement to register certain charges; certain formalities of transfer[2]; and the lex situs rule[3]. These special rules cannot in general be disapplied or modified by contract[4]. Because the application of these rules to electronic settlement may be inconvenient or uncertain, legislative support is generally required to create legally robust settlement systems. This slows down the reform of the post-trade infrastructure to the pace of the public sector. Moreover, these rules may differ from country to country, and therefore harmonised legislation may be needed[5]. This was one of the main areas considered by the Legal Certainty Group in its August 2008 report to the EU Commission[6], and is also considered in the ECON Report in 2011 (see Chapter 7, para **7.187** n 1).

1   Personal rights (eg such as those arising under a contract of sale) are enforceable only against the person who owes them (eg the seller). In contrast, property rights are generally enforceable against the world at large (with the possible exception of the good faith buyer of the assets subject to those rights without notice of them). This is why, after settlement, the buyer is generally able to assert its rights in purchased securities against the liquidator and creditors of the insolvent seller.

2   These also serve as anti-fraud measures. In the UK, see ss 53(1)(c) and 136 of the Law of Property Act 1925, discussed in Chapter 2.

3   This rule also serves the interest of commercial convenience, as discussed in Chapter 5.

4   This is because of course it would be unfair by a private contract to prejudice the rights of third parties.

5   As discussed in Chapter 5, the application of the lex situs rule to intermediated securities has presented a particular challenge, which a number of legislative initiatives seek to address.

6   Legal Certainty Group *Second Advice of the Legal Certainty Group – Solutions to Legal Barriers related to Post trading within the EU*, August 2008.

Insolvency

8.101 Participant insolvency may have systemic implications for the post-trade infrastructure. In simple terms, it is important to ensure that the insolvency of one participant does not cause liquidity and/or credit problems for other participants, causing them to default in turn. Such consequential problems might arise for a range of reasons under the insolvency law of the defaulting participant. For example, payments and deliveries (in settlement of transactions or under collateralised lending arrangements) which the defaulting participant has made prior to the date of insolvency might be reversed under preference and other displacement rules. Also, payments and deliveries made by the defaulting participant after the moment of insolvency may be avoided as post-insolvency dispositions. As clearing and settlement systems may admit participants from many different countries, a particular concern is the widely varying provisions of the different national insolvency laws[1]. This lack of harmonisation has long been a major source of legal risk.

1   Regulation 1346/2000/EC of 29 May 2000 on insolvency proceedings (the 'Insolvency Regulation') refers, in Recital 11, to the 'widely differing substantive laws' of insolvency within the EU.

8.102   The treatment of the assets of an insolvent person is governed by the mandatory provisions of insolvency law. Any contractual provision which purports to modify such mandatory provisions is generally ineffective[1]. It is therefore necessary to ensure that the laws that would govern the insolvency of market participants do not conflict with the rules of the relevant clearing and settlement systems. Provisions contained in a number of EU measures, discussed in Chapter 5 and very briefly below, seek to address this risk. Two particular sensitivities are collateral and netting.

1   *British Eagle International Airlines Ltd v Compagnie Nationale Air France* [1975] 1 WLR 758, [1975] 2 All ER 390.

Collateral

8.103   The central premise of clearing is that the CCP is able to absorb credit risk without compromising its own financial stability. In order to achieve this, the CCP relies on a number of measures including, importantly, taking collateral from its members. Equally, settlement systems which assume credit exposures to their members seek to collateralise these exposures using the assets credited to members' accounts. The effect of successful collateral arrangements is to enable the CCP or settlement system to recover sums owed to it by disposing of the collateral assets, thus avoiding the need to prove as unsecured creditor in the member's insolvency. While helpful for the collateral taker, this of course involves a cost for the general creditors of the insolvent as it depletes the assets available to them. For this reason, insolvency law in each jurisdiction has wide powers to cut across collateral arrangements which are considered to be unfair to general creditors, as discussed in more detail in Chapter 4. The law reform initiatives very briefly discussed below seek to address this risk.

Netting

8.104   The netting of obligations is essential to clearing, both in day-to-day operations[1] and under default rules. In effect, the netting of obligations owed to and from a member involves the use of the member's rights against the CCP to meet its liability to the CCP. Like collateral, netting protects the CCP but involves a cost for the general creditors of an insolvent member, by depriving them of the benefit of the insolvent's netted rights. In order to avoid unfairness to general creditors, each system of insolvency law carefully defines the circumstances in which insolvency netting is permitted.

1   In trade netting discussed above.

8.105   Interbank netting schemes were considered in detail in the 1990 Lamfalussy Netting Report[1]. Although this report focused on private interbank netting schemes, it has served as a benchmark for the risk analysis of netting in the wider financial markets[2]. It recommends a number of minimum standards, the first of which is that 'Netting schemes should have a well-founded legal basis under all relevant jurisdictions'[3]. The call for legal certainty in netting has been stressed elsewhere[4]. Legally unreliable netting is worse than no netting, as it obscures the true measure of credit exposure[5]. Potential insolvency-related challenges to netting include the unavailability of insolvency set off[6]; insolvency displacement under preference or similar rules[7]; and zero hour rules[8]. (See Chapter 4 for a discussion of these terms, and Chapter 5 for a discussion of law reform initiatives which address these risks.) The increased focus on netting as an important tool for counterparty protection can be seen in the approach by EMIR which requires central counterparty clearing for certain OTC derivative transactions (see para **8.92** above).

1   *Report of the Committee on Interbank Netting Schemes of the Central Banks of the Group of Ten Countries* (the 'Lamfalussy Netting Report'). This followed and in part responded to Group of Experts on Payment Systems of the central banks of the Group of Ten countries, BIS *The Report on Netting Schemes* (the 'Angell Report') of 1989.

2   Lamfalussy Netting Report, p 4. See also Hills et al, para **8.27** n 4 above, at 125.

3   Lamfalussy Netting Report, p 17. See also p 11.

4   See 1995 G30/ISSA Recommendations, p 23; and Giovannini Reports in 2001 and 2003 regarding Barrier 14.

5   See Lamfalussy Netting Report, pp 2, 11.

6   Many sets of default rules rely on multilateral netting, which is not generally permitted under the normal principles of insolvency law, and requires special legislative support.

7   Which might displace previously netting positions.

8   See Lamfalussy Netting Report, p 11.

The conflict of laws

8.106   These challenges are increased in the case of remote clearing and international settlement by the conflict of laws. The rules of domestic law on which CCPs and settlement systems rely differ from jurisdiction to jurisdiction. In a cross-border situation, therefore, the outcome of a dispute may depend on the rules for determining which of the potentially relevant systems of domestic law applies. These rules are called conflict of laws rules. The application of traditional conflict of laws rules to the post-trade infrastructure may be unclear[1]. This has hindered the achievement of legal certainty[2], particularly in relation to collateral[3] and netting[4]. However, the need to address this challenge in clearing[5] and settlement[6] has been stressed, and has generated a number of relevant law reform initiatives.

1   Unfortunately, the conflict of laws rules have traditionally also differed from jurisdiction to jurisdiction, so that the outcome of certain cross-border disputes has been highly dependent upon where they are heard; this has rendered them inherently unpredictable.

2   See Bank for International Settlements *Cross-Border Securities Settlement*, May 1994, Basle, and the ESF Submission on the ISD, p 2.

3   See the Lamfalussy Securities Markets Report, p 85.

4   See the Lamfalussy Netting Report, p 11. In the absence of harmonisation, the Lamfalussy Netting Report recommends that the legal basis of cross-border netting arrangements should be considered under '(a) the law of the country in which the counterparty is chartered and, if the counterparty is a branch of a foreign bank, then also under the law of the jurisdiction in which the branch is located; (b) the law that governs the individual transactions subject to the netting scheme; and (c) the law that governs any contract or agreement necessary to effect the netting' (p 18).

5   See the EU Commission's ISD Consultation Document, p 35.

6   See CPSS/IOSCO Principles, p 25.

Law reform initiatives

8.107   Many of the law reform initiatives discussed below relate directly or indirectly to insolvency. Historically, efforts to harmonise substantive insolvency law internationally have met with incomplete success. This is not surprising, because national insolvency laws reflect the policy priorities of each jurisdiction. Moreover, the insolvency sensitivities mentioned above are generally designed to protect general creditors of the insolvent, and reflect important policy concerns. However, securities settlement systems are often linked to wholesale payment systems, and the systemic propagation of liquidity and credit problems through settlement systems might pose a threat to the financial system[1]. For this reason, the policy case has been made to disapply some of the normal provisions of insolvency law in favour of major clearing and settlement systems, in order to address systemic risk.

1   See Recital 2 of the Settlement Finality Directive (discussed below).

The Settlement Finality Directive[1]

8.108   The Settlement Finality Directive was designed to reduce systemic risk in EU payment and securities settlement systems[2]. It displaces a number of the provisions of insolvency law that might otherwise disturb the smooth operation of such systems following the insolvency of a participant[3]. In order to benefit from the Settlement Finality Directive, a system must be designated by a member state and notified to the Commission[4]. (Lawyers in London had speculated that some major custodians might apply to the FSA for recognition as a designated system for the purposes of the Settlement Finality Directive, but at the date of writing none have done so.) The Settlement Finality Directive's provisions include the following. Transfer orders[5] and netting[6] will be binding and enforceable despite the insolvency of a participant[7], providing they occur before the moment of insolvency[8]. This is notwithstanding insolvency displacement rules[9]. Member states may provide for the defaulting participant's assets to be used to meet its settlement obligations on the day of insolvency[10]. Collateral giver insolvency shall not affect a collateral taker (being a central bank[11] or a participant taking collateral in connection with the system[12]).

1   Directive 98/26/EC of the European Parliament and of the Council of 19 May 1998 on settlement finality in payment and securities settlement systems. See also Chapter 5, para **5.57**.

2   Recital 1 indicates that the original inspiration of the Settlement Finality Directive was the discussion of systemic risk in wholesale payment systems in the Lamfalussy Netting Report.

3   See Recital 4. In the UK, it builds on the pre-existing provisions of Pt VII of the Companies Act 1989.

4   Articles 1(a), 2(a) and 10. For the UK designation procedure, see Pt II of The Financial Markets and Insolvency (Settlement Finality) Regulations 1999 (SI 1999/2979). The CREST system is a designated system for the purposes of the Directive, see further Chapter 9, para **9.53–9.56**.

5   'Transfer order' is defined to include instructions for the transfer of cash and securities: art 2(i).

6   Whether on default or otherwise: see art 2(k).

7   Article 3(1).

8   Or after but on the same day as the opening of insolvency proceedings, provided the settlement system can prove it was unaware of the opening of proceedings: art 3(1).

9   Article 3(2).

10 Article 4.

11 Whether the central bank of a member state or the ECB.

12 Article 9(1).

8.109   While CCPs could benefit from the existing provisions of the Settlement Finality Directive, the Directive was not designed with CCPs in mind, and the ESF called for revised provisions to cover, in particular, wider aspects of CCP default rules, and non-insolvency displacement[1]. Following a proposal to amend the Settlement Finality Directive (published by the European Commission in April 2008[2]) which was intended to clarify various aspects of this Directive, including application to clearing systems, the Directive was amended in 2009 by Directive

2009/44/EC of the European Parliament and of the Council of 6 May 2009 amending Directive 98/26/EC on settlement finality in payment and securities settlement systems and Directive 2002/47/EC on financial collateral arrangements as regards linked systems and credit claims[3]. This was implemented in the UK by the Financial Markets and Insolvency (Settlement Finality and Financial Collateral Arrangements) (Amendment) Regulations 2010 (SI 2010/2993).

1   Submission on ISD, p 7.
2   European Commission *Proposal for a Directive of the European Parliament and of the Council amending Directive 98/26/EC on settlement finality in payment and securities settlement systems and Directive 2002/47/EC on financial collateral arrangements as regards linked systems and credit claims*, COM(2008) 213 final.
3   The main purpose of the amendments was clarificatory, including in relation to requirements regarding interoperable systems.

EU Insolvency Regulation and Banking Winding Up Directive

8.110 The EU Insolvency Regulation provides[1] that the impact of insolvency on rights of and obligations to settlement systems is governed by the law of the relevant settlement system. In the Banking Winding Up Directive[2] (which applies to credit institutions) art 27 protects transactions carried out on regulated markets; this will in turn protect clearing and settlement systems to which those markets are attached. Further, the EU Insolvency Regulation and the Banking Winding Up Directive do much to harmonise the rules for insolvency jurisdiction and recognition in Europe, and clarify choice of law rules concerning the availability of set off and post-insolvency dispositions of (interests in) securities. See Chapter 5 for further discussion.

1   In art 9. See also art 8 of the Settlement Finality Directive.
2   Directive 2001/24/EC of the European Parliament and of the Council of 4 April 2001 on the reorganisation and winding up of credit institutions.

Financial Collateral Directive

8.111 The Financial Collateral Directive[1] is discussed in Chapter 4. While the Directive's scope is not addressed primarily to the post-trade infrastructure, it builds on the Settlement Finality Directive in addressing the legal risk associated with wholesale cash and securities collateral, primarily by harmonising and liberalising the provisions of national insolvency laws within the EU.

1   Directive 2002/47/EC of the European Parliament and of the Council of 6 June 2002 on financial collateral arrangements.

Hague Convention

8.112 The Hague Convention on the Law Applicable to Certain Rights in Respect of Securities held with an Intermediary is discussed in Chapter 5 (see paras **5.59–5.61**). It builds on the Settlement Finality Directive by extending the concept of PRIMA to all dealings in intermediated securities.

European Securities Code

8.113 In its communication *Clearing and settlement in the European Union, main policy issues and future challenges*[1], the European Commission consulted on the desirability of developing a European securities code[2]. In view of the challenges involved[3], the Commission suggested that this is not an option for the short term. The challenges are of course considerable, especially in the context of the different views of legal systems on such fundamental issues as the nature of ownership of property, and appropriate priorities in an insolvency situation. An often quoted ideal is the enviable level of legal certainty achieved in the US securities markets; this of course required enormous effort in the preparation and revision of art 8 of the US Uniform Commercial Code. It is possible that a European Securities Code could be developed over the medium to long term[4], and the proposed Securities Law Directive (see Chapter 7, paras **7.177–7.193**) might do so, provided its aims are not too ambitious. The Legal Certainty Group report (see para **8.78** above) and the UNIDROIT Convention (see Chapter 5) might have prompted a similar result, but at present such initiatives seem unlikely to progress further.

1   COM(2002) 257.

2   *Clearing and settlement in the European Union, main policy issues and future challenges*, p 12:

'Given the substantial divergence in the legal treatment of securities across the EU, it has been suggested that the optimal solution would ... require achieving a uniform legal treatment of securities across the EU. This implies creating a special legal regime for securities – a "uniform securities code".'

See the European Securities Forum Contribution on the Joint CESR/ECB Consultation on Clearing and Settlement, 2002:

'One key area where a pan-EU instrument would serve is harmonisation of member states' diverse securities laws (ie property laws as they relate to securities) which have the effect of complicating all inter-member state securities activity involving EU securities and thus constitute barriers to a single market. Harmonisation needs to embrace payment finality laws, securities payment finality laws, bankruptcy laws and transfer of ownership laws. We understand that the US authorities solved some similar difficulties with a superordinate "universal security code"' (ESF comment on consultation question 2.1).

3   *Clearing and settlement in the European Union, main policy issues and future challenges*, p 12:

'Such a regime would be far from easy to design, especially for equities, because of the many links with national property, company, succession and insolvency law in Member States.'

4   Such a Code would complement the Council Regulation 2157/2001/EC of 8 October 2001 on the Statute for a European company ('SE').

Lisbon Treaty 2009

8.114 A development likely to have a long-term, if indirect, effect on the future evolution of post-trade arrangements is the Lisbon Treaty which entered into force in December 2009. Since member states and the European Parliament can as a result delegate power to the European Commission to adopt delegated acts and implementing legislation, the European Commission can be given much wider power to introduce legislation more quickly without detailed input from member state representatives. As may be seen already, the amount of EU legislation is ever-increasing, and this seems likely to continue. One obvious consequence seems to be that more EU legislation will seen in the form of Regulations having direct effect rather than requiring national implementing measures. This should in theory mean that there will be less divergence in the interpretation of EU requirements in member states, but in practice there will inevitably still be questions of how relevant provisions and terms are to be interpreted and applied in any particular jurisdiction, and it seems likely that many jurisdictions will be tempted to have regard to their own particular history of approach to particular concepts or case-law. As has been seen from the application and interpretation of the Financial Collateral Directive as implemented in English law (see Chapter 4, para **4.102**), where terms have a well-known background under local law, it is by no means certain that a local law judge will always recognise the relevance of interpretation by reference to European concepts[1]. It is to be hoped that in the future, with more background and case-law regarding interpretation of the concepts used in European legislation, there will be more harmonisation of approach as well as legislative wording, but it seems likely that there is a long way to go before this is achieved.

1   'Amongst the 27 Member States of the EU not two legal frameworks are the same. Terminology varies considerably and legal concepts are intimately linked with each language and Member States' legal framework. Therefore, it would be insufficient to translate, for example, the relevant national word for "property" into the other EU languages assuming that the legal understanding would be exactly the same'. 'Cross-border issues of securities law: European efforts to support securities markets with a coherent legal framework', the EU Parliament's Committee on Economic and Monetary Affairs (ECON), May 2011, p 8.

CHAPTER 9

UK settlement systems

CREST[1]

Introduction

9.1 CREST is an electronic system for the paperless settlement of transactions in registered securities in London[2]. (Trade confirmation takes place outside CREST, although pre-settlement matching occurs within CREST; types of transactions settled include transfers, repos and securities loans and corporate actions.) CREST offers dematerialisation[3], payments by reference to central bank money for pounds sterling and euro, an assured payments system for US dollars, and can handle corporate actions.

1   The name is not an acronym. This chapter considers certain aspects of the CREST system as at 13 September 2012, but does not seek to provide a detailed or exhaustive analysis of the whole system. For further detail see the Euroclear UK & Ireland section of the Euroclear website (www.euroclear.com). Although the CREST system is now part of the Euroclear group, and the Euroclear website generally refers to 'Euroclear UK & Ireland' or 'EUI' in more recent publications, the terms 'CREST' and 'the CREST system' are still commonly used and remain in various documents therefore are retained for certain purposes in this chapter.

2   Bearer securities are ineligible. However, securities which are bearer in paper form such as allotment letters may be dematerialised if a register is created: see CREST *The Business Description*, Bank of England, December 1994, p 14.

3   That is, the removal of the certificates and instruments of transfer which are otherwise generally necessary to permit UK registered securities to be evidenced and transferred. The Group of Thirty Securities Clearance and Settlement Study of 1989 (the 'G30 Report') defined dematerialisation as: 'The elimination of physical certificates or documents of title which represent ownership of securities so that securities exist only as computer records.'

9.2 At the time of writing, the only securities which are eligible for transfer through CREST are registered securities constituted under the laws of England and Wales, Scotland or Northern Ireland, the Republic of Ireland, the Isle of Man, Jersey or Guernsey[1]. This is because the legal rights and obligations applicable to securities held through CREST derive from specific legislation, therefore CREST cannot settle securities issued subject to the law of a particular jurisdiction unless the relevant legislation has been passed in that jurisdiction. UK shares and other securities are covered by the CREST Regulations (see para **9.4** below), and equivalent regulations have been made in the Republic of Ireland, the Isle of Man and Jersey to provide for the transfer of securities issued in such jurisdictions through CREST[2].

1   Generally, see Chapter 7 of the CREST Rules.

2   The Irish Companies Act 1990 (Uncertificated Securities) Regulations 1996, as amended (SI 1996/68) and other relevant regulations made under s 239 of the Companies Act 1990; the Isle of Man Companies Act 1992 Uncertificated Securities Regulations 2005 (SI 2005/754) and other relevant regulations made under s 28 of the Companies Act 1992; and the Companies (Jersey) Law 1991 Companies (Uncertificated Securities) (Jersey) Order 1999 (SI 1999/9462) and other relevant regulations in Jersey. (Note that there is no similar legislation in Guernsey, therefore although Guernsey securities are admissible to CREST provided there is appropriate provision in the articles of association of the issuing company, 'Guernsey shares are not participating securities as defined in the CREST Regulations'. See CREST Rule 8.) Thus in principle only securities issued in, and with a register of title in, the UK, Republic of Ireland, Isle of Man, Jersey or Guernsey are eligible for settlement in CREST, although securities issued in other jurisdictions may be brought into CREST through depositary receipt schemes or the CREST DI arrangements (see paras **9.69–9.74** below).

9.3 Use of CREST is in principle[1] optional both for issuers and investors[2], although this will depend on the terms of issue of the relevant shares or securities[3].

1 In practice, listed securities (other than certain types of listed debt securities and fixed income securities) are required to be capable of electronic settlement by the Listing Rules of the Financial Services Authority ('FSA') (see LR 6.1.23R). This provision was introduced in September 1997.

2 Note that membership is relatively unrestricted, although in practice a person's ability to obtain direct membership will be limited by whether it is able to maintain the appropriate computer access (but see discussion at paras **9.36–9.39** below regarding sponsored membership) or to appoint a settlement bank (see paras **9.12–9.24** below). See also para 25 of Sch 1 to the CREST Regulations, and the CREST Rules, Part I, Rule 1 regarding admission of users and participants. There is no restriction on membership of non-UK persons, although an appropriate legal opinion will be required (Rule 1 of the CREST Rules, Section 1.2), and the computer system giving CREST access must be installed and maintained in Belgium, France, Germany, Guernsey, Ireland, the Isle of Man, Jersey, the Netherlands, Sweden, Switzerland, one of the UK jurisdictions, one of the jurisdictions of the US, the province of Ontario, Canada, or (subject to Euroclear UK and Ireland Limited's prior consent) another EU member state (Rule 1 of the CREST Rules, Section 2.2).

3 Issuing companies may elect whether to make their securities eligible for CREST, and may also issue what the Regulations call 'wholly dematerialised securities' (see Rule 7 of the CREST Rules, Section 6), namely securities or shares the terms of issue for which provide that such instruments may only be held in uncertificated form and only transferred through CREST. Unless the securities are wholly dematerialised securities, investors in CREST-eligible securities may elect whether their securities should be held in uncertificated form in CREST, or in certificated form outside it, ie certificated securities may be brought into CREST, and uncertificated securities may be recertificated.

9.4 CREST is owned and operated by Euroclear UK and Ireland Limited ('EUI')[1], formerly CRESTCo Limited, which in turn is owned by Euroclear SA/NV. The CREST system is operated by EUI in accordance with the Uncertificated Securities Regulations 2001, as amended[2] (the 'CREST Regulations')[3].

1 CRESTCo Limited was acquired by Euroclear in September 2002 (see para **9.125** n 1 below). CREST was originally set up following the creation of a task-force by the Bank of England which proposed the CREST system in June 1993.

2 SI 2001/3755.

3 The earlier regulations were the Uncertificated Securities Regulations 1995 (SI 1995/3272), as amended by the Uncertificated Securities (Amendment) Regulations 2000 (SI 2000/1682), which were revoked by SI 2001/3755 as from 26 November 2001. In this chapter, unless otherwise specified, any reference to a 'CREST Regulation' means a regulation forming part of SI 2001/3755. The particular terms which apply to participants in the CREST system (in addition to the terms of membership or other agreements entered into with EUI) are set out in the CREST Manual, consisting of the CREST Reference Manual, CREST International Manual, CREST Central Counterparty Service Manual, CREST Rules, CCSS Operations Manual, and CREST Glossary of Terms (which includes the Glossaries to the CREST International Manual and to the CREST Central Counterparty Service Manual). For general reference, the CREST Rules and CREST Reference Manual are a good starting point, together with the general CREST Terms and Conditions (as distinct from the CREST Personal Member Terms and Conditions, see para **9.36** n 2 below) which form part of a CREST member's agreement with EUI. Any reference to CREST documentation in this chapter means the applicable forms available on the CREST website, www.euroclear.com, Euroclear UK and Ireland section, as at 13 September 2012.

Core legal structure

Dematerialisation

9.5 Outside CREST, UK company legislation generally requires companies to issue share certificates[1] and to register transfers only on receipt of instruments of transfer[2]. Dematerialisation is based on the CREST Regulations[3]. SI 2001/3755 is not limited to CREST and does not mention it by name. Accordingly, competing systems (including the continental settlement systems) are in principle free to apply for recognition under SI 2001/3755 to settle UK shares and other registrable securities, and it may be argued that the form of SI 2001/3755 is thus beneficial in not stifling competition. However, a parallel system to CREST has not been set up in the UK to date, perhaps because possible competitors prefer to avoid creating the systems necessary to handle the complex corporate actions associated with UK equities, and detailed procedures tracking applicable stamp duty and stamp duty reserve tax ('SDRT') rates. The implications of the CREST system becoming part of the Euroclear group are discussed further in paras **9.125–9.134** below, but this chapter focuses on CREST, therefore, for the sake of convenience, this chapter refers to the system contemplated by SI 2001/3755 as CREST.

1   Companies Act 2006, s 769.

2   Companies Act 2006, s 770.

3   The CREST Regulations were made under s 207 of the Companies Act 1989 (now repealed but replaced by s 785 of the Companies Act 2006), which allowed the Secretary of State to make provision 'enabling title to securities to be evidenced and transferred without a written instrument'. (See also CREST Regulation 2(1)). CREST Regulation 14 expressly permits the electronic transfer of title. (This is broadly comparable to the old statutory provision which permitted the dematerialisation of gilts within the old Central Gilts Office system (the 'CGO')).

Legal and equitable ownership

9.6   Legal title to CREST securities is prima facie determined, both inside and outside the system, by registration[1]. The usual statutory requirements for written transfers are expressly disapplied[2].

1   See Companies Act 2006, s 127 and CREST Regulation 24(1).

2   Law of Property Act 1925, s 53(1)(c) and s 136 are disapplied by CREST Regulation 38(5).

Settlement structure – UK securities

9.7   Currently[1], in relation to securities constituted under or governed by the laws of England and Wales, Northern Ireland or Scotland and admitted to CREST under the CREST Regulations[2] ('UK Securities'), the relevant records maintained by CREST of entries in CREST accounts constitute part of the register of legal title for such securities. Such UK Securities are therefore in dematerialised form, and held and transferred through CREST. As a result, there is no need to update the register of title separately in relation to such securities to reflect the transfer across CREST accounts (unlike non-UK securities, regarding which see para **9.11** below).

1   Since 26 November 2001. Prior to this date, transfers of UK securities across CREST accounts resulted in an instruction to the relevant registrar to update the register of title, in the same way as described for non-UK securities below.

2   Rather than, for example, the equivalent Irish legislation.

9.8   Since the CREST records are the register of title for UK securities so recorded (the 'operator register of securities'), a transfer from one CREST account to another CREST account of itself transfers legal title (rather than creating an equitable interest which is followed by transfer of legal title when the register of title is updated). The relevant issuer is required to maintain a duplicate record of this CREST register of title (the duplicate record being known as the 'record (of securities)', as well as a register of holders of certificated securities (the 'issuer register of securities')[1]. These arrangements apply to shares as well as registrable securities other than shares, and 'public sector securities'[2].

1   See CREST Regulations 20–22.

2   Defined to mean 'UK Government securities [securities 'issued by Her Majesty's Government in the United Kingdom or by a Northern Ireland department'] and local authority securities' (CREST Regulation 3, Definitions).

9.9 The CREST Rules set out further detail regarding the electronic transfer of title[1]. The CREST Rules state that the operator register of securities consists of, effectively, the CREST Accounts of all CREST Members which record the relevant securities, and the Corporate Action delivery data[2].

> 1   It is important to note that currently these arrangements only apply to securities admitted to CREST pursuant to the CREST Regulations in the UK. Securities admitted under, for example, the relevant Irish legislation relating to CREST, are still subject to the two stage procedure for transfer of title, as explained in para **9.11** below.
>
> 2   CREST Rule 14, Part B, Section 2 in relation to UK securities:
>
> '...the records referred to below comprise the Operator register of securities:
>
> > 2.1   the stock accounts of all Members to which are credited units of the relevant participating security;
> >
> > 2.2   Corporate Action Data;
> >
> > 2.3   the names and addresses of all Members, determined by reference to the Name and Address Database;
> >
> > 2.4   the CSD List;
> >
> > 2.5   the stock postings held on the Local Record;
> >
> > 2.6   the list maintained by EUI of participants admitted as CREST IPAs; and
> >
> > 2.7   those parts of the Local Record archive which store the information referred to in paragraphs 2.1 to 2.8 above (and the information required by each previous version of this Rule in relation to the period for which such version was in force) for the period of 20 years from the date on which a relevant Member ceased to hold the relevant participating security.'

9.10 The arrangements for CREST registration of title to UK Securities raise certain interesting issues, some of which are discussed in paras **9.136–9.140** below.

Settlement structure – non-UK securities

9.11 In relation to CREST eligible securities other than UK securities (namely, securities issued under the laws of the Republic of Ireland, Isle of Man, Guernsey and Jersey), transfers of securities through the CREST system result in an electronic notification through the CREST system to the registrar of the issuer of the securities to update the register of title. Thus, in addition to being named in the register of the issuer of the securities as holder of the relevant securities, CREST participants have a record of their securities in accounts at CREST[1]. Registrars are required to register a CREST transfer within two hours of the corresponding change in the CREST records, and in order to protect the transferee from the credit risk of the transferor during this short interval, the book entry transfer across the relevant CREST accounts gives the transferee equitable ownership of the securities pending transfer of legal title taking place upon the update of the register of title[2].

> 1   CREST securities accounts are regularly reconciled to the issuer's register under this system.
>
> 2   See generally CREST Rule 14, Part A, Sections 3–8, and CREST Reference Manual, Chapter 5. These requirements apply as a result of the relevant local legislation relating to CREST, as well as the CREST manual, except in the case of Guernsey where the requirements which would otherwise appear in local legislation are set out in Rule 8 of the CREST Rules relating specifically to the admission to CREST of Guernsey securities.

Payments

9.12 The currencies in which payment obligations may be recorded in the CREST system are sterling, euro and US dollars. Since the CREST system is not a bank, no CREST accounts are bank accounts, and therefore records of payments made between CREST accounts do not reflect debts owed to the relevant CREST member by EUI. Where, for example, a payment is required to be recorded through CREST as having been made in connection with a transfer of securities settled through CREST against payment, the payment by the relevant CREST member will be recorded as a debit to such CREST member's cash memorandum account ('CMA') and a credit to the other CREST member's CMA. These records in the relevant CMAs discharge[1] the obligation of the transferee to pay the transferor in respect of the securities transferred, and replace this payment obligation with an obligation for the transferee's settlement bank to pay the transferor's settlement bank[2]. A CMA shows at any one time the net amount of payment obligations which the CREST member's settlement bank has incurred on behalf of that CREST member (if a negative balance) or which such bank is owed for the benefit of the CREST member (if a positive balance), and therefore the amount which the CREST member is owed by its settlement bank (or owes to its settlement bank) at that time[3].

1   CREST Terms and Conditions, Condition 13. This means that the CREST member to which payment is due cannot seek payment from the paying CREST member, even if it does not receive payment in due course from its own settlement bank, or its settlement bank does not receive payment from the paying CREST member's settlement bank.
2   CREST Reference Manual, Chapter 6, Section 6.
3   The payment obligation of the settlement bank is calculated by reference to the CMA of the CREST member for which it acts, in which the payment obligations referable to the member's purchases and sales are recorded. 'Each CREST member has at least one CMA, on which the CREST system records CREST payments made by or to that CREST member upon the occurrence of the relevant Payment Settlement Events.' (CREST Reference Manual, Chapter 6, Section 2.) This will include payments such as amounts due in respect of transfers of securities against payment, and payments of commission, stamp duty or SDRT, and dividends.

9.13 Every CREST participant is required to have appointed a settlement bank[1] as a condition of admission into CREST[2] and must confirm this in the CREST Application Form.

1   For requirements regarding admission of CREST settlement banks, see CREST Rule 16.
2   CREST Reference Manual, Chapter 6, Section 1.

9.14 Each CREST member is required by CREST to have a settlement bank for each relevant currency[1] which the CREST member will wish to receive or transfer through CREST. (A CREST member which is itself a settlement bank may act as its own settlement bank.) The CREST member will have a CMA for each such currency which will record obligations or entitlements in that currency, and the balance recorded in such account will change during the day, as payment obligations of or to such CREST member are created through CREST, for example, by settlement of a transfer of securities against payment.

1   CREST Reference Manual, Chapter 6, Section 2, states that: 'Each member can have only one settlement bank per designated currency but could use the same bank as settlement bank for a number of designated currencies.'

9.15 Since a settlement bank incurs debt obligations, or is owed amounts, for the account of a CREST member for which it acts as settlement bank, it will need to recover from, or pay the amount due to, the CREST member. Payments between the settlement bank and the CREST member will be settled outside CREST as a commercial matter between the bank and the CREST member (usually by the operation of bank accounts associated with the relevant CMAs).

REAL TIME GROSS SETTLEMENT[1]

9.16 This is the mechanism for the transfer between settlement banks of the sterling and euro amounts which they are required to pay as a result of incurring payment obligations on behalf of the CREST members for which they act as settlement bank (as recorded in the relevant CMAs). For payments in sterling and euro, settlement banks make payments to each other through their accounts with the relevant central bank[2] during the day on a real-time basis as credits and debits are made to the relevant CMAs of each CREST member for which the settlement banks provide services.

1   Since 26 November 2001. Prior to this date, the assured payment arrangements applied to these currencies as well as US dollars (see paras **9.21–9.23** below).

2   The Bank of England for sterling, and the Central Bank of Ireland for euro. The euro payment services were provided by the Bank of England prior to 14 April 2008, but were transferred to the Central Bank of Ireland in advance of the Bank of England ceasing to be a participant in TARGET, the real-time gross settlement system for euro payments (TARGET ceased to operate on 16 May 2008, and was fully replaced by TARGET2 on 19 May 2008; this followed the phased migration to TARGET2 which began on 19 November 2007).

9.17   Where a CREST member makes a transfer against payment through CREST, securities cease to be recorded in the transferor's CREST account and are recorded in the transferee's CREST account in return for the creation of a payment obligation owed by the transferee's settlement bank to the transferor's settlement bank (as recorded by a credit to the CMA of the transferor CREST member and a debit to the CMA of the transferee CREST member)[1]. The settlement bank's payment obligation will be satisfied not at the end of the day but at the same time as the records are made in the relevant CMAs. This happens by the creation of an irrevocable and unconditional undertaking by the central bank to credit the payment amount (the amount of the debit to the CMA, which is to be paid by the transferee's settlement bank) to the relevant account of the transferor's settlement bank. This means the central bank undertakes to credit the relevant account of the transferor's settlement bank with the central bank, and to make a corresponding debit to the relevant account of the transferee's settlement bank with the central bank. The undertaking given by the central bank in reality precedes the actual debits and credits to the central bank accounts, but takes effect on the creation of the relevant debits, and because the undertaking is irrevocable and is given by the central bank, the transferor in effect receives, in return for the transfer of legal title to securities, an enhanced claim against its settlement bank. This is because although it still has a claim against its settlement bank, such settlement bank now takes the credit risk of a central bank rather than credit risk on the transferee or its settlement bank. Consequently, the transferor is not exposed to the insolvency of the transferee or the transferee's settlement bank (although is still exposed to the insolvency of its own settlement bank). The central bank will make sure funds are available from each settlement bank to meet its obligations for CREST payments, and will earmark funds on the relevant central bank account of each settlement bank (so that the settlement bank cannot remove such funds) in advance, but the undertaking from the central bank is 'entered into unconditionally' therefore is not affected by the value of the funds earmarked (CREST Reference Manual, Chapter 6, Section 6, subsection headed 'RTGS payment mechanism').

1   It would be impossible for all CREST participants to have accounts with the Bank of England. The transfer of legal title through CREST therefore cannot literally take place against transfer to the seller of central bank money, thus the payment obligation created is that of a settlement bank, not the central bank. It is arguable that this is in some respects an advantage for CREST participants, since there is a choice of providers for settlement bank services.

9.18   Agreements are in place between settlement banks and CREST (and between the central banks and the settlement banks) in relation to the Real Time Gross Settlement ('RTGS') payment process and the linking of CREST and RTGS systems, and such concepts are also set out in relevant provisions of the general CREST Terms and Conditions and the CREST Manual.

9.19 Because settlement depends on the availability to the settlement bank of funds at the central bank, it is essential that settlement banks ensure they have sufficient funds or collateral with the central bank.

9.20 In relation to the Bank of England[1], settlement banks can generate additional liquidity by transferring assets to the Bank of England under a repo transaction[2]. The assets used for the repo may be the settlement bank's own assets, or the assets being purchased by the relevant CREST member in an 'auto-collateralisation' procedure, where such CREST member enters into a repo with the settlement bank and the settlement bank uses the assets transferred under such repo to enter into a repo with the Bank of England on a back-to-back basis[3]. Where securities subject to the repo are sold by the relevant CREST member, CREST may use securities in the CREST member's available balance, or unwind the repo, triggering a redelivery of the stock by the Bank of England and a simultaneous repayment to the Bank of England by the relevant settlement bank[4]. These arrangements will normally only be permitted to provide intra-day liquidity and therefore will be unwound at the end of the day. This auto-collateralisation facility is only available for certain types of securities[5], and CREST settlement banks will need appropriate documentation in place with the Bank of England for this purpose, namely an RTGS CREST Master Auto-Collateralising Repurchase Agreement. A similar agreement is required between the CREST member and its settlement bank to enable the CREST member to have similar auto-collateralisation arrangements in place with its settlement bank, and, where necessary, to transfer securities to the settlement bank for on-transfer to the Bank of England under the settlement bank's auto-collateralisation arrangements[6]. This facility is available only where the relevant securities are held by the CREST member as principal or the underlying owner has consented to use of the securities in this manner. In addition, auto-collateralisation will only apply to sterling transactions over the minimum value specified by the Bank of England.

1   The Central Bank of Ireland does not provide a similar service for euros.

2   CREST Reference Manual Chapter 7, Section 8 'Auto-collateralisation arrangements'. Prior to 2012, the collateralisation by repo happened automatically where purchases were eligible for self-collateralisation, even if additional liquidity was not in fact required. The new auto-collateralisation service is more sophisticated and provides additional liquidity only where this is needed. See CREST White Paper 'Enhancing Central Bank Money – Improving liquidity efficiency', October 2011. See also the CREST 'CCI/Single Platform update', 2 July 2010, in which it was stated: 'Single Platform Central Bank Money will deliver 'demand-driven' autocollateralisation to Euroclear UK & Ireland settlement banks in place of the existing 'supply-driven' self-collateralisation repo (SCR) model. This development is focused on the settlement banks to improve their liquidity usage (and reduce cost) compared to the current SCR model. We expect to launch Single Platform Central Bank Money at the end of Q2 2011.'

3   CREST Reference Manual, Chapter 7, Section 8: 'The SB auto-collateralisation arrangements will seek automatically to create autocollateralising repo (SCR) transaction(s), which instruct and settle the movement of securities from the RTGS settlement bank's settlement bank repo member (or a settlement bank linked member) to the Bank of England's repo member, wherever: • a transaction of a client-member (or a settlement bank linked member) has a sterling consideration; and • the settlement bank of the cash debit party has insufficient liquidity in its LMA to settle the transaction. All transaction types that include a sterling CREST payment are capable of initiating the automatic creation of auto-collateralising repo (SCR) transaction(s) by the SB autocollateralisation process.'

4   In a purchase of securities involving auto-collateralisation by both the relevant CREST member and its settlement bank, there is a transfer on the CREST accounts of the securities from seller to purchaser, and the creation of an obligation on the purchaser's settlement bank to make payment to the seller's settlement bank. The purchased securities will be transferred under a repo from the purchaser to its settlement bank, and the settlement bank makes a payment to the purchaser. The settlement bank in turn transfers the securities to the Bank of England and the Bank of England provides payment under the repo to the settlement bank by enabling the settlement bank to make payment to the seller's settlement bank. All such repos will be automatically unwound at the end of the day if they have not been unwound earlier (if this is not possible, the unwind deliveries will be scheduled for settlement on the following business day). In a transfer of securities (for a sale or DBV) where the securities have been used in a self-collateralisation repo as described above, CREST will identify the transactions

which require the stock and may either use stock from the CREST member's available balance and leave the repo in place, or automatically return the repo securities to the relevant CREST member by procuring a redelivery by the Bank of England to the settlement bank, redelivery by the settlement bank to the CREST member, and delivery by the CREST member to the relevant purchaser, at the same time as repayment under the repo by the settlement bank to the Bank of England, repayment by the CREST member to the settlement bank, and payment (by debit and credit of CREST cash memorandum accounts) from the purchaser to the seller.

5   See the Bank of England's RTGS Reference Manual.

6   Note the differences in CREST procedures. In relation to the auto-collateralisation between client and settlement bank, 'The client auto-collateralisation arrangements: (a) are triggered by a member's purchase of eligible securities against sterling, regardless of their need for additional credit (known as "on-supply"); (b) will repo the securities (i.e. those which are the subject of the member's purchase) from the member to their RTGS settlement bank (known as "on-flow"); and (c) result in cash consideration equivalent to the settlement bank margined value of the securities being credited to the CMA of the member.' In relation to the auto-collateralisation between settlement bank and the Bank of England, 'The SB auto-collateralisation arrangements: (a) are triggered when a settlement bank has insufficient liquidity in their LMA to fund the settlement of an underlying client-member (or a settlement bank linked member) transaction against sterling (known as "on-demand"); (b) will repo securities from the settlement bank repo member (or a settlement bank linked member) to the Bank of England's repo membership, where the repoed securities are either: (i) the subject of the underlying transaction (known as "on-flow"), which may be either a client-member purchase (where the securities are transferred from the member via client auto-collateralisation to the settlement bank repo member) or a settlement bank linked member purchase; or (ii) not the subject of the underlying transaction, but are held by the settlement bank repo member or the settlement bank linked member (known as "onstock"); and (c) result in a liquidity credit for the settlement bank equivalent to the central bank repo value of the securities.' CREST Reference Manual, Chapter 7, Section 8

ASSURED PAYMENTS SYSTEM

9.21   CREST has an assured payment system for payments in US dollars. The RTGS mechanism for payments in sterling or euro is discussed at paras **9.16–9.20** above. Like the RTGS process, when book entry settlement takes place within CREST so that the CMA of the paying CREST member is debited and the CMA of the CREST member receiving payment is credited, the settlement bank of the paying CREST member becomes irrevocably and unconditionally obliged to pay the relevant amount to the settlement bank of the CREST member receiving payment[1], and the creation of the assured payment obligation (when the respective CMAs are debited and credited) discharges any payment obligation of the transferee.

1   The assured payments obligation is contained in the settlement bank agreement entered into bilaterally by each settlement bank and EUI and also in the assured payments agreement entered into multilaterally by EUI and all the settlement banks. New settlement banks are bound by the terms of the assured payments agreement under a deed of adherence.

9.22   The assured payment system was originally introduced because 'it was judged essential to have a payments system that would provide assurance of payment …'[1]. However, the system does not eliminate credit risk for the seller of securities. It merely replaces the credit risk of the buyer of securities with that of both the settlement bank of the buyer and the settlement bank of the seller[2].

1   Gilt edged settlement. Phase 2 of the CGO Service, Bank of England Quarterly Bulletin, February 1987. (The CREST assured payments system was modelled on that used by the old Central Gilts Office (the 'CGO').)

2   This assumes that the buyer's settlement bank does not agree to accept the risk of non-payment by the seller's settlement bank (such acceptance would be unusual). The arrangement is for the buyer's settlement bank to pay the seller's settlement bank, and for the seller's settlement bank in turn to pay the seller. If any link in this chain fails, the seller will not be paid. As between the seller's settlement bank and the seller, under the usual terms of the agreement between such parties, the settlement bank's duty to pay the seller is likely to be limited to sums it actually receives, and to require reimbursement of the settlement bank by the seller of any payments made by the settlement bank without corresponding receipt of payment. The Bank of England has no legal obligation to stand behind a defaulting settlement bank.

9.23 Inter-settlement bank payments are made through CHAPS or other appropriate system outside CREST[1]. Unlike the RTGS mechanism, payment between settlement banks does not take place on an ongoing basis in central bank funds, but instead the net payment obligation of one settlement bank to another will be paid at the end of day in the manner which the paying and receiving settlement banks agree with each other. As a result, under the assured payments system, settlement banks are exposed to each other's credit risk intra-day[2]. If one settlement bank fails to pay another, it will be in breach of its obligations under the CREST Manual and the relevant terms agreed with EUI and each other settlement bank, but the unpaid settlement bank will only have an unsecured claim against the defaulting settlement bank for the net amount due as calculated at the end of the day. Settlement banks may protect themselves against exposure to clients by setting a suitable debit cap and/or by taking a charge over clients' assets within CREST[3] (see paras **9.42–9.45** below) but cannot limit their exposure to other settlement banks.

1 While in practice settlement is on a multilateral net basis, the arrangements escape the rule in *British Eagle* [1975] 2 All ER 390 (broadly that contractual netting arrangements that purport to vary statutory insolvency netting are not effective in the event of insolvency) because the contractual payment obligations are calculated on a bilateral net basis, in accordance with r 4.90 of the Insolvency Rules 1986 (SI 1986/1925).

2 It is understood that when CREST was first set up, the banks demanded a link to RTGS as a condition of acting as CREST settlement banks; in view of operational difficulties with providing this from the outset, CREST at that time could only agree to offer RTGS as soon as practicable.

3 CREST settlement bank charges (referred to as 'system charges') are protected by Pt VII of the Companies Act 1989, as applied by the Financial Market and Insolvency Regulations 1996 (SI 1996/1469), as amended by the CREST Regulations. Protections include (broadly) disapplication of: restrictions on enforcement of security interests in the chargor's administration, the power of an administrator to deal with charged property and avoidance of property disposition. (By way of background, it is understood that when the CGO (on which CREST was based) was set up, the settlement banks were uneasy with the limited liability involved in the assured payments system, particularly when the Insolvency Act 1986 restricted the value of a floating charge where the chargor goes into administration, hence requested the application of Pt VII.) See also discussion regarding the effect of the Settlement Finality Directive at paras **9.53–9.56** below.

DELIVERY VERSUS PAYMENT

9.24 CREST offers delivery versus payment or 'DVP'[1]. In all forms of DVP, a settlement event is synchronised with a payment event. However, the important question is the exact nature of the settlement event and payment event. If the settlement event is not the passing of legal title but the passing of an equitable interest with legal title to follow, there is a risk that final settlement may not actually occur, for example, if the transferor is insolvent. This issue does not arise where securities are subject to full electronic transfer of title, where legal title is transferred by debit from one CREST account and credit to another, as discussed above (see paras **9.7–9.9** above), but a transfer could still be reversed in certain circumstances, for example, where fraud is involved. Where electronic transfer of title does not apply, the CREST procedure requires updating of the register within two hours of transfer across CREST accounts (see para **9.11** above) therefore there is only a short period in which insolvency might arise and prevent registration, but it is nevertheless a potential issue. As explained above, the creation of the undertaking to pay by a buyer's settlement bank is irrevocable and discharges the buyer of the obligation to pay. However, the seller still has certain exposures in place of exposure to the buyer. Under the assured payment mechanism, the seller is exposed to the credit risk of the buyer's settlement bank, or indeed its own settlement bank, and may not receive payment if either the buyer's settlement bank, or its own settlement bank, becomes insolvent. Under the RTGS mechanism, exposure to the insolvency of the buyer's settlement bank is removed, but exposure to the seller's own settlement bank still remains.

1   See further discussion of DVP in Chapter 8.

Regulation

EUI

9.25 EUI is regulated as a recognised clearing house ('RCH'[1]) by the FSA[2]. In addition EUI has been approved and is subject to supervision by the FSA as operator of CREST in accordance with Part 2 of the CREST Regulations, and in respect of any non-clearing activities[3] is an exempt person for the purposes of the Financial Services and Markets Act 2000 ('FSMA 2000')[4].

1   For the purposes of s 285 of FSMA 2000.

2   Such recognition was originally obtained in order to settle transactions executed on the London Stock Exchange, since under the requirements for recognition of a recognised investment exchange ('RIE') for the purposes of s 36 of the Financial Services Act 1986 (now repealed), the London Stock Exchange was required under Sch 4, para 2(4) to clear transactions either itself or through an RCH. This approach was in reality slightly odd since the CREST system is not a clearing house as such term is usually understood, but a settlement system. An entity wishing to become a RIE or RCH must now apply for recognition in accordance with Pt XVIII of FSMA 2000, and upon becoming so recognised, will be subject to the FSA Recognised Investment Exchanges and Recognised Clearing Houses sourcebook ('REC'). The REC rules applicable to RIEs do not require use of an RCH but contain general requirements to the effect that 'satisfactory arrangements' must be made for settlement, and RIE members must be allowed to use any settlement facility they wish (provided that appropriate links with the RIE exist to enable 'efficient and economic settlement' and the RIE is satisfied that 'the smooth and orderly functioning of the financial markets will be maintained' (REC 2.8.1, 2.8.1A). This reflects the requirements of Directive 2004/39/EC of the European Parliament and of the Council of 21 April 2004 on markets in financial instruments ('MiFID') regarding unrestricted access to clearing and settlement systems.

3   ie any activities listed in the Financial Services and Markets Act 2000 (Regulated Activities) Order 2001 (SI 2001/544), as amended, carried out otherwise than in the context of clearing.

4   Under the Financial Services and Markets Act 2000 (Exemption) Order 2001 (SI 2001/1201), as amended, reg 5 and Pt III of the Schedule to that Order.

9.26 EUI is an approved reporting mechanism ('ARM') for the purposes of FSA transaction reporting[1] but note the restriction relating to CREST: 'Firms will not be able to submit transaction reports for: (i) non-exchange instruments (OTC); and (ii) instruments identified using the Alternative Instrument Identifier (AII) codes.'[2]

1   FSA Supervision sourcebook ('SUP') requires firms to report details of certain transactions to the FSA (SUP 17.1.4R) and relieves a firm of this obligation if the transaction is reported directly to the FSA by an ARM (SUP 17.2.3R).

2   From FSA list of ARMs, see www.fsa.gov.uk, section 'Doing business with us', subsection 'Being regulated', information regarding 'Reporting requirements' and 'Transaction reporting'.

9.27 EUI will not assist with the observance of US regulatory holding restrictions, essentially because this would be inconsistent with the securities being freely transferable and fungible in CREST[1], but does have procedures regarding settlement discipline[2]. Custodians should monitor this exposure and ensure they have adequate indemnities in their customer documentation.

1   See CREST Blue Book *Corporate actions standardisation* (November 2004), Chapter entitled 'Common issues', section 3.

2   See CREST Rule 6, and CREST White Book *CREST Settlement Discipline: Overview of rules and common questions*, October 2009.

9.28 The CREST system has the benefit of designation for the purposes of the Settlement Finality Directive[1].

1 Directive 98/26/EC of the European Parliament and of the Council of 19 May 1998 on settlement finality in payment and securities settlement systems. See further detail at paras **9.53–9.56** below and also Chapter 8, paras **8.108–8.109**.

CREST PARTICIPANTS

9.29 In general, participation in CREST does not of itself necessitate authorisation under FSMA 2000. However, CREST members may require authorisation if they are providing sponsor or custody services. In particular, persons acting as CREST sponsors (see paras **9.36–9.39** below) require authorisation for the purposes of FSMA 2000 in order to be able to send dematerialised instructions through CREST on behalf of sponsored members for whom they act as CREST sponsor[1]. In addition, irrespective of CREST, a CREST member who holds the securities in its CREST accounts not for its own benefit but for third parties is acting as a custodian and (subject to any exemptions) will require authorisation under FSMA 2000 if providing such custody services in the UK[2].

1 See the Financial Services and Markets Act 2000 (Regulated Activities) Order 2001, art 45.

2 See Chapter 7 in relation to regulatory issues for custodians.

SDRT

9.30 SDRT rather than stamp duty is likely to be primarily the issue on a transfer of dematerialised chargeable securities within CREST[1].

1 Unless of course the transfer is itself exempt or zero rated. The following are indicative of CREST's approach to these issues (but see further in Chapter 10 in relation to the Inland Revenue approach):

'The CREST system incorporates functionality to allow stamp duty due to the UK or Irish tax authorities to be collected on transfers of chargeable securities occurring as the result of settlements in the system' and 'The CREST system collects ... SDRT on behalf of HMRC and Stamp Duty on behalf of the Irish Revenue Commissioners ... from the purchaser (or his agent) on all transfers in the CREST system at the standard percentage rates of the stampable consideration ... Certain securities (principally fixed-interest securities) are exempt from stamp duty. The CREST system will recognise these by means of exempt flags linked (by the CREST system) to their ISIN codes' (CREST Reference Manual, Chapter 8, Section 1).

'UK-chargeable securities held on behalf of exempt bodies such as charities should be held in one or more member accounts with an exempt member account tax status. Transfers into such accounts will be automatically exempted from duty. HMRC have stipulated that where two or more charities are pooled within a single member account, the designation of that account should begin "CH ..." (where this is not possible for any reason, the member should notify HMRC). In addition, HMRC require the inclusion of charity reference numbers on the associated legs of transfers destined for charities, in particular where custodians acquire securities on behalf of charities.' (CREST Reference Manual, Chapter 8, Section 2).

Custody accounts

9.31 Three main options are available to custodians holding securities in CREST: (i) The custodian's name (or that of its nominee) may appear on the register of title with a general (but not specific) client designation (pooled accounts); (ii) the custodian's name (or that of its nominee) may appear on the register of title with a specific client designation (designated accounts); (iii) the client's name (or that of its nominee) may appear on the register (sponsored membership).

9.32 It should be noted that where a sponsor provides services to a sponsored member (see paras **9.36–9.39** below), the sponsored member's name is on the register of title, therefore technically the sponsor is not acting as custodian for those securities because it is not holding legal title on behalf of the client (although it may be acting as custodian of other securities, or providing administrative assistance).

Pooled accounts

9.33 In many cases, the securities of more than one client will be pooled in a single account maintained by a custodian CREST member. A single debit cap (see explanation in paras **9.44–9.46** below) will permit efficiencies in the use of credit[1]. In the absence of effective trust arrangements between the custodian and its client, pooling may pose certain risks concerning the beneficial title of clients. A further risk is that a shortfall attributable to the business of one custody client may be borne by another custody client[2].

1   Since clients who are net sellers of securities on any day can fund clients who are net purchasers.

2   See Chapter 3 for discussion of pooling and issues arising.

Designated accounts

9.34 Individual designation may be desired by clients to avoid the above risks, or by the custodian for tax planning[1]. This is permitted within the holding of a CREST member by the use of separate accounts. CREST notes these different accounts against the name of the member in the operator register[2]. Also, it is possible for one person to have more than one CREST membership. Such designation[3] may make corporate actions easier to handle, reducing the incidence of fractional entitlements.

1   For example, to segregate different securities attracting different rates of SDRT.

2   'A designation may be an alphanumeric but should not give any indication of the identity of any beneficial owner ... Where a member ... has more than one member account, each member account is reflected on the register (and, in the case of UK Securities other than eligible debt securities, the issuer's record). Member accounts can therefore be used to segregate one type of holding from another ...' (CREST Reference Manual, Chapter 2, Section 5).

3   It is unclear how such designations in the register of UK shares accord with Companies Act 2006, s 126 (which replaced the similar wording in Companies Act 1985, s 360, with effect from 1 October 2009), which provides that 'No notice of any trust, expressed, implied or constructive, shall be entered on the register of members of a company registered in England and Wales or Northern Ireland, or be receivable by the registrar'. Related provisions are included in CREST Rule 7, Section 2.9.2. The correct view may be that such designations are ineffective against the issuer (so that it is not fixed with notice of custody trusts) but are effective against the liquidator of the custodian (so that it cannot make the custody assets available to creditors of the custodian on the basis that any custody trust fails for want of certainty of subject matter). Independently of CREST, it has long been customary for company registrars to note special designations on the register beside members' names.

9.35 However, even where a custodial trust is effective as against the custodian member and its liquidator, it will not be effective against EUI, which will not assist any custody client in claims against a custodian member[1].

1   CREST Regulation 23(3) provides that: 'No notice of any trust, expressed, implied or constructive, shall be entered on an Operator register of securities, or a part of such a register, or be receivable by an Operator.'

Sponsored membership[1]

9.36 Certain custody clients may wish to have their names on the register of the issuer in place of the custodian, and may therefore wish to be sponsored CREST members[2]. Sponsored members have CREST accounts in their own names[3] and are therefore the registered holders of CREST securities. However, their sponsor (the custodian, although when providing this service not holding securities as custodian) will maintain the electronic links with CREST and operate their CREST accounts on the client's behalf[4]. The arrangement is comparable to the administration by a custodian of certificated securities registered in the client's name through the use of a power of attorney. It protects the client from the custodian's insolvency but not from its fraud[5].

1   See CREST Reference Manual, Chapter 2, Section 2.

2   In practice, the sponsor could be the client's broker or some other services provider rather than its custodian. Sponsored membership may be particularly attractive to pension funds or other entities concerned to remain the legal owner of the relevant securities held through CREST. The CREST website contains considerable information about persons wishing to be 'personal members' using a CREST sponsor. See www.euroclear.com, Euroclear UK & Ireland section, under the heading 'About', the information regarding 'Becoming a client', in particular in relation to Private Individuals. The information available includes a list of stockbrokers willing to act as sponsors. There are specific CREST Personal Member Terms and Conditions which are in a form which is slightly different from the general CREST Terms and Conditions (although the content is essentially the same).

3   Sponsored members must enter into an agreement (the CREST Terms and Conditions (which apply equally to members and sponsored members) and the CREST admission agreement) with EUI as well as a settlement bank agreement with a CREST settlement bank, and a commercial agreement with the sponsor. Where the sponsored member is a nominee, it may instead enter into a sponsored member (nominee) admission agreement (together with the CREST Terms and Conditions); this differs from the normal sponsored membership arrangements principally in that the CREST Terms and Conditions require undertakings and warranties to be given by the nominee's parent.

4   In CREST terminology, the sponsored member is a participant and the sponsor is a user.

5   Fraud risk may be reduced by specifying daily withdrawal limits.

9.37 Sponsored members must appoint their own settlement banks[1], and custodians may be expected to arrange for this banking facility (or provide it themselves if already acting as a CREST settlement bank) and prepare the documentation as part of the custody package. Since a sponsored member has a separate settlement bank arrangement, sponsored members will have a separate debit cap[2]. The use of different debit caps for different custody clients may have the benefit of shielding one client from settlement gridlock attributable to excess purchases by another client; a disadvantage is that netting between one client's purchases and another's sales will not be available to the custodian for the purposes of calculating headroom[3].

1   Bank of England *CREST: The Business Description*, December 1994, indicated (at p 31) that: 'A sponsored member will often be able to grant a charge over his assets in CREST for the benefit of the [settlement] bank, which should ensure that he will normally have no difficulty in obtaining an adequate amount of intra-day credit for his account to be operated within CREST.'

2   In the case of private investors becoming sponsored members of CREST through their brokers, a zero debit cap was envisaged, on the basis that purchases are settled initially into the broker's CREST account, and then (after the client has put the broker in funds outside CREST) transferred free of payment into the client's CREST account.

    This approach may be adopted by custodians, who may operate a settlement account with an adequate debit cap for the initial settlement of client trades, and then (following payment outside CREST) transfer securities free of payment to the client's sponsored member accounts. This would enable the custodian to concentrate credit in one account and keep control of the banking side of settlement.

3   See further discussion of debit caps and headroom at paras **9.44–9.46** below. It may not be feasible for custodians to take the alternative approach of deferring the settlement of the initial purchase until they are put in funds by clients, for the following reason. In settlement, the giver of both cash and securities can specify the priority of the trade and this will determine the order in which it is settled. A zero priority on securities will in effect freeze the transfer of securities until the priority is lifted. However, on the cash side of any transaction, at the end of the settlement day a zero priority is automatically raised. (See eg the following statement in CREST Reference Manual, Chapter 4,

Section 11: 'For DvP transactions, the priority given on the cash side will not have an effect on the sequence of the transaction.') Thus, the securities side of a transaction can be frozen, but the cash side cannot. Therefore a custodian wishing to defer a purchase until it is put in funds by its client faces the problem that it is committed to the purchase as soon as the trade is matched. (The automatic raising of zero priorities on cash transfers was introduced in response to market consultation.)

Custodians may even be willing to transfer free to a sponsored member's account in advance of payment outside CREST, as they may be in a position to freeze securities in that account in exercise of any lien taken in their commercial documentation with the sponsored member (the sponsor's agreement does not require the sponsor to agree with EUI that it will obey all instructions from the sponsored member). The same may be true for designated accounts.

9.38 Sponsored members may not wish to handle their own corporate actions. Even though the client's name is on the register, the issuer could be instructed to direct any mailings to the address of the custodian on the client's behalf (but this will not assist if corporate actions are processed directly through CREST). However, this may be inconvenient for the custodian, who will be required to respond to any election separately (whether through CREST or otherwise) for each sponsored member, and not once for a global holding.

9.39 The role of sponsor involves certain risks. A sponsor is obliged[1] to notify CREST immediately upon becoming aware of the occurrence of events affecting the sponsored member's ability to transfer title to CREST securities, although it is not clear that it would know of such an event[2]. In addition, similar concerns about confidentiality and risk arise for the sponsor as for the custodian member (see paras **9.42–9.65** below). The drafting of the commercial agreement between the sponsor and its sponsored member (the terms of which are left to the parties to decide) is of great importance in limiting the risk of the custodian where acting as sponsor.

1   Under Clause 7, CREST Sponsor Terms and Conditions.

2   The provision was included on the basis that it might. 'The obligations placed on the sponsored member to notify the Operator of anything which might give rise to a risk of a bad delivery or of any insolvency, is repeated in the Sponsor's Agreement, given that the sponsor may often be the first to learn of his client's situation' (Bank of England *CREST Membership Agreements*, July 1995, p 7).

Visibility

9.40 Concern has been expressed[1] at the extent of intermediation of the holdings of private investors and the consequent lack of 'shareholder visibility', ie the ability of issuers readily to identify investors in their shares[2].

1   By, among others, ProShare, a lobby group for small investors.

2   The development of CREST prompted further discussion of loss of shareholder visibility, or the ability of issuers to identify investors by reference to the register. While investigation of beneficial ownership of public companies is possible under Companies Act 2006, s 793, this procedure is cumbersome. Ready identification of investors is generally more important to issuers in the UK than on the continent, because of the higher UK incidence of hostile takeovers. On the other hand, for some years there has been concern about how the ultimate beneficial owner of shares can influence the exercise of the rights represented by the shares which it holds through a chain of intermediaries. This has resulted in certain provisions introduced in the Companies Act 2006, namely ss 145–153 which came into force on 1 October 2007. See further in Chapter 6, paras **6.84–6.85**, and Chapter 7, paras **7.177–7.193** regarding the proposed Securities Law Directive.

9.41 While rapid rolling settlement may encourage the use of nominees, it has been argued that sponsored membership offsets this, and 'any net losses of visibility will be small'[1]. It should also be noted that in some cases there are commercial and practical arguments as to why lack of visibility can be useful; some clients of custodians may have legitimate and compelling reasons to wish to be invisible[2]. However, there has been growth in the use of personal membership (either directly or through sponsored membership) of CREST which, because of the fact that CREST is not a system based on immobilisation, means such persons are 'visible' as holders of securities.

1   Bank of England *CREST: The Business Description*, December 1994, p 93.

2   For example, high net worth individuals may wish to keep the extent of their wealth confidential for security reasons, and holders of shares in companies in sensitive areas may need to avoid pressure group action.

Risk

Credit

9.42   Credit may be a major risk issue for a custodian providing services in CREST, both in terms of the need to ensure sufficient credit or headroom will be available promptly with the custodian's settlement bank in order to be able settle clients' trades, and the need to control credit exposures to clients.

9.43   As a general point, if the settlement bank of a purchaser defaults, neither EUI nor the vendor's settlement bank is obliged to make good the loss to the vendor[1]. Custodians should ensure the terms of client documentation have the result that, in the event of settlement bank default, the custodian is not obliged to make good any shortfall, and that the custodian's only obligation is to account for sums actually received[2].

1   Section 5.2.1 of the CREST Terms and Conditions in effect excludes any duty on EUI in relation to the risk of the default of other CREST members or settlement banks.

2   Where inter-settlement bank payments are made on a net basis, allocating cash shortfalls to particular clients may be a complex matter. It is not necessarily the case that shortfalls can be allocated pro rata between clients.

HEADROOM

9.44   Through the payment mechanisms, the settlement bank of a purchaser of securities will assume personal liability for the payment of the purchase price. CREST settlement banks can generally be collateralised (where the participant owns the securities in its account) by taking security over the assets held in CREST[1], permitting collateralised capped assured payments ('CCAP')[2]. However, because of the significant legal difficulties which arise where custodians seek to charge assets beneficially owned by their clients, CCAP may not be available to custodians[3].

1   CREST provides facilities for the maintenance of margin, ie the monitoring of the value of securities charged as collateral in relation to a settlement bank's exposures.

2   See CREST Reference Manual, Chapter 6, Section 3.

3   Briefly, the custodian is not empowered to charge the assets without the consent of the client. Under the rule nemo dat quod non habet (none can give that which it does not own), where a security interest is purportedly given without the consent of the beneficial owner of the charged assets, the chargee may have a valid security interest if it can show that it acted as bona fide purchaser of the legal estate for value without notice of the lack of consent. A chargee can be treated as a purchaser for this purpose, but only if it takes a legal security interest. A charge is always equitable, so that the settlement banks cannot be protected by this doctrine, and will always be vulnerable if the true owners did not consent to the charge. For example, the client may not be free to give such authority because of fiduciary, regulatory or constitutional restraints on it. In addition, where the assets of more than one client are held together in one CREST account, the granting of a charge would result in one client's assets being used to secure exposures referable to the business of another client. It is hard to envisage how authority could properly be given for a charge to be granted in such circumstances.

9.45   Settlement banks may control their CREST exposures by imposing debit caps, ie limits on the volumes of net purchases they will permit a participant to settle on any day[1]. Such caps are not usual in settlement systems, and might be regarded as a cause for concern. A member is in practice free to delay the settlement of a purchase by ensuring that it has insufficient headroom to settle it. Moreover, the possibility of gridlock must be present. At times of volume surge (following privatisations or in market crashes) such caps might lead to the very settlement backlogs that, in the mid-1980s, prompted the search for a better settlement system[2]. CREST does not monitor the exhaustion or withdrawal of credit caps; where headroom is exhausted, back-ups will occur, prompting members to seek to resolve the problem amongst themselves, but in addition, EUI will monitor settlement and impose fines or other sanctions for breach of the rules designed to maintain timely and orderly settlement[3]. Because of the interdependencies of settlement credit and the fact that EUI does not regulate the matter, the ability of the system to function depends on each member taking a responsible approach.

1   'Each cap is set by only one settlement bank and relates to only one member. A settlement bank may set a zero cap.' And 'Every member must have at least one CMA [cash memorandum accounts within CREST] cap. The same cap can cover a number of CMAs in different designated currencies and payment types belonging to the same member, provided that the same settlement bank is associated with each CMA and has specified the base currency of that cap ... The CMA cap allows a settlement bank to control the amount of intra-day credit available to a member. The cap represents the maximum cumulative net debit position on his CMA(s) that a member can run during the settlement day.' (CREST Reference Manual, Chapter 6, Section 3).

'A member's CMA cap and current CMA position(s) are checked before the system debits the CMA to ensure that the cap is not breached upon the occurrence of the relevant Payment Settlement Event. Where a CREST payment for a particular transaction would cause the cap to be breached, that transaction remains unsettled until there is sufficient headroom within the cap' (CREST Reference Manual, Chapter 6, Section 3). However, 'The technical netting process is a system feature designed to resolve situations of settlement gridlock which can arise where delivery of one type of scarce resource (either securities or headroom) is dependent upon receipt of another scarce resource (also either securities or headroom)' (CREST Reference Manual, Chapter 5, Section 6).

'CREST will ensure that the cap is not breached. Banks may be willing to provide more credit if the customer can provide more collateral ... Those with inadequate credit will be more likely to have settlement delays and fails ...' (*Intra-day Credit and Caps in CREST*, April 1995).

2   On the other hand, it might be argued that the problem is not peculiar to CREST, as insufficient credit within a market will always impede settlement in practice, and a member can agree with its settlement bank a change to the relevant cap where necessary (although the settlement bank can only change the cap within the timing permitted by the CREST timetable).

3   CREST Rule 6, Settlement Discipline.

9.46   Custodians must also consider the risk that heavy buying by one client may affect its ability to settle purchases for another client[1].

1   Unless the custodian opens separate designated client accounts and negotiates separate debit caps for them, all clients will share the same cap (see the CREST Reference Manual, Chapter 6, Section 3). Custodians could address this in the custody agreement by imposing volume limits on clients, and making express disclosures about the possibility of delays, but in practice may ensure the cap is very large in order to cover most anticipated settlement requirements.

CREDIT EXPOSURES TO CLIENTS

9.47   Outside CREST, credit arrangements with clients may be undocumented, with informal overdrafts arising in the course of settlement[1] and credit limits being unadvised to clients. However, the involvement of settlement banks and debit caps in CREST precludes such an informal approach. Where custodians operate pooled accounts, they cannot rely on the debit cap effectively to control credit exposures to *particular* clients[2]. Internal credit controls, based on the custodian's own books and not merely on the pooled accounts of CREST, will be necessary.

1   The custodian might simply pay the purchase price on behalf of its clients and then seek to be put in funds to the extent of any overdraft.

2   This is because where client A is a net buyer and other clients are net sellers, an overall debit cap will not prevent client A in effect buying securities with the proceeds of the other clients' sales, nor relieve the custodian from the obligation of repaying to the other clients those proceeds of sale.

9.48 However, provided custody documentation grants custodians effective security interests over their clients' securities, these exposures may be effectively collateralised by virtue of DVP within CREST.

Bad deliveries and fraudulent transfers

9.49 It is not suggested that dematerialisation increases fraud or bad deliveries. Paper-based fraud has occurred in the City, and CREST arguably provides a more secure environment. However, the custodian and its clients should note the types of CREST transfers that are permitted to fail by the CREST system, as well as the types that are allowed to proceed.

BAD DELIVERIES[1]

9.50 For CREST eligible securities subject to the electronic transfer of title arrangements described at paras **9.7–9.10** above, the major protection against bad deliveries in CREST is the fact that the transfer between CREST accounts transfers legal title. For CREST eligible securities not subject to the electronic transfer of title arrangements, legal title will be granted within two hours of the transfer across CREST accounts[2]. A further protection is that certificated securities being dematerialised and transferred into CREST will not be credited to a member account until registered[3]. However, the risk cannot be excluded that some CREST settled trades will not proceed to registration, for example, where the securities in question are affected by a court order[4] or insolvency[5], but subject always to the application of the Settlement Finality Directive as discussed below. Note that the Bank of England will not stand behind a transferee's rights in relation to gilts[6], and the Registrar of Government Stock[7] has the right to refuse to give effect to any transfer unless it is furnished with such evidence as it may require of the transferor's right to make the transfer[8]. CREST Regulation 28 contemplates and permits bad deliveries, in the sense that the general requirement of participating issuers to register book entry transfers is disapplied in certain circumstances.

1   'a transfer of title from one member's uncertificated holding to another member's uncertificated holding which cannot be effected on the register in response to an RUR' (CREST Rule 12). This cannot apply to securities where the entity on the member's CREST account itself constitutes title to the securities. However, although CREST Rule 12 states that the bad delivery rule 'applies to securities which have been admitted to CREST pursuant to the Irish Regulations, Isle of Man Regulations or the Jersey Regulations and to CREST Guernsey securities, as defined in CREST Rule 8', this Rule 12 also states that the bad delivery rule 'may also (at EUI's discretion) be applied to securities admitted to the CREST system pursuant to the UK Regulations if it were to become necessary to rectify an Operator register of securities'.

2   CREST also seeks to reduce the risk of bad deliveries by providing (in CREST Rule 7, Section 2.9.2) that the constitutional documents of issuers of CREST eligible securities must not permit notice of trusts or other interests to be entered on the register. This is presumably intended to reduce tracing claims by reducing notice of beneficial interests.

3   CREST Reference Manual, Chapter 3: 'The paper interface'.

4   That is, a charging order, stop order or stop notice.

5   CREST Regulation 31(8) states that the provisions of CREST Regulation 31 do not take effect to confer a proprietary interest if to do so 'would otherwise be void by or under any enactment or rule of law'. (Arguably, this was necessary because s 207(4) of the Companies Act 1989 provided (broadly) that regulations to be made under s 207 should leave unchanged 'so far as practicable' rights and obligations in relation to uncertificated securities; there is no equivalent of such wording in s 785 of the Companies Act 2006.) It should be noted that no direct financial criteria are imposed

on CREST members in order to reduce the risk of member insolvency (see for example, the terms applicable to CREST Personal Members – see para **9.36** n 2 above). It may be argued that the obligation for all CREST members to appoint a settlement bank operates indirectly to exclude bad credit risks from membership, since a settlement bank is unlikely to wish to provide settlement bank services to a person who is not a good credit risk. In any case 'EUI does not owe the Member any duty in relation to the admission of any person as a system-member …' (CREST Terms and Conditions, Section 5.2.1) and similarly EUI states in Section 6.1.7 of Part 2 of the CREST Personal Member Terms & Conditions: 'we do not owe you any duty in relation to the admission of any person as a system-member …'

6 In such circumstances the Bank of England is protected from liability by provision in reg 3 of the Stock Transfer (Gilt-edged Securities) (CGO Service) Regulations 1985 (SI 1985/1144), as amended, that a CGO credit is not a representation that the member has title to the securities. Note that when CRESTCo Ltd took over operation of the CGO in 1999, references to the CGO became in effect references to CREST – see Stock Transfer (Gilt-edged Securities) (CGO Service) (Amendment) Regulations 1999 (SI 1999/1208).

7 Originally the Bank of England, but since December 2004 Computershare Investor Services plc.

8 Government Stock Regulations 2004 (SI 2004/1611), reg 16.

9.51 Where custody client A purchases securities, it may expect to be able to sell them immediately they are credited to the custodian's CREST account. If electronic transfer of title does not apply, such sale may occur in advance of registration. The risk is therefore present that if the first transfer fails after A has on-sold the securities, a shortfall will arise[1]. If the account also contains the securities of clients B, C and D, these clients bear A's shortfall (in effect, the custodian has lent the securities of B, C and D to A). In order to avoid breach of duty to its clients, the custodian should disclose these risks to B, C and D[2]. It should also consider collateralising the exposure to A.

1 A potential source of bad deliveries is indicated by the note to CREST Rule 7, Section 2.4 which states that securities admitted to CREST must be freely transferable, but includes a note stating that in exceptional circumstances 'a security may be permitted to be transferred through the CREST system where the security is transferable in limited circumstances', but 'In such cases EUI does not supervise compliance with the limitations'. As a result, non-compliant transfers (possibly subject to reversal by court order or even ineffective under the articles of the issuer) may be permitted. The CREST Terms and Conditions seek to limit risk by requiring the member to warrant, represent and undertake that it will not bring into CREST any securities if it is aware of any defect in its title (Section 9.1.2; and the equivalent section of the CREST Personal Member Terms & Conditions, Part 1, is Condition 2.2.5). If the member becomes aware of a stop notice or court order, or if other circumstances occur that might affect the member's ability to transfer securities through CREST, it is required immediately to notify CREST under the CREST Terms and Conditions. There will be a shortfall if A's account does not contain additional securities sufficient to absorb the debit.

2 In practice, the custodian would look to A immediately to eliminate the shortfall and, if A failed to do so, would buy securities in the market to make good the account, looking to A to repay the purchase price, but an issue arises if A is insolvent and therefore cannot make good the shortfall. It should be noted that the FSA rules applicable to all custodians prior to 1 November 2007 tried to draw attention to this type of problem arising in relation to the pooled assets, by requiring custodians to notify clients if assets were held on a pooled basis, and to explain to retail clients what this means. However, somewhat oddly, the relevant FSA rules implementing MiFID (Directive 2004/39/EC) which rules took effect on 1 November 2007 (and which from 1 January 2009 apply to custody in a non-MiFID context as well as a MiFID context), do not require any notification of pooling to professional clients. See further Chapter 7, para **7.46–7.48**.

9.52 Custodians face further risk (in relation to bad stock held for their clients) under the CREST Terms and Conditions, which provide[1] in effect that CREST may take action to seek to avert a bad delivery at the risk of the member and with the benefit of an indemnity from the member.

1 CREST Terms and Conditions, Section 14.2.

9.53 CREST members do have the benefit of the fact that the CREST system is a designated system in the UK and in Ireland for the purposes of the Settlement Finality Directive[1]. It should be noted that because technically securities are settled in the CREST system pursuant to the legislation in certain different jurisdictions (see para **9.2** above), the detailed provisions regarding designation of the CREST system, as reflected in Chapter 13 of the CREST Rules, designate for the purposes of the Directive particular aspects of the CREST system known as the 'CREST UK system'[2] and the 'CREST Irish system'[3].

1   Directive 98/26/EC. Implemented in the UK in 1999 by the Financial Markets and Insolvency (Settlement Finality) Regulations 1999 (SI 1999/2979), as amended, and in Ireland by equivalent legislation.
2   Broadly, the aspects of the CREST system applicable to transfer orders for any securities unless such orders are securities are subject to the laws of a jurisdiction which is not an EU member state.
3   Broadly, the aspects of the CREST system applicable to settlement of Irish securities and related payments.

9.54   As a result, conflict with various insolvency rules will not invalidate a CREST transfer order, CREST default arrangements or 'a contract for the purpose of realising collateral security in connection with participation in' CREST[1] (this will assist settlement banks taking charges over assets of CREST members). For the purposes of the application of these Regulations, 'collateral security' includes, broadly, any assets (including money) provided under a charge, repo or otherwise in order to secure rights arising in connection with the designated system, and 'transfer order' means, very broadly, an instruction by a system participant to pay or transfer securities to another person[2]. Although this suggests that irrevocable settlement instructions in CREST will proceed to settlement despite the insolvency of one of the parties to the transaction to be settled, the position is not straightforward (and even if this were the case, there remains the practical problem for counterparties to a CREST member where such member's CREST accounts are frozen due to the member's insolvency, see para **9.83** below).

1   See Regulation 14(1) of the Financial Markets and Insolvency (Settlement Finality) Regulations 1999 (SI 1999/2979), as amended.
2   Chapter 13 of the CREST Rules sets out in detail what constitutes a 'transfer order' for the purposes of the CREST system, the point at which such order enters the CREST system, and the time at which the order becomes irrevocable. Chapter 13 also contains the CREST default arrangements.

9.55   Under CREST Rules 13, a transfer order is irrevocable 'from the time at which the order of the relevant transaction type is or becomes incapable of being amended or deleted in accordance with the procedures of the CREST UK and Irish system for the time being (which are explained in the CREST Manual) by the single input of an instruction from the participant who wishes to amend or delete the order.'[1] Moreover, 'A participant or any third party (including without limitation any liquidator or other insolvency office-holder of a participant or a receiver other than an administrative receiver) shall not revoke, or purport or attempt to revoke, any transfer order from the time at which it becomes irrevocable'[2]. This suggests that once a transfer order is irrevocable, the CREST system will process settlement of the relevant payment or transfer of securities, regardless of the insolvency of one of the CREST members which is party to such transfer. However, as indicated by the note following Rule 13, section 6 (and as demonstrated following commencement of the administration in relation to Lehman Brothers International (Europe)[3], in practice CREST is likely to immediately block any transfers to or from the CREST accounts of the insolvent entity, and instruct the insolvency official acting for the insolvent entity and the counterparties to transfers awaiting settlement to delete the unsettled transfer orders by matching instructions.

1   CREST Rule 13, Section 3
2   CREST Rule 13, Section 4.
3   See in particular EUI operational bulletin No. 1510, dated 8 October 2008.

9.56 As a result, the position is that, pursuant to the application of the Settlement Finality Regulations, transfer orders which have settled prior to the account freeze imposed by CREST will not be unwound, but transfer orders which have not proceeded to settlement will not be settled and will in due course be required to be cancelled (unless EUI is satisfied that relevant conditions are satisfied for the re-enabling of the frozen CREST accounts, for example, if EUI is satisfied that 'systemic or other types of risk that arise by reason of the participation of the defaulting participant in the CREST UK system or the CREST Irish system would be limited or otherwise mitigated by re-enabling its participation' and 'such re-enablement, and any settlement which may be effected as a result of such re-enablement, will not cause EUI to be in breach of any direction or requirement of any regulatory authority or body to whose jurisdiction it is subject' and 'such re-enablement, and any settlement which may be effected as a result of such re-enablement, will be consistent with the effect and operation of the default rules (within the meaning of Part VII of the Companies Act 1989) of any relevant exchange or clearing house'[1].

1 CREST Rule 13, paragraph 2 of Notes following Section 6.

FRAUDULENT TRANSFERS

9.57 The dematerialisation of forged securities should not give rise to bad deliveries because securities are not credited to CREST accounts until registered in the name of the CREST transferee[1]. In the case of UK Securities, following the delivery of a dematerialisation notice, the issuer is required to delete the relevant entry from the issuer register of securities and CREST will subsequently enter the name of the relevant system-member on the relevant CREST account which constitutes the register of title for this purpose.

1 See para **9.50** above in relation to absence of bad deliveries for UK Securities.

9.58 While the circumstances in which the CREST Regulations permit issuers to omit to register CREST transfers include (very broadly) notice of fraud against a participant or a sponsored member, and in the case of UK Securities CREST may refuse to register for similar reasons[1], the relevant circumstances do not include notice of fraud against an indirect beneficial owner of CREST securities. There is no protection for frauds outside the system. The difficulty with this is that the system reduces the issuer's ability to respond to such fraud. Even if an issuer's registrar had actual notice of such a fraud against a custody client, it would apparently have to register the fraudulent transfer and, in the case of UK Securities, would have no opportunity to notify EUI not to register the transfer (subject to the possibility of obtaining a court order)[2]. Clients may therefore be particularly exposed to custodian fraud in such circumstances[3]. Equally, custodians bear the risk of fraudulent transfers affecting their client securities[4].

1 CREST Regulations 27(4)(d) and 35(5)(a)(i)–(iii).

2 While issuers could in effect escape liability for complying with their registration requirements in respect of instructions affected by fraud against the operator, a participant or a sponsored member under Regulation 35(4) and (8) of the CREST Regulations, this does not apply to UK Securities but only to securities where the CREST account does not constitute the record of title. Even in relation to non-UK Securities, the limitation of liability does not extend to circumstances where indirect beneficial owners are defrauded, and for UK Securities there is still the question of what liabilities may apply to the issuer in respect of the actions of CREST (see paras **9.137–9.140** below).

   This may leave issuers exposed to claims from defrauded custody clients, where the issuer or CREST knowingly registered a fraudulent transfer because it was required to do so under the Regulations. (In practice it is perhaps unlikely that CREST could be shown to have registered such a transfer with knowledge of the relevant fraud.)

   Where an issuer has actual notice of such a fraud, it may decide to seek a court order against itself or CREST forbidding registration; CREST is required to refuse to register where prohibited by a court order under CREST Regulation 27(2)(a).

UK settlement systems

Rectification of registers in relation to uncertificated securities are only permitted pursuant to a court order or with the consent of EUI. CREST Rule 11, Section 4 indicates that consent will not be given where, after consultation, any affected CREST member objects to the proposed rectification. This consultation process can take five business days in accordance with CREST Rule 11, Section 6.

CREST Regulation 36 imposes certain compensation obligations on the operator of CREST for losses in certain circumstances, but these are limited to £50,000 for 'each such forged dematerialised instruction, induced amendment to an Operator register of securities, or induced Operator-instruction' (CREST Regulation 36(6)) and do not affect the liability of any other person for losses associated with CREST (CREST Regulation 36(8)).

3   Where they become aware of such a fraud, their only option may be to seek a court order to prevent registration; this may be difficult if little time is available. Unless compelled by a court order, no assistance may be available from CREST, as it is not bound by notice of any trusts and therefore need not recognise the rights of custody clients: CREST Regulation 40(3).

4   Section 9.1.1 of the CREST Terms and Conditions requires the CREST member to represent (broadly) that any form of transfer presented by it bringing stock into and out of CREST will be validly executed. Where such transfers are executed by clients or third parties, the custodian may not be in a position to confirm this.

UNSCRAMBLING BAD DELIVERIES

9.59 CREST Rule 12 makes provision for the unscrambling of bad deliveries[1]. Depending on the circumstances, bad deliveries will be (a) reversed, (b) replaced or (c) addressed by tracing, which may be summarised as follows.

(a) Reversals: broadly speaking, where sufficient securities remain in the account of the transferee, CREST will reverse the bad delivery at the price for which it was made[2]. Reversals raise the following exposures in relation to the return of the purchase price. Reversal is dependent on the availability of sufficient 'headroom' in the cash memorandum account of the original transferor, which is placed under an absolute obligation to increase this if necessary[3]. This raises concerns for the custodian. If transfers through CREST from the custodian's clients fail, the custodian may be absolutely required to obtain additional credit and therefore unable to resist commercially unreasonable terms from its settlement bank. Even where the custodian acts as its own settlement bank, the CREST Rules may require it to return the purchase price even if its clients have spent it, exposing it to their credit. If transfers through CREST to the custodian's clients fail, the custodian's ability to recover the purchase price for its clients will depend on the debit caps of the transferor[4].

In cases where the original purchase price cannot be determined[5] EUI seeks to unscramble the securities side of the transaction without assisting the transferee in getting its money back[6]. This may expose the custodian to other CREST members, unless this credit risk can be transferred to the custodian's clients by provision in the custody agreement.

(b) Replacement: in cases where insufficient securities remain in the transferee's account to reverse the book entry, 'The Original Transferor shall procure the free delivery (if necessary from a third party) to the Original Transferee of the relevant amount of registrable securities within two hours of being notified by EUI of the bad delivery'[7]. Custodians may need to consider their operational ability to comply with the strict time limits, and may wish to take express indemnities from their clients in respect of this exposure.

(c) Tracing: the above techniques depend in some measure on participant cooperation and therefore may fail to resolve the bad delivery[8]. In these cases, tracing may be necessary for the following reasons. Where A transfers securities to B through CREST, B may also transfer those securities to C before the first transfer is registered (this will not arise where electronic transfer of title applies) or rejected by the registrar and hence the potential arises for the 'domino effect', considered in CREST Rule 12, Section 2.2.2[9]. CREST securities are fungible[10] and there is therefore a need for rules for allocating bad deliveries across accounts, akin to the equitable tracing rules. CREST Rule 12, Section 7 specifies a tracing methodology[11].

1   Bad deliveries are CREST transfers that do not proceed to registration: see discussion at paras **9.50–9.56** above.
2   CREST Rule 12, Section 1.3.2.
3   CREST Rule 12, Section 8.3.1.
4   Custodians should consider expressly disclosing this risk to clients.
5   The original price would only be undeterminable in rare cases involving 'complex deliveries', for example, corporate actions involving the transfer of more than one parcel of stock against a cash payment. In such cases, it may not be possible to determine how much of the cash was attributable to a particular parcel of stock.
6   CREST Rule 12, Sections 4 and 6.
7   CREST Rule 12, Section 5.3 (and similar wording in Section 6.4).
8   For example, CREST Rule 12, Sections 5.3 and 6.4 contractually require the original bad transferor to provide replacement stock. As the major source of bad deliveries may be transferor insolvency, new securities may not be available to satisfy these Rules at the time they are needed.
9   See also CREST Rule 12, Sections 5.2 and 6.2.
10 CREST Rule 7, Section 2.7: 'All units of the security must be in all respects identical ...' and Section 2.8: 'The units of the security must not be numbered or otherwise identifiable individually'.
11 Based on transaction order and size. It represents a departure from normal equitable tracing rules under English law.

9.60   A member who was not the source of the bad stock may be required to make good the shortfall, if the burden is allocated to it. While this measure of systemic risk may be inevitable in any clearing system, custodians may wish to ensure that it is borne, not by them, but by their clients, through adequate disclosure in the custody agreement[1].

1   CREST Rule 12, Sections 5.4 and 6.5 require EUI, if new securities are not forthcoming from the original bad transferor within two hours, to notify 'the members affected' of the bad delivery and provide relevant information 'so as to enable them to make such applications (whether to the court or otherwise) as they think fit'.

Custody agreements

9.61   Should custodians offering services through CREST include specific drafting in their custody agreements? In the old CGO membership agreement, a CGO participant holding assets on behalf of another was required to obtain from its client an acknowledgment and authority in a prescribed form[1]. Because of the operational difficulty in obtaining the positive consent of existing clients to new terms, custodians usually prefer to minimise the introduction of new provisions for existing customers[2]. It may be possible effectively to bind existing customers with new provisions concerning CREST by unilateral notice in cases where the notice of new provisions is given to the client before the custodian begins providing services in CREST[3].

1   See paras **9.141–9.142** below.
2   The original draft CREST Membership Agreement (July 1995) prescribed specific wording which custodian members were to be required to include in their custody agreements (adopting the approach of the CGO). Custodian institutions resisted this obligation and wished to be able to confine

themselves to writing to clients in relation to CREST without obtaining client responses. Also, in general custodians prefer to rely on clients' consent in generic terms in existing documentation to the custodian using clearing systems on the terms of those systems. However, there are risks with this approach for the reasons discussed below. (It is interesting to note that following the merger of the CGO into CREST, some custodians required clients to sign up to a new copy of the wording formerly required for CGO purposes but this time referring to *all* securities transferred through CREST, rather than only the instruments formerly held through the CGO, even though technically such wording was no longer required.)

3   On the basis that services provided through CREST are a new addition not envisaged in existing documentation, and that the client, by permitting the custodian to use CREST on the disclosed basis, has accepted the new terms by conduct. However, the efficacy of this approach must be considered on a case-by-case basis.

9.62   In any case, specific additional drafting is recommended for custodians for a number of reasons. First, the custodian owes duties of confidentiality to its clients both as banker and as fiduciary. General law relieves these duties of confidentiality where there is a legal duty of disclosure. However, many of the disclosure provisions in the CREST agreements binding the custodian as CREST member are wider than this. Therefore, in order for the custodian not to be in breach of its duties of confidentiality to its clients, its disclosure obligations under the CREST agreements should be drawn to clients' attention, and their consent obtained in the custody agreement.

9.63   Since participation in CREST presents certain specific issues (as discussed in this section), the cautious approach, in order to protect the custodian from liability for client losses attributable to particular risks associated with CREST, would be to disclose to clients, and obtain their consent to, such risks. While the CREST Regulations relieve trustee participants from liability associated with the absence of DVP within CREST[1], other CREST risks may involve the custodian in liability to clients who suffer loss in consequence of such risks. A custodian's ability to recover any damages from EUI is extremely limited by the relevant provisions of the CREST Terms and Conditions[2]. Special provision in the custody agreement would be appropriate to protect the custodian from liability to its clients in connection with the use of CREST.

1   For non-UK Securities and US dollar assured payment: CREST Regulation 40.
2   See, for example, CREST Terms and Conditions Sections 5.1.2, 5.2.1–5.2.6, 6.6, 7.5, 8.1, 8.2, 11.1, 12.2, 12.3, 13.3, 14.2, and 16.5. As indicated above, CREST Regulation 36 provides for compensation orders to be made against EUI in relation to (broadly) fraudulent CREST instructions, but limitations on the quantum of compensation (GBP50,000 maximum) and the circumstances in which it is available reduce the value of this provision.

9.64   In addition, specific drafting is arguably necessary in order to discharge a custodian's contractual obligations to EUI. The CREST Terms and Conditions require[1] the custodian member (broadly) to obtain the consent of clients to aspects of CREST that may affect the clients[2]. The best way of complying with this requirement is to give clients express disclosure of relevant risks and to obtain a signed acknowledgment and consent to such risks. In addition, the CREST Terms and Conditions oblige the custodian 'so far as it is able' to prevent clients making adverse claims against transferred securities so as to prevent registration[3]. It is not clear how this can be achieved otherwise than by express contractual provision binding clients.

1   CREST Terms and Conditions, Section 5.2.6.
2   Enforcing the commercial argument that such provision is necessary to protect the custodian.
3   CREST Terms and Conditions, Section 10.1.2. Since this may be clients' only effective recourse in the case of fraud, it may be hard to obtain their consent to such provision in the custody documentation. The custodian's obligation to CREST is not limited by reasonableness, and (where custody clients have suffered fraud) may cut across the custodian's commercial relationship with its clients.

9.65 As all members (including custodians) are obliged to indemnify EUI in respect of (broadly) the member's CREST business[1], a corresponding indemnity to the custodian from the client would be advisable. Such an indemnity would ideally also expressly cover the liability of the custodian member to make good any shortfalls in CREST accounts[2] and the potential liability of the custodian associated with its warranty that all CREST transfers it settles can take place free of third party claims[3]. In addition, it would be advisable for custodians to consider whether their collateral arrangements are sufficient in view of the personal liabilities they may bear as CREST members. Where custodians access CREST through nominees (ie the nominee rather than the custodian is the CREST member), care should be taken to ensure that any indemnities and collateral arrangements provided to the custodian also cover liabilities of the nominee.

1   CREST Terms and Conditions, Section 17.11.
2   CREST Terms and Conditions, Section 11.1.2.
3   CREST Terms and Conditions, Section 10.1.1.

Cross-border issues

9.66 As discussed in Chapter 5, it is a general rule of private international law that formalities necessary for the transfer of assets are determined by the law of the place where the assets are situated (lex situs). Lex situs of registered securities is generally the law of the jurisdiction in which the principal register is located[1]. Because a UK statutory instrument cannot alter foreign law, the CREST Regulations cannot dematerialise foreign securities.

1   See Chapter 5.

9.67 One method of bringing foreign securities into CREST is to have local legislation achieving the same result as the CREST Regulations, as discussed below. A pragmatic alternative is to turn foreign securities into UK securities, by repackaging them under depositary receipt programmes. Special provisions relating to the admission of depositary receipts into CREST ('Depository Interests') are set out in CREST Rule 9, requiring inter alia the issuance of the Depository Interests under the laws of (and the maintenance of the register of title in) England and Wales, Northern Ireland, Scotland, Ireland, the Isle of Man or Jersey, as appropriate. (Note not Guernsey: see explanation of the special position regarding Guernsey at para **9.2** n 2 above.) Other repackaging arrangements include the CREST CDI structure described at paras **9.69–9.74** below, and structures such as exchange-traded funds ('ETFs').

9.68 The taxation of depositary receipts in CREST is an important issue[1].

1   See Chapter 10.

International securities[1]

9.69 As explained in para **9.2** above, the only securities which are eligible for transfer through CREST are registered securities constituted under the laws of England and Wales, Scotland or Northern Ireland, the Republic of Ireland, the Isle of Man, Jersey or Guernsey[2]. This is because relevant legislation has been enacted in each case[3]. Securities created under other legal systems can only be transferred through CREST if repackaged as securities constituted under appropriate law[4], or if held through CREST by use of the links between CREST and other settlement systems[5].

1   For further details see the CREST publication 'Euroclear UK & Ireland international service description', July 2012; and the CREST International Manual.
2   See para **9.2** n 2 above for the relevant legislation in each such jurisdiction.
3   Except for Guernsey. See para **9.2** n 2 above.
4   For example, an English law depositary receipt established in accordance with the Uncertificated Securities Regulations 2001 (SI 2001/3755) and the CREST Manual, in particular see CREST Rules 7 and 9.
5   At the time of writing such links exist with the following central securities depositories: SIX SIS AG ('SIS') in Switzerland, the Depository Trust and Clearing Corporation in the US, and Euroclear Bank SA/NV in Belgium. These arrangements allow CREST members to hold and settle securities issued under the laws of the following countries (although in certain cases only in restricted circumstances): Australia, Austria, Belgium, Bermuda, British Virgin Islands, Canada, Cayman Islands, Denmark, Finland, France, Germany, Greece, Italy, Luxembourg, the Netherlands, Norway, Portugal, Spain, Sweden, Switzerland and the US, as well as any securities held through the Euroclear international settlement system, and Clearstream Banking, Luxembourg. Many of these jurisdictions are available as a result of the sub-custodian network of SIS. See the CREST International Manual, and he CREST publication 'Euroclear UK & Ireland international service description', July 2012.

9.70 Securities which would not otherwise be eligible for transfer through CREST may be held by a CREST member through CREST if the relevant securities can be held in a settlement system with which CREST has a link. The precise details of settlement through links with other systems (including the types of securities which can be transferred via the link, and whether transfers can only occur free of payment) will depend on the nature of the relevant linked system and the way the link has been set up. Broadly speaking, the arrangements for the acquisition of an international security by a CREST member from a counterparty who is not a CREST member operate as follows[1].

1   Further details can be found on the CREST website (www.euroclear.com, Euroclear UK & Ireland section): see in particular the CREST International Manual and the CREST publication 'Euroclear UK & Ireland international service description', July 2012.

9.71 The international securities are transferred into the account of the relevant nominee entity[1] (or its delegate) in the other settlement system, and the nominee holds its rights to such securities on behalf of CREST Depository Limited under an English law trust. CREST Depository Limited issues dematerialised depository interests ('CDIs') representing its beneficial interest in the underlying securities held by the nominee, and holds such beneficial interest and associated rights against the nominee on trust for the registered holders of the CDIs pursuant to an English law trust established by the Deed Poll. The CDIs are securities constituted by the Deed Poll governed by English law and are eligible for holding and transfer in CREST. The relevant CREST member's holding of CDIs is recorded in such CREST member's CREST account, which constitutes the register of title for such CDIs.

1   CREST International Nominees Limited (this entity and CREST Depository Limited are wholly owned subsidiaries of EUI).

9.72 In each such case, the relevant nominee (or its delegate) will hold assets in the settlement system subject to such system's terms of participation, and where the nominee is using a delegate, the nominee will be subject to the relevant terms on which the delegate holds the assets for the nominee.

9.73 Generally, CDIs are only issued in uncertificated form, are not treated as different from the underlying securities for the purposes of listing and have the same ISIN (as well as size and price) as the underlying securities.

9.74 Where participants in a relevant linked settlement system wish to hold CREST-eligible securities, such securities can be transferred from the relevant transferring CREST member into the CREST account of the settlement system, and such system will then hold those securities for the participant in such system subject to its usual terms.

Collateral and securities lending

9.75 An important use of CREST eligible securities (shares or other securities, including public sector securities such as gilts) is to serve as collateral, whether for securities lending or for other exposures. The involvement of custodians in collateral arrangements is discussed in Chapter 4.

9.76 CREST securities may serve as collateral in a variety of ways, both under arrangements within and outside the CREST system. However, in all cases it is important to appreciate that CREST does not create security interests (or outright collateral transfers); it merely facilitates delivery for the purposes of creation of security interests (although certain functions are designed particularly to help create security interests, such as arrangements for escrow balances, securities lending and repos, and DBVs, as discussed below). Any security interest in (or outright collateral transfer of) CREST securities must be created by documentation between the parties (although in some circumstances may arise by operation of law).

Security interests

9.77 As discussed in Chapter 4, a wide range of security interests are available under English law, varying in the degrees of formality involved and the robustness of the protection given to the security holder.

LEGAL MORTGAGES (CREST TRANSFERS)

9.78 Under a legal mortgage, legal title to assets is transferred by way of security, with the mortgagor retaining only the equity of redemption (ie the right to have the assets back free from the security interest upon the discharge of the secured obligations). Mortgagors are of course subject to the fraud risk of mortgagees who improperly dispose of the mortgaged securities, whether the transfer of title occurs within CREST or outside it.

9.79 SDRT does not arise in respect of a legal mortgage effected by a delivery through CREST, but fixed rate stamp duty of £5 will be payable in connection with the procedure required. Various information is available through the CREST website (see eg the CREST publication 'UK Stamp Duty Reserve Tax: reliefs for principal traders' (August 2011)), but in particular 'HMRC have explained that a "transfer by way of security for a loan" can be executed through the CREST system using flag 5 provided the transfer is accompanied by a letter of direction which is duly stamped with £5 fixed duty. CREST transaction flag 5 applies to this and certain other transfers on which stamp duty at a fixed rate would apply to transfers in materialised form' (CREST Reference Manual, Chapter 8, Section 2, penultimate paragraph of 'Data flags' sub-section). (See further discussion at Chapter 10.)

EQUITABLE MORTGAGE (ESCROW BALANCE)

9.80 Prior to CREST, much of the security that was given over English equities was by way of an equitable charge, which arose upon the deposit with the chargee of share certificates and signed but undated transfer forms. With dematerialisation in CREST, this is not possible, and a need arises for the functional equivalent of an equitable mortgage of shares, ie a rapid and informal method of using shares as security which does not involve re-registering them.

9.81 This is offered by the escrow balance, an arrangement which involves blocking securities in a sub-account of the collateral giver's account, where they are subject to the control of the collateral taker[1]. The movement of securities to an escrow balance does not transfer legal title to the collateral taker and therefore does not appear on the register of the issuer[2]. As with an equitable charge outside CREST where a collateral taker is given control over the charged assets, the collateral giver is exposed to the risk that collateral taker will dispose of the collateral before it is entitled to do so under the terms of the relevant charge (the CREST system will not monitor or prevent this).

1   See CREST Reference Manual, Chapter 7, Section 3. CREST refers to the mortgagee as an 'escrow agent'. (Note that escrow accounts are also used for other functions, such as processing corporate actions.)
2   Some care should be taken in the relevant charge documentation to cover appropriately corporate action events or similar issues affecting the securities in the escrow balance, since, for example, a transformation of the securities in the escrow balance (other than under the CREST automatic transformation process) will result in credit of the new securities to the available balance not the escrow balance, and if for some reason the securities are recertificated, the certificates will be sent to the relevant CREST member not to the escrow agent.

9.82 The crucial question is whether the interest of the security taker over securities in the escrow balance is enforceable following the insolvency of the security giver. Broadly speaking, it will be enforceable if the interest is proprietary, and will not be enforceable if it is merely contractual[1]. Placing of securities in the escrow balance of itself probably does not confer a property interest in the escrow agent[2]. It is therefore important to document any security interest using the escrow balance carefully, to ensure that a proprietary security interest is conferred.

1   Because of the restriction in Insolvency Act 1986, s 127, on dispositions of a company's property after the commencement of winding up.
2   The escrow balance is also used for corporate actions, in which case no property is conferred.

9.83 A further issue arises in the insolvency of the CREST member granting security over its assets. In such case, there will normally be an automatic freezing of CREST accounts imposed by EUI, in which case the chargee will be unable to exercise its control over the escrow balance until the relevant liquidator has been appointed and taken control of the insolvent entity's CREST accounts. This could present significant problems for a chargee who needs to enforce quickly[1].

1   This is less of an issue for settlement banks taking security, as the CREST Reference Manual provides for special procedures: CREST Reference Manual, Chapter 6, Section 7.

9.84 The CREST Terms and Conditions[1] place responsibility on the CREST member for the suitability and adequate use of the escrow balance. For a custodian, this may mean ensuring that no client fails to take effective security through the escrow balance, which would be a very wide responsibility, in view of the possibility that the collateral agent's interest may be merely contractual.

1   Condition 12.

9.85 An obvious limitation of the escrow balance is that CREST securities can only be encumbered in this way in favour of CREST participants. If the relevant collateral taker is not a CREST member, it would need to appoint a person who is a CREST member to act as its security agent, holding the control rights in respect of the collateral on behalf of the collateral taker.

CHARGES

9.86 CREST members (and their clients) are free to charge their interests in their CREST member accounts in the ordinary way (subject to any negative pledge given to a settlement bank to support a settlement bank charge). If charged securities remain in the chargor's account, a floating charge may be created, although it should be noted that floating charges created by UK corporates are registrable[1].

1 Under Companies Act 2006, s 860, unless within the scope of the Financial Collateral Arrangements (No 2) Regulations 2003, as amended (SI 2003/3226) ('Financial Collateral Regulations') (see Chapter 4, para **4.85**). And see also discussion of further developments regarding the registration requirements in the UK (Chapter 4, paras **4.50–4.54**).

PLEDGES

9.87 A pledge involves the transfer of possession of a tangible asset, and therefore cannot be given in respect of shares, which are intangible. Although share certificates are capable of pledge, the pledge is irrelevant for dematerialised securities.

Securities lending and repos

9.88 Provisions[1] are available in CREST to facilitate the use of dematerialised securities in securities lending or repo transactions as loaned securities or securities collateral, and mark to market revaluations[2]. It should be noted that although the CREST system facilitates the settlement of bilateral securities lending (or repo) arrangements entered into by CREST members outside CREST, EUI is not a party to, or involved in arranging or monitoring, securities lending arrangements between CREST members.

1 See CREST White Paper Securities lending and collateral transfers in CREST, December 2004.
2 'While EUI believes that the functionality has been designed to be consistent with the principles of the Global Master Securities Lending Agreement (2010) (and its precursors), the CREST system does not monitor or enforce compliance with the terms of that or any other agreement or with any other applicable regulatory or other requirement ... Stock lending functionality may also be used in the context of a sale and repurchase agreement ("repo") executed, ordinarily, pursuant to the terms of the TBMA/ISMA Global Master Repurchase Agreement, although there are transaction types and related functionality specifically available to support settlement under repo agreements ... As with stock loans, EUI does not monitor compliance with the terms of this agreement.' (CREST Reference Manual, Chapter 7, Section 1: note that Chapter 7 uses the terms 'stock loan' to refer to both repos and securities lending transactions.)

CASH COLLATERAL

9.89 Where securities are transferred within CREST by way of a stock loan, and the transfer is made against payment within CREST, the payment obligation constitutes the cash collateral.

9.90 Where CREST transfers are identified as stock loans, special facilities are available to handle automatic redeliveries[1] and the margining of cash collateral[2].

1 While there is no need for the lender to give instructions for the return, the automatic return instruction is given zero priority so that the borrower will need to intervene to lift the priority to permit settlement. (See CREST Reference Manual, Chapter 7, Section 1, Stock loan returns.)
2 CREST Reference Manual, Chapter 7, Section 1, Stock loan revaluations. In CREST these margin adjustments are automatically made through the payments system.

SECURITIES COLLATERAL: DELIVERY BY VALUE ('DBV')

9.91 Where CREST securities are to be delivered as collateral[1], automatic collateral selection is available by using the delivery by value ('DBV') facility.

A member may instruct CREST to transfer securities from its account by way of collateral to another member's account. The aggregate value of the collateral to be delivered is specified, but not the individual securities, and the CREST system selects the securities to be delivered[2]. Where CREST securities are provided by a DBV, the securities are registered in the name of the collateral taker[3].

1   In practice, a sequential combination of cash and securities collateral may be used, as follows. Following a request from a borrower for securities, a broker may obtain the securities from a lending institution. The securities will be transferred from the account of the lender to that of the broker, and then on into the account of the borrower. In respect of each of these transfers, the payment obligation of the transferee will serve as cash collateral. During the currency of the loan, the borrower may wish to use the cash that has been provided by way of collateral to the broker. The brokers may be willing to release this money against the provision of further collateral. Outside CREST, this further collateral may be provided in the form of Stock Exchange short-term certificates or other securities. Within CREST, it may be provided by DBV (the assured payment for the DBV constituting the return of the cash). DBV is only provided once daily towards the end of the settlement process. Intraday, borrowers may rely on cash collateral. Towards the end of the day, the borrower can recover the cash by substituting securities through DBV.

2   Although the parties must specify the DBV Class (the category of securities to be included in the DBV, eg FTSE 100, FTSE 250, all British Government Securities, Eurotop 300, US Securities, etc), and each DBV will exclusively relate to one category; also, DBVs may optionally be subject to a 10 per cent concentration restriction and DBV takers may exclude certain securities which they are prevented from holding. See the CREST Reference Manual, Chapter 7, Section 2.

3   This was not the case in the CGO but was introduced with the original two-hour registration time frame in CREST (as opposed to the old three-day cycle in the CGO). Moreover, whereas transfer of title in CGO was based on contract, the basis of transfer of title in CREST is statutory (CREST Regulation 24) and (unlike in the old CGO) linked to registration.

   The collateral taker is exempt from the requirements of the FSA's Disclosure Rules and Transparency Rules sourcebook ('DTRs'), Chapter 5, relating to the disclosure of voting rights held as shareholder, provided that the collateral taker 'does not declare any intention of exercising (and does not exercise) the voting rights attaching to such shares' (DTR 5.1.3R(5)). The DTRs also contain appropriate disclosure exemptions for lenders and borrower in stock loan transactions (see DTR 5.1.1R(5) and 5.1.3R(6)).

9.92 For an overnight DBV, securities are only delivered as collateral at the end of the day and are automatically 'redelivered'[1] on the next business day[2]. New DBV collateral must be put up by the borrower daily; the amount of daily DBV collateral will need to be adjusted to reflect the margining requirements of the securities lending arrangement. In contrast, a term DBV may have a maturity of up to two years. It should be noted that the CREST system does not link a DBV which is used to provide collateral to the relevant stock loan which it collateralises. The parties will therefore need to monitor and control such arrangements themselves.

1   Strictly, the 'redelivery' is not of the same securities but of equivalent securities; DBV securities are delivered outright and not by way of security.

2   Unless countermanding instructions are given by the collateral taker wishing to enforce the collateral.

9.93 It may be operationally convenient to have a separate DBV account, although this is not necessary[1].

1   It might be argued that the placing of DBV securities in a special account exposes the arrangement to the risk of recharacterisation as a charge (which might in turn be void for want of registration) as opposed to an outright transfer. However, provided there is no obligation on the DBV recipient to use a special account, and no restriction on its freedom to take the securities out of that account or to block their 'redelivery', this should not be a problem, as it does not imply any retained property in the DBV securities by their provider by way of a charge.

Corporate actions[1]

9.94 CREST may be used to execute corporate actions[2]. Whether or not to use this CREST functionality is the choice of the relevant company and its agent. Where a company does choose to make use of the CREST facilities, EUI requires that the relevant procedures should be followed in order to achieve a standard approach in the CREST system but EUI will not monitor the details of the process, for example, compliance by CREST members with deadlines. Corporate action details provided by the issuers or their agents are held in the CREST system and a range of special transaction types are available for use in corporate actions[3]. However, compliance with the terms of a stock event (eg deadlines for acceptance) is not the responsibility of, and not monitored or enforced by, EUI.

1   See CREST Reference Manual, Chapter 7, Section 4.

2   It was here that Taurus (the system proposed in the early 1990s) came to grief, and it has been argued that the need to handle complex stock events (together with stamp duty) has deterred the continental European clearers from competing for the settlement of UK equities.

3   These are: complex (many to many) deliveries; unmatched stock events; registrar's adjustments; transfers to escrow; transfers from escrow; escrow account adjustment; and dividend/interest payment.

Central sponsor arrangements[1]

9.95 The central sponsor arrangements were launched on 26 February 2001 and originally concerned trades by members of the London Stock Exchange on SETS (the London Stock Exchange electronic order book).

1   This is of course a broad summary only. For further detail see the CREST Central Counterparty Service Manual, and the CREST Reference Manual, Chapter 4, Sections 4, 4A, 4B and 4C.

9.96 CREST provides settlement services for trades on the London Stock Exchange (SETS, SETSqx and SEAQ), SIX Swiss Exchange ('SIX'), and the Irish Stock Exchange (the 'ISE'), in each case in relation to securities which are eligible for the CREST central counterparty services[1].

1   The exchange known as virt-x (formerly Tradepoint) was operated by virt-x Exchange Limited, then became SWX Europe Ltd in 2008, and in April 2009 all business was transferred to SIX.

9.97 Both LCH. Clearnet Limited ('LCH') and SIS x-clear AG ('x-clear') act as a central counterparty clearing trades on SETS, SETSqx, and SIX. Eurex Clearing AG ('ECAG') acts as central counterparty clearing trades on the ISE. Since in the clearing process the central counterparty becomes party to two matching transactions with clearing members, the resulting delivery obligations between the central party and each clearing member will need to be settled through an appropriate settlement mechanism.

9.98 Where settlement takes place through CREST, matching instructions for settlement by transfers through CREST are required in the normal way. The central sponsor mechanism is the process by which the matching instructions to be given by both central counterparty and by clearing member can be given automatically by the relevant CREST central sponsor.

9.99 CRESTCo acts as CREST central sponsor for LCH and x-clear in relation to trades on SETS and SETSqx, therefore will input the appropriate trade data and procure that settlement instructions are given on behalf of LCH or x-clear, as appropriate. In contrast, for trades on SIX which are cleared by LCH, LCH acts as its own CREST central sponsor and itself inputs into CREST the relevant settlement instructions. For trades on SIX which are cleared by x-clear, SIX SIS AG acts as CREST central sponsor therefore will input into CREST settlement instructions on behalf of x-clear. In relation to trades on the ISE which are cleared by ECAG, ECAG acts as its own CREST central sponsor and inputs into CREST its settlement instructions. In each case, under the CREST Rules the relevant central counterparty is automatically deemed to have chosen that settlement of its obligations takes place on a net basis.

9.100 The matching delivery instructions to be given by the relevant clearing member which is a CREST Member (or the CREST Member acting as settlement agent for the clearing member if the clearing member does not itself hold securities in a CREST account) can be input into CREST directly by such person or on its behalf by a CREST central sponsor where such person so elects. The available CREST central sponsors are, respectively: for SETS or SETSqx trades, CRESTCo; for SIX trades cleared through LCH, LCH; for SIX trades cleared through x-clear, SIX SIS AG; and for ISE trades, ECAG.

9.101 If the CREST Member has chosen to use the netting process, matching of delivery instructions is followed by netting of the delivery obligations between the CREST Member and the relevant central counterparty will be netted, and the net delivery instructions are then created and must be matched in CREST.

9.102 Where there are two possible central counterparties providing clearing services for the same exchange, there will be extra steps in the settlement process if the relevant clearing members involved in the trade are members of different clearing systems. If B sells to A on the relevant exchange, A (or the clearing member it uses) may clear through central counterparty X and B (or the clearing member it uses) may clear through central counterparty Y. For the purposes of this example, assume A and B are both clearing members. In such case, the contracts which arise will consist of a contract between B as seller and Y (as central counterparty) as buyer, a contract between Y as seller and X (as central counterparty) as buyer, and a contract between X (as central counterparty) as seller and A as buyer. In this context, because Y is contracting with X where X acts as central counterparty, Y must also be a clearing member of X. Assuming that both B and A have elected to use the relevant CREST central sponsor service, the delivery/receipt instructions on behalf of B and Y as central counterparty will be given by the entity acting as CREST central sponsor for Y, and the delivery/receipt instructions on behalf of Y as a clearing member of X, X as central counterparty and A will be given by the entity acting as CREST central sponsor for X.

9.103 With the new opportunities under MiFID for the creation of MTFs (multilateral trading facilities), CREST is also providing a similar (but more limited) form of clearing support services to entities acting as central counterparties for trades on MTFs which settle in CREST. The particular systems discussed in the CREST Reference Manual (Chapter 4, Section 4B) at present include (in addition to the RepoClear Service operated by LCH) Turquoise[1], BATS Chi-X Europe[2], Nasdaq OMX[3], NYSE Arca Europe, Smartpool and Pipeline[4].

1   Turquoise: operated by Turquoise Global Holdings Limited. European Central Counterparty Limited ('EuroCCP') acts as central counterparty for trades on Turquoise. EuroCCP is also a CREST member therefore receives and delivers securities itself, and Citibank, NA acts as CREST central sponsor for EuroCCP and for any CREST members who act as settlement agent for clearing members of Turquoise and have elected to use Citibank, NA as CREST central sponsor for this purpose.

2   BATS Chi-X Europe (BATS Europe and Chi-X Europe merged in 2011): operated by BATS Trading Limited. European Multilateral Clearing Facility NV ('EMCF'), EuroCCP, LCH and x-clear act as central counterparties for trades on BATS Chi-X Europe. Fortis Bank (Nederland) NV is the entity which as a CREST member receives and delivers securities on behalf of EMCF. Fortis Bank Global Clearing NV acts as CREST central sponsor for Fortis Bank (Nederland) NV and for any CREST members who act as settlement agent for clearing members of BATS Chi-X Europe and have elected to use Fortis Bank Global Clearing NV as CREST central sponsor for this purpose.

3   Nasdaq OMX: operated by Nasdaq OMX Europe Limited. European Multilateral Clearing Facility NV ('EMCF') acts as central counterparty for trades on Nasdaq OMX, Fortis Bank (Nederland) NV is the entity which as a CREST member receives and delivers securities on behalf of EMCF, and Fortis Bank Global Clearing NV acts as CREST central sponsor for Fortis Bank (Nederland) NV and for any CREST members who act as settlement agent for clearing members of Nasdaq OMX and have elected to use Fortis Bank Global Clearing NV as CREST central sponsor for this purpose.

4   NYSE Arca Europe, Smartpool and Pipeline: these are operated, respectively, by Euronext Amsterdam NV, Smartpool Trading Limited and Pipeline Limited. EuroCCP acts as central counterparty for trades on each of these systems, and as a CREST member receives and delivers securities itself. Citibank, NA acts as CREST central sponsor for EuroCCP and for any CREST members who act as settlement agent for clearing members of these systems and have elected to use Citibank, NA as CREST central sponsor for this purpose.

9.104 It should be noted that while CREST facilitates the giving of the settlement instructions by providing the central sponsor service, EUI is not a party to the transactions between the central counterparty and transaction counterparties.

9.105 Initially, the central counterparty settlement service operated on the basis that the trades settled on an 'as dealt' or 'gross' basis, but in due course the option of settlement netting was introduced[1].

1   Optional settlement netting launched 1 July 2002.

Funds

9.106 From September 2009, CREST has provided services for the settlement of transfers of both cash and fund units in UK investment funds[1]. The CREST system does not maintain the register of title for fund units but maintains 'a record of notional balances of units held by members' which are required to be 'be reconciled on a daily basis against the actual legal register'[2]. It is important to note that the notional balances 'do not constitute or evidence any legal or equitable interest in investment fund units.'[3] Transfer instructions through CREST will result in payment by credits and debits in respect of the relevant Cash Memorandum Accounts in the usual way, but the change in the notional balance of fund units does not change ownership of such units. The CREST system will generate an instruction to the relevant registrar for the fund to update the register of legal title, and the registrar is expected to retrieve such information and update the register of title accordingly and confirm to the CREST system. However, the registrar has no obligation to do so.

1   See 'Euroclear UK & Ireland funds settlement', October 2009, and CREST Reference Manual, Chapter 13.
2   CREST Reference Manual, Chapter 13. Section 1.
3   CREST Reference Manual, Chapter 13, Section 1.

Gilts

9.107 The paperless settlement of gilt-edged securities[1] takes place through CREST in essentially the same way as other CREST-eligible securities, removing the need for stock certificates and stock transfer forms necessary to evidence and transfer gilts outside CREST. Outside CREST written instruments are required for the transfer of government stock[2]. Dematerialisation is based on the Stock Transfer (Gilt-Edged Securities) (CGO Service) Regulations 1985[3], as amended (the '1985 Regulations') made under the Stock Transfer Act 1982, as amended, although holding and transfer are subject to the CREST Regulations.

1   Registered securities issued in the UK by certain other entities (such as the European Bank for Reconstruction and Development) can also be settled in CREST (see the Stock Transfer Act 1982 and the Stock Transfer (Specified Securities) Order 1991 (SI 1991/340)).

2   The Government Stock Regulations 2004 (SI 2004/1611) (see in particular reg 15) permit government stock to be transferred either by written instrument according to the Stock Transfer Act 1963, or through a system operated pursuant to the CREST Regulations.

3   SI 1985/1144.

9.108   Gilts are registered debt securities, denominated in sterling, issued by the Debt Management Office ('DMO') on behalf of HM Treasury. Market liquidity is provided by gilt-edged market-makers ('GEMMs') who continuously quote two-way prices for gilts. GEMMs deal with each other electronically on a no-names basis through inter-dealer brokers. For a short discussion of stock lending and repos in the gilts market, see paras **9.112–9.118** below[1].

1   Formerly, dematerialised gilts settled through the CGO, an electronic system established in 1986 as a joint initiative by the Bank of England and the London Stock Exchange, then operated by CRESTCo Ltd in 1999 and finally merged into CREST with effect from 3 July 2000. The Registrar of Government Stock (the Bank of England prior to December 2004, and thereafter Computershare Investor Service plc) continues to maintain the register for all gilts (whether held in paper from or through CREST). See CREST Regulation 21(3).

9.109   Ninety per cent of gilts are held in dematerialised form. CREST's payments systems provides for the payment of the cash consideration for transfers through settlement banks. Dividends are paid outside CREST to registered holders. Although all gilts are eligible for CREST settlement, investors may elect to hold their gilts in certificated form[1] unless, as discussed earlier, pursuant to the CREST Regulations the relevant instruments have been issued in wholly dematerialised form[2].

1   Unless issued on a wholly dematerialised basis, certificated gilts may be dematerialised in CREST, and uncertificated gilts may be recertificated.

2   Gilt strips are wholly dematerialised; it is understood that HM Treasury intends that in due course gilts should all be issued on a wholly dematerialised basis.

Transfer of title

9.110   Transfer of legal title and payments in relation to gilts are handled by the CREST system in the same way as other CREST eligible UK securities. (See paras **9.7–9.10** and **9.16–9.24** above) Although the register of title is now constituted by the relevant CREST account records, the corresponding record of register entries is still maintained by the Registrar of Government Stock[1].

1   CREST Regulation 21(3), and see para **9.108** n1 above.

Stamp duty and SDRT

9.111   Transfers of gilts (within and outside CREST) are exempt from stamp duty and SDRT[1].

1   See further in Chapter 10 for the exemption from stamp duty for transfers of gilts, and the position with respect to SDRT.

Gilt title finance (stock lending and repos)

RESTRICTED AND FREE MARKET

9.112   Until January 1996 the rules of the London Stock Exchange prohibited gilt repos, and restricted gilt stock lending to GEMMs[1] and Stock Exchange Money Brokers ('SEMBs') serving GEMMs[2]. The purpose of permitted borrowing was limited to the filling of a short position.

1   And discount houses for stock up to seven years' maturity.

2   GEMMs incur short positions in the course of their market making. To cover these short positions, they must borrow stock. Until January 1996, they were only permitted to borrow from SEMBs who in turn borrowed stock from Inland Revenue approved institutional lenders. The restrictions meant in effect that only GEMMs could go short in gilts, and that therefore only they could make a market in gilts.

9.113 In January 1994 the Bank of England developed arrangements for supplying liquidity in the banking system through the use of gilt repos between the Bank of England and market counterparties[1].

1   Back-to-back repos between the Bank of England's counterparties and other gilt holders were also permitted.

9.114 On 2 January 1996 an open gilt stock lending and repo market was introduced by changes in the Stock Exchange rules[1]. GEMMs continue to be obliged to quote continuous two-way prices on gilts, but now any market participant is free to engage in stock lending or repos of gilts with any counterparty for any purpose.

1   The ability to borrow gilts ceased to be confined to GEMMs; the permitted purpose of borrowing ceased to be limited to covering a short position and gilt repo transactions were permitted.

STOCK LENDING

9.115 The former restriction of gilt stock lending to GEMMs and SEMBs has now been relaxed, and the role of SEMBs has dropped away[1]. However, GEMMs continue to dominate gilt stock lending.

1   The Stock Exchange Rules no longer refer to this category and the CREST Reference Manual does not. Many participants in gilt stock lending enter into their transactions directly, without using intermediaries.

9.116 The borrowed stock is transferred in each case through CREST. Certain institutional lenders may prefer to hold securities instead of cash for investment and risk management reasons[1]. They therefore often require alternative collateral in the form of DBVs. In addition, GEMMs may have surplus gilts but not surplus cash, preferring to 'borrow back' the cash collateral and substitute gilts through the DBV system. A DBV against payment provides for the return of the cash collateral.

1   In the past, certain institutional lenders faced tax problems with cash collateral, but these are largely historic.

9.117 As noted in para **9.92**, overnight DBVs are automatically returned on the next business day, therefore in such cases it is necessary to 'roll over' or redeliver DBVs on a daily basis during the currency of the loan.

REPOS

9.118 Certain enhancements to the old CGO system were introduced to assist the new repo market. Further information about the gilts market is available on the DMO website[1].

1   See www.dmo.gov.uk.

Eligible debt securities

9.119 Money market instruments issued in dematerialised form (eligible debt securities or 'EDSs') (effectively therefore registered instruments) can be held through CREST[1]. The arrangements for EDSs are slightly different from gilts and registered securities due to differences in the relevant markets. The original UK settlement system for money market instruments (the 'Central Moneymarkets Office' or 'CMO') was designed to facilitate rapid issuance and transfer of short-term bearer negotiable debt instruments, typically traded over the counter for same day settlement and used for short term funding and investment. EDSs typically need to be issued quickly therefore the procedure for introducing new issuances into CREST is different from the application procedure which applies to other types of CREST-eligible securities[2].

1   Before CREST took over this function, the CMO (launched by the Bank of England in 1990) was the depositary and electronic settlement system for sterling bearer money market securities (such as treasury bills, bank bills and certificates of deposit). The CMO held the physical instruments as bailee (transfers of interests in the instruments were in practice transfer of claims against CMO as bailee which passed by attornment). From September 1994, it was possible for instruments to be issued into the CMO in dematerialised form on the basis of documentation intended to replicate contractually the rights existing for physical instruments. In order to merge the CMO system into CREST, all money market instruments needed to become dematerialised, so that they would only be issued and recorded in the CREST system. Money market instruments were gradually migrated into CREST on this basis, with the result that (as from 15 September 2003) all new EDSs to be held in a settlement system must be issued in dematerialised form and held through CREST (although issuers can if they choose issue physical instruments to be held outside the system). The CMO finally shut down mid October 2003.

2   See in particular the CREST Rules, Rule 7 and Appendix 2.

PAPER-INTERFACE AND NEGOTIABILITY

9.120 A useful aspect of physical bearer instruments is the concept of negotiability[1]. This is not relevant to registered instruments[2]. It is of course still possible to issue and hold physical money market instruments outside CREST, and holders may be able to deposit physical instruments in exchange for dematerialised instruments held through CREST, but this will be dealt with by and at the option of the appropriate Issuing and Paying Agent for the relevant money market instruments rather than by the central CREST service.

1   As discussed in Chapter 2, a negotiable instrument has two attractive features. First, it is transferable without formalities. Second, honest acquisition confers good title (even if the transferor did not have good title), ie the holder in due course takes free from prior equities in the title of the transferor. Physical instruments held within the CMO were negotiable instruments, with CMO members having constructive possession and transferring it by attornment, but it is not clear this was the case for dematerialised instruments in the CMO.

2   The Bank of England and EUI consulted leading counsel (Mr Richard Sykes QC) on the effect of the loss of negotiability for EDSs (see the Bank of England Consultation Paper 'The Future of Money Market Instruments', November 1999, and, in particular, Appendix II). Mr Sykes was of the view that a holder of a dematerialised EDS through CREST was not in a worse position than the holder of a negotiable instrument, not least on the basis that reg 29 of the Uncertificated Securities Regulations 1995 (SI 1995/3272) (Regulation 35 of the current CREST Regulations is in essentially the same form) has the result that where a transfer follows a properly authenticated dematerialised instruction, such transfer cannot be reversed even if it can be shown that the relevant authenticated dematerialised instruction was in fact forged or unauthorised. It is therefore arguable that transfer of dematerialised EDSs through CREST at the least provides better protection than transfer of dematerialised EDSs through the CMO because there is the benefit of statutory provision rather than just contractual arrangements. However, there is also the argument that the CREST arrangements do not necessarily give the same protection as exists for transfer of negotiable instruments. For further discussion of the CMO issues, see ch 9 of Joanna Benjamin *Interests in Securities* (2000, Oxford University Press).

9.121 The Issuing and Paying Agent is a specific type of CREST Participant relevant to EDSs. It is responsible for the input of an issuance of EDSs into the CREST system (similar to the way lodging agents did in the CMO). The issuer's agent is intended to have control over the issuance of EDSs through CREST: hence the issuance, allocation of an ISIN number, and transfer to third parties can happen very rapidly through CREST[1], rather than applications for admissions of securities to

CREST being processed centrally within CREST as happens for gilts and equities. The record of title to EDSs is maintained by the CREST system, in the same way as for equities, but the administration in connection with such register is handled by the relevant Issuing and Paying Agent, not EUI.

1   Very important given the fact that large numbers of issues are lodged each day.

FUNGIBILITY

9.122   EDSs in CREST are issued not as separate identifiable instruments but as fungible instruments[1]. This is significant for any person holding EDSs on behalf of another, because it is not possible to identify the particular instruments held for a particular client but only that a proportion of an undivided whole is held[2]. This may not necessarily be of concern to a custodian, depending on how it holds assets for its client, but may be relevant if clear identification is important to the custodian or its clients. It should be noted that the usual CREST account facilities are available in relation to EDSs; therefore if necessary EDSs can be held through designated accounts or sponsored member accounts[3].

1   CREST Consultation Papers 'Money Market Instruments in CREST', January 2001 and 'Money Market Instruments in CREST – Frequently asked questions', February 2008. This was not necessarily the case for physical instruments in the CMO, since when such instruments were lodged, each was mechanically stamped with a distinctive number which was quoted in every subsequent transfer and withdrawal of the instruments.
2   See further discussion of issues arising in Chapter 3.
3   See paras **9.34–9.39** above.

COLLATERAL

9.123   An important use of EDSs is as collateral. For EDSs in CREST, the collateral arrangements are the same as those which apply currently to all CREST eligible securities[1], and therefore involve outright transfer of EDSs. If this is a concern for entities providing or taking EDSs as collateral, the parties could agree to impose additional restrictions by contract[2], or another option would be to pledge physical instruments outside CREST (but this is unlikely to be appealing because it would reintroduce the administration issues of dealing with paper).

1   See paras **9.75–9.93** above.
2   See discussion of escrow balance arrangements at paras **9.80–9.85** above.

SETTLEMENT AND PAYMENT

9.124   The RTGS payment mechanism in central bank funds for sterling and euro is available for EDS transfers, and the US dollar currency assured payment facility is also available. In contrast, in the CMO, payment arrangements involved settlement banks in a structure similar to assured payment, settling end of day (not RTGS), but the relevant documentation did not provide that payments were assured or irrevocable, therefore settlement banks were able to reverse payments.

CREST – further developments

9.125   With the continuing concern to speed up settlement and make systems more efficient, a major area of concern is how the current fragmented arrangements consisting of many different systems will change in the future. Views on the way forward vary: for example, both Euroclear and Clearstream have a large number of system links but increasingly have focused on joining forces with existing systems as far as possible, whereas CREST has historically concentrated on creating cross-border links with other systems (see discussion at paras **9.69–9.74** above). Whichever approach is preferred, one major focus is to increase efficiency by reducing administration and effectively maintaining one point of access to a central system through which the participant can access settlement for as wide a variety of securities as possible. At the same time, there is also a concern to maintain a range of settlement options in order to encourage competition and freedom of choice, and it is not always clear how to reconcile these concepts appropriately. In this context, it is useful to consider the merger of CREST with Euroclear[1], the proposed 'Single Platform' for the Euroclear group[2], and the potential issues involved.

1   On 4 July 2002, the boards of Euroclear and EUI announced that the terms of the proposed merger had been agreed, and this was approved by shareholders at meetings on 14 and 16 August 2002. The merger proposal was reviewed in accordance with the UK Fair Trading Act 1973, but the Secretary of State for Trade and Industry decided not to refer the merger to the UK Competition Commission, and subsequently at the UK High Court hearing on 19 September 2002 the scheme was sanctioned by the court. The merger completed on 23 September 2002.

2   See the various discussion papers and operational explanations available on the Euroclear website, for example: 'Update Paper – Single Platform Custody Blueprint – Edition 1', 6 November 2006; 'Update Paper – Single Platform Settlement Blueprint – Edition 1', 3 December 2007; 'Update Paper – ESES Blueprint – Edition 6', 13 February 2008; and 'Single Platform – Corporate actions – Domestic Service', 9 July 2008.

9.126 Although EUI is now part of the Euroclear group[1], the CREST system has in effect become another service available from the Euroclear stable of services[2]. The challenge of merging different systems created under different systems of law is of course quite considerable, particularly where the underlying basis of settlement or governing legal system differs. For example, the international service provided by Euroclear Bank under Belgian law[3] involves the holding by Euroclear Bank of a variety of securities, which may be issued under and subject to the law of many different jurisdictions. Euroclear Bank holds the relevant securities pursuant to Belgian law[4] in an arrangement akin to a trust under English law, so that effectively a person holding securities through Euroclear Bank has exchanged rights under the laws governing the underlying security for a repackaged asset (a type of securities entitlement) in the form of a Belgian law interest in the securities held by Euroclear Bank. This 'interest' (under Belgian law, a form of co-ownership right in the pool of fungible securities recorded in the books of Euroclear Bank) is subject to the relevant Belgian legislation as well as the contractual terms of participation in Euroclear entered into with Euroclear Bank ('Terms and Conditions governing the use of the Euroclear System' and related documentation which are governed by Belgian law). In contrast, as discussed in the earlier paragraphs, securities held through CREST are not held by EUI as an intermediary but are registered securities title to which is acquired by registration of the relevant CREST member in a CREST account (for UK securities) or register of title (for non-UK securities), in each case subject to the provisions of the appropriate legislation in the UK, Ireland or certain other jurisdictions. Similarly, securities held through Euroclear France, Euroclear Belgium, Euroclear Nederland, Euroclear Sweden and Euroclear Finland are subject to the relevant arrangements for registration of title governed by, respectively, French law, Belgian law, Dutch law, Swedish law and Finnish law. How can these various arrangements 'merge' effectively?

1   EUI is a wholly owned subsidiary of Euroclear SA/NV.

2   See in particular CREST/Euroclear press release, 4 July 2002; CREST press release, 18 July 2002 and the paper published in July 2002 by CREST and Euroclear, 'Delivering a domestic market for Europe'.

3   For the purposes of this discussion, when referring to the international settlement service provided by Euroclear, reference is made to Euroclear Bank. When referring to the domestic settlement service relating to Belgian securities, reference is made to Euroclear Belgium.

4   The Belgian Royal Decree No 62 of November 1967, as amended (including amendment by the law of 2 August 2002 on the oversight of the financial sector: art 133).

9.127 The answer seems to be that while significant efforts are being made to coordinate systems and harmonise various operational aspects, the Euroclear group has not attempted radical changes to the legal nature of existing ownership structures. Although the ultimate aim is for a system participant to have one securities account, one interface with the system and one payment or settlement relationship, essentially the same services are provided independently by CREST and the other domestic Euroclear systems and will remain available. An early discussion paper[1] noted specifically that 'European consolidation of settlement will be successful only if it offers the full range of services already enjoyed by customers without diminution of service provision' and that: 'A single platform which operated a single, rigid, settlement and custody service would not meet the needs of all its customers.'

1   'Delivering a domestic market for Europe', July 2002.

9.128 The Euroclear Single Platform is being set up in several phases. The first stage was the creation of the 'Single Settlement Engine' (or 'SSE') which, broadly, is intended to provide the initial level of common operational systems for Euroclear Bank, CREST, Euroclear Belgium, Euroclear France and Euroclear Nederland. Euroclear France started using the SSE in May 2006, CREST in August 2006 and Euroclear Bank in January 2007. Euroclear Belgium and Euroclear Nederland connected to the SSE in January 2009 as part of the next phase, the Euroclear Settlement of Euronextzone Securities (or 'ESES').

9.129 The ESES is described as 'an integrated settlement platform for the Straight-Through Processing (STP) of trades from Euronext Single Order Book, for local and remote Euronext members, and for the processing of OTC trades. ESES allows Euroclear Belgium, Euroclear France and Euroclear Nederland (the Belgian, French and Dutch CSDs, respectively) to use a common settlement and custody platform on which most of the system functionalities, market rules and practices for the three markets are largely harmonised'[1]. In effect, the ESES creates one settlement platform from what was originally three settlement platforms. Importantly, the ESES creates a 'common settlement and custody platform', makes use of the SSE to settle all transfers requiring settlement through Euroclear Belgium, Euroclear France or Euroclear Nederland, and enables 'ESES clients ... to operate all their settlement transactions through one operational facility'[2]. However, this structure does not replace or amend the underlying legal arrangements in each jurisdiction, as 'any client using the ESES platform will hold Belgian securities directly in Euroclear Belgium, French securities directly in Euroclear France and Dutch securities directly in Euroclear Nederland' and 'clients will need to enter into a contractual relationship with each CSD in which they intend to hold securities' (broadly in the form of common terms created for the ESES with certain country-specific rules for each CSD) although: 'Clients who already have a contractual relationship with a CSD of the ESE platform are not requested to sign the new documentation.'[3] The SSE maintains records of securities which 'mirror ... the legal records of each group CSD for the securities holding' but 'Finality will be achieved upon the update of legal records' rather than the SSE mirror records[4]. As such, the ESES system is not intended to affect the legal nature of a CSD member's entitlement to securities.

1   Euroclear publication 'Update Paper – ESES Blueprint – Edition 6', 13 February 2008.
2   Ibid.
3   Ibid.
4   Ibid.

9.130 The ESES platform was launched for members of the Euroclear France system in November 2007, was connected to the TARGET2 euro payment system in February 2008 and incorporated Euroclear Belgium and Euroclear Nederland in January 2009.

9.131 Another significant aspect of the creation of the ESES platform is the consideration given to harmonising the approaches of the different CSDs. For example, Euroclear Belgium, Euroclear France and Euroclear Nederland have historically had different rules regarding the types of person permitted to access each such CSD and the time at which unilateral revocation of settlement instructions can no longer be made. A consistent approach has been agreed for these CSDs for the purposes of the ESES platform. In contrast, certain aspects of specific CSDs will be retained where providing a operational benefit, for example, the existing links which Euroclear France has with other CSDs[1]. It is not wholly clear how the merged settlement service copes with the significant difference between the CREST approach to admission of participants and the approach of other Euroclear group entities[2].

1   See further discussion in 'Update Paper – ESES Blueprint – Edition 6', 13 February 2008.

2   Historically, Euroclear restricted participation to, broadly, large financial institutions (Euroclear requires participants to meet its criteria in relation to matters such as financial resources, technological ability, system requirements and market reputation), and, broadly, only credit institutions and inter-professional institutions (eg clearing houses and foreign CSDs) were permitted to participate in Euroclear Netherlands (formerly Necigef). In contrast, whereas (although in practice participation may be limited by the influence of factors such as the need to set up computer access to CREST and to appoint a settlement bank) CREST has, broadly, permitted participation by any individual or institution which is able to comply with the relevant operational and fee arrangements. (Arguably, the process of vetting potential CREST participants has ended up in the hands of the CREST settlement banks (or, possibly, sponsors where relevant), since a person cannot become a CREST member without appointing a settlement bank, and a bank will in practice not enter into an agreement with such person without going through its normal counterparty and credit checks. It should of course be remembered that while a settlement bank may choose to provide services on the basis of the protection provided by the settlement bank charge, this is no guarantee that the relevant person is creditworthy or a reputable counterparty, and EUI takes no responsibility for this.) At present, for the purposes of the Single Platform, it appears that CREST's approach is preserved in relation to the CREST system: 'In regards to the individual membership [ie individuals holding directly], it is expected that it will remain a specific feature of Euroclear UK and Ireland which will not be extended to the other group CSDs.' 'Update paper – Single Platform Settlement Blueprint – Edition 1', 3 December 2007, Chapter 3, section 3.3.1.

9.132 The final phases of the creation of the Single Platform were intended to be the introduction of Single Platform Custody as an interim phase, to be followed by Single Platform Settlement (at which stage, the interim ESES platform and the CREST legacy system would be decommissioned). The intention was that Single Platform Custody would be introduced for Euroclear Bank in the fourth quarter of 2009, followed by the joining of the ESES CSDs and then finally CREST. Thus the intended final result was essentially one point of access to a number of different settlement systems, with harmonised processes for instructions and ongoing functions such as corporate actions, although the four underlying domestic CSDs governed by different laws will remain in existence as will the international CSD operated by Euroclear Bank[1]. As part of this process, the Common Communication Interface ('CCI') which provides access to ESES was made available in relation to CREST in 2011. However, different arrangements are inevitably necessary to reflect the difference requirements of the different systems. In particular, since the Bank of England decided not to outsource GBP to the T2S platform, 'Euroclear UK & Ireland will not outsource the GBP Central Bank Money settlement functionality to the T2S platform. Given the costs involved in directly or indirectly linking Euroclear UK & Ireland to the T2S platform for EUR settlement, and following consultation with the Irish securities market, it is planned that Irish securities will be made available on the

T2S platform via an ESES CSD acting as an investor CSD. As such, the adaptation work has been discontinued for Euroclear UK & Ireland.'[2]

1   'One of the main principles of the Single Platform is to set up a "multi-jurisdictional" (or "direct holding") model for the group CSDs through which each participant will be able to directly access the primary CSD for group securities. This means that any CSD participant will hold Belgian securities directly in Euroclear Belgium, French securities directly in Euroclear France, Dutch securities directly in Euroclear Nederland and UK, Irish, Jersey, Guernsey and Isle of Man dematerialised securities directly in CREST under the jurisdiction laws of those countries.' 'Update Paper – Single Platform Custody Blueprint – Edition 1', 6 November 2006, Chapter 4, section 4.3.1.

2   CREST White paper 'T2S Euroclear adaptation plan to T2S', December 2011.

9.133   System participants are able to obtain what is termed a 'domestic service' by signing up to terms governed by, for example, French law for the service from Euroclear France, and English law for the service from what is currently EUI. This at least means that the arrangements with the relevant local central securities depositary for holding direct title to securities issued in France or the UK are governed by the appropriate local legal system[1] as well as the applicable regulatory requirements of the local regulator. Specific services which are unique to a particular system also remain available (where required in the relevant market), such as the DBV arrangements in CREST. In addition to the domestic services, participants can sign up separately in order to obtain the 'full service' provided under Belgian law which, as discussed above, is based on the concept of Euroclear holding relevant rights in securities for participants subject to Belgian law.

1   Note that the merger of EUI into Euroclear includes the CREST service for all CREST-eligible securities as described at para **9.2** above, such as Irish, Jersey, Guernsey and Isle of Man securities.

9.134   As a system development, the merger is arguably of assistance to participants, who can deal with what is effectively one system using one account (or set of accounts). However, different agreements governed by different laws will remain in existence with each underlying CSD and this may require some care in the harmonisation process to minimise scope for conflicts of terms or inconsistencies, particularly if issues arise in the event of insolvency or fraud (see discussion in Chapter 5). In practice it may be easier to reach conclusions or at least some pragmatic solution in the event of conflicting claims, given that the arrangements will be intra-group if not with the same system entity, but this may raise its own issues concerning competition, transparency of arrangements or related matters.

Conclusions

9.135   The legal aspects of CREST were at the outset drafted with a light hand. An early consultative paper stated, 'the government wishes to rely as far as practicable on the existing legal framework affecting shareholdings'. The deliverable was not law reform, but an effective settlement system. One result of this approach is that key legal aspects of the system were left to the contractual provisions to be developed between different players involved in CREST. For custodians, the negotiation of sponsorship and custody agreements, together with the terms of settlement bank facilities, is of primary importance. Another important point is that the CREST system was not intended to provide solutions to all possible issues from the outset, but by starting with a fairly simple model with which the market was familiar (from the old CGO system), it has been possible to develop additional functions over time with appropriate consultation with CREST participants, leading to significant developments such as electronic transfer of title, the RTGS payments arrangements and electronic proxy voting. It remains to be seen to what extent further Euroclear developments, such as the harmonisation process forming part of the Single Platform development discussed in paras **9.125–9.134** above, will affect the way in which the services provided by the CREST system develop further.

FURTHER ISSUES FOR CONSIDERATION IN RELATION TO CREST

Operator register of title, record of title and issuer register

9.136 The following lists certain specific legal issues which may be of interest in the context of the CREST system arrangements.

(a) An issuer of UK Securities maintains a register of holders of shares in certificated form, but in relation to uncertificated shares only has a duplicate record of the register of title maintained by CREST. The public cannot examine the CREST records: therefore this presents potential problems for due diligence[1].

(b) Under CREST Regulation 24, although the operator register or issuer register is prima facie evidence of 'any matters which are by these Regulations directed or authorised to be inserted in it', this is not true for the issuer register to the extent that it is inconsistent with the operator register. Consequently, although the issuer register in theory governs title to certificated shares, if the CREST register records a different position, it would not do so (and this would not be obvious to anyone looking at the issuer register). In principle, it is difficult to see why there would be an inconsistency given that the issuer register records only certificated shares, but there could be difficulties in some cases, for example, where shares were being transferred from certificated to uncertificated form, or vice versa. Again, this could cause difficulties for persons inspecting the issuer register but unaware of inconsistencies with the operator register.

(c) Also in CREST Regulation 24, it is stated that a person's name in the issuer register will not be prima facie evidence that such person is a member of the company unless the issuer register shows such person to be a holder of certificated shares, or the operator register shows such person to be a holder of uncertificated shares, or such person is deemed to be a member of the company (as discussed at (e) below). This creates the same issues as noted in (b).

(d) It is unclear what the position is where the CREST register and the company's duplicate record are inconsistent[2]. Note that Schedule 4, paragraph 5(2) of the CREST Regulations requires that the issuer record should be 'regularly reconciled with the Operator register of members' unless 'it is impracticable to do so by virtue of circumstances beyond its control'. There is no reference in the CREST Regulations as to what is meant by 'regularly reconciled' (although see the standard CREST Registrars Agreement), but paragraph 5(3) has the effect that, provided the issuer record is 'regularly reconciled' with the operator register, the company will not be liable for any action taken on the assumption that the record details 'accord with' the operator register details[3].

(e) Where there is a transfer of uncertificated shares to a person who will hold in certificated form, the relevant entry on the operator register will be deleted and an appropriate entry made on the issuer register in due course. There will in principle be a period during which there is no record of the ownership of the relevant shares on either the operator register or the issuer register (although presumably the transferring party will still (briefly) appear in the issuer record until the issuer register is updated). CREST Regulation 31 provides that, until the transferee is entered on the issuer register, the transferor will retain legal title but the transferee acquires (at the time of the deletion from the operator register) an equitable interest in the relevant securities being transferred. In CREST Regulation 32, which relates to the conversion of shares from uncertificated to

284 *The Law of Global Custody*

certificated form (ie shares come out of CREST but are held by the same person) it is specifically stated that 'During any period between the deletion of any entry in an Operator register of securities ... and the making of the entry in an issuer register of securities ... the relevant system-member shall retain title to the units of the security ... notwithstanding the deletion of any entry in the Operator register of securities; and ... where those units are shares, the relevant system-member shall be deemed to continue to be a member of the company'[4]. These are important exceptions to current company law (Companies Act 2006, s 112) where a person is only a member of a company if entered on the register of that company.

(f) CREST Regulation 33 relates to the conversion of securities into uncertificated form. Again there appears to be a potential timing issue regarding register entries. The relevant issuer is required to give a dematerialisation notice to CREST in the circumstances specified in this CREST Regulation (including where a system-member requests conversion of securities from certificated to uncertificated form), and upon doing so, to delete the relevant securities from the issuer register. The operator is required to enter the relevant system-member in the operator register, but the only obligation of the operator regarding notification to the relevant issuer is to notify whether or not the registration has been made on the operator register 'Within 2 months of receiving a dematerialisation notice'. In principle, the issuer could check the register at an early stage, and presumably in practice the relevant system-member would be aware quite quickly whether or not the relevant securities were recorded in its CREST account, but this information will not be available to the public, except to the extent that the issuer's record notes this[5]. This is a potential issue where the making of an entry on the register is time critical[6].

(g) CREST Regulation 33 has wording similar to CREST Regulation 32 in that it states that the relevant system-member will 'retain title to the units of the security specified in the dematerialisation notice notwithstanding the deletion of any entry in any issuer register of securities' and in relation to shares shall 'be deemed to continue to be a member of the company'[7]. This raises issue similar to those discussed in (e).

1   The company and its registrar do have the right to inspect CREST's register, and could therefore be required to certify as to the accuracy of the duplicate record, but arguably this does not give the same protection as an independent examination of the register. In addition, as discussed in relation to CREST Regulations 31 and 32 below, there may be intervals where shares are not registered in either the operator register or the issuer register (such shares may still appear in the issuer record but, as noted, this is not a record of title).

2   The idea is that the company should be subject to the same obligations and liabilities in relation to the maintenance of the duplicate record of uncertificated shares as apply to the maintenance of the register of certificated shares, but if a problem is caused by CREST, is there any recourse? For example, if the CREST register shows more securities than are actually in issue, is the company required to issue more securities to remove the shortfall? The normal position under English law is that a company is liable for statements on the register, and is generally regarded as estopped from arguing that the number of shares shown in the register as being in issue is wrong; therefore the company is required to issue more shares to eliminate any shortfall. There is no indication that this normal rule would not apply: therefore in principle an issuer accepts the same liability for CREST as maintainer of the operator register in this respect as it does in relation to the actions of itself (or its registrar) in relation to maintaining the register of certificated shares.

3   In wording comparable to Companies Act 2006, s 115, an issuer with more than 50 members is required to maintain a single record of when people become, or cease to be, members, whether they hold shares in certificated or uncertificated form (CREST Regulations, Schedule 4, paragraph 7(1)).

4   CREST Regulation 32(6).

5   Although presumably the issuer's record will only be updated once it is confirmed that the relevant securities have been registered on the operator register.

6   Note also CREST Regulation 34(1), where CREST's obligation to enter names on the register of securities is subject to the rules of CREST, which raises similar issues.

7   Note that, unlike under CREST Regulation 31 (transfer from uncertificated to certificated form), the transferee where securities are being converted and received in uncertificated form following a transfer does not receive equitable title, and the transferor remains the relevant holder until the transferee's name is entered on the operator register.

Capacity and liability of registrar

9.137   It is useful to consider the role of the registrar in relation to UK securities held through CREST.

9.138   Is CREST maintaining part of the register as agent of the company?[1] CREST Regulation 20(1) states that in relation to shares issued by a company participating in CREST 'there shall be (a) a register maintained by the participating issuer ... and ... a register maintained by the Operator'. It is also stated in CREST Regulation 20(4) that: 'References in any enactment or instrument to a company's register of members shall, unless the context otherwise requires, be construed in relation to a company which is a participating issuer as referring to the company's issuer register of members and Operator register of members.' However, there is no clear indication whether the company ceases to be responsible for the functions to be carried out by the operator, or whether the operator is maintaining the register as agent of the company.

1   The primary obligation to maintain the whole register under the Companies Act 2006 is disapplied (see CREST Regulation 23(1)(b)) but it is unclear if the company may have liability for CREST if CREST does not maintain the register properly; although see para **9.136** n 2 above.

9.139   It should be noted that in Schedule 4 to the CREST Regulations it is stated that s 113 of the Companies Act 2006 (obligations to maintain register) does not apply[1] to a company which is a participating issuer. As a result, if an issuer has any securities in uncertificated form, its obligations regarding maintenance of the register will be under the CREST Regulations rather than the Companies Act 1985. The same is true for certain other parts of the Companies Act 1985, for example, s 114 (location of register).

1   CREST Regulations, Schedule 4, paragraph 2(4). Section 113(8) will apply in the sense that the company and its officers may still a face a fine for non-compliance with obligations in relation to maintenance of the register, although such obligations arise under Schedule 4, paragraph 2, rather than s 113.

9.140   CREST will not be subject to the same liability for failure to maintain the register correctly as the company, given the extent of the exclusions of liability by CREST[1]. It should also be noted that the CREST Terms and Conditions (which all members sign up to) state that CREST will only be liable if negligent, fraudulent or in wilful default (and such limitation is intended to apply to all claims in contract, tort, misrepresentation, breach of any other duty imposed by law or in any other way), but the maximum liability for all claims (not just claims from an individual CREST member) arising from the same event is capped[2]. Therefore, in practice, if there were ever a major problem and many claimants, each claimant might well recover very little.

1   For example, CREST Regulation 23(1): 'The obligations of an Operator to maintain and to keep and enter up any register of securities, imposed by these Regulations ... shall not give rise to any form of duty or liability enforceable by civil proceedings for breach of statutory duty.' However, Schedule 4, paragraphs 18 and 19 indicate that certain fines for failure to maintain the Operator register properly will apply to CREST and its officers. Commentary notes in the HM Treasury consultation paper 'Modernising Securities Settlement' (produced in connection with the first draft of the present Regulations) indicated the intention that CREST should still be liable for its own fraud or negligence without limitation, but this is not clear from CREST Regulation 23.

2   At the time of writing the cap was £40,000,000 (or £20,000,000 where liability of EUI arises out of an act, omission or event prior to 3 July 2000) (see CREST Terms and Conditions, Section 17.6 and Schedule 5 (definition of 'Liability Cap')).

EXTRACT FROM OLD CGO MEMBERSHIP AGREEMENT

9.141 The wording in para **9.142** is quoted by way of example of the type of specific wording formerly required by system rules (the CMO required something similar[1]). The terms of Clause 3(16)(a)(i) of the old CGO Membership Agreement were compatible with custody arrangements, as they provided, not that the stock was free from third party equities, but that it could be dealt with free from such equities.

1   See also discussion in paras **9.61–9.65**.

9.142 Clause 3(16) of the CGO Membership Agreement:

'If and whenever the CGO Member acts or proposes to act as nominee or agent for another person ("a principal") in relation to stock held or to be held on, or transactions over, CGO Accounts of the CGO Member, to obtain from that principal before beginning to act as nominee or agent for that principal:

(a) an acknowledgment that the holding of stock for the account of that principal on the CGO Accounts of the CGO Member and all transactions over those CGO Accounts or otherwise in relation to facilities relating to the CGO Member's membership of the CGO Service will be subject to all of the provisions of this Agreement and to the CGO Rules and in particular (but without limiting the generality of the foregoing):

   (i) that the stock is to be introduced into the CGO only if it has been purchased or is held on terms authorising the holder to deal with it free from any proprietary or equitable interest of any other person and in particular free from any unpaid vendor's lien; and

   (ii) that the Bank of England and its servant, and agents, with certain limited exceptions expressly provided for in this Agreement, are exempt from liability caused directly by or indirectly by the provision or operation of the CGO Service or any part thereof, or by any loss, interruption or failure in the provision or operation of the CGO Service or any part thereof, and entitling the Bank of England without liability to act without further enquiry on instructions or information or purported instructions or information received through the CGO Service or otherwise in accordance with the CGO Manual; and

(b) an authority for the CGO Member on behalf of that principal to do all such acts and things and execute all such documents as may be required to enable the CGO Member fully to observe and perform its obligations under this Agreement and the CGO Rules, and enter into any arrangement which the CGO Member considers proper for the purpose of facilitating clearance of or settlement of transactions effected on behalf of the principal through the CGO.'

CHAPTER 10*

UK taxation

INTRODUCTION

10.1 This chapter is intended to outline some of the main UK tax considerations which may arise in the context of custody arrangements.

* This chapter was written by Gerald Montagu, who is a consultant at Davenport Lyons, to whom Madeleine Yates is grateful.

10.2 It should perhaps be stressed that a global custodian may, depending upon the precise circumstances, be subject to taxation liabilities and/or compliance obligations (such as information reporting requirements) in more than one jurisdiction with respect to securities held by the custodian. The focus here is solely on UK tax law as it is likely to relate to custody assets (rather than for example the direct tax position of the global custodian itself). Although not dealt with here, a global custodian will need to consider its own direct tax position and to familiarise itself with the taxation regime in each of the jurisdictions which may seek to impose a taxing right with respect to assets which it holds in custody.

10.3 Stamp duty and each charge to tax are examined in turn to give a brief overview of how stamp duty and each tax is levied, in order that some specific practical issues which arise can then be addressed. The discussion is not comprehensive, but it is hoped that it will serve to highlight certain areas where difficulties can arise.

10.4 Tax treatment is essentially parasitic on underlying legal relationships and property rights. Whether, for example, a document is chargeable to duty, a payment is liable to deduction of income (ie withholding) tax, or a custodian is directly assessable for income tax as an agent/trustee of an investor can depend (as appropriate) upon the legal effect of a document, the nature of a payment and the precise circumstances in which a custodian is acting. Difficulties associated with the interpretation of tax law and HM Revenue and Customs practice apart, the precise nature of the rights and obligations enjoyed by and owed to participants in the financial markets form an essential foundation for any tax analysis. Shortage of space prevents a detailed analysis of how all these pieces may be fitted together, but it is important to keep in mind that the taxation aspects covered in this chapter cannot be understood outside the context of the legal analysis in the other chapters of this book.

10.5 In order to avoid unnecessary confusion, it is worth noting that a word or phrase may have a precise meaning in the context of a particular duty or tax which differs from the meaning accorded to that word or phrase in other contexts. With regard to the terminology used in other chapters of this book, references are made to a 'clearance' service (and clearing systems) which are described as settlement systems[1]. However, in the context of the charges to UK stamp duty and stamp duty reserve tax ('SDRT'), which are discussed below, a clearance service (such as Clearstream, Euroclear or The Depositary Trust Company ('DTC')) is regarded by HM Revenue and Customs as a system for holding securities and settling transactions, whereas HM Revenue and Customs characterise an entity such as CREST as a settlement system through which transfers of securities are settled[2]. Consequently, the use of the term 'settlement' and 'clearing' by HM Revenue and Customs in the context of these stamp duty and SDRT charges differs from the customary market use of such terms; the latter simply equates settlement with delivery, and clearing with the pre-settlement of credit exposure, usually by the use of a central counterparty (as discussed in Chapter 9).

1   See Chapter 9.
2   See further para **10.22** below.

STAMP DUTY

10.6 Stamp duty is a duty on instruments[1] (rather than a tax on transactions). An instrument is within the charge to duty if it is executed in the UK, or relates (wherever it is executed) to any property situated in, or any matter or thing done or to be done in the UK[2]. There is, as a matter of stamp duty law per se, generally no obligation to pay duty, as the payment of duty is not generally enforceable as a debt due to the Crown[3]. In practice, however, duty must be paid if a document is to be registered in the UK[4] or if an instrument is to be produced in evidence, or available for any purpose whatever, in civil proceedings in the UK[5]. If duty is not paid within 30 days of an instrument being executed, interest runs at a rate set periodically[6]. Additionally, a penalty is payable if an instrument is not presented for stamping within 30 days of execution (if an instrument is executed in the UK), or is not so presented within 30 days of the day on which the instrument is first received into the UK (if an instrument is executed outside the UK). If an instrument is presented for stamping within one year of the end of the 30-day period the penalty is the lesser of £300 and the amount of duty due; thereafter the penalty is the higher of £300 and the amount of duty due[7].

1   It follows that where a book entry system is in use (eg in the context of a settlement system like CREST, or a clearance system such as Clearstream) no stamp duty should be chargeable on a transfer as no stampable instrument is produced; see further para **10.24** n 1 below.

2   Stamp Act 1891, s 14(4). 'The provision ... speaks of an instrument "relating to" certain subjects. There is no expression more general or far reaching than that', per McNaughton J in *IRC v Maple & Co (Paris) Ltd* [1908] AC 22.

3   If, however, duty chargeable under Finance Act 1999, Sch 15, para 2 on stock constituted by or transferable by means of a bearer instrument is not paid on the first transfer of such stock in the UK, each person in the UK who transfers the stock by means of the instrument or is concerned as broker or agent in any such transfer is jointly and severally liable to the Crown for the duty chargeable, interest on the unpaid duty from the date of the transfer in question until the date on which duty is paid, and severally liable to a penalty not exceeding £300 and the amount of the duty chargeable (Finance Act 1999, Sch 15, para 23).

4   If an instrument is not duly stamped, a person whose office it is to enrol, register or enter in or upon any rolls, books or records an instrument is liable to a penalty (Stamp Act 1891, s 17).

5   Stamp Act 1891, s 14(4). In August 2001, the Professional Standards Committee of the Bar Council, after consultation with the Chancery judges, announced that a 1956 Bar Council ruling under which it had been unprofessional (other than in revenue cases) for a barrister to take a stamp duty objection, was obsolete. There is therefore now no longer any rule of practice or conduct that it is unprofessional for an advocate to take a stamp objection.

6   Stamp Act 1891, s 15A(3). The rate is set using a formula set out in Finance Act 1989, s 178 and changed following decisions made by the Bank of England Marketing Policy Committees (Taxes (Interest Rate) Regulations 1989 (SI 1989/1297), reg 3 as amended by Taxes and Duties (Interest Rate) (Amendment) Regulations 2008 (SI 2008/3234)). Interest under £25 is disregarded and is not payable; where interest is payable it is rounded down to the nearest £5: Stamp Act 1891, s 15A(4).

7   Stamp Act 1891, s 15B.

10.7 Stamp duty is charged under various heads; in the context of the financial markets (and hence situations likely to be regularly encountered by custodians), the following heads of charges are particularly relevant.

Bearer instrument[1]

10.8 Duty is chargeable (at the rate of 1.5 per cent) on:

(a) the issue of a bearer instrument in the UK and on the issue of a bearer instrument outside the UK by or on behalf of a UK company[2]; and

(b) (if there is no charge on issue under (a)) on the first transfer in the UK of stock constituted by or transferred by means of a bearer instrument if either duty would be chargeable on a transfer on sale if the transfer were effected by means of an instrument other than a bearer instrument, or the stock constituted by or transferable by means of a bearer instrument consists of units under a unit trust scheme[3].

1   The evolution of this charge to duty shadows the withering of exchange control. For the use of bearer securities and how their increased popularity was a consequence of the rolling back of exchange control in 1963 and its abolition in 1979, see Joanna Benjamin *Interests in Securities: A Proprietary Law Analysis of the International Securities Markets* (2000, Oxford University Press), p 32 n 6. For a narrative treatment against a broader canvass, see also David Kynaston *The City of London: IV A Club No More 1945–2000* (2001, Pimlico), pp 98–9, 562, 581, 600.

2   A 'UK company' is defined as a body corporate formed or established in the UK: Finance Act 1999, Sch 15, para 11.

3   Finance Act 1999, Sch 15, paras 1–2.

10.9 In practice, payment of duty under this head of charge is rarely encountered with respect to issues of debt securities. An exemption is available, for example, if either the stock constituted by or transferable by means of a bearer instrument falls within the statutory definition of loan capital[1], or stock is expressed in a currency other than sterling[2]. Duty is, therefore, likely to be an issue only where a sterling denominated bearer instrument does not qualify as loan capital[3].

1   Finance Act 1986, s 79(2); loan capital is defined to mean (s 78(7)):

   '(a) any debenture stock, corporation stock or funded debt by whatever name known, issued by a body corporate or other body of persons (which here includes a local authority and any body whether formed or established in the UK or elsewhere);

   (b) any capital raised by such a body if the capital is borrowed or has the character of borrowed money, and whether it is in the form of stock or any other form;

   (c) stock or marketable securities issued by a government of any country or territory outside the UK; and

   (d) any capital raised under arrangements which fall within section 48A of the Finance Act 2005 or section 507 of the Corporation Tax Act 2009 (alternative finance investment bonds)'.

   Section 48A was repealed by the Taxation (International and Other Provisions) Act 2010; the rewritten provisions are section 564G of the Income Tax Act 2007 and section 151N of the Taxation of Chargeable Gains Act 1992.

2   Finance Act 1999, Sch 15, para 17.

3   The exemption provided for foreign loan securities by Finance Act 1999, Sch 15, para 13 is not often relied upon in practice, as it is a requirement (in addition to the loan being expressed in a currency other than sterling) that a bearer instrument (a) is not offered for subscription in the UK, or (b) offered for subscription with a view to an offer for sale in the UK of securities in respect of the loan. Such restrictions are clearly incompatible with the marketing of many securities traded on the international capital markets.

Transfer on sale

10.10 Duty is chargeable (at the rate of 0.5 per cent in the case of stock or marketable securities) on a transfer on sale of property for stampable consideration[1] unless the stampable consideration is under £1,000 and the instrument is certified accordingly[2].

1 Finance Act 1999, Sch 13, paras 1–4. Stampable consideration takes the form of cash, stock, marketable securities and debt: Stamp Act 1891, ss 55, 57. The amount of duty payable is rounded up to the nearest £5: Finance Act 1999, s 112.

2 Finance Act 1999, Sch 13, para 1(3A) (introduced by Finance Act 2008 s 98).

The certificate states:

'I/we certify that the transaction effected by this instrument does not for part of a larger transaction or series of transactions in respect of which the amount or value, or aggregate amount or value, of the consideration exceeds £1,000.'

Exempt loan capital

10.11 Duty is not chargeable on the transfer of a bearer instrument by delivery provided that, as one would expect to be the case, no documentary transfer is produced[1]. There is an exemption from all stamp duties for an instrument which transfers exempt loan capital[2]. A security will qualify for this exemption if it is loan capital (within the scope of the statutory definition[3]) and is therefore essentially 'vanilla' debt without any (equity-like) disqualifying features[4]. If an instrument transfers an interest in securities, and the securities themselves are within the loan capital exemption, that instrument is also exempt from all stamp duties[5].

1 A physical bearer instrument should by its nature be transferable only by delivery, depending of course on all the circumstances. It is, however, conceivable that a document characterised as an instrument transferring an immobilised or dematerialised bearer security (or transferring such a security in contemplation of the sale of that security (Finance Act 1965, s 90)) could be stampable as a transfer on sale.

2 Finance Act 1986, s 79(4).

3 See para **10.9** n 1 above.

4 An instrument will not qualify as exempt loan capital which 'at the time the instrument is executed, carries a right (exercisable then or later) of conversion into shares or other securities, or to the acquisition of shares or other securities, including loan capital of the same description' (Finance Act 1986, s 79(5)), or:

'... at the time the instrument is executed or any earlier time, carries or has carried:

(a) a right to interest the amount of which exceeds a reasonable commercial return on the nominal amount of the capital,

(b) a right to interest the amount of which falls or has fallen to be determined to any extent by reference to the results of, or of any part of, a business or to the value of any property, or

(c) a right on repayment to an amount which exceeds the nominal amount of the capital and is not reasonably comparable with what is generally repayable (in respect of a similar nominal amount of capital) under the terms of issue of loan capital listed on the Financial Services Authority's Official List' (Finance Act 1986, s 79(6)).

In the case of alternative finance investment bonds s 79(6) has effect as if (a) above is omitted, for (c) there is substituted a requirement that an alternative finance investment bond does not carry and has not carried a right at the end of the bond term to a payment that exceeds the aggregate of the amount paid for the issue of the bond and the notional payment amount (ie the amount of payments which would have represented a reasonable commercial return on the bond over the bond term less the amount of payments actually made), and references to 'additional payments' are substituted for references to 'interest' (Finance Act 1986, s 79(8A), introduced by Finance Act 2008).

Finance Act 1986, s 79(7A) (introduced by Finance Act 2000) provides that an instrument is not regarded as falling within (b) above by reason only that loan capital carries a right to interest which (i) reduces in the event of the results of the business or part of the business improving, or the value of any property increasing, or (ii) increases in the event of the results of a business or part of a business deteriorating, or the value of any property diminishing.

Finance Act 1986 s 79(7B) (introduced by Finance Act 2008) further provides that a capital market instrument will not be treated as exempt loan capital by virtue of (b) above by reason only that the capital market investment concerned carries or has carried a right to interest which ceases or reduces if, or to the extent that, the issuer, after meeting or providing for other obligations specified in the capital market arrangement concerned, has insufficient funds available from that capital market arrangement to pay all or part of the interest otherwise due.

5   Finance Act 1987, s 50.

Call options

10.12   It should be noted that a call option is also chargeable to duty under this head of charge because such an option is treated as a transfer of property in its own right[1]. Care should therefore be taken that an issuer's right to redeem securities is a term of debt securities rather than a separate option (as a separate option could constitute a chargeable document on the day on which it is granted). The type of difficulties which can arise in this area have been attested by the discussions which took place between the Inland Revenue (the predecessor of HM Revenue and Customs)[2] and the Financial Services Authority before the launch in September 2002 by the London Stock Exchange of a covered warrants market under (what is now) Section 19 (*Securitised derivatives*) of the Financial Services Authority's Listing Rules. In the course of those discussions the view was put forward that the issue of such global warrants might give rise to a stamp duty charge under the *Wimpey* principle[3]. However, the Inland Revenue is understood to have given the Financial Services Authority sufficient reassurance that no stamp duty should be chargeable with respect to the issue of a global covered warrant listed under Listing Rule 19 for the UKLA's Listing Rules to launch the new market and the rationale for this position is now that such covered warrants are cash settled (rather than being physically settled by the delivery of securities to which a warrant relates).

1   *George Wimpey & Co Ltd v IRC* [1975] 1 WLR 995, [1975] 2 All ER 45.

2   HM Revenue and Customs took over the functions previously carried out by the Inland Revenue and HM Customs and Excise on 18 April 2005: see Commissioners for Revenue and Customs Act 2005, s 5.

3   *Financial Times*, 18 September 2002, p 2.

10.13   This leaves open the position on the grant of a warrant or option which is designed to be physically settled, and this may become relevant where an option relates to stock or a marketable security which is not exempt loan capital[1]. There appears, however, to be a helpful constraint on the ambit of the *Wimpey* principle in that a central feature of that case was that it concerned a call option which could be completed by the conveyance to the holder of the option of property (land) which existed at the time the option was granted.

HM Revenue and Customs acknowledges a restriction on the breadth of SA 1891, s 60 which is grounded upon an early twentieth century case[2] where it was indicated that no charge to duty should arise under SA 1891, s 60 unless the sale of an option is capable of being completed by transfer or conveyance[3]. Consequently, stamp duty should not be chargeable under the *Wimpey* principle or s 60 where (as is often the case) a warrant relates to securities which have not been issued when the warrant is granted. Where, however, the securities which are the subject of an option exist at the time of grant, s 60 and the *Wimpey* principle would seem to be point and it would seem that it may only be possible to avoid a payment of duty if there is no stampable consideration for the grant of the option or warrant[4].

1   Where an issuer is to have the right to redeem its security, that right to redeem should be drafted as a term of debt securities rather than a separate option to avoid this minefield.

2   *Great Northern Railway Company v IRC* [1902] 1 KB 416.

3   HM Revenue and Customs's Stamp Tax Manual, para 4.329.

4   It may be arguable that the *Wimpey* principle is restricted to options over land.

The rationale for this approach is that if the approach which the court adopted in Wimpey were to be applied in relation to a ordinary contract, that contract could be regarded as vesting property in a promisee and this would entirely erode the dividing line established by *IRC v G Angus & Co* (1889) 23 QBD 579) between contract and transfer because the an instrument vesting such property in the promisee would be dutiable in the same way (subject to any differences in the value of stampable consideration) as a transfer to the promisee would be.

This line of reasoning reaches out to some non-stamp duty cases concerning options over land (*London and South Western Railway Company v Gomm* (1882) 20 Ch D 562, and *Spiro v Glencrown Properties* [1991] Ch 537) indicate that the grant of option over land operates to create a trust over the land which can be defeased at the behest of the beneficiary of that trust. Unfortunately, these land law cases are under-pinned by the equitable principles of specific performance and it has been held that specific performance cannot be obtained in relation to fungible property (see, for example *Re Goldcorp Exchange Limited (in receivership)* [1995] 1 AC 74).

Fungible property includes cash and quoted shares. *Hunter v Moss* ([1993] 1 WLR 934, [1994] 1 WLR 452, CA) is authority that equity can establish a trust over shares in a private company, but although this case has been followed the reasoning of both the Judge in the High Court and the Court of Appeal seems flawed (see paras **3.36–3.40**).

In any event, it would hardly be a satisfactory result if the stamp duty treatment of the grant of an option were to depend upon either:

(a) whether that option related to stock or marketable securities:

   (i)   which are publicly listed (which could not be subject to stamp duty under the *Wimpey* principle as such an option could not be completed by specific performance); or

   (ii) which are not publicly listed, perhaps because the issuer is a private limited company which is not permitted by company law to offer its shares to the public (which could be subject to stamp duty under the Wimpey principle as such an option could, following *Hunter v Moss*, be completed by specific performance); or

(b) that option is over stock or marketable securities which are separately identifiable by virtue of being held in a blocked account (which could be subject to stamp duty under the Wimpey principle as such an option could be completed by specific performance on the basis that such securities were sufficiently 'identifiable'; see para 3.41).

Other exemptions

10.14   In addition to the exemption for exempt loan capital referred to above, a transfer of shares in government or parliamentary stocks or funds or strips of such stocks or funds, and a renounceable letter of allotment, letter of rights or other similar instrument where the rights under the letter or other instrument are renounceable not later than six months after its issue, are each exempt from duty under the transfer head of charge[1].

1   Finance Act 1999, Sch 13, para 24.

10.15   There is also an exemption for an instrument which transfers stock in accordance with a repo or stock loan where either:

(a) (i)   either of the parties to the arrangement is authorised under the law of an EEA State to provide any of the investment services or activities listed in Section A 2 or 3 of Annex I (execution of orders on behalf of clients and dealing on own account) of the MiFID Directive in relation to the stock of the kind concerned (irrespective of whether either of the parties to the arrangement is authorised under the MiFID Directive); and

    (ii) stock of the kind is regularly traded on a regulated market; or

(b) (i)   the arrangement is effected on a multilateral trading facility or a recognised foreign exchange[1]; and

    (ii) stock of that kind is regularly traded on that market facility or exchange[2].

Where the only reason that the above conditions are not fulfilled is that after securities have been transferred and either party to the arrangement become insolvent on or after 1 September 2008 and it becomes apparent that, as a result of that insolvency, securities will not be retransferred in accordance with the arrangement (and the parties are not 'connected' for the purposes of section 1122 of the Corporation Tax Act 2010), Finance Act 1986, s 80D provides if the solvent party acquires replacement securities within 30 days of the insolvency occurring, then stamp duty is not chargeable on any instrument transferring those replacement securities to the solvent party or its nominee (equally, stamp duty is not chargeable on an instrument transferring replacement securities if no collateral is provided under the arrangement).

1 An arrangement is 'effected on a market, facility, or exchange, if (and only if) it is subject to the rules of the market, facility or exchange, and is reported to the market, facility or exchange in accordance with the rules of the market, facility, or exchange; Finance Act 1986, s 80C(6). See also para **10.35** n 1 below.

2 Finance Act 1986, s 80C, as amended by Finance Act 2007, Sch 21. Note that the exemption is not available if:

 (a) the arrangement would not have been entered into by persons dealing with each other at arm's length, or

 (b) under the arrangement any of the benefits or risks arising from fluctuations, before the transfer to 'B' (the stock lender/repo seller) (or his or her nominee) takes place, in the market value of the stock accrues to, or falls on, 'A' (the stock borrower/repo buyer).

Depositary receipts

10.16 No ad valorem stamp duty is in practice usually paid on a transfer of a depositary receipt, as a depositary receipt is usually represented by a book entry maintained by a depositary, with the register being kept, and any transfer documents executed and kept, outside the UK. Notwithstanding that in practice this is often the position, it is arguable that a depositary receipt in respect of a security issued by a UK incorporated company can be said to relate to property situate in the UK. As trading in a depositary receipt ultimately determines title to an economic interest (and, in a customary depositary receipt structure, is generally thought to constitute a transfer of an equitable interest)[1] in the underlying securities, it is conceivable that, if circumstances were to arise in which a depositary receipt holder wished to prove title to an underlying security, a documentary record of an instruction to a depositary to transfer a depositary receipt might need to be produced in evidence before a court in the UK. In such a case it may be arguable[2] that that instruction, or a print-out of the depositary's records, could be a stampable document (as, respectively, a transfer on sale, or as a memorandum of a transfer on sale)[3]. A well-advised depositary will try to ensure, in the unlikely event that the intermediation structure of which it forms part were to unravel in such a fashion (eg in circumstances in which a depositary's customer sought to acquire the actual underlying security to which a depositary receipt related), that any stamping is undertaken by others.

1 Cf *HSBC Holdings PLC and The Bank of New York Mellon Corporation v HMRC* ([2012] UKFTT 163 (TC)) where the First-tier Tribunal formed the view that the holder of a American Depositary Receipt issued under New York Law did not enjoy an equitable interest in an underlying security. It may be open to question whether the First-tier Tribunal was correct in this regard, and, as a practical matter, HM Revenue and Customs has indicated in Revenue and Customs Brief 14/12 that HM Revenue and Customs generally intends to continue to treat the holder of an ADR as beneficially entitled to an interest in the underlying security.

2 Much will depend upon the precise nature and legal effect of the documentation; cf for example, para **10.58** n 1 below.

3 Under what is sometimes called the 'memorandum rule' a memorandum of an agreement which is brought into existence to implement the transfer of property which that instrument purports to record

is stampable as if it were an agreement to transfer or convey that property: *Lord Braybooke v A-G* (1861) 9 HL Cas 150; *Wigan Coal and Iron Co Ltd v IRC* [1945] 1 All ER 392; *Associated British Engineering Ltd v IRC* [1941] 1 KB 15; *IRC v Clarkson-Webb* [1933] 1 KB 507; *Horsfall v Hey* (1848) 2 Exch 778; *Garnett v IRC* (1899) 81 LT 633.

Transfer of any other kind

10.17 No duty is payable on a transfer of any other kind (ie otherwise than on sale)[1]. Some examples of such a transfer include where the consideration for a sale does not comprise stampable consideration[2], and where legal title alone is transferred.

1 Finance Act 2008, s 99, Sch 32 abolished the charge to fixed duty of £5 with respect to instruments executed on or after 13 March 2008 and not stamped before 19 March 2008.
2 See para **10.10** n 1 above.

10.18 If an instrument transfers securities of a UK incorporated company to a UK resident company, the business (or part of the business) of which is exclusively that of holding shares, stock or other marketable securities as nominee or agent for a provider of clearance services, to another company which fulfils the same requirements, stamp duty is not chargeable on that instrument (whereas ad valorem duty at the rate of 1.5 per cent may be chargeable under the clearance service charge – see further below)[1]. A similar provision operates in respect of an instrument which transfers relevant securities from one nominee or agent of an issuer of depositary receipts to another such nominee or agent of the issuer of depositary receipts: no stamp duty is chargeable on such an instrument (whereas ad valorem duty at the rate of 1.5 per cent may be chargeable under the depositary receipt charge to duty)[2]. Equally no stamp duty is chargeable on an instrument which transfers securities of a company incorporated in the UK between a depository receipt system and a clearance system (provided that, in the case of a transfer from a clearance system an election is not force under s 97A immediately before the transfer)[3].

1 Finance Act 1986, s 70(9), as amended by Finance Act 2008, Sch 32, para 7.
2 Finance Act 1986, s 67(9), as amended by Finance Act 2008, Sch 32, para 6.
3 Finance Act 1986, s 72A, as amended by Finance Act 2008, Sch 32, para 8.

10.19 There is also an exemption which provides that stamp duty is not chargeable on an instrument which effects a transfer of securities if the transferee is a member of an electronic transfer system (eg a system such as CREST which enables title to securities to be transferred and evidenced without a written instrument in accordance with the Uncertificated Securities Regulations 2001[1]). For the exemption to apply, an instrument must be in a form which will, in accordance with the rules of that system, ensure that securities are changed from being held in certificated form to being held in uncertificated form so that title to them may become transferable by means of that system[2].

1 SI 2001/3755.
2 Finance Act 1996, s 186. See also Stamp Taxes Manual, March 2002, paras 10.36–10.40.

Contract or agreement chargeable as a transfer on sale

10.20 An agreement for the sale of an interest in securities is stampable as a transfer on sale, unless (i) the securities qualify as stock[1] or marketable securities[2], or (ii) the securities constitute property situated outside the UK, and (in either case) the agreement is for the sale of legal and equitable title to those securities[3].

1 For the definition of 'stock' see Stamp Act 1891, s 122: 'stock' includes:

'...any share in any stocks or funds transferable at the Bank of England or at the Bank of Ireland, any strip (within the meaning of Finance Act 1942, section 47) of any such stocks or funds, and any share in the stocks or funds of any foreign or colonial state or government, or any capital stock or funded debt of any county council, corporation, company, or society in the UK, or of any foreign or colonial corporation, company or society.'

2 For the definition of 'marketable security' see Stamp Act 1891, s 122: 'marketable security' means 'a security of such a description as to be capable of being sold in any stock market in the UK'. This phrase has been glossed as referring to securities which are capable 'according to the use and practice of stock markets, of being there sold and bought', per Shand J in *Texas Land and Cattle Co Ltd v IRC* (1888) 16 R 69 (see also *Speyer Bros v IRC* [1908] AC 92, HL). If a security could be admitted to trading on a stock exchange, but is not so admitted, this should not prevent that security constituting a marketable security. In order to be a security an instrument must also create an obligation (*Brown Shipley & Co v IRC* [1895] 2 QB 598) and whether a certificate for registered debenture stock constitutes a marketable security depends upon whether a contract between the debenture holder and the company issuing the debenture are enshrined within the certificate; a contract was so enshrined in *Re Dunderland Iron Ore Co Ltd* [1909] 1 Ch 446 but not in *Noakes v IRC* (1900) 83 LT 714. Hypothecation is not necessary for a security to constitute a marketable security (*Speyer Bros v IRC* [1907] 1 KB 246 (where there was no hypothecation); *Deddington Steamship Co Ltd v IRC* [1911] 2 KB 1001 (where there was hypothecation)).

3 Finance Act 1999 Sch 13, para 7.

Depositary receipt and clearance service charge – EU law aspects

10.21 One recurrent theme which runs through the stamp duty (and SDRT) analysis below is the implications of the ECJ's judgement in *HSBC Holdings Plc and Vidacos Nominees Ltd v. Commissioners for Her Majesty's Revenue & Customs*[1]. It may, therefore be helpful to summarise the facts of that case:

- HSBC made an offer to acquire shares in the French bank Crédit Commercial de France ('CCF'); shareholders in CCF where given the choice of consideration in the form of cash or of HSBC shares.

- It was a requirement of obtaining a listing in Paris that the newly issued shares HSBC shares should be transferred into the French clearance service (SICO-VAM).

- SDRT was charged at 1.5 per cent of the value of the shares on entry into the clearing system (representing about £27 million of SDRT).

- over 40 per cent of the HSBC shares were, after less than two weeks, withdrawn from SICOVAM and traded within CREST, incurring further SDRT at the normal rate of 0.5 per cent.

- shareholders who continued to hold their shares through SICOVAM, suffered a further 1.5 per cent SDRT charge on the issue of scrip dividends, this liability was satisfied by a reduction in the number of shares issued to shareholders to whom the script issue was made in SICOVAM.

The EU's Capital Duty Directive[2] prohibits the imposition of tax on the issue of 'stocks, shares or other securities of the same type, or of the certificates representing such securities'. HM Revenue and Customs countered that article 12 of the Capital Duty Directive which allows duties on the transfer of securities, permitted the 1.5% charge as it represented advance payment for future transfers of the shares within the clearing system. The ECJ rejected HM Revenue and Customs's argument for the following reasons:

(a) the 'principal' charge to SDRT is payable by different taxable persons (viz: the transferee in the case of each particular transfer) each of whom pays 0.5% whereas the clearance service charge is paid (in practice) by the issuer/transferor of the securities and is paid at the rate of 1.5%; and

(b) the 1.5 per cent charge is calculated on a different basis from the 'principal' charge of 0.5 per cent on a transfer.

The ECJ acknowledged that what took place was a 'transfer' (rather than an 'issue' of such shares), but held that Article 11(a) would be devoid of any sensible meaning if the first acquisition of securities could not regarded as being encompassed within the word 'issue'.

The Government responded to the ECJ's judgement by introducing an anti-avoidance rule in the Finance Act 2010. With respect to a transfer of a chargeable securities on or after 1 October 2009, FA 1986, s 97C1 (as inserted by the Finance Act 2010 s 54), provides that where chargeable securities are:

(a) issued to a nominee for an EU depositary receipt issuer or an EU clearance service'; and

(b) subsequently transferred 'from'[3] such a nominee 'to'[4] the nominee for a non-EU depositary receipt issuer (or clearance service),

the charge to SDRT is not disapplied by any of the usual exemptions if:

(i) the chargeable securities have not previously been transferred; or

(ii) any previous transfer was exempt (ie by virtue of FA 1986, ss 90(5), 95(1), 97(1) or 97B(1)).

It seems far from unarguable that the approach adopted by FA 2010 amendments is necessarily EU compliant, and the position appears likely to be tested further in light of a group litigation order granted by the High Court on 21 October 2010[5].

These developments have been followed by a ruling of the First-tier Tribunal in *HSBC Holdings PLC and The Bank of New York Mellon Corporation v HMRC*[6] where it was held that the 1.5% SDRT charge on the issue of shares to a non-EU issuer of ADRs (American Depositary Receipts) infringed Directive 69/335/EEC and article 56 of the Treaty of the Functioning of the European Union. In the wake of this decision HM Revenue and Customs announced that:

> 'In reaching its decision the Tribunal held that the Capital Duty Directive applies to issuers situated in the EU irrespective of where their investors are located. Acceptance of the decision means that HMRC will no longer seek to impose SDRT at the rate of 1.5 per cent on issues of UK shares [sic] to depositary receipt issuers and clearance services outside the EU. Following the decision of the European Court of Justice in '*HSBC Holdings plc and Vidacos Nominees Limited v Commissioners for HMRC (C-569-07)*', which held that SDRT charges on issues of UK shares to clearance services (and, by extension, depositary receipt issuers) within the EU is unlawful, the overall effect is now that 1.5 per cent SDRT is no longer applicable to issues of UK shares and securities to such entities anywhere in the world.
>
> HM Revenue and Customs does not consider that the Tribunal's decision has any impact upon transfers (on sale or otherwise than on sale) of shares and securities to depositary receipt systems or clearance services that are not an integral part of an issue of share capital. The Stamp Duty and Stamp Duty Reserve Tax charges under sections 67, 70, 93 and 96 therefore continue to apply to such transactions.'

1   Case 569-07.

2   The original Directive, Directive 69/335, has been recast as Directive 2008/7/EC.

3   A transfer is made 'from' an EU clearance service if it is from a company which is incorporated under the law of a member State and at the time of the transfer falls within FA 1986, s 67(6) (having a business of issuing depositary receipts) or s 70(6) (having a clearance service business); see FA 1986, s 97C(4)(a).

4   A transfer is made 'to' an EU clearance service if it is from a company which is incorporated outside the member States and at the time of the transfer falls within FA 1986, s 67(6) (having a business of issuing depositary receipts) or s 70(6) (having a clearance service business); see FA 1986, s 97C(4)(b).

5   The order is in respect of claims for restitution or damages where:

   (a) the charge to stamp duty at the rate of 1.5% pursuant to FA 1986, ss 67 or 70, arising on the transfer or relevant securities to a depositary receipt issuer or a clearance service provider (wherever located); or

   (b) the charge to SDRT at the rate of 1.5% pursuant to FA 1986, ss 93 or 96, arising on (i) the issue of chargeable securities to a depositary receipt issuer or a clearance service provider or located outside the EU, or (ii) the transfer of existing chargeable securities to a depositary receipt issuer or a clearance service provider (wherever located);

   are said to contravene Directive 69/335/EEC articles 10 and/or 11, and/or the Treaty of the Functioning of the European Union, and/or Directive 88/361/EEC.

   The group litigation order provides for the court to resolve whether:

   - claims for restitution are excluded by statute;
   - claims in respect of duty or tax paid more than six years before claims were issued are time barred;
   - the charges to duty and tax referred to above are contrary to EU law; and
   - a claimant is entitled to claim compound interest (by way of restitution) and/or damages.

6   [2012] UKFTT 163 (TC).

Depositary receipts

10.22 There is a charge to duty (at the rate of 1.5 per cent) on an instrument which transfers the securities of a company incorporated in the UK to certain persons, including a person whose business is exclusively that of holding relevant securities as a nominee or agent for a person whose business is or includes issuing depositary receipts[1]. This charge, however, does not bite on the issue of a security to a depositary (although there may be a charge under the bearer instrument head of charge). This charge on the transfer of securities to a depositary at triple the usual 0.5 per cent rate of duty was introduced to compensate the Exchequer for the loss of duty (or SDRT) which would, in the absence of the issue of depositary receipts, have been chargeable on future transfers of the underlying securities to which the depositary receipts relate.

1   Finance Act 1986, s 67.

10.23 A transfer of exempt loan capital, which is exempt from all stamp duties, is exempt from this charge. Irrespective of whether the loan capital is available, no chargeable instrument should be produced if a bearer instrument is transferred by delivery to a depositary prior to the issue of depositary receipts. This charge is, therefore, only likely to be in point where depositary receipts are issued in respect of the registered securities of a UK incorporated company which do not benefit from the loan capital exemption.

In light of the ECJ's ruling in *HSBC Holdings Plc and Vidacos Nominees Ltd v. Commissioners for Her Majesty's Revenue & Customs*[1] HM Revenue and Customs does not now attempt to seek to apply this 1.5 per cent stamp duty charge when 'shares'[2] are transferred to an EU depositary receipt system[3]. On 27 April 2012, in light of the First-tier Tribunal's decision in *HSBC Holdings PLC and The Bank of New York Mellon Corporation v HMRC*[4], HM Revenue and Customs accepted that the imposition of a charge to SDRT on the issue of securities to a depositary where that transfer represents 'an integral part of an issue of share capital' is incompatible with EU law[5].

1   (C560-07).

2   Presumably, this is 'short-hand' for any relevant chargeable security.

3   'Stamp Duty and Stamp Duty Reserve Tax Anti-Avoidance: Transfers of shares to depositary receipt systems and clearance services', PBRN 17 (9 December 2009).

4   [2012] UKFTT 163 (TC).

5   *SDRT – HSBC Holdings PLC and the Bank of New York Mellon Corporation v HMRC*: First-Tier Tax Tribunal decision – further announcement (27 April 2012).

Clearance service[1]

10.24 There may be a charge to duty (at the rate of 1.5 per cent) on an instrument which transfers shares in stock, or marketable securities of a company incorporated in the UK to certain persons, including a person whose business is exclusively that of holding shares, stock or other marketable securities as a nominee or agent for a person whose business is or includes the provision of clearance services for the purchase and sale of shares, stock and marketable securities[2]. HM Revenue and Customs takes the view that CREST is not a clearance service for the purposes of this charge to duty (or the equivalent charge to SDRT). HM Revenue and Custom's Stamp Taxes Manual states that CREST is a settlement system and not a clearance service (and that it is not a trading exchange, a custodian or a clearance service)[3]. The rationale for drawing this distinction is that a clearance service is a system for holding securities and settling transactions in those securities by book entry and 'the securities may be held indefinitely within the system despite changes in beneficial ownership and are held either by the company operating the clearance system or its nominee'[4]. Most European settlement systems (other than in the UK, Ireland and the Nordic states) operate on an intermediated basis, as discussed in Chapter 9.

1   See paras **10.1–10.5** above in relation to the distinction between the terminology used in relation to stamp duty and the terminology used elsewhere in this book.

2   Finance Act 1986, s 70.

3   Stamp Taxes Manual, March 2002, para 10.16.

4   Stamp Taxes Manual, March 2002, para 14.10.

One-off charge

10.25 Where applicable, there is a one-off charge on the issue or transfer to a clearance service at triple the usual 0.5 per cent rate of duty that was (like the depositary receipt charge) introduced to compensate the Exchequer for the loss of duty (or SDRT) which would, in the absence of transfer by clearing system book entries, have been chargeable on future transfers of the underlying securities which have been placed in a clearing system. Indeed, the drive for the introduction of the clearance service charge came, in large part, from market players seeking to create a level playing field between issuers of depositary receipts and operators of clearing systems[1].

1   See further para **10.42** n 2 below.

Election to pay stamp duty or SDRT

10.26 The operator of a clearance service may, however, elect that instead of the clearance service charge applying, stamp duty (or, more probably, SDRT) will be charged on any agreement to transfer of securities[1]; the Board of HM Revenue and Customs may require, as a condition for approving such an election, that the operator makes and maintains such arrangements as the Board considers necessary for the collection of duty in respect of such transfers[2]. If such an election is made, no charge to duty is made under the clearance service charge (nor under the sister charge to SDRT in respect of a transfer to a clearance service)[3]. Furthermore, if an election is made, there should be no charge to duty on the issue of securities into the clearance service; and the better view is that any instrument transferring a security to the depositary/nominee for the operator of a clearance service will not be chargeable with ad valorem stamp duty (as no economic interest moves to the nominee for the clearing system, there is no 'sale' of a security).

1   As discussed in Chapter 8, paras **8.6–8.10**, where securities are immobilised or dematerialised transfers are made through book entries in the accounts maintained by the system for its participants. Consequently, where a security is held in a clearance system there is not likely to be any documentary transfers of those securities when secondary market trading takes place between investors. No dutiable instrument may be created in the course of executing such trades, but SDRT is likely to arise in respect of an agreement to transfer chargeable securities: see further below.

2   See further para **10.44** n 7 below.

3   Finance 1986, s 97A(3).

Exempt agreements to transfer

10.27 A transfer of exempt loan capital, which is exempt from all stamp duties, is exempt from this charge and, where the exemption for such loan capital is not available, no chargeable instrument should be produced if a bearer instrument is transferred by delivery to the provider of a clearance service. This charge is, therefore, only likely to be in point where registered securities of a UK incorporated company which do not benefit from the loan capital exemption are transferred to a nominee for a clearance system.

In light of the ECJ's ruling in *HSBC Holdings Plc and Vidacos Nominees Ltd v. Commissioners for Her Majesty's Revenue & Customs*[1] HM Revenue and Customs does not now attempt to seek to apply this 1.5 per cent stamp duty charge when 'shares'[2] are transferred to an EU clearance service[3]. On 27 April 2012, in light of the First-tier Tribunal's decision in *HSBC Holdings PLC and The Bank of New York Mellon Corporation v HMRC*[4], HMRC accepted that the imposition of a charge to SDRT on the issue of securities to a clearance service where that transfer represents 'an integral part of an issue of share capital' is incompatible with EU law[5].

1   (C560-07).

2   Presumably, this is 'short-hand' for any relevant chargeable security.

3   'Stamp Duty and Stamp Duty Reserve Tax Anti-Avoidance: Transfers of shares to depositary receipt systems and clearance services', PBRN 17 (9 December 2009).

4   [2012] UKFTT 163 (TC).

5   SDRT – *HSBC Holdings PLC and the Bank of New York Mellon Corporation v HMRC*: First-Tier Tax Tribunal decision – further announcement (27 April 2012).

Investors

10.28 Generally speaking, stamp duty is likely to be principally of concern to a person wishing to prove title to securities: in many cases this will be the investor[1]. An issuer and the arranger/lead manager in respect of an issue of securities usually co-operate to ensure that no duty is payable on the issue of a security and that the characteristics of a security are such that an investor can trade in the security, or in interests in that security, without duty necessarily being payable. Thus, for example, a written instruction to transfer an American depositary receipt ('ADR') issued in respect of a registered equity share of a company which is incorporated in the UK (and where the register is in the UK) may well be within the charge to stamp duty as it relates to property, namely a share, situated in the UK. Provided, however, that the share to which the depositary receipt relates remains with the depositary and an investor trades the depositary receipt in respect of the share and is not obliged to prove title before a court in the UK, duty need not be paid on a written instruction to transfer a depositary receipt. Any duty payable on the transfer of such a share to a depositary (or a clearing system) should as a commercial matter be borne by the issuer of the securities; as an indemnity in respect of stamp duty may be void[2], a depositary (or clearing system) should customarily seek a covenant from the issuer that the issuer will ensure that a stampable document is duly stamped.

1   Note, however, the rules in relation to bearer instrument duty: see para **10.6** n 2 above.

   A person whose business is or includes the provision of clearance services for the purchase and sale of relevant securities incorporated in the UK must notify the Commissioners of HM Revenue and Customs within one month of first providing such clearance services; a person whose business includes holding relevant securities as nominee or agent for the operator of a clearance service is under a similar notification duty and this duty must be fulfilled within one month of first holding such securities as nominee or agent for such purposes.

   A company incorporated in the UK which becomes aware that the operator of a clearance system, or the agent or nominee for such a person, holds shares in that company must also notify the Commissioners within one month of becoming aware of such a fact. If an operator, or an agent or nominee for such an operator fails to comply with this duty, the operator, agent or nominee is liable for a penalty not exceeding £1,000; in the case of a company the penalty for non-compliance may not exceed £100. See Finance Act 1986, s 71.

2   Stamp Act 1891, s 117.

Custodians

10.29   A custodian needs to be sensitive to stamp duty considerations as it may hold stampable documents and may, indeed, if it issues depositary receipts or 'custody receipts' (as such instruments are sometimes referred to in the US) be liable to pay a depositary receipt charge. In certain circumstances a custodian's clients may be concerned to understand a custodian's operating procedures in order to ascertain whether they might involve the unnecessary production of documentation which would be stampable and, if so, whether the production of such documentation can be avoided. Generally speaking, however, other than in the case of an instrument liable to duty under the bearer instrument head of charge, a custodian should not itself directly incur liability for the stamping of instruments in its custody[1]. A custodian in the UK is, however, obliged to satisfy itself in registering title to property that an instrument of transfer is duly stamped; otherwise it will infringe s 17 of the Stamp Act 1891 on entering on a register a transfer to which an unstamped instrument relates[2].

1   Whether a document is stampable depends upon the precise contents of that document, for example:

   (a)   it should be the case that an instruction from a client to make the appropriate entries under a book entry system pursuant to an agreement which that client has reached with another party to transfer an interest in securities represented by account entries, should not be stampable. Such an instruction, if in writing, represents a contractual request to the custodian – it does not transfer property, nor should it be regarded as a memorandum of agreement to transfer property (since it was not produced for the purposes of recording the agreement and bringing it into effect as between the parties, but merely between an account holder and the custodian); and

   (b)   a written transfer of registered securities is stampable.

   Stamp Act 1891, s 5 provides that 'all the facts and circumstances' affecting the chargeability of an instrument must be fully and accurately set forth in that instrument; otherwise a person who executes an instrument or is concerned with its preparation with an intent to defraud the Crown incurs a penalty not exceeding £3,000 (see also *Parinv (Hatfield) v IRC* [1996] STC 933; affd [1998] STC 305, CA; Inland Revenue press release, August 1997).

2   The penalty may not exceed £300.

Evidence

10.30 A custodian should also be concerned to ensure that it will not be obliged to have to pay duty in order to have an instrument by which it is appointed stamped, so that such an instrument can be produced in evidence in civil proceedings before a court in the UK[1]. Although one would normally expect a custodian's clients, rather than a custodian, to wish to stamp an instrument (or to have it stamped) to prove title to property which is held in custody by the custodian, circumstances could arise where a person providing custody services wishes for its own purposes to produce a document before a court: such circumstances could include the enforcement of covenants given to the custodian or where a custodian (eg if the custodian is a trustee) seeks a declaration from the court as to its duties with respect to the custody assets. Although an indemnity for stamp duty may be void under s 117 of the Stamp Act 1891, a covenant to ensure that duty is paid may be enforceable and a covenant of this type is often included in documents[2]. A custodian may obtain further comfort that the instrument by which it is appointed is not stampable if, as in many capital market transactions, lawyers for the issuer or the arranger give a written opinion to the effect that transaction documents (including the instrument of appointment) are not stampable (and the trustee is an addressee of such an opinion).

1 An instrument of appointment, such as a custody agreement, should not be stampable with ad valorem duty provided that it does not contain:
   (a) a transfer of beneficial ownership (or an equitable interest in) property;
   (b) an agreement to transfer beneficial ownership of (or an equitable interest in) property;
   (c) an option to transfer beneficial ownership of (or an equitable interest in) property; or
   (d) an agreement to grant an option.

2 If, for example, a trust deed is only stampable with fixed duty (£5 or 50p) (ie did not constitute a transfer on sale, but was executed prior to 13 March 2008 and not stamped before 19 March 2008 and was a simple transfer of legal title to property) a custodian trustee might have been content to rely on a right to recover expenses (including duty) from trust property (this right should have been expressly stated in a well-drafted trust deed, but if no express right was included a right to recover properly incurred expenses is implied under Trustee Act 2000, s 31). Note that industry standard custody agreements allow the custodian to collect amounts to cover their expenses out of the custody assets, as discussed at Chapter 6, para **6.52** n 1.

STAMP DUTY RESERVE TAX (SDRT)

Chargeable securities

10.31 SDRT (unlike stamp duty) is a tax on transactions and is enforceable as a debt due to the Crown. SDRT is chargeable in relation to chargeable securities[1]. Chargeable securities are defined as[2]:

(a) stocks, shares or loan capital[3];

(b) interests in, or in dividends or other rights arising out of, stocks, shares or loan capital;

(c) rights to allotments of or to subscribe for, or options to acquire[4], stocks, shares or loan capital; and

(d) units under a unit trust scheme[5].

1 There is a distinction between the person who is liable for SDRT in the case of each charge to tax, and the 'accountable person' who may be obliged to account to HM Revenue and Customs within set time limits (with respect to the principal charge to SDRT (other than where securities are in CREST, as to which see para **10.33** below), normally the seventh day in the month after the month in which an agreement which is chargeable to SDRT is made) for the SDRT. For a list identifying accountable

persons and the time limits within which tax must be paid (without interest or penalties becoming payable) and other rules relating to the collection and enforcement of SDRT, see the Stamp Duty Reserve Tax Regulations 1986 (SI 1986/1711), as amended.

2   Finance Act 1986, s 99(3).

3   'Loan capital' is 'capital raised which is borrowed or has the character of borrowed money' (*A-G v South Wales Electrical Power Distribution Co* [1920] 1 KB 552, CA) or 'funded debt' (*Reed International v IRC* [1976] AC 336, [1975] 3 WLR 413, [1975] 3 All ER 218).

In the *South Wales* case the Court of Appeal offered guidance as to what constitutes capital raised which is borrowed or has the character of borrowed money. That case concerned the issue by a company of 'warrants' in lieu of interest which had fallen due on debenture stock issued by that company (such that warrants bore interest and fell due after a specified date). In holding that such warrants did not constitute capital raised which is borrowed or has the character of borrowed money, Atkin LJ stated that 'this case is really determined by a consideration of the nature of the transaction' (at 557) (see similarly the tone of Younger LJ's judgment at 560 and Lord Sterndale MR at 555). HM Revenue and Customs takes the view that the definition of loan capital is intended to cover 'any loan, for a specific period, however short'.

There is no statutory definition of 'funded debt'. Lord Wilberforce expressed the view in *Reed International v IRC* [1976] AC 336 at 361B that:

'It may be that no precise definition can be given, but I think that at any rate a debt is funded if it has some degree of permanence or long term character and some other indicia such as would be expected by a creditor, repayment of whose debt is to be postponed. Amongst such indicia would be payment of stipulated interest, a premium on redemption, security through a sinking fund or periodical drawings, or by a charge on specific revenues, the assignment of a definite order of priority as compared with other debts, the possibility of transfer in separate amounts.'

The other members of the Judicial Committee which heard Reed agreed with Lord Wilberforce, and Viscount Dilhorne added the observation that 'something more is needed in addition to the debt being permanent or semi-permanent or long term for it to be regarded as funded'.

4   This can embrace a warrant which carries a right to acquire a security which is not itself a chargeable security. Whether a warrant will be regarded as an 'option to acquire' will depend upon the rights enjoyed by the owner of that option. For example, an 'American style' warrant under the terms of which an investor may, on exercise, demand physical settlement is likely to be a chargeable security. A warrant which is treated as a chargeable security as an 'option to acquire' is also likely to be chargeable to stamp duty on issue under the principle outlined by the House of Lords in *George Wimpey & Co Ltd v IRC* [1975] 2 All ER 45: see para **10.12** above.

5   Prior to amendments made by the Finance Act 1987 to s 57 of the Finance Act 1946 which brought the definition of 'unit trust scheme' into line with that in the Financial Services Act 1986, there was a concern that global and immobilised securities could be regarded as unit trusts and therefore qualify as chargeable securities.

This point was of concern in a SDRT context as a unit trust is structured as issues and redemptions of units in order to avoid stamp duty on secondary market transactions (transfers to a manager are subject to special provisions in Finance Act 1999, Sch 19). No stamp duty arises on the transfer of a dematerialised security (as it is a duty on instruments) but the principal charge to SDRT which arises on agreements to transfer chargeable securities could apply if a dematerialised security were a chargeable security. Historically, unit trust instrument duty was chargeable on the creation of a unit trust scheme and, prior to the abolition of this duty in 1988 (and the alteration of the definition of unit trust scheme in 1987), there was therefore a concern that a global and/or immobilised security could give rise to unit trust instrument duty.

Prior to the 1987 amendments Finance Act 1946, s 57(1) had defined 'unit trust scheme' to mean 'any arrangements made for the purpose, or having the effect of providing, for persons having funds available for investment, facilities for the participation by them, as beneficiaries under a trust, in any profits or income arising from the acquisition, holding, management or disposal of any property whatsoever'. The current definition in Finance Act 1999, Sch 19, para 14 tracks the definition of 'unit trust scheme' in Financial Services and Markets Act 2000, s 237(1), which replaced the Financial Services Act 1986 provision. This definition provides that 'unit trust scheme' means 'a collective investment scheme under which the property is held on trust for the participants'.

Immobilised and global securities do not per se generally fall within the Financial Services and Markets Act 2000 definition. First, it is arguable that arrangements for immobilised securities and global securities do not satisfy this primary definition of a unit trust scheme, as the purpose and effect of such arrangements is not participation in and receipt of profits or income. Although that may be the purpose and effect of investment in the underlying issue, the purpose and effect of interposing an intermediary to create immobilised securities or global securities is the achievement of settlement efficiencies and (where securities are to be offered for sale to US persons) compliance with US securities restrictions. Second, immobilised global securities are taken out of the definition by Financial Services and Markets Act 2000, s 235(2) which provides that 'the arrangements must be such that the persons who are to participate ("participants") do not have day to day control over the management of the property in question...'.

Excluded securities

10.32 Certain securities, including the following are excluded from being chargeable securities:

(a) securities which are exempt from all stamp duties (this includes exempt loan capital and gilts (irrespective of whether a transfer of gilts is within CREST)[1];

(b) securities issued or raised by a body corporate[2] not incorporated in the UK, where the securities are not registered in a register kept in the UK by or on behalf of the issuer (and, in the case of a Societas Europaea, the Societas Europaea does not have its registered office in the UK) and in the case of shares which are paired those shares are not paired shares issued by a body corporate incorporated in the UK[3];

(c) a depositary receipt for stocks or shares[4];

(d) a UK depositary interest in foreign securities[5]; and

(e) a unit under a unit trust scheme, if either –

(i) all the trustees of the scheme are resident outside the UK and the unit is not registered in a register kept in the UK by or on behalf of the trustees of the scheme; or

(ii) under the terms of the scheme the trust property can only be invested in exempt investments[6].

1 Finance Act 1986, s 99(5)–(5ZA).

2 On the meaning of 'body corporate', see G F H Montagu 'Is a foreign state a body corporate?' (2001) 6 *British Tax Review* 421–48, as reissued with minor (albeit not quite complete) corrections in 2002 to more closely reflect the final proofs.

3 Finance Act 1986, s 99(4)–(4A).

4 Finance Act 1986, s 99(6). A 'depositary receipt for stocks or shares' is an instrument acknowledging:

(a) that a person holds stocks or shares or evidence of the right to receive them, and

(b) that another person is entitled to rights, whether expressed as units or otherwise, in or in relation to stocks or shares of the same kind, including the right to receive such stocks or shares (or evidence of the right to receive them) from the person mentioned in (a) above.

However, a 'depositary receipt for stocks or shares' does not include an instrument acknowledging rights in or in relation to stocks or shares if they are issued or sold under terms providing for payment in instalments and for the issue of the instrument as evidence that an instalment has been paid. See Finance Act 1986, s 99(7).

5 Finance Act 1999, s 119 and the Stamp Duty Reserve Tax (UK Depositary Interests in Foreign Securities) Regulations 1999 (SI 1999/2383, as amended by SIs 2000/1871, 2001/3779, 2007/12 and 2008/954). A UK depositary interest is a depositary interest which is issued in the UK or registered in a register kept in the UK. A 'depositary interest' is defined as a security which:

(a) consists of the rights of a person in or relating to securities of a particular kind which, or entitlements to which, are held on trust for the benefit of that person by another person; and

(b) under the terms of its issue, can only be transferred in accordance with regulations under Companies Act 2006, s 785 (provision enabling procedures for evidencing and transferring title) or by means of a transfer within Finance Act 1996, s 186(1) (transfer of securities to a member of electronic transfer system).

'Foreign securities' are securities within Uncertificated Securities Regulations 2001 (SI 2001/3755), reg 3(1) which:

(a) are issued or raised by a body corporate that is not incorporated, and whose central management and control is not exercised, in the UK;

(b) are not registered in a register kept in the UK by or on behalf of the body corporate by which they are issued or raised;

(c) are of the same class in the body corporate as securities which:

(i) are listed on a recognised stock exchange; or

(ii) would have been treated as so listed immediately before 28 November 2001.

6   Finance Act 1986, s 99(5A). An investment is an exempt investment if (s 99(5B) as amended by Finance Act 2011, s 84 with effect from 24 July 2011):

(a) in the case of an investment other than an interest under a collective investment scheme, if and only if it is not an investment on the transfer of which ad valorem stamp duty would be chargeable, on the acquisition of which stamp duty land tax would be chargeable, and it is not a chargeable security;

(b) in the case of an interest under a collective investment scheme, unless more than 20% of the market value of the investments in which the property subject to the scheme is invested is attributable to investments which are not exempt investments; and

(c) in the case of a derivative, it relates wholly to one or more exempt investment; and

(d) funds held for the purposes of day-to-day management of a unit trust scheme are not regarded as investments.

Charges to SDRT

10.33 There are three charges to SDRT.

Principal charge

10.34 This charge arises where a person (A) agrees with another person (B) to transfer chargeable securities (whether or not to B) for consideration in money or money's worth[1]. Tax is chargeable at the rate of 0.5 per cent of the consideration in money or money's worth. Person B is liable for SDRT chargeable under the principal charge[2]. However, where chargeable securities have been dematerialised within CREST, CRESTCo, as operator of a 'relevant system' for the purposes of the Stamp Duty Reserve Tax Regulations 1986[3], is (except where different arrangements are authorised by the Board of HM Revenue and Customs) generally required on or before the accountable date, to notify HM Revenue and Customs of each charge to tax which has arisen and to pay the tax due[4].

1   Finance Act 1987, s 87.

2   Finance Act 1986 s 91(1).

3   SI 1986/1711.

4   Stamp Duty Reserve Tax Regulations 1986, reg 4A. CRESTCo may, on making a claim, be relieved of its liability to account for and pay tax (and any interest on that tax) if it proves to the Board of the HM Revenue and Customs' satisfaction that it has taken without success all reasonable steps to recover from the person liable for the tax in respect of which CRESTCo is obliged to account under reg 4A: reg 7.

For an outline of HM Revenue and Customs' approach to administering SDRT through CREST see the Stamp Taxes Manual, March 2002, paras 10.21–10.35 and see also Stamp Duty Reserve Tax in CREST – a guide to market practice (Euroclear, December 2011).

SDRT is charged, and exemptions from SDRT are generally given effect to, by means of a 'transaction stamp status ("TSS") flag' or 'exception flag' which is inputed by a CREST participant with respect to each transaction. The main flags are:

'P'	0.5% ad valorem SDRT	This is the default flag if no input is specified.
'R'	1.5% ad valorem SDRT	
'O'	No SDRT	On a transfer between nominees, or between a nominee and a beneficial owner, without a transfer of beneficial ownership
'S'	No SDRT	On a transfer to an exempt charity
'T'	No SDRT	SDRT paid inside CREST on another CREST transaction
'U'	No SDRT	Stamp duty paid outside CREST on a physical document (including a form 169); or SDRT payable outside CREST on corporate action
'W'	No SDRT	Issuing house exemption on new issue
'3'	No SDRT	Intra-group transfer entitled to relief from stamp duty under s 42 of the Finance Act 1930 (as amended), a letter of direction having been adjudicated by the Stamp Office.
'4'	No SDRT	Stock loan return or transfer of delivery by value ('DBV') (see Chapter 9, para **9.89**) collateral relating to loans
'5'	No SDRT	A letter of direction having been executed (eg pension scheme merger, purchase of life insurance policy or transfer by way of security for a loan)
'6'	No SDRT	Merger of authorised units, or the conversion/amalgamation of authorised unit trusts/open-ended investment companies
'7'	No SDRT	Security on an overseas register.

A CREST participant is obliged to keep evidence to support an exemption when it inputs an exemption flag. In an unusual case where one of the flags is not suitable and a statutory exemption is available, either (where a paper transfer attracts fixed stamp duty) use of a paper transfer (rather than settling the transfer through CREST) should be considered or a repayment of SDRT can be sought from HM Revenue and Customs.

Where a repayment is claimed, the CREST Transaction ID, individual SDRT claim amount, trade date, and relevant repayment code must be submitted to HM Revenue and Custom's SDRT Operations Unit. For HM Revenue and Custom's practice with respect to reclaims of SDRT, see Stamp Taxes' Customer Newsletter – Stamp Duty Reserve Tax (SDRT), No 1, July 2002, as supplemented by Customer Newsletter – Stamp Duty Reserve Tax (SDRT), No 3, April 2003.

EXEMPTIONS

10.35 There are a number of exemptions from the principal charge. For example, these include exemptions which apply to:

(a) certain repos and security loans[1];

(b) intermediaries[2];

(c) an agreement to transfer a non-UK bearer instrument[3];

(d) an agreement to transfer a UK bearer instrument where (amongst other things):

   (i) the agreement is not made in contemplation of, or part of, an agreement for a takeover of the body corporate which issued the instrument;

   (ii) a chargeable security (or a depositary receipt for the chargeable securities)[4] is listed on a recognised stock exchange[5].

1   Finance Act 1986, s 89AA (as amended by Stamp Duty Reserve Tax (Amendment of section 89AA of the Finance Act 1986) Regulations 2008 (SI 2008/3236). The exemption applies where a person (P) has entered into an arrangement with another person (Q) under which Q is to transfer chargeable securities of a particular kind to P or his or her nominee, and chargeable securities of the same kind and amount are to be transferred by P or his or her nominee to Q or his or her nominee and certain conditions are fulfilled. The conditions are that either:

   (a) (i)   the agreement is effected on a regulated market, a multilateral treading facility or a recognised foreign exchange;

   (ii) securities of the kind concerned are regularly traded on that market, facility or exchange; and

   (iii) the chargeable securities are transferred to P or his or her nominee and Q or his or her nominee in pursuance of the arrangement; or

   (b) P or Q are authorised under the MiFID Directive to execute orders on behalf of clients and deal on its own account, securities of that kind are regularly traded as a regulated market, and chargable securities are transferred to P or his nominee and Q or his nominee in pursuance of the arrangement.

   Where the only reason that the above conditions are not fulfilled is that after Q has transferred securities either P or Q become insolvent on or after 1 September 2008 and it becomes apparent that, as a result of that insolvency, securities will not be transferred to Q or Q's nominee in accordance with the arrangement (and P and Q are not 'connected' for the purposes of section 1122 of the Corporation Tax Act 2010), Finance Act 1986, s 89AB provides that a charge under s 87 is not to arise. If the solvent party acquires replacement securities within 30 days of the insolvency occurring, then s 87 also does not apply in respect of any agreement to transfer those replacement securities to the solvent party or its nominee (equally, s 87 does not apply if no collateral is provided under the arrangement and there is an agreement to transfer replacement securities).

   In order to be 'effected' on a market, facility, or exchange, an agreement must be subject to the rules of that market, facility or exchange and reported in accordance with the rules of that market, facility, or exchange (with respect to securities admitted to trading on the London Stock Exchange, see The Rules of the London Stock Exchange; especially Chapters 2 and 8).

   HM Revenue and Customs regards the requirement for a transaction to be 'reported' in accordance with the rules of the relevant exchange, multilateral trading facility or market as being satisfied if the transaction is reported in accordance with the MiFID Directive; see 'Stamp Duty & Stamp Duty Reserve Tax: Intermediary and Stock Lending Reliefs – FA 2007 Changes' para 4.2 p 5 which is available at www.hmrc.gov.uk/so/sdrt-guidance-mifid.pdf and effectively supersedes the out-dated guidance in the Stamp Taxes Manual.

   HM Revenue and Customs regards a security as being 'regularly traded' if it is admitted to trading on the relevant market, multilateral trading facility or exchange. HM Revenue and Customs looks, for example, to lists of regularly traded shares held in CREST and maintained by the appropriate market; ibid para 3.6 p 3. Euroclear maintains a list of 'regularly traded' securities (as well as a separate list of s-approved intermediaries).

   An arrangement does not fall within the exemption if it is not such an agreement as would be entered into by persons dealing with each other at arm's length, or under the arrangement any of the benefits or risks arising from fluctuations before the transfer to Q or his or her nominee takes place in the market value of the chargeable securities accrues to, or fall on, P.

2   Finance Act 1986, s 88A(1)–(1C) (as substituted by the Finance Act 2007) exempt from the principal charge to SDRT any agreement to transfer securities of a particular kind to B or his or her nominee if (a) B is a member of an a regulated market on which securities of that kind are regularly traded and B is an intermediary recognised in accordance with arrangements approved by HM Revenue and Customs; (b) B is a member of a multilateral trading facility or a recognised foreign exchange on which securities of that kind are regularly traded, B is an intermediary and is recognised as an intermediary by the exchange in accordance with arrangements agreed with HM Revenue and Customs, and the agreement is effected on the facility or exchange; (c) B is an intermediary who is approved by HM Revenue and Customs, and securities of that kind are regularly traded on a regulated market; or (d) B is an intermediary who is approved by HM Revenue and Customs, and securities of that kind are regularly traded on a multilateral trading facility or recognised investment exchange the agreement is effected on the facility or exchange.

   Finance Act 1986, s 88A(2A)–(2C) (as substituted by the Finance Act 2007) similarly exempt any agreement to transfer securities of a particular kind to B or his or her nominee if: (a) B is a member of a regulated market, a multilateral trading facility or a recognised foreign options exchange (or is approved by HM Revenue and Customs); (b) options to buy or sell securities of that kind are regularly traded on that market, facility or exchange and are listed by or quoted on that market, facility or exchange; (c) (where B has not been approved by HM Revenue and Customs) B is an options intermediary and is recognised as an options intermediary by that market, facility or exchange in accordance with arrangements approved by HM Revenue and Customs; and (d) (i) securities of that kind are regularly traded on a regulated market, or (ii) the agreement is effected on a regulated market, a multilateral trading facility or a recognised foreign options exchange on which securities of that kind are regularly traded, or is effected on such an exchange pursuant to the exercise of the relevant option and options to buy or sell securities of that kind are regularly traded on that market, facility or exchange and are listed by or quoted on that market, facility and exchange.

An 'intermediary' (or an options intermediary) is essentially a person who carries on a bona fide business of dealing in chargeable securities and does not carry on an excluded business. Excluded businesses include a business which consists wholly or mainly on making or managing investments, insurance business, managing or acting as trustee in relation to a pension scheme or operating or acting as trustee for a collective investment scheme (Finance Act 1986, s 88A(4)–(5)). The equivalent stamp duty exemptions are in Finance Act 1986, s 80A.

HM Revenue and Customs can only 'approve' a person for the purpose of these exemptions for intermediaries if that person is authorised under the law of a European Economic Area ('EEA') state to provide certain investment services or activities (executions of orders on behalf of clients and dealing on own account) in Annex 1 of the MiFID Directive. For the operation of this exemption by Euroclear, see Euroclear's Update Paper Miscellaneous items on the Single Platform – Service description, July 2008, para 10.1.1. and

There are also exemptions, made by the Treasury using powers conferred by the Finance Act 1991 (s 116 with respect to stamp duty, and s 117 with respect to SDRT as, in each case, amended by Finance Act 2010, s 65), which prevent multiple charges arising due to the mechanics of particular exchanges where a transaction is entered into by a recognised intermediary (eg a central counterparty or a clearing member on an exchange) on an exchange and that intermediary has entered into appropriate arrangements with HM Revenue and Customs. The relevant regulations are:

- Stamp duty and Stamp Duty Reserve Tax (Eurex Clearing AG) Regulations 2011 (SI 2011/666).
- Stamp duty and Stamp Duty Reserve Tax (European Central Counterparty Limited) Regulations 2011 (SI 2011/667).
- Stamp duty and Stamp Duty Reserve Tax (European Multilateral Clearing Facility NV) Regulations 2011 (SI 2011/668).
- Stamp duty and Stamp Duty Reserve Tax (LCH.Clearnet Limited) Regulations 2011 (SI 2011/669).
- Stamp duty and Stamp Duty Reserve Tax (Six X-Clear AG) Regulations 2011 (SI 2011/670).

3   Finance Act 1986, s 90(3)(a).
4   See para **10.38** n 1 below (Finance Act 1986, s 90(6)).
5   Finance Act 1986, s 90(3A)–(3F).

10.36 There is also an exemption from the principal charge for an agreement which gives rise to a charge to SDRT under the depositary receipt charge or the clearance service charge (discussed below), or where when an agreement is made and the Board of HM Revenue and Customs is satisfied that chargeable securities are held for the purpose of a business which consists of holding stock, shares or marketable securities as nominee for a clearance service provider, or when an agreement is for the transfer of a depositary receipt for chargeable securities[1]. An agreement to transfer securities to a body of persons established for charitable purposes, or certain other categories of exempt persons, is also exempt[2].

1   Finance Act 1986, s 90(4)–(6); note that this exemption may be disapplied by FA 1986, s 97C as to which see **10.21** above.
2   Finance Act 1986, s 90(7).

DOUBLE CHARGE

10.37 Although it is possible in certain circumstances for there to be a double charge, to SDRT under the principal charge and to stamp duty under the transfer on sale head of charge, such a result is often avoided by the cancellation of an SDRT charge (and the refund of any SDRT which has been paid) if an instrument is executed pursuant to an agreement to transfer chargeable securities and that instrument is duly stamped[1].

1   Finance Act 1986, s 92.

10.38 Where an instrument is not chargeable to stamp duty on the dematerialisation of chargeable securities by virtue of s 186 of the Finance Act 1986[1], any SDRT which has been paid may be reclaimed (within the relevant time limits) and if SDRT has not been paid the principal charge to SDRT charge is cancelled[2].

1   See paras **10.17–10.19** above.
2   Finance Act 1986, s 88(1A).

Depositary receipt charge

10.39 There is a charge to SDRT where in pursuance of an arrangement a person (a 'Depositary') whose business is or includes issuing depositary receipts for chargeable securities[1] has issued or issues a depositary receipt for chargeable securities; chargeable securities of the same kind and amount are transferred or issued to the Depositary or a person (a 'Custodian') whose business is or includes holding chargeable securities as nominee or agent for the Depositary; and chargeable securities are appropriated towards the eventual satisfaction of the entitlement of the receipt holder to receive chargeable securities[2]. The rate of SDRT applicable is 1.5 per cent[3]. If ad valorem stamp duty is payable on an instrument effecting the transfer of securities, then the amount of SDRT payable is reduced by the amount of stamp duty[4]. The person liable for the SDRT is the person who issues depositary receipts, but if that person is not resident in the UK and does not have a branch or agency in the UK, the person to whom the securities are transferred is liable for the tax[5].

1   A 'depositary receipt for chargeable securities' is an instrument acknowledging (a) that a person holds chargeable securities or evidence of the right to receive them, and (b) that another person is entitled to rights, whether expressed as units or otherwise, in or in relation to chargeable securities of the same kind, including the right to receive such chargeable securities (or evidence of the right to receive them) from the person mentioned in (a) above. However, a 'depositary receipts for chargeable securities' does not include an instrument acknowledging rights in or in relation to chargeable securities if they are issued or sold under terms providing for payment in instalments and for the issue of the instrument as evidence that an instalment has been paid. See Finance Act 1986, s 94(1).
2   Finance Act 1986, s 93(1)–(3).
3   Finance Act 1986, s 93(4).
4   Finance Act 1986, s 93(7).
5   Finance Act 1986, s 93(8)–(9).

EXEMPTIONS

10.40 There are various exemptions from the depositary receipt charge. There is no charge to tax:

(a) on a transfer by, or to, a company which is an agent for the depositary and is a UK resident company[1];

(b) on a transfer, issue, or appropriation of a UK bearer instrument except in the case of[2]:

    (i) a renounceable letter of allotment which is exempt from stamp duty[3], or

(ii) a non-sterling bearer instrument which does not raise new capital[4] and is not issued in exchange for an instrument raising new capital[5];

(c) on an issue by a company (X) of securities in exchange for shares in another company (Y) where either[6]:

(i) X has control of Y; or

(ii) X will have control of Y due to the exchange or an offer, as a result of which the exchange is made and the shares in Y are held under a depositary receipt scheme;

(d) on the transfer or issue of certain replacement securities[7].

In light of the ECJ's ruling in *HSBC Holdings Plc and Vidacos Nominees Ltd v. Commissioners for Her Majesty's Revenue & Customs*[8] HM Revenue and Customs does not now attempt to seek to apply this 1.5 per cent stamp duty charge when 'shares'[9] are transferred to an EU depositary receipt issuer[10]. On 27 April 2012, in light of the First-tier Tribunal's decision in *HSBC Holdings PLC and The Bank of New York Mellon Corporation v HMRC*[11], HM Revenue and Customs accepted that the imposition of a charge to SDRT on the issue of securities to a depositary where that transfer represents 'an integral part of an issue of share capital' is incompatible with EU law[12].

1   Finance Act 1986, s 95(1).
2   Finance Act 1986, s 95(2)–(2D).
3   Finance Act 1999, Sch 15, para 16.
4   An instrument which raises new capital includes an instrument issued in connection with relevant securities which are subscribed for only in cash. A 'relevant security' is a security the holders of which have a right to a dividend at a fixed rate (but no other right to share in profits), or loan capital (as defined in Finance Act 1986, s 78), and which does not carry any rights by which securities which are not relevant securities may be obtained.
5   For example, an instrument issued in conjunction with the issue of relevant securities by a company in exchange for relevant securities issued by another company and immediately before exchange an instrument would have been regarded as raising new capital.
6   Finance Act 1986, s 95(3)–(5).
7   Finance Act 1986, s 96(2). Tax is charged on a percentage, where securities are issued, of their price when issued; or where securities are transferred for consideration in money or money's worth of the amount or value of consideration; and in any other case, the value of the securities.
8   (C560-07).
9   Presumably, this is 'short-hand' for any relevant chargeable security.
10 'Stamp Duty and Stamp Duty Reserve Tax Anti-Avoidance: Transfers of shares to depositary receipt systems and clearance services', PBRN 17 (9 December 2009).
11 [2012] UKFTT 163 (TC).
12 SDRT – *HSBC Holdings PLC and the Bank of New York Mellon Corporation v HMRC*: First-Tier Tax Tribunal decision – further announcement (27 April 2012).

10.41 For practical purposes, the exemption at (b) is the most frequently in point. Effectively, that exemption confines the depositary receipt charge in respect of bearer securities to the issue of depositary receipts for certain non-sterling bearer instruments issued by UK incorporated companies[1]. The logic appears to be that where a bearer instrument benefits from an exemption from stamp duty under the bearer instrument head of charge it would not be appropriate to impose an SDRT charge on the issue of depositary receipts. The somewhat gothic nature of the provisions, which are designed to ensure that the issue of depositary receipts for such foreign currency denominated bearer securities only escape a charge to duty if the securities represent genuine loan capital, is attributable to some arrangements which certain UK incorporated companies employed in the past to minimise stamp duty/SDRT by means of using foreign currency denominated bearer securities in the context of mergers and acquisitions.

1   Note that, for these purposes, the definition of chargeable securities is narrowed so as to exclude from the definition (and hence from the depositary receipt charge and clearance system charge) any capital raised by a company not incorporated in the UK: Finance Act 1986, s 99(10).

TRANSFERS BETWEEN DEPOSITARY RECEIPT AND CLEARANCE SYSTEMS

10.42   There is no charge under the depositary receipt charge in relation to a transfer between a depositary receipt system and a clearance system[1]. Note, however, that if chargeable securities remain in a clearing system and a depositary receipt is issued in respect of chargeable securities it would appear that a depositary receipt charge could arise (even if a clearance service charge had already arisen in respect of the chargeable securities)[2].

1   Finance Act 1986, s 97B. This section does not apply to a transfer from a clearance system if at the time of the transfer an election for the alternative system of charge under Finance Act 1986, s 97A is in force, or if FA 1986, s 97C is engaged, as to which see **10.21** above.

2   Any such harsh result may be attributable to the history of the depositary receipt charge and the clearance service charge. The depositary receipt charge was originally mooted to protect the Exchequer from the perceived loss of revenue when American depositary receipts ('ADRs') were issued in respect of multiples of securities issued by UK companies and subsequently transferred without there being a transfer of the underlying securities. The clearance service charge was introduced so as to create a level playing field between issuers of ADRs into the US market and distribution to investors in the European markets, where it is more usual to trade interests in underlying securities held through the medium of a clearing system than to trade depositary receipts.

Clearance service[1]

CLEARERS

10.43   There is a charge to SDRT where in pursuance of an arrangement a person (a 'clearer') whose business is or includes the provision of clearance services for the purchase and sale of chargeable securities has entered into an agreement to provide such services for another person, and in pursuance of that arrangement, chargeable securities are transferred or issued to the clearer or a person whose business is or includes holding chargeable securities as nominee for the clearer. The mechanics of the clearance service charge are similar to those of the depositary receipt charge. Thus, the rate of SDRT applicable is 1.5 per cent[2]. If ad valorem stamp duty is payable on an instrument effecting the transfer of securities, then the amount of SDRT payable is reduced by the amount of stamp duty[3]. The person liable for the SDRT is the clearer but, if that person is not resident in the UK and does not have a branch or agency in the UK, the person to whom the securities are transferred is liable for the tax[4].

1   See para **10.5** above in relation to the distinction between the terminology used in relation to SDRT and the terminology used elsewhere in this book.

2   Finance Act 1986, s 93(4).

3   Finance Act 1986, s 96(5).

4   Finance Act 1986, s 96(6)–(7).

EXEMPTIONS

10.44   The exemptions from the clearance service charge to SDRT are also similar to those which are available in respect of the depositary receipt charge[1]. However, as an alternative to such exemptions, the operator of a clearance system may, with the approval of the Board of HM Revenue and Customs, elect for an alternative system of charge to apply[2]. If an election is made[3], the clearance service charge to SDRT will not apply when a security is issued or transferred into the clearance system, but the principal charge will apply to an agreement to transfer the chargeable securities[4] (although the better view is that no tax is actually payable under the principal charge in respect of the agreement to transfer a security to a depositary/nominee for a clearing system, on the basis that such an agreement is not an agreement to transfer a chargeable security for consideration in money or money's worth)[5]. Both Euroclear[6] and Clearstream are understood to have made an election under s 97A of the Finance Act 1986[7]. As discussed above, there is no charge under the depositary receipt charge in relation to a transfer between a depositary receipt system and a clearance system[8].

In light of the ECJ's ruling in *HSBC Holdings Plc and Vidacos Nominees Ltd v. Commissioners for Her Majesty's Revenue & Customs*[9] HM Revenue and Customs does not now attempt to seek to apply this 1.5 per cent stamp duty charge when 'shares'[10] are transferred to an EU clearance service[11]. On 27 April 2012, in light of the First-tier Tribunal's decision in *HSBC Holdings PLC and The Bank of New York Mellon Corporation v HMRC*[12], HM Revenue and Customs accepted that the imposition of a charge to SDRT on the issue of securities to a clearance service where that transfer represents 'an integral part of an issue of share capital' is incompatible with EU law[13].

1 Finance Act 1986, ss 97 (ableit that this exemption may be disapplied by FA 1986, s 97C as to which see **10.21** above), 97AA.

2 Finance Act 1986, s 97AA.

3 HM Revenue and Customs, as of September 2011, took the view that:

(a) the following National Central Securities Depositaries were unelected clearance services: Euroclear Netherlands, Euroclear Belgium, Euroclear France, VPC in Sweden, VPS in Norway and VGP in Denmark; and

(b) each of the following International Central Securities Depositaries has made a s 97A election for part of its system: Clearstream in Frankfurt, Euroclear Bank in Belgium, and Sega Intersettle in Switzerland.

For this practice see M J Quinlan *Sergeant and Sims: Stamp Duties* (First published 2000, Issue 16 September 2008, Lexis Nexis Butterworths), Part 13.2. The author is grateful to Michael Quinlan for clarifying the source of the authority for this information.

For the position in relation to Euroclear (which has elected for the alternative system of charge to apply in respect of certain securities) see n 6 below.

4 Finance Act 1986, s 97A(3) disapplies the exemption from the principal charge to SDRT in s 90(5).

5 Note that the stamp duty clearance service charge is also disapplied if an election for the alternative system of charge is made.

6 Euroclear UK made an election for the alternative system of charge in 1999 for certain uncertified equity securities which are, in HM Revenue and Customs parlance, 'settled' through CREST.

With effect from 7 June 2002 Euroclear Bank introduced a more general policy with regard to accepting CREST-eligible UK equities subject to the SDRT 1.5 per cent clearance service charge. By default the alternative system of charge (ie under the s 97A election) will continue to apply and Euroclear will identify securities accepted under the s 97A election by using an International Securities Identifying Number ('ISIN') and a first Common Code. A participant may, however, submit a request that the alternative system of charge should not apply: in such a case securities will be identified by a second Common Code only. In addition to identifying the applicable SDRT regime by reference to the ISIN/Common Code, Euroclear will add the applicable SDRT rate to the name of the security.

Separate accounts are used by Euroclear to enable a participant to hold and transfer UK equities under the 1.5 per cent charge or the alternative system of charge (and, apparently, to convert from one regime to the other when dealing with a counterparty which uses a different regime from that used by a participant). Where the 1.5 per cent regime applies, SDRT is charged to a participant and Euroclear communicates this to a participant by means of a corporate action notification (DACE notice). Where securities are transferred between two clients of a participant without giving rise to a debit or credit in a participant's securities clearance account, then on the actual settlement date of the transfer in the participant's books the participant sends a duly completed report of the internal transfer to Euroclear Bank SA/NV via authenticated SWIFT message or tested telex on the actual

312 *The Law of Global Custody*

settlement date of each transfer in a participant's books: see further *Euroclear Newsletter 2002-N-03*, 20 May 2002, the 'UK' section in Euroclear's *Participant User Guide: Market Links*, 20 May 2002, and *Euroclear Newsletter 2007-N-042*, 18 June 2007 (in particular, for the forms to be used for reporting an internal transfer, a certificate for exemption from UK stamp duty to be used where a transfer is exempt, and a summary of the documentation to retained by a participant for the period of six years from the settlement date of a transaction).

Euroclear France and Euroclear Nederland hold CREST-eligible securities through Euroclear Bank's SDRT account (securities account 56XKJ in CREST). In the context of the Euroclear Settlement of Euronext-zone Securities ('ESES') a transaction between two ESES parties is settled within Euroclear Bank's global position with CREST, and a SDRT liability does not arise for the ESES delivering party. This treatment is accorded to a clear international delivery order ('IDO') or a clear international import order ('IIO'), or a cross-border IDO (ie where securities are transferred out of Euroclear Bank's CREST account to the account of another CREST party). In the case of a cross-border IIO, an ESES party should ensure that its counterparty credits Euroclear Bank's 1.5 per cent SDRT account with the SDRT due and correctly inputs the stamp duty flag to account for the SDRT due in its delivery instruction in the CREST system. A security which is a chargeable security for SDRT purposes is not eligible for the bridge between Euroclear Bank and Clearstream Banking Luxembourg. See further, Euroclear's *ESES International Links*, version 4.1, 16 January 2009, para 4.17.23.

It is envisaged that when Euroclear implements Single Platform Settlement (originally scheduled to have been completed by 2011 but understood to have been delayed in the wake of the abandonment of the Common Communication Interface (referred to as the 'CCI') in favour of Euroclear Connect which incorporates the Euroclear Access Application (referred to as the 'E2A')), the UK domestic service on the Single Platform will continue unaffected, see Euroclear's *Update Paper, Miscellaneous items on the Single Platform – Service description*, July 2008, paras 3 and 10.1. In order to allow participants to deal in securities with any counterparty within the Euroclear group without borders, SDRT eligible securities will no longer be eligible within Euroclear France and Euroclear Nederland (except in the case (i) of a cross-border merger between a UK company and, respectively, a French or Dutch company – where it will continue to be possible to settle a security SDRT free on the basis that the issuer picks up the 1.5 per cent SDRT charge, or (ii) where an investor picks up the 1.5 per cent charge), ibid, para 3.2.

7   It appears that whether an election is acceptable to the Commissioners of HM Revenue and Customs, and the extent of any such election which is accepted, will depend in each case upon the circumstances. However, HM Revenue and Customs has indicated that some of the main issues to be considered in this context are (Stamp Taxes Manual (March 2002), para 14.14):

- comparability with the procedures for accounting for SDRT through CREST;
- ensuring that all chargeable transactions are reported and duty paid;
- considering how higher rate charges and any reliefs would be administered;
- ensuring a flow of information for audit purposes that is accessible in the UK;
- preventing participants operating clearing services under cover of the arrangement;
- the need for an overseas clearance service to appoint a UK fiscal representative; and
- noting that s 97A enables HM Revenue and Customs to terminate the election on notice.

8   Finance Act 1986, s 97B. This section does not apply to a transfer from a clearance system if at the time of the transfer an election for the alternative system of charge under s 97A is in force.

9   (C560-07).

10 Presumably, this is 'short-hand' for any relevant chargeable security.

11 'Stamp Duty and Stamp Duty Reserve Tax Anti-Avoidance: Transfers of shares to depositary receipt systems and clearance services', PBRN 17 (9 December 2009).

12 [2012] UKFTT 163 (TC).

13 SDRT – *HSBC Holdings PLC and the Bank of New York Mellon Corporation v HMRC*: First-Tier Tax Tribunal decision – further announcement (27 April 2012).

Settlements and direct assessment

10.45 Although settlements rarely arise in practice, care needs to be taken to ensure that a settlement does not arise for income tax[1], capital gains tax[2] or inheritance tax[3] purposes.

1   An income tax settlement should not arise unless a trust is established by virtue of any act of bounty: *Bulmer v CIR* [1967] Ch 145, [1966] 3 WLR 672, [1966] 3 All ER 801; *IRC v Plummer* [1979] STC 793.

    If a settlement were to arise, the trustees of the settlement would be assessable in respect of accumulated or discretionary income in excess of £1,000 a year at the trust rate (50 per cent at the time of writing) or at the dividend trust rate (42.5 per cent at the time of writing) in respect of dividend income (Income Tax Act 2007, ss 9, 479, 491). Dividend income in relation to trustees includes: income chargeable under Chapter 3 of Part 4 of Income Tax (Trading and Other Income) Act 2005 (dividends etc from UK resident companies), equivalent foreign income from non-UK resident companies, and stock dividends from UK resident companies (Income Tax Act 2007, s 19).

2   A capital gains tax settlement will not arise provided that property is held under a 'bare trust' (Taxation of Chargeable Gains Act 1992, s 68).

    Property is held under a 'bare trust' only if the beneficiary is 'absolutely entitled' against the trustee; if there is more than one beneficiary, the beneficiaries must be 'jointly ... absolutely entitled' against the trustee (Taxation of Chargeable Gains Act 1992, s 60(1)).

    There are four leading cases on the meaning of 'jointly absolutely entitled' in this context: *Kidson v MacDonald* (1973) 49 TC 503; *Stephenson v Barclays Bank Trust Co Ltd* (1974) 50 TC 374; *Booth v Ellard* (1980) 53 TC 393; and *Jenkins v Brown* (1989) 62 TC 226. These form a unified line of authority; each decision followed and applied each of the previous ones:

    (a) 'absolutely': beneficiaries must be entitled together to put an end to the trust and call for a transfer of the trust property; and

    (b) 'jointly': interests must be 'concurrent' (ie not successive) and 'in common' (ie must relate to a common pool of property); the interests must be 'the same', meaning 'a similarity of interests in quality, not equality in quantity ... each has, pro rata to the size of his ... holding, the same sorts of rights'.

    In *Anders Utkilens Rederi A/S v O/Y Lovisa Stevedoring Co A/B and Keller Bryant Transport Co Ltd* [1985] STC 301 at 307, Goulding J rejected an approach which seemed to him 'altogether too technical and refined' and acknowledged the importance of what he termed 'common sense and commercial reality' in applying this legislation.

    The rate of capital gains tax, at the time of writing, is generally 28 per cent although a 18 per cent rate can apply if an individual is not chargeable to tax at the higher rate or dividend upper rate in respect of any of his or her income (Taxation of Chargeable Gains Act 1992, s 4 (as substituted by the Finance (No.2) Act 2010)).

3   Although the prospect of a capital markets issue of securities giving rise to inheritance tax can initially induce incredulity, it is possible to create such a settlement as, despite the name of the tax and associations with the death of individuals, inheritance tax is a tax which may arise on chargeable transfers of value from an individual's estate both during life and on death. An inheritance settlement will be created (Inheritance Tax Act 1984, s 43) if property (other than excluded property falling within s 48):

    (a) is held in trust for persons in succession or for any person subject to a contingency;

    (b) held by a trustee on trust to accumulate the whole or part of any income of the property or with power to make payments out of that income at the discretion of the trustee or some other person, with or without power to accumulate surplus income; or

    (c) charged or burdened (other than for full consideration paid to the settlor) with the payment of any annuity or other periodical payment payable for a life or any other limited or terminable period.

    Inheritance tax may be chargeable on settled property in certain circumstances including, where a transfer of value is made out of the settlement and, at the rate of 10 per cent, on the tenth anniversary of the date on which the settlement commenced and subsequent ten-yearly intervals (Inheritance Tax Act 1984, s 64).

10.46 A person in the UK, such as a custodian, may be assessable for income tax (a) as a trustee or agent under s 687 and s 689 of the Income Tax (Trading and Other Income) Act 2005, or (b) if he or she is a UK representative of a person who is not resident in the UK and carries out a trade, profession or vocation through the custodian, under provisions in the Chapter 2B of Part 14 of the Income Tax Act 2007.

Income Tax (Trading and Other Income) Act 2005, ss 687 and 689

10.47 Section 689 of the Income Tax (Trading and Other Income) Act 2005 provides that a person who receives or is entitled to income which is chargeable to tax is liable to income tax. Tax is chargeable on such a person as the representative of the beneficial owner of the income[1]. At current tax rates, a custodian can be assessed to tax at a number of different rates depending upon the nature of a security in respect of which income arises and the identity of an investor[2]. It is, however, arguable that given all the layers of intermediation which may occur between a custodian and the ultimate investor in securities a strict operation of this section would not be feasible, as in many cases a custodian would not have knowledge, and would not have any means to gain knowledge, as to the beneficial owner of each security in a custody portfolio. In reality, if a custodian were chargeable under ss 687 and 689, the basis on which a custodian should comply with the rules governing self assessment for income tax and a practical basis upon which tax is or may be assessed should be discussed with HM Revenue and Customs.

1   See *Williams v Singer* [1921] 1 AC 65, where Viscount Cave said that a trustee needed 'actual receipt and control' of income if it were to be chargeable to tax in respect of that income; *Reid's Trustees v IRC* (1929) 14 TC 512; *Kelly v Rogers* (1935) 19 TC 692. HM Revenue and Customs Residency has issued guidance stating that a bare trustee is not obliged to complete a self-assessment return: see www.hmrc.gov.uk/cnr/nr_trusts.htm#13.

2   A person assessable in a representative capacity is generally assessable (subject, arguably, to the provisions of any applicable double taxation treaty or Income Tax Act 2007, s 81 which limits the income tax chargeable on certain types of disregarded income to which a person resident outside the UK is beneficially entitled) at the basic rate (currently 20 per cent). However, an individual receiving savings income up to the starting rate limit (currently £2,710) is only liable to income tax at the starting rate of 10 per cent to the extent that such an individual does not have non-savings income above the starting rate limit (Income Tax Act 2007, s 12).

Where securities are beneficially owned by a person within the charge to corporation tax (ie a UK tax resident company or a company which carries on a trade through a permanent establishment in the UK and the securities are used by, or held for, the permanent establishment) a person in the UK who receives or is entitled to such income is not liable to assessment under ss 687 and 689 to income which is within the charge to corporation tax by virtue of Corporation Tax Act 2009, s 3(1)–(2).

If, as generally should not be the case in relation to a custodian operating in the financial markets, income is to be accumulated by or payable at the discretion of a custodian or any other person, the trust rate, currently 50 per cent, will apply, other than in respect of income to which the dividend trust rate applies. See para **10.45** n 1 above.

10.48 The forerunner of ss 687 and 689 dates back to the Taxes Act 1842, long before the rise of global electronic securities markets. In the context of a security trust arrangement (where a secured asset is held on trust for a class of collateral takers), a security trustee is not thought (in leading Counsel's view) to be assessable under ss 687 and 689 prior to the enforcement of the security. Whether a party in a depositary receipt structure is treated as receiving or entitled to income will depend upon the nature of the transaction and the drafting of the documentation: the position is not always so clear cut and HM Revenue and Customs is known to have taken the view that in certain circumstances a depositary receipt structure can involve a separate and independent obligation owed by a depositary trustee to the recipient holder, which may give rise to a charge to tax under ss 687 and 689. This is an area in which professional advice should always be sought.

UK representatives and disregarded income

10.49 A UK representative of a person who is not resident in the UK and conducts a trade, profession or vocation in the UK through a branch or agency (in the case of an individual) or a permanent establishment (in the case of a company) can be subject to obligations and liabilities in respect of income tax, corporation tax and chargeable gains tax[1]. Generally speaking, a custodian should not be liable to assessment as a UK representative of a person who is not resident in the UK and who conducts a trade, profession or vocation in the UK through such a custodian.

1   Income Tax Act 2007, Part 14 Chapter 2B (in the case of income tax), Taxation of Chargeable Gains Act 1992, Part 7A Chapter 1, and Corporation Tax Act 2010, Part 22 Chapter 6 (in the case of a corporation tax).

10.50   Sections 811 and 814 of the Income Tax Act 2007 provide that income received by a UK representative of such a person is, in many cases, disregarded income and therefore outside the charge to income tax. Disregarded income includes disregarded savings and investment income (dividends and stock dividends from UK resident companies, and (except for relevant foreign income as defined in Income Tax Act 2007, s 989) interest, purchased life annuity payments, profits from deeply discounted securities, distributions from unauthorised unit trusts, and transactions in deposits[1]) and disregarded annual payments[2].

1   Income Tax Act 2007, s 825.

2   Income Tax Act 2007, s 826.

10.51   There are also special exemptions in s 814(4) of the Income Tax Act 2007 and s 1146 of the Corporation Tax Act 2010, which provide that a person in the UK who acts as an investment manager for a person who is not resident in the UK is not to be treated as a UK representative of such a non-resident. If a custodian, in addition to providing custody services, offers investment management services, professional advice should be sought with a view to ensuring, if possible, that in performing such investment management services the custodian's activities fall within the scope of the investment manager exemption. The requirements necessary to fall within this exemption are complex and HM Revenue and Customs has issued *Statement of Practice 1/01* (revised in July 2007) setting out its approach to the treatment of investment managers and their overseas clients.

ENFORCEMENT IN THE UK OF TAX ASSESSED UNDER THE LAWS OF ANOTHER JURISDICTION

10.52   It used to be an established principle of English law that the courts in England and Wales would not enforce a foreign revenue law, either directly or indirectly[1]. Similarly, an English court used not to permit an action to be brought before it to collect the taxes of a foreign country[2].

1   *Rossano v Manufacturers' Life Insurance Co* [1963] 2 QB 352.

2   *Government of India, Ministry of Finance (Revenue Division) v Taylor* [1955] AC 491, [1955] 2 WLR 303, [1955] 1 All ER 292; *QRS 1 Aps v Frandsen* [1999] STC 616.

10.53   Consequently, a custodian for the most part used not to need to be concerned as to whether enforcement proceedings could be taken against assets in its care in respect of unpaid foreign tax. Inroads into this principle have, however, been made by the EU and the way has been prepared for it to be further eroded by Part 9 of the Finance Act 2006.

10.54   Initially, the EU assault related only to value added tax and certain other indirect taxes sought by the tax authorities in other member states of the EU and enabled such taxes to be recovered as if such taxes were a debt due to the Crown[1]. However, the Finance Act 2002[2] implemented a new 'Mutual Assistance Recovery Directive'[3] intended to 'improve'[4] existing procedures for recovery of indirect taxes under an older Directive[5] and which extended the mutual assistance provisions to cover direct taxes (income tax, corporation tax, capital gains tax and petroleum revenue tax)[6]. Under the legislation introduced by the Finance Act 2002, the UK tax authorities could, pursuant to UK law and after consultation with the EU member state seeking to recover tax in the UK, allow a debtor time to pay or authorise payment by instalments[7]. This legislation was updated on 1 January 2012 by the MARD Regulations[8] which sought to implement into UK law Directive 2010/24/EU. This legislation might have an impact on a custodian operating from an EU member state other than the UK, if it had not paid tax it owed on its own account in such a member state (and equivalent legislation should cause the provisions of the New Directive to be enacted into the national law of each of the EU member states so that tax unpaid in the UK could be enforced against a custodian's own assets in another EU member state). Equally, however, a custodian may need to be aware of the possibility that, although assets held in the UK cannot be subject under these provisions to enforcement proceedings in the UK to collect tax which a custodian's client has not paid under the laws of a non-EU jurisdiction, such assets may be subject to enforcement proceedings in the UK where a client has not (or is alleged not to have) paid tax in the relevant non-EU jurisdiction.

1   Finance Act 1977, s 11, implementing Directive 76/308/EEC.

2   Finance Act 2002, s 134, Sch 39 (Recovery of taxes etc due in other member states); see also the Recovery of Duties and Taxes etc Due in Other Member States (Corresponding UK Claims, Procedure and Supplementary) Regulations 2004 (SI 2004/674) and Finance (No 2) Act 2005, s 68.

3   Directive 2001/44/EC (the 'New Directive').

4   Press Release IR/CEI, 17 April 2002.

5   Directive 76/308/EEC (the 'Old Directive'); the Old Directive was replaced on 26 May 2008 by Directive 2008/551/EC.

6   Article 7 of the New Directive states that a revenue authority of another EU member state may address a request to recover unpaid tax to the relevant UK tax authority and that such a request must be accompanied by an official or certified copy of the instrument permitting its enforcement, issued in the EU member state and, if appropriate, by the original or a certified copy of other documents necessary for recovery. The Old Directive provided guidelines (preserved under the New Directive) on the procedures the EU member state must undertake to recover the tax. Article 7(2)(a) and (b) of the Old Directive (as replaced in 2008) provide that the EU member state may not make a request for recovery unless the claim and/or the instrument permitting its enforcement are not contested by the relevant UK tax authority and the EU member state in which the liability has arisen has applied appropriate recovery procedures which have not resulted in the payment in full of the unpaid tax.

7   Note that interest will be charged for late payment under the laws, regulations and administrative provisions in force in the UK and shall be remitted to the EU member state seeking to recover the tax.

8   MARD Regulations 2011 (SI 2011/2931).

10.55 The Finance Act 2006 introduced into UK law powers under which arrangements relating to international tax enforcement can have effect in the UK[1]. Such arrangements relate to the exchange of information foreseeably relevant to the administration enforcement or recovery of any UK or foreign tax, the recovery debt relating to any UK or foreign tax and/or the service of documents relating to any UK or foreign tax[2]. It is worth noting in this context that in *Commissioners of HMRC and Commissioner for South African Revenue Service v Ben Nevis (Holdings) Limited, Metlinka Trading Limited and HSBC Trustee (Guernsey) Limited*[3] the High Court considered the position in relation to liabilities to South African tax, amounting to some £222 million, which had arisen during 1998, 1999 and 2000. It was claimed that as a result of investigations being carried out by the South African Revenue Service into Ben Nevis Holdings Limited's ('Ben Nevis') affairs, Ben Nevis had transferred all its assets to Metlinka Trading Limited ('Metlinka'), at the behest of the beneficiary of a trust which owned the shares in both Ben Nevis and Metlinka and of which the trustee was HSBC Trustee (Guernsey) Limited ('HSBCG'). Pelling QC, sitting as a judge of the High Court:

(a) refused to accept that prior to the coming into force of the Finance Act 2006, article 25A (introduced by a 2010 Protocol to the treaty) of the double taxation convention between the UK and the Republic of South Africa entered into in 2002 was *ultra vires* and void[4],

(b) was not persuaded that Finance Act 2006 s 173 and/or the statutory instrument enacting the 2010 Protocol were *ultra vires* to the extent a tax debt arose before these provisions came into force[5];

(c) held that there was 'no tenable' basis for arguing that the application of article 25A to a pre-existing tax debt infringed article 1 of the First Protocol of the European Convention of Human Rights[6];

(d) refused to allow the South African Revenue Service to pursue a claim under the Insolvency Act 1986, s 423 against Ben Nevis, Metlinka or HSBCG[7];

(e) decided that HM Revenue and Customs had failed to demonstrate an 'arguable basis' for seeking permission to serve proceedings in Guernsey against HSBCG. The Judge found that no tenable claim had been identified against HSBCG and that it was 'neither here nor there' that HSBCG was trustee of the trust. Neither the suggestion that to make orders granted against Ben Nevis and Metlinka effective nor the possibility that HSBCG might have documentation regarding the circumstances of the transfer of an asset of Ben Nevis to Metlinka were considered sufficient to justify service out of the UK on HSBCG[8].

1   Finance Act 2006, s 173.

2   See further the Recovery of Foreign Taxes Regulations 2007 (SI 2007/3507) (as amended by the Recovery of Foreign Taxes (Amendment) Regulations 2010 (SI 2010/794).

 At the time of writing, provisions enabling a debt relating to foreign tax to be recovered in the UK had been included in a number of agreements, including the:

 (i)   Double Taxation Relief and International Tax Enforcement (Faroes) Order 2007 (SI 2007/3469), art 26;

 (ii) Protocol to the UK/New Zealand Double Taxation Convention signed on 7 November 2007 which provides for the insertion of a new art 25A (Assistance in the Collection of Taxes) into the Convention for the Avoidance of Double Taxation between the UK and New Zealand signed on 4 August 1983, implemented by the Double Taxation Relief and International Tax Enforcement (Taxes on Income and Capital) (New Zealand) Order 2008 (SI 2008/1793); and

 (iii) Double Taxation Convention signed on 26 September 2008 by the UK and the Netherlands, art 27.

3   [2012] EWHC 1807.

4   Interestingly, the Judge declined to apply the Vienna Convention on the Law of Treaties as an aid to construing the double tax convention between the UK and South Africa because, although the UK is a signatory to the Vienna Convention, the Republic of South Africa is not; see [2012] EWHC 1807 para 24.

5   [2012] EWHC 1807 para 45.

6   [2012] EWHC 1807 para 47.

7   [2012] EWHC 1807 para 55.

8   [2012] EWHC 1807 paras 57–60.

SITUS

10.56 The situs of an asset can be relevant in a number of different contexts for tax purposes, and in particular the situs of a security can determine whether that security:

318 *The Law of Global Custody*

(a) is 'excluded property' for inheritance tax purposes[1]; and

(b) is remitted to the UK for capital gains tax purposes[2].

The question can therefore arise as to what the situs is of a security which is in the care of a custodian.

Situs is a private international law, rather than a tax law concept, and for inheritance tax purposes situs is generally determined in accordance with private international law rules[3]. Specific legislation sets out a statutory code which determines where an asset is to be treated as located for the capital gains tax purposes, and where that code is silent private international law principles apply.

The following paragraphs examine the general rules which apply in respect of inheritance tax and capital gains tax, in each case considering the position in relation to a share or debenture before turning to the position where such an asset is held through a clearing system, depositary, or in CREST.

First, however, it may be helpful to note that special statutory rules apply in the case of securities issued by the International Monetary Fund, the International Bank for Reconstruction and Development, the International Finance Corporation, the International Development Association, the Asian Development Bank, the African Development Bank, the European Coal and Steel Community, the European Atomic Energy Community, the European Investment Bank, the European Bank for Reconstruction and Development[4]. Essentially, securities issued by these organisations are treated as having a situs outside the UK unless they are in bearer form and physically located in the UK. Securities issued by the Inter-American Development Bank are treated as having a situs outside the UK[5] and the OECD Support Fund Act 1975 makes similar provision in respect of a security issued by that fund.

---

1 The general scheme of inheritance tax operates by imposing a charge to tax by reference to the value transferred by a chargeable transfer. A transfer of value is defined by section 3(1) of the Inheritance Tax Act 1984, as a disposition as a result of which the value of a person's estate is reduced and s 3(2) of the Act provides that for these purposes the value of excluded property which ceases to form part of a person's estate is to be ignored. Section 6(1) states that 'property situated outside the United Kingdom is excluded property if the person beneficially entitled to that property is an individual domiciled outside the United Kingdom'. Consequently, a disposition of property with a situs outside the UK by a person who at the time of that disposition is not domiciled (or deemed to be domiciled) in the UK does not give rise to a charge to inheritance tax.

   There are also rules (Inheritance Act 1984, ss 64–65) which impose a charge to tax at various times in respect of relevant property which is comprised in (or taken out of) a settlement for inheritance tax purposes. The definition of 'relevant property' in section 58 of the Act states that excluded property is not included as part of relevant property and section 48(3) provides that where property comprised in a settlement is situated outside the UK, that property is excluded property unless the settlor was domiciled in the UK when the settlement was made. It follows, that the situs of a security can be a key factor in determining whether the value of that security is chargeable to inheritance tax as that tax applies to property comprised in a settlement.

2 Where an individual is domiciled outside the UK (or is not ordinarily resident in the UK) but is resident in the UK and elects to be taxed on the remittance basis (and, potentially, pays a remittance base charge of up to £50,000), capital (and income) is only subject to capital gains tax (or income tax) to the extent it is remitted to the UK. Consequently, the situs of an asset can be extremely important because where property (or income) has a situs outside the UK, a liability to capital gain tax (or income tax) only arises if that property (or income) is remitted to the UK.

   The scope of what constitutes a remittance was very considerably broadened by provisions introduced by the Finance Act 2008 (Income Tax Act 2007, ss 809A–809Z7). However, the rigour of these rules has been modified by the Finance Act 2012 which helpfully introduced rules (Income Tax Act 2007, ss 809VA–809VO) permitting a remittance basis taxpayer, subject to certain strict conditions being met, to invest in shares (including securities issued by, or a loan made to, a certain companies (broadly, a company, or parent company of a group, whose shares are not listed on a recognised stock exchange and which carries on a commercial trade) incorporated in the UK and make a claim for the making of that investment not to be treated as constituting a remittance for income tax or capital gains tax purposes.

3   The position which generally obtains at private international may be overridden by a double taxation treaty where that treaty confers an exemption from which operates by reference to the situs of property; see, for example, the treaties between the UK and France and between the UK and Italy.

4   See (with respect to inheritance tax) Finance Act 1984,s 126 and HM Revenue and Customs Manual IHT 27141 and (with respect to tax on capital gains) Taxation of Chargeable Gains Act 1992, s 265 and HM Revenue and Customs Manual CG 12440.

5   By virtue of Finance Act 1976, s 131 for inheritance tax purposes and Taxation of Chargeable Gains Act 1992, s 266 for capital gains purposes.

10.57 The rules of private international law provide that the situs of (and, consequently, for inheritance tax purposes the situs of):

(a) a registered share is located where the register is[1] (and, if there is a branch register, where a register is required by law to be kept)[2];

(b) a bearer share is located where the certificate evidencing the share is held[3];

(c) a bond (including a quoted Eurobond in bearer form) or debenture under seal, as a speciality debt, is generally situated where the document which constitutes the debt is to be found[4].

Where securities are held through intermediaries or depositary arrangements there is, however, a divergence between the position under private international law and HM Revenue and Customs' practice.

The Law Commission has concluded that 'provided that the choice of law rules applied to the different intermediated securities are clear, the lender need only concern itself with the perfection requirements of the jurisdiction in which the account is located rather than the requirements of each of the jurisdictions applicable to the various underlying securities'[5] – and the situs of an investor's asset is therefore where the intermediary with whom the investor has a contractual relationship is located as this is the jurisdiction the intermediated security can be dealt with.

HM Revenue and Customs on, the other hand, takes the view that the situs of a security held through a clearing system (eg Euroclear and Clearstream) is determined by the terms of issue of that security; HM Revenue and Customs treats any intermediary as an agent of the investor unless the terms on which a security is issued provide otherwise so as to 'look through the intermediary and treat the beneficiary-investor as owning the underlying Eurobonds or similar fungibles'[6].

As discussed above[7], the CREST register is where legal title to securities constituted under the law of England, Scotland or Northern Ireland – and the situs of such securities therefore lies in England[8] when a company issues a share which is dematerialised within CREST. Where securities issued by a company incorporated in the Republic of Ireland, the Isle of Man, Guernsey or Jersey are dematerialised within CREST legal title is established by reference to the register maintained by the issuer in accordance with law of its incorporation (transfers being settled through CREST) so that the situs of such securities is not altered as a result of securities being settled through CREST.

1   HM Revenue and Customs Manual, IHT 27121; HM Revenue and Customs cites *Attorney General v Higgins* (1857) 2 H&N 339 as authority for this proposition.

In relation to a letter of allotment, cf *Young v Phillips* 58 TC 232 where it was held that the situs of a letter of allotment issued by a company with a share register in the UK was held be in the UK (rather than where the letter of allotment was located).

2   HM Revenue and Customs Manual, IHT 27122, 27122, 27125 and 27127; the Manual also provides guidance in respect of duplicate registers, where a list is maintained but that list not affect legal title to a security and transfer offices.

3   *R v Williams* [1942] AC 541, PC. The Privy Council glossed an earlier decision (*Brassard v Smith* [1925] AC 371) in which it had been held that the test is 'where can shares be effectively dealt with'

by saying that this was a reference to 'where the shares can be effectively dealt with as between the shareholder and the company, so that the transferee will become legally entitled to al the rights of a member'.

4   *Attorney General v Bouwens* (1838) 4M&W 171, as approved in *Attorney General v Winans (No.2)* [1910] AC 27. See also HM Revenue and Customs Manual, 27076 and 27079.

5   'The UNIDROIT Convention on the Substantive Rules regarding Intermediated Securities Further Updated Advice to HM Treasury' (May 2008), para 21.6.

6   HM Revenue and Customs Manual, IHT 27077.

7   Chapter 9 above.

8   At the time of writing it is not thought that it should make any difference for tax purposes whether the situs of a dematerialised security is in England or another constituent kingdom of the UK. It would appear that this position should not be altered by the Scotland Act 2012, because although that Act provides for a variable rate of Scottish income tax to be imposed by the Scottish Parliament with respect to the non-savings income of an individual resident in Scotland, the rules relating to the situs of securities are generally not relevant for income tax purposes.

10.58 The position is slightly different for capital gains purposes because instead of reliance being place on the private international concepts, specific statutory provisions address the situs of assets. The legislation provides that[1]:

(a) shares or debentures (defined to include a security[2]) issued by municipal or governmental authority, or by any body created by such an authority, are situated in the country of that authority[3];

(b) shares or debentures of a company incorporated in any part of the UK, are situated in the UK; and

(c) registered shares or debentures are situated where they are registered and, if registered in more than one place, where the principal register is situated.

The situs of a bearer security, as an type of 'intangible asset' is in the UK if at the time it is created it is governed by, otherwise subject to or enforceable under the law of any part of the UK[4] (referred to as being 'subject to UK law'). These rules are supplemented by a rule that where an asset is comprised of a co-ownership interest, the situs of that asset is determined on the basis that the asset is wholly owned by the person holding the interest in that asset[5]. Where the statute is silent, namely in the case of bearer securities which are not subject to UK law, private international law principles apply and the situs of a bearer bond is where the document constituting the bond is located[6]. HM Revenue and Customs tends to adopt a fairly pragmatic approach to applying these rules in the case of intermediated securities issued by non-UK incorporated companies, and this is the case notwithstanding that as a matter of statutory construction the position may not be entirely clear[7] and that the First-tier Tribunal has recently illustrated through a finding of fact that a holder of an ADR issued under New York law did not own a beneficial interest in underlying the security to which the ADR related[8]. In Revenue & Customs Brief 14/12 HM Revenue and Customs noted that a finding of the First-tier Tribunal was not binding and published a draft of some amended guidance. The amended guidance applies where a depositary receipt can be exchanged for the underlying shares on demand by the depositary receipt holder, any dividends, subject to a handling fee, flow through to the depositary receipt holder, and the holder of shares in depositary receipt form may at any time cancel the arrangement by asking for delivery of the share certificates in respect of their underlying shares, and surrendering the depositary receipt at a local branch of the depositary. In such cases:

> **'UK-issued DRs**
>
> Where a DR is issued in the UK the HM Revenue and Customs view is that the holder of a DR is the beneficial owner of the underlying shares. ...

DRs issued outside UK

Where a DR is issued outside the UK the question of whether the holder of the DR is the beneficial owner of the underlying shares will be determined by reference to the law of the territory in which the DR is issued. Information on beneficial ownership may be provided to investors by the depositary.

Beneficial ownership not conclusively determined by overseas law

Where beneficial ownership of the underlying shares cannot conclusively be determined by reference to the law governing the arrangements relating to the issue of the DRs, for tax purposes HM Revenue and Customs will continue to determine beneficial ownership according to its understanding of the principles of UK law. This means that HM Revenue and Customs will continue to apply its longstanding practice of regarding the holder of a DR as holding the beneficial interest in the underlying shares.

The ADRs referred to in the HSBC decision fall into this category.

Beneficial ownership determined by overseas law

Where the relevant law means that the holder of a DR is not the beneficial owner of the underlying shares the practical implications include that:

- a transfer of shares by a shareholder to a depositary in exchange for an issue of DRs is a disposal of the shares for capital gains purposes because the shareholder loses beneficial ownership of the shares
- a disposal of the DRs is not a disposal of the underlying shares …'

Securities constituted under the law of England, Scotland or Northern Ireland which are dematerialised in CREST have a situs in England when a company issues a share which is dematerialised within CREST. Where securities issued by a company incorporated in the Republic of Ireland, the Isle of Man, Guernsey or Jersey is dematerialised within CREST legal title is established by reference to the register maintained by the issuer in accordance with law of its incorporation (transfers being settled through CREST) so that the situs of such securities is not altered as a result of securities being settled through CREST.

1 Taxation of Chargeable Gains Act 1992, s 275(1)(d), (da) and (c).

2 Taxation of Chargeable Gains Act 1992, s 275(2)(b).

3 HM Revenue and Customs points out at HM Revenue and Customs Manual, CGT 12440 that this applies to both registered and bearer securities.

4 Taxation of Chargeable Gains Act 1992, s 275A(3) and s 275B(2).

5 Taxation of Chargeable Gains Act 1992, s 275C.

6 HM Revenue and Customs Manual, CG 12440.

7 J Kessler, QC takes the view that the statutory situs rules referred to above, reinforced by Taxation of Chargeable Gains Act 1992, s 60, result in the situs of an intermediated security being located where a registered maintained by the intermediary is located; see J Kessler, *Taxation of Non-Residents and Foreign Domiciliaries 2011–2012* (Keyhaven, Publications PLC, Oxford) 10th ed. Vol 3, para 71.9. However, the premise of this argument appears to be that, unlike the case with shares (Companies Act 2006, s 744), company law does not require a register (in the sense of a list which determines or provides proof of ownership) to be kept of debenture holders – and that a register maintained by an intermediary should therefore be properly be regarded as a register of debentures. It is respectfully suggested, on the other hand, that a register maintained by an intermediary strictly records the rights of an investor against the intermediary (see, for example, the Law Commission's analysis referred to at **10.57** above) and does not acknowledge any indebtedness on behalf of the intermediary to the investor; on this basis one is left with the investor holding an intangible right against the intermediary and a position, the suspicion that the position should not be that dissimilar to that in respect of IHT and that HM Revenue and Customs' pragmatic practice probably best accommodates the position.

8 *HSBC Holdings PLC and The Bank of New York Mellon Corporation v HMRC* ([2012] UKFTT 163 (TC)).

WITHHOLDING TAX

10.59 There is no generic definition of withholding tax in UK tax law. A withholding tax may be said, in UK tax law terms, to constitute the imposition on a person making a payment or collecting a receipt, of a liability to deduct or account for income tax (which represents the liability, or part of the liability, to income tax of the person beneficially entitled to the payment or receipt). UK withholding[1] was significantly simplified by the abolition with respect to payments made and receipts collected on or after 6 April 2001 of the paying and collecting agent rules which applied to foreign dividends paid or received by agents in the UK[2]. Withholding has (under pressure, at least in part, to find a political comprise acceptable both to EU institutions and the City of London to perceived tax evasion in respect of savings income)[3], in many respects (other than in respect of UK source[4] annual[5] interest[6] or annual qualifying payments[7]) given way to information reporting.

1   Simplification has also resulted from the abolition of advance corporation tax in respect of distributions made on or after 6 April 1999 and the consequent disappearance of complex provisions dealing with the credit which used to arise in respect of advance corporation tax ('ACT') paid by companies within the charge to UK corporation tax. For UK tax purposes ACT represented an advance payment in respect of a company's corporation tax liability which was, subject to certain limitations, creditable against that company's liability to mainstream corporation tax.

2   Broadly speaking, these rules applied to the payment or receipt by a person in the UK of a dividend, interest, annual payment or annuity paid by a body of persons established outside the UK or out of funds outside the UK. The paying and collecting agent rules, which enjoyed their final statutory incarnation under provisions enacted by the Finance Act 1996, dated back to the nineteenth century when provisions applied to what were then known as 'foreign and colonial dividends'.

3   Other influences have also been at work. The (phased) introduction of payment on account of corporation tax for accounting periods ending on or after 1 July 1999 reduced the cashflow advantage to the Exchequer which withholding in respect of foreign dividends used to entail.

4   Whether interest has a UK source is determined by reference to a 'basket' test. The characteristics of each borrowing are considered to determine whether a sufficiently strong nexus with the UK is formed for an interest payment to be regarded as having a UK source. Unfortunately, case law in this area is somewhat obscure and it is difficult in certain respects to reconcile it with HM Revenue and Customs guidance: *Westminster Bank Executor and Trustee Co (Channel Islands) Ltd v National Bank of Greece SA* (1970) 46 TC 472; HM Revenue and Custom's Savings and Investment Manual, paras 9090 and 9095.

   HM Revenue and Customs considers that the most important factor is the residence of the debtor and the location of its assets. Other factors which HM Revenue and Customs highlight are the place of performance of the contract and the method of payment, the competent jurisdiction for legal action, the proper law of the contract, and the residence of the guarantor and of any security for the debt. HM Revenue and Customs considers that a company is regarded for these purposes as being resident where it carries on business. Interest paid by a UK resident company is regarded as not having a UK source if an overseas branch enters into the agreement overseas, the loan is for the business of that branch, the branch pays the interest from its income and the loan is enforceable in the jurisdiction in which the branch is located. Conversely, a UK branch of a foreign company can be regarded as paying UK source interest if there is a similar nexus between the UK branch and the loan.

   In October 2012 HM Revenue and Customs published a response document indicating that the Finance Bill 2013 would include a provision to amend ITA 2007, s 874 to make it clear that the location of the agreement or deed evidencing a debt has no bearing on whether interest has a UK source; see 'Possible changes to income tax rules on interest: Summary of Responses' (October 2012), para 3.16. The draft Finance Bill 2013, published on 11 December 2012 did indeed include such a provision which operated by means of inserting a new ITA 2007, s 874(6A) which states that in determining whether a payment of interest arises in the UK, no account is to be taken of the location of any deed which records the obligation to pay the interest.

   For a fuller discussion see *Norfolk and Montagu on the Taxation of Interest and Debt Finance* (Looseleaf, Bloomsbury Professional) Issue 24, Chapter 3.

5   Interest is 'annual' interest for these purposes if is payable with respect to a borrowing with a term of a year or more. This is a factual test and turns on the intention of the parties. Consequently, if, for example, a borrowing has a term of less than a year and there is provision for it to be rolled over

beyond a year, or the parties contemplate that the loan will not be repaid within the year, then interest will be treated as annual interest. In this context, care should to be taken in the context of putting in place a programme for issuing interest bearing commercial paper.

In March 2012 HM Revenue and Customs published a consultation document proposing that the distinction between yearly and non-yearly interest should be dispensed with; see 'Possible changes to income tax rules on interest' (27 March 2012), para 4.7. In the light of substantial lobbying, HM Revenue and Customs has announced that the Government does not intend to proceed with the abolition of the concept of yearly interest; see 'Possible changes to income tax rules on interest: Summary of Responses' (October 2012), para 3.13.

6   There is no statutory definition of interest for UK tax purposes, although the meaning of the word has been considered in a number of cases. The classic description, by Rowlatt J in *Bennett v Ogston* (1930) 15 TC 374 at 374, is 'payment by time for the use of money'. More recently, Megarry J in *The Euro Hotel (Belgravia) Limited* (1975) SITC 293 at 301I–302B said:

'It seems to me that running through the cases there is the concept that as a general rule two requirements must be satisfied in order for a payment to amount to interest, and a fortiori to amount to "interest of money". First, there must be a sum of money by reference to which the payment which is said to be interest is to be ascertained. The payment cannot be "interest of money" unless there is the requisite "money" for the payment to be said to be "interest of". Plainly, there are sums of "money" in the present case. Second, those sums of money must be sums that are due to the person entitled to the alleged interest; and it is this latter requirement that is mainly in issue before me. I do not, of course, say that in every case these two requirements are exhaustive, or that they are inescapable.'

Payment of a premium is treated as interest for UK taxation purposes, although a discount is not treated as interest (and is, therefore, not subject to withholding) (*Lomax v Peter Dixon* (1943) 25 TC 353). Note also, for example, that payment of a price differential under a repo agreement, while not interest, is deemed to be a payment of interest on a deemed loan for the purposes of the Taxes Acts (Income Tax Act 2007, s 578) and such interest may, accordingly, be subject to withholding (Income Tax Act 2007, ss 919 and 920).

7   A qualifying annual payment is a payment which is:

(a)   an income and not a capital payment;

(b)   pure income profit in the hands of the payee; and

(c)   made under a legally binding obligation.

The term 'qualifying annual payment' is defined by Income Tax Act 2007, s 899. In a global custody context the type of annual payment which is most likely to be relevant, will fall within Income Tax (Trading and Other Income) Act 2005, s 683.

10.60   Legislation has traditionally maintained a distinction between withholding tax imposed on payers and paying agents, on one hand, and that imposed upon collecting agents, on the other[1]. This distinction remains important (notwithstanding that it does not play a role in the EU Savings Directive on the taxation of savings income[2]). The following analysis is divided into a section on payers and paying agents and a section on collecting agents. Although a global custodian is more likely to be a collecting agent, an awareness of the rules governing payers and paying agents may also be relevant to a global custodian.

1   There is no generally applicable statutory definition of a paying or collecting agent, although the (repealed) paying and collecting agent rules included detailed provisions by reference to which it was possible to ascertain whether in performing a particular function a person was regarded for the purposes of that legislation as acting as a paying or collecting agent. Typically, however, a paying agent is appointed by an obligor to make payments on the obligor's behalf and a collecting agent is appointed by a payee, lender or investor. A collecting agent may, of course, make payments to its customer, but the function it performs (in the capacity of agent or trustee) is to ensure that payments are received (or assets realised) on behalf of its customer.

2   Directive 2003/48/EC.

Payers and paying agents

10.61   Where a payment of UK source annual interest is paid, otherwise than in a fiduciary or representative capacity, by a company (other than a building society) or a local authority[1], or by or on behalf of a partnership of which a company is a member, or by any person to another person whose usual place of abode is outside the UK, the payer is obliged to deduct income tax at the lower rate (20 per cent at the time of writing)[2], unless an exemption applying a direction to make gross payment is obtained from HM Revenue and Customs Residency[3], or the payment is an excepted payment within ss 933–937 of the Income Tax Act 2007.

1   The meaning of 'local authority' for these purposes is defined by Income Tax Act 2007, s 999.

2   Income Tax Act 2007, s 874.

3   HM Revenue and Customs Residency is charged with administering the Board of HM Revenue and Customs' power under the Double Taxation Relief (Taxes on Income) (General) Regulations 1970 (1970/488) to issue a direction authorising gross payment where a recipient of interest is entitled to relief under a double taxation agreement in respect of that interest.

EUROBONDS

10.62 In the context of the global custody business, the exemption which has most relevance is that for interest paid in respect of quoted Eurobonds[1]. For interest payments made on or after 6 April 2001[2], this exemption applies to payments made in respect of a security issued by a company which carries a right to interest and is (and continues to be) listed on a recognised stock exchange[3]. This position reflects changes introduced by the Finance Act 2000 and amounts to significant deregulation, as it removed difficulties previously associated with reconciling, on the one hand, the requirement (abolished by the Finance Act 2000 with effect from 6 April 2001) that, for the quoted Eurobond exemption to apply in respect of a payment, a security had to be in bearer form with, on the other hand, US tax and regulatory requirements that a security should not be in bearer form. Along with the need for a quoted Eurobond to be in bearer form, certain administrative requirements were also abolished. These requirements concerned the location of paying agents; stated that in certain instances an investor should be tax resident outside the UK in order to receive gross payment (and should produce a declaration to evidence the same) and specified the recognised clearing systems[4] in which a quoted Eurobond could be held. In March 2012 HM Revenue and Customs published a consultation document proposing that the quoted Eurobond exemption should be restricted so as not to apply where a bond is issued on a recognised stock exchange to the member of the same group as the issue and there is no substantial trading in respect of that bond; industry lobbied hard against this proposal because of the additional complexity and compliance burden which would have involved, and in October 2012 HM Revenue and Customs announced that legislation to restrict the restrict the availability of the quoted Eurobond exemption in a group context would not be brought forward[5].

1   Income Tax Act 2007, s 882. A 'recognised stock exchange' has, since amendments introduced by Finance Act 2007 took effect, been defined as any market of a recognised investment exchange (as defined in Financial Services and Markets 2000, s 235) designated by HM Revenue and Customs and any market outside the UK which HM Revenue and Customs designates (Income Tax Act 2007, s 1005). In order for a security to be listed on a recognised stock exchange, a security must be admitted to trading on an exchange and included in the official list: Revenue and Customs Brief 21/08.

2   The modified rules apply to payments made on or after 6 April 2001, even if a security was issued prior to that date.

3   Income Tax Act 2007, s 987.

4   Euroclear, Clearstream (Luxembourg) and the Depositary Trust Company were 'recognised clearing systems'. The abolition of the concept of a recognised clearing system has opened the way for a gross paying quoted Eurobond to be cleared (namely 'settled' as used in other chapters of this book; see paras **10.1–10.5** above for an explanation of this terminology) through other clearing systems (such as Monte Titoli, SICOVAM).

5   'Possible changes to income tax rules on interest: Summary of Responses' (October 2012), para 4.9. HM Revenue and Customs also indicated that it had noted representations made on the wider question of the extent to which tax is withheld from interest in a cross border context, and would consider this further.

DISAPPLICATION OF THE DUTY TO DEDUCT INCOME TAX

10.63 Section 85 of the Finance Act 2001 introduced further provisions, subsequently extended by the Finance Act 2002 and rewritten by the Income Tax Act 2007, which disapply the obligation to withhold or deduct income tax from certain payments of UK source annual interest (and annual payments) by a company or local authority where the company authority or partnership has a reasonable belief that the payment is an excepted payment[1]. A payment may be a 'excepted payment' if it is made to:

(a) a company which is tax resident for UK tax purposes in the UK[2];

(b) a company not so resident which carries on a trade in the UK through a permanent establishment and income which that payment constitutes income in that person's hands which is chargeable to corporation tax as part of the profits of that permanent establishment[3];

(c) certain other entities[4]; or

(d) a partnership every member of which falls within (a) to (b) (or certain entities within (c) above)[5] or the European Investment Bank Fund[6].

1   Income Tax Act 2007, s 930.
2   Income Tax Act 2007, s 933.
3   Income Tax Act 2007, s 934.
4   The other categories of entity referred to in (c) above include (Income Tax Act 2007, ss 935–936):
    (a) specified tax-exempt bodies. A local authority, a health service body, a public office or department of the Crown, a charity, certain scientific research organisations, the UK Atomic Energy Authority, the National Radiological Protection Board, an administrator or trustees of certain pension schemes;
    (b) a nominee or manager of an individual savings account; and
    (c) a society or institution which receives the payment in respect of a tax-exempt special savings account.
5   Income Tax Act 2007, s 937. The entities which may not be included in a partnership, if such a partnership is to be entitled to receive gross payments, are (a) a nominee or manager of an individual savings account, and (b) a society or institution which receives the payment in respect of a tax-exempt special savings account.
6   Income Tax Act 2007, s 937(6).

10.64 The effect of these provisions on global custodians is expected to be limited (as a custodian has not generally been obliged to withhold or deduct income tax from receipts of UK source interest, as in many cases it receives interest but it is not a person through whom a payment of interest is made) and is examined below under 'collecting agents'[1].

1   The possible application of this legislation is not assisted, from the perspective of a paying agent, by Income Tax Act 2007, s 930(9), which states that reference to 'the company by which a payment is made' does not include 'a company acting as agent or trustee for another person'. Although one might suspect that it would be logical for a paying agent to be able to form a reasonable belief as to the entitlement of a payee to receive gross payment, the effect of this subsection appears to cast some doubt as to whether a paying agent would be entitled to pay gross if it formed a reasonable belief that the payee was entitled to gross payment.

Collecting agents

10.65 As a result of the repeal by the Finance Act 2000 of the collecting agent rules with respect to receipts collected on or after 6 April 2001, there is no liability upon a collecting agent in the UK to withhold or deduct UK income tax from a receipt it receives in its capacity as collecting agent.

10.66 Although the rules in s 874 of the Income Tax Act 2007 which apply to a payer (or a paying agent) making a payment of UK source annual interest do not apply to a collecting agent, the rules relating to 'paying agents' may have an indirect impact on the business of some custodians.

EUROBONDS

10.67 The lifting of the requirement that a quoted Eurobond be in bearer form for a payment of interest made in respect of a quoted Eurobond to be made gross, removed at a stroke the difficulties which custodians had previously faced in satisfying the requirement that a security be in bearer form for UK tax purposes, while at the same time (eg if the security were to be offered for sale to US persons) qualifying as a registered security for the purposes of the Tax Equity and Fiscal Responsibility Act 1993 for US purposes.

'REASONABLE BELIEF' TEST

10.68 Furthermore, s 85 of the Finance Act 2001 introduced further provisions, subsequently expanded by the Finance Act 2002[1] and rewritten by the Income Tax Act 2007, which may apply where the financial asset in custody is not a quoted Eurobond, and these new provisions may in the future have an impact on the manner in which a custodian performs services where the payer has a reasonable belief that the person beneficially entitled to that payment is entitled to gross payment[2]. In introducing a 'reasonable belief' test, rather than an objective set of conditions, these provisions broke new ground. It is understood that part of HM Revenue and Custom's preference for a reasonable belief test was due to its desire to give a payer some flexibility in the manner in which the payer satisfies itself that the conditions for gross payment are met; rather than a direct representation or warranty from an investor as to its status and the manner in which it holds a financial asset a payer may be able to form a reasonable belief based upon an assurance given to it by an investor's custodian/collecting agent. It is not entirely clear precisely in what circumstances, in HM Revenue and Custom's view, a payer will be able to form a reasonable belief that gross payment is appropriate[3]. Market reaction is also likely to influence the extent to which custodians are prepared to become involved in helping a payer to form a reasonable belief. As a payer is usually obliged as a matter of contract to pay gross unless required by law to deduct tax, an investor who can supply sufficient information to a payer for that payer to form a reasonable belief that the conditions for gross payment are fulfilled would appear (unless a payer is to risk breach of contract) to be in a position to compel a payer to pay gross. With the many layers of intermediation common in the capital markets it seems unlikely that as a practical matter these provisions will generally find wide application (as a depositary for a global bond is extremely unlikely to have any information as to the identity of the ultimate beneficial owner of an interest in that security), although where a registrar keeps a register of holders of securities it may be (if a registrar has the benefit of an appropriate representation from a holder of its status and as to its beneficial ownership of a security) that a registrar can assist a borrower (and, if appropriate, its paying agent) in arriving at a reasonable belief that payment should be made gross[4].

1   Income Tax Act 2007, s 930.

2   For the categories of payee entitled to gross payment see para **10.60** above.

3   On 30 March 2001 the Inland Revenue issued some initial guidance to accompany the publication of clause 83 of the Finance Bill 2001. Subsequently, in the *Tax Bulletin* (August 2001), the Inland Revenue issued further guidance. This guidance indicates that what constitutes grounds for 'reasonable belief' will vary depending upon the relationship between the payer and the payee. The Revenue suggested that where a payment is made between associated companies, the payer is in a good position to know whether the payee meets the conditions for gross payment. Conversely, where the payer and payee are not known to each other, a payer may want to obtain documentary evidence of the payee's status. Such evidence may take the form of a statement signed by an appropriate officer of the payer company containing either confirmation that the payee meets the conditions for gross payment or, if the payee is a nominee, confirmation that the beneficial owner of income meets the conditions for gross payment. The Revenue stated that if a payer is in any doubt as to the accuracy or trustworthiness of such evidence, the payer will not have reasonable grounds for believing the payee is entitled to receive payment gross and should deduct tax from a payment to that payee. It remains to be seen whether the Revenue will accept that if evidence supplied is inaccurate (eg there is a typographical error or the wording of such a confirmation does not precisely track the statute) but a payer has no reason to suspect bad faith on the payee's part, a payer can be regarded as having the requisite reasonable belief to make gross payment. The Revenue has also stressed that it is willing to work with market operators in drawing up guidance for specific markets. For the Revenue's mission to 'be seen to enable as well as to regulate', see Sir Nicholas Montagu 'The Reality of Today's Revenue' (2002) *The Tax Journal*, 29 July, pp 4–6.

4   In March 2001 the Inland Revenue undertook a consultation exercise as to whether, where a collecting agent is involved in a chain of payments and it is necessary to seek the tax which should have been deducted, the tax could be sought from the collecting agent (if resident in the UK) instead of from the payer: Inland Revenue press release *REV BN13*, 7 March 2001. The Revenue asked: 'Would such a system be an advantage? It is, however, worth noting that, unless a collection mechanism were optional and suitable protection was built in for a collecting agent, such a change could amount to an extension of the obligation to withhold UK tax to collecting agents (whereas this obligation currently, as observed above, only applies to paying agents). As the Finance Act 2002 extended the legislation originally introduced by the Finance Act 2001, but did not provide for the introduction of such a system, it seems likely that, at least for the moment, HM Revenue and Customs has concluded against taking any steps to introduce such a regime.

INFORMATION REPORTING

10.69 In the March 2000 Budget the UK Government took a policy decision, subsequently enshrined in the Finance Act 2000, that a system of information reporting should replace the paying and collecting agent rules (the abolition of which has been referred to above)[1]. The broad rationale behind this approach is that the tax base can be protected, and tax paid by the individual who is the beneficial owner of income, if the fiscal authority with jurisdiction to charge the beneficial owner income possesses information that such income has been received by that individual; in such a case there is, consequently, no need to impose an obligation on a third party (the payer, a paying or a collecting agent) to deduct income tax (which effectively represents tax payable by the beneficial owner of the income) from a payment or receipt.

1   A relatively contemporaneous instance of this emphasis upon information exchange may be found in art 27 of the double taxation agreement between the UK and the US which was signed on 24 July 2001. The treaty provides that information relating to persons who are not resident in either the UK or the US may be exchanged (art 27(1)). Information may be exchanged even where the contracting state providing the information does not require the information for its own tax purposes (art 27(2)). If specifically requested to do so by the competent authority of a contracting state, the competent authority of the other contracting state will provide information in the form of authenticated copies of unedited original documents (art 27(4)).

10.70 Under the information reporting regime any person by or through whom interest[1] is paid (irrespective of whether tax is deducted from that payment) and any person by whom any such interest is received must notify HM Revenue and Customs of certain information in relation to that payment (this information includes the amount of the payment, the name and address of the person (the 'investor') whom interest is paid to or on whose behalf interest is received)[2]. These provisions apply irrespective of whether an investor is resident in the UK for UK taxation purposes. Where an investor is not resident in the UK, the details provided to the HM Revenue and Customs may, in certain cases, be passed by HM Revenue and Customs to the tax authorities of the jurisdiction in which an investor is resident for taxation purposes.

1   'Interest' is defined for these purposes as any dividend in respect of a share in a building society, any amount to which a person holding a deeply discounted security (as defined by Income Tax (Trading and Other Income Act) 2005, ss 430–436) is entitled on the redemption of that security, a foreign dividend (a 'foreign dividend' is any annual payment, interest or dividend payable out of, or in respect of, the stocks, funds, shares or securities of a body of persons that is not resident in the UK or a government or public or local authority of a country outside the UK) and alternative finance return: Finance Act 2011, Schedule 23 para 12(2); also the Data-gathering Powers (Relevant Data) Regulations 2012 (SI 2012/847).

These provisions do not apply to payments or receipts representing redemption proceeds in respect of discounted securities or foreign dividends (not including foreign interest) made or received prior to 6 April 2002, repo interest, manufactured payments, or the redemption proceeds of deeply discounted securities or foreign dividends (which are not foreign interest; if a financial institution cannot immediately identify whether a foreign dividend is interest that payment is not reportable); see HM Revenue and Custom's *Type 18 RETURNS 2012/2013 (formerly returns made under section 17 of the Taxes Management Act 1970) – Guidance Notes for returns of Interest from Banks, Building Societies and other Deposit-takers under Schedule 23 to the Finance Act 2011*, para 4.5.

Although it may be arguable that payments in respect of a guarantee do not constitute 'interest', it is thought that for compliance purposes it may be prudent to regard a payment made in respect of a guarantee as being within these provisions.

2   A person who has responsibility for reporting may report payments/receipts in respect either of all individuals or of individuals with an address in a 'fully reportable country'. 'Fully reportable countries', at the time of writing, are Australia, Canada, Japan, New Zealand, Norway, South Korea, USA and UK dependencies, etc of Anguilla, Bermuda, Cayman Islands and Turks & Caicos Islands; see http://www.hmrc.gov.uk/esd-guidance/fr-countries-2012-13.pdf.

10.71   There are a number of circumstances in which information need not be supplied to HM Revenue and Customs. The most important of these is where there is a payment to, or a receipt for, a person who is not an individual (in whatever capacity the individual concerned is acting)[1]. Another significant exclusion relates to a payment in respect of a payment plan such as an individual saving account[2]. (There is also no requirement to report where a person passively collects interest: eg where a bank does no more than clear a cheque or arranges for a cheque to be cleared, but takes no step to secure the payment of monies.) HM Revenue and Customs has published guidance notes indicating how it approaches the implementation of the reporting requirements[3].

1   HM Revenue and Customs, *Type 18 RETURNS 2012/2013 (formerly returns made under section 17 of the Taxes Management Act 1970) – Guidance Notes for returns of Interest from Banks, Building Societies and other Deposit-takers under Schedule 23 to the Finance Act 2011*, para 4.1–4.3.

2   HM Revenue and Customs, *Type 18 RETURNS 2012/2013 (formerly returns made under section 17 of the Taxes Management Act 1970) – Guidance Notes for returns of Interest from Banks, Building Societies and other Deposit-takers under Schedule 23 to the Finance Act 2011*, para 4.5.

3   *Type 18 RETURNS 2012/2013 (formerly returns made under section 17 of the Taxes Management Act 1970) – Guidance Notes for returns of Interest from Banks, Building Societies and other Deposit-takers under Schedule 23 to the Finance Act 2011*.

Where HM Revenue and Customs issues a notice requiring an annual return to be submitted, that notice is usually issued in the February before the end of the relevant tax year.

An annual return must usually be submitted by whichever is the later of 30 June following the end of the tax year to which a notice relates, or four months after the issue of the notice. If, however, a s 18 annual return is combined with a return under the EU Savings Directive (Directive 2003/48/EC), and a notice requiring an EUSD return is issued after 31 May, the time limit for submitting the combined return is 30 days from the date of the EUSD notice.

EUROPEAN UNION DIRECTIVE ON THE TAXATION OF SAVINGS INCOME

10.72 The European Union's Directive on the taxation of savings income in the form of interest payments[1] (the 'EUSD') came into force on 1 July 2005. The EUSD is designed to secure that at least a minimum effective rate of tax is paid on all interest and similar savings income earned by individuals who are resident in EU member states. On 13 November 2008, following a review of the manner in which the EUSD had been operating since July 2005[2], the EU Commission adopted a proposal to amend the EUSD with a view to closing perceived loopholes and eliminating tax evasion[3]. It is unclear at the time of writing whether that proposal will be implemented, or if it is adopted whether it will be subject to significant amendment. However, that proposal, in the form in which it was published in November 2008, is discussed below.

1 Directive 2003/481/EC.

2 *Report from the Commission to the Council in accordance with Article 18 of Council Directive 2003/48/EC on taxation of saving income in the form of interest payments*, SEC (2008) 2420, 16 September 2008.

3 'Taxation of savings: The European Commission proposes changes to eliminate tax evasion', 13 November 2008 (IP/08/1697); for the proposal itself see: *Proposal for a Council Directive amending Directive 2003/48/EC on taxation of savings income in the form of interest payments*, COM (2008) 727 (the 'Commission Proposal').

10.73 Where a 'paying agent'[1] established in any EU member state makes an 'interest payment'[2] to an individual resident in another member state and who is the 'beneficial owner'[3] of that interest payment, that paying agent is required to notify the competent authority in the member state in which that paying agent is established, and that authority is required to supply details of that payment to the competent authority of the other member state[4].

1 For these purposes, the term 'paying agent' is widely defined to include both the principal obligor under a debt obligation; a paying agent in the normal sense of that term; and an agent (a 'paying agent on receipt') who receives interest, discounts or premiums on behalf of an individual beneficially entitled to such interest, discount or premium. Note that the use of the term 'paying agent' (Directive 2003/48/EC, art 4) in this context is much broader than has traditionally been the case in UK tax law: see para **10.57** above.

2 The term 'interest payment' is defined to include:

   (i) interest relating to a debt claim of any kind (including income from government securities and bonds or debentures; but not penalty charges for late payment);

   (ii) interest accrued or capitalised at the sale, refund or redemption of a debt claim;

   (iii) income distributed by a an undertaking for Collective Investment in Transferable Securities ('UCITS') authorised in accordance with Directive 85/611/EC (the 'UCITS Directive'), an entity which opts to be treated as a UCITS under EUSD, art 4(3), or an undertaking (a 'UCITS equivalent') for collective investment established in a territory outside the member states; and

   (iv) income realised on the sale, refund, or redemption of shares or units in an entity or undertaking within (iii) above if that entity or undertaking invests directly or indirectly more than 40 per cent of its assets in debt claims within (i) and (ii) above.

   See Directive 2003/48/EC, art 6.

3 A paying agent is required to take 'reasonable steps' to establish the identity of the beneficial owner of interest, and if it is not able to identify the beneficial owner is required to treat an individual to whom it makes a payment as a the 'beneficial owner'; see Directive 2003/48/EC, art 2(2).

4 Directive 2003/48/EC, art 4(3).

Transitional period

10.74 During a transitional period Austria, Belgium and Luxembourg may, instead of supplying information on savings income to the tax authorities of other member states (and notwithstanding that they are entitled to receive such information from other member states), operate a withholding tax[1].

1 Directive 2003/48/EC art 10(1). Austria, Belgium and Luxembourg may each elect to move from a withholding regime to an information reporting regime at any time during the transitional period: Directive 2003/48/EC art 10(3).

During 2005 and 2006, 45 per cent of the revenue raised pursuant to the EUSD was collected by Switzerland, and 22 per cent by Luxembourg. In these years, Germany received € 192.7 million, Italy € 112.9 million, and Belgium more than € 71 million.

10.75 A paying agent established in Austria, Belgium or Luxembourg must, during this transitional period, unless an individual elects to follow an information reporting procedure (see next paragraph), withhold tax from any interest payment paid to an individual resident in another member state. The withholding tax is levied at a rate of 15 per cent for payments made prior to 1 July 2008, at a rate of 20 per cent for payments made on or after 1 July 2008 and prior to 1 July 2011, and at the rate of 35 per cent for payments made on or after 1 July 2011[1].

1 Directive 2003/48/EC, art 11.

10.76 The EUSD requires Austria and Luxembourg[1] to allow one or two procedures under which an individual may elect to report interest income (rather than receive that income subject to deduction of tax). One of these procedures (the 'voluntary disclosure procedure') involves an individual authorising the paying agent to disclose details of the income to the tax authority of his or her state of residence. The other procedure (the 'certification procedure') involves an individual presenting a certificate obtained from the tax authority of his or her state of residence confirming that those authorities are aware of the payment due to the individual; such a certificate must be issued within two months of an individual requesting it and may be valid for a period not exceeding three years[2].

1 And, for payments prior to 1 January 2010, Belgium.
2 Directive 2003/48/EC, art 13.

10.77 The transitional period will shall cease to apply at the end of the first full fiscal year following the later of the date on which an agreement comes into force (i) with the unanimous consent of Switzerland, Liechtenstein, San Marino, Monaco and Andorra to the exchange of information and the imposition by those countries of withholding tax at the rate which applies at the relevant time during the transitional period, and (ii) the US is committed (in the unanimous view of the European Council) to the exchange of information upon request in accordance with OECD Model Tax Agreement on the Exchange of Information on Tax Matters released on by the OECD on 18 April 2002[1].

1 Directive 2003/48/EC, art 10(2). Most of the agreements that have been entered into between with other jurisdictions are unilateral (eg Anguilla and Cayman Islands) in that information is given to member states, or the withholding tax levied is shared with member states (Andorra, Liechtenstein, Monaco, San Marino, Switzerland and Turks & Caicos Islands). Agreements have been entered into, on a bilateral basis, to share information only with Montserrat and Aruba, and withholding tax only with Jersey, Guernsey, the Isle of Man, British Virgin Islands and the Netherlands Antilles (which was dissolved on 1 October 2010, with Curacao and St Martine becoming autonomous countries within the Kingdom of the Netherlands and the other remaining parts of the Netherland Antilles becoming provinces of the Kingdom of the Netherlands).

10.78 During the transitional period (at least until 31 December 2010)[1] domestic and international bonds and other negotiable debt securities issued before 1 March

2001, or issued under a prospectus approved by a competent authority before that date, were exempt from the withholding tax provisions of the EUSD. Similarly, there is no requirement for the EUSD to be applied to payments made in respect of securities issued before 1 March 2001 or to payments in respect of securities issued before 1 March 2002 and fungible with securities issued before 1 March 2001[2]. Securities issued on or after 1 March 2002 are fully within the scope of the EUSD.

1   Exemption from the EUSD only continues to apply after 31 December 2010 where negotiable debt securities which contain gross-up and early redemption clauses, and where the paying agent is established in a member state applying the withholding tax under art 11 of the EUSD and that paying agent pays interest to, or secures the payment of interest for the immediate benefit of, a beneficial owner resident in another member state: Directive 2003/48/EC, art 15(1).

2   Directive 2003/48/EC, art 15.

   Note, however, that if there is a further issue on or after 1 March 2002 of a negotiable debt security issued by a government or a related entity acting as a public authority or whose role is recognised by an international tax treaty (as defined in the Annex to the EUSD) under a prospectus approved before that date, both the original issue and the further issue are brought within the scope of the EUSD.

Reform of the EUSD

10.79 Article 18 of the EUSD places the EU Commission under an obligation to report to the Council of Ministers every three years with respect to the operation of the EUSD. In September 2008 the Commission published the first of these reports in which it concluded that the EUSD has, broadly, been implemented successfully. The EU Commission disclosed that it has begun infringement proceedings against just two member states which it believes have not implemented the EUSD correctly into national law[1]. Although the EU Commission seems to believe that the EUSD has not distorted the market to a material extent, its concedes that its analysis 'suffers from many shortcomings linked to legal provisions of the [EUSD], to severe data limitations and to technical issues'[2]. At the time of writing these proposals[3] appear to have become rather stuck in a political quagmire and these proposals remain pending awaiting an agreement amongst the EU's member states. On 2 March 2012, after a second three-year period had elapsed, the EU Commission issued a second report on the function of the Directive in which it concluded that[4]:

> '... the updating of the Directive ... in terms of product scope as well as transactions and economic operators covered, is urgently needed in order to address the existing possibilities for circumvention, including those arising from triangular situations which involve jurisdictions both within and outside the scope of the Savings Agreements. A consensus on the Proposal and the adoption of a negotiating mandate for equivalent provisions in these Agreements are necessary in order to promote transparency and good governance in tax matters both within and outside the EU.'

1   Commission Report, para 1.

2   In one case, article 4(3) of the EUSD, which is intended to permit a non-UCITS to opt to be treated as a UCITS and therefore as a paying agent, may not have been properly transposed into national law.

   In the other case, a member state has taken the position that the EUSD does not apply if a beneficial owner is exempt from tax in the member state in which he or she is resident.

   See the draft Commission Staff Working Document (as referred to in the Commission Report) para 1.

3   Little progress appears to have been made since the Danish Presidency suggested a compromise text for a new Directive on 25 November 2009 – 'Proposal for a Council Directive amending Directive 2003/48/EC on taxation of savings income in the form of interest payments – Political agreement', 16473/1/09 REV 1.

4   Report from the Commission to the Council in accordance with Article 18 of Council Directive 2003/48/EC on taxation of savings income in the form of interest payments, COM (2012) 65 final.

Implementation of the EUSD by the UK

10.80 The regulations implementing the EUSD require a person who is established in the UK, and makes 'savings income payments'[1] in the course of his or her business or profession for the immediate benefit of a 'relevant payee'[2] or to a 'residual entity'[3] established in a 'prescribed territory'[4], to notify HM Revenue and Customs in writing within 14 days of the end of the tax year in which a payment is made/received that that person needs to make a report (unless HM Revenue and Customs has already notified it of the need to make a report[5]). A report must contain information specified in the implementing regulations[6].

1   The definition of 'savings income payments' accords with the equivalent definition adopted by the EUSD. However, it is worth noting that the UK has implemented the EUSD such that:

- income distributed by a UCITS established in the UK or another member state, or a UCITS equivalent established in a territory which has also implemented a 15 per cent threshold, is savings income only if the relevant UCITS or UCITS equivalent has invested more than 15 per cent of its assets in debt claims other than grandfathered bonds; and

- income realised on the sale, refund or redemption of shares or units in a UCITS or UCITS equivalent is savings income only if that entity or undertaking invests directly or indirectly more than 40 per cent (25 per cent from 1 January 2011) of its assets in debt claims.

See the Reporting of Savings Income Information Regulations 2003 (SI 2003/3297), reg 8.

2   A 'relevant payee' is a person resident in a prescribed territory who is an individual and does not provide evidence to the paying agent that he or she falls within a certain category specified in the regulations: Reporting of Savings Income Information Regulations 2003 (SI 2003/3297), reg 7.

3   A 'residual entity' is a body of persons or an organisation (but not an individual) which is not:

- a legal person (other than in Finland an *'avoin yhtiö* (AY)', a *'kommandittiyhtiö* (KY)*löppet bolag*' and *Kommanditbolag*', and in Sweden a *'handelsbolag* (HB)' and a *'kommanditbolag* (KB))';

- taxed under the general arrangements for business taxation;

- a UCITS or UCITS equivalent; or

- an elective UCITS (ie an entity which has opted to be treated as a UCITS).

See the Reporting of Savings Income Information Regulations 2003 (SI 2003/3297), reg 4.

4   At the time of writing, all EU member states (other than the UK), Bonaire, Curacao, Gibraltar, Aruba, the British Virgin Islands, Guernsey, the Isle of Man, Jersey, Montserrat, Saba, St Eustatius, St Maarten are 'prescribed territories': Savings Income Reporting Guidance Notes (updated November 2011), para 74.

5   Reporting of Savings Income Information Regulations 2003 (SI 2003/3297), reg 3.

6   Reporting of Savings Income Information Regulations 2003 (SI 2003/3297), regs 9–13.

10.81 The UK has also entered into non-reciprocal arrangements with Anguilla, the Cayman Islands and the Turks & Caicos Islands in accordance with which each of these territories applies equivalent measures to the EUSD, but in the case of each of these 'relevant territories' the UK is not required to supply information to the competent authorities in those territories. These 'relevant territories' are important in the context of determining whether a distribution paid by a UCITS equivalent is savings income which must be reported by a paying agent established in the UK. In particular, the Cayman Islands has negotiated an agreement with the UK under which a fund established in the Cayman Islands which is *not* licensed under s 5 of the Cayman Islands' Mutual Fund Law (2007 revision) is regarded as not being an 'UCITS equivalent' and, therefore, as not generating savings income payments. It is understood that funds licensed with the Cayman Islands Monetary Authority under s 5 of the Mutual Funds Law (2007 revision) are rarely used (save eg where a fund desires a minimum subscription level of less than US$50,000 and does not wish

UK taxation 333

to employ a Cayman licensed administrator) and made up (as of early 2008) only approximately 1.3 per cent of the total funds registered in the Cayman Islands.

FATCA

Overview

10.82 'FATCA' is an acronym used to describe the 'Foreign Accounts Tax Compliance' provisions of the United States' Hiring Incentives to Restore Employment Act 2010 which are intended to promote compliance by US persons[1] and Specified US persons[2] ('Relevant US Persons'). FATCA requires non-US financial institutions to report information relating to accounts held by Relevant US Persons to the Internal Revenue Service ('IRS') or to impose withholding at the rate of 30%.

The implementation of FATCA has presented institutions with both practical difficulties (eg in putting in place the procedures and systems to enable them to comply with FATCA reporting obligations) and legal difficulties because the law (eg relating to data protection) of certain non-US jurisdictions prohibits the sharing of data with an entity such as the IRS which is established outside those jurisdictions[3,4]. In order to address these legal obstacles the G5 countries (France, Germany, Italy, Spain and the UK) published a model intergovernmental agreement on 26 July 2012, and on 12 September 2012 the UK and the US signed a joint agreement to improve international tax compliance and to implement FATCA (the 'UK IGA') which is closely based on the G5 model agreement. It is understood that Switzerland and Japan also intend to enter into agreements with the US (albeit based on a different model to that adopted by the G5).

The UK IGA seeks to enable institutions to comply with FATCA by requiring them to report information to HM Revenue and Customs[5] pursuant to legislation which is to be introduced by the Finance Act 2013; HM Revenue and Customs will, in turn, report information to the IRS under the automatic exchange of information provisions of the double taxation treaty between the US and the UK[6].

The discussion below is restricted to the terms of the UK IGA (rather than the FATCA provisions themselves) and is also limited to the obligations which are to be imposed under UK law as provided for by the terms of the UK IGA[7]. Draft UK legislation was expected to be published too close to this book going to press to be reflected here, and reference is therefore made where appropriate to a consultation document published by HM Revenue and Customs in September 2012[8].

The UK IGA acknowledges that, to some extent, the arrangements it provides for represent a 'work in progress' and provision is made:

- for implementing rules (as yet unspecified) to prevent the UK IGA being circumvented by financial institutions[9];
- for the US government to further improve transparency and enhance its exchange relationship with the UK with a view to achieving 'equivalent levels of reciprocal automatic information exchange'[10];
- for the development of a 'practical and effective' alternative approach in relation to foreign passthru payment and gross proceeds withholding which minimises the compliance burden[11];
- for the development of a common model for information exchange (including reporting and due diligence standards) with other members of the OECD and the EU[12];

- for consultations to take place, prior to 31 December 2016, in good faith to amend the UK IGA to reflect progress made in relation to the three previous bullet points[13];

- for Annex II to the UK IGA, which lists Non-Reporting UK Financial Institutions and Products, to be amended, as and when appropriate, following agreement between HM Revenue and Customs and the IRS[14]; and

- for the UK to be granted the benefit of any more favourable terms which the US may agree with any other jurisdiction in relation to FATCA (a 'Partner Jurisdiction')[15].

1   A 'US person' is defined as a:
   (i)   a US citizen;
   (ii) a US resident individual;
   (iii) a partnership or a corporation organised under the laws of the US (or on State of the US);
   (iv) a trust over (a)which a US court would have jurisdiction under applicable law to make an order concerning substantially all issues regarding administration of the trust, (b) over which a US person has authority to control substantial decisions; or
   (v)   an estate of a decedent this is a citizen or resident of the US.

   See UK IGA, art 1(ff).

2   A 'Specified US person' is, broadly speaking, defined as a US person other than:
   (i)   a company whose common stock is regularly traded on a securities market (or a company which is a member of an expanded affiliated group as such a company);
   (ii) the US (or a wholly owned agency or instrumentality of the US) or any State of the US;
   (iii) an organisation exempt from tax under section 501(a) of the US Internal Revenue Code (the 'US Code') or an individual retirement plan;
   (iv) a bank, a real estate investment trust, a regulated investment company, an entity registered with the Securities and Exchange Commission under the Investment Company Act 1940;
   (v)   a common trust fund, a trust which is exempt from tax under section 664(c) of the Code or which is described in 4979(a)(1) of the US Code;
   (vi) a dealer in securities, commodities, or derivative financial instruments which is registered as such under the laws of the US or the laws of any State; or
   (vi) a broker as defined in section 6045(c) of the Code.

   See UK IGA, art 1(gg).

3   FATCA also offers taxing jurisdictions an opportunity to considerably enhance the information they obtain from other jurisdictions. This has not gone unnoticed and the Government announced on 5 December 2012 that it intends to enter into agreements with other jurisdiction providing for similar information exchange to that provided for under the UK IGA; see HM Treasury, Autumn Statement 2012 (Cm 8480), para 1.174. The attraction of this from HMRC's perspective is obvious: once the mechanism has been put in place to obtain the necessary information from UK financial institutions it should be relatively straight forward to exchange that information with other jurisdictions in order to obtain enhanced information about offshore accounts maintained by UK resident persons.

4   On 14 November 2012, the IRS published a template for a 'Model 2' agreement with these jurisdictions; see http://www.treasury.gov/resource-center/tax-policy/treaties/ Documents/FATCA-Model-2-Agreement-to-Implement-11-14-2012.pdf.

   The Model 2 agreement requires a non-US jurisdiction to 'require and enable' financial institutions which are subject to its jurisdiction to register directly with the IRS and report annually to the IRS. Unlike the Model 1 agreement, the Model 2 agreement:

   - does not restrict the responsibility to make a FATCA withholding to 'withholding qualified intermediaries and other entities which choose to collect US withholding tax; and

   - does not suspend (pending any further agreement) obligations in respect of foreign pass-thru payments or gross proceeds withholding.

5   UK IGA, arts 2–3.

The core obligation to withhold under FATCA in respect of FDAP payments and certain gross proceeds applies to payments made on or after 1 January 2014. The FATCA provisions themselves refer to United States Fixed, Determinable, Annual, or Periodical ('FDAP') income which equates to all income, except gains derived from the sale of real or personal property (including market discount and option premiums, but not including original issue discount) and items of income excluded from gross income, without regard to the US or foreign status of the owner of the income, such as tax exempt municipal bond interest and qualified scholarship income.

IRS Notice 2011-53 provides guidance with respect to the manner in which a foreign financial institution may enter into a direct agreement with the IRS in order to comply with FATCA as a participating financial institution which (generally) reports information rather than withholds tax. Such an agreement must be entered into on or before 30 June 2013 if an institution wishes to be identified as a participating FFI and therefore avoid FATCA withholding when that withholding begins on 1 January 2014.

Payments of the gross proceeds of property which can potentially produce income or dividends will be potentially subject to FATCA withholding if made on or after 1 January 2017 (see IRS Announcement 2012-42, para V).

The IRS has acknowledged that uncertainty arising from the length of time it is taking to finalise the relevant regulations has been causing increasing concern because institutions have been unsure as to their obligations and it has been difficult for parties to allocate risk appropriately in contractual documentation. In order to address these difficulties, the IRS announced (see IRS Announcement 2012-42, para VI) that the following additional categories of 'grandfathered obligations' will be included in the final implementing regulations:

- an obligation that produces, or could produce, a foreign pass-thru payment and that cannot produce a withholdable payment (ie because the payment does not have a US source), provided that obligation is outstanding six months after the final regulations defining the term 'foreign pass-thru payment' are filed with the Federal Register. This date is likely to be mid-2013 at the earliest;

- any instrument that gives rise to a withholdable payment, solely because that instrument is treated as giving rise to a dividend; and

- any obligation to make a payment with respect to (including, it would seem, manufactured interest), or to repay, collateral posted to secure obligations under a notional principal contract (eg a derivative) that is itself a grandfathered obligation. It appears that this safe harbour may not cover the posting or return of collateral – and if this turns out to be the case, this may cause difficulties where a derivative is itself grandfathered.

For a useful portal to IRS pronouncements, see http://www.irs.gov/Businesses/Corporations/Foreign-Account-Tax-Compliance-Act-(FATCA).

6   The Double Taxation Relief (Taxes on Income) (The United States of America) Order 2002 (SI 2002/2848), art 27.

7   Cf. the obligation, imposed on the US by UK IGA, art 2(2)(b) to obtain and exchange information in relation to accounts held by a Reportable US Financial Institutions in relation to the UK Reportable Accounts.

8   HMRC, 'Implementing the UK-US FATCA Agreement' (18 September 2012) (the 'FATFA Condoc').

On 18 December 2012, HMRC did indeed publish a response document to the FATCA Condoc ('Implementing the UK-US FATCA Agreement: Summary of Responses' (18 December 2012)), a draft of the relevant regulations (International Tax Compliance (United States of America) Regulations 2013) and draft guidance relating to those regulations ('Implementation of International Compliance (United States of America) Regulations 2013: Guidance Notes').

It is anticipated that during the lifetime of this edition the position in relation to the implementation of FATCA will develop fast – and readers who would like to access an updated discussion are referred to Chapter 8 of the looseleaf work *Norfolk and Montagu on the Taxation of Interest and Debt Finance* (Bloomsbury Professional) which covers FATCA in more depth than space will allow here and which it is intended will be updated every six months (and more frequently if required).

9   UK IGA, art 5, para 4.

10 UK IGA, art 6, para 1.

11 UK IGA, art 6, para 2.
12 UK IGA, art 6, para 3.
13 UK IGA, art 10, para 3.
14 UK IGA, Annex II.
15 UK IGA, art 7.

Compliance under the UK IGA

10.83 The UK IGA identifies a Custodial Institution, a Depositary Institution[1], an Investment Entity[2] or a Specified Insurance Company as a 'Financial Institution'. In the context of this book, the definition of 'Custodial Institution' is most likely to be relevant – and that is 'an entity that holds, as a substantial proportion of its business, financial assets for the account of others'[3].

A UK Financial Institution (referred to in the UK IGA as a 'Reporting United Kingdom Financial Institution') (a 'UK RFI'), which is not a Non-Reporting United Kingdom Financial Institution[4], will be treated as having complied with its FATCA obligations if it complies with its obligations under UK law to report information to HM Revenue and Customs as envisaged by articles 2 and 3 of the UK IGA[5] and:

(a) in 2015 and 2016 reports, annually, to HM Revenue and Customs the name of each Non-participating Financial Institution[6] to which it has made payments (and the aggregate amount of such payments);

(b) complies with the registration requirements applicable to Financial Institutions in other jurisdictions which enter into IGAs with the US;

(c) withholds 30% of any US Source Withholdable Payment[7] to any Non-participating Financial Institution to the extent that it: (i) is acting as a qualified intermediary (for the purposes of section 1441 of the Code) which has elected to assume primary withholding responsibility[8], (ii) a foreign partnership which has elected to act as a withholding foreign partnership (for the purposes of sections 1441 and 1471 of the Code); or (iii) a foreign trust which has elected to act as a withholding foreign trust (for the purposes of sections 1441 and 1471 of the Code); and

(d) if an institution is not within (c) above, and makes a payment of, or acts as an intermediary in respect of, a US Source Withholdable Payment to a Non-participating Financial Institution, its provides to the immediate payor the information required for withholding and reporting to occur with respect to that payment.

Where a UK RFI satisfies each of these conditions, it will not be subject to an obligation to withhold tax under section 1471 of the Code unless the IRS identifies it as a Non-participating Financial Institution. Furthermore, if an accountholder is a 'recalcitrant account holder'[9], a UK RFI will not be required to withhold tax or close the account if the IRS receives certain information with respect to that account[10].

A Non-Reporting UK Financial Reporting Entity[11] and a retirement plan specified in Annex II of the IGA[12] is treated as a deemed-compliant Foreign Financial Intermediary or as an exempt beneficial owner for FATCA purposes.

Where a UK RFI meets the requirements outlined above, or a Non-Reporting UK Financial Institution, has a Related Entity or branch which operates in a jurisdiction the laws of which prevent the requirements or a UK RFI or a deemed-compliant FFI from being satisfied, or is an entity is a retirement plan, that institution is to be treated[13] as complying with the terms of the UK IGA and as a deemed-compliant FFI or an exempt beneficial owner for the purposes of section 1471 of the Code, provided that, where a UK RFI or Non-Reporting UK Financial Institution has a Related Entity or branch, each Related Entity or branch[14]:

(a) is treated as a separate Non-participating Financial Institution for reporting and withholding purposes and that entity or branch identifies itself to withholding agents as a Nonparticipating Financial Institution;

(b) identifies its US accounts and reports information as required under section 1471 of the Code to the extent permitted by the laws which apply to it; and

(c) does not specifically solicit US accounts held by persons that are not resident in the jurisdiction where it is located or accounts held by Non-participating Financial Institutions that are established in other jurisdictions, and is not used by the UK Financial Institution to circumvent its obligations under the UK IGA or under section 1471 of the Code.

The UK IGA also includes provisions governing minor or administrative errors[15], and significant non-compliance[16].

An entity may out-source its obligations under the UK IGA to a third party, but the responsibility for compliance may not be passed to a third party[17].

1   An entity which accepts deposits in the ordinary course of banking or similar business; see UK IGA, art 1(i).

2   An entity which conducts as a business (or is managed by an entity which conducts as a business) on behalf of a customer:

   (a) trading in money market instruments; foreign exchange; exchange, index rate and interest instruments; transferable securities or commodity futures trading;

   (b) individual and collective portfolio management; and/or

   (c) otherwise investing, administering, or managing funds or money on behalf of other persons.

   It is intended that an entity which is not required to comply with anti-money laundering regulations in the UK should not qualify as an Investment Entity (eg HM Revenue and Customs envisages that 'most' family trusts should not be included, but professionally managed trusts will be included); see FATCA Condoc, para 3.9.

   HM Revenue and Customs has acknowledged that multiple reporting by sub-funds and umbrella funds would not be desirable, and has suggested that centralising reporting at the level of an umbrella fund following the approach suggested by IRS Notice 2011-34 might be appropriate. Although HM Revenue and Customs intends that a fund (rather than a manager) should be treated as the 'Financial Institution' and therefore have responsibility for reporting, it envisages that a report may actually be made by a manager (ie as the manager, rather than the fund, is likely to have the necessary information). See FATCA Condoc, paras 3.10–3.14.

3   A 'substantial proportion' equates to 20% or more of an entity's gross income during the shorter of: (i) the three-year period ending on 31 December prior to the year in which a determination is being made; or (ii) the period during which the entity has been in existence; see UK IGA, art 1(h). HM Revenue and Customs has indicated in the FATFA Condoc (at para 3.5) that UK tax law is to be used to determine whether an entity's gross income.

4   A 'Non-Reporting United Kingdom Financial Institution' means:

   (a) a UK Governmental Organisation (ie a devolved administration or local authority);

   (b) the Bank of England (and its wholly owned subsidiaries);

   (c) International Organisations (eg the IMF, the World Bank, the IBRD, the IFC, the IDA, the EU and various development banks);

   (d) a pension scheme or retirement agreement established in the UK and described in article 3 of the UK/US double taxation convention;

   (e) certain deemed compliant institutions (eg an entity registered as a charity with the Charity Commission or with HM Revenue and Customs, or a community amateur sports club registered with HM Revenue and Customs);

   (f) an institution with a local client base (eg a credit union, an industrial and provident society, a friendly society, a building society, a mutual society, an investment trust company, a venture capital trust); and

(g) an institution which is licensed and regulated under UK law, which has no place of business outside the UK, which does not solicit account holders outside the UK (a website does not count as solicitation provided that it is does not specifically indicate that services are provided to non-residents or targets/solicits US customers), which is subject to information reporting or withholding obligations under UK law, 98% of whose accounts (by value) are held by residents of an EU member state, which implements procedures to monitor accounts prior to 1 January 2014, which reviews accounts opened prior to those procedures being implemented, and which has related entities (by reference to over 50% by votes or value; but HM Revenue and Customs may treat entities as not related if they are not members of the same expanded affiliated group as defined by section 1471(e)(2) of the Code) each of which is incorporated in the UK and qualifies under this paragraph (g).

In addition, in order to qualify as a Non-Reporting United Kingdom Financial Institution, an institution must meet certain compliance requirements which are described at the end of this section relating to FATCA and it must also be the case that each of its Related Entities are incorporated or organised in the UK and meet the requirements for Non-Reporting United Kingdom Financial Institution reporting status.

See UK IGA Annex II, paras 1–2.

5   UK IGA, art 4 para 1.

6   A 'Non-participating Financial Institution' is an institution as defined in regulations issued by the US Treasury (this does not include UK Financial Institution or an institution established in a Partner jurisdiction unless that institution is guilty of significant non-compliance).

7   'US Source Withholdable Payment' is defined, widely, to mean 'any payment of interest (including any original issue discount), dividends, rents, salaries, wages, premiums, annuities, compensations, remunerations, emoluments, and other fixed or determinable annual or periodical gains, profits, and income, if such payment is from sources within the United States', but so as not to include any payment that is not treated as a withholdable payment in relevant U.S. Treasury Regulations; see UK IGA, art 1(1)(jj).

8   HM Revenue and Customs does not expect a UK Financial Institution to meet this criterion, on the basis that many qualifying intermediaries are understood not to have elected to assume primary withholding responsibility; see FATCA Condoc, para 3.39.

9   As defined in section 1471(1)(d) of the Code.

10 That information is set out in the UK IGA at article 2, para 2(a) – and must be provided within the timeframe specified by the UK IGA, art 3.

11 UK IGA, art 4, para 4.

12 UK IGA, art 4, para 3.

13 This treatment continues for an indefinite period, and this position represents a relaxation from the position under FATCA itself; see FATCA Condoc, para 3.43.

14 UK IGA, art 4, para 5.

15 UK IGA, art 5, para 1.

16 UK IGA, art 5, para 2. If non-compliance is not resolved within 18 months of a UK RFI being notified of the non-compliance, the institution will be treated as a Nonparticipating Financial Institution (and named as such on a list which the IRS will make available).

HM Revenue and Customs' 'initial thoughts' are that the following would constitute significant non-compliance:

- the intentional provision of substantially incorrect information;
- the deliberate or negligent omission of required information;
- ongoing or repeated failure to register, supply accurate information, or establish appropriate governance or due diligence processes; and
- repeated fairlure to file a return, or repeated late filing.

See FATCA Condoc, para 3.50.

17 UK IGA, art 5, para 3.

Account identification and review obligations for UK RFIs

10.84 Annex I to the UK IGA sets out in some detail the processes and procedures which a UK RFI will need to apply to identify US Reportable Accounts[1].

It is worth noting that where the way in which the rules apply is determined, in part, by reference to the balance or value of accounts and that special account aggregation rules apply to prevent the rules from being manipulated. All the accounts maintained by a UK RFI or its Related Entities must be aggregated to the extent that the institution's computer systems link those accounts by reference to a data element such as a client number of taxpayer identification number and allow balances to be aggregated; the entire balance or value of a jointly held individual account is attributed to each joint holder for these purposes[2].

A brief summary of the requirements to identify, review and report in respect of accounts is set out below:

1 The UK IGA, Annex I, para I(c) permits HM Revenue and Customs to allow UK RFIs, as an alternative to the detailed rules set out in Annex I itself, to rely on the procedures described in relevant US Treasury Regulations to establish whether an account is a US Reportable Account or an account held by a Non-participating Financial Institution. HM Revenue and Customs has indicated that it is considering whether to permit procedures specified in the relevant US Treasury regulations where those procedures would be less burdensome; see FATCA Condoc, para 4.3.

2 In relation to individual accounts (and jointly held accounts), see UK IGA, Annex I, para VI C(1); in relation to entity accounts, see UK IGA, Annex I, para VI C(2).

Pre-existing accounts held by individuals and opened on or before 31 December 2013

10.85 An account with a balance or value on 31 December 2013 that does not exceed $50,000 does not need to be reviewed, identified, or reported[1].

However, where, on 31 December 2013, an account the balance or value of an account exceeds $50,000, a UK RFI will be required to review data which it can search electronically to identify any of the following 'US indicia'[2]:

- a US citizen or resident is the account holder;
- an unambiguous indication that the account holder was born in the US;
- a current US mailing address or residence address;
- a current US telephone number;
- standing instructions to transfer funds to an account maintained in the US;
- a currently effective power or attorney or signatory authority granted to a person with an address in the US; and/or
- an 'in-care-of' or 'hold-mail' address that is the sole address on file for the account holder (in the case of a lower value account an 'in-care-of' address outside the US is not regarded as an indication of a US nexus).

If none of these indicia are revealed, a UK RFI need not take any further action with respect to an account, unless 'US indicia' arise as a result of a change of circumstances[3].

Where, however, one (or more) of these US indicia is identified a UK RFI is required to treat that account as a US Reportable Account, unless the UK RFI elects to take advantage of a safe harbour which will be available with respect to particular US indicia on the following basis[4]:

- US place of birth

  The UK RFI has previously reviewed and maintained a record of, or obtains:

  (i) a self-certification that the account holder is neither a US citizen nor a US resident for tax purposes (eg on an IRS Form W-8 or other similar agreed form);

  (ii) a non-US passport or other identification issued by a government which identifies the account holder as being a citizen or national or a country other than the US; and

  (iii) a copy of (a) an account holder's Certification of Loss of Nationality of the United States, or (b) a reasonable explanation of the reason the account holder does not have such a certificate or the reason the account holder did not obtain US citizenship at birth.

- US mailing or residence address, US telephone number(s) (being the only telephone number(s) associated with the account)

  The UK RFI has previously reviewed and maintained a record of, or obtains:

  (i) a self-certification that the account holder is neither a US citizen nor a US resident for tax purposes (eg on an IRS Form W-8 or other similar agreed form);

  (ii) a non-US passport or other identification issued by a government which identifies the account holder as being a citizen or national or a country other than the US.

- Standing instructions to transfer funds to an account maintained in the US

  The UK RFI has previously reviewed and maintained a record of, or obtains:

  (i) a self-certification that the account holder is neither a US citizen nor a US resident for tax purposes (eg on an IRS Form W-8 or other similar agreed form); and

  (ii) certain documentary evidence establishing the account holder's non-US status.

- Power of attorney, etc with a US address, 'in-care-of' etc address in the US which is the only address for the account holder, or US telephone number(s) (if a non-US telephone number is also associated with the account)

  The UK RFI has previously reviewed and maintained a record of, or obtains:

  (i) a self-certification that the account holder is neither a US citizen nor a US resident for tax purposes (eg on an IRS Form W-8 or other similar agreed form); or

  (ii) documentary evidence establishing the account holder's non-US status.

A UK RFI must complete its review of 'Lower Value Accounts' by 31 December 2015[5]; such accounts which have been identified as US Reportable Accounts (other than a Depositary Account with a value of less than $50,000) will continue to have this status unless an account holder ceases to be a Specified US Person[6].

Where a pre-existing individual account has a balance or value which exceeds $1 million on 31 December 2013 (referred to as a 'High Value' account) an enhanced review procedure applies. In addition to the electronic search described above[7], a further search of paper records[8] will be required where a UK RFI's electronic records do not include sufficient information[9]. Furthermore, where a relationship manager has actual knowledge that an account holder is a Specified US person, that account must also be treated as a US Reportable Account[10].

The review procedure in respect of High Value Accounts must be completed by 31 December 2014, and information relating to such accounts must be reported with respect to the calendar years 2013 and 2014[11].

If an account becomes a High Value Account on or after 1 January 2014, but is a High Value Account on the last day of a subsequent calendar year, a UK RFI has six months in which to subject that account to an enhanced review[12].

Once an account has been the subject of an enhanced review, then unless there is a change of circumstances in relation to the account as a result of which US indicia become associated with it, the review which must be undertaken by a UK RFI in relation to that account is limited to a checking whether the relationship manager has actual knowledge of any US indicia[13].

1 UK IGA, Annex I, para II A.

2 UK IGA, Annex I, para II B(1).

3 UK IGA, Annex I, para II B(2) and D(5).

  If there is such a chance in circumstance, a UK RFI must treat an account as a US Reportable Account unless the UK RFI elects to take advantage of the safe harbour described below; see UK IGA, Annex I para II C(2).

4 UK IGA, Annex I para II B(3)–(4).

5 UK IGA, Annex I para II C(1).

  A 'Lower Value' account is an account with a balance or value in excess of $50,000 ($250,000 for a Cash Value Insurance Contract or an Annuity Contract) but not in excess of £1 million.

6 UK IGA, Annex I para II C(3).

7 UK IGA, Annex I para II D(1).

8 This involves a review of the current customer master file, and to the extent not contained in that file the following documents obtained by the UK RFI in the previous five years which relate to any of the US indicia:

  (a) the most recent documentary evidence associated with the account;

  (b) the most recent account opening contract/documentation;

  (c) the most recent documentation obtained for money-laundering/know you client ('KCY') or any other regulatory purposes;

  (d) any power of attorney or signature authority forms currently in effect; and

  (e) any standing instructions to transfer funds currently in effect.

  See UK IGA, Annex I, para II D(2).

9 Electronic records contain sufficient information if they include fields for and capture the following information:

  (a) the account holder's nationality or residence status;

  (b) the account holder's residence address and mailing address;

  (c) the account holder's telephone number(s);

  (d) whether there are any standing instructions to transfer funds to any other account (including at another branch of the UK RFI);

  (e) whether there is a current 'in-care-of' or 'hold-mail' address for the account holder; and

  (f) whether there is any power of attorney or signatory authority for the account holder.

  See UK IGA, Annex I, para II D(2)–(3).

10 UK IGA, Annex I, para II D(4).

11 UK IGA, Annex I, para II E(1).

12   UK IGA, Annex I, para II E(2).

13   UK IGA, Annex I, para II E(3)–(4).

>   A UK RFI is required to implement procedures to ensure that a relationship manager identifies any change in circumstances and obtains appropriate documentation relating to that change from an account holder; see UK IGA, Annex I, para II E(5).

Pre-existing Entity Accounts

10.86 Where the account balance or value does not exceed $250,000 on 31 December 2013, a UK RFI is not required to review, identify or report in respect of that account, although a review will need to take place if the balance subsequently exceeds $1 million[1]. Where, however, an account does not meet the hurdle for a review to take place on 31 December 2013, but meets that hurdle at the end of a subsequent calendar year, a UK RFI must conduct this review within the six months which follow the end of that subsequent calendar year[2].

Where review is required, a UK RFI must determine whether the account holder is[3]:

(a)   a US Person[4];

If information indicates that an account holder is a Specified US Person, the account must be treated as a US Reportable Account unless the UK RFI either (i) obtains a self-certification[5], or (ii) determines from publicly available information, that the account holder is not a Specified US Person.

(b)   a UK Financial Institution or Financial Institution established in a Partner Jurisdiction[6];

(c)   a participating FFI[7], a deemed compliant FFI, an exempt beneficial owner, or an excepted FFI[8]; or

A UK RFI is required to treat an entity as a Non-participating Financial Institution unless it obtains a self-certification from the entity that it is a deemed-compliant FFI, an exempt beneficial owner, or an excepted FFI, or (in the case of a participating FFI or registered deemed-compliant FFI, verifies that entity's FATCA identifying number on a list to be published by the IRS)[9].

(d)   an Active[10] NFFE[11] or a Passive[12] NFFE.

In the case of a NFFE, a UK RFI must identify: (i) whether the NFFE has Controlling Persons[13], (ii) whether that entity is a passive NFFE[14], and (iii) whether any Controlling Person is a citizen or resident of the US[15].

This review must be completed by 31 December 2015 in respect of pre-existing entity accounts which have a balance or value which exceeds $250,000 on 31 December 2013[16]. Where, at the end of a subsequent calendar year, the balance of value of an account exceeds $1 million (and did not exceed $1 million on a previous 31 December) a review of the account must be completed within six months following the end of that subsequent calendar year[17].

Reference is made above to the concept of 'Controlling Person' and this signifies the natural person(s) who exercise control over an entity and is interpreted in a manner consistent with the Recommendations of the Financial Action Task Force[18]. In the case of a trust, this means the settlor, the trustees, the protector (if any), the beneficiaries or class of beneficiaries, and any other natural person exercising ultimate effective control over the trust, and in the case of a legal arrangement other than a trust, such term means persons in equivalent or similar positions[19].

1   UK IGA, Annex I para IV A–B.

The UK IGA provides for the UK to introduce the ability for a UK RFI to elect to conduct a review of accounts which have a lower balance or floor. HM Revenue and Customs has indicated that it is concerned that if it were to provide for such an election to be made, a UK RFI might be in breach of its data protection obligations if it were to make such an election and review/report all its accounts.

2   UK IGA, Annex I, para IV E(2).
3   UK IGA, Annex I, para IV D.
4   The review relates to information maintained for regulatory purposes.
5   A UK RFI is required to review an account if, as a result of a change of circumstances, it knows or has reason to know that a self-certification is incorrect or unreliable; see UK IGA, Annex I, para IV D(3).
6   The review relates to information maintained for regulatory purposes.

If an entity falls within this category, no further review or reporting is required.

7   The IRS will publish a list identifying Non-participating Financial Institutions who are have engaged in non-compliant conduct.
8   These are all terms defined in the relevant US Treasury regulations.
9   UK IGA, Annex I para V D(3)(c).
10 An Active NFFE is a NFFE where:

   (a) less than 50% of the NFFE's gross income for the preceding calendar year or other appropriate reporting period is passive income and less than 50% of the assets held by the NFFE during the preceding calendar year or other appropriate reporting period are assets that produce or are held for the production of passive income;

   (b) the stock of the NFFE is regularly traded on an established securities market or the NFFE is a Related Entity of an Entity the stock of which is traded on an established securities market;

   (c) the NFFE is organised in a US Territory and all of the owners of the payee are bona fide residents of that US Territory;

   (d) the NFFE is a non-US government, a government of a US Territory, an international organisation, a non-US central bank of issue, or an Entity wholly owned by one or more of the foregoing;

   (e) substantially all of the activities of the NFFE consist of holding (in whole or in part) the outstanding stock of, and providing financing and services to, one or more subsidiaries that engage in trades or businesses other than the business of a Financial Institution.

   However, an NFFE does not qualify for this status if the NFFE functions (or holds itself out) as an investment fund, such as a private equity fund, venture capital fund, leveraged buyout fund or any investment vehicle whose purpose is to acquire or fund companies and then hold interests in those companies as capital assets for investment purposes;

   (f) the NFFE is not yet operating a business and has no prior operating history, but is investing capital into assets with the intent to operate a business other than that of a Financial Institution; provided, that the NFFE shall not qualify for this exception after the date that is 24 months after the date of the initial organisation of the NFFE;

   (g) the NFFE was not a Financial Institution in the past five years, and is in the process of liquidating its assets or is reorganising with the intent to continue or recommence operations in a business other than that of a Financial Institution;

   (h) the NFFE primarily engages in financing and hedging transactions with or for Related Entities that are not Financial Institutions, and does not provide financing or hedging services to any Entity that is not a Related Entity, provided that the group of any such Related Entities is primarily engaged in a business other than that of a Financial Institution; or

   (i) the NFFE meets all of the following requirements:

       (1) it is established and maintained in its country of residence exclusively for religious, charitable, scientific, artistic, cultural, or educational purposes;

       (2) it is exempt from income tax in its country of residence;

       (3) it has no shareholders or members who have a proprietary or beneficial interest in its income or assets;

(4) the applicable laws of the Entity's country of residence or the Entity's formation documents do not permit any income or assets of the Entity to be distributed to, or applied for the benefit of, a private person or non-charitable Entity other than pursuant to the conduct of the Entity's charitable activities, or as payment of reasonable compensation for services rendered, or as payment representing the fair market value of property which the Entity has purchased; and

(5) the applicable laws of the Entity's country of residence or the Entity's formation documents require that, upon the Entity's liquidation or dissolution, all of its assets be distributed to a governmental Entity or other non-profit organisation, or escheat to the government of the Entity's country of residence or any political subdivision thereof.

See UK IGA, Annex I para VI B(4).

11 An 'NFFE' is any Non-US Entity that is not a Foreign Financial Institution (including a Non-US Entity that is resident in the UK or a Partner Jurisdiction and is not a Financial Institution); the acronym seems more confusing than it need be, for the order of the letters suggests a 'non-foreign' institution, whereas what is actually referred to is a foreign institution which is not a financial institution (ie the 'N' relates to the second 'F' rather than the first 'F').

12 A 'Passive NFFE' is any NFFE which is not an Active NFFE.

13 A UK RFI may rely, for this purpose, on KYC data.

14 A UK RFI must obtain a self-certification (eg IRS Form W-8 or W-9), or information which is in its possession or publicly available, from which it can 'reasonably determine' that the entity is an Active NFFE.

15 UK IGA, Annex I, para V D(4).

A UK RFI may rely on KYC data if the account balance does not exceed $1 million, or if a self-certification if the account balance does exceed $1 million.

16 UK IGA, Annex I, para V E(1).

17 UK IGA, Annex I, para V D(2).

18 See 'International Standards on Combating Money Laundering and Financing Terrorism and Proliferation: The FATF Recommendations' (February, 2012).

19 UK IGA, art 1(1)(mm).

New Individual Accounts opened on or after 1 January 2014

10.87 The way in which provisions of the UK IGA apply depends upon the nature of the institution concerned. In the case of a Custodial Institution, a UK RFI must obtain a self-certification from the account holder which will allow the UK RFI to determine whether the account holder is resident in the US for tax purposes and to confirm the reasonableness of that self-certification by reference to other information obtained by the UK RFI as part of the account opening process[1]. Where the account holder is resident in the US, a UK RFI is required to treat the account as a US Reportable Account and to ensure that the self-certification includes the account holder's US tax payer identification number ('US TIN')[2]. If a change of circumstances causes a UK RFI to know, or have reason to know, that a self-certification is incorrect or unreliable, the UK RFI must either obtain a valid self-certification or treat the account as a US Reportable Account[3].

1 UK IGA, Annex I, para III B.

2 UK IGA, Annex I, para III C.

IRS Form W-9, or any other similar agreed form, may act as such self-certification.

3 UK IGA, Annex I, para III D.

New Entity Accounts opened on or after 1 January 2014

10.88 A UK RFI must determine whether the account holder is[1]:

(a) a Specified US Person;

(b) a UK Financial Institution or Financial Institution established in another jurisdiction which has entered into an intergovernmental agreement with the US with respect to FATCA (a 'Partner Jurisdiction');

(c) a participating FFI, a deemed compliant FFI, an exempt beneficial owner, or an excepted FFI; or

(d) an Active NFFE or a Passive NFFE.

A UK RFI can determine that an account holder is an Active NFFE, a UK (or other Partner Jurisdiction) Financial Institution using information which is in its possession or which is publicly available[2]. In other cases the UK RFI must obtain a self-certification to establish the status[3] of an entity or of that entity's Controlling Persons.

An account is classified as not being a US Reportable Account, and no reporting is required in respect of an account, if the account holder is: (i) a US Person but is not a Specified US Person; (ii) a Non-participating Financial Institution, a UK Financial Institution or other Partner Jurisdiction Financial Institution; (iii) a participating FFI, a deemed-compliant FFI, an exempt beneficial owner, or an excepted FFI; (iv) an Active NFFE; or (v) a Passive NFFE none of the Controlling Persons of which is a U.S. citizen or resident[4].

Where the account holder is a Non-participating Financial Institution, then the account is also not a US Reportable Account, but payments to the account holder must be reported as contemplated in paragraph 1(b) of article 4 of the UK IGA[5].

1 UK IGA, Annex I, para V A.
2 UK IGA, Annex I, para V B.
3 UK IGA, Annex I, para V C.
   In the case of a Passive NFFE, the status of any Controlling Persons must be identified by reference to a self-certification from the account holder or the relevant Controlling Person.
4 UK IGA, Annex I, para V C(3).
5 UK IGA, Annex I, para V C(4).

Reporting obligations for UK RFIs

US Reportable Accounts

10.89 An account is treated as a US Reportable Account if:

(a) in the case of an individual account open on 31 December 2013, a UK RFI has identified as a result of its review (or identifies as a result of a change in circumstances) one or more US indicia and the UK RFI has not elected to avail itself of the safeharbour described above[1];

(b) in the case of an individual account opened on or after 1 January 2014, a UK RFI has identified as a result of its review (or identifies as a result of a change in circumstances) one or more US indicia[2];

(c) in the case of an entity account open on 31 December 2013, a UK RFI has identified that the accountholder is[3]:

   (i) a Specified US Person;

   (ii) a Passive NFFE which has one or more Controlling Persons who is a US citizen or a US resident[4].

If a Non-US entity is identified as a Financial Institution, its account is not a US Reportable Account[5].

(d) in the case of an entity account opened on or after 1 January 2014, a UK RFI identifies that the accountholder is[6]:

   (i) a Specified US Person;

   (ii) a Passive NFFE which has one or more Controlling Persons who is a US citizen or a US resident.

A UK RFI will be required to report, in relation to each US Reportable Account which is a Custodial Account[7] (specifying the currency in which each relevant amount is denominated)[8]:

(a) the name, address, and US TIN of each Specified US Person that is an account holder and, in the case of a Non-US Entity that is identified as having one or more Controlling Persons that is a Specified US Person, the name, address, and US TIN (if any) of such entity and each such Specified US Person;

(b) the account number (or functional equivalent in the absence of an account number);

(c) the account balance or value as of the end of the relevant calendar year or other appropriate reporting period or, if the account was closed during such year, immediately before closure;

(d) the total gross amount of interest, the total gross amount of dividends, and the total gross amount of other income generated with respect to the assets held in the account, in each case paid or credited to the account (or with respect to the account) during the calendar year or other appropriate reporting period; and

(e) the total gross proceeds from the sale or redemption of property paid or credited to the account during the calendar year or other appropriate reporting period with respect to which the Reporting United Kingdom Financial Institution acted as a custodian, broker, nominee, or otherwise as an agent for the account holder.

The UK IGA provides, helpfully, that the amount and characterisation of payments made with respect to a U.S. Reportable Account may be determined in accordance with the principles of the UK's tax laws[9].

Transitional rules are designed to ease the burden initially placed on a UK RFI in relation to US Reportable Accounts by providing that the information to be obtained and exchanged[10]:

- with respect to 2013 and 2014 is only the information described in (a)–(c) above; and

- with respect to 2015 is the information does not include gross proceeds referred to in (e) above.

Where an account was open on 31 December 2013 (ie an account is a pre-existing account), if the US TIN is not held in the records of the UK RFI, a UK RFI will be required to provide the date of birth of the relevant person assuming that it has that information[11].

Information which relates to the 2013 calendar year will be given to the IRS by HM Revenue and Customs no later than 30 September 2015; in relation to subsequent years HM Revenue and Customs will transmit information to the IRS no later than 9 months after the end of the relevant calendar year[12]. HM Revenue and Customs has indicated that (subject, possibly, to some transitional arrangements[13]) it intends to require a UK RFI to report information to it by 31 March following the end of a calendar year.

1   UK IGA, Annex I, para II B(3)–(4) (for pre-existing accounts), para II C(2) (for pre-existing accounts which are Lower Value accounts), para II D(5)(b) and para II E(2) (for pre-existing accounts which are High Value accounts).

2   UK IGA, Annex I, para III (C)–(D).
3   UK IGA, Annex I, para IV D(1)(b) (for pre-existing accounts).
4   UK IGA, Annex I, para IV C.
5   UK IGA, Annex I, para IV D(4)(d).
6   UK IGA, Annex I, para V C(4).
7   UK IGA, art 2(2).
8   UK IGA, art 3(2).
9   UK IGA, art 3(1).
10 UK IGA, art 3(3)(a).
11 UK IGA, art 3(4).
12 UK IGA, art 3(5).
13 At the time of writing, HM Revenue and Customs is giving consideration as to whether data in relation to 2013 should be reported before 31 March 2015, and data relating to 2014 should be reported before 30 June 2015; see FATCA Condoc, para 3.32.

Reporting in relation to payments to Non-participating Financial Institutions

10.90 In addition to reporting the details referred to above in relation to US Reportable Accounts, a UK RFI will be required to report to HM Revenue and Customs for 2105 and 2016, the name of each Non-participating Financial Institution to which a UK RFI makes a payment in a calendar year and the aggregate amount of the payments to that institution[1]. HM Revenue and Customs intends that these reports should be made to it by 31 March 2016 (in respect of 2015) and 31 March 2017 (in respect of 2016)[2].

1   UK IGA, art 4(1)(b).
2   FATCA Condoc, para 3.35.

Account review, monitoring and reporting by a UK Non-reporting Financial Institution

10.91 A UK Non-reporting Financial Institution must review accounts opened prior to 1 January 2014 to identify accounts which could not be opened on or after that date (see below) with a view to any such accounts being either: (i) reported to HM Revenue and Customs as though that institution were a UK RFI, or (ii) closed[1].

A UK Non-reporting Financial Institution must ensure, from 1 January 2014, that no account is opened for[2]:

(a) a Specified US Person, unless that person is UK resident (an account for a person who is UK resident when an account is opened and ceases to be UK resident does not satisfy this requirement); or

(b) a Non-participating Financial Institution as defined in regulations issued by the US Treasury (this does not include UK Financial Institution or an institution established in another Partner jurisdiction unless that institution is guilty of significant non-compliance); or

(c) a Passive NFFE controlled by natural persons (this includes a trust (or equivalent entity), by reference to the settlor, the trustees, a protector, the beneficiaries or any other person exercising effective control over the trust) who are US citizens or residents.

Where an account that is held by an individual who is not a resident of the UK or by an entity, and that account is opened prior to the date that the Financial Institution implements the procedures described in the previous paragraph (and which must be implemented no later than 1 January 2014), the Financial Institution must review that account in accordance with the procedures described in Annex I of the UK IGA which are applicable to Pre-existing Accounts in order to identify any US Reportable Account and any account held by a Non-participating Financial Institution. Any such account which is identified must be closed or reported to HM Revenue and Customs as though the Financial Institution were a UK RFI[3].

1   UK IGA, Annex II, para 2(g).
2   UK IGA, Annex II, para 2(f).
3   UK IGA, Annex II, para 2(h).

VALUE ADDED TAX

10.92   A taxable person[1] who makes taxable supplies in the UK must account to HM Revenue and Customs for value added tax in respect of supplies of goods and services which that person makes. If, in an accounting period, the amount of supplies made by a taxable person (outputs) exceeds the taxable supplies received by that person (inputs) and attributable to those outputs, a sum equal to the amount by which the outputs exceeds inputs must be paid to HM Revenue and Customs. Where, however, inputs which are attributable to outputs exceed those outputs for an accounting period a sum equal to the excess may be reclaimed from HM Revenue and Customs. The rate at which tax is chargeable depends upon the nature of a particular supply: a supply can be exempt, zero rated, taxable (generally) at 20 per cent. For the financial services industry (including providers of custodian services), where supplies are often exempt, a recurrent difficulty is that inputs attributable to exempt outputs are not recoverable from HM Revenue and Customs.

1   A taxable person is a person who is, or is required under the Value Added Tax Act 1994 to be, registered (s 3). A person becomes liable to be registered if the value of its taxable supplies in the past year exceeds £77,000 or there are reasonable grounds for believing that the value of its taxable supplies in the following 30 days will exceed £77,000 (Sch 1, para 1(1)).

Scope

10.93   Before considering whether a supply of financial services is exempt or standard rated, it is necessary to check whether a supply is within the scope of UK value added tax. The place of supply rules are complex, but the starting point for general purposes tends to be that services are supplied where the supplier is established (and will be supplied in the UK if a supplier has a business establishment in the UK with which the supplies are connected). However, in certain cases supplies are treated as being supplied where received and may therefore be outside the scope of UK value added tax if supplied to a recipient who belongs in a jurisdiction which is not European Union member state – banking, financial and insurance services are types of services to which such a treatment applies[1].

1   Value Added Tax Act 1994, Sch 4A, para 16(2).

Exemptions

10.94   The services which a custodian provides are likely to be exempt or standard rated. A supply of financial services is exempt if it falls within one the categories set out in Group 5 of Value Added Tax Act 1994, Sch 9[1]. This Group includes:

(a) the issue, transfer or receipt of, or any dealing with, money, any security for money or any note or order for the payment of money;

(b) the making of any advance or the granting of any credit;

(c) the management of credit by the person granting it;

(d) the issue, transfer or receipt of, or any dealing with, any security or secondary security, being shares, stocks, bonds, notes (other than promissory notes), debentures, debenture stock or shares in any oil royalty, certain bearer documents and letters of allotment;

(e) the underwriting of an issue within (a) above or a transaction within (d) above;

(f) the provision of intermediary services in relation to (a)–(d) above by a person acting in an intermediary capacity: intermediary services consist of the bringing together, with a view to the provision of financial services, of persons who are or may be seeking to receive such services and persons who provide financial services;

(g) the management of an authorised open ended investment company, an authorised unit trust scheme, certain Gibraltar collection investment schemes (or sub-funds), certain individually recognised overseas schemes (or sub-funds), recognised collective investment schemes authorised is a designated country or territory (or sub-funds), certain recognised collective scheme constituted in another EEA state (or sub-funds); and

(h) the management of a closed-ended collective investment undertaking.

1   This legislation has, at the time of writing, been amended by seven statutory instruments, most recently (with effect from 1 October 2008) by the Value Added Tax (Finance) (No.2) Order 2008 (SI 2008/2547).

10.95 HM Revenue and Customs has agreed with the British Bankers' Association an extensive taxonomy of financial services which sets out the appropriate treatment for many types[1]. HM Revenue and Customs holds the view that although safe custody services are taxable supplies, global custody in securities are a package of services which may include safe custody, the collection of interest/dividends dealing with scrip and rights issues and payment against delivery of stock and that this package constitutes an exempt supply[2].

1   The *Blue Book*, which is updated periodically in line with changes to the law and practice.
2   Notice 701/49, November 2011, para 6.6.

10.96 A custodian can, as a practical matter, insulate itself with regard to the risk that value added tax must, or will in future, be payable in respect of its fees or that (where supplies are not exempt) the rate of value added tax may alter. This is achieved by including an express statement in an agreement regulating the custodian's remuneration that fees and amounts expressed to be payable to a custodian are exclusive of any value added tax which may be chargeable (and that, if value added tax is due, an amount equal to the value added tax due in respect of a supply will be paid when the fees or other amounts fall due).

CHAPTER 11

Conclusions

PRECEDING CHAPTERS

11.1 This work has sought to provide guidance on the legal concepts underlying the service known as global custody and related securities arrangements. Chapter 1 gives an overview of the global custody industry and the legal context in which it operates, introducing fundamental operational and legal concepts. Chapter 2 discusses electronic intermediation in the securities markets and considers the impact of this on the legal nature of traditional securities. It argues that the asset of the investor in the electronic intermediated environment comprises equitable, indirect co-proprietary rights, which are called by the authors 'interests in securities'.

11.2 Chapter 3 considers the custody relationship in the electronic environment. It argues that, with respect to client cash accounts, a custodian which is a bank is generally a debtor and that, with respect to client securities accounts, a custodian is generally a trustee. In relation to global client accounts, a valid trust may be established in favour of clients generally, preferably using express wording, but shortfall risk remains. Chapter 4 relates to the use of the custody portfolio as collateral, considering in turn the collateralisation of the global custodian's own exposures to the client, and those of third parties. Different legal collateral structures are considered, together with the particular legal sensitivities in each case. Recent industry and law reform developments are discussed.

11.3 Cross-border questions are discussed in Chapter 5, with special reference to sub-custodian insolvency and cross-border collateral arrangements. Chapter 6 considers the global custodian's duties, looking in turn at the use of limitation clauses; contractual, tortious and trustee duties; liability for third parties; particular clauses; indemnities for breach of duty; and corporate actions. The UK and international regulatory regime in which global custodians operate is discussed in Chapter 7.

11.4 Chapter 8 surveys the post-trade infrastructure, giving an overview of developments in clearing and settlement; considering risk management in the industry; the process of consolidation; and underlying legal principles. CREST is discussed in Chapter 9, and Chapter 10 considers certain UK taxation aspects of global custody.

MANAGING LEGAL RISK

11.5 A priority for all those involved in the global custody industry, and more generally in the international securities markets, is managing legal risk. It is important to be able to determine, with as much certainty as possible, the rights, duties and liabilities of global custodians, their clients and counterparties, and all those dealing with them, including collateral takers. This work has sought to make some progress towards that objective.

11.6 Two challenges in particular still exist. First, practice has moved ahead of settled law with the computerisation of the securities markets. This has cut across traditional legal analysis. It has been argued that computerised interests in securities cannot be negotiable instruments (Chapter 2) and that the lack of a tangible subject matter takes custody beyond the scope of bailment (Chapter 3). Second, international portfolios of securities raise complex conflict of laws issues. A particular sensitivity is intermediation, where the asset of the client corresponds to a number of different account entries maintained by the international chain of intermediaries through whom the client's asset is held. This is discussed in Chapter 5.

INTERESTS IN SECURITIES

11.7 This work has indicated that legal analysis must follow contemporary operational practice. As indicated in Chapter 3, the client's interest in the securities making up the investment portfolio is characteristically unallocated and indirect. Rather than owning particular securities, the client has commingled rights in a fungible bulk, often held on a cross-border basis through one or more intermediaries. A client cannot in general enforce these rights directly, but only through the global custodian. However, the client's rights are protected in the insolvency of the global custodian, and in this sense they are proprietary. These rights have been referred to as 'interests in securities'. Although interests in securities confer the same economic benefits and burdens[1] as direct and allocated ownership of the underlying securities, they are legally distinct from them. This distinction is significant in relation to the rights of the client against the custodian[2], to priorities[3], and to collateral structures[4], particularly cross-border collateral structures[5].

1   For example, the client owning interests in securities suffers a capital loss when the value of the underlying securities drops.
2   Which arise under a trust relationship and not a bailment. See Chapter 2.
3   The client's interest is equitable; equitable interests generally suffer weaker priority than competing legal interests. See Chapter 4.
4   An equitable asset cannot be subject to a legal security interest. See Chapter 4.
5   See the discussion of PRIMA in Chapter 5.

11.8 The above analysis also informs the concept of securities entitlements, introduced in the US by the revised art 8 (Investment Securities) of the Uniform Commercial Code. With both English law interests in securities and US securities entitlements, the interest of the investor is enforceable only through the intermediary, ring-fenced in the intermediary's insolvency and generally located, for conflict of laws purposes, in the jurisdiction of the intermediary. The practical advantages of this approach are clear. The investor is protected from custodian credit risk, and the legal analysis of cross-border collateral is simplified. It is argued in this work that the position achieved by statute in the US is available under the general principles of English law.

11.9 However, in order to put the matter beyond doubt, and also to address and clarify important issues of priority, security of transfer and perfection, as well as creating consistency in different jurisdictions, various initiatives have been attempted, including the UNIDROIT Convention and the prospective Securities Law Directive (discussed in Chapter 5). Some of aspects of these proposals will inevitably create new issues, as well as resolving some issues, but it is hoped that some degree of further certainty and harmonisation of approach will be achieved on this subject.

THE FUTURE?

11.10 As has been indicated, the global custody industry is a moving target. The underlying systems and operational arrangements, as well as the legal and regulatory framework, are constantly changing. Existing trends that seem likely to continue include, in particular: increased focus on certainty of the rights of custody clients and protection of client assets (particularly in the event of insolvency), and the consolidation of the trading and post-trading infrastructure, particularly within Europe. The earlier idea of one central counterparty to service all European markets seems to have been superseded by the ideas of flexibility and customer choice, notwithstanding potential netting benefits (particularly in the equity markets, where mixed participation involves a wide range of credit exposures). The amount of European legislation seeking to achieve legal and regulatory consolidation in various areas is constantly increasing, but inevitably, because of the number of different legal and regulatory regimes involved, faces greater challenges for implementation than, for example, comparable developments in the US.

11.11 One very clear tendency in the custody markets is the focus on the protection of assets held by a custodian for its clients, and the level of service provided by custodians. This is understandable in view of the upheavals and difficulties in all areas of the financial markets, and in particular the wish for clients to recover their assets quickly in the context of various high profile insolvency cases. Nevertheless, it is important not to lose sight of the fundamental question of the nature of the custody service, and what the custody client is doing when holding assets with a custodian. Holding securities will inevitably involve a degree of risk, given the possibility of the issuer of the securities becoming insolvent so that the securities are worthless, or the securities becoming difficult to sell for a variety of other reasons. It would be wholly unreasonable to suggest that a custodian has the function of protecting its client against all risks associated with investing in a particular market, and arguably it is the client's responsibility to decide whether it is willing to accept the relevant risks, or to take appropriate measures for protection, such as insurance or relevant hedging transactions. As regards the services provided by the custodian, only certain aspects will be within the control of the custodian. There will of course always be arguments about where the line should be drawn regarding liabilities which are risks to be borne by the client, and liabilities which should be accepted by the custodian. However, ultimately, as with any service, the question is what benefit is being provided by the custodian, what is the cost of this and what are the custodian and its client willing to agree in the particular context in which they are operating. A 'one size fits all' approach is dangerous because it lacks flexibility to reflect the requirements of different clients, structures and areas of the market. Greater liability of a custodian to a client will inevitably have a cost which arguably should be borne by the client since it is a substantial benefit for the client.

11.12 In addition, a new issue which is likely to draw significant attention in the future is the increasing burden (of which FATCA constitutes the principal, but not the only, aspect) placed on custodians to assist tax authorities in seeking to track (and then tax) the assets of individuals and other entities which are regarded as being subject to tax under the laws of the jurisdiction in which those tax authorities are competent to collect tax.

11.13 Any entity providing or receiving custody services in the financial markets needs to be aware of existing legal requirements and potential issues, and also needs to keep up to speed with new initiatives, in order to remain competitive. In the midst of continuous changes in market conditions and regulatory developments, this book can inevitably only serve as a snapshot at the time of writing, but it is hoped that it will provide a useful starting point for consideration of the issues discussed.

Bibliography

Adams, D, *Banking and Capital Markets* (2008) College of Law Publishing

Austen-Peters, A O, *Custody of Investments* (2000) Oxford University Press

Bank for International Settlements *Central Bank Payment and Settlement Services with respect to Cross-Border and Multi-Currency Transactions* (1993)

— *Collateral in Wholesale Financial Markets: Recent Trends* (March 2001)

— *Cross-Border Securities Settlement* (May 1995)

— *Delivery Versus Payment in Securities Settlement Systems* (1992)

— *The New Basel Capital Accord* (January 2001)

— *Report of the Committee on Interbank Netting Schemes of the Central Banks of the Group of Ten Countries* ('Lamfalussy Netting Report') (1990)

— *Report on Netting Schemes* ('The Angell Report') (1989)

— *Settlement Risk in Foreign Exchange Transactions* (1996)

Bank for International Settlements and CPSS *Core Principles for Systemically Important Payment Systems* (2001)

— *The Interdependencies of payment and settlement systems* (June 2008)

Bank for International Settlements and IOSCO *Disclosure Framework for Securities Settlement Systems* (1997)

Bank of England *CREST: The Business Description* (December 1994)

— *The Future of Money Market Instruments* (November 1999)

— *Sponsored Membership of CREST for the Private Investor* (April 1995)

Basel Committee on Banking Supervision *International Convergence of Capital Measurement and Capital Standards: A Revised Framework* (updated November 2005)

Beale, H (ed) *Chitty on Contracts* (29th edn, 2004) Sweet & Maxwell

Beaves, A, 'Global Custody – A Tentative Analysis of Property and Contract' in Palmer and McEndrick (eds) *Interests in Goods* (2nd edn, 1998) LLP

Benjamin, J, *Interests in Securities* (2000) Oxford University Press

— 'Custody: an English Law Analysis' (1994) 9 JIBFL 121

— 'Negotiability and Computerisation' (1995) 10 JIBFL 253

— 'Recharacterisation and Conflict of Laws' in Butterworths Journal of International Banking and Financial Law (December 1997)

Bernasconi, C, *The Law Applicable to Dispositions of Securities Held through Indirect Holding Systems*, Hague Conference on Private International Law (January 2001)

Birks, P, 'Mixtures' in Palmer and McKendrick (eds) *Interests in Goods* (2nd edn, 1998) LLP

— *Overview: Tracing, Claiming and Defences, Laundering and Tracing* (1995) Clarendon

Black, J, *Rules and Regulators* (1997) Oxford University Press

Blackstone *Commentaries*, Book II

Brown, J, 'Recovery wakes up to extreme risk' *Euromoney* (November 2001)

Burrows, A (ed) *English Private Law* (2008) Oxford University Press

Civil Justice Council *Improving Access to Justice through Collective Actions* (2008)

CESR-ECB *Standards for Securities Clearing and Settlement in the European Union* (October 2004)

Collins, L, et al (eds) *Dicey and Morris on the Conflict of Laws* (14th edn, 2006) Sweet & Maxwell

CMO Reference Manual

CPSS/IOSCO *Joint Task Force Recommendations for Securities Settlement Systems* (2001)

CREST *Reference Manual*

Devonport, K and Turing, D, 'Reducing risk and costs in cross-border transactions: Are Hague and UNIDROIT missing pieces in the puzzle?' (2007) 1 *Journal of Securities Operations & Custody* 1

Dixon, M, Bridge, S, et al *Megarry and Wade The Law of Real Property* (7th edn, 2008) Sweet & Maxwell

DTCC *Central Counterparties: Development, Cooperation and Consolidation – A White Paper to the Industry on the Future of CCPs* (October 2000)

— *Straight-Through Processing: A White Paper to the Industry on T+1* (June 2000)

ECSDA *The European Central Securities Depositories Association's First Annual Status Report Relating to its Standards for the Removal of Giovannini Barriers 4 and 7* (April 2005)

Euroclear *Comments from Euroclear to the Basel Committee on Banking supervision on the New Basel Capital Accord* (31 May 2001)

— *ESES International Links* (August 2007) version 2.2

— *Participant User Guide: Market Links* (20 May 2002)

— *Update Paper Miscellaneous items on the Single Platform – Service description* (July 2008)

European Commission *Clearing and settlement in the European Union; Main policy issues and future challenges* (May 2002)

— *Final Report of the Committee of Wise Men on the Regulation of European Securities* Markets (15 February 2001) ('Lamfalussy Securities Market Report')

— *Financial Services: Implementing the Framework for Financial Markets: Action Plan*, COM (1999) 232

— *Proposal for a Directive of the European Parliament and of the Council amending Directive 98/26/EC on settlement finality in payment and securities settlement systems and Directive 2002/47/EC on financial collateral arrangements as regards linked systems and credit claims*, COM (2008) 213

European Securities Forum *Contribution on the Joint CESR/ECB Consultation on Clearing and Settlement* (2002)

— *EuroCCP; ESF's Blueprint for a Single Pan-European Central Counterparty* (2000)

Ewart, J S, 'Negotiability and Estoppel' (1900) 14 LQR 135

Fédération Internationale Des Bourses de Valeurs *Clearing and Settlement Best Practices* (1996)

— *Improving International Settlement* (1989)

Financial Services Authority Handbook

Finn, P D, *Fiduciary Obligations* (1977) Law Book Co, Sydney

— *The Fiduciary Principle, Equity, Fiduciaries and Trusts* (1989) Carswell

Fletcher, I F, *Insolvency in Private International Law* (2nd edn, 2005) Oxford University Press

— 'International Insolvency: Recent Cases' (1997) JBL 471

Giovannini Group *Cross-Border Clearing and Settlement Arrangements in the European Union* (November 2001)

— *Second Report on EU Clearing and Settlement Arrangements* (April 2003)

Goode, R M, *Legal Problems of Credit and Security* (3rd edn, 2003) Sweet & Maxwell

— 'Ownership and Obligation in Commercial Transactions' (1987) 103 LQR 433

— 'The Nature and Transfer of Rights in Dematerialised and Immobilised Securities' (1996) 10 JIBFL 162

Goode, R, Kanda, H and Kreuzer, K, Explanatory Report on the 2006 Hague Securities Convention (2005) Koninklijke Brill NV

Gray, K, 'Property in Thin Air' (1991) CLJ 252

Group of 30 *Clearance and Settlement in the World's Securities Markets* (1989)

— *Global Clearing and Settlement: Final Monitoring Report* (May 2006)

Group of 30 Steering & Working Committees of *Global Clearing & Settlements Study Group Global Clearing and Settlements: A Plan of Action* (January 2003)

Guiliano and Lagarde Report on the Rome Convention

Guynn, R, Modernising Securities Ownership, Transfer and Pledging Laws (1996) IBA

Hayton, D J, *Underhill & Hayton on the Law relating to Trusts and Trustees* (17th edn, 2006) Butterworths

— 'Developing the Law of Trusts for the Twenty-First Century' (1990) 106 LQR 87

— 'The Irreducible Core of Trusteeship' [1996] JTCP

— 'Uncertainty of Subject-Matter of Trusts' (1994) 110 LQR 335

Hayton, D J and Mitchell, C, *Hayton and Marshall: Commentary and Cases on the Law of Trusts and Equitable Remedies* (12th edn, 2005) Sweet & Maxwell

Hayton, D J, Kortmann, S C J J, and Verhagen, H L E (eds) *Principles of European Trust Law* (1999) Kluwer

HM Revenue and Customs *Corporate Finance Manual*

— *Guidance Notes for TMA section 18 return 2007/2008*

HM Treasury *Domestic and International Initiatives Concerning Conflict of Law Issues Relating to Securities: Consultation Document* (July 2001)

— *Updating the Myners principles: a consultation* (March 2008)

Hills, B, et al 'Central Counterparty Clearing Houses and Financial Stability' (June 1999) *Bank of England Financial Stability Review* 124

Hohfeld, W N, *Fundamental Legal Conceptions* (1964) (first printed 1919) Yale University Press; (reprinted 2000) The Lawbook Exchange, Ltd

— *Manufactured Payments on Overseas Securities Guidance Notes* (December 2003)

— *Stamp Office Manual* (March 2002)

— *Stamp Taxes' Customer Newsletter* – Stamp Duty Reserve Tax (SDRT), No 1 (July 2002)

— *Customer Newsletter* – Stamp Duty Reserve Tax (SDRT), No 3 (April 2003)

— *Tax Bulletin* (August 2001)

International Organisation of Securities Commissions *Client Asset Protection* (1996)

— *Report of the Technical Committee on Clearing and Settlement* (1990)

International Society of Securities Administrators *Report on Cross-Border Settlement and Custody* (1992)

Jowitt's Dictionary of English Law (2nd edn, 1985) Sweet & Maxwell

Kennett, W, 'The Brussels I Regulation' (2001) ICLQ 725

Kirby, A, 'Global Straight-Through Processing is this Year's Imperative for Custodian Banks and their Clients' (6 January 2000) www.gstpa.org

Kynaston, D, *The City of London: IV A Club No More 1945–2000* (2001) Pimlico

Law Commission *Fiduciary Duties and Regulatory Rules* (1995) Law Com No 236

— *Registration of Security Interests: Company Charges and Property other than Land* (2002) Consultation paper No 164

— *Trustee Exemption Clauses* (2003) Consultation paper No 171

— *The UNIDROIT Convention on Substantive Rules regarding International Securities – Further Updated Advice to HM Treasury* (2008)

Lee, R, *What is an Exchange? The Automation, Management, and Regulation of the Financial Markets* (1998) Oxford University Press

Legal Certainty Group *Second Advice of the Legal Certainty Group – Solutions to Legal Barriers related to Post trading within the EU* (August 2008)

London Business School *Custodianship and the Protection of Client Property* (July 1994)

Micheler E, 'Farewell Quasi-Negotiability; Legal Title and Transfer of Shares in a Paperless World' (2002) JBL 358

Mokal, R J, 'Priority as Pathology: The Pari Passu Myth' (2001) 69(3) CLJ 581

Montagu, G F H, 'Is a foreign state a body corporate?' (2001) *British Tax Review*, vol 6

Montagu, N, 'The Reality of Today's Revenue' *The Tax Journal* (29 July 2002)

Mooney, C W, 'Beyond Negotiability' (1990) 12 Cardozo LR 305

Morgan Guaranty Trust Company Report *Cross-Border Clearance, Settlement and Custody: Beyond the G30 Recommendations* (1993)

Mowbray, J, et al *Lewin On Trusts* (18th edn, 2008) Sweet & Maxwell

Myners, P, *Institutional Investment in the United Kingdom: A Review* (4 March 2001)

National Association of Pension Funds *Institutional Investment in the UK: six years on. Report and recommendations* (November 2007)

Palmer, N E, *Bailment* (2nd edn, 1991) Sweet & Maxwell

— *Liability of Bankers as Custodians of Client Property* (1979)

Palmer, N and McKendrick, E (eds) *Interests in Goods* (2nd edn, 1998) LLP

Pickering, A, *A simpler way to better pensions; An independent report by Alan Pickering* (2002)

Pollock, F, *An Essay on Possession in the Common Law* (1888) Clarendon

Potok (ed) *Cross Border Collateral: Legal Risk and the Conflict of Laws* (2002) Tottel Publishing

Prime, T, *International Bonds and Certificates of Deposit* (1990) Butterworths

Quinlan, M J, *Sergeant and Sims: Stamp Duties* (13th edn)

Rogers, J S, 'Policy Perspectives on the Revised UCC Article 8' (1996) 6 UCLALR 1413

Rogers, W, *Winfield and Jolowicz on Tort* (17th edn, 2006) Sweet & Maxwell

Rogerson, P J, 'The Situs of Debts in the conflict of Laws – Illogical, Unnecessary and Misleading' (1990) CLJ 441

Ryan, R, 'Taking Security Over Investment Portfolios held in Global Custody' (1990) 10 JIBL 404

Sandler Review *Medium and Long-Term Retail Savings in the UK: A Review* (2002)

Schwarcz, S L, 'Intermediary Risk in a Global Economy' (2001) 50 Duke LJ 1541

Smart, P, *Cross-Border Insolvency* (3rd edn, 2006) Bloomsbury Professional

Snell's Principles of Equity (31st edn, 2005) Sweet & Maxwell

Squires, S J, 'Something old, something new ...' *The Tax Journal* (9 April 2001)

SWIFT *Elimination of Giovannini Barrier One – Final Protocol recommendation* (March 2006)

— *The Proposal for the Removal of Barrier 1 of the Giovannini Report* (January 2005)

Tennekoon, R C, *The Law and Regulation of International Finance* (3rd edn, 2006) Tottel Publishing

Tsien, P, 'Present Problems and Future Possibilities for Central Counterparties' in Marcus Evans Conference Proceedings *Trading in Europe: Assessing the Future for Central Counterparties* (1 and 2 October 2001)

Turing, D, 'The EU Collateral Directive' (2002) 5 JIBFL 187

Valdez, S, *An Introduction to Global Financial Markets* (4th edn, 2003) Macmillan

Virgos, M and Schmit, E, *Report on the Convention on Insolvency Proceedings* (1996)

Wood, P, *Comparative Financial Law* (1995) Sweet & Maxwell

Worthington, S, *Personal Property Law; Text and Materials* (2000) Hart Publishing

— *Proprietary Interests in Commercial Transactions* (1996) Clarendon

— 'Shares and Shareholders: Property, Power and Entitlement, Part 1' (2001) Comp Law 22(9)

— 'Sorting out ownership interests in a Bulk: Gifts, Sales and Trusts' (1999) JBL 1

Youdan, T G (ed) *The Fiduciary Principle, Equity, Fiduciaries and Trusts* (1989) Carswell

Index

[*all references are to paragraph number*]

Accounts
  cash
    debtor/creditor principle, 3.3–3.4
    trust over cash, 3.5–3.9
  generally, 3.2
'Act honestly, fairly and professionally'
  regulatory duties, and, 7.29
Actions and claims
  legal categories of assets, and, 1.37–1.38
'Administration'
  regulatory duties, and, 7.18–7.19
AIFMD (Directive 2011/61/EC)
  depositary's liability for loss, 7.165–7.170
  global custody industry, and, 1.9
  implications for depositary's delegates, 7.171–7.176
  regulatory duties, and, 7.164–7.176
Allocation question
  cases, 3.30–3.46
  conclusions, 3.47–3.49
  equitable tenancy in common, 3.42
  equivalent redelivery, 3.24–3.26
  fungible custody, 3.24–3.26
  Hunter v Moss, 3.37–3.41
  introduction, 3.23
  Re Goldcorp Exchange Ltd (in receivership), 3.35–3.36
  Re London Wine (Shippers) Ltd, 3.31–3.32
  Re Stapylton Fletcher Ltd, 3.33–3.34
  requirement for allocation, 3.27–3.29
  shortfalls, and, 3.55
Asset categories
  fundamental concepts, and, 1.37–1.38
Assured payments system
  CREST, and, 9.21–9.23

Back-office functions
  global custody industry, and, 1.8
Bailment
  custody relationship in electronic environment, and, 3.10–3.22
  sub-custodian insolvency, and, 5.31–5.32
Banking Winding Up Directive (2001/24/EC)
  generally, 5.21
  place of the relevant intermediary account (PRIMA), and, 5.58
  post-trade infrastructure, and, 8.110

Banks
  international securities portfolios, and, 1.2
Basel III
  global custody industry, and, 1.9
Batch settlement
  risk management, and, 8.39
Bearer securities
  computerised bearer securities
    generally, 2.17
    introduction, 2.14
    negotiability,
  Eurobonds, and, 2.14
  introduction, 2.14
  nature of securities, and, 1.23
  negotiability of computerised securities
    arguments against, 2.18–2.28
    benefits of, 2.29–2.34
    ease of transfer, 2.30–2.31
    indirect nature, 2.18–2.19
    intangibility, 2.20–2.24
    introduction, 2.15–2.16
    law merchant, and, 2.17
    security of transfer, 2.32–2.33
  stamp duty, and, 10.8–10.9
  traditional bearer securities
    generally, 2.14
    negotiability, 2.16
Book entry transfer
  post-trade infrastructure, and, 8.6–8.10
Building societies
  international securities portfolios, and, 1.2

Call options
  stamp duty, and, 10.12–10.13
Cash
  debtor/creditor principle, 3.3–3.4
  trust over cash, 3.5–3.9
  UNIDROIT, and, 5.68
Central counterparty
  consolidation of services, 8.90–8.98
  generally, 8.12
  straight through processing, 8.46–8.47
Central Securities Depositories
  consolidation of settlement, and, 8.89
Central sponsor arrangements
  CREST, and, 9.95–9.105
Charges
  CREST, and, 9.86

Charities
international securities portfolios, and, 1.2
Choice of law
See also Conflict of laws
generally, 5.25–5.28
property rights, 5.48–5.50
Choses in action
legal categories of assets, and, 1.37–1.38
Choses in possession
legal categories of assets, and, 1.37–1.38
Claims
legal categories of assets, and, 1.37–1.38
Clearance and Settlement in the World's Securities Markets (1989, G30)
book entry transfer, and, 8.8
generally, 8.56–8.57
introduction, 2.5
Clearance service
election to pay stamp duty, 10.26
EU law aspects, 10.21
exempt agreements to transfer, 10.27
generally, 10.24
one-off charge, 10.25
stamp duty reserve tax, and
  exemptions, 10.44
  generally, 10.43
Clearing
central counterparty, 8.12
consolidation of services, 8.90–8.98
fundamental concepts, and, 1.26
generally, 8.3
netting, 8.13–8.15
post-trade infrastructure, and, 8.11–8.15
Clearing and Settlement Advisory and Monitoring Expert Group (CESAME)
generally, 8.64
Clearstream
consolidation of settlement, and, 8.88
Client Assets sourcebook (CASS)
regulatory duties, and, 7.21
Client classification
regulatory duties, and, 7.33
Client money
adequate arrangements, 7.92–7.94
application of rules, 7.61
BCOBS, 7.83–7.84
case law
  adequate arrangements, 7.92–7.94
  application of trusts, 7.87–7.91
  commingling, 7.95–7.97
  deductions from client money, 7.102–7.108
  introduction, 7.85–7.86
  MiFID, and, 7.98–7.99
  reconciliations, 7.100
  reliability of Client Money Rules, 7.101
  set-off rights, 7.92–7.94
commingling, 7.95–7.97

Client money – *contd*
deductions, 7.102–7.108
developments, 7.109–7.116
disapplication of rules, 7.62–7.65
holding of cash by custodian, 7.66–7.67
introduction, 7.58–7.60
MiFID, and, 7.98–7.99
opting-out, 7.68–7.73
prior written notice, 7.77
reconciliations, 7.100
reliability of Rules, 7.101
set-off
  case law, 7.92–7.94
  generally, 7.83–7.84
trustee firms, 7.74–7.75
trusts, 7.87–7.91
unclaimed funds, 7.78–7.82
use of non-approved bank, 7.76
Client's right of action
breach of FSA rules, 7.141
breach of regulatory requirements, 7.142–7.143
introduction, 7.139–7.140
COBS
regulatory duties, and, 7.21
Collateralisation
collateral management products,
  in favour of global custodian, 4.18–4.22
  in favour of third parties 4.15–4.17
collateral structures
  insolvency displacement, 4.37–4.39
  introduction, 4.36
  margining, 4.40
  marking to market, 4.40
  priorities, 4.43–4.46
  substitution, 4.41–4.42
conflict of laws, and, 5.39–5.41
credit limits, 4.70
credit risk, 4.4–4.5
CREST, and
  introduction, 9.75–9.76
  repos, 9.88–9.93
  securities lending, 9.88–9.93
  security interests, 9.77–9.87
cross-border issues
  conflict of laws, 5.39–5.41
  Hague Convention on Securities held with an Intermediary, 5.59–5.61
  overview, 5.38
  place of the relevant intermediary account (PRIMA), 5.54–5.58
  property rights, 5.42–5.53
  Securities Law Directive, 5.69–5.72
  set-off, 5.73
  UNIDROIT, 5.62–5.68
custodian's settlement exposures, 4.12–4.14
financial assets, 4.10

Collateralisation – *contd*
Financial Collateral Directive (2002/47/EC)
  background, 4.80
  criteria, 4.95–4.98
  enforcement, 4.89–4.90
  floating charges, 4.99–4.106
  formal requirements, 4.84–4.85
  general comments, 4.111–4.112
  governing law, 4.108–4.110
  implementation in UK, 4.79
  insolvency protection, 4.86–4.88
  introduction, 4.79
  overview, 4.81–4.83
  policy issues, 4.107
  recharacterisation risk, 4.93–4.94
  right of use, 4.91–4.92
financial institutions as collateral takers, 4.6–4.9
floating charges
  favour of global custodian, in, 4.71
  favour of prime broker, in, 4.75
  Financial Collateral Directive, 4.99–4.106
freedom to deal, 4.69
fundamental concepts, and, 1.33–1.36
global custodian, and
  collateral management products, 4.15–4.22
  custodian's settlement exposures, 4.12–4.14
  introduction, 4.11
governing law, 4.108–4.110
insolvency, and, 4.4
insolvency displacement, 4.37–4.39
insolvency protection, 4.86–4.88
insolvency set-off, 4.58–4.59
Insurance Winding-Up Directive, 4.8
intermediation, 4.66–4.67
introduction, 4.1–4.3
legal structures
  introduction, 4.23
  outright collateral transfers, 4.30–4.32
  security interests, 4.24–4.29
lex situs, 4.66–4.67
liens, and, 4.72
margining, 4.40
marking to market, 4.40
meaning, 4.4
nature, 4.4–4.5
netting, 4.60–4.62
outright collateral transfers
  generally, 4.57–4.65
  insolvency set-off, 4.58–4.59
  introduction, 4.30
  netting, 4.60–4.62
  recharacterisation risk, 4.63–4.64
prime brokerage, 4.18–4.22
priorities, 4.43–4.46
purpose, 4.2–4.3

Collateralisation – *contd*
recharacterisation risk
  Financial Collateral Directive, 4.93–4.94
  generally, 4.63–4.64
regulatory duties, and
  CASS Resolution Pack, 7.121–7.122
  compliance, 7.119
  extension of rules, 7.120
  introduction, 7.117–7.118
regulatory restrictions, 4.76–4.78
right of use
  Financial Collateral Directive, 4.91–4.92
  generally, 4.75
security interests
  generally, 4.24–4.29
  perfection, 4.48–4.49
  registration, 4.50–4.54
  right of use, 4.55–4.56
  sensitivities, 4.47–4.56
sensitivities
  all types of collateral assets, for, 4.35–4.65
  collateral comprising securities held in custody, for, 4.65–4.75
  collateral structures, 4.36–4.46
  favour of global custodian, in, 4.68–4.72
  favour of prime broker, in, 4.73–4.75
  insolvency displacement, 4.37–4.39
  intermediation, 4.66–4.67
  introduction, 4.33–4.34
  lex situs, 4.66–4.67
  margining, 4.40
  marking to market, 4.40
  outright collateral transfers, 4.57–4.65
  priorities, 4.43–4.46
  security interests, 4.47–4.56
  substitution, 4.41–4.42
straight through processing, 8.48
structures
  insolvency displacement, 4.37–4.39
  introduction, 4.36
  margining, 4.40
  marking to market, 4.40
  priorities, 4.43–4.46
  substitution, 4.41–4.42
substitution, 4.41–4.42
Commingling
client money, and, 7.95–7.97
custody relationship in electronic environment, and, 3.51–3.54
Computerisation
custody relationship, and, 3.12
fundamental concepts, and, 1.24
Computerised bearer securities
generally, 2.17
introduction, 2.14
negotiability,
  arguments against, 2.18–2.28

Computerised bearer securities – *contd*
  negotiability – *contd*
    benefits of, 2.29–2.34
    ease of transfer, 2.30–2.31
    indirect nature, 2.18–2.19
    intangibility, 2.20–2.24
    introduction, 2.15–2.16
    law merchant, and, 2.17
    security of transfer, 2.32–2.33
Concurrent liability
  global custodians, and, 6.22
Conduct of Business Rules
  regulatory duties, and, 7.21
Confirmation
  generally, 8.3
Conflict of laws
  choice of law, 5.25–5.28
  collateral, and, 5.39–5.41
  enforcement, 5.29
  insolvency jurisdiction
    Banking Winding Up Directive, 5.21
    English courts, 5.22–5.24
    European regulation, 5.17–5.18
    introduction, 5.15–5.16
    recognition of proceedings, 5.19–5.20
  introduction, 5.5–5.6
  jurisdiction
    insolvency, 5.15–5.24
    non-insolvency, 5.9–5.14
    overview, 5.7–5.8
  non-insolvency jurisdiction
    Brussels Regulation, 5.11
    common law regime, 5.12–5.14
    generally, 5.9–5.10
Conflicts of interest
  fiduciary duty, and, 6.47–6.50
Consequential damages
  global custodian's duties, and, 6.72
Consolidation
  CCP services, of, 8.90–8.98
  clearing, of, 8.90–8.98
  current fragmentation, 8.86–8.87
  introduction, 8.85
  settlement, of, 8.88–8.89
Contractual duties
  global custodians, and, 6.16–6.19
Control
  regulatory duties, and, 7.123–7.126
Corporate actions
  client issues, 6.80–6.85
  CREST, and, 9.94
  custodian issues, 6.86–6.90
  generally, 6.78–6.79
  introduction, 6.76
  meaning, 6.77
Credit risk
  CREST, and, 9.42–9.48
  principal risk, 8.22
  replacement cost risk, 8.23–8.24
CREST
  assured payments system, 9.21–9.23

CREST – *contd*
  capacity of registrar, 9.137–9.140
  cash collateral, 9.89–9.90
  central sponsor arrangements, 9.95–9.105
  CGO membership agreement, 9.141–9.142
  charges, 9.86
  collateral
    introduction, 9.75–9.76
    repos, 9.88–9.93
    securities lending, 9.88–9.93
    security interests, 9.77–9.87
  computerised securities, and, 2.35
  conclusions, 9.135
  corporate actions, 9.94
  credit risk, 9.42–9.48
  CREST transfers, 9.78–9.79
  cross border issues, 9.66–9.68
  custody accounts
    designated accounts, 9.34–9.35
    introduction, 9.31–9.32
    pooled accounts, 9.33
    sponsored membership, 9.36–9.39
    visibility, 9.40–9.41
  custody agreements, 9.61–9.65
  delivery by value, 9.91–9.93
  delivery versus payment, 9.24
  dematerialisation, 9.5
  designated accounts, 9.34–9.35
  eligible debt securities
    collateral, 9.123
    fungibility, 9.122
    introduction, 9.119
    negotiability, 9.120–9.121
    paper interface, 9.120–9.121
    payment, 9.124
    settlement, 9.124
  eligible securities, 9.2
  equitable mortgages, 9.80–9.85
  equitable ownership, 9.6
  escrow balance, 9.80–9.85
  Euroclear UK and Ireland, 9.25–9.28
  fraudulent transfers, 9.57–9.58
  funds, 9.106
  further developments, 9.125–9.134
  further issues for consideration, 9.136–9.140
  gilts
    eligible debt securities, 9.119–9.124
    introduction, 9.107–9.109
    repos, 9.118
    stamp duty, 9.111
    stock lending, 9.115–9.117
    title finance, 9.112–9.114
    transfer of title, 9.110
  international securities, 9.69–9.74
  introduction, 9.1–9.4
  issue register, 9.136
  legal mortgages, 9.78–9.79
  legal ownership, 9.6

CREST – *contd*
legal structure
  dematerialisation, 9.5
  equitable ownership, 9.6
  legal ownership, 9.6
  payments, 9.12–9.24
  regulation, 9.25–9.30
  settlement structure, 9.7–9.11
liability of registrar, 9.137–9.140
operator register of title, 9.136
owners, 9.4
payments
  assured payments system, 9.21–9.23
  delivery versus payment, 9.24
  introduction, 9.12–9.15
  real time gross settlement, 9.16–9.20
pledges, 9.87
pooled accounts, 9.33
record of title, 9.136
registered computerised securities, and, 2.35
regulation
  CREST participants, 9.29
  Euroclear UK and Ireland, 9.25–9.28
  SDTT, 9.30
replacement of bad deliveries, 9.59
repos
  cash collateral, 9.89–9.90
  delivery by value, 9.91–9.93
  gilts, and, 9.118
  introduction, 9.88
  securities collateral, 9.91–9.92
reversal of bad deliveries, 9.59
risk
  bad deliveries, 9.49–9.60
  credit risk, 9.42–9.48
  custody agreements, 9.61–9.65
  fraudulent transfers, 9.57–9.58
securities lending
  cash collateral, 9.89–9.90
  delivery by value, 9.91–9.93
  introduction, 9.88
  securities collateral, 9.91–9.92
security interests
  charges, 9.86
  CREST transfers, 9.78–9.79
  equitable mortgages, 9.80–9.85
  escrow balance, 9.80–9.85
  introduction, 9.77
  legal mortgages, 9.78–9.79
  pledges, 9.87
settlement structure
  non-UK securities, 9.11
  UK securities, 9.7–9.10
sponsored membership, 9.36–9.39
stamp duty reserve tax
  generally, 9.30
  gilts, and, 9.111
stock lending, 9.115–9.117
tracing of bad deliveries, 9.59
use, 9.3

Cross-border collateral
conflict of laws, 5.39–5.41
Hague Convention on Securities held with an Intermediary, 5.59–5.61
overview, 5.38
place of the relevant intermediary account (PRIMA)
  generally, 5.54–5.56
  other supporting measures, 5.58
  Settlement Finality Directive, 5.57–5.58
property rights
  choice of law, 5.48–5.50
  intangible assets, in, 5.43–5.45
  introduction, 5.42
  jurisdiction, 5.46–5.47
  lex situs, 5.48–5.53
Securities Law Directive, 5.69–5.72
set-off, 5.73
UNIDROIT
  cash, 5.68
  conceptual issues, 5.66–5.67
  generally, 5.62–5.65
  interests in securities, 5.68

Cross-border issues
collateral
  conflict of laws, 5.39–5.41
  Hague Convention on Securities held with an Intermediary, 5.59–5.61
  overview, 5.38
  place of the relevant intermediary account (PRIMA), 5.54–5.58
  property rights, 5.42–5.53
  Securities Law Directive, 5.69–5.72
  set-off, 5.73
  UNIDROIT, 5.62–5.68
conflict of laws
  choice of law, 5.25–5.28
  enforcement, 5.29
  introduction, 5.5–5.6
  jurisdiction, 5.7–5.24
CREST, and, 9.66–9.68
introduction, 5.1–5.4
risk management, and, 8.30
sub-custodian insolvency
  bailment, 5.31–5.32
  introduction, 5.30
  local ring-fence opinions, 5.35–5.36
  other risks, 5.37
  risks, 5.33–5.34
  trust, 5.31–5.32

Custodian-trustee
accounts, 3.2
allocation question
  cases, 3.30–3.46
  conclusions, 3.47–3.49
  equitable tenancy in common, 3.42
  equivalent redelivery, 3.24–3.26
  fungible custody, 3.24–3.26
  Hunter v Moss, 3.37–3.41
  introduction, 3.23

Custodian-trustee – *contd*
 allocation question – *contd*
  Re Goldcorp Exchange Ltd (in receivership), 3.35–3.36
  Re London Wine (Shippers) Ltd, 3.31–3.32
  Re Stapylton Fletcher Ltd, 3.33–3.34
  requirement for allocation, 3.27–3.29
 bailment, 3.10–3.22
 cash
  debtor/creditor principle, 3.3–3.4
  trust over cash, 3.5–3.9
 interests in securities
  introduction, 3.10–3.13
  possession, 3.14–3.15
  trust, 3.16–3.22
 introduction, 3.1
 possession, 3.14–3.15
 shortfalls
  allocation, 3.55
  commingled accounts, and, 3.51–3.54
  introduction, 3.50
 trust assets, 3.16–3.22
Custody
 electronic environment, in
  See also Custodian-trustee
  accounts, 3.2
  allocation question, 3.23–3.49
  bailment, 3.10–3.22
  cash, 3.3–3.9
  interests in securities, 3.10–3.22
  introduction, 3.1
  possession, 3.14–3.15
  shortfalls, 3.50–3.55
  trust assets, 3.16–3.22
 regulatory activities, and, 7.2–7.4
Custody accounts
 designated accounts, 9.34–9.35
 introduction, 9.31–9.32
 pooled accounts, 9.33
 sponsored membership, 9.36–9.39
 visibility, 9.40–9.41
Custody services
 affiliates, 7.57
 content of agreements, 7.36–7.37
 introduction, 7.34
 lien, 7.41–7.44
 maintenance of records, 7.45
 protection of client assets, 7.38
 registration of title, 7.49–7.56
 risk warnings, 7.46–7.48
 set-off rights, 7.41–7.44
 stock lending, 7.39–7.40
 sub-custodians, 7.35

Debt and equity
 nature of securities, and, 1.21–1.22
Debtor/creditor principle
 cash, and, 3.3–3.4
Delivery and payment
 post-trade infrastructure, and, 8.5

Delivery by value
 CREST, and, 9.91–9.93
Delivery versus Payment (DVP)
 CREST, and, 9.24
 finality, 8.37–8.38
 introduction, 8.32
 models, 8.33–8.34
 qualities, 8.35–8.36
Dematerialisation
 book entry transfer, 2.6
 CREST, and, 9.5
 definition, 2.10
 generally, 2.10–2.13
 introduction, 2.5
Depositary receipts
 EU law aspects, 10.21
 generally, 10.22–10.23
 stamp duty reserve tax, and
  exemptions, 10.40–10.41
  generally, 10.39
  transfers between receipt and clearance system, 10.42
 transfer on sale, 10.16
Depositor protection scheme
 cash, and, 3.3
Depositors' money
 custody relationship in electronic environment, and, 3.3
Directive 2002/47/EC (Financial Collateral)
 background, 4.80
 criteria, 4.95–4.98
 enforcement, 4.89–4.90
 floating charges, 4.99–4.106
 formal requirements, 4.84–4.85
 general comments, 4.111–4.112
 governing law, 4.108–4.110
 implementation in UK, 4.79
 insolvency protection, 4.86–4.88
 introduction, 4.79
 overview, 4.81–4.83
 place of the relevant intermediary account (PRIMA), and, 5.58
 policy issues, 4.107
 post-trade infrastructure, and, 8.111
 recharacterisation risk, 4.93–4.94
 right of use, 4.91–4.92
Directive 2004/39/ EC (MiFID)
 global custody industry, and, 1.9
Directive 2009/65/EC (UCITS IV)
 global custody industry, and, 1.9
Directive 2011/61/EC (AIFMD)
 global custody industry, and, 1.9
Duty of care
 global custodians, and, 6.28–6.35
 trustees, and
  case law, 6.30–6.31
  introduction, 6.28
  limitation clauses, 6.32–6.35
  statute, under, 6.29

Duty defining clauses
See also Global custodian's duties
generally, 6.2–6.3

EEA passport arrangements
regulatory duties, and, 7.145–7.150
Educational bodies
international securities portfolios, and, 1.2
Electronic environment
bearer securities
  computerised securities, 2.17
  introduction, 2.14
  negotiability, 2.15–2.34
custodian as trustee
  accounts, 3.2
  allocation question, 3.23–3.49
  bailment, 3.10–3.22
  cash, 3.3–3.9
  interests in securities, 3.10–3.22
  introduction, 3.1
  possession, 3.14–3.15
  shortfalls, 3.50–3.55
  trust assets, 3.16–3.22
dematerialisation
  book entry transfer, 2.6
  definition, 2.10
  generally, 2.10–2.13
  introduction, 2.5
immobilisation
  book entry transfer, 2.6
  definition, 2.7
  generally, 2.7–2.9
  introduction, 2.5
interests in securities, 2.37–2.40
introduction, 2.1–2.4
legal nature of custody relationship, and
  accounts, 3.2
  allocation question, 3.23–3.49
  bailment, 3.10–3.22
  cash, 3.3–3.9
  interests in securities, 3.10–3.22
  introduction, 3.1
  possession, 3.14–3.15
  shortfalls, 3.50–3.55
  trust assets, 3.16–3.22
legal nature of investors' assets, and
  bearer securities, 2.14–2.34
  dematerialisation, 2.10–2.13
  immobilisation, 2.7–2.9
  introduction, 2.5–2.6
  registered computerised securities, 2.35–2.36
registered computerised securities, 2.35–2.36
Eligible debt securities
collateral, 9.123
fungibility, 9.122
introduction, 9.119
negotiability, 9.120–9.121
paper interface, 9.120–9.121

Eligible debt securities – *contd*
payment, 9.124
settlement, 9.124
EMIR (Regulation EU No 648/2012)
consolidation of clearing, and, 8.92
global custody industry, and, 1.9
Enforcement
conflict of laws, and, 5.29
Equitable mortgages
CREST, and, 9.80–9.85
Equitable ownership
CREST, and, 9.6
Equitable tenancy in common
allocation question, and, 3.42
Equity
nature of securities, and, 1.21–1.22
Erroneous instructions
global custodian's duties, and, 6.73
Escrow balance
CREST, and, 9.80–9.85
EU Insolvency Regulation
jurisdiction, and, 5.21
post-trade infrastructure, and, 8.110
Eurobonds
bearer securities, and, 2.14
withholding tax, and
  collecting agents, 10.67
  payers and paying agents, 10.62
Euroclear
CREST, and, 9.25–9.28
generally, 8.88
regulation, 9.25–9.28
European Market Infrastructure Regulation (EU No 648/2012)
global custody industry, and, 1.9
European Securities Code
post-trade infrastructure, and, 8.113–8.114

FATCA
account identification
  introduction, 10.84
  new entity accounts, 10.88
  new individual accounts, 10.87
  pre-existing accounts held by individuals, 10.85
  pre-existing entity accounts, 10.86
account review
  UK non-reporting financial institutions, 10.91
  UK reporting financial institutions, 10.84
compliance under UK IGA, 10.83
overview, 10.82
payments to non-participating financial institutions, 10.90
reporting obligations
  UK non-reporting financial institutions, 10.91
  UK reporting financial institutions, 10.89–10.90

FATCA – *contd*
  review obligations
    UK non-reporting financial institutions, 10.91
    UK reporting financial institutions, 10.84
  US reportable accounts, 10.89
Fiduciary duty
  global custodians, and, 6.40
  trustees, and
    conflicts of interest, 6.47–6.50
    generally, 6.36–6.37
    limitation clauses, 6.41–6.46
    nature, 6.38–6.39
    secret profits, 6.51–6.55
Financial Collateral Directive (2002/47/EC)
  background, 4.80
  criteria, 4.95–4.98
  enforcement, 4.89–4.90
  floating charges, 4.99–4.106
  formal requirements, 4.84–4.85
  general comments, 4.111–4.112
  governing law, 4.108–4.110
  implementation in UK, 4.79
  insolvency protection, 4.86–4.88
  introduction, 4.79
  overview, 4.81–4.83
  place of the relevant intermediary account (PRIMA), and, 5.58
  policy issues, 4.107
  post-trade infrastructure, and, 8.111
  recharacterisation risk, 4.93–4.94
  right of use, 4.91–4.92
Financial Conduct Authority
  regulatory duties, and, 7.6–7.9
Financial Services Action Plan
  consolidation of clearing, and, 8.86
Financial Services Authority
  regulatory duties, and, 7.5
Floating charges
  favour of global custodian, in, 4.71
  favour of prime broker, in, 4.75
  Financial Collateral Directive, 4.99–4.106
Force majeure
  global custodian's duties, and, 6.71
Foreign Accounts Tax Compliance (FATCA)
  account identification, 10.84–10.88
  account review, 10.91
  compliance under UK IGA, 10.83
  overview, 10.82
  reporting obligations, 10.89–10.90
  review obligations, 10.84
Fraud
  limitation of liability, and, 6.8
Fraudulent transactions
  liability for third parties, and, 6.64–6.68
Fraudulent transfers
  CREST, and, 9.57–9.58

Freehold land
  legal categories of assets, and, 1.37–1.38
FSA Principles
  regulatory duties, and, 7.23
Fundamental concepts
  asset categories, 1.37–1.38
  clearing, 1.26
  collateralisation, 1.33–1.36
  computerisation, 1.24
  introduction, 1.16–1.17
  nature of securities, 1.20–1.23
  personal rights, 1.29
  private legal rights, 1.28–1.32
  property rights, 1.30–1.32
  settlement, 1.27
  trading, 1.25
Fungible custody
  allocation question, and, 3.24–3.26

G30 report
  book entry transfer, and, 8.8
  generally, 8.56–8.57
  introduction, 2.5
Gilts
  eligible debt securities, 9.119–9.124
  introduction, 9.107–9.109
  repos, 9.118
  stamp duty, 9.111
  stock lending, 9.115–9.117
  title finance, 9.112–9.114
  transfer of title, 9.110
Giovanni Report (2001)
  consolidation of clearing, and, 8.86
  generally, 8.60
Giovanni Report (2003)
  generally, 8.62–8.63
Global custodian
  See also Global custodian's duties
  collateralisation, and
    collateral management products, 4.15–4.22
    custodian's settlement exposures, 4.12–4.14
    introduction, 4.11
Global custodian's duties
  care, of
    case law, 6.30–6.31
    introduction, 6.28
    limitation clauses, 6.32–6.35
    statute, under, 6.29
  consequential damages, 6.72
  contractual duties, 6.16–6.19
  corporate actions, and
    client issues, 6.80–6.85
    custodian issues, 6.86–6.90
    generally, 6.78–6.79
    introduction, 6.76
    meaning, 6.77
  duty defining clauses, 6.2–6.3

Global custodian's duties – *contd*
  duty of care
    case law, 6.30–6.31
    introduction, 6.28
    limitation clauses, 6.32–6.35
    statute, under, 6.29
  erroneous instructions, 6.73
  fiduciary duty
    conflicts of interest, 6.47–6.50
    generally, 6.36–6.37
    global custodians, and, 6.40
    limitation clauses, 6.41–6.46
    nature, 6.38–6.39
    secret profits, 6.51–6.55
  force majeure, 6.71
  indemnities for breach of duty, 6.75
  information, 6.74
  introduction, 6.1
  liability for third parties
    fraudulent instructions, 6.64–6.68
    introduction, 6.56
    nexus, 6.69
    sub-custodians, 6.57–6.63
  limitation of liability
    generally, 6.5–6.8
    gross negligence, 6.9
    negligence, 6.9
    statutory restrictions, 6.11–6.15
    UCTA 1977, 6.11–6.14
    UTCCR, 6.15
    wilful default, 6.10
  overview, 6.2–6.4
  particular clauses
    consequential damages, 6.72
    erroneous instructions, 6.73
    force majeure, 6.71
    information, 6.74
    introduction, 6.70
  third party rights, 6.19
  tortious duty of care, 6.20–6.23
  trustees, as
    duty of care, 6.28–6.35
    fiduciary duty, 6.36–6.55
    generally, 6.24–6.27
Global custody
  background, 1.6
  challenges and opportunities, 1.7–1.9
  computerisation, 1.24
  development of services, 1.10
  fundamental concepts
    asset categories, 1.37–1.38
    clearing, 1.26
    collateralisation, 1.33–1.34
    computerisation, 1.24
    introduction, 1.16–1.17
    nature of securities, 1.20–1.23
    personal rights, 1.29
    possession, 1.35–1.36
    private legal rights, 1.28–1.32
    property rights, 1.30–1.32
    settlement, 1.27

Global custody – *contd*
  fundamental concepts – *contd*
    trading, 1.25
  meaning
    generally, 1.1
    global custody, 1.4–1.5
    international securities portfolios, 1.2–1.3
  nature of securities
    bearer securities, 1.23
    debt and equity, 1.21–1.22
    introduction, 1.20
    registered securities, 1.23
  opportunities, 1.7–1.9
  other functions, 1.11–1.12
Global custody contract
  consequential damages, 6.72
  duty defining clauses, 6.2–6.3
  erroneous instructions, 6.73
  force majeure, 6.71
  indemnities for breach of duty, 6.75
  information, 6.74
  introduction, 6.1
  limitation of liability clause
    generally, 6.5–6.8
    gross negligence, 6.9
    negligence, 6.9
    statutory restrictions, 6.11–6.15
    UCTA 1977, 6.11–6.14
    UTCCR, 6.15
    wilful default, 6.10
  overview, 6.2–6.4
  particular clauses
    consequential damages, 6.72
    erroneous instructions, 6.73
    force majeure, 6.71
    information, 6.74
    introduction, 6.70
Goods
  legal categories of assets, and, 1.37–1.38
Governing law
  collateralisation, and, 4.108–4.110
Gross negligence
  limitation of liability, and, 6.9

Hague Convention on Law Applicable to Certain Rights in Respect of Securities
  cross-border collateral, and, 5.59–5.61
  post-trade infrastructure, and, 8.112
High Level Standards
  regulatory duties, and, 7.23

Immobilisation
  book entry transfer, 2.6
  definition, 2.7
  generally, 2.7–2.9
  introduction, 2.5
Indemnities for breach of duty
  global custodians, and, 6.75

Information
  global custodian's duties, and, 6.74
Insolvency
  Banking Winding Up Directive, 5.21
  collateralisation
    generally, 8.103
    introduction, 4.4
  conflict of laws, 8.106
  jurisdiction
    Banking Winding Up Directive, 5.21
    English courts, 5.22–5.24
    European regulation, 5.17–5.18
    introduction, 5.15–5.16
    recognition of proceedings, 5.19–5.20
  netting, 8.104–8.105
  post-trade infrastructure, and
    collateral, 8.103
    conflict of laws, 8.106
    introduction, 8.101–8.102
    netting, 8.104–8.105
  recognition of proceedings, 5.19–5.20
  sub-custodian
    bailment, 5.31–5.32
    introduction, 5.30
    local ring-fence opinions, 5.35–5.36
    other risks, 5.37
    risks, 5.33–5.34
    trust, 5.31–5.32
Insolvency displacement
  collateralisation, and, 4.37–4.39
Insolvency jurisdiction
  Banking Winding Up Directive, 5.21
  English courts, 5.22–5.24
  European regulation, 5.17–5.18
  introduction, 5.15–5.16
  recognition of proceedings, 5.19–5.20
Insolvency protection
  collateralisation, and, 4.86–4.88
Insolvency set-off
  collateralisation, and, 4.58–4.59
Insurance companies
  international securities portfolios, and, 1.2
Insurance Winding-Up Directive
  collateralisation, and, 4.8
Intangible personal assets
  legal categories of assets, and, 1.37–1.38
  property rights, and, 5.43–5.45
Interests in securities
  custody relationship in electronic environment, and
    introduction, 3.10–3.13
    possession, 3.14–3.15
    trust, 3.16–3.22
  generally, 2.37–2.40
  UNIDROIT, and, 5.68
Intermediation
  collateralisation, and, 4.66–4.67
International securities portfolios
  generally, 1.2–1.3

Investment Bank Special Administration Regulations 2011
  custody relationship in electronic environment, and, 3.13
  return of custody assets, and, 1.8
Jurisdiction
  insolvency
    Banking Winding Up Directive, 5.21
    English courts, 5.22–5.24
    European regulation, 5.17–5.18
    introduction, 5.15–5.16
    recognition of proceedings, 5.19–5.20
  non-insolvency
    Brussels Regulation, 5.11
    common law regime, 5.12–5.14
    generally, 5.9–5.10
    overview, 5.7–5.8
Lamfalussy Securities Market Report
  consolidation of clearing, and, 8.86
Land
  legal categories of assets, and, 1.37–1.38
Legal mortgages
  CREST, and, 9.78–9.79
Legal nature of custody relationship
  See also Custodian-trustee
  accounts, 3.2
  allocation question, 3.23–3.49
  bailment, 3.10–3.22
  cash, 3.3–3.9
  interests in securities, 3.10–3.22
  introduction, 3.1
  possession, 3.14–3.15
  shortfalls, 3.50–3.55
  trust assets, 3.16–3.22
Legal nature of investors' assets
  bearer securities
    computerised securities, 2.17
    introduction, 2.14
    negotiability, 2.15–2.34
  dematerialisation
    book entry transfer, 2.6
    definition, 2.10
    generally, 2.10–2.13
    introduction, 2.5
  immobilisation
    book entry transfer, 2.6
    definition, 2.7
    generally, 2.7–2.9
    introduction, 2.5
  introduction, 2.5–2.6
  registered computerised securities, 2.35–2.36
Legal risk
  risk management, and, 8.28
Lehman Brothers
  custody relationship in electronic environment, and, 3.13
  return of custody assets, and, 1.8

Index 371

Lex situs
  collateralisation, and, 4.66–4.67
  property rights, and, 5.48–5.53
Liability for third parties
  fraudulent instructions, 6.64–6.68
  introduction, 6.56
  nexus, 6.69
  sub-custodians, 6.57–6.63
Liens
  collateralisation, and, 4.72
Limitation of liability
  duty of care, and, 6.32–6.35
  fiduciary duty, and, 6.41–6.46
  generally, 6.5–6.8
  gross negligence, 6.9
  negligence, 6.9
  statutory restrictions
    UCTA 1977, 6.11–6.14
    UTCCR, 6.15
  wilful default, 6.10
Liquidity risk
  risk management, and, 8.25–8.26
Living wills
  global custody industry, and, 1.9

Managed funds
  international securities portfolios, and, 1.2
Margining
  collateralisation, and, 4.40
Market-market clearing
  risk management, and, 8.55
Marking to market
  collateralisation, and, 4.40
MF Global Ltd
  return of custody assets, and, 1.8
Middle-office functions
  global custody industry, and, 1.8
MiFID (Directive 2004/39/EC)
  client money, and, 7.98–7.99
  global custody industry, and, 1.9
  regulatory duties, and, 7.10–7.14
MiFID 2 (draft Directive)
  regulatory duties, and, 7.14

Negligence
  limitation of liability, and, 6.9
Negotiability
  computerised bearer securities
    arguments against, 2.18–2.28
    benefits of, 2.29–2.34
    ease of transfer, 2.30–2.31
    indirect nature, 2.18–2.19
    intangibility, 2.20–2.24
    introduction, 2.15–2.16
    law merchant, and, 2.17
    security of transfer, 2.32–2.33
  traditional bearer securities, 2.16
Netting
  collateralisation, and, 4.60–4.62
  post-trade infrastructure, and, 8.13–8.15

Nominees
  regulatory duties, and, 7.20

Operational risk
  generally, 8.27
  legal risk, 8.28
Outright collateral transfers
  generally, 4.57–4.65
  insolvency set-off, 4.58–4.59
  introduction, 4.30
  netting, 4.60–4.62
  recharacterisation risk, 4.63–4.64
Outsourcing
  regulatory duties, and, 7.130–7.138

Payment
  CREST, and
    assured payments system, 9.21–9.23
    delivery versus payment, 9.24
    introduction, 9.12–9.15
    real time gross settlement, 9.16–9.20
  post-trade infrastructure, and, 8.5
Pension funds
  international securities portfolios, and, 1.2
Personal assets
  legal categories of assets, and, 1.37–1.38
Personal rights
  fundamental concepts, and, 1.29
Place of the relevant intermediary account (PRIMA)
  generally, 5.54–5.56
  other supporting measures, 5.58
  Settlement Finality Directive, 5.57–5.58
Pledges
  CREST, and, 9.87
Pooled accounts
  CREST, and, 9.33
Possession
  custody relationship in electronic environment, and, 3.14–3.15
  fundamental concepts, and, 1.35–1.36
Post-trade infrastructure
  background, 8.2
  Banking Winding Up Directive, 8.110
  book entry transfer, 8.6–8.10
  central counterparty
    consolidation of services, 8.90–8.98
    generally, 8.12
    challenges, 8.16–8.19
  clearing
    central counterparty, 8.12
    consolidation of services, 8.90–8.98
    introduction, 8.11
    netting, 8.13–8.15
  consolidation
    CCP services, of, 8.90–8.98
    clearing, of, 8.90–8.98
    current fragmentation, 8.86–8.87
    introduction, 8.85
    settlement, of, 8.88–8.89

Post-trade infrastructure – *contd*
  credit risk
    principal risk, 8.22
    replacement cost risk, 8.23–8.24
  delivery and payment, 8.5
  Delivery versus Payment (DVP)
    finality, 8.37–8.38
    introduction, 8.32
    models, 8.33–8.34
    qualities, 8.35–8.36
  EU Insolvency Regulation, 8.110
  European Securities Code, 8.113–8.114
  Financial Collateral Directive, 8.111
  Hague Convention on Law Applicable to Certain Rights in Respect of Securities, 8.112
  insolvency
    collateral, 8.103
    conflict of laws, 8.106
    introduction, 8.101–8.102
    netting, 8.104–8.105
  introduction, 8.1
  legal principles
    insolvency, 8.101–8.106
    introduction, 8.99
    law reform initiatives, 8.107–8.114
    property rights, 8.100
  liquidity risk, 8.25–8.26
  nature of clearing
    central counterparty, 8.12
    introduction, 8.11
    netting, 8.13–8.15
  nature of settlement
    book entry transfer, 8.6–8.10
    delivery and payment, 8.5
    introduction, 8.4
  netting, 8.13–8.15
  operational risk
    generally, 8.27
    legal risk, 8.28
  overview, 8.3
  payment, 8.5
  property rights, 8.100
  risk management
    basic techniques, 8.31–8.39
    batch settlement, 8.39
    credit risk, 8.22–8.24
    cross-border trades, 8.30
    derivatives to cash securities, 8.54
    DVP, 8.32–8.38
    introduction, 8.20
    key risks, 8.21–8.30
    leading studies and reports, 8.56–8.84
    liquidity risk, 8.25–8.26
    market-market clearing, 8.55
    operational risk, 8.27–8.28
    remote clearing, 8.55
    shorter settlement cycles, 8.39
    STP, 8.41–8.55
    system risk, 8.29
    studies and reports, 8.56–8.84

Post-trade infrastructure – *contd*
  risk management – *contd*
    T+1, 8.40
    vertical silo, 8.55
  settlement
    book entry transfer, 8.6–8.10
    consolidation of services, 8.88–8.89
    delivery and payment, 8.5
    introduction, 8.4
  Settlement Finance Directive, 8.108–8.109
  straight through processing (STP)
    benefits of clearing for market participants, 8.51–8.52
    central counterparty, 8.46–8.47
    collateralisation, 8.48
    default provisions, 8.49–8.50
    development of clearing, 8.53
    generally, 8.41–8.45
    system risk, 8.29
    T+1, 8.40
Prime brokerage
  collateralisation, and, 4.18–4.22
  regulatory duties, and, 7.154–7.158
Principal risk
  risk management, and, 8.22
Private legal rights
  fundamental concepts, and
    introduction, 1.28
    personal rights, 1.29
    property rights, 1.30–1.32
Property rights
  cross-border collateral, and
    choice of law, 5.48–5.50
    intangible assets, in, 5.43–5.45
    introduction, 5.42
    jurisdiction, 5.46–5.47
    lex situs, 5.48–5.53
  fundamental concepts, and, 1.30–1.32
  post-trade infrastructure, and, 8.100
Protection of client assets
  custody services, 7.38
  generally, 7.30–7.31
Prudential Regulatory Authority
  regulatory duties, and, 7.6–7.9

Real assets
  legal categories of assets, and, 1.37–1.38
Recharacterisation risk
  Financial Collateral Directive, 4.93–4.94
  generally, 4.63–4.64
Registered securities
  electronic environment, and, 2.35–2.36
  nature of securities, and, 1.23
Regulation on OTC derivatives, central counterparties and trade repositories (EU/648/2012)
  consolidation of clearing, and, 8.92
  global custody industry, and, 1.9

Regulatory duties
  'act honestly, fairly and
    professionally', 7.29
  'administration', 7.18–7.19
  AIFMD
    depositary's liability for loss, 7.165–7.170
    implications for depositary's
      delegates, 7.171–7.176
    introduction, 7.164
  background
    FSA 1986, 7.2
    FSMA 2000, 7.3–7.4
  Client Assets sourcebook (CASS), 7.21
  client classification, 7.33
  client money
    application of rules, 7.61
    BCOBS, 7.83–7.84
    case law, 7.85–7.108
    developments, 7.109–7.116
    disapplication of rules, 7.62–7.65
    holding of cash by custodian, 7.66–7.67
    introduction, 7.58–7.60
    opting-out, 7.68–7.73
    prior written notice, 7.77
    set-off, 7.83–7.84
    trustee firms, 7.74–7.75
    unclaimed funds, 7.78–7.82
    use of non-approved bank, 7.76
  client's right of action, and
    breach of FSA rules, 7.141
    breach of regulatory
      requirements, 7.142–7.143
    introduction, 7.139–7.140
  COBS, 7.21
  collateral
    CASS Resolution Pack, 7.121–7.122
    compliance, 7.119
    extension of rules, 7.120
    introduction, 7.117–7.118
  Conduct of Business Rules, 7.21
  control, 7.123–7.126
  custody, 7.2–7.4
  custody services
    affiliates, 7.57
    content of agreements, 7.36–7.37
    introduction, 7.34
    lien, 7.41–7.44
    maintenance of records, 7.45
    protection of client assets, 7.38
    registration of title, 7.49–7.56
    risk warnings, 7.46–7.48
    set-off rights, 7.41–7.44
    stock lending, 7.39–7.40
    sub-custodians, 7.35
  EEA passport arrangements, 7.145–7.150
  Financial Conduct Authority, 7.6–7.9
  Financial Services Authority, 7.5
  FSA Principles, 7.23

Regulatory duties – *contd*
  further changes to CASS, 7.159–7.161
  general principles, 7.23–7.29
  general provisions, 7.32
  High Level Standards, 7.23
  indirect holders' rights, 7.151–7.153
  international developments
    AIFMD, 7.164–7.176
    depositary's liability for loss, 7.165–7.170
    implications for depositary's
      delegates, 7.171–7.176
    introduction, 7.162–7.163
  introduction, 7.1
  MiFID, 7.10–7.14
  MiFID 2, 7.14
  nominees, 7.20
  outsourcing, 7.130–7.138
  prime brokerage, 7.154–7.158
  protection of client assets
    custody services, 7.38
    generally, 7.30–7.31
  Prudential Regulatory Authority, 7.6–7.9
  regulated activities, 7.15–7.16
  relevant rules, 7.21–7.22
  'safeguarding', 7.18–7.19
  Securities Law Directive
    further developments, 7.187–7.188
    future, 7.192–7.193
    introduction, 7.177
    loss of securities, 7.182–7.184
    nature of ownership, 7.189
    non-discrimination as to securities
      rights, 7.185–7.186
    omnibus accounts, 7.191
    rights granted to persons other than
      legal owner, 7.178–7.181
    rights of use, 7.190
  specified activities, 7.17
  trustees, 7.127–7.129
  'treating customers fairly' (TCF), 7.25–7.27
  unclaimed assets, 7.144
  Unfair Contract Terms Regulatory Guide (UNFCOG), 7.28

Remote clearing
  risk management, and, 8.55

Replacement cost risk
  risk management, and, 8.23–8.24

Repos
  cash collateral, 9.89–9.90
  delivery by value, 9.91–9.93
  gilts, and, 9.118
  introduction, 9.88
  securities collateral, 9.91–9.92

Risk management
  basic techniques
    DVP, 8.32–8.38
    introduction, 8.31–8.39
    batch settlement, 8.39

Risk management – *contd*
  credit risk
    principal risk, 8.22
    replacement cost risk, 8.23–8.24
  CREST, and
    bad deliveries, 9.49–9.60
    credit risk, 9.42–9.48
    custody agreements, 9.61–9.65
    fraudulent transfers, 9.57–9.58
  cross-border trades, 8.30
  derivatives to cash securities, 8.54
  Delivery versus Payment (DVP)
    finality, 8.37–8.38
    introduction, 8.32
    models, 8.33–8.34
    qualities, 8.35–8.36
  introduction, 8.20
  key risks
    credit risk, 8.22–8.24
    cross-border trades, in, 8.30
    introduction, 8.21–8.30
    liquidity risk, 8.25–8.26
    operational risk, 8.27–8.28
    system risk, 8.29
  leading studies and reports, 8.56–8.84
  legal risk, 8.28
  liquidity risk, 8.25–8.26
  market-market clearing, 8.55
  operational risk
    generally, 8.27
    legal risk, 8.28
  principal risk, 8.22
  remote clearing, 8.55
  replacement cost risk, 8.23–8.24
  shorter settlement cycles, 8.39
  straight through processing (STP)
    benefits of clearing for market
      participants, 8.51–8.52
    central counterparty, 8.46–8.47
    collateralisation, 8.48
    default provisions, 8.49–8.50
    development of clearing, 8.53
    generally, 8.41–8.45
  system risk, 8.29
  studies and reports, 8.56–8.84
  T+1, 8.40
  vertical silo, 8.55

'Safeguarding'
  regulatory duties, and, 7.18–7.19
Secret profits
  fiduciary duty, and, 6.51–6.55
Securities
  nature
    bearer securities, 1.23
    debt and equity, 1.21–1.22
    introduction, 1.20
    registered securities, 1.23
Securities Law Directive (EU draft)
  cross-border collateral, and, 5.69–5.72
  further developments, 7.187–7.188

Securities Law Directive (EU draft) – *contd*
  future, 7.192–7.193
  introduction, 7.177
  loss of securities, 7.182–7.184
  nature of ownership, 7.189
  non-discrimination as to securities
    rights, 7.185–7.186
  omnibus accounts, 7.191
  regulatory duties, and, 7.177–7.193
  rights granted to persons other than legal
    owner, 7.178–7.181
  rights of use, 7.190
Securities lending
  cash collateral, 9.89–9.90
  delivery by value, 9.91–9.93
  introduction, 9.88
  securities collateral, 9.91–9.92
Security interests
  charges, 9.86
  CREST transfers, 9.78–9.79
  equitable mortgages, 9.80–9.85
  escrow balance, 9.80–9.85
  introduction, 9.77
  legal mortgages, 9.78–9.79
  pledges, 9.87
Set-off
  client money, and
    case law, 7.92–7.94
    generally, 7.83–7.84
  cross-border collateral, and, 5.73
Settlement
  book entry transfer
    generally, 8.6–8.10
    introduction, 2.6
  consolidation of services, 8.88–8.89
  CREST
    central sponsor arrangements, 9.95–9.105
    CGO membership agreement, 9.141–9.142
    collateral, 9.75–9.93
    conclusions, 9.135
    corporate actions, 9.94
    cross border issues, 9.66–9.68
    custody accounts, 9.31–9.41
    funds, 9.106
    further developments, 9.125–9.134
    further issues for consideration, 9.136–9.140
    gilts, 9.107–9.117
    international securities, 9.69–9.74
    introduction, 9.1–9.4
    legal structure, 9.5–9.30
    repos, 9.118–9.124
    risk, 9.42–9.65
  delivery and payment, 8.5
  dematerialisation
    book entry transfer, 2.6
    definition, 2.10
    generally, 2.10–2.13
    introduction, 2.5

Settlement – *contd*
  fundamental concepts, and, 1.27
  generally, 8.3
  immobilisation
    book entry transfer, 2.6
    definition, 2.7
    generally, 2.7–2.9
    introduction, 2.5
  introduction, 2.5
  post-trade infrastructure, and
    book entry transfer, 8.6–8.10
    consolidation of services, 8.88–8.89
    delivery and payment, 8.5
    introduction, 8.4
Settlement Finality Directive (98/26/EC)
  post-trade infrastructure, and, 8.108–8.109
Settlement interval
  generally, 8.3
Stamp duty
  bearer instrument, 10.8–10.9
  call options, 10.12–10.13
  clearance service
    election to pay stamp duty, 10.26
    EU law aspects, 10.21
    exempt agreements to transfer, 10.27
    generally, 10.24
    one-off charge, 10.25
  contract chargeable as transfer on sale, 10.20
  custodians, 10.29
  depositary receipts
    EU law aspects, 10.21
    generally, 10.22–10.23
    transfer on sale, 10.16
  evidence, 10.30
  exempt loan capital, 10.11
  introduction, 10.6–10.7
  investors, 10.28
  other exemptions, 10.14–10.15
  transfer of other kinds, 10.17–10.19
  transfer on sale
    call options, 10.12–10.13
    depositary receipts, 10.16
    exempt loan capital, 10.11
    introduction, 10.10
    other exemptions, 10.14–10.15
Stamp duty reserve tax (SDRT)
  chargeable securities, 10.31
  charges
    clearance service charge, 10.43–10.44
    depositary receipt charge, 10.39–10.42
    introduction, 10.33
    principal charge, 10.34–10.38
  clearance service charge
    exemptions, 10.44
    generally, 10.43
  CREST, and
    generally, 9.30
    gilts, and, 9.111

Stamp duty reserve tax (SDRT) – *contd*
  depositary receipt charge
    exemptions, 10.40–10.41
    generally, 10.39
    transfers between receipt and clearance system, 10.42
  double charge, 10.37–10.38
  excluded securities, 10.32
  principal charge
    double charge, 10.37–10.38
    exemptions, 10.35–10.36
    generally, 10.34
  settlements, 10.45–10.51
Stock lending
  CREST, and, 9.115–9.117
Straight through processing (STP)
  benefits of clearing for market participants, 8.51–8.52
  central counterparty, 8.46–8.47
  collateralisation, 8.48
  default provisions, 8.49–8.50
  development of clearing, 8.53
  generally, 8.41–8.45
Stock lending
  CREST, and, 9.115–9.117
Sub-custodians
  insolvency, and
    bailment, 5.31–5.32
    introduction, 5.30
    local ring-fence opinions, 5.35–5.36
    other risks, 5.37
    risks, 5.33–5.34
    trust, 5.31–5.32
  liability for third parties, and, 6.57–6.63
System risk
  post-trade infrastructure, and, 8.29

T+1
  risk management, and, 8.40
Tangible personal assets
  legal categories of assets, and, 1.37–1.38
Taxation
  enforcement in UK assessment under laws of another jurisdiction, 10.52–10.55
  Foreign Accounts Tax Compliance (FATCA)
    account identification, 10.84–10.88
    account review, 10.91
    compliance under UK IGA, 10.83
    overview, 10.82
    reporting obligations, 10.89–10.90
    review obligations, 10.84
  introduction, 10.1–10.5
  situs, 10.56–10.58
  stamp duty
    bearer instrument, 10.8–10.9
    call options, 10.12–10.13
    clearance service, 10.24–10.27
    contract chargeable on transfer on sale, 10.20
    custodians, 10.29

Taxation – *contd*
  stamp duty – *contd*
    depositary receipts, 10.16, 10.22–10.23
    EU law aspects, 10.21
    evidence, 10.30
    exempt loan capital, 10.11
    introduction, 10.6–10.7
    investors, 10.28
    other exemptions, 10.14–10.15
    transfer of other kinds, 10.17–10.19
    transfer on sale, 10.10–10.16
  stamp duty reserve tax (SDRT)
    chargeable securities, 10.31
    charges, 10.33–10.44
    clearance service, 10.43–10.44
    depositary receipt charge, 10.39–10.42
    excluded securities, 10.32
    principal charge, 10.34–10.38
    settlements, 10.45–10.51
  value added tax
    exemptions, 10.94–10.96
    introduction, 10.92
    scope, 10.93
  withholding tax
    collecting agents, 10.65–10.68
    Directive on taxation of savings income, 10.72–10.81
    generally, 10.59–10.60
    information reporting, 10.69–10.71
    payers and paying agents, 10.61–10.64
Third parties
  liability for
    fraudulent instructions, 6.64–6.68
    introduction, 6.56
    nexus, 6.69
    sub-custodians, 6.57–6.63
Third party rights
  global custodian's duties, and, 6.19
Torts
  duty of care, 6.20–6.23
Tracing
  CREST, and, 9.59
Trading
  fundamental concepts, and, 1.25
Traditional bearer securities
  bailment, and, 3.10
  generally, 2.14
  negotiability, 2.16
  stamp duty, and, 10.8–10.9
Transfer on sale
  call options, 10.12–10.13
  depositary receipts, 10.16
  exempt loan capital, 10.11
  introduction, 10.10
  other exemptions, 10.14–10.15
Trust assets
  custody relationship in electronic environment, and, 3.16–3.22
Trustees
  client money, and, 7.74–7.75

Trustees – *contd*
  custodians as
    accounts, 3.2
    allocation question, 3.23–3.49
    bailment, 3.10–3.22
    cash, 3.3–3.9
    interests in securities, 3.10–3.22
    introduction, 3.1
    possession, 3.14–3.15
    shortfalls, 3.50–3.55
    trust assets, 3.16–3.22
  duty of care
    case law, 6.30–6.31
    introduction, 6.28
    limitation clauses, 6.32–6.35
    statute, under, 6.29
  fiduciary duty
    conflicts of interest, 6.47–6.50
    generally, 6.36–6.37
    global custodians, and, 6.40
    limitation clauses, 6.41–6.46
    nature, 6.38–6.39
    secret profits, 6.51–6.55
  generally, 6.24–6.27
  regulatory duties, and, 7.127–7.129
'Treating customers fairly' (TCF)
  regulatory duties, and, 7.25–7.27
Trusts
  client money, and, 7.87–7.91

Unclaimed funds and assets
  client money, and, 7.78–7.82
  regulatory duties, and, 7.144
Undertakings for collective investment in transferable securities (UCITS)
  global custody industry, and, 1.9
Unfair Contract Terms Act (UCTA) 1977
  limitation of liability, and, 6.11–6.14
Unfair Contract Terms Regulatory Guide (UNFCOG)
  regulatory duties, and, 7.28
Unfair Terms in Consumer Contracts Regulations (UTCCR) 1999
  limitation of liability, and, 6.15
UNIDROIT
  cross-border collateral, and,
    cash, 5.68
    conceptual issues, 5.66–5.67
    generally, 5.62–5.65
    interests in securities, 5.68
Universities
  international securities portfolios, and, 1.2

Value added tax
  exemptions, 10.94–10.96
  introduction, 10.92
  scope, 10.93
Vertical silo
  risk management, and, 8.55

Wilful default
  limitation of liability, and, 6.10
Withholding tax
  collecting agents
    Eurobonds, 10.67
    introduction, 10.65–10.66
    'reasinable belief' test, 10.68
  Directive on taxation of savings income, 10.72–10.81
  disapplication of duty to deduct income tax, 10.63–10.64

Withholding tax – *contd*
  Eurobonds
    collecting agents, 10.67
    payers and paying agents, 10.62
  generally, 10.59–10.60
  information reporting, 10.69–10.71
  payers and paying agents
    disapplication of duty to deduct income tax, 10.63–10.64
    Eurobonds, 10.62
    introduction, 10.61